Biographical
Dictionary Of The Left

Biographical Dictionary Of The Left

Volume III

by

Francis X. Gannon

WESTERN ISLANDS

BOSTON   LOS ANGELES

Published by

Western Islands
Belmont, Massachusetts 02178

Library of Congress Catalog Card Number 76-12821
Manufactured in the United States of America

TABLE OF CONTENTS

A FOREWORD BY THE PUBLISHER

It is our present expectation that this *Biographical Dictionary Of The Left* will consist of eight volumes in this Western Islands edition, and will contain in all about twenty-five hundred names. As an aid to the reader and as an important preface to the biographies included, each volume will begin with a section on organizations of the Left.

Because of the urgent need for such a reference dictionary, we shall bring out each compilation of about three hundred sketches as soon as it is ready, in the same format as this volume. All of the names in any one volume will be alphabetized into one sequence between its covers. This will require extra work by the reader in searching for a particular entry. But it is far more practicable, and will make the early volumes far more useful, than if we followed the alternative procedure – as did the French *Encyclopédistes*, for instance – of having each volume simply move further down the total alphabet. As an aid to the reader, we have included in Volume Three a cumulative index of the organizations and individuals covered in all of the first three volumes.

Each volume is being prepared by, or under the careful supervision of, Dr. Francis X. Gannon, head of the Research Department of The John Birch Society. Dr. Gannon, who received his Ph.D. in History from Georgetown University, has long been a worthy disciple of his great teacher, the eminent historian Charles Callan Tansill. Sound scholarship in his chosen field, and unimpeachable accuracy in every line he writes, have been imperative considerations for Dr. Gannon, as they were for Dr. Tansill before him.

Believing that it is better to err a hundred times on the side of restraint and understatement than to err even once, no matter how slightly, on the side of abuse or exaggeration, Dr. Gannon will give you in these volumes as much dependable information concerning contemporary leaders of the liberal-left persuasion as space, time, and other practical limitations will permit. And we send this third volume forth in continuance of the tremendous project which we hope will result in a series of reference books that will prove useful to all patriotic students of the planned and subversive confusion which now engulfs us all.

Editorial Staff, Western Islands

INTRODUCTION

There is a Left in America. That is a fact of life. To deny it is to deny the existence of a far-flung establishment whose members have been working tirelessly for decades to Socialize or — if you please — Sovietize the United States.

To determine why any particular individual may have become a leftist is not the purpose of this study. He may have arrived on the Left motivated by genuine idealism, incurable do-goodism, scholarly curiosity, compassionate brotherhood, or by a sentiment no more harmful than desire for adventure. Or his motives may have been of a crasser nature: financial, political, or social opportunism; dedication to Socialism or Communism; or some variant of these alien totalitarian systems.

What does matter for this report is that the individual has been and is on the Left, working for leftist causes. A pattern of his past and present positions, his media and affiliations, his causes — domestic and foreign — and his activities can be recognized.

The leftist has come from Ivy League, state, and sectarian universities and colleges. He has received Rhodes and Fulbright scholarships; Guggenheim and Nieman fellowships; Carnegie and Ford and 20th Century Fund grants; Pulitzer and Nobel prizes; Sidney Hillman and Freedom House awards; and sinecures at foundations or university and government research centers. He has had his plays or books reviewed favorably in the *New York Times*, the *New Republic, Time*, and the *Nation.* He has studied abroad at the London School of Economics or at Oxford or graduate schools in New Delhi or Geneva. He has joined the NAACP, the Council on Foreign Relations, the Union for Democratic Action — later Americans for Democratic Action — or one or many Communist fronts.

The leftist has been in government offices on federal, state, and local levels — through election or appointment, or in consultative or advisory capacities; in radio and television, in commercial and educational films, on newspapers and magazines, on trade organs and scholarly journals — as commentator, editor, producer, director, publisher, writer, cartoonist, reviewer; in religion — all creeds — preaching, writing, and politicking; on university and college campuses — as teacher, administrator, researcher, scholar-in-residence, and student activist; in organized labor; in business and trade associations; in the recently developed "think" factories, which are government-financed research projects involving the most critical problems of diplomacy, economics, military strategy, and national security; and in the arts — as illustrator, painter, sculptor, playwright, novelist, poet, and entertainer.

After Franklin Roosevelt inaugurated the New Deal, the leftist was to be found in the higher echelons of Henry Wallace's Department of Agriculture, the Treasury Department of Henry Morgenthau and Harry Dexter White, the National Labor Relations Board, the Office of Education, the State Department, and Frances Perkins' Department of Labor. Some leftists even moved into the White House, and others wormed their way onto congressional committee staffs.

In the circumstances immediately surrounding World War II, the leftist sought his niche in the Office of Price Administration, the Office of Strategic Services, the Office of War Information, the War Production Board, and the Board of Economic Warfare. Later, the leftist was to be found in the Central Intelligence Agency; on the United Nations staff; in the foreign aid programs (under their ever-changing names); in the Alliance for Progress, the Office of Economic Opportunity, the Peace Corps, and the Department of Health, Education, and Welfare.

Look for the leftist in the AFL-CIO, on the Supreme Court, in the Foreign Policy Association, in the American Assembly, in the National Council of Churches, at the New School for Social Research, in the Brookings Institute, in Chambers of Commerce, in gubernatorial mansions, on Wall Street, in Congress, in the Anti-Defamation League, in the Institute for American Democracy, in mental health associations, in American Friends of Vietnam, in the Republican and Democrat parties, and marching side-by-side with black powerites, trampling upon others' civil rights and violating law and order.

The causes of the American leftist on the domestic scene have been directed toward the exaltation of society and the state by attacks upon individual and family dignity and property rights. The leftist has promoted confiscatory taxation, deficit spending, deliberate inflation, and wilful debauchery of the entire monetary system. Fraudulent and compulsory insurance schemes have been presented as social security; federal control and dominance of education as aid; dictatorial ukases as judicial decisions.

The leftist has preached that Joe McCarthy had to go — Alger Hiss was framed — Owen Lattimore was an objective scholar — Jomo Kenyatta is a statesman — Titoism is a gentle kind of Communism — Castro and Sukarno and Ben Bella were George Washington reincarnated — the United Nations is mankind's best and last hope — *extreme* leftists and extreme rightists are equally dangerous — the U.S. Constitution was written for horse and buggy days — the Communists have mellowed — loyalty oaths attack academic freedom — better-Red-than-dead — congressional committees are inquisitorial except when presided over by Fulbright or Celler or Symington — and the Third World War (a nuclear holocaust) is just around the corner unless the military-industrial complex can be ground to bits in a Pentagon computer.

In the State Department and elsewhere, the leftist has not turned his back on Alger Hiss, and the Department's leftward foreign policy has been the work of Dean Acheson's protégés, George Kennan's disciples, and the Institute of Pacific Relations veterans led by Dean Rusk. Derogated as fantasies are Communist aggression and Communist subversion. Business as usual with Communist enemies is encouraged in time of hot war, which the leftist calls cold. Red China should be extended formal diplomatic recognition and brought into the "peace-loving" United Nations. The leftist wants nuclear treaties and disarmament; dialogues with the Communists; a United Nations "peacekeeping" force; and, most of all, Peaceful Coexistence with the Communist tyrants who are irrevocably bent on world conquest.

The leftist is not necessarily — though he may be — scribbling the latest party line in the pages of *The Worker* or grinding out revolutionary tracts in a dank cellar or dusty loft. The Left is far more inclusive than a hard-core of disciplined members of the Communist Party. There are legions of leftists who have gravitated — not merely through coincidence — toward common bases of activity. The leftist is here in America in greater numbers, more secure in his influence, and accelerating his program faster, than ever before. He may deny that he is part of any establishment, but his denials will be more heated if he is accused of "rightism." In the following biographical sketches, we present the leftist in his environment.

Francis X. Gannon
Belmont, Massachusetts 02178

NOTE TO THE READER

Phrases contained in quotation marks, characterizing various organizations and publications, are quoted from *Guide to Subversive Organizations and Publications,* prepared and released by the Committee on Un-American Activities of the U.S. House of Representatives, December 1, 1961. The reports in this publication are in turn verbatim quotations from reports of Federal government and Congressional authorities, namely, the committee itself (HCUA), the Senate Judiciary Committee and its Internal Security Subcommittee, and the Subversive Activities Control Board; and from letters to the Loyalty Review Board from United States Attorneys General Francis Biddle, Tom Clark, and J. Howard McGrath; and also from reports of State or (then) territorial investigating committees (California, Hawaii, Massachusetts, New York, Ohio).

It should be noted that no revision of this Guide, first published in 1957, has been issued since 1961.

Organizations Of The Left

BUSINESS EXECUTIVES MOVE FOR VIETNAM PEACE
BUSINESSMEN'S EDUCATIONAL FUND
MILITARY INDUSTRIAL RESEARCH SURVEY
THE WASHINGTON WATCH

On February 8, 1967, in the *Washington Post*, there appeared a half-page advertisement in the form of an open letter to President Lyndon Johnson "from Business Executives." Under the heading, "Stop the War, Mr. President," the advertisement read: "We, the undersigned American business executives, most of whom have served at least once in the Armed Services of the United States, protest against the escalation of the war in Vietnam. We believe that this war is against our national interest and world interest. We feel this on moral and practical grounds . . . ."

The advertisement was the work of Henry E. Niles, chairman of the board of the Baltimore Life Insurance Company. He had recruited a number of business executives who shared his antipathy toward the Vietnam War. On September 27, 1967, Niles and his associates organized as Business Executives Move for Vietnam Peace (BEM).

Prior to 1967, Niles had signed a few anti-Vietnam War advertisements. He had been affiliated with the ultra-leftist United World Federalists. He had served on the advisory council of the Peace Research Institute, one of the most prestigious organizations in the entire leftist-pacifist movement. Within his family, his daughter Alice had been a pacifist since at least 1949. Her husband, Staughton Lynd, was and remains one of America's better-known revolutionary pacifists.

In the early days of BEM, Niles served as co-chairman of the group, along with Harold Willens, president of the Factory Equipment Supply Company of Los Angeles. According to the *Chicago Tribune* of October 1, 1967, Willens "has raised millions of dollars in financial support for the controversial Center for the Study of Democratic Institutions in Santa Barbara, California." As of 1967, Willens was on the council of advisors of radio station KPFA, which is part of the ultra-leftist Pacifica Foundation radio complex. Willens told the *Chicago Tribune* that the BEM was first discussed on May 28, 1966, at a meeting held in the office of Charles G. Simpson, general manager of the Philadelphia Gas

1

Works. Of the original organizing group, Willens said that at least 50 were members of the exclusive President's Club of $1,000 contributors to the Democratic Party. Willens also told the *Chicago Tribune* that at the first major meeting in Washington, D.C., of the BEM, about 900 were in attendance, most of whom, he said, were "reluctant to join any of the established peace groups because of possible harm to their corporate image."

One of the first major press notices BEM received was in the *Wall Street Journal*. The story appeared on the eve of BEM's first major meeting. In a dispatch by Jerry Landauer, Niles was quoted as saying: "This isn't a one-shot thing. We're going to keep going until this war is over. We have a responsibility to be heard before it's too late." Landauer also wrote that Niles said he would prefer a Red-run South Vietnam to the risk of wider war. A spokesman for BEM told Landauer: "We're not the kooks, the picketers or the Dr. Spocks. We're level-headed middle-level businessmen."

Among the early organizers of BEM were Augustin H. Parker, chairman of the Old Colony Trust Company of Boston; Joseph E. McDowell, president of Servomation; John B. Prendergrast Jr., vice-president of Southern Cross Industries; Max Palevsky, president of Scientific Data Systems; Randolph T. Compton, vice-president of Kidder, Peabody & Company, stockbrokers; Erwin A. Salk, president of Salk, Ward & Salk, Inc.; Marriner S. Eccles, chairman of Utah Construction & Mining Company; Edward M. Keating, president of the ultra-leftist *Ramparts* magazine; and Gerard Piel, president of the ultra-leftist *Scientific American.*

Shortly after BEM was formally organized, Harold Willens established a BEM adjunct, the Businessmen's Educational Fund (BEF). The BEF was established as a tax-exempt organization. During the first year of its existence, its main activity was the free distribution of Richard J. Barnet's *The Economy of Death*, an all-out attack upon the elusive "military-industrial complex."

On January 11, 1968, the BEF announced the formation of the Military Industrial Research Survey (MIRS). The MIRS was an attempt to bring professional military judgment onto the side of BEM. For this purpose, Niles and Willens announced the formation of a military group including a retired general, three brigadier generals, and a rear admiral: General David M. Shoup and Brigadier General Samuel B. Griffith II,

2

retired from the U.S. Marines; Brigadier General William W. Ford and Brigadier General Robert L. Hughes, retired from the U.S. Army; and Rear Admiral Arnold E. True, retired from the U.S. Navy. The Board of Trustees for MIRS had Willens as chairman and included as members J. Sinclair Armstrong, a New York banker; G. Sterling Grumman, president of G.S. Grumman & Associates of Boston; Edwin Janss Jr., president of Janss Corporation of Los Angeles; McDowell of Servomation; Palevsky of Scientific Data Systems; J.R. Parten, an oil producer from Houston; Alfred P. Slaner, president of Kayser-Roth Corporation of New York; and Gordon B. Sherman, president of Midas-International Corporation.

In its promotional literature, BEM included a reprint of an article from the *Atlantic Monthly* ("The New American Militarism," April 19, 1969), written by General Shoup, in which he warned of "the burgeoning military establishment and associated industries (that) fuel it. Anti-Communism provides the climate which nurtures it." Even before MIRS was formed, Shoup had publicly criticized American involvement in the Vietnam War. (Gordon Sherman, a trustee of MIRS and chairman of the Chicago branch of BEM, told *Chicago Today* of November 11, 1969, that "militarism has taken root like a cancer in the U.S." Sherman said: "To support it [the military complex] we speak of menacing enemies far away waiting to destroy us. Everything we do is done innocently in the name of defense. Meanwhile, we corrupt the opportunity which rests solely with us to take the leadership in a world running out of time – a world whose needs are ignored, whose hopes are aborted by our rampant, self-righteous irresponsibility . . . .")

On February 6, 1968, BEM inaugurated a newsletter, *The Washington Watch*. In charge of the newsletter was Tristram Coffin, whose *The Passion of the Hawks*, published in 1964, was a venomous and defamatory attack upon the highly elusive military-industrial complex. After a few issues of *The Washington Watch*, the BEM offered a disclaimer on the first page of the publication: "The views expressed by Mr. Coffin are his own and Business Executives Move for Vietnam Peace does not necessarily endorse them." The disclaimer was really meaningless since at the time it appeared, the masthead described *The Washington Watch* as "a private newsletter circulated to members and supporters of Business Executives Move for Vietnam Peace," and of course the newsletter continued to be financed by BEM.

3

BUSINESS EXECUTIVES MOVE FOR VIETNAM PEACE

In the *New York Times* of February 27, 1968, Gladwyn Hill wrote that BEM had 1,600 members. Co-chairman Willens told Hill that BEM was nonpartisan. "We aren't even necessarily anti-Johnson," said Willens. "We're for exactly the same objective our Government says it's for: negotiated settlement. But the course the Administration has been pursuing plainly hasn't brought us any closer to that goal. We feel it's become mainly a matter of passionate self-righteousness and personal pride to a little handful of men in Washington.

"As businessmen we feel that when a policy hasn't proved productive after a reasonable trial it's sheer nonsense not to change it. We don't believe in unilateral, precipitate withdrawal — the realities of the situation have made that impractical. But we're for a policy of de-escalation aimed at total disengagement."

On March 16, 1968, BEM received a highly favorable puff in the influential *Business Week* magazine. The author of the piece made mountains of accomplishments out of molehills of BEM anti-war newspaper advertisements, which were not substantially different from those emanating from groups of lawyers, educators, students, scientists, and assorted leftist and pacifist groups. Although the rhetoric and strategy of BEM were substantially imitative of other anti-war groups, *Business Week* presented BEM as rather unique: "Opposition to the Vietnam war has typically had an unscrubbed look. Its bearded, beaded, and flowered ranks have busily raised the love-in to national celebrity, and all but drowned out the presence of other, more sober voices raised against the war. These voices are now being increasingly heard; the peace movement last week was taking on a new, gray-flannel respectability.

"The Business Executives Move for Vietnam Peace (BEM), launched nationally just six months ago to persuade the Johnson Administration to reverse its Vietnam policy, has set itself on a new, bold course. In newspaper advertisements and press conferences in a score of cities late last week, the group appealed for broader support in the U.S. business community. Its aim is to intensify pressure on Washington for gradual de-escalation and eventual disengagement in Vietnam."

Co-chairman Harold Willens was quoted by *Business Week* as saying that BEM had entered "phase two" of its bold, new effort. "Phase one," said Willens, "entailed contacting the President directly." Phase one was never realized but Willens did have a 45-minute audience with presidential adviser Walt W. Rostow. "He didn't move me," said Willens, "any more than I moved him."

Officials of BEM who were interviewed by *Business Week* indicated that they were still looking for support from executives from major corporations. The *Business Week* writer summarized the reaction experienced by BEM: "Most of the group's membership so far comes from top executives of medium-sized companies, although there are a few of national fame. Prominent among them are Marriner S. Eccles, former chairman of the Federal Reserve Board, and Theodore O. Yntema, retired Ford Motor Co. executive.

"So far, the companies of BEM executives have been tolerant of their anti-war activities. Only three executives have been asked to delete their company names from group promotions. None has lost a customer he knows of.

"Acceptance of the organization for what it claims to be – a group of responsible businessmen patriotically opposed to the conduct of the war – has not come without a hitch. As recently as last December, New York leaders were told there was no room at the Overseas Press Club for them. Club spokesmen later admitted that 'Business Executives Move for Vietnam Peace' had sounded too improbable.

"Background: BEM is hardly New Left or uncompromisingly pacifist. Members – about 60 per cent are Democrats, the rest Republicans."

In the business and finance section of the Sunday edition of the *New York Times* (March 17, 1968), generous linage was given to an interview conducted by Robert A. Wright with four leaders of the New York chapter of BEM: Herbert A. Brandon, owner of Brandon Publications; Ernest R. Chanes, president of Consolidated Water Conditioning Corporation; Louis M. Gersten, owner of Rostrum, Inc.; and Norman Eisner, owner of Lincoln Graphic Arts. Without identifying the individual respondents, Wright provided a partial transcript of the collective interview: "Q. – Do you have businessmen joining your group who formerly would not have? A. – I would say that not only in the organization itself, where many people have now joined who never were joiners or active in organizations that were trying to make changes in the features of American life, but in my own industry, I have found people coming to me because I have been outspoken. Q. – Do you have any idea why these people have changed their minds? A. – The impact of the war in Vietnam is now being felt in greater and greater circles. It's detrimental to business. It is now extending itself into the lives of the middle-class families as more and more boys become involved. Q. – What about the defense suppliers and the larger businesses? A. – Insofar as the big defense establishments are concerned, they are tied up in the war effort, not necessarily because that is the best and only way they can make a profit in running their businesses, but they are tied up because the defense establishment has become a $100-billion purchasing operation, which becomes one of their largest customers. They steer clear of any direct controversy about the war. Q. – And why haven't these larger businessmen been willing to join groups such as yours? A. – We've been told by a number of the major business members that we do have that there are many people in such positions today who share the views of the B.E.M., and although they may be earning $200,000 a year, they're still hired managers, and therefore they are not in the same position of freedom without potential loss of their position to come out for such a position. This is why Theodore Yntema, who was chief financial officer of the Ford Motor Company, can now do so because he is retired.

"Q. – Have the so-called organization men indicated that they would like you to speak for them in this matter? A. – In fact [John Kenneth] Galbraith made that comment. That the middle group of executives in big business is afraid to make the move until a large number of businessmen appear on the scene and pave the way for them. Q. – More and more leaders of big business are taking a larger social role and encouraging their managers to do the same. Are they still afraid nonetheless? A. – The organization man is the most conservative man in American society. He's got a good position in the establishment and he hesitates to do anything to rock the boat and endanger his position. However, the more big businessmen and smaller and middle businessmen, such as our organization represents, come out in the open and prepare the way for them, it will be more conducive to them to take a role in this operation. Q. – They're still using you as sort of middle men to speak up. Is that right? A. – Yes. Yes. That's quite true. However, there's been a change all the way through. It's only a few years ago that we ran some ads in the *New York Times* and we found that even the small businessmen at that time were not eager to use their company names. There's been a tremendous movement, right up on the line.

6

"Q. — I notice that there are some generals in your organization as well as businessmen. A. — Yes, just like the comment that was made before, that it's a hell of a lot easier for retired corporation executives to become part of our movement, so it is apparently with the military. I'm sure that there's a great part of the military that don't go along with the Johnson policy, but it's impossible for them to speak out. Q. — Is the motivation in this group a business one? Has your business been hurt by the war? A. — Our chief motivation is not that our businesses are being hurt. Our chief motivation is a moral one and an ideological one. Q. — Have there been any pressures put upon you not to get into this? Any pressure in terms of orders? A. — Well, I haven't had any real pressures, despite the fact that I publish a shipping magazine. And the major advertisers are American steamship lines, which are very heavily involved in the carriage of goods to Vietnam. And none of them has indicated any kind of opposition to the editorials that I have run against the war in Vietnam, despite the fact that they are business oriented to that. Q. — Is your organization interested in November's election, or are you just as interested in changing President Johnson's mind before then? A. — We'll attempt to influence the Johnson Administration to bring about an end to the war in Vietnam. At the same time we are engaging wherever possible in political activity to exert the political pressure that we hope the Johnson Administration will respond to. In the event that he doesn't respond to it, the gathering political force, under our influence, will be used to defeat him in the November elections."

In the *New York Times* of July 5, 1968, Gladwin Hill reported that Harold Willens had indicated that BEM might drop its nonpartisan role in order to support an acceptable nominee of either major party. Said Willens: "At the moment we can't endorse any particular candidate because our membership includes both Democrats and Republicans. But we'd consider our hard work well spent if, for instance, the Republican nomination went to Governor Rockefeller and the Democratic nomination to Senator McCarthy, rather than to more militant entries on both sides."

Willens also told Hill that if there were a decided contrast in the views of the major party nominees, the BEM might support that party whose candidate held the better policy on the Vietnam War. Willens also said that the BEM was applying pressure on major financial contributors of both parties to withhold convention support from "any candidate who does not adopt a clear-cut, easily understandable political solution to the Vietnam War."

In 1968 and 1969, the BEM continued to grow and continued to place advertisements in newspapers. As a recruiting measure, they employed David Schoenbrun, a leftist commentator who spoke to business groups throughout the country and who appeared in a 30-minute BEM film which was shown to groups when Mr. Schoenbrun was unable to make a personal appearance.

In 1969, the BEM became quite impatient with the Nixon Administration's Vietnam policy. One of the most dramatic examples of this impatience was the BEM's active participation in the Vietnam Moratorium demonstrations, which were thoroughly saturated by leftist and pacifist groups. On November 12, 1969, in the *New York Times*, the BEM ran a full-page advertisement with the headline: "That Effete Corps of Impudent Snobs is About to Do It Again." In the text of the advertisement, BEM said: "There is nothing impudent about honest disagreement. What is impudent, what is really cheeky, is to cover all those who observed the Moratorium with one large vituperative blanket.

"We, Business Executives Move for Vietnam Peace (BEM), were out there. And we neither hate barbers, our fathers, nor the establishment. We are very much part of the·establishment. All 2,600 of us across the country are owners, officers or major executives of companies. It is our collective, pin-striped opinion that the war makes no moral, economic, or legal sense. The country is in a war never duly declared by Congress, taking place largely because we ignored the 1954 Geneva Agreements, and continuing mainly on its own insane momentum to the detriment of more valid and honorable social problems here at home.

"If you agree with us, we'd like to see you out there November 13, 14, and 15 [at the Vietnam Moratorium demonstrations]. Never mind what you do for a living or how you dress. We impudent snobs have to stick together. But if you're a business executive, we're asking for more than your attendance. Help us pay for more ads. Help us make our message felt in government. Speak before groups. Lend our cause the well-earned respect and prestige your name would bestow on it. We know how to make things run, how to make money. Let us see if we know how to make peace."

BEM fliers circulated at the time of the November 1969 Vietnam Moratorium did not differ substantially in their content from those distributed by scores of leftist and pacifist groups. The emotional language, the righteous presumptions, and the statistics were the same. The text of one flier read: "Here is our answer, Mr. Nixon. We listened to your speech of November 3rd. We listened carefully, and as we listened we hoped for some word, some phrase, some expression that offered us an end to the Vietnam War. We listened, Mr. Nixon, but we heard nothing. We heard nothing because — in spite of your rhetoric — you said nothing.

"You said nothing to assure us that a day would come that we could count on when no more American soldiers would be killed in jungles 12,000 miles from home. (Close to 50,000 have already died.) You said nothing to assure us that a certain day would soon come when no more American soldiers would be wounded in a war Congress has yet to declare. (Over 250,000 are already maimed, blinded, crippled.) You said nothing to assure us that on a given day an end would be put to this conflict which has drained our country's resources (106 billion dollars thus far) and prevented attention to our critical domestic needs.

"Actually, Mr. Nixon, you did say certain things, either by word or innuendo. And from what you said, we infer the following: You intend to continue the war indefinitely if you deem it necessary; You allow for the chance that you may increase our military involvement; You now — without equivocation — identify yourself and your administration with the conduct of the war, and accept responsibility for its course; And you urge that no Americans oppose your attitude or actions, insinuating that those who do are at best 'misled' and at worst 'unpatriotic.'

"Our answer, Mr. Nixon, is that we completely reject your stance on this issue that cuts to the core of our national well-being. We reject it and we resent it . . . and we represent millions of loyal and patriotic Americans. Millions of Americans who — in growing numbers — are sickened in mind and spirit by what is happening to our country. Millions of Americans whose creed is this: 'Not my country right or wrong; my country — when right — to be defended; my country — when wrong — to be set right.'

"That is our answer, Mr. Nixon. And to give voice to our answer we shall again gather as we did on October 15th, to again protest the carnage of Vietnam. We are inviting citizens who share our feelings to join us. We shall listen to community leaders speak out against the war, and during the entire day we shall wear black armbands to signify our grief and sorrow. We shall protest, Mr. Nixon, and we shall continue to protest until our voice is heeded and our country is again at peace. That is our answer, Mr. Nixon."

Henry Niles, chairman and founder of BEM, wrote and distributed at least two editions of a pamphlet titled *Ten Myths About Vietnam.* The pamphlet was replete with inaccuracies, absurdities, misinterpretations, unsubstantiated statistics, and liberal-leftist cliché's. He insisted that the Vietnamese conflict was "essentially a civil war. It is not aggression by a separate country." He said, "We are supporting a government which is headed mainly by persons who are from North Vietnam and who fought in the 1940's and in the 1950's alongside the French against the independence movement of their own countrymen." He showed no indication that he had ever heard of the mass exodus from North to South Vietnam by those fleeing from the real and threatened persecution of Ho chi Minh's regime. Niles said: "We support a regime [in South Vietnam] which was elected by less than a majority of the voters in an election the fairness of which has been questioned." Niles gave no indication that such conditions were not uncommon in the United States and in other nations throughout the free world. He raised the usual argument that the U.S. bombing of North Vietnam had not stopped the flow of men and supplies southward, but he never indicated that he knew that bombing targets were highly selective and that bombing efforts by U.S. forces were deliberately contrived to avoid dealing crushing blows to North Vietnam's war industries or the strategic supply port of Haiphong.

Niles said: "The war [in Vietnam] itself is a bloodbath beyond any savagery in modern times." He conveniently forgot the savagery of Stalin, Hitler, Castro, Ho chi Minh, Khrushchev, Mao Tse-tung, and Chou En-lai. He displayed his ignorance of Asia and Communism when he wrote such statements as: "The major force in Asia is Asian nationalism." — "The revolutionary forces of Asia are mainly nationalist with a touch of Marxism adapted to local conditions." — "Our war against Communism is strengthening it by uniting diverse and antagonistic Communist groups."

The leading lights of BEM include a number of individuals who have had previous affiliations with leftist and/or pacifist organizations. They include Thomas B. Adams of Boston, Roger P. Sonnabend, Stewart Mott (a financial angel to leftists and leftist projects), Theodore O. Yntema, Max Palevsky of Xerox (a company that has lavished support on leftist projects), Jerome Grossman (head of Massachusetts PAX and a leader of nationwide leftist protests), and J. Sinclair Armstrong of United States Trust Company (a disarmament buff). The diplomatic sponsors of BEM are certifiable leftist-liberals: Benjamin V. Cohen, John Kenneth Galbraith, Roger Hilsman, and Edwin O. Reischauer.

In 1971, BEM became increasingly more active in the political arena as its leaders decided to move away from the routine of newspaper advertisement protests, featuring long columns of names. *Human Events* (February 13, 1971) reported on a radio series of free recorded commentaries distributed by BEM: "The series, entitled 'In the Public Interest,' will feature prominent liberals and radicals with token participation by conservatives.

"Robert Maslow, the producer and syndicator of the series, cheerfully acknowledges the series will be 'lop-sided, not two-sided.' The only reason for the sprinkling of conservatives, he related, is to satisfy Internal Revenue Service regulations governing tax-exempt groups.

"Aside from the war in Viet Nam, the broadcasts — each one to be four minutes long — will cover such subjects as defense spending, hunger, disarmament, youth problems, the news media and women's liberation.

"Some of the featured speakers Maslow says he has recruited include former Sen. Eugene McCarthy (D.-Minn.), Donald Duncan, ex-Green Beret turned peacenik, I.F. Stone, the leftist publisher of *I.F. Stone's Weekly* and Sen. Edmund Muskie (D.-Maine).

"*Human Events* discovered last week that BEF's radio project is being conducted out of the Washington offices of the tax-exempt Institute for American Democracy, Inc. [an anti-anti-Communist witch-hunting offshoot of the defamatory Anti-Defamation League], which is supposedly in the business of ferreting out 'extremist' groups. The IAD, however, normally goes after any group to the right of Edmund Muskie.

"Maslow said that the IAD is allowing the BEF to use the office space and phones for free because 'they dig what we are doing.' "

In April 1971, at a two-day meeting of the BEM's national council,

11

Representative Paul McCloskey was urged to enter the presidential primary in New Hampshire. McCloskey, whose commitment to the far left's position on the Vietnam War has made him a virtual renegade from the Republican Party, was assured of support by the BEM leaders.

On October 1, 1971, BEM engaged in one of its bizarre undertakings when it held an "American Peace Awards" ceremony in Chicago. Among the recipients of the awards were such renowned leftists as Daniel Ellsberg, David Schoenbrun, former U.S. Senator Wayne Morse, George Wald, John Kerry of Vietnam Veterans Against the War, and folksinger Joan Baez, who shocked a few in the audience by twice throwing the American flag on the stage floor.

In 1971, Henry Niles, the chairman of BEM, became a special adviser to John Gardner, the head of Common Cause, which has become a leading leftist political pressure group. In 1971, Ben Peckin and Irwin Salk of BEM endorsed the People's Peace Treaty, a Hanoi-inspired project that achieved high priority in the 1971 activities of America's ultra-leftists.

COMMITTEE FOR INDEPENDENT POLITICAL ACTION
NATIONAL CONFERENCE FOR NEW POLITICS
CALIFORNIANS FOR LIBERAL REPRESENTATION
COMMUNITY FOR NEW POLITICS
PEACE AND FREEDOM PARTY

In August 1965, radicals Julian Bond, Simon Casady, and Stokely Carmichael held a meeting of white and black militants in Santa Barbara, California. The meeting was held under the financial and ideological auspices of the ultra-leftist Center for the Study of Democratic Institutions. At the conclusion of their meeting, the radical militants issued a call for a new politics to "the unrepresented, the exploited, the alienated and the manipulated." The call was, in effect, a design for a third political party that would unite the entire Left.

In January 1966, the leaders of the Santa Barbara meeting went to an organizing conference in Chicago of the Committee for Independent Political Action (CIPA). Plans for the CIPA's organization had been described by Austin Wehrwein in the *New York Times* of December 9, 1965: "The first steps have been taken toward the formation of a political movement that would link civil rights, various student protests and opposition to the war in Vietnam, a policy statement disclosed today. An organization meeting has been called for January 15.

"Candidates representing the new, militant left-wing movement will probably be entered in next year's Congressional contests here . . . . Committee officials . . . said protests and demonstrations had already created a 'sizable protest community' and the time had come for direct political action. The policy statement said the election of candidates on 'an essentially radical program' was possible . . . .

"The organizers of the new united front include Paul Booth, national secretary of the Students for a Democratic Society; Dick Gregory, the Negro comedian; Tim Black, president of the Negro American Labor Council; Lutheran, Congregational and Roman Catholic clergymen active in civil rights; Prof. Robert Havighurst, a University of Chicago professor who wrote a report critical of the integration pace in Chicago schools; representatives of peace groups and representatives of Voters of Illinois, an affiliate of Americans for Democratic Action."

On December 10, 1965, the CIPA issued a policy statement calling for "a full-speed program for civil rights, an effective approach to full employment, a sustained fight for civil liberties, and a major campaign for a peaceful foreign policy." The CIPA noted that there had developed in recent years "a sizeable protest community, seeking new ways to freedom, jobs and peace," and that the protesters had engaged in vigils, marches, and sit-ins and other types of demonstrations. The CIPA, however, would concentrate upon an electoral arm of protest, and this strategy was described in the policy statement: "The various protest movements are anti-establishment in the sense that they believe that social change must come about through a confrontation with those who defend the status quo. Sometimes they influence persons in power and sometimes they do not. Their chance of influencing persons in power is increased if they enter politics and work actively for a candidate. The protest movement needs an electoral arm.

"If the candidates of the establishment are not 'good' enough, then independent political action is needed. Running an independent candidate, even if he cannot be elected, helps educate the public. And occasionally an independent candidate can be elected. More often, though, an independent political movement can swing enough votes to elect a good candidate from one of the regular parties.

"It is now time to get a truly independent and anti-establishment political movement going. The undersigned feel that it is time to make the voice of independents felt at the ballot box . . . ."

The CIPA policy statement was issued over the signatures of such well-known leftists as Paul Booth, Rennie Davis, Dick Gregory, Robert Havighurst, Paul Lauter, Sidney Lens, Lucy Montgomery, Jack Spiegel, and Quentin Young. Havighurst and Gregory served as co-chairmen of the organizing conference. The conferees numbered about 800 and included Communists, white and black militants, and leaders of such ultra-radical organizations as Women Strike for Peace, the American Friends Service Committee, the Student Nonviolent Coordinating Committee, Voters of Illinois (a branch of Americans for Democratic Action), and Martin L. King's Southern Christian Leadership Conference.

Among those who addressed the CIPA conference were Monroe Sharp, director in Chicago of the Student Nonviolent Coordinating Committee; Charlie Cobb, the field secretary of the Student Nonviolent Coordinating Committee; Sidney Lens, a veteran radical with close connections to the Communist regime in Cuba; James Bevel of the Southern Christian Leadership Conference; and Paul Lauter of the American Friends Service Committee. Prior to the conference, Lauter had emphasized the necessity of implementing direct action protests with electoral politics: ". . . All over the country those in the 'liberal-radical' spectrum are·turning with new vigor and hope and fresh ideas and techniques to independent electoral politics. The forms of such political activity have varied enormously − from the civil rights voter registration origins of the Mississippi Freedom Democratic Party, to work in the Democratic precincts of Detroit, to statewide organization of liberals in California. However diverse . . . these activities . . . have shown a number of things about independent electoral politics.

"To begin with, men and women devoted to peace, civil rights, jobs, to an essentially radical program, can be elected. John Conyers won a seat in Congress in Detroit despite strong opposition by establishment liberals. Julian Bond, longtime SNCC staff worker, was elected to the Georgia legislature last spring . . . .

"One reason for such electoral success is that the Movements have energized many people who were not previously active in political decision-making in this country. Negroes, academics, housewives, clergymen more and more have participated in the politics of protest. That participation can be carried over into electoral politics.

"Put another way, there have been creative relationships developed between Movement-style political protest and electoral political activity, and these can be expanded . . . the Movement has much to gain in electing new men to office. For protest activities can succeed in pressuring reluctant politicians to pass some laws to relieve the pressure. But only the combination of direct action where necessary and the election of new men . . . representing new constituencies can assure implementation and extension of laws like the Voting Rights and Rent Subsidy bills, and the adoption of new policies aimed at true social change . . . ."

The CIPA prepared a comprehensive political platform for its candidates to guide them on foreign, national, state and city policies. On foreign policy: "(1) Renounce America's policy of unilateral intervention in the internal affairs of other countries and reaffirm our support for the right of people everywhere to determine their own forms of government. (2) End the war in Vietnam and bring American troops home. Negotiate directly with the National Liberation Front for internationally supervised free elections. (3) Support an expanded and strengthened United Nations, cease all military assistance to dictatorships, and redirect foreign aid to the building of free and prosperous societies. (4) Establish diplomatic relations with all countries, curb the influence of American corporations on American foreign policy, and support the right of foreign countries to national sovereignty over foreign investment. (5) Take advantage of the decreased international tensions that would result from a new American foreign policy to press for a genuine international agreement on disarmament."

On national policy: "(1) The people who live in our society should participate in the social, economic and political decisions which affect their lives and the lives of their children. (2) Reallocate our national priorities and finance a real war on poverty, slums, disease, and ignorance by diverting funds from our $60,000,000,000 war budget. (3) Reduce federal tax rates by closing loopholes for high income brackets and initiating progressive corporate and capital gains tax. (4) Extend federal labor legislation and social security benefits to agricultural workers and workers in other inter-state industries not presently covered. (5) Define 'maximum feasible participation' of the poor in the war on poverty as meaning a minimum of 51% on all war on poverty advisory boards. Take administration and control of war on poverty out of politics. (6) Repeal all anti-labor sections of the Kennedy-Landrum-Griffin Act and the Taft-Hartley (particularly section 14b). (7) Enact a $2.00 an hour minimum wage and assert the right (nòt privilege) of every family to a minimum guaranteed annual income of $5,000. (8) No wage increase restrictions from government without corporate profit restrictions. Take wage increases from corporate profits, not the consumer's pocket. (9) Social planning now for automation to prevent future unemployment and to allow all to share the wealth of increased productivity. (10) Extend compulsory medical insurance (Medicare) to all citizens and enact a progressive tax scale for the social security system. (11) Integrate public schools as directed by the Supreme Court in 1954, and initiate a policy of enforcing federal voting rights legislation. (12) Protect the consumer through federal truth-in-packing and truth-in-lending legislation. (13) Assert our commitment to freedom and civil liberties through repeal of the McCarran Act [Internal Security Act] and the Emergency Detention Act, by the abolition of HUAC [House Committee on Un-American Activities], the Senate Internal Security Subcommittee, and all travel bans, and by placing military justice under the review of civilian courts. (14) Restructure the draft system to eliminate social inequity and provide for those who object to specific wars on reason of conscience or higher law. Seek the eventual termination of compulsory conscription. (15) Guarantee independent and minor party political candidates equal access to all news media."

. On state and city policy: "(1) A total restructuring of city and state systems of taxation is required. The sales tax must be replaced by a progressive income tax. Flat rate property taxation should be replaced by progressive property tax. All tax exemptions from income and investment properties of educational and religious organizations should be repealed to prevent the destruction of the tax base. State corporate taxes should have a progressive scale. Tax value assessment must be removed from the influence of politics. (2) Enactment and enforcement of a comprehensive open occupancy law, an end to block-busting, and the location of public low income housing in other than Negro and slum neighborhoods. (3) Abolition of exploitative credit and interest rates. Establishment of a state credit agency serving those currently blacklisted by the private credit and banking industry to provide funds for the purchase and improvement of real estate at reasonable prices. (4) The integration of . . . schools, establishment of a directly elected school board by school districts, and the extension of pre-school education in low income areas. (5) Creation of a civilian review board for the police department. (6) An end to the construction of 'high rise slums' and co-op management by tenants of public low income housing. (7) The enforcement of housing and zoning codes, and the extension of all public services (e.g., street repair, rodent control, public transportation) to all neighborhoods of the city. (8) Recognition by the public aid department of welfare recipients unions and the extension of welfare as a right of all citizens, not a gift. The abolition of means tests, invasions of privacy, and the coercion of welfare recipients by the threat (real or imagined) of withheld payments. (9) Recognition of the right of public employes to strike and to union representation . . . . (12) Reduction of the voting age to 18."

The major effect of the Chicago organizing conference was that a political coalition emerged. The CIPA, pulled together by Dick Gregory, and the Santa Barbara group, led by Julian Bond, decided to call themselves the National Conference for New Politics (NCNP).

In the spring of 1966, the NCNP began a fund-raising effort "to support the campaigns of peace and civil rights candidates in the 1966 elections." One of the first efforts was in the form of a newspaper advertisement ("Your Taxes Pay for War — Will You Pay for Peace?"). The favorite arguments of the doves were a part of the theme: The Vietnam War threatens every family, therefore: "Will our sons go to war or to school? Will our tax dollars be used to wipe out slums at home or villages in Vietnam?" The body of the advertisement read: "The killing of Americans and Vietnamese will not stop unless the opponents of this war, and of the bankrupt foreign policy which it reflects, can turn their dissent into real political power. Fortunately, across the nation, local alliances of issues-oriented liberals, student activists, peace and civil rights workers, and grass-roots movements of the poor are being formed for the tangible ends of winning elections.

"In Oregon, Howard Morgan, former Federal Power Commissioner, is running for the Democratic nomination for the U.S. Senate against a supporter of Administration policy in Vietnam. Morgan is supported by Senator Wayne Morse. Simultaneously, former Congressman Charles

Porter, who has a distinguished record of peace activity, is running for Congress in the 4th district.

"In California, there are 30 anti-war candidates, ranging from incumbent Congressmen George Brown, Phil Burton and Don Edwards to newcomers Ed Keating, Bob Scheer, and Stanley Sheinbaum of *Ramparts* magazine and, from the Watts area of Los Angeles, David Scott, candidate for the State Assembly, who says, 'There will be no welfare as long as there is warfare.'

"In Mississippi, Alabama, Georgia and North Carolina, Negro candidates for local office, ranging from sheriff to state assemblyman to Congressman, are awakening the energies of people long denied any share in shaping their own future, and are now reconstructing the whole of Southern politics.

"In New York State, many vigorous opponents of the war in Vietnam — among them Ted Weiss, reform City Councilman, and Mel Dubin, recent candidate for Controller on Congressman Ryan's ticket — are challenging incumbent Democrats on peace and poverty. In Massachusetts, Thomas Boylston Adams is leading a peace campaign for the U.S. Senate with considerable support from within the Democratic Party.

"Other politically viable campaigns, equally important and promising, are building. The National Conference for New Politics has been created to assist in these developments. The Conference is not an organization established to compete with other groups. Rather it is a cooperative effort solely to provide financial, research, and human resources to those candidates who will speak clearly for peace and for a domestic program commensurate with the great wealth of our country and the needs of its citizens.

"Political campaigns are staggeringly expensive; but we are persuaded that many Americans care deeply enough about the issue of war or peace that they will make great sacrifices to insure that in the next Congress Senators Morse and Gruening, Fulbright and Young, and the few other bold spirits no longer stand alone. Moreover, we believe that they understand the great opportunity offered by the insurgent politics in the South and the ghettos of the urban North and that they will not allow these to fail for lack of funds.

"We have already helped significantly in New York, Oregon, Alabama, and Mississippi, where several thousand dollars in early funds have provided the means to keep campaigns rolling effectively. However, much more is needed. Your money may be the one way in which we can realistically overcome the sense of hopelessness which the real war in Vietnam and the 'half-war' on poverty both engender.

"Since we have a clear obligation to make certain that debate continues on Vietnam policy, and because the nation is as one precinct on this issue, we would hope that individuals will contribute regardless of geographical areas. The allocation of funds shall be determined by the signers of this appeal in consultation with Congressional supporters and the NCNP National Council."

The leaders of the NCNP, in May 1966, were named as Julian Bond, Simon Casady, Rev. William Sloane Coffin Jr. (chaplain at Yale University), and Benjamin Spock. At the same time, the NCNP's national council included: Josiah Beeman, national committeeman of the Californian Federation of Young Democrats; Paul Booth, secretary of Students for a Democratic Society; Stokely Carmichael, chairman of the Student Nonviolent Coordinating Committee; W.H. "Ping" Ferry (vice president), Hallock Hoffman (secretary-treasurer), and Irving Laucks (consultant) of the Center for the Study of Democratic Institutions; Martin Peretz and Lucy Montgomery, financial angels of the Left; Harvard faculty members Pitirim Sorokin, Mark de Wolf Howe, Everett Mendelsohn, H. Stuart Hughes, Barrington Moore Jr., and Samuel Bowles; old-time radical Sidney Lens; Erich Fromm, psychoanalyst; Robert S. Browne of Fairleigh-Dickinson University; Warren Hinckle, executive editor of *Ramparts* magazine; Jerome Grossman, head of Massachusetts PAX; Victoria Gray of the Mississippi Freedom Democratic Party; Alfred Hassler, executive secretary of the Fellowship of Reconciliation; Herbert Marcuse, "prophet of the New Left" and mentor of Angela Davis; Stewart Meacham of the American Friends Service Committee; Sumner Rosen of the American Federation of State, County, and Municipal Employees; Edward Gottlieb of the War Resisters League and the American Federation of Teachers; Robert Silvers, editor of the *New York Review of Books*; Harold Taylor, former president of Sarah Lawrence College; Arthur Waskow of the Institute for Policy Studies; literary figures Nat Hentoff and Lenore Marshall; old-time leftist writer Carey McWilliams; Albert Szent-Györgyi, Nobel prize winner and longtime leftist-pacifist; and Robert Schwartz of the National Committee for a Sane Nuclear Policy.

During the summer of 1966, others joined the national council of the NCNP, including Paul Albert of the California Democratic Council; Grenville Clark of the United World Federalists; Ronnie Dugger, editor of the *Texas Observer*; Richard Hudson of *War/Peace Report*; Don Rothenberg of Californians for Liberal Representation; and Michael P. Wood of the National Student Association.

The Communists showed an early interest in the NCNP. On June 18, 1966, the *National Guardian* reported: "The organization developed out of a year of meetings and talks looking forward to the support of candidates in local campaigns who have accepted 'new politics.' A statement of purpose defines the new politics as 'a politics of ordinary people who want to control democratically the decisions that affect their lives . . . .' This new politics is built by people who demand that our nation fulfill its pledge to abolish racial discrimination and poverty; who understand the necessity of ending the cold war and American military intervention abroad, and creating world disarmament and a decent relationship with societies undertaking revolutionary change; who want to end the depletion of our resources by an ever-growing military budget and use our enormous productive capacity to meet the staggering social needs that led to Watts, for ending the public squalor that disfigures our cities, our suburbs and our countryside, and for building a good society at home and abroad . . . ."

The Communist Party's *People's World* reported on a June meeting of the NCNP and noted with approval the four demands issued by the NCNP: "(1) The end of the Vietnam war, the cold war and all U.S. intervention abroad; (2) The abolition of racial discrimination; (3) World disarmament and a decent relationship with societies undertaking revolutionary change; (4) Use of present military appropriations to meet the staggering social needs of the country."

By mid-June of 1966, the NCNP decided to launch a major fund-raising drive, using recent political successes as a means of attracting a hoped-for $500,000 campaign fund. Julian Bond and Simon Casady wrote in a solicitation letter: "The outcry throughout the world over the bombing of Hanoi and Haiphong is causing countless numbers of Americans to question our Vietnam policy. Their doubts can be turned into dissenting votes if we continue to carry our message directly to the voters.

"The National Conference for New Politics was founded to enable those who work for peace, civil rights and an end to poverty to register the greatest impact by concentrating money and manpower on direct political action in selected campaigns. We have achieved encouraging results in the primaries just concluded.

"In California, eight critics of our Vietnam policy were nominated for Congress in the Democratic primaries. Six other Congressional challengers made strong showings and ran close seconds; among these were Philip Drath (45 per cent of the vote), Robert Scheer (45 per cent), Edward Keating (47 per cent), Stanley Sheinbaum (41 per cent) and Arthur Carstens. In many cases, work in the communities has continued with the hope of building large 'New Politics' constituencies.

"In Oregon, two Congressional candidates and three state legislature candidates who are Vietnam critics won nomination.

"In New York, five Congressmen who are Vietnam critics won renomination. In addition, Jerome Wilson, a Congressional peace candidate, overwhelmed his opponent by a 3 to 1 vote. Seymour Posner, candidate for the Assembly and running on a peace platform, won nomination with 60 per cent of the vote. A major Congressional peace candidate, Mel Dubin, came so close to defeating the incumbent that the election is now being contested in the courts. In the 19th CD, where Theodore Weiss campaigned on a strong anti-war platform, the June primary was also contested in court. It is even more encouraging that the New York State Supreme Court has ordered a new primary in this district.

"In Mississippi, the Freedom Democratic Party ran five candidates for Congress and one for the Senate, an impressive effort. The MFDP outpolled the regular Democrats in Jefferson and Claiborne Counties, the FDP Senatorial candidate, Reverend Clifton Whitley, is continuing the struggle, running as an independent candidate against Senator James O. Eastland in the general elections. In Sunflower County, Eastland's home, approximately 70 per cent of the Negroes voted.

"In Alabama, there were 54 Negro candidates for office, more than at any time since Reconstruction. In at least 7 counties, including Lowndes County, Negro voter registration now outnumbers white registration. There were four Negro winners in the run-off primaries held on May 31; three in Macon County, including Lucius Amerson, candidate for sheriff whose election is almost assured, and in Greene County, where Negroes still cannot attend white schools, a candidate for the County School Board.

"The National Conference for New Politics is concerned not only with the candidate but with his constituency as well. We are encouraged to find that many peace and civil rights candidates who made strong showings in their first bids for office are now seeking to build viable grass roots organizations in their districts to continue effectively the challenge in November and in 1968. NCNP has created a Committee on 1968 to explore methods of keeping peace and social change energies alive after the 1966 election. The National Conference for New Politics has contributed not only to campaigns but also to grass roots organizing efforts in New Jersey, Mississippi and Alabama.

"We believe the results of the primaries just concluded prove the value of encouraging those who work for peace, civil rights and an end to poverty to support key campaigns throughout the country. More than ever, we see our efforts toward greater political effectiveness as the best means of bringing the voice of the people into our local, county, state and national legislatures.

"Over 1,800 donors have contributed to the National Conference for New Politics to support some of these candidates and other effective programs. In fact, demand for financial help during the primaries was far beyond our resources, and a sharply intensified program to raise additional funds for the forthcoming elections is already under way. We are continuously reviewing the needs of approved candidates and will allocate support in keeping with our ability.

"Your financial support will be translated immediately into the activities of the National Conference for New Politics. Although contributions are not tax-deductible, they may be the one way in which we can overcome the sense of hopelessness which the real war in Vietnam and the 'half-war' on poverty both engender . . . ."

The satisfaction of Bond and Casady with the results of the California primaries was shared by the Communist Party. In the Party's *Political Affairs* for September 1966, it was written: "The primary, which showed the increasing polarization of the California electorate under the strains of the escalating war in Vietnam and the unresolved problems of the new stage of the Negro struggle, had as its truly encouraging feature the phenomenal vote for the peace candidates. Incumbent congressional candidates who have notedly criticized the war, Philip Burton of San Francisco, Don Edwards of San Jose and George Brown of Los Angeles, won decisively. But even more significant, the new peace candidates uniformly registered in the neighborhood of 40-45 per cent of the vote in the Democratic primary. Besides the widely publicized campaign for Congress of Robert Scheer in the Berkeley-Oakland area, there were five other such peace candidates for Congress including two in Los Angeles, as well as several candidates for the State Senate and Assembly. Included among the peace votes must be the fact that, as one paper put it, 'More than 85,000 people in Los Angeles voted for a peace candidate who is a well known Communist Party leader — Dorothy Healey . . . running for the nonpartisan office of Los Angeles County Tax Assessor.' . . . The campaign provided an opening to broad sections of the non-Communist left as well as to youth. On campuses where she had previously spoken on the Communist Party generally, Comrade Healey was invited to return and speak on her campaign by such organizations as Students for a Democratic Society, CORE and the DuBois Clubs. Non-Communist youth were among her major campaign workers and literature distributors . . . . What was the significance of the vote? The 86,000 vote was the highest ever attained by a Communist in California for any office where the Communist was not the only candidate challenging the incumbent . . . . The vote was definitely not an anti-incumbent vote. Two other anti-incumbent candidates were on the ballot, one (O'Connor) getting some 240,000, while the other got less than Comrade Healey . . . ."

The success of the leftist candidates in California was due in great part to Don Rothenberg, a member of the NCNP's national council, who worked through Californians for Liberal Representation (CLR). The California Senate Fact-Finding Committee on Un-American Activities reported on Rothenberg in its 1970 Report: "Rothenberg, born July 19, 1924, in Brooklyn, New York, came to California from Cleveland, Ohio, in February 1966. His application for a telephone (526-0210), the one listed for him on the accompanying exhibit, was filed in Berkeley February 16, 1966, and he stated he had recently arrived from Cleveland and was employed by the Californians for Liberal Representation. In testimony before the House Committee on Un-American Activities in Dayton, Ohio, on September 14, 1954, Rothenberg stated that he was then state director of the Ohio Progressive Party. Records of the House Committee on Un-American Activities for August 25, 1966, show that he had been the finance director for the National Rosenberg Committee, later known as the

23

National Committee to Secure Justice for the Rosenbergs and Morton Sobell. Ethel and Julius Rosenberg were executed as spies for the Soviet Union, and Sobell is still serving time on his conviction as a spy. Testifying before the House Committee on Un-American Activities on June 11, 1951, Mrs. Mary Stalcup Markward, formerly secretary of the Washington, D.C., unit of the Communist Party, stated that Rothenberg had been a member of a Communist cell in Washington in 1943, and that he had been a District of Columbia organizer for the Southern Conference for Human Welfare, a Communist front. His subsequent activities have followed the same pattern, according to records of various dates of the House Committee on Un-American Activities, and of the Ohio Un-American Activities Committee.

"Rothenberg, while still active in Californians for Liberal Representation (at this writing, April 1967) is also listed on the masthead of *Ramparts* magazine (March 1967) as assistant to the publisher. Edward Keating, publisher of *Ramparts*, was one of the candidates for Congress endorsed by Californians for Liberal Representation (CLR). He also took an active part in CLR . . . ."

The 1970 Report described some of Rothenberg's CLR associates and circumstances surrounding the 1966 primaries: "As to other members of the CLR, Arthur Bierman, San Francisco State College, and Franklyn Brann were signers of the statement supporting the Free Speech Movement. Malcolm Burnstein was one of the FSM attorneys, and was at one time a member of the firm of Edises and Treuhaft, identified Communist attorneys. Insofar as Richard Strohman is concerned, he has been active in leftist activities on the campus of the University of California. Marshall Windmiller, San Francisco State College, was a contributor to the *People's World* of March 11, 1967, and has long been identified with liberal-to-left causes in the bay area. Thomas Winnett was a member of the Finance Committee in the Scheer-for-Congress campaign.

"However, none of the others approaches Don Rothenberg in importance. A party member of his experience and apparent capabilities can direct the activities of several organizations simultaneously.

"Two more 'peace' candidates were later added to the roster of those endorsed by CLR: Dr. Carlton Goodlett, onetime candidate for Governor, and Robert Treuhaft, for district attorney, Alameda County (nonpartisan). Both lost.

"Soon after the election was over three CLR-endorsed candidates called a press conference to announce that their fight would continue. They were Philip Drath, Edward M. Keating and Robert Scheer. They included in their group the absent Robert Treuhaft, William Bennett and Franklyn Brann of the Californians for Liberal Representation. Scheer led off with the statement: 'I care nothing for the loyalty of the Democratic Party. I'm not a Democrat; I'm a human being.'

"The following day, Simon Casady, identifying himself as co-chairman of the National Conference for New Politics, told the news media that his organization planned to develop 'a skilled cadre of campaign workers to move in where they are needed,' and that the issue on which candidates would concentrate would be ending the war in Vietnam, abolishing racial discrimination and poverty, redirecting national funds from the military to 'social needs'; and 'a decent relationship with societies undertaking revolutionary change.' These then, were the planks of the platform of the National Conference for New Politics.

"Robert Scheer moved quickly after [losing in] the primary to build a permanent organization around his campaign staff, workers and contributors."

In Scheer's renewed campaign, on July 25, 1966, he announced the formation of the Community for New Politics which was, in effect, a California adjunct of the NCNP. Said Scheer in his announcement: "Our campaign was founded on assumptions which are at odds with mainstream American politics. We are concerned with issues and not personalities. We were committed to development of community dialogue and involvement, and not merely to electoral victory. The fact that we obtained an unexpectedly large vote does not change this commitment, but rather reinforces it. The Community for New Politics was formed to carry out this commitment. We are, in fact, in a very favorable position to implement a 'new politics.' The campaign produced strong community ties and the beginnings of a serious program. If we succeed in new politics, it will serve as a much needed mode for American political life. If we fail to seriously attempt it we betray not only the larger community but our most significant hopes as well. This will be a more difficult period than that which preceded the election — it requires all of our support."

In September 1966, Scheer revealed that his Community for New

Politics would work alongside Californians for Liberal Representation to promote a statewide conference on New Politics. The conference, held from September 30 until October 2, was given support from practically every leftwing organization in California. The sponsors of the conference were California's most prominent old and new leftists, including Bettina Aptheker, Jim Berland, Carl Bloice, Farrell Broslawsky, Arthur Carstens, Simon Casady, Mark Comfort, Phil Drath, H. Bruce Franklin, Rev. Stephen H. Fritchman, Dr. Carlton Goodlett, John R. Haag, Terence Hallinan, Timothy F. Harding, Warren Hinkle, Prof. Donald Kalish, Edward Keating, Pierre Mandel, Linus Pauling, Irving Sarnoff, Stanley Sheinbaum, Robert Treuhaft, Rev. W. Hazaiah Williams, and Marshall Windmiller.

To the conferees, Scheer propounded a list of questions which were obviously rhetorical in nature: "What bold, effective action can we take, on a statewide level, against the war in Vietnam? — How can we convince thousands more Californians to join us in action against the war? — Can the peace movement work effectively with civil rights and other movements to stop the war? How? — How can the anti-war forces in this state consolidate enough power to have an impact which will change policy?

"How can Mexican-Americans and Negroes gain greater political power in this state? — How do we begin to implement effective solutions to the problems of the ghetto? — How can we win significant minority representation at all levels of the political power structure? — What does 'Black Power' mean for California? — Can Negroes and Mexican-Americans work together for mutual gains? On what issues? What will the role of the white liberal be in this struggle?

"How can liberals in labor and the community at large work together more effectively for economic justice? — What can be done about escalating prices, taxes, rents and insurance rates? — How can we work for full employment and/or guaranteed annual income? — How can the poor gain greater control of anti-poverty programs?

"What actions can we take to protect our right to dissent while also expanding our civil liberties? — How can we effectively combat right-wing influences? — How can movements concerned with civil liberties relate to each other?

"What are our choices in the November elections? — On which issues do we judge our support of candidates? — Should we support Governor

Brown? Is there an alternative? — Should we concentrate on the State legislative and Congressional elections in November?

"How can we prepare for electoral action in 1967, 1968 and beyond? — Can we use existing political machinery for effective action on issues? — What can we do to build and support grass-roots political organizations? — How can we find and develop candidates who will truly represent us?

"How can we organize effectively on a statewide level? — Can we coordinate existing statewide, local and 'single issue' groups? — Should we concentrate on strengthening existing groups? — Should we attempt to build a new organization? — How should we deal with the possibilities for third party politics in this state?"

In the November 1966 elections in California, Scheer and his fellow CNP candidates were unsuccessful. Scheer, however, kept the CNP intact and decided to concentrate on the April 1967 municipal elections in Berkeley. On the formal CNP slate were Robert Avakian, Ronald Dellums, Howard Harawitz, Robert Kaldenbach, J.B. Neilands, and Hazaiah Williams — all of whom had strong leftist credentials. Communists and their fellow travelers were active supporters of the CNP candidates. And the ideological position of the CNP was adequately described in an advertisement placed in the March 31, 1967 issue of the *Berkeley Barb*: "This country has been in the grips of hysterical anti-communism for 20 years. This hysteria has been responsible for McCarthyism, FBI harassment, CIA intrusion into domestic institutions and the insane and reactionary foreign policy which produced the war in Vietnam. A rational approach to Communism and revolution is a prerequisite to a peaceful world.

"The CNP refuses to practice guilt by association or red-baiting. We welcome as members all who will work for an end to the Vietnam war, conversion of our war economy to peaceful production, a solution to the critical domestic problems of racism and poverty and unemployment, and the development of a more democratic society . . . ."

In the Berkeley elections, Dellums and Williams were successful and the other CNP candidates, although losers, made respectable showings. In 1970, as a New Politics candidate, Dellums was elected to the U.S. House of Representatives.

In 1966, on the national scene, the NCNP concentrated its energies upon the congressional elections — "a test of confidence in Lyndon

27

Johnson." In its campaign literature, the NCNP said: "The November elections pose a test of confidence in Lyndon Johnson. Every vote cast for an opponent of the war in Viet Nam is a vote against the belligerent foreign policy of the Johnson administration and the deceptions with which it has undermined democratic institutions.

"In the Congressional districts around the country, a grass roots movement for peace is challenging the destructive consensus of the cold war; in many of these, electoral victory can now transform dissent into real political power.

"Almost alone in Washington, a handful of Senators and Congressmen has been seeking to put the issues of this war before the people. They must be joined by others on all levels of government and throughout the country. This will not happen unless Americans care deeply enough to support 'new politics' candidates against the 'old politics' of military intervention abroad and racial and economic injustice at home.

"The National Conference for New Politics is assisting issues-oriented liberals, peace and civil rights activists and anti-poverty organizations who are striving to win elections. It is a co-operative effort to provide financial, research and human resources to those candidacies and constituencies speaking clearly for peace and a full scale assault on the root causes of poverty. It is now abundantly clear that the cost of the war has doomed hopes of any meaningful attack on our slums and ghettos. We can no longer be satisfied with politicians who whisper sentiments for peace in private that they fear to utter in public."

Most of the congressional candidates supported by the NCNP were Democrats, including incumbent Representatives George Brown, Philip Burton, and Donald Edwards of California; John Conyers of Michigan; John Dow and William Fitts Ryan of New York; Edith Green of Oregon; and Robert Kastenmeier of Wisconsin. Others running as Democrats included former Representative Charles O. Porter of Oregon, Sheldon Clark of Ohio, Lawrence Sherman of California, and Charles Tsapatsaris of Massachusetts. In several states, the NCNP supported Liberals and Independents. The eight incumbents supported by the NCNP were reelected.

In 1967, the NCNP arrived at the peak of its power when it held a Labor Day convention in Chicago. The formal "Call to Convention" was written by Arthur Waskow: "This is the American present: We need doctors and decent houses and decent food in Harlem and in Harlems everywhere, because slums breed an infant mortality rate twice that in middle-class America. Yet we spend our money on napalm that burns Vietnamese children to death. In order to make children die abroad, we let children die at home. And the President says we have chosen the lesser evil, to avert a greater evil. What greater evil? That both the children of Vietnam and the children of Harlem should grow up and be free?

"Who created the American present? Did the people of Harlem decide that their children should die? Did the people of Vietnam decide to have Americans kill their children? Did our young men – high school students, college students, drop-outs – decide to spend their youth killing and being killed, instead of teaching and being taught, healing and being healed, loving and being loved? Did even our solid middle-class adults decide to make America the scourge of the world? We think not; but it happened. Was it an accident? An aberration? Did it happen because the President usurped power? What happened to the 'checks and balances'? Do the people of Harlem, the younger men, and the solid citizens have a right to make those decisions? Do the people of Vietnam have that right? All Mankind has a right to membership in the body politic; all men have a right to power, to share in making the decisions that affect their lives.

"Who runs the American present? We do not feel that we now can govern our government. We do not feel that we can even govern our own private institutions – the ones we work in – for our own good: our schools, our hospitals, our stores, our factories, our transportation systems. Who decided that our schools should be dreary, ugly prisons of body and mind, instead of arenas of discovery and conflict of ideas? We didn't. Who decided that strip mining should wipe out towns in Appalachia? We didn't. Who decided to put a man on the moon, to give 80 billion a year to the military establishment, instead of making our country a healthy and creative place to live and raise children? We didn't. Whoever runs America, it is not the American people.

"We intend to build a different American future. We intend to end the destruction of Vietnam. We intend to end the destruction of scores of other countries by the economic and political pressures of the great powers to keep them poor and powerless. We intend to abolish the

29

armies that consume the world's substance. We intend to begin the building of 'Mankind' — which we know our children will have to continue. We intend to end poverty, fear and despair at home. We intend to end the bribery and subversion of our private associations, unions and churches by the secret agencies of 'our' own government. We intend to make our government accountable to us. We intend to make our own workplaces accountable to us. We intend to make the election process meaningful again. We intend to make it available to those who have always been excluded from it. We intend to use other kinds of tactics of creative disorder: sit-ins and marches, rent strikes and labor strikes and school boycotts. We plan to invent our own institutions, to found neighborhood governments based on neighborhood power; to open new kinds of schools and grocery stores and medical centers, new sorts of law firms and social work agencies and research institutes and to transform the old ones. We will not be trapped inside the old parties; and we will not be trapped outside of them. And if we should build a party, it will be not merely a party, but a movement.

"We intend to start now. Many of us started years ago. But we will start again now. We will start again next year, too. We will always be starting, because our vision of the future that we intend to build will constantly be changing as we learn from our new experience, and new people join us. We are making one such new start now, because we are coming together in convention. All of us in the new politics, coming together on the basis of one member, one vote. We who sign this Call see ourselves as midwives only. You are the fathers and mothers of the new politics, just as all of us are its children; reborn in the last few years in the travail of America. We ask all of you to join us to decide how to start again. We want to talk about 1968 and beyond. We start with one commitment! Don't mourn for America — organize!"

The "Call to Convention" was a steering committee composed of Julian Bond, Paul Booth, Carlton Goodlett, Victoria Gray, Jerome Grossman, Lucy Montgomery, Robert Scheer, Stanley Sheinbaum, Andrew Young of the Southern Christian Leadership Conference, Ivanhoe Donaldson of the Student Nonviolent Coordinating Committee, Richard Hatcher (soon to be elected Mayor of Gary, Indiana), William Clay (soon to be elected to Congress from St. Louis), and Myles Horton of the Highlander Center. New members of the NCNP's national council added since 1966 included Donna Allen and Martin L. King Jr. The executive director of the NCNP was William F. Pepper. The coordinator was Michael Wood, formerly of the National Student Association.

Prior to the convention, Michael Wood, writing in the first edition of *New Politics News*, summarized six issues which delegates were expected to discuss: "(1) *Candidates in Presidential Primaries of Democratic Party.* The Republican Party will offer no alternative to Lyndon Johnson's war policy in 1968. Still, we must defeat both the policy and Johnson. Thus, our responsibility can be met only by conducting a crusade in the Presidential Primaries of the Democratic Party. The new politics movement should enter either 'favorite son' candidates in each state with a primary, or a unified national ticket in all the primaries. If Johnson is beat in enough states, and delegations committed to anti-war candidates are elected from enough states, then at the Democratic National Convention uncommitted delegates from other states might well switch support from Johnson to a 'dark horse' peace candidate. The people of the United States would then have a genuine alternative: an anti-war candidate from the Democratic Party, a pro-war candidate from the Republican Party. This view assumes that the anti-war sentiment among Democrats is great enough to defeat Johnson in at least two or three critical states, and that Johnson's falling popularity with rank-and-file Democratic Party workers is enough greater than his power of incumbency that significant numbers of delegates would desert Johnson on the first ballot of the Democratic Convention. This view rejects the feasibility of a third party effort.

"(2) *King-Spock: Third Party Presidential Ticket.* This view agrees with the first that the Republican Party will not be a Peace Party in 1968, but further asserts that, because of incumbency, Johnson can't be beaten at the Democratic Convention, even were he defeated in a number of significant primaries. The American people deserve an alternative, and only a third party can give them one. The most logical Presidential ticket would be Drs. Martin Luther King and Benjamin Spock, who represent between them the combined forces of the civil rights and peace movements while appealing both to Negroes and vast segments of the middle class. Some who hold this view hope that enough votes (perhaps in a four-way race, including Wallace), would be cast for King-Spock to win a plurality, and thus the election. Others don't believe that King-Spock could be elected, but do believe that they would deny the Democratic Party most of its leftwing and a substantial portion of its Negro Vote, without which John Kennedy would have lost the big cities and the election in 1960. This would defeat Johnson and elect a Republican, while allowing the new politics to build its own movement around its own ideas, rather than supporting the Republican philosophy and the Republican machine. Some of this view believe that the Republicans, as the party out of power, are less committed to the policy of escalation in Vietnam and might be persuaded to make peace. Some regard providing an alternative to Johnson in Nov. '68 as a tactical move that does not involve a commitment now to a permanent third party, others see it as clear opening shot in creating such a third party. Still another argument is that participating in a real national presidential campaign would activate people in communities all over America, including those less politically developed, would encourage local candidacies and organizations where these might not otherwise occur, and open new manpower and financial resources for the national and local effort.

"(3) *Local Candidates.* This school of thought holds that the new politics is too poorly organized to be a significant factor in the 1968 Presidential elections; it rejects both of the previous alternatives. The Democratic Party will not only stand firmly behind Johnson, but is irretrievably committed to the cold war and machine politics. While a third party — or rather, a second party, inasmuch as the Democratic and Republican parties are as Tweedle Dee and Tweedle Dum when it comes to basic change — is desirable, any effort to form one now would be premature. Even assuming that a third party could be established in enough states and could attract enough votes to defeat Johnson in 1968, an assumption this view would question seriously, the effort would be penny-wise and pound-foolish. The vast demands it would create on the movement would be so great as to divert available energies and money from the vital task of organizing strong local constituencies. In the history of the United States, premature attempts to run a third-party candidate for the Presidency have broken the backs of emergent movements. This view's priority continues to be to offer candidates at the local level on the basis of multi-issue political programs that clearly offer the people alternatives to the old poli-

32

tics. They feel no compulsion to enter the Presidential arena at this time, an arena in which the cards are stacked in favor of the two major candidates. At a later date the new politics will be strong enough to launch a third party on a permanent basis.

"(4) *Coordinated Campaign of Local Elections.* This view is the same as the previous one, calling for local candidacies, but makes one additional assumption: the new-politics movement, as well as the peace movement, is beginning to feel a need for some kind of national editorial opposition to Johnson in 1968. In order to avoid the inevitable defeat of a third party Presidential effort, a nationally coordinated campaign of local candidacies should be advanced by the new politics to fill the need for national expression. Local candidates would assemble in convention to express common opposition to the policies of both major parties and to adopt a common minimal platform. Common colors and slogans would be adopted to further establish the national identity and a national secretariat would be established to serve as national spokesman for the coordinated campaigns. The secretariat would also provide basic services in the way of research, printing, and fund raising. It would preach the gospel of grass-roots democracy: Presidential elections can only reflect sentiments that already exist at the grass roots; fundamental social change can be generated only by organizing from the ground up. The New Politics, in this view, should await a later date for entry into Presidential politics.

"(5) *Favorite Son Presidential Campaigns in Separate States.* This view shares the organizational perspective of No. 3 and No. 4, does not feel a need for nationally identified electoral actions yet identifies strategic objectives attainable through Presidential politics at the state level. The new politics, in this view, should select a few key industrial states and run 'favorite sons' of the new politics for President in the main election. Thus, Simon Casady might head a ticket in California, Dick Gregory in Illinois, and Adam Clayton Powell in New York. By running separate tickets in separate states, the new politics would stress the strategic nature of the campaigns, while not allowing its efforts to be judged a failure for not having taken over the White House. The strategic objectives are (1) the defeat of Johnson; and (2) the denial of a large percentage of the Negro vote – highly important to the Democratic Party in recent elections – to the Democratic Party,

33

thereby developing an independent Negro vote with an ability to bargain with the various powers that be.

"(6) *King-Spock: 'If not nominated, I'll run; if not elected, I'll serve.'* This view shares the perspective of No. 4, which calls for a coordinated campaign of local candidates. Yet, it would add the super-structure of a mock Presidential campaign to enhance the national visibility of local new politics. A mock election, while pointing out the fraudulent nature of the choices offered by the two major parties, would not allow the new politics to be roundly defeated in the lists at the national level. On election day, regardless of the votes accumulated by the other two parties, the vote claimed for King-Spock would be the total vote cast for new politics candidates in local elections. During the campaign, Drs. King and Spock would barnstorm the country, like any other Presidential campaign, encouraging all those who truly desire peace abroad and a new society at home to join with the new politics movement in campaigns at the local level. This view holds that vast new constituencies could be activated around this program, especially in younger middle class circles."

In pre-convention issues of *New Politics News*, various radicals submitted position papers to be considered by the would-be delegates. Martin Peretz of Harvard University, a generous financial benefactor to many leftist causes, wrote of his concern that the convention might become the place "where the lefts engaged in mutual vituperation and in fratricide, where ideological absolutism displaced both theory and concrete analysis." He was of the opinion that radicals had failed to recruit the masses of American people because there had been too much reliance upon slogans, physical demonstrations, intimidation, and threats. He felt that electoral politics was the soundest policy and the means of achieving radical goals. He wrote: "There are millions of Americans ready to vote for peace and hundreds of thousands eager to work and educate for the corollary program of social reconstruction. The new world will not come tomorrow; but how are our people to know what we would intend it to be? We have not even hinted at what we mean by 'radical social change.' That is why more people have not even responded to the challenge we think we have laid down."

Peretz suggested a six-point program for the radicals to follow: "(1) We require electoral campaigns aimed first of all at an end to the war in Vietnam and a prompt return home of our troops. (2) We must retrieve that long-discarded plan of full employment in a full-production economy as the only solution to the immoral priorities of corporate capitalism and its misuse of national wealth. (3) We should call and plan for the construction of dozens of new cities in the vast stretches of empty land in our country as the only way to break out of the prison of our urban areas and revive the dignity of creative and adventurous work. (4) We must point to the immoral and regressive nature of our tax system as an offense to human values and as an indefensible reward for non-earned and inherited capital. The present system should be replaced by a tax system, limiting incomes now and reducing income inequalities drastically from generation to generation.

"(5) We must face up to the vast amounts of public power held in private hands. The concentration of wealth, influence, and opinion control in the possession of the relative few is the most vexing problem for our society; and no ready and very acceptable solution is available from any other extant social order. All the same, I am persuaded that even sheer and bold description of corporate concentration can radicalize our citizenry sufficiently to make it search for radical answers. What is very clear, however, is that land reform in many rural areas of America is as indispensable as it is in Viet Nam. (6) We must illumine the structural and functional inadequacies of the present federal system. But this is a long-term and total issue. Localism, as now proffered on the left, opens the country to the entrenchment of reactionary power. In community after community, let us say Cicero as an example, localism would mean a provincial and primitive fascism. Moreover, without an enrichment of the idea of material responsibility, localism will prove to be the creation of new forms of exploitation. We dare not become the chief purveyors of a program for the poor that will amount at best only to a redistribution of poverty and the establishment of new bureaucracies at its helm."

Professor Curtis MacDougall of Northwestern University, a veteran of the 1948 Progressive Party of Henry Wallace, was most pessimistic of any third-party success for the NCNP. He considered professional politicians as vital to any success and he could not anticipate that office-holders would desert either the Republican or Democrat parties no matter how sympathetic they were to radical politics.

Rennie Davis and Staughton Lynd were co-authors of a position paper which advised the disbanding of the NCNP. They gave as their

35

reasons: "NCNP is perceived by black radicals and by the poor as an organization controlled by, and interesting to, the white middle-class. That perception seems to us correct . . . . Whether its orientation is to national or local electoral action, NCNP represents a turn toward electoral politics without first having built a base through non-electoral organizing. We think this is the wrong way to organize anyone, and particularly disastrous when the people at the top are white middle-class intellectuals and those whom the Movement most wants to organize are not. We believe black people must lead an American radical Movement and that national organization will become appropriate only when regional radical networks, with black leadership, call it into being."

Sidney Lens of the NCNP's national council issued two warnings to the delegates. In the first, he said that the NCNP should run candidates for local as well as national office and, in the beginning, exert more energies for the local candidates. In his second warning, he advised strongly against too much reliance upon electoral politics. Lens wrote: "The New Politics convention is a major step forward not only for the enlightened elements in the United States but for the nation itself, and by extension the world. It is a beacon against the darkness of Vietnam, the arms race, resurgent colonialist attitudes, continued racism, and the hoax of antipoverty. It can be an immeasurable step towards introducing maturity into the American political system. But it will not only fail, it will be − as the new word has it − 'counter-productive' unless it measures electoral politics against the whole political spectrum.

"The rest of the spectrum includes simple pressures such as letter-writing; more sustained pressures such as lobbying; dissent such as teach-ins, mass meetings, and written discussion of the issues; protest such as vigils, demonstrations, marches, parades; resistance such as civil disobedience, sit-ins, lie-ins, refusal of induction; and finally, as in 1776 when all else failed, revolution . . . . New Politics will be effective only to the extent that it not only canvasses, campaigns and votes, but marches, vigils, protests and commits civil disobedience."

Jack Spiegel, a trade union organizer who had been affiliated closely with the Communist Party since the early 1930's, was enthusiastically in favor of the NCNP convention and was hopeful that it would launch a third party. He wrote: "Should an independent Peace and Freedom ticket be decided on, no sector of the movement will be harmed. On the contrary – all can benefit by it. It could have far-reaching consequences for peace and freedom throughout the land and around the world; it would not be the millenium, but an advance, and an important step toward it. It could become the means of reaching nation-wide audiences with the inspiring message and a program of Peace and Freedom, and thereby set new millions into motion and into organization."

Paul Booth of the NCNP's national council and a top official of the Marxist-oriented Students for a Democratic Society offered the convention one of the most militant position papers. He felt that a third party movement was a bit premature. Yet, at the same time, he believed that a third party movement could serve as a rallying point for radicals.

Booth wrote of priorities for the insurgent movements represented in the NCNP: "One priority for the anti-war movement is to break out of the strait-jacket that confines it to the intellectual middle class. An electoral campaign practically forces it to do that, pushing its adherents into unfamiliar neighborhoods in search of allies and supporters. But there are other priorities which do not fit so neatly into an electoral context: (1) Protesting the election of pro-war candidates to national office. An anti-war campaign for President will receive about as many votes as protest campaigns for the House and Senate received in 1966 – up to 3 per cent or possibly 4 per cent on a third line, or 10-20 per cent in the Democratic primaries. And the protest is muted in the secret voting places. A boycott has similar problems. I believe that massive demonstrations at the national party conventions are one preferable course of action. As well, NCNP should pledge to organize a protest in Washington on January 20, 1969, if a war President is to be inaugurated that day; this will have particular weight if we tie this pledge to the likely event that anti-war candidates will be ruled off the ballot in several states.

"(2) Deepening its attack on the institutional roots of the war, in imperialist economic practices and in the military-industrial complex. Certainly this would be forwarded by candidates who articulate these facts. But this is no substitute for other means of raising these facts: direct action (a march on the CIA headquarters, a sit-in at the Green Beret camp, draft resistance); journalism of exposure (U.S. penetration of Latin-American economies, the CIA, the real meaning of foreign aid); etc. A Negro candidate for President could give important boosts to efforts to organize the Negro community on a permanent basis if he chose to. His speeches in the local churches could tell the people that voting was not enough, that they had to participate in the ongoing programs of the welfare unions and neighborhood organizations he identified. New groups springing up for the campaign work would represent a break with the Democratic Party, and might well be turned into permanent organizations. The campaign might also project nationally a fundamental program for change in the conditions of American Negroes. Scattered community movements around public welfare, urban renewal, slum housing, and schools, have frequently been blunted by the need for national programs to affect local conditions. It is a national decision that keeps the appropriations for low-cost public housing at a pitifully low level. National standards for welfare assistance, for public housing admission, and for enforcement of civil rights laws are part of the problem. The federal income tax law could be an object for attack. For those questions of the ghetto that are fundamentally problems of the distributions of income and resources, a national program is needed. So a campaign that would propose a tax program, a guaranteed income program, a housing program, and a schools program, that would involve genuine redistribution from the propertied rich to the poor, would be serving an important function."

Those who organized the NCNP were conspicuously patronizing toward black militants. On August 6, 1967, the NCNP's executive board adopted a "Resolution on the Rebellions." It read: "We share the feelings of powerlessness that led to black uprisings in cities across the nation. We understand these uprisings as revolts against the condition of abject poverty and as attempts to combat police oppression. We saw, in our own land, the shooting and killing of women and children in their homes and of young men in the streets. We condemn the cruel and primitive social system that places property values above human values, demonstrated by the behavior of police, the intervention of federal troops, and the wanton use of military force by the national guard.

"We believe that there can be no peace in our cities until police forces stop being occupation armies in black and other poor communities. This requires the transfer of power from the police to the people of the local communities. This solution to the misuse of police power is necessary throughout the nation. We believe the country cannot live in peace until there is a major transfer of resources and energies away from the conduct of despicable foreign wars and toward the total reconstruction of our cities. While massive allocations of funds are essential to this job, the decisions of how such funds shall be used must rest with the community people themselves. We have long called for an end to economic exploitation of the poor in our cities; but the failure of liberal solutions to this ill now convinces us that collective ownership of property and control of local business within the ghettoes must now be vested in the people."

In a pre-convention issue of *New Politics News*, a racist diatribe delivered by Floyd McKissick to a recent National Black Power Conference was offered to the delegates because it "contributes much to the dialog on perspectives for New Politics." In the course of his speech, McKissick said: "Every day, Black People around the world see hunger, suffering, despair, disease and hatred. They see a world of oppression, presided over by a few white people dominating the masses of powerless colored people – on every continent. Black Men have gained a special insight, an almost 'privileged' perception. It is an insight acquired over years of oppression, years without freedom.

"White men live in a totally different reality from Black Men. Their thought processes are molded by experiences foreign to Black Men. Because white men cannot understand Black People or the way they feel and think – they are afraid. The white man knows that he has been the oppressor and, for that, he is guilty. His guilt makes him fear. White people without fear of Blacks are white people without guilt. White supremacy reigns in such distant and exotic places as Europe and South Africa. But the true bastion of white supremacy, that country which makes it all possible, is the United States of America . . . .

"The Black and colored masses are regarded merely as chattel – with a difference. We are mere consumers. And by our consumption of the goods and services of this nation – this economic, political system, we furnish the margin of profit on which the system survives. The system of white supremacy and its manipulators are dedicated to the proposition that the system must be maintained at all cost – even at the expense of Total Destruction of Black and colored peoples in the United States and around the world – that system which exploits, denies, debases and destroys – destroys humanity, values, morality and non-white cultures . . . .

"With the climate existing in the United States, we would be foolish, as leaders, to think that Black People are not being politically oppressed. If Black People got political power, they might be able to merge their values with the values of the dominant culture. And the white man wants to protect his values – particularly his economic values. The materialism which has distorted his dealings with the entire world . . . .

"We cannot let those [genocidal] patterns which have already been applied so successfully around the world and which are already in motion in this country – be carried to their logical, ultimate conclusion. These patterns must be halted now. And we must be the ones to do it. We cannot expect help from anyone but ourselves. Even our friends in the peace movement find it too easy to look thousands of miles away from home and, with much indignation, see the extermination of the Vietnamese. On the other hand, they cannot see ten blocks away, where many Black People are the Walking Dead – dead in mind and spirit, because of lack of hope and lack of chance. We cannot look elsewhere for help. We cannot lean on the crutch of religion. We cannot depend on phony 'coalitions.' We must work out our own methods. We must draw our own conclusions."

The DuBois Club, created by the Communist Party, submitted a position paper and recited the usual litany of leftist complaints: "The primary political issue of our time is the war policy executed by Lyndon Johnson and endorsed by both major parties, and the crises that flow from that policy – the unwarranted intervention of our military, political, and economic power into Vietnam and in scores of other countries throughout the world; the growing expenditure of tax dollars into the war drive and the resulting cutback in funds for the abolition of poverty, for education, housing and the eradication of disease; the drafting of our young men to kill and be killed for no good reason; the growing attacks on the American labor movement; the rise of racism and the genocidal oppression of minorities in America; the growth of inflation and taxation; the denial of civil liberties and increasing corruption in public and private life; the intervention of militarism and big business in American education; and the bribery and subversion of private organizations in our country by secret agencies of our own government."

The DuBois Clubs were in complete support of a third party ticket for 1968 — a Peace and Freedom Party. This was the Communist Party's line as Gus Hall, general chairman of the Party, indicated in the August 1967 issue of *Political Affairs*: "One of the most realistic and promising national movements for mass independent politics is the coalition of independent groupings gathered together under the designation of the National Conference for New Politics.

"Thus far it is a coming together of important forces from the Civil Rights Movement, various sections of the Peace Movement, some trade union groups, organizations and leaders in the anti-poverty struggles, student groups, Civil Liberties organizations and some organized farm groups. It is a movement that has attracted forces from both the independent movements of the past and the New Left groups.

"The New Politics movement is politically and ideologically, as well as organizationally, independent of the two old parties. In local electoral campaigns, it has supported candidates running through the apparatus of the two-party system, as well as candidates running as independents. But it is truly independent of the two-party system, the question of how it runs candidates for political office becomes secondary.

"This is a young movement with tremendous potential. It opens up the avenue for a political alliance of the different mass dreams of struggle, a path that can lead away from separate, fragmented and isolated political movements. It is a movement engaged both in expressing an electoral protest and seeking electoral victories. It has the potential of becoming a winning coalition of electoral forces."

Invited to participate and/or to observe at the NCNP convention were the leaders of such national organizations as Clergy and Laymen Concerned About Vietnam, the National Committee for a Sane Nuclear Policy, the Congress of Racial Equality, the Council for a Livable World, the Resistance, the Inter-University Committee for Debate on Foreign Policy, the Southern Christian Leadership Conference, Spring Mobilization, the Student Mobilization Committee to End the War in Vietnam, the Student Nonviolent Coordinating Committee, Students for a Democratic Society, the W.E.B. DuBois Clubs of America, Women's International League for Peace and Freedom, Women Strike for Peace, Vietnam Summer, the Southern Conference Educational Fund, Californians for Liberal Representation, the Catholic Peace Fellowship, the Fellowship of Reconciliation, Resist, the Medical

Committee for Human Rights, the Committee for Nonviolent Action, state and local branches of the Committee for Independent Political Action, Community for New Politics, PAX, Cesar Chavez's United Farm Workers Organization, the Peace and Freedom Party, peace groups, draft-resister groups, and various "independent" political groups. Also invited as observers were the staffs of leftist publications including *Liberation, Dissent, New University Thought, Studies on the Left, War/Peace Report, National Guardian, Texas Observer, Nation, New York Review of Books, Ramparts,* and *I.F. Stone's Weekly.*

The Communist Party of the United States, which had been more or less stifled on the third-party issue since 1948, was naturally attracted to the NCNP's convention. An extraordinary set of correspondence from Communist Party leaders to convention officials was revealed by Senator James Eastland, chairman of the Senate Internal Security Subcommittee. On July 24, 1967, Arnold Johnson wrote to Convention Coordinator Michael Wood: "In the *New Politics News* with all the information on the forthcoming convention there is a notice that 'deadline for application from groups and individuals wishing to be accredited at the July 29-30 Steering Committee meeting is July 28th.' On this basis I assume that you are accepting applications and I trust that you will consider this letter as an application to attend and be accredited at the July 29-30 meeting.

"As to a bit of information, I am a member of the national board of the Communist Party, U.S.A. and have a responsibility in the areas of political action and peace as well as in the total field of politics. I have been active on the leading committees of the National Coordinating Committee to End the War in Vietnam and more recently, on the Spring Mobilization Committee and its continuing work.

"In the past I was the district organizer of the Communist Party in Ohio from 1940 to 1947 during which time I ran for School Board in Cleveland in 1943 and received some 47,000 votes and in 1945 when I got some 60,000 votes. I have also run for other offices. I became the National Legislative Director of the Communist Party, U.S.A. in 1947 and since then have been on the staff of the national office of the Party except for a brief 3-year sentence under the Smith Act from 1955-1957.

"I make this application to participate in a Steering Committee meeting in an individual capacity with the understanding, of course, that my organizational affiliation is with the Communist Party, U.S.A. I trust the above information is sufficient and that you will let me know the time and place of the Steering Committee meeting by air mail."

On July 24, Johnson also wrote to William Pepper, executive director of the NCNP, expressing the hope that his application for accreditation to the convention's Steering Committee would receive favorable consideration.

On July 25, 1967, Johnson again wrote to Wood: "I am enclosing herewith a copy of the *Worker* of July 16 because I feel you should have directly from us the editorial on the New Politics Convention, as well as other references to the call to your Convention contained in this particular issue. I trust that you will also be interested in the section of Gus Hall's report to a recent meeting of the Communist Party which deals with the question of political action. I am also sending a copy of this to William Pepper."

On August 11, 1967, David Rubin, the national organization secretary of the Communist Party, wrote to Wood: "In accord with the purposes of the Convention as outlined in the Call to the Convention and the Rules and Procedures as presented in *New Politics News*, the following have been elected as delegates of the National Committee of the Communist Party, U.S.A. to attend the Convention: Arnold Johnson, Claude Lightfoot, Gilbert Green, Roscoe Proctor, Thomas Dennis and Mike Zagarell. While we are confident that our policy and activities which can be documented by many publications does not need extensive elaboration, yet we are enclosing copies of pamphlets which can be used for reference.

"We have designated our delegation as representative of our National Committee of 80 members so as to avoid any concept that we are seeking to influence the Convention by the voting strength of our total membership throughout the country. Arnold Johnson and Gilbert Green will be in Chicago from August 28 to attend any preliminary meetings and to confer and cooperate on all matters in which we may have an interest."

Timothy J. Wheeler, who attended the NCNP convention on assignment, said in *National Review* (September 19, 1967) that the Communists flooded the convention. Wheeler presented his own astute observations along with those of others: "For a supposedly New Left affair, the Old Leftists of the Communist Party got a piece of the action early. Labor columnist Victor Riesel reported, 'At the last of its secret sessions, [the Communist Party's] general secretary, Gus Hall, point by point, stratagem by stratagem, laid out the tactics for intense infiltration of the National Conference for New Politics . . . . Hall told his own comrades at the closed, and hitherto unreported, National Committee session that the Chicago parley will have 2,000 delegates. [Almost 4,000 delegates eventually attended.] Since there really is no way to control credentials at this political launching pad, Gus Hall plans to have quite a bloc present.' And so he did.

"Public instructions to the comrades, through the Communist press, were delicately worded but precise. For instance, a *Worker* editorial ('Open and Democratic') pointed out, 'Practically anyone [This Means You!] interested in peace and freedom . . . can come to be heard and participate in the making of decisions — either as delegate or observer. All one has to do is get his union, his shopmates, his neighbors, his organization or his church group to pick him as their delegate . . . . With such an opportunity, there is no doubt that hundreds of delegates from every community in the nation will be at the New Politics convention in Chicago.'

"Such instructions, and publicity for the convention, were greatly facilitated by the proximity of the New Politics convention headquarters in Chicago (27 East Monroe) and the Midwest offices of the *Worker* (27 East Monroe), run by Ted Pearson. Traffic between the offices was heavy. Somebody from the *Worker* office was forever coming over for an interview with the NCNP staffers (a number of such interviews by Pearson and by Mike Davidow appeared in the *Worker*), or to help with the drudge work.

"Meanwhile, backstage, the Dialogue between the CPUSA and the NCNP proceeded, not noticeably troubled by the New Left-Old Left enmities the press is so fond of reporting. Example: '[Students for a Democratic Society leader Paul] Booth conceded that there might be Communists in his 5,000-member organization, but he rejected suggestions that the Communist Party might have infiltrated SDS. He said it was the other way around. Three SDS observers will attend the forthcoming convention of the Communist Party . . . and through lobbying would help the party's young generation of some 500 newly recruited members to "democratize and radicalize" the Communist Party . . . . Patronizing remarks about the Communist Party, which was pictured as a coterie of "tired bureaucrats and doctrinaires" were heard also from other young members of antiwar groups.' (Paul Hoffman, the *New York Times*, June 10, 1966.)"

The *Chicago Tribune* (August 31, 1967) reported: "Federal and local security officers who are closely observing proceedings of the Convention said several hundred known Communists are attending as delegates or observers." Gary Allen, who attended the convention on assignment from *American Opinion*, and Wheeler of *National Review* encountered a good share of the Communist representation, including Mike Eisencher, midwest director of the DuBois Clubs; Joseph Brandt, general manager of the *Worker*; John Abt, general counsel for the Communist Party; Ishmael Flory, Lulu Saffold, and Alfred McPherson of the Afro-American Heritage Association; Dorothy Healey of California; LeRoy Wollins, Rose Chernin, John Rossen, Richard Criley and Jack Kling of Chicago; Dorothy Hayes of the Women's International League for Peace and Freedom; Jesse Prosten, Charles Spencer, and George Powers from organized labor; Don Hammerquist from the Oregon Society for New Action Politics; Lou Diskin, manager of the Communist Party's bookstore in Chicago and also manager of the literature room at the Convention; Frank Wilkinson of the National Committee to Abolish the House Un-American Activities Committee; Hunter Pitts O'Dell, aide to Martin L. King Jr.; Carl Braden from the Southern Conference Educational Fund; William Howard Melish of Brooklyn; and the delegates from the Communist Party hierarchy: Thomas Dennis of Detroit, Arnold Johnson, Gilbert Green, and Mike Zagarell of New York, Claude Lightfoot and James West of Chicago, and Roscoe Proctor of Oakland.

Martin L. King Jr., keynote speaker at the Convention, was asked by a reporter if he thought the NCNP had been infiltrated by Communists. He responded: "I am not aware of any Communist influence or infiltration of the group. And as a Baptist preacher I am strongly opposed to that philosophy." King was a logical choice for keynoter. He was being suggested by many as the presidential candidate on a Peace and Freedom ticket. He was one of the first to allege that American Negroes were being used as cannon fodder in Vietnam. He was one of the first to allege that the war in Vietnam was depriving American Negroes of their handouts from the federal government in the United States. He was one of the first to encourage a merger of energies between civil rights agitators and peaceniks. (On February 25, 1967, at Los Angeles, King said: "A war in which children are incinerated, in which American soldiers die in mounting numbers, is a war that mutilates the conscience. These casualties are enough to cause all men to rise up with righteous indignation and oppose the very nature of this war . . . . The greatest irony and tragedy of all is that our nation, which initiated so much of the revolutionary spirit of the modern world, is now cast in the mold of being an arch anti-revolutionary. We are engaged in a war that seeks to turn the clock of history back and perpetuate white colonialism . . . . The bombs in Vietnam explode at home: they destroy the hopes and possibilities for a decent America . . . . Those of us who love peace must organize as effectively as the war hawks. As they spread the propaganda of war we must spread the propaganda of peace. We must combine the fervor of the civil rights movement with the peace movement. We must demonstrate, teach, and preach until the foundations of our nation are shaken . . . ."

In his keynote address to the NCNP convention, King delivered the pure Communist line: "These are revolutionary times. All over the globe men are revolting against old systems of exploitation and oppression, and out of the wombs of a frail world new systems of justice and equality are being born . . . . We in the West must support these revolutions . . . a morbid fear of Communism [has made Americans] the arch anti-revolutionaries. This has driven many to feel that only Marxism has the revolutionary spirit. Communism is a judgment of our failure . . . .

"We have deluded ourselves into believing the myth that capitalism grew and prospered out of this Protestant ethic of hard work and sacrifices. The fact is that capitalism was built on the exploitation and suffering of black slaves and continues to thrive on the exploitation of the poor — both black and white . . . . The way to end poverty is to end the exploitation of the poor, ensure them a fair share of the government's services and the nation's natural resources . . . .

"We must recognize that the problems of neither racial nor economic injustice can be solved without a radical redistribution of political and economic power."

Early in the convention proceedings, the Communists realized that black militants did not regard King as a suitable presidential candidate. Then, many of the black militants and many of the younger white

COMMITTEE FOR INDEPENDENT POLITICAL ACTION

activists let it be known that they opposed the formation of a national third party. Under such circumstances, the Communists dropped King's candidacy and the third-party plans. Eventually, the convention voted against a national third-party ticket but voted in favor of independent presidential slates wherever local groups felt that they could wage a productive campaign.

The Communists were especially anxious not to antagonize the black militants who attended the convention in great force. They were there from the Congress of Racial Equality, the Student Nonviolent Coordinating Committee, and the Revolutionary Action Movement. The most militant black leaders were on the scene: Floyd McKissick, H. Rap Brown, and James Forman.

During the first three days of the convention, the black militants boycotted the proceedings and held their own Black Caucus. When they did make their first appearance in the convention's general session, they presented a list of thirteen demands in the form of an ultimatum: the demands would be completely accepted by the convention or else the Black Caucus would leave.

By an overwhelming vote, the demands were given the convention's vote of approval. The demands were: "We, as Black people, believe that a United States system that is committed to the practice of genocide, social degradation, the denial of political and cultural self-determination of Black people, cannot reform itself; there must be revolutionary change. Revolutionary change does not mean systematic exclusion of Blacks from the decision-making process as was done here in this convention. This exclusion raises serious doubts that white people are serious about revolutionary change. Therefore, responding to our revolutionary consciousness, we demand that this conference: (1.) Respond to the importance of Black participation by regrouping all committees, giving fifty per cent representation to Black people. (2.) Make the conference slogan not peace and freedom, but freedom and peace. (3.) Support the concept of self-determination for Black people. (4.) Give total and unquestionable support to all national people's liberation wars in Africa, Asia and Latin America, particularly Vietnam, Mozambique, Angola, South Africa, and Venezuela. (5.) Condemn the imperialistic Zionist war; this condemnation does not imply anti-Semitism. (6.) Condemn the further disenfranchisement of the people of Harlem and demand the immediate reseating of Adam C.

Powell, the duly elected representative of the Harlem people. Powell must immediately be restored to his former Chairmanship of the House Committee on Health, Education and Welfare. (7.) Assist indigenous local freedom and political organizations in voter registration, political education, and the election of Black candidates whom Black people select. (8.) Give support to Black control of the political, economic, religious, and social institutions in Black communities. (9.) Call upon all 'so-called' freedom loving white people who wish to strike a blow for humanity to unshackle their minds from old conceptual structures and deal anew with the Twentieth Century facts of Black liberation efforts. (10.) Make immediate reparation for the historic, physical, sexual, mental and economic exploitation of Black people. (11.) We strongly suggest that white civilizing committees be established immediately in all white communities to civilize and humanize the savage and beast-like character that runs rampant throughout America, as exemplified by George Lincoln Rockwells and Lyndon Baines Johnsons. (12.) Go on record as supporting all resolutions issuing from the recent National Conference on Black Power in Newark, New Jersey. [One of the resolutions called for the study of a plan to establish two nations in the United States – one for whites, one for blacks.] (13.) Support the Conyers Bill to rebuild Detroit Black communities destroyed by Gestapo police tactics and Army occupation."

After the convention surrendered to the black militants by voting for the thirteen demands, the blacks demanded and received 50 per cent of the delegates' voting power. The black militant takeover of the NCNP was for all practical purposes complete and the white delegates were content to listen to outrageous black militant harangues, such as that delivered by James Forman, who arrived on the scene with bodyguards and a retinue of followers. Said Forman: "We are not Americans, we are Africans . . . . Those of us who have been trained to fight in Vietnam, for example, and do not want to fight and live in this country, may very soon have to form a Black International and return to Africa to fight or die for the liberation of the Mother Country. Africa is our home! One Africa, One People! . . . We Blacks, and we alone, have the responsibility to wage our own war of liberation as we see fit. No one, absolutely no one in the world or the United States, has the right to dictate to us the forms of our struggle. We insist on our right to define the manner in which we will fight our aggressors. It is our right, our responsibility, and anyone who doesn't like it can go to hell .... The dispossessed must assume direction and give leadership to the New Politics. If you're not going to support, you go on your merry way, and we're going to liberate you whether you want to be liberated or not .... Black Power is a threat to white power .... We are prepared to wage a struggle to take that power .... If Johnson is willing to use napalm in Vietnam, you know what he is prepared to do to us niggers in America."

In the aftermath of the NCNP convention, the NCNP more or less faded out of sight. A few feeble gestures were made, mostly through newspaper advertisements, to revive the enthusiasm that prevailed before the black militants made a shambles out of the convention. But there was no hope.

The one positive result of the NCNP convention was the formation of the Peace and Freedom Party. It all began in California where Robert Avakian of *Ramparts* magazine, Professor J.B. Nielands of the University of California at Berkeley, and Professor Farrel Broslawsky of San Fernando State College announced that, as members of the Peace and Freedom Party, they would attempt to place a presidential candidate on the 1968 California ballot.

On September 17, 1967, at San Luis Obispo, about 200 individuals met to plan the future strategy of the Peace and Freedom Party. The leaders at the meeting were Avakian, Jack Weinberg, a former leader of Berkeley's Free [Filthy] Speech Movement, and Al Moreno of the Community for New Politics.

A short time after the San Luis Obispo meeting, leaders of the Community for New Politics urged its members to join the Peace and Freedom Party. The signers included Avakian, Peter Franck, Saul Landau, Barbara Garson, Weinberg, Franz Schurman, Robert Scheer, Stephen Smale, Malcolm Burnstein, Howard Jeter, and Broslawsky. Broslawsky wrote: "Active support for the Peace and Freedom Party cuts across sectarian lines and tactical divisions. Radical political militants supporting the Party include Bob Avakian, Mike Hannon, Paul Jacobs, Mal Burnstein, Jack Weinberg, and Robert Scheer. To date, the Peace and Freedom Party has provided a focal point for electoral activity on the part of radicals, intellectuals, discontented middle-class individuals and anti-war activists."

Jack Weinberg became state coordinator for the Peace and Freedom

Party and he was successful in getting enough voters registered to place the Party on the California ballot. Other early leaders of the Party included Paul Jacobs, John Haag of the DuBois Clubs, Hursel Alexander and Frank Pestana of the Communist Party, and Mario Savio, the original leader of the Berkeley Free Speech Movement.

In April 1968, the Peace and Freedom Party formed a working coalition with the Black Panthers, and Eldridge Cleaver, Black Panther leader, was named to the Peace and Freedom's steering committee. The merger with the Black Panthers caused wholesale defections from the Peace and Freedom Party, but nevertheless the Party compiled a slate of candidates: Cleaver for President; Haag for State Senate; Ben Dobbs, an old-time Communist, Weinberg, Haag, and Sherman Pearl for Congress; and Paul Jacobs for U.S. Senate.

In the meantime, the Peace and Freedom Party was organized in other states, but not to the same extent as in California. In August 1968, Peace and Freedom delegations from various states held a two-day convention at Ann Arbor, Michigan, where Eldridge Cleaver was nominated as the Peace and Freedom presidential candidate. (The New York Peace and Freedom Party endorsed Cleaver's candidacy a month earlier.)

Along the way, the Communist Party leaders became disaffected with the Peace and Freedom Party, which it characterized as "ultra-leftist." The Communists boycotted the Peace and Freedom national and state conventions and nominated their own presidential candidate.

Peace and Freedom literature said of Cleaver: "For the first time in many years, we have an opportunity to reach millions of people who are beginning to look for an alternative to Establishment politics, through the nomination of Eldridge Cleaver for president." The Peace and Freedom platform was simple: "Power to the people — Black Power to black people."

Cleaver's campaign oratory was candid and radical: "What we need in America is radical political machinery that is able to move in two directions at the same time, able to harness two, on the surface, different sets of political dynamics — the liberation struggle in the black community and the class struggle in the white community . . . . We believe that the coalition formed between the Black Panther Party and Peace and Freedom Party in California is the foundation of this new and needed machinery . . . .

"The Democratic party and the Republican party are both criminal organizations and they should be destroyed. I don't believe that it's possible for black people to have a good life under a capitalist system . . . .

"The pigs of the power structure say the people are impotent, that we can't control things anymore, that we have to leave things to pigs like Dean Rusk or that Texas pig in the White House. As long as there are people on this Earth they will always be able to take control of their own destiny and pull down the pigs of the power structure. They say, if you want a bad example, look to China. Well I ain't gonna look to China. I done looked to China. And I see Mao Tse-tung took up a gun, took the coolies away from the rickshaw, and now he's got the hydrogen bomb. And I say that's all right.

"They got parole officers out here to monitor me. Up in San Francisco they told 'em to come in here and listen to my speech, to see if I violate my parole, you dig? Well, I don't know what to do about that. As far as I'm concerned, pigs of the power structure's on parole . . . . But there are more people than there are pigs, and the people got more guns than the pigs got guns. I don't say give me liberty or give me death; I say 'Give me liberty or I gonna pick up a gun.'

"I am not a freak for violence. Guns is ugly. People is what's beautiful, and when you use a gun to kill a person you doin' something that's ugly. But there are two forms of violence — violence to liberate yourself and violence visited on you to keep you in your place. We have to make a choice between continuing to be the victim, or decide to take our freedom . . . . If you ain't part of the solution, you part of the problem, you dig? There's no more middle ground. We gonna provide a situation that's gonna force the Babylonians to deal with it.

"Speaking of pigs, I was asked about Ronald Reagan. There's a punk who can read anything they put in front of him and remember it. Then he trots out in front of a microphone and recalls it. Take away all those script writers and bring him out here with nothing and he will revert to his nature and say 'oink' . . . . There gonna be blood on the streets of Babylon."

In the 1968 presidential election, Cleaver received 36,375 recorded votes in only six states: Arizona (217); California (27,707); Iowa (1,322); Michigan (4,585); Minnesota (935); and Washington (1,609). After the 1968 election, the Peace and Freedom Party became almost totally inactive except in California, where it made a vain attempt to elect candidates for Congress and the state legislature.

COMMITTEE OF LIAISON WITH FAMILIES
OF SERVICEMEN DETAINED IN NORTH VIETNAM

On October 28, 1969, William Kunstler, the famed ultra-radical attorney, announced in a press conference that the New Mobilization Committee to End the War in Vietnam [New Mobe] was going to establish an office and a staff for the purpose of receiving names of American prisoners of war held by the North Vietnamese. When the names were received by the new office, they would be relayed to the relatives of the POWs. Kunstler said that the new office was being established at the request of North Vietnamese officials who had talked to Kunstler during a recent trip he had made to Paris.

On December 16, 1969, it was reported in the press media that Cora Weiss was in Hanoi "negotiating" for the disclosure of American POW names. Mrs. Weiss, a co-chairman of New Mobe, was in Hanoi at the invitation of the North Vietnamese government.

On January 15, 1970, in Chicago, four New Mobe officials (David Dellinger, Cora Weiss, Stewart Meacham, and Richard Fernandez) held a press conference and issued a press release which read: "In an unprecedented move, six anti-war activists announced today the formation of a Committee of Liaison with Families of Servicemen Detained in North Vietnam. The Committee will, according to Mrs. Cora Weiss, a co-chairman of the new group and a housewife from Riverdale, N.Y., 'facilitate communication between servicemen held in North Vietnam and their relatives in the United States.'

"Specifically, 'the Committee will receive letters from the captured American pilots,' according to Mrs. Weiss, 'and immediately forward them to the addressee. Also,' she continued, 'we will forward inquiries from families in the United States to the North Vietnamese authorities and they will attempt to confirm the status of their missing relatives.'

"According to Mrs. Weiss, 'the North Vietnamese have agreed to send and receive one letter per month between airmen known to be held in North Vietnam and relatives in this country. Letters sent from the U.S.,' she continued, 'should be addressed to prisoner, serial number, Camp of Detention for U.S. Pilots Captured in the DRV (Democratic Republic of Vietnam), Via Moscow, Soviet Union.'

Packages, Mrs. Weiss added, are not to exceed six pounds. Mrs. Weiss noted that the Committee will forward letters for the families to North Vietnam if requested by relatives to do so.

"Dave Dellinger, the other co-chairman of the Committee and presently being tried on conspiracy charges in Chicago, outlined the background of previous prisoner releases to the American peace movement and said that 'It is understandable that the North Vietnamese indicate their confidence in the American people through the peace movement in this way.' 'We who are on this Committee,' he continued, 'firmly believe that the safe return of American pilots held in North Vietnam can only come with a decision on the part of the U.S. government to withdraw from Vietnam.'

"Mr. Dellinger decried the U.S. government for its ignoring the fate of thousands of prisoners in jails in South Vietnam who, with full knowledge and assistance of American personnel, are subjected to grotesque tortures, as has been frequently documented, most authoritatively by Congressman John Conyers and the Rev. Robert Drinan, Dean of Boston College Law School, in a recent survey of South Vietnamese prisons.

"Another member of the Committee, Stewart Meacham, Peace Education Secretary of the American Friends Service Committee, said that 'Lou Schneider of the AFSC has recently been given a packet of 69 letters in Hanoi from servicemen and those letters will soon arrive from Hong Kong in New York, and will immediately be sent to the addressees.' Mr. Meacham said that 'the 69 letters en route to the U.S. were written by 64 prisoners and the Committee can presently confirm the names of 182 airmen held by the North Vietnamese, or reported to be dead or unknown.' Mr. Meacham emphasized that the list (available upon request) of 182 names was neither final nor comprehensive. He said that 'While these names are known to us, there are undoubtedly others known to their families.' "

In January 1970, families of American POW's held in Vietnam received invitations to attend a press conference at the Cannon House Office Building in Washington, D.C. The invitations were sent out by Women Strike for Peace, and read: "You are invited to meet Cora Weiss and members of Congress to hear her first-hand report from Hanoi.

"Mrs. Weiss went to Hanoi for 17 days in December at the invitation of the Vietnam Women's Union. She had extensive interviews with the

North Vietnamese Prime Minister, with captured U.S. pilots, and with survivors from My Lai. She also travelled through bombed-out villages in North Vietnam, 'seeing firsthand what this nation has wrought.' The 138 letters from imprisoned G.I.s that the women brought back were in some cases the first word their families had received from them in several years.

"Cora Weiss, a leader of Women Strike for Peace, was Co-Chairman of the recent Mobilization March on Washington."

Robert M. Horner, chief investigator of the House Internal Security Committee, has testified concerning the press conference held by Mrs. Weiss. Said Horner: "She opened the conference by expressing criticism of the United States for the massacres which she alleged had been committed by U.S. troops in Vietnam, and said the United States Commander-in-Chief should be held responsible. She described alleged massacres and atrocities which she attributed to U.S. troops and said these had occurred in early 1969. Her source for this information was a document headed, 'The following was received from the Provisional Revolutionary Government of South Vietnam.' She described her inspection of North Vietnamese prison camps in Hanoi and quoted a North Vietnamese official as stating that North Vietnam would not negotiate concerning the treatment of prisoners until the U.S. withdraws all troops completely and recognizes a coalition government of South Vietnam. She said the antiwar movement would handle communications between the prisoners of war and their families . . . . She went on to question the accuracy of the information furnished by [former POWs] Navy Lieutenant Robert Frishman and Seaman Douglas Hegdahl, both of whom described the inhumane treatment given prisoners of war in North Vietnam in their testimony before this committee [HISC] in December of 1969. With respect to the arm injury sustained by Lieutenant Frishman, she commented that since he was caught as a war criminal he was lucky to have an arm at all. She also discussed the excellent living conditions she observed in the North Vietnamese prison camp described as the 'Hanoi Hilton,' but refused to be drawn into a discussion as to whether this represented typical treatment of American prisoners of war in North Vietnam."

In January 1970, the families of American POWs had received an information sheet from CL. The information sheet was of interest on many points: (1) The CL attempted to give the impression that its members had met with their anti-war civilian counterparts of North Vietnam rather than having met exclusively with officials of the North Vietnamese regime. (2) The usual Communist line about the Communists being at war against the U.S. government rather than the American people was emphasized. (3) The CL stressed that the American peaceniks who trafficked with the enemy are the embodiment of American idealism in the eyes of the North Vietnamese. (4) The CL accepted without criticism North Vietnamese charges of atrocities on the part of U.S. and South Vietnamese troops against POWs.

The information sheet read: "*Background*: In the course of the Vietnam war, links have been built between the people of Vietnam and Americans who oppose the war through numerous meetings and conferences. These meetings have taken place in Europe, Canada, Cuba and Southeast Asia and have included people from both the Democratic Republic of Vietnam (North Vietnam) and the National Liberation Front of South Vietnam (now part of the Provisional Revolutionary Government).

"In these meetings the Vietnamese have always stressed a distinction between the U.S. government, whom they hold responsible for the policy of war, and the U.S. people, whom they believe still value the goals upon which this country was founded — independence, justice, freedom and equality. This same distinction is evident to those Americans who have visited North Vietnam and found that even though the nation is armed to defend itself, the people are encouraged by their government to believe that the American people are basically decent and humane.

"It is therefore understandable that the Vietnamese should indicate their basic confidence in the American people through the peace movement which they believe embodies American ideals, rather than the government. And in the past, the Vietnamese have asked the peace movement to receive U.S. servicemen — primarily pilots whose planes were shot down — when the North Vietnamese government has decided to release them. On three separate occasions — February, 1968, July, 1968, and July, 1969 — the peace movement has gone to Hanoi and returned with released servicemen; on one occasion an American peace activist went to Phnom Penh, Cambodia to receive three released NLF captives.

"In addition, Americans visiting Hanoi have frequently carried letters there at the request of families, and have brought back letters from servicemen. There have also been occasions when American peace activists have met prisoners, and talked with them.

"*Functions of the Committee*: A Committee of Liaison has now been established as an extension of these past efforts at the request of the North Vietnamese. As on past occasions, the peace movement is responding to a request by the Vietnamese to meet a specific, immediate need and is not in any sense representing the government of North Vietnam.

"The Committee will seek to facilitate communication between families in the U.S. and servicemen now imprisoned in North Vietnam. Basically, the Committee will receive letters from servicemen and forward them through the domestic mails, thereby decreasing, we hope, past problems in the receipt of such mail. We will also forward letters to North Vietnam at the request of relatives. Families are of course still free to send letters and parcels directly but should note that the instructions on mailing previously issued by the State Department are wrong. The correct address is: name of serviceman, serial number, Camp of Detention of U.S. Pilots Captured in the D.R.V., Hanoi, Democratic Republic of Vietnam, via Moscow, U.S.S.R.

"Requests for information about servicemen from families who are uncertain if their relatives are being held in North Vietnam should be submitted to the Committee, but there is no certainty when and if the North Vietnamese will be able to respond. The Committee will of course transmit immediately any information that it receives to the family.

"*Clarification*: Two clarifications are in order: first, it should be noted that the Committee will be dealing solely with the government of North Vietnam and will not have any information on men held in South Vietnam by the Provisional Revolutionary Government. Nor will we be able to provide information at this time concerning men held in Laos or any other Southeast Asian country where U.S. troops and aircraft are presently involved in combat missions.

"Secondly, the Committee will function entirely apart from the U.S. government. The U.S. government has frequently made it more difficult for the Vietnamese to be open to the concerns of American families by using the families' genuine desires as a propaganda ploy. The government has further attempted to provoke an angry response from the

Vietnamese by publicizing unsubstantiated and inflammatory testimony from fliers already released: apparently, the government has decided to jeopardize existing communications and the possibility of future releases for the sake of propaganda aimed at prolonging the war. The North Vietnamese are also very aware that the U.S. government's claims of humanitarian concerns are contradicted by the well-documented policy of torture and brutality practiced on prisoners taken in the South by U.S. and Saigon troops.

"In addition to all these factors, there is the simple fact that the resolution of the fate of all the servicemen now held in North Vietnam waits ultimately upon a U.S. decision to end the war and withdraw all its forces and material.

"*Who We Are*: We firmly believe that the safe return of these men and the half million others that the U.S. maintains in South Vietnam, Laos, Thailand and aboard naval vessels — who can also be viewed as prisoners, prisoners of their own government since many have been sent to fight in a war against the dictates of their own conscience — can only come with a decision on the part of the U.S. government to withdraw from Vietnam. Because of this conviction, we who are serving on this Committee will continue our efforts to create popular pressure strong enough to force the government to withdraw.

"We are active in a variety of organizations committed to ending the war: American Friends Service Committee, the New Mobilization Committee to End the War in Vietnam, Clergy and Laymen Concerned About Vietnam, Women Strike for Peace, The Conspiracy, and Women Against Daddy Warbucks. The Committee is supported by donations from individuals and organizations, and welcomes any gifts to sustain its work."

In practice, the CL, which posed as a humanitarian group, achieved a monopoly on the exchange of letters between POWs and their families. They used the monopoly to exploit the sufferings of the families and the prisoners. Whenever they did obtain a batch of letters from Hanoi, they announced the event in the glare of publicity, complete with press conferences and television cameras. They built up themselves and the North Vietnamese as humanitarians. They used every opportunity, relating to the exchange of letters, to publicize the fact that the North Vietnamese appreciated and wanted more of "peace" demonstrations in the United States.

The CL, in its distribution of letters from POWs, customarily sent a covering letter to the family and used the covering letter to spread their 'peace' message. A typical example of such extraneous messages was to be found in a letter from CL to Mrs. Dale Ross, wife of a POW: "We are very pleased to be able to perform this service and hope that you will feel free to be in touch with us if you have any questions. In the meantime we continue to work for the immediate and complete withdrawal of all U.S. troops from Vietnam; to bring an end to the fighting, killing and capturing and to hasten the day when all families will be reunited, American and Vietnamese."

A similar message was in a letter from CL to Mrs. Edwin Shuman, wife of a POW: "In closing we wish to express the deep hope that the U.S. government will come to its senses, withdraw its armed forces from Vietnam, and thus make it possible for the families, both American and Vietnamese which have been separated as a result of this cruel war, to be reunited."

Families of POWs were harassed by the CL, which attempted to get the families to join the CL in its "peace" movement antics. The CL deliberately delayed delivery of letters and attempted to use the contents of the letters in publicity ploys.

Representative Richard Ichord (D.-Mo.), chairman of HISC, has said of the CL: "I don't know the motivations of all of these people who serve on the committee [CL]. I think I can speak with some assurance of being right as to the motivation of Dave Dellinger and Rennie Davis ... They [have] made it quite clear ... that they hate this country and everything it stands for and they sympathize with the North Vietnamese ... but I can only say, and I think it is time that the news media start recognizing the fact, that this is the cruelest act that could possibly be perpetrated upon spouses, upon wives of American servicemen now being held in Vietnam. I think it is time that the news media start recognizing this for what it is. This is a product of sick minds, extremely sick minds . . . ."

Representative William J. Scherle (R.-Iowa) said: "How a little band of traitors – and that is exactly what they are, this Committee of Liaison – can degrade and humiliate this country to the extent where they have forced us into the background and taken command of this country, as far as negotiations are concerned, and established contact with a foreign power which is our enemy is totally incomprehensible to me .... To think that we have a band of people — and this is treason, that is all it could be — that would utilize the sacrifices made by our POWs .... It doesn't even border on treason; it goes much further than that."

On the CL with co-chairman David Dellinger and Cora Weiss are treasurer Anne Bennett, who has been affiliated with New Mobe and Women Strike for Peace; Rennard (Rennie) Davis, a New Mobe official, who has been a fund-raiser for the Communist Party's W.E.B. DuBois Clubs; Norman Fruchter, who has had close association with Communists in this country and abroad; Maggie Geddes, who has participated in destructive raids against Selective Service offices; Steve Halliwell, who has participated in Communist-sponsored activities abroad; Richard J. Barnet, an accomplished apologist for the Hanoi regime; Donald Kalish, who has described himself as far to the left of the Communist Party; Stewart Meacham, one of the busiest radical demonstration leaders in the country; Franz Schurmann, a long-time apologist for Red China and the Viet Cong; Ethel Taylor, a sponsor of the GI Civil Liberties Defense Committee, a creation of the Trotskyite Young Socialist Alliance; Barbara Webster, David Dellinger's secretary; and Trudi Young, a national coordinator for New Mobe.

COMMITTEE OF RESPONSIBILITY

In 1967, the Committee of Responsibility was established ostensibly for a highly commendable purpose: to bring to the United States war-wounded Vietnamese children, especially those in need of orthopedic, plastic, or general surgery and subsequent physical therapy. In four years, the CR brought 76 Vietnamese children to the United States. Then, in 1971, South Vietnam's Ministry of Health, which had cooperated with CR, decided that CR should not limit its services "only to the sphere of those children injured by war," and suggested that CR concentrate on the development of treatment facilities in Vietnam rather than remove children who could only be saved by the sophisticated medical treatment available in the United States. CR's insistence that it could treat only war-wounded children, and extend the treatment only in the United States, led the South Vietnamese Ministry of Health to say that CR "cannot distinguish or categorize war casualties" and absolutely cannot "exploit unfortunate children for political purposes."

COMMITTEE TO DEFEND THE CONSPIRACY

In CR's own literature, there is strong evidence that the organization's laudable purpose was, from the beginning, a respectable front for many individuals whose overriding concern was not wounded children but rather the get-out-of-Southeast Asia campaign being promoted by all elements of the American left. In their first solicitations for funds, the CR embellished their advertisements with quotations from the ultra-leftist U.S. Senator George McGovern and the ultra-leftist *Ramparts* magazine. In CR's list of honorary chairmen, three out of seven names belonged to extremely active leftwing-pacifists — John C. Bennett, Bishop Paul Moore, and Benjamin Spock. On the board of directors was William F. Pepper, better known as the executive director of the ultra-leftist National Conference for New Politics. Sponsors of CR included a number of individuals whose affiliations with the extreme Left were so extensive that any reasonable observer would question the ideological-political orientation of any group to which they all belonged. They included Allan M. Butler of the Center for the Study of Democratic Institutions; Stanley Cobb of Harvard Medical School; Rev. William Sloane Coffin Jr., chaplain at Yale University; Edward U. Condon of the University of Colorado; Rabbi Roland Gittelsohn of Boston; Rev. Donald S. Harrington, Liberal Party leader in New York; Donald Kalish of the University of California at Los Angeles (who by his own admission is "to the left of the Communist Party"); Rabbi Edward E. Klein of New York; Salvador Luria of Massachusetts Institute of Technology; Everett Mendelsohn of Harvard University; Anatol Rapoport of the University of Michigan; Rev. Peter J. Riga of St. Mary's College in California, and Albert Szent-Györgyi of the Woods Hole Marine Biological Laboratories in Massachusetts.

As early as 1969, the CR openly allied itself with the Communist-saturated Vietnam Moratorium "in demanding unilateral withdrawal of American troops, and an immediate end to the slaughter of Vietnamese and American lives." Such an alliance was no surprise since so many of CR's leaders have been expressing the same sentiments for several years. The real surprise was that the South Vietnamese Minister of Health ever allowed this group to work in Vietnam.

COMMITTEE TO DEFEND THE CONSPIRACY

In 1968, the Democratic National Convention in Chicago was the scene of riots that were unparalleled in the history of American politics.

In the aftermath of the riots, indictments were drawn against eight individuals who were charged with violating the anti-riot provisions of the Civil Rights Act of 1968. The defendants in the case became widely known as "The Conspiracy." They were David Dellinger, Rennard Davis, and John Froines, officials of the National Mobilization Committee to End the War in Vietnam; Thomas Hayden, a founder of Students for a Democratic Society; Bobby Seale, a top official of the Black Panthers; Abbie Hoffman and Jerry Rubin of the Youth International Party (Yippies); and Lee Weiner, a graduate student from Northwestern University.

In the year between the riots and the trial of The Conspiracy, the eight defendants became heroes of a cause supported by both the old Left and the so-called New Left. The Communist press, the underground press, and the liberal press bombarded readers with pre-trial propaganda that portrayed the members of The Conspiracy as martyrs for the great American traditions of free speech and peaceable assembly. The bleeding hearts of the academy, the legal fraternity, the clergy, the Congress, and the members of The Conspiracy pleaded for the support of the American people, by utilizing every means of communication, in the fight against the alleged forces of repression, the police statists, the "law and order" extremists.

A Committee to Defend the Conspiracy was formed and issued a "Statement of Concern" that was unrestrained in its hysterical and inflammatory language. The usual fright-words were sprinkled liberally throughout the statement: police state – police violence – totalitarian – repression – horrors of Dachau, Auschwitz, and Belsen.

On the eve of the trial of the eight defendants, the Committee to Defend the Conspiracy called for demonstrators to appear at the U.S. District Court in Chicago and solicited funds for the defense of the alleged conspirators by printing the Statement of Concern as newspaper advertisements: "Tomorrow, September 24, 1969, eight American citizens will go on trial on 'Conspiracy' charges as a result of the Democratic Convention in Chicago. They have been indicted under an antiquated conspiracy statute, and the controversial 'Anti-Riot' provision of the new Civil Rights Act of 1968.

"However, what is on trial here are not merely the eight defendants. What is on trial are the rights of the individual to politically dissent, the viability of our democracy, and the future of our children.

"In this decade, countless of Americans have participated (and in some instances lost their lives) in organized demonstrations and protests — boycotts, freedom rides, community organizing, and the peace movement. Their efforts have revitalized democratic politics. Yet civil authorities, unable to cope with a changing social and political tide, have consistently employed police violence to suppress 'the right of the people peaceably to assemble.' The spectres of conspiracy, incitement, and riot have been invoked again and again.

"The 1968 'Anti-Riot Law' is a unique piece of legislation which makes it a federal crime to cross state lines with 'intent' to promote civil disorder. By using the word 'intent,' it establishes guilt not based on physical action, but upon the assumption that the person perpetrated the act within the framework of his own mind (ie: he thought about it). But more important, it subverts the First Amendment guarantee of free assembly by equating organized political protest with organized violence and premeditated incitement. The inclusion of a militant black leader, whose involvement in the demonstration was almost incidental, underlines the punitive nature of this kind of legislation.

"Potentially, this law is the foundation for a police state in America. There were many members of congress who, realizing the disastrous long-term effects of the 'Anti-Riot Law,' were courageous enough to stand up against it. Among those were Senators [Robert F.] Kennedy (D.-N.Y.), [Edward M.] Kennedy (D.-Mass.), [Edward W.] Brooke (R.-Mass.), and [Jacob] Javits (R.-N.Y.), and Representatives [Sidney R.] Yates (D.-Ill.), [Frank] Annunzio (D.-Ill.), [Emanuel] Celler (D.-N.Y.), [John] Conyers (D.-Mich.), [Robert W.] Kastenmeier (D.-Wis.), and [Henry S.] Reuss (D.-Wis.).

"But over these votes of protest, congress passed the bill anyway — just as it will pass additional oppressive legislation now being proposed, unless the American people unite against such totalitarian measures.

"The time to fight repression is when it first begins — even when the initial victims of such repression are people with whom we may not agree. Remember, the horrors of Dachau, Auschwitz, and Belsen didn't happen overnight. They were a direct result of a people who had become apathetic to the suppression of political dissent — a people who felt 'Law and Order' was of greater importance than Reason and Justice.

"The Committee to Defend the Conspiracy was established as a result of the Federal Government's prosecution. It is pledged to support the constitutional challenge of the 'Anti-Riot Act' and the Federal Conspiracy statute, both of which are now at issue in this precedent setting case."

In support of the Statement of Concern was a representative cross-section of the Left, including Gar Alperovitz, Richard Avedon, John C. Bennett, Leonard Bernstein, Julian Bond, Carter Burden, Noam Chomsky, Blair Clark, Judy Collins, John Conyers Jr., Harvey Cox, Ossie Davis, Ruby Dee, Don Edwards, Jules Feiffer, Allen Ginsberg, Paul Goodman, Andrew Hacker, Michael Harrington, Robert J. Havighurst, Joseph Heller, Nat Hentoff, John Hersey, Jane Jacobs, Christopher Jencks, Donald Kalish, Elia Kazan, Jonathan Kozol, Christopher Lasch, Sidney Lens, Helen Merrell Lynd, Dwight MacDonald, Norman Mailer, Stewart Meacham, Jack Newfield, Michael Novak, Conor Cruise O'Brien, Marcus Raskin, Pete Seeger, Roger L. Shinn, Tom Smothers, Susan Sontag, Terry Southern, Albert Szent-Györgyi, Benjamin Spock, I.F. Stone, Harold Taylor, Arthur Waskow, Peter and Cora Weiss, Robert Paul Wolff, Howard Zinn, William T. Baird, Carl W. Condit, Msgr. John J. Egan, Dick Gregory, Staughton Lynd, Curtis D. MacDougall, Dr. Victor Obenhaus, Al Raby, Theodor Rosebury, Alexander Calder, Jack Spiegel, and Rev. C.T. Vivian.

DECLARATION OF CONSCIENCE

In the midst of the leftist-pacifist anti–Vietnam War agitation of the 1960's, four organizations joined together in a project, Declaration of Conscience, which was based on a mixture of hysteria, falsehoods, and tortuous reasoning. The organizations were the Catholic Worker, the Committee for Nonviolent Action, the Student Peace Union, and the War Resisters League.

The "Declaration" read: "Because the use of the military resources of the United States in Vietnam and elsewhere suppresses the aspirations of the people for political independence and economic freedom; Because inhuman torture and senseless killing are being carried out by forces armed, uniformed, trained and financed by the United States; Because we believe that all peoples of the earth, including both Americans and non-Americans, have an inalienable right to life, liberty, and the peaceful pursuit of happiness in their own way;

and Because we think that positive steps must be taken to put an end to the threat of nuclear catastrophe and death by chemical or biological warfare, whether these result from accident or escalation — We hereby declare our conscientious refusal to cooperate with the United States government in the prosecution of the war in Vietnam.

"We encourage those who can conscientiously do so to refuse to serve in the armed forces and to ask for discharge if they are already in. Those of us who are subject to the draft ourselves declare our own intention to refuse to serve. We urge others to refuse and refuse ourselves to take part in the manufacture or transportation of military equipment, or to work in the fields of military research and weapons development. We shall encourage the development of other nonviolent acts, including acts which involve civil disobedience, in order to stop the flow of American soldiers and munitions to Vietnam."

Appended to the "Declaration" was a note of warning: "Signing or distributing this Declaration of Conscience might be construed as a violation of the Universal Military Training and Service Act, which prohibits advising persons facing the draft to refuse service. Penalties of up to 5 years imprisonment, and/or a fine of $5,000 are provided. While prosecutions under this provision of the law almost never occur, persons signing or distributing this declaration should face the possibility of serious consequences."

Leading the signers of the "Declaration" were the brothers Rev. Daniel Berrigan and Rev. Philip Berrigan, who were then emerging on the radical scene as leaders in the anti-Vietnam War, anti-draft agitation movement. They were joined in the "Declaration" project by a group of individuals whose ties to orthodox Communist circles or Trotskyite Communist circles stripped the project of any claims to idealistically or religiously motivated pacifism. They included Kay Boyle, William C. Davidon, David Dellinger, Ralph DiGia, W.H. "Ping" Ferry, Maxwell Geismar, Paul Goodman, Paul Jacobs, Irving Laucks, Sidney Lens, John Lewis, Staughton Lynd, Bradford Lyttle, Milton Mayer, Stewart Meacham, Lucy Montgomery, A.J. Muste, Otto Nathan, Linus Pauling, A. Philip Randolph, Bayard Rustin, and Harvey Swados.

To justify their "Declaration," the signers quoted Communist Norodom Sihanouk of Cambodia: "The more the Americans fight Communism in the way they are fighting it in South Vietnam, the more they'll spread Communism over the region. It is still not too late to stop the war and save South Vietnam from a complete Communization."

A ridiculous statement by C.L. Sulzberger of the *New York Times* was used to dispel fears of Red China's ties with Hanoi: "Ho [chi Minh] worries about Washington's ultimate triumph — the threat of wholesale escalation. Destructive air raids could upset Ho's wobbly economy and invite intervention by Peking's infantry. The last thing Ho wants is Chinese occupation." Richard Starnes of the *New York World Telegram* was cited as an authority on the supply of arms from North Vietnam and China to the Viet Cong: "There is not one shred of credible evidence that the bulk of munitions used by the Vietcong originate in the north. At the outset, the Vietcong used crude homemade weapons, but the bulk of their arms now are captured or otherwise acquired from the woefully inept defenders of South Vietnam."

Other authorities cited by the "Declaration" signers were fellow-traveler Arthur Miller, the ultra-liberal U.S. Senator Wayne Morse, and Walter Lippmann, the veteran Socialist pundit.

In its full context, the supporting argumentation of the "Declaration" is indistinguishable from the propaganda emanating from North Vietnam: "It is not easy for Americans to believe that the mess in Vietnam is as bad as it is. The news is of military coups and demonstrations by the Vietnamese people against the U.S.-backed government; of the torture of 13-year-old boys and the spraying of poisons from the air to destroy crops and livestock; of the napalm bombing of native villages and the herding of civilians into stockaded villages, which are essentially concentration camps. The news is of military defeat and senseless deaths.

"Most Americans are used to thinking that the United States stands for freedom, democracy and peace — and that if the United States gets involved in a foreign war it is on the side of the people. It has taken Americans a long time to realize that this is not the case in Vietnam. Now that we have the facts, we have no honorable choice but to insist on an immediate withdrawal of American troops and an end to all military aid to the Saigon government . . . .

"It may well be that some form of Communism will come to Southeast Asia, whether the United States continues to intervene or not. But in any case, the United States does not have the right to tell the people of Southeast Asia what form of government they must have, any more than the Russians or Chinese do. Continuation of the war increases the danger of domestic [Saigon-created] totalitarianism or additional foreign intervention . . . .

"Every day that the United States continues to intervene increases the danger of intervention by the Chinese, since China and Vietnam are neighbors. The war in Vietnam could escalate into general war with China and World War III.

"There are other things at stake in the continued American aggression [*sic*] in Vietnam in addition to the lives and freedom of the Vietnamese people, important as these are. It is perhaps impossible for most Americans to compare their present responsibility to speak out against the war in Vietnam with the responsibility of the Germans to speak out in the early days of Hitler. Everyone knows that we have no Hitlers here, in power or close to power. But one wonders what limits there are to the atrocities Americans will go along with, so long as they are explained, however falsely, as necessary for the maintenance of democracy . . . .

"The prospects for the future are terrifying if those of us who live in the most powerful nation in the world, a nation loaded with money and overkill, fail to do what we say the Germans should have done when atrocities were being committed in their name and with their knowledge.

"We must insist on immediate withdrawal of all U.S. troops from Vietnam, even though the situation may remain a tragic one. Many problems will remain, but withdrawal of U.S. troops will provide the only chance that the people of South Vietnam can become masters of their own destiny. Then the way will be open for genuine negotiations about the problems of Southeast Asia, as distinct from manipulation by outside powers, and for friendly aid to the stricken peoples of the region, if they ask for it. This is the only peace with honor that is possible in Vietnam. End the War in Vietnam."

If the "Declaration" promoters were to be believed, the Americans, not the North Vietnamese, are the aggressors in South Vietnam; the war is "civil" and not a war of aggression; atrocities are committed solely by the Americans and their allies, and not by the North Vietnamese; the Saigon regime, not the Viet Cong, oppresses the South Vietnamese people; and the Viet Cong is a separate entity from the Hanoi regime rather than the regime's fighting arm. There is no admission, direct or indirect, that the Soviet Union and its satellites have been the manufacturers and distributors of the greater part of the war machine used against the United States forces and their allies. There is no mention of American prisoners of war and their inhumane treatment at the hands of the Hanoi Communists. There is criticism of Saigon's, but not of North Vietnam's elections. There is criticism of Saigon's alleged censorship of press and radio but not of North Vietnam's police state control of all communications media. And most important, the signers of the "Declaration" are willing to sacrifice South Vietnam to Communist control ("the situation may remain a tragic one") in exchange for an American withdrawal — a withdrawal from an unfinished war, in which, despite the "Declaration" protests, an American military victory was never sought.

EMERGENCY CONFERENCE COMMITTEE

For more than two decades, Communists and their leftist-liberal dupes in the United States have been urging the United States government to approve the so-called Genocide Convention of the United Nations. In the pro-Genocide Convention propaganda there has always been a conspicuous omission of any mention of the genocide perpetrated by the Soviet Union and Red China. In a remarkable example of perversion, the ultra-left has accused the United States of accomplished and planned genocide. The accusation has been made a part of the current and massive campaign of instigation of racist warfare in the United States.

In the October 17, 1970 issue of the Communist Party's *Daily World*, there appeared a "Petition to the United Nations to End Genocide." The petition was issued by the newly-formed Emergency Conference Committee. It said: "We, the undersigned citizens of the United States, gravely concerned with the continued racist persecution, conscious and unconscious, and centuries-old denial of Constitutional rights and respect for human dignity to men, women and children of Red, Brown, Yellow and Black Americans, assert that:

"The savage police activities, based upon official policies of Federal, State and City governments, has resulted in innumerable beatings, frame-ups, arrests and murders of Black Americans, the classical example of which is the Black Panther Party. The murderous attacks on Black youth in Chicago, Illinois; Orangeburg, South Carolina; Augusta,

67

Georgia; Jackson, Mississippi; and the innumerable beatings, legal frame-ups of Brown, Red, Yellow and Black youths are not only in violation of their legal rights, but as well of this government's commitment under the Charter of the United Nations.

"The Genocide Convention adopted by the General Assembly of the United Nations on December 9, 1948, defines as genocide 'killing members of the group and any intent to destroy in whole or in part a national racial or ethnic or religious group.' And further, according to the Convention, 'Causing serious bodily or mental harm to members of the group' is Genocide.

"We assert that the Genocide Convention has been flagrantly violated by the Government of the United States. We further assert that the United Nations has jurisdiction in this matter, to hold otherwise is to repudiate its position regarding apartheid in South Africa and as well its universal Declaration of Human Rights, and its Convention for the Prevention and Punishment of Genocide.

"The racist planned and unplanned terror suffered by more than 40 millions of Black, Brown, Red and Yellow citizens of the United States cannot be regarded solely as a domestic issue. The continuance of these practices threatens the struggle of mankind throughout the world to achieve peace, security and dignity.

"On the basis of simple justice, it is time for the United Nations to call for universal action to apply economic and political sanctions against the United States Government until such time as the United States will abide by the Genocide Convention and the Declaration of Human Rights."

The viciously anti-United States petition was sponsored by such renowned ultra-leftists as Rev. Ralph Abernathy; Coretta King; Congresswoman Shirley Chisholm; entertainers Ossie Davis, Ruby Dee, and Dick Gregory; attorneys Arthur Kinoy and Charles Garry; Anne and Carl Braden of the Southern Conference Educational Fund; Frank Wilkinson; Frank A. Anglin Jr.; Angie Dickerson; Richard Criley; Carlton Goodlett; Donald Kalish; Black Panther leader Huey Newton; Dalton Trumbo; Irving Sarnoff; and Jack Spiegel.

GI CIVIL LIBERTIES DEFENSE COMMITTEE

The GI Civil Liberties Defense Committee was established in 1969 and has always been staffed by the Young Socialist Alliance, an arm of the Troskyite Socialist Workers Party (. . . "A subversive and Communist organization which seeks to alter the form of government of the United States by unconstitutional means." — "A dissident Communist group not affiliated with the Communist International nor officially recognized by either the Communist hierarchy in Moscow or the Communist Party, U.S.A. Essentially, however, both the official and unofficial groups base themselves upon the teachings of Marx, Engels, and Lenin. The Socialist Workers Party are followers of Leon Trotsky, who was expelled from the Russian Communist Party").

The Committee has described its aims: "The purpose of the GI Civil Liberties Defense Committee is to defend the rights of American citizens in uniform to freedom of speech, freedom of the press, freedom of assembly and association, and the right to petition the government for a redress of grievances. It supports the right of GIs to use these and all other constitutionally guaranteed liberties to express their opinions on public affairs and political issues, including the war in Vietnam.

"It extends this support by obtaining legal counsel for GIs whose rights are violated and by publicizing their cases. Toward this end it raises funds and solicits the endorsement and support of all those who uphold the constitutional rights of American servicemen."

The Committee's sponsors are drawn from the ultra-left: Carl Barus of Swarthmore College, Fred J. Carrier of Villanova University, William C. Davidon of Resist, Allen Fleishman of the National Lawyers Guild, author Maxwell Geismar, Rev. David Gracie of the Episcopal Peace Fellowship, Communist Terence Hallinan, Fred Hampton of the Black Panthers, Donald Kalish from "left of the Communist Party," Clark Kissinger of the Communist weekly *Guardian*, Sue Larson of Barnard College, Eleanor Leacock of Brooklyn Polytechnic Institute, Sandra Levinson of the ultra-leftist *Ramparts* magazine, Irving Sarnoff of the Peace Action Council of Southern California, Ernest A. Smith of Hunter College, Benjamin Spock, Paul M. Sweezy of the ultra-leftist *Monthly Review*, Ethel Taylor of Women Strike for Peace, and Maurice Zeitlin of the University of Wisconsin.

INDIVIDUALS AGAINST THE CRIME OF SILENCE

According to its own literature, Individuals Against the Crime of Silence "is an outgrowth of an idea by Herbert D. Magidson, who expressed the plan to a group of 25 men, from the Los Angeles area, of considerable and diversified skills in the areas of behavioral sciences, law, international relations, business, education, clergy, and experience in the peace movements.

"The idea was refined and put down in the form of the Declaration, which was presented to the Secretary General of the United Nations through Undersecretary C.V. Narasimhan, *Chef de Cabinet* of the United Nations. The Declaration was accepted and is part of the permanent archives of the United Nations. A letter from Mr. Narasimhan to this effect is in the possession of the IACS. The United Nations also agreed to regularly receive reports of the total numbers of signatories to the Declaration as part of its permanent archives. It was arranged with the United Nations that the individual signed counterparts of this Declaration are to be held at the office of the IACS.

"The individual signatures will be collected through distribution and mailings of the Declaration and by ads of it in major publications.

"The office of the IACS receives individual signatures and processes them, and then returns to everyone who signs a current letter of its activities, the emblem, a wallet-sized registration card and additional Declarations, plus four special letters – one to the President, two to the U.S. senators, and one to the U.S. congressman. These letters advise that the signatory, a constituent, has signed his name to the Declaration (which is repeated in the letters) to be on permanent record with the Declaration to the United Nations. The letters also state that the office of the IACS will advise each representative regularly of the growing number of signatories. The signer is urged to also sign and mail these special four letters to Washington immediately."

By 1971, the IACS claimed that 150,000 individuals had signed the Declaration, which reads: "A Declaration to Our Fellow Citizens of the United States, to the Peoples of the World and to Future Generations: (1) We are appalled and angered by the conduct of our country in Vietnam. (2) In the name of liberty, we have unleashed the awesome arsenal of the greatest military power in the world upon a small agricultural nation, killing, burning and mutilating its people. In the name of peace, we are creating a desert. In the name of security, we are inviting world conflagration. (3) We, the signers of this declaration, believe this war to be immoral. We believe it to be illegal. We must oppose it. (4) At Nuremberg, after World War II, we tried, convicted and executed men for the crime of obeying their government, when that government demanded of them crimes against humanity. Millions more, who were not tried, were still guilty of the crime of silence. (5) We have a commitment to the laws and principles we carefully forged in the American Constitution, at the Nuremberg Trials, and in the United Nations Charter. And our own deep democratic traditions and our dedication to the ideal of human decency among men demand that we speak out.

"We therefore wish to declare our names to the Office of the Secretary General of the United Nations, both as permanent witness to our opposition to the war in Vietnam and as a demonstration that the conscience of America is not dead."

In its literature promoting the Declaration, the IACS noted: "On September 23, 1965, a Memorandum of Law was incorporated in the Congressional Record of the 89th Congress of the United States of America, in which eighty leading American attorneys, after careful analysis of our position and actions in the Vietnam War, came to the conclusion that we are violating the following accords: The Charter of the United Nations, The Geneva Accords of 1954, the United States Constitution."

The attempt to place the prestige of the Congress behind the Declaration was clumsy at its best and phony at its worst. The "Memorandum of Law," referred to by IACS, was inserted in the Congressional Record by Senator Wayne Morse of Oregon, whose leftist credentials are impeccable. The "eighty leading American attorneys" who prepared the "Memorandum of Law" were the Lawyers Committee on American Policy toward Vietnam. The honorary chairman of the Lawyers Committee is Robert W. Kenny, possessor of an extraordinary history of affiliations with the Communist Party and a past president of the National Lawyers Guild ("the foremost legal bulwark of the Communist Party, its front organizations, and controlled unions"). The executive committee of the Lawyers Committee is composed of William L. Standard, chairman; Carey McWilliams, vice-chairman; and Joseph Crown, secretary. Among the leading lights of the Lawyers Committee are Raphael Konigsberg who has pleaded the Fifth Amendment when asked about his Communist Party membership, and John Abt, general counsel of the Communist Party. Vice-chairman McWilliams' Communist front affiliations are almost legendary. Secretary Crown, chairman

Standard, and committee members Richard Falk and Stanley Swerdlow have represented the Lawyers Committee at the Soviet-controlled Stockholm Conferences on Vietnam.

The publicized signers of the IACS's Declaration include the usual leftist representation from the entertainment field — Ben Gazzara, Carl Reiner, Janice Rule, Robert Ryan, Dick Van Dyke, and Robert Vaughn; the leftist clergy — Rev. Daniel Berrigan, Rev. Philip Berrigan, Rev. William H. DuBay, Rev. Stephen H. Fritchman, and Rabbi Richard N. Levy; authors and literary figures — James Baldwin, Ring Lardner Jr., Norman Mailer, and Louis Untermeyer; academicians — Robert McAfee Brown, Jerome Frank, Donald Kalish, Hans Morgenthau, and Robert Simmons; and assorted other leftists — James Farmer, W.H. "Ping" Ferry, Hugh B. Hester, Edward M. Keating, Henry E. Niles, Linus Pauling, Benjamin Spock, David Schoenbrun, and Harvey Wheeler.

INTER-UNIVERSITY COMMITTEE FOR A PUBLIC HEARING ON VIETNAM

INTER-UNIVERSITY COMMITTEE FOR DEBATE ON FOREIGN POLICY

On March 24, 1965, the teach-in movement began at the University of Michigan. The movement was initiated by Eric J. Wolf, professor of anthropology, William A. Gamson, assistant professor of sociology, and Arnold S. Kaufman, associate professor of philosophy. The teach-in group was organized as the Inter-University Committee for a Public Hearing on Vietnam [I-UC]. I-UC defined a teach-in: "A teach-in is a critical examination by members of the academic community of fateful Government policies and of policy alternatives. It is conceived as a natural extension of scholars' responsibilities as teachers and citizens in a time of public crisis. Professors, it ought to be known, have not been cloistered in ivory towers. Many have been engaged by the Government for advice on political and scientific matters; many conduct research of direct use to the Nation. This kind of public service has always been deemed respectable. But it is just as respectable to offer results of thought and scholarship that conflict with current lines of policy. Indeed, dissent in a democratic forum, is the highest form of cooperation."

In a staff study ("The Anti-Vietnam Agitation and the Teach-In Movement") prepared for the Senate Internal Security Subcommittee, the first teach-in was described: "An estimated 2,500 persons attended this meeting, which was jazzed up with a kaleidoscopic series of lectures, rallies, and seminars, punctuated by folksinging and bomb scares . . . . Films of the Vietnam war made by the Vietcong and smuggled into this country were shown to the students. Later on, the Vietcong representative in Algiers, Huyn Van Tam, was to boast that he had received a $100 contribution for the purchase of medical supplies from an unidentified group of students at the University of Michigan (*Chicago Tribune*, August 3, 1965)."

In its evaluation of the first and subsequent teach-ins, the staff study said: "In reality, the great majority of the teach-ins (there were a few notable exceptions to this rule) have had absolutely nothing in common with the procedures of fair debate or the process of education. In practice they were a combination of an indoctrination session, a political protest demonstration, an endurance contest, and a variety show.

"At most of the teach-ins the administration's point of view was given only token representation. The great majority of the speakers, by deliberate design, were critics of the administration. At many of the teach-ins, spokesmen for the administration's policy were subjected to booing and hissing and catcalling, so that it was impossible for them to make a coherent presentation of their case.

"Communist propaganda films were frequently shown. Communist literature was frequently distributed. People of known Communist background were frequently involved. And at virtually every teach-in, the anti-administration speakers vied with each other in their extremist denunciations of administration policy."

After its success with the March 24th and subsequent teach-ins, I-UC planned a major teach-in in Washington, D.C. The University of Michigan group solicited sponsors for the national teach-in at Washington. In a letter to academicians, I-UC said: "The escalation of the Vietnam War has brought about a mobilization of public protest unprecedented in the history of the Cold War. In the academic community, a form of protest has appeared spontaneously and is spreading from campus to campus — the teach-in. These teach-ins are organized by local faculties and students. The usual format includes presentations by authorities on Southeast Asian Affairs, intensive analyses of the events leading up to the present crisis, and explorations of alternatives to the present policy.

"On May 15th we propose to hold a national version of these local conferences in Washington, D.C. The national conference will be essentially a confrontation between scholars and scientists on the one hand, and on the other, members of the government and those former members of the academic community who are presently advising the government on Vietnam policy. Members of the government and their advisors will be invited to explain the rationale behind the present policy on Southeast Asia and to answer certain questions, for example: (1) Under what conditions would our government agree to a cease fire? (2) What sort of government would be acceptable to the United States in South Vietnam? Would the participation of the National Liberation Front be acceptable under any conditions? (3) Are the continued bombing attacks on North Vietnam likely to achieve the stated objectives? (4) What types of provisions have been made or are planned to ascertain the wishes of the Vietnamese people? (5) How does the war in Southeast Asia affect the relations between the United States and our allies? (6) What is the effect of the present war on other undeveloped nations? (7) How is the present war affecting Sino-Soviet relations? (8) What role should the United Nations play in resolving the present conflict? (9) Is the National Liberation Front primarily an indigenous resistance movement against an unpopular government? If so, should the United States be engaged in suppressing that movement?

"In addition to directing these questions to the government and its advisors, we shall invite senators and congressmen to participate in seminars on a variety of topics related to the Vietnam situation in all its ramifications. We shall bring together experts on the history, the economy and the political structure of Southeast Asia; on guerrilla warfare; on relations between China and North Vietnam; on the National Liberation Front, SEATO, public opinion in South Vietnam, and related topics.

"We are attempting to recruit a large representative group of scholars and scientists to sponsor the National Teach-In. Sponsorship implies only a deep concern with the present situation in Southeast Asia and a conviction that questions related to peace and war should be open to responsible debate. Sponsorship does not entail the endorsement of any particular scheme for settling the situation in Vietnam. This is precisely what we are searching for."

The original members of I-UC, in almost all instances, had shut off all real debate on the Vietnam War. Through their writings, public utterances, and affiliations, almost all of them were committed to United States withdrawal from Vietnam. Almost all were either officials or members of some leftist-pacifist organization. Almost without exception, very few of the original sponsors had any extensive diplomatic or military experience or special expertise on Vietnam or Southeast Asia. Among the original sponsors, more than a few had a history of deep involvement with Communist fronts. The original sponsors included: from the University of Pennsylvania, Russell Ackoff (operations research) and Joseph Stokes Jr. (medicine); from the University of Chicago, Robert Adams (anthropology) and Hans Morgenthau (political science); from Harvard University, Gordon Allport (psychology), Rupert Emerson (government), Roderick Firth (philosophy), H. Stuart Hughes (history), Bernard Lown (medicine), Henry A. Murray (psychology), Talcott Parsons (sociology), David Riesman (sociology), B.F. Skinner (psychology), and George Wald (biology); from the University of Michigan, Robert G. Angell (sociology), Kenneth Boulding (economics), Richard Brandt (philosophy), Samuel Eldersveld (political science), William B. Harvey (law), Daniel Katz (psychology), Herbert C. Kelman (psychology), Theodore M. Newcomb (psychology), Anatol Rapoport (mathematical biology), Albert Reiss (sociology), J. David Singer (political science), Lawrence B. Slobodkin (biology), James N. Spuhler (anthropology), and Eric R. Wolf (anthropology); from Stanford University, Christian Bay (political science), Robert McAfee Brown (religion), Claude Buss (history), Karel De Leeuw (mathematics), Robert Finn (mathematics), Albert Guerard (English), Lincoln Moses (statistics), R. Nevitt Sanford (psychology), Charles Stein (statistics), and Gordon Wright (history); from Union Theological Seminary, John C. Bennett (president); from Western College for Women, T. Arthur Bisson (intercultural studies); from the University of California at Berkeley, David Blackwell (statistics), Henry Helson (mathematics), Morris Hirsch (mathematics), David Krech (psychology), Jerzy Neyman (statistics), Henry Scheffé (statistics), Mark Schorer (English), Elizabeth L. Scott (statistics), and Stephen Smale (mathematics); from The Center for the Study of Democratic

Institutions, Scott Buchanan, W.H. "Ping" Ferry, and Robert M. Hutchins; from Washington University of St. Louis, Barry Commoner (botany); from the University of Wisconsin, Merle Curti (history), William R. Taylor (history), and William A. Williams (history); from Yale University, Robert Dahl (political science), Karl W. Deutsch (political science), Thomas I. Emerson (law), and Harold Lasswell (political science); from the University of Missouri, Arthur Dunham (social work); from Northwestern University, Richard Ellmann (English); from The Johns Hopkins University, Jerome Frank (psychiatry); from the Colgate-Rochester Divinity School, George Hall (social ethics) and William Hamilton (theology); from the Worcester Foundation, Hudson Hoagland (biology); from Michigan State University, Abba Lerner (economics) and Herbert Weisinger (English); from the Massachusetts Institute of Technology, Salvadore Luria (biology); from Sarah Lawrence College, Helen Merrell Lynd (philosophy); from Columbia University, Robert S. Lynd (sociology), Robert K. Merton (sociology), and Ernest Nagel (philosophy); from the editorial board of *Scientific American*, James R. Newman (mathematics); from the University of Wisconsin, William G. Rice (law) and Ragner Rollefson (physics); from Indiana University, Roger W. Russell (psychology); from Cornell University, Philip Morrison (physics); from Chicago Theological Seminary, Howard Schomer (president); from the University of Illinois, Julian H. Steward (anthropology); from the Woods Hole Marine Biological Laboratories, Albert Szent-Györgyi (physiology); and from the University of Virginia, Quincy Wright (political science).

In its preparation for the national teach-in, I-UC invited Presidential Assistant McGeorge Bundy to participate. Bundy not only accepted the invitation but also agreed to the stipulation that his companion speaker for the Administration's viewpoint would be chosen by I-UC from a panel of speakers submitted by Bundy. He also agreed that the chairmen for most of the panel sessions would be designated by I-UC.

In his preparation for the teach-in, Bundy sought as his co-speakers Max Lerner, John P. Roche, and Arthur M. Schlesinger Jr. Lerner's affiliations with Communist fronts and socialist groups and his persistent pro-Soviet views evidently qualified him, in Bundy's opinion, to defend U.S. involvement in Vietnam. Roche's experience as national chairman and vice-chairman of the ultra-radical Americans for Democratic Action and his affiliation with the National Committee for a Sane

Nuclear Policy apparently qualified him as a hawk on Vietnam. But the choices of Lerner and Roche were academic, since both men declined Bundy's invitation. On the other hand, Schlesinger did accept, and he eventually became the leadoff spokesman "for" the Administration in the teach-in. As a matter of fact, Schlesinger made his presentation without the help of Bundy, who at the very last moment declined to attend the teach-in.

Schlesinger predictably used the opportunity to blast the Administration, especially Secretary of State Dean Rusk. He criticized President Johnson's involvement in the Dominican Republic. He denounced U.S. policy in Vietnam, dating back to 1954, which included the policies of the Eisenhower Administration and the two administrations in which he worked, the Kennedy and Johnson Administrations. By his choice of Schlesinger, Bundy threw gunpowder into the fire. Throughout the course of the May 15th teach-in during the morning, afternoon, and evening sessions, the pro-Administration panelists were not much different from Schlesinger. Without exception, they merely defended the no-win policy faithfully pursued by the Johnson Administration. They carefully avoided any advocacy of a military victory in Vietnam. They preached about negotiation and peace. The pro-Administration spokesmen included Zbygniew Brzezinski, Wesley Fishel, Robert A. Scalapino, Paul Kattenberg, Benjamin Schwartz, Herbert Spivack, Thomas Conlon, William Jorden, Leo Cherne, Daniel Ellsberg, Samuel Huntington, Paul Seabury, and Walt W. Rostow.

Ranged against the Administration was a carefully selected group of agitators, including Hans J. Morgenthau, the British Marxist Isaac Deutscher, George Kahin, Mary Wright, William A. Williams, French citizen Bernard Fall, Denna F. Fleming, Marcus Raskin, Staughton Lynd, Anatol Rapoport, Seymour Melman, Robert Scheer, Robert Browne, and Felix Greene, a well-known propagandist for Mao Tse-tung.

Several thousand people attended the May 15th teach-in. The proceedings were carried on closed circuit television to 129 colleges and universities. Portions of the teach-in were also carried by the National Educational Television Network to its 91 affiliates, and by at least 30 radio stations.

Meg Greenfield, writing in *Reporter* magazine ("After the Washington Teach-In," June 3, 1965), offered her eyewitness observations of the proceedings: "The audience of course was preponderantly academic, both by profession and in style. Everyone on both sides seemed to have a favorite historical analogy at the ready; excessively courteous titles were dispensed ("Mr. Ho chi Minh"); the grim and sidewise joke, particularly as it was offered up by Morgenthau ("the noble war we are fighting," the "poor victim of aggression"), rarely failed to get a laugh. And, not surprisingly, people who had traveled hundreds and even thousands of miles to register a protest were overwhelmingly inclined to the view that (1) the Government was acting out of unexampled malignity and (2) it had caused us to be hated with renewed fervor around the world. Indeed, the mere expression of either of these sentiments tended to produce an outpouring of cheers and applause that went beyond agreement to something like exultation and which was reminiscent of nothing so much as the happy automatic shout with which New York's Democratic Party workers in the election of 1960 used to greet Carmine De Sapio's every dark announcement that the Nation's economy was on the verge of collapse.

"Among the sponsors and supporters of the teach-in were veterans of the peace movement, which has primarily concerned itself with disarmament in the past decade and which has focused rather suddenly and late on the problem of Vietnam – A.J. Muste, Seymour Melman, Arthur Waskow, Kenneth Boulding, Herbert Kelman, Staughton Lynd. Some, such as the economist, Paul Sweezy, who in 1949 was arguing the perniciousness and futility of the Marshall plan at the Waldorf-Astoria world peace conference, have been making their dire predictions at these conventions for almost 20 years. Others who were present in large numbers probably weren't 20 years old – students from high schools and universities in the Washington area. The meeting was notable for the dearth of big names from the world of arts and letters and even more notable for its heavy weighting of sociologists, physical scientists, and, above all, psychologists. There were, for instance, 181 professors of psychology as compared with 78 political scientists in the roster of teach-in sponsors.

"Despite the emphasis that the teach-in's leaders placed on facts and expertise, it remained essentially an apolitical – or even an antipolitical – affair. Speaker after speaker professed not to understand why, if the Government was engaged in negotiations, it could not tell the people all about them. Much of the argument seemed to be based on a psychiatric explanation of the behavior of Communist countries coupled with a kind of mote-and-beam moral logic by which the United States was disqualified from making even the simplist political judgments."

Reporter Bruce Biossat of the *Washington Daily News*, another eyewitness to the teach-in, wrote: "The participants in overwhelming majority made it plain they came seeking confirmation of their pre-Washington judgments that administration policy in Vietnam is almost wholly wrong. Contrary arguments no matter how seemingly well buttressed with fact, were generally greeted with skepticism, scorn, or derision . . . . In the whole fifteen and one half hours I did not hear from the lips of any critic a single approving word about U.S. policy in Vietnam or anywhere else. The Government was portrayed as stupid, ignorant, arrogant, secretive, and persistently wrongheaded."

On May 17, 1965, in an editorial ("Lesson in Democracy"), the *New York Times* expressed its delight in the anti-American spectacle — the national teach-in: "The academic community has given the American people — and their Government — a badly needed reminder that democratic discussion is both important and useful for the defense of democracy. Professors and students in all parts of the country spent most of Saturday listening in — by radio, television, and special telephone — on what was surely the most comprehensive and civilized public debate on the Vietnamese war in all the decade since the United States became involved in the conflict there . . . . The academicians on both sides conducted themselves with a dignity and respect for fact that contrasted favorably with the emotionalism that too often passes for discussion in foreign affairs among champions and critics of Government policy alike . . . .

"Whether any large number of minds — young or old — were changed by the hundreds of thousands of words the debaters exchanged is less consequential than this reaffirmation of the right of all citizens in a democracy to participate in shaping official policy through the full and unhampered interchange of ideas. Nothing could do more to erase the distinction between our system and totalitarianism than the notion that the Government has a monopoly of wisdom and any questioning or criticism is subversive. The teach-ins have helped to keep that crucial distinction alive."

In the Senate Internal Security Subcommittee's staff study, a summary of conclusions was presented: "(1) The great majority of those who have participated in anti-Vietnam demonstrations and in teach-ins are loyal Americans who differ with Administration policy in Vietnam for a variety of reasons, ranging from purely strategic considerations to pacifism. (2) The Communists have traditionally sought to infiltrate and exploit all organizations dedicated to peace; and a reading of the official Communist press and of confidential directives to party members makes it clear that the CPUSA and its affiliates have given all-out support to the anti-Vietnam demonstrations and teach-ins, have directed their members to participate in them, and have sought to influence them in the interests of Communist expansion.

"(3) While leaders of other pacifist organizations like the National Committee for a Sane Nuclear Policy have sought to protect themselves by demarcating their own position from that of the Communists and by establishing certain criteria and certain controls to protect their organization against Communist infiltration, there is nothing in the public record to suggest that the leaders of the anti-Vietnam agitation and of the teach-in movement have similarly sought to demarcate their position on Vietnam from the Communist position on Vietnam or to repudiate Communist support or to establish criteria and controls designed to prevent Communist infiltration and exploitation of their movement. (4) In the absence of any such effort by the non-Communist leaders of the movement to prevent or limit Communist infiltration or participation, a significant number of people of known Communist background or with long records of association with Communist fronts have been able to play a prominent role in the movement. (5) The control of the anti-Vietnam movement has clearly passed from the hands of the moderate elements who may have controlled it at one time, into the hands of Communists and extremist elements who are openly sympathetic to the Vietcong and openly hostile to the United States, and who call for massive civil disobedience . . . . (6) The great majority of the teach-ins have had absolutely nothing in common with procedures of fair debate or the process of education. In practice, they were a combination of an indoctrination session, a political protest demonstration, an endurance contest, and a variety show. The proceedings were characterized by extremist statements and the open distribution of Communist literature.

"(7) The national teach-in in Washington on May 15 was characterized by a plausible effort at impartiality during the morning and afternoon sessions, but in the summary session that evening all pretense at impartiality was abandoned in favor of a totalitarian one-sidedness, with panelist after panelist and speaker after speaker excoriating the administration and calling for the mobilization of a national movement of protest. The national teach-in sessions of May 15, 1965, received complete support from the Communist and pro-Communist publications in the United States like the *Worker*, the *People's World*, the *National Guardian*, and the *Militant*. The national teach-in of May 15, 1965, was arranged in a manner that left an impression condemnatory of U.S. policy in Vietnam. (8) The evidence is overwhelming that the world Communist apparatus — in the United States, in Moscow, in Peiping, in Hanoi, in Havana, and elsewhere — have been able to exploit the anti-Vietnam agitation and the teach-in movement for the purpose of confusing their own people, for the purpose of fostering the impression that the majority of the American people are opposed to the administration's policy in Vietnam, and for the purpose of attacking the morale of American servicemen in Vietnam.

"(9) It is also clear from numerous statements by Communist spokesmen that many of them believe their own propaganda and that they are convinced that American public opinion will compel the Johnson Administration to pull out of Vietnam and leave the field to Communism. (10) What all this adds up to is a global effort on the part of the Communist apparatus to force the withdrawal of American troops from Vietnam by means of a massive psychological warfare attack. In this effort, the Communists are exploiting all the idealism of honest critics to bolster their position, just as they used Communist-front groups to bolster their position in various crisis situations in the thirties and forties. In many cases, the personnel is the same. The only thing which has changed is the cause — and even this is the same if we consider that the greater cause of all Communist activity in America is to bolster the international gains of world Communism, by urging Americans that what occurs in Vietnam, or Korea, or Berlin, or Greece, or Turkey, is essentially none of our business."

In the staff study, there was presented a 46-page section devoted to the Communist affiliations and sympathies of some I-UC sponsors and speakers. The material was far from being comprehensive on any one individual, but enough was presented to indicate that neither the affiliations nor the sympathies could be blamed upon either innocence or gullibility. The individuals included in the 46-page section were Thomas A. Bisson of Western College for Women, Derk Bodde of the University of Pennsylvania, Oliver Edmund Clubb of Columbia University, Nathaniel Coburn of the University of Michigan, Denna F. Fleming, formerly of Vanderbilt University, Waldo Frank, Robert J. Havighurst of the University of Chicago, Halstead Holman of Stanford University, Matthew Josephson, Thomas I. Emerson of Yale University, Sidney Lens, Oliver Loud of Antioch College, Helen M. Lynd of Sarah Lawrence College, Robert S. Lynd of Columbia University, Staughton Lynd of Yale University, Harry Magdoff of the New School for Social Research, John W. Somerville, Philip Morrison of Cornell University, Melba Phillips of the University of Chicago, Anatol Rapoport of the University of Michigan, Anton Refregier, Theodor Rosebury of Washington University in St. Louis, Harry Slochower of the New School for Social Research, Sidney Socolar of Columbia University, Colston E. Warne of Amherst College, and William A. Williams of the University of Wisconsin.

In the Communist Party's *Worker*, Mike Davidow expressed pleasure at the national teach-in. Davidow wrote: "The teach-in held last week in Washington by college professors and heard by millions on TV and radio blazed trails both in exposing Washington's bankrupt policy in Vietnam, the Dominican Republic, and, elsewhere abroad, and in establishing a new technique of popular discussion . . . . One felt the sting of true patriotism in the sharp criticism of the Johnson Administration's foreign policy.

"The teach-in reflected determination to make America a place where all can live in pride. It was evident that many levels of opposition to the Administration's course existed among the participants of the teach-in. The great majority consider that what is happening in Vietnam and the Dominican Republic is 'unjustifiable.' Therein lies the reason that little headway was made by Administration spokesmen like Walter W. Rostow and Arthur Schlesinger, who took the place of McGeorge Bundy, special Presidential Assistant . . . .

"Another large group, as a result of their disenchantment with U.S. policy in Vietnam, have begun to scrutinize and challenge the entire course of U.S. foreign policy. Perhaps the smallest segment, but a significant one, seems to be refusing to close its eyes to the probability that all this basically stems from the imperialistic nature of our foreign policy.

"The teach-in, by its very objective, many-sided probing of issues, provides the natural medium for the exchange of all views. It is a 'marketplace for ideas' as well as an avenue of protest. As long as it maintains that character, it will continue to unite all levels of views. Its academic objectivity is its strength. The Administration unquestionably views with alarm the success of this new and dynamic movement, and above all the danger of its spreading. For what the teach-in above all demonstrated was that the present policy in Vietnam, the Dominican Republic, and the entire U.S. foreign policy can't stand debate. With the exception of Senators Wayne Morse and Ernest Gruening, there has been no real debate in Congress of the Johnson doctrine.

"The teach-in is a revolt on the campus against the bipartisan misrepresentation of world reaction to its foreign policy and of the rising opposition at home. More, it views discussion and debate in a dynamic way, as a potent instrument for reversing the disastrous course in Vietnam. Its refusal to accept as final Bundy's cancellation of his commitment to debate seems to be in line with this concept. The proponents of the teach-in are, of course, right in their concept of the power to debate at this moment. For when disturbing and disgraceful deeds are done in darkness, light can become a galvanizing force."

The Soviet Union's *International Affairs* of May 20, 1965, commented on the national teach-in: "Voices full of emotion resounded in the hall of the hotel. They demanded that an end be put to the bombings of North Vietnam, that the troops be immediately withdrawn from South Vietnam, that the negative policy of anti-Communism be abandoned.

"The nationwide debate in Washington, as well as the meetings at the universities and colleges of the country, Comrade Vishnevskiy points out, however, the efforts of official propaganda try to play down their significance, mean an important turning point in the consciousness of the 'silent generation,' as the youth of the United States has usually been regarded. They reflect the growing concern and alarm about the extension of the American armed intervention in Southeast Asia.

"Of course there are still many people in the United States who are deceived and fooled by the official propaganda. But something else is indisputable too: the number of Americans taking a stand against the policy of the Administration in Vietnam is increasing every day, as the last Gallup poll has shown."

In the June 15, 1965 issue of Moscow's *Izvestiya*, there appeared an article ("Not All Is Quiet In America") by an allegedly American journalist, Herman Brown. The article, although containing many inaccuracies, indicated the Soviet government's pleasure over the national teach-in. Wrote "Brown": "In the early fifties when McCarthyism was setting the tone in U.S. life, it was quiet in the lecture halls of the large American universities. Both teachers and students kept silent. Truman's government was preparing the people for the Korean War – it was necessary to shut the people's mouths. Communists were jailed and liberal artists, teachers, and state officials – anybody who dared even to think, let alone talk, of friendship with the Soviet people and of peace – were subjected to persecution. There was a time when thousands of political émigrés asked for asylum in the United States. In the stern years of McCarthyism all this changed. Even now it is possible in various parts of the world to find Americans who left the United States at that time. Tens of thousands of youngsters were sent to Korea. They killed the children of a people who were struggling for their independence, and many Americans found their graves thousands of miles away from home.

"Fifteen years have passed and once more tens of thousands of American youths are being thrown into remote regions. Once more they are fighting a people who want freedom and independence. They are bombing foreign cities, destroying the crops maturing in the fields, destroying villages, and killing women, children, and old men. At the same time hundreds of Americans are dying in the rice paddies of South Vietnam. America is plunging more and more deeply into the mud of the war in Southeast Asia. Times have changed, however, and America is not what it was. The American people have derived some lessons from their own history in the past 15 years, and America has broken its silence.

"The struggle against American intervention in South Vietnam and against the bombing of North Vietnam has above all expanded at the universities. A great dialogue is now being conducted there – the dialogue about peace. Its slogans are 'Get out of the blood-stained mud in Vietnam,' 'Stop the aggression against the Dominican Republic,' and 'Peace.'

"The dialogue has spread to 50 universities in various parts of the country: states of the middle west — Michigan, Illinois, Wisconsin; the northern states — New York, New Jersey, Pennsylvania; New England — Massachusetts, Connecticut, Rhode Island; in the west — California, Washington, Oregon; and even in the south — for example, in Texas. Tens of thousands of students and thousands of teachers are participating in this great debate, and it is showing a distinctly anti-military nature.

"America's academic world is not limiting itself to mere discussions: Students and teachers are picketing government institutions, organizing demonstrations, and conducting mass meetings. They are waking up the people.

"Paid advertisements in large newspapers and in university students' publications are another form of appealing to the people and of mobilizing them. In early May in the *New York Times* Sunday issue, a paid advertisement appeared which occupied almost three-quarters of a page. The advertisement contained an appeal to President Johnson to stop the war in Vietnam. The signatures of more than 1,000 university teachers from New England were attached to the appeal.

"In recent months such advertisements have appeared rather frequently in newspapers, and they are not only published by professors. Such advertisements are publicized by artists from the stage and screen, and they are signed by scientists, psychologists, physicians dancers, musicians, artists, and others. The advertisements are paid for by those signing them.

"The struggle of the university teachers and students together with other popular representatives had two climaxes. One was on April 17 in Washington. On that day 30,000 people flocked together in the American capital as a sign of protest against the war in Vietnam. People from all parts of the country — from east and west, north and south — arrived there. Some 30,000 people, mainly youths, chiefly students, went out to demonstrate.

"Four weeks later, on Saturday, May 15, also in Washington, the protest movement acquired the nature of a nationwide dispute on the dirty war.' The dialog was organized by the 'university committee for the public hearing of the Vietnam case.' The main discussion took place in the big hall of the Sheraton Hotel in Washington. Several government representatives supported by some teachers, spoke in defense of the

85

government policy. Professors Hans Morgenthau, Stanley Millet, Mary Wright, and William Williams spoke against the policy of the Johnson government. Professor George Kahin of Cornell University was the main leader of this group. Many other outstanding scientific figures supported the group. The discussion continued the whole day, from early morning till an hour past midnight . . . .

"Although the struggle against war is of a most dramatic nature in university circles, it also is being conducted in other places and by other strata of the populace. The organization 'Women Fight for Peace,' for example, which sprung up some four or five years ago, is participating in every anti-militaristic action in the country. It frequently organizes anti-war demonstrations. This is a very peculiar organization, without a membership in the proper sense of the word. Meetings, conferences, and all sorts of gatherings are convened by telephone or by word of mouth, communicating information on the meeting or on some other planned action.

"There also are trade unions which are participating actively in the anti-war struggle . . . . It is necessary to emphasize the role of the Communist Party, which for many years has waged persistently and consistently a struggle for peace and the peaceful coexistence of countries with different social systems. Hundreds of organizations of the progressive-radical front are also active in the same direction.

"The outburst of indignation against the American invasion in South Vietnam and the Dominican Republic was not unexpected. It constitutes a natural consequence of the events in the country of the past five years. I have in mind the heroic struggle of the Negro population for civil rights, for equal rights with white Americans. The struggle of 20 million Negroes, supported by tens of thousands of white citizens, for the right to work, for the right to vote and to be elected, and for human dignity has revolutionized American life. This struggle already has produced its heroes and martyrs. The skirmishes of the Negro population with the reactionaries have set many Americans thinking and made them violate the vow of silence. America has begun to think and to act."

In the aftermath of the May 15th national teach-in, the leaders of I-UC decided to make teach-ins a continuous activity. They formed the Inter-University Committee for Debate on Foreign Policy [I-UCD]. The executive council of the new structure included Douglas F. Dowd of

Cornell University as president, Julian Gendell of the University of Michigan as treasurer, and four vice-presidents: Thompson Bradley of Swarthmore College, Stanley Diamond of Syracuse University, Arnold Kaufman of Tuskegee Institute, Charles Haynie of Franklin and Marshall College, and Robert Browne of Fairleigh-Dickinson College.

On the national board of the newly-formed I-UCD were six individuals who had served on the original I-UC: Barry Commoner of Washington University, Philip Morrison of the Massachusetts Institute of Technology, Anatol Rapoport of the University of Michigan, Stephen Smale of the University of California, William A. Williams of the University of Wisconsin, and Eric Wolf of the University of Michigan. New members of the national board included from the University of Oregon, David Aberle; from Cornell University, Andreas Albrecht, Robert Greenblatt, and Joe H. Griffith; from the University of California, Inge P. Bell, Peter Lackowski, Michael Shub, Richard Strohman, and Howard G. Tucker; from Arizona State University, Henry M. Bracken and Robert L. Rein'l; from Washington University, Robert Buckhout; from San Fernando Valley State College, Vern L. Bullough and Joseph A. Ernst; from Massachusetts Institute of Technology, Noam Chomsky and Steven Chorover; from Syracuse University, Ronald Corwin, Oliver E. Clubb Jr., and Lawrence Krader; from Haverford College, William Davidon; from the University of Connecticut, Jack M. Davis; from California State College, Gene L. Dinielli, Roger Dittman, Timothy F. Harding, Roy K. Heintz, Frank Lindenfield, Bernard J. Somers, and Alva F. Yano; from Stanford University, Charles Drekmeier, John E. Rue, and Marc Sapir; from Columbia University, Morton Fried; from Bryn Mawr College, Richard B. DuBoff; from Carleton College, T. Fuse; from the University of Michigan, William Gamson, Richard D. Mann, Dennis Roseman, and Marshall Sahlins; from the University of Texas, George Goss and Anthony Leeds; from Hunter College, Irving Howe; from Riverside City College, Edna Infante; from Claremont Men's College, John W. Israel; from Vanderbilt University, David Kotelchuck; from the City College of New York, Sandra Levinson; from Yale University, Staughton Lynd and Mary Wright; from Adelphi College, Stanley Millet; from the University of Pennsylvania, Jonathan Mirsky and Robert Rutman; from Albion College, Arthur W. Munk; from Goucher College, William Neumann; from Rensselaer Polytechnic Institute, Ashakant Nimbark;

from Western Reserve University, Sidney Peck and Benjamin Spock; from Harvard University, Hilary Putnam; from Tuskegee Institute, Thomas Robischon; from the Illinois Institute of Technology, Bernard Rosenthal; from the University of Wisconsin, Joan W. Scott; from the Center for the Study of Democratic Institutions, Stanley Sheinbaum; from the New School for Social Research, A.J. Vidich; from the Institute for Policy Studies, Peter Weiss; from San Francisco State College, Marshall Windmiller; and from Boston University, Howard Zinn.

The newly-formed I-UCD published a "Statement of Purpose": "We are dismayed by the U.S. Administration's failure to generate informed public discussion of foreign policy. Our aim is to counteract the tendencies that have brought this condition about in ways appropriate to our function as educators and students, so that this country can, for the first time, make foreign policy on the basis of fact and moral principle rather than solely on the basis of myth and exclusive concern with national interest in its narrowest sense."

In its most recent self-description, I-UCD says that it "Serves as information center for local groups on campuses and in communities. Urges that the United States cease the bombing of North Vietnam, halt troop build-up, and otherwise refrain from further escalation of the war in Vietnam; allow the South Vietnamese an expression of popular will; make clear U.S. willingness to negotiate with the National Liberation Front; allow the National Liberation Front to participate in a South Vietnamese government. Encourages support for political candidates who oppose the war in Vietnam. Organizes teach-in movements on national and local levels. Conducts research on revolutionary and nationalist movements abroad, the extension of the war in Vietnam, etc. Co-sponsors National Dialogue Program to provide literature, films, tapes, and other material for use in public discussions on the war. Provides speakers to lecture and debate on domestic and foreign policy. Conducts and contributes to conferences on China, Southeast Asia, and relevant topics."

LEAGUE OF WOMEN VOTERS

The League of Women Voters (known until 1946 as the National League of Women Voters) was organized as a corporation on September 15, 1923 in Washington, D.C. The original plan of the LWV was first mentioned by Carrie Chapman Catt when she addressed the annual convention of the New York State Woman Suffrage Party on December 3, 1918. Said Mrs. Catt: "The women voters of the world have a unique opportunity at this time to render a signal and immortal service to the liberty and welfare of humanity. The call for help comes from the distressed nationalities of Middle Europe, struggling forward to representative institutions . . . . The women voters of the world – and they number millions – united, insistent, can do for the women of those struggling new republics what no men ever have done for them. The leaders among them may be encouraged and aided in unnumbered ways."

In 1921, Mrs. Maud Wood Park, chairman of the National League of Women Voters, described the origin of the LWV: "The history of the National League of Women Voters is brief; first a plan in the mind of a great woman, our Hononary Chairman, Mrs. Carrie Chapman Catt; then a year of wise experiment under the leadership of Mrs. C.H. Brooks and the fostering care of the National American Woman Suffrage Association; after that a notable convention to complete organization as an independent body."

On February 14, 1920, Carrie Chapman Catt addressed the first congress of the LWV. For about a year, the LWV was a sort of auxiliary of the National American Woman Suffrage Association, which Mrs. Catt served as president from 1915 until 1947. Her group had been in the vanguard of those fighting for ratification of the 19th Amendment to the Constitution of the United States – the women's suffrage amendment. In her address to the LWV, Mrs. Catt said: "You will discover that having the vote isn't bringing the millenium in one election. Probably when you enter the party of your choice you will find yourself in a sort of political penumbra where most of the men are. These men will be glad to see you and you will be flattered by their warm welcome and will think how nice it is to be free at last. Perhaps if you stay there long enough . . . you will think how charming it is to be a partisan; but if you stay still longer and move around enough, keeping your eyes wide open, you will discover a little denser group, which we might call the numbra [umbra] of the political party. You won't be so welcome there. Those are the people who are planning the platforms and picking out the candidates and doing the work which you and the men voters are expected to sanction at the polls. You won't be so welcome there, but that is the place to be. And if you stay there long enough and are active enough, you will see something else — the real thing in the center, with the door locked tight, and you will have a long, hard fight before you get behind that door, for there is the engine that moves the wheels of your party machinery . . . . If you really want women's votes to count, make your way there.

"In the League of Women Voters we have this anomaly: We are going to be a semi-political organization. We want to do political things. We want legislation. We are going to educate for citizenship. In that body we must be nonpartisan and all partisan. Democrats from Alabama and Republicans from New Hampshire must be friends and work together for the same things and without doubt of each other's sincerity. Yet these Republicans of New Hampshire must get inside the Republican Party and the Democrats of Alabama, in spite of some recent events, must get inside the Democratic Party. They must convert their respective parties to have confidence in women, confidence in the League of Women Voters, but I must further warn you that only about one man in twenty-five will be big enough to understand that you, a Republican, can work with you, a Democrat, in a non-partisan organization and be loyal to your respective parties at the same time . . . . If we are going to trail behind the Democratic and Republican parties about five years, and our program is going to be about that much behind that of the dominant political parties, we might as well quit before we begin. If the League of Women Voters hasn't the vision to see what is coming and what ought to come, and be five years ahead of the political parties, I doubt if it is worth the trouble to go on . . . . Let no one of us lose sight of the fact that power to build a higher welfare for all lies within the parties and not without."

In her peroration, Mrs. Catt said: "To sail between the Scylla of narrowminded partisanship on the left and the Charybdis of ultra-conservatism on the right, is the appointed task of the League of Women Voters; through that narrow and uncomfortable passage it must sail to wreck upon the rocks or to glorious victory."

The newly formed LWV wasted no time responding to the exhortations of Mrs. Catt. In May 1920, the LWV issued a campaign bulletin favoring the Department of Education Bill, which was then under consideration by the Congress. In its bulletin, the LWV instructed its members: "Get into the parties . . . . Democratic women, you need the help of your Republican sisters. Republican women, you will succeed only if you join hands with the Democratic members working from within. Neither side could win without the other, but by team work in behalf of the legislative measures in which women believe, the League of Women Voters will become invincible.

"Before the League assembles for the Convention of 1921, the United States will be far on the road to equality of opportunity of education for men, for women and for children, native and foreign born. This is to be accomplished through the medium of the public schools by means of federal and state legislation promoted and engineered by the members of the National League of Women Voters in the various states of the Union.

"Members of the League of Women Voters should become trained propagandists for the education of public opinion as to the importance of this (Education) Bill, using the same methods which won the . . . [19th] Amendment."

In an article ("How Far to the Left Is the League of Women Voters?" *National Republic*, August 1954), Felix Wittmer provided sketches of the activities of Mrs. Catt and other early leaders of the LWV: "A veteran pacifist and internationalist, Mrs. Catt throughout the years was an easy target of those who use our gullible 'liberals' as sponsors of the Marxian fronts. During the Spanish Civil War, in the 1930's, she sponsored the Coordinating Committee to Lift the Embargo, 'one of the numerous Communist front enterprises which were organized around the Communists' agitation over the Spanish civil war' (Special Committee on Un-American Activities, House of Representatives, 78th Congress, 2nd Session, on H. Res. 282). Signing a petition, 'Lift the Embargo Now,' which appeared in the *New York Times* of January 31, 1939, Mrs. Catt found herself in the company of such old-timers of the pro-Communist causes as Marc Blitzstein, Rockwell Kent, Emil Lengyel and others. The *Daily Worker* of February 10, 1944, page 3, listed her as sponsoring the Committee of Women of the National Council of American-Soviet Friendship, in sending recorded messages to women of the Soviet Union. She also joined another Communist front in petitioning in behalf of Harry Bridges, in 1942.

"Jane Addams, world famous pacifist who has been prominent in the history of the League of Women Voters, was on the Advisory Board

91

of Russian Reconstruction Farms, cited as a Communist enterprise which was directed by Harold Ware, son of the Communist, Mother Bloor, and organizer of the first Communist spy cell in our Government. She was one of the key agitators for recognition of Russia in 1933.

"Emily Newell Blair, another League of Women Voters stalwart, sponsored the League of Women Shoppers, 'an organization which this committee found to be a Communist-controlled front by indisputable documentary evidence obtained from the files of the Communist Party in Philadelphia' (Special Committee on Un-American Activities, Report, March 29, 1944, page 121). She was also active in the 'Spanish Refugee' groups in 1939 and was chairman of the Consumers Federation of District of Columbia in 1938.

"Julia Clifford Lathrop, outstanding figure in the League of Women Voters, served on the advisory council of the American Society for Cultural Relations with Russia. Mrs. Henry Goddard Leach, idol of the League of Women Voters, publicly appealed in behalf of the Soviet Russian people before we were actively involved in World War II, and she was director of the American-Russian Institute in 1936. The toxicologist, Alice Hamilton, veteran of the League of Women Voters, may without exaggeration be characterized as a veteran of the Communist fronts. The American Committee to Save Refugees, Russian Reconstruction Farms, Consumers National Federation, Friends of the Soviet Union, National Council of American-Soviet Friendship, and the National Federation for Constitutional Liberties figure among the many pro-Communist outfits which she has sponsored. While, as a national committeewoman of the American Committee for Democracy and Intellectual Freedom, she petitioned for the discontinuation of the House Un-American Activities Committee, Professor Hamilton sponsored the Schneiderman Defense Committee and the Citizens' Committee to Free Earl Browder.

"During the Nazi-Soviet alliance, this shining light of the League of Women Voters, according to the *Daily Worker* of September 17, 1940, pages 1 and 5, was one of forty-five who urged President Roosevelt and Attorney General Robert H. Jackson to release from jail the leaders of the Communist-controlled International Fur and Leather Workers, who through strikes had sabotaged our aid to the free world. This was after the fall of France when a Nazi invasion of England 'vas a strong possibility. Along this line, on March 5, 1941, three and a half months before Hitler attacked his Soviet ally, Dr. Hamilton, in a full-page spread in the *Daily Worker*, along with other Soviet sympathizers defended the Communist Party."

In 1948, two astute critics of the LWV, Lucille Cardin Crain and Anne Burrows Hamilton, in their pamphlet, "Packaged Thinking for Women," provided an exposé of the leftist measures supported by the LWV in its first quarter of a century of activities. They pointed out that the LWV was one of twenty-one organizations with membership in the Women's Joint Congressional Committee, which was founded in 1920 as "a clearing house for the legislative work of national organizations engaged in promoting federal measures pertaining to the general welfare." The Crain-Hamilton pamphlet revealed that the Women's Joint Congressional Committee was the source of "packaged thinking" for its member organizations, including the LWV. In the parallel histories of the LWV and the Women's Joint Congressional Committee, there were parallel concerns in lobbying activities. The Crain-Hamilton pamphlet provided a summary of the activities: "During the twenty-seven years the Women's Joint Congressional Committee has functioned, its legislative committees have done active work in connection with legislation of many kinds, such as: support for the Women's Bureau in the United States Department of Labor; the Bureau of Human Nutrition and Home Economics in the United States Department of Agriculture; the Office of Education and Children's Bureau in the Federal Security Agency; the Food and Drug Administration; appropriations for maternal and child welfare; the Child Labor Amendment; entrance of the United States into the United Nations; revision of the Neutrality Act; reciprocal trade agreements; revision of the Food and Drug Act; suffrage for the District of Columbia; federal-aid-to-education; and school lunch bills; and opposition to the so-called Equal Rights Amendment."

While the LWV was affiliated with the Women's Joint Congressional Committee, it also was a member of the Program Information Exchange. The PIE was founded in 1944 as a clearing house for opinion-forming groups. It boasted that its membership represented the means of reaching fifty-six million people. The head of the PIE was Evans Clark, an old-time Socialist and Communist fronter. Clark, through the PIE, was able to present socialist-oriented packaged thinking to the LWV, the American Association of University Women, the YWCA, the National Council of Jewish Women, and the National Association of Business and Professional Women's Clubs — all of which were coincidentally members of the Women's Joint Congressional Committee. Clark's clearing house was financed by the Carnegie Endowment for International Peace, the Twentieth Century Fund, the Federal Council of Churches, and the American Association of University Women — all of which were oriented definitely leftward. Through the LWV's membership in the PIE, it became affiliated with such leftist-oriented organizations as the Political Action Committee of the CIO, the Institute of Pacific Relations, the War Resisters League, the Foreign Policy Association, the Commission to Study the Organization of Peace, the National Citizens Political Action Committee, the Council on Foreign Relations, the Progressive Citizens of America, and the Advertising Council.

In the late 1940's, in its own literature, the LWV all but admitted that it was working for a socialist America. It tried to forestall criticism for such efforts: "Careless use of the words 'communistic' and 'socialistic' has marked much of our debate in the past, and because of the emotional connotations of these words, they can blind us to the actual situation under discussion. We must not be misled by the bogey of 'planned economy.'" Planned economy was far from being a bogey; it was a very real objective of the LWV, which urged its members to support legislation for "governmental policies which prevent inflation and deflation and stimulate maximum production and employment." The LWV certainly regarded government as necessarily paternalistic: "Government for the people requires the assumption of responsibility for social problems which affect the general welfare." — "We must take such steps as will establish democracy as the most successful form of government in allowing maximum freedom for the individual while at the same time assuring the essential needs of life such as education, housing, and the opportunity for employment security." Democracy to the LWV meant socialist housing programs, socialist medical care programs, socialist birth-to-death social security, socialist governmental-created full employment programs, and socialist governmental-controlled and financed education. But even such comprehensive "democracy" was not enough for the LWV; it actively supported organizations working for world citizenship in world government — world "democracy."

From its very beginnings, the LWV worked for the comprehensive concept of "international cooperation." The most important application of the concept was the LWV's formal endorsement of United States membership in the League of Nations in 1932. The endorsement remained as a continuing plank of the LWV's platform until the League of Nations collapsed without the United States ever having joined it.

When the League of Nations faded out of interest, the LWV's internationalist energies concentrated upon support of the World Bank, the International Monetary Fund, the United Nations Rehabilitation and Reconstruction Administration (UNRRA), and the Dumbarton Oaks Conference, from which emerged an agreement by the Soviet Union, the United Kingdom, and the United States to establish the United Nations Organization.

In 1945, the LWV participated on a consulting basis at the San Francisco organizing conference of the United Nations. In March 1964, the LWV reviewed its pro-UN history: "From that day [1945] to this the League has given unswerving support to the United Nations and has examined its strengths and weaknesses with a friendly but critical eye. Realizing that no organization which reflects today's tense and troubled times can be free from conflicts of interest, occasionally acrimonious debate, and some mistakes, we have been heartened by the success of the United Nations in peacekeeping and in contributing to creation of the basic conditions for a peaceful and stable world through economic and social programs."

In truth, during the first nineteen years of the United Nations' existence, the LWV followed the guidelines presented to it by the Program Information Exchange in 1947: "Uneasiness about Russian policies and the veto, heard behind the scenes, is played down and will be by most organizations. Idea is that United States-Russian [sic] cooperation, cornerstone of the United Nations structure, must not be undercut by public distrust."

In 1962, in convention, the LWV "decided to re-examine and re-evaluate the U.S. system as it is today, to determine what U.S. policies could strengthen that system, and to consider the appropriate relationship between the United Nations and U.S. foreign policy." (For more than a decade the LWV had in its "Continuing Responsibilities" program: "U.S. support of the United Nations and its specialized agencies, including adequate financial contributions, increased use, and improved procedures; U.S. support of measures designed to keep the peace through the United Nations and regional defense arrangements, and U.S. support of measures to promote international economic development and technical assistance [programs of the UN]." Related "continuing responsibilities" were: "Cooperation with other nations in solving international problems and promoting world peace [and] development of international organization and international law to achieve permanent means of cooperation.")

It is difficult to escape the conclusion that between 1962 and 1964 there was absolutely no need for the LWV's members to study any further on the matter of the United Nations. The collective mind of the LWV was closed to any and all criticism of the United Nations. In the September 1962 issue of the LWV's *The National Voter*, there was an apologia for the UN which included an incredible amount of misinformation, distorted history, outright lies, and fuzzy thinking. This all appeared under the heading "Questions and Answers on the U.N." The text read:

"The talkathon of the dis-united nations starts today in the U.N. building that looks like a tombstone. We hope it will be one and mark the demise of the U.N. – the sooner the better for the U.S.A.

"The above is a composite of remarks made by different persons at different times. How do you refute such defeatist, destructive criticism? Here are simple factual answers to a few of the questions most frequently asked. Q. Do the Russians run the United Nations? A. It would be impossible for any one nation to 'run' the United Nations. There are 104 member states. Each state has one vote. The best way to measure Soviet dominance or the lack of it is to see what resolutions are passed by the United Nations and which nations support or oppose them. In the Sixteenth Session of the General Assembly (September 1961 to June 1962), as in previous sessions, all major resolutions proposed by the United States were approved. The record shows that the United States and the Asian and African nations were on the same side most of the time, with the Soviet bloc on the opposite side and losing consistently. In the Security Council the United States, like the Soviet Union and the other permanent members (China, France, Great Britain), has the power of the veto. We can veto any resolution which appears to be contrary to U.S. interests. Since the United Nations has been in existence the United States has never used the veto; the Russians have used it 100 times.

"Q. Is the U.N. Secretariat a nest of Communist spies? A. The professional staff of the Secretariat is recruited on as wide a geographical basis as possible, as required by the U.N. Charter. It includes nationals from practically every member nation. About 52 percent of the professional staff are from NATO nations, including the United States; adding other allies of and countries friendly to the United States, the proportion increases to 72 percent. About half the general service staff are U.S. nationals. Any member of the staff found to be a spy is dismissed.

"Q. Do the Soviets control U.N. military affairs? A. First, U.N. involvement with military matters, with the exception of Korea, has been minimal. There is no U.N. military or police force as envisioned in the Charter. Second, U.N. forces (troops from middle-sized and small powers only) now in the Middle East and in the Congo are the responsibility of the Secretary General, acting under direction of the General Assembly or the Security Council. None of the Secretary General's military advisers is from a Communist nation.

"Q. Can the United Nations draft our boys to fight anywhere in the World? A. The United States can veto any Security Council action concerning the use of armed force. The General Assembly can recommend police action, but the decision to send troops to help make up such a police force is voluntary with each country. In any event, the U.N. practice has been not to use troops from the United States or Russia or any of the major powers but only from the small and middle-sized powers.

"Q. Why should, for example, Iceland with 170,000 people have the same vote as the United States with 180,000,000? A. U.N. membership is based on the 'principle of the sovereign equality of its members' — one nation, one vote. Equal voting power in the General Assembly is greatly cherished by the smallest and by the newest nations, who tend to use their votes responsibly. While all U.N. members have equal votes in the Assembly, equal influence is another matter. It is apparent to anyone that the greater powers have the greater influence. In the Security Council, voting is modified to a large extent by the veto power.

"Q. Do we pay more than our share of U.N. expenses? A. Assessments are determined in line with a scale drawn up by a committee of the General Assembly with reference to each nation's 'capacity to pay.' The 1946 assessment on the United States was 39.89 percent of the U.N. regular budget and the assessment has steadily decreased since that time. In 1961 we paid 32.5 percent; in 1962, 32.02 percent. The U.N. goal is a maximum of 30 percent of the regular budget from any one nation. In 1961 the assessments on the United States for the budgets of some of the Specialized Agencies were the same as for the regular budget, but for most of these budgets our assessments were less. In 1961 we contributed a little over one half of the costs of the voluntary programs. Since 1957 we have paid 49 percent of the special assessments for the peacekeeping operations in the Middle East and in the Congo. The 1961 U.S. contribution to the United Nations amounted to about two tenths of one percent of the total U.S. federal budget. This does not seem out of line with our status as the richest nation in the world and with our responsibilities as a leader of the world.

"Q. Are we turning U.S. foreign policy over to the United Nations? A. U.S. foreign policy is made in Washington – in the final analysis, by the President of the United States. It may be carried out in a variety of ways: country to country; through regional groups such as the Organization of American States, which includes Latin American nations and the United States; through various international organizations, of which the United Nations is the most inclusive. It is not a question of 'turning over' policy to the United Nations. It is a question of whether working through the United Nations is the most practical way to implement a certain U.S. policy at a given time.

"Q. Wouldn't we be better off in a Council of Free Nations than in the United Nations? A. The choice is not 'either/or.' If U.S. foreign policy is to achieve its objectives we must be a part of the free-world community (there are many groups organized on this basis, and we belong to most of them) and we must be a part of the international community (the United Nations). We need to work closely with those with whom we have the most in common. We must also work with those whose views may differ from ours, for it is better to try to resolve the differences than to let them build up until they explode into war."

At its 1964 convention, the LWV reported on the results of its decision to re-examine and re-evaluate the U.N. system: "Results of two years of concentrated study are: broadening of League positions to include support of the principle of one-nation-one-vote in the General Assembly and of continuing negotiations to reduce the risk of war; greater appreciation of the role of the United Nations in keeping the peace and awareness of the necessity for improving its ability for doing so; insight into the problems created by the rapid increase in membership; recognition of the vitality that the new member nations have brought to the organization; deepened understanding of the mutual interests of the United States and the United Nations; strong reaffirmation of support for the U.N. system."

Germane to what LWV means by "two years of concentrated study" to arrive at a position on the United Nations or any issue is an understanding of the LWV's structure and modus operandi. In its own recruiting literature, the LWV says: *"Democratic Procedure*: Members consciously practice democracy within the League. Majority opinion prevails, but minority opinion is welcome. The League strives for substantial agreement on a position, not for unanimity.

"Study, Discussion, Action: Full facts, the pros and cons, are studied before the League takes a position. Members participate in discussion in small units and in large meetings; everyone has an opportunity to express an opinion. When a position is reached through consensus of membership, the League and the members as individuals work to implement that position. League action methods include testifying at public hearings, and the use of public forums, panel discussions, mass media, League publications, and letters to local, state, and national officials.

"How Program is Selected: The League works on governmental issues which arise out of needs of the community, the state, the nation. The membership chooses the program.

"Six months before the biennial national Convention, local Leagues begin a discussion of issues and send in recommendations for the national program. The national Board considers them and sends a 'Proposed Program' to Leagues for a second round of discussion. Final decisions are made by a majority vote of delegates in Convention. State and local programs are selected by the same general democratic procedure as is the national program.

"The League does not try to cover the civic waterfront but selects a few important issues at a time. The program is divided into two parts: *Current Agenda* — subjects for concentrated study and concerted action; *Continuing Responsibilities* — positions on issues to which the League has given sustained attention and on which it may continue to take action. *Principles* — government principles supported by the League as a whole — give authority for the adoption of local, state, and national Current Agendas."

Members of LWV belong to local leagues at the community level. The local leagues belong to state Leagues. Every other year, the local leagues assemble in a national convention. At the national convention, the LWV puts its "democracy" to work as it adopts its position on various issues. In truth, the positions are not the deliberate opinions of the members from either the local or state level. The positions are the work of the LWV's National Board. Prior to the national convention, there is no vote on the positions. The National Board does go through the formality of recommending study materials to local leagues. Members do discuss the issues. Local leagues are encouraged to send to the National Board opinions about the issues under study, but no vote is taken and it is the National Board, using what it claims is a consensus as a guide, that determines what position the LWV shall take on any particular issue. The impression is given to the members, when they have arrived at the convention, that their approval of various positions has already been noted in the correspondence of local and state leagues to the National Board. At the convention, no additions or amendments to a position statement may be debated unless two-thirds of the members present vote in favor of such a debate. It means, in effect, that the national convention is a rubber-stamp affair, as a majority vote is sufficient to approve what the National Board presents as its program. Deviations from this cut-and-dried procedure have been rare in the history of LWV's conventions.

At the 1964 convention, when the LWV re-affirmed and broadened its support of the United Nations, it provided explanatory details which in every single respect reflected the views of the liberal-internationalist organizations — and they are myriad — whose sole purpose is to propagandize for the United Nations.

In explanation of its expanded United Nations position, the League said: "(1) *Improving peacekeeping procedures.* By its 'presence' the United Nations has kept the peace in many places and in many ways. Observation, fact-finding, conciliation at an early stage have frequently kept international disputes from blowing up into bitter conflict that would have jeopardized world peace. For instance, with the help of the United Nations such conflicts have been avoided in perpetually troubled Kashmire and in West New Guinea. The League attaches great importance to U.S. preventive diplomacy as well as to the necessity for advance planning for military or police action if it should become necessary, as it did in the Congo and the Middle East.

"(2) *Upholding the principle of collective financial responsibility for administration, peacekeeping, and development.* The sharing of the costs of the world organization by member states, commensurate with their ability to pay, is a basic principle of the Charter — a principle essential to the operation of the United Nations. No country, because of the size of its financial contribution, should be able to dominate the United Nations. It was the spirit of mutual responsibility for peace and development which led to the formation of the world body and which makes the United Nations effective in today's world. Only in such rare instances as the Congo operation has U.S. financial support approached a share proportionate to our percentage of the world's wealth. Our country may in the future need to make our contribution to peacekeeping costs a more consistent reflection of our resources.

"(3) *Continuing negotiations to reduce the risk of war.* League support of efforts to reduce the risk of war evolves from an historic League belief that nations must find means other than war to solve world problems. Changing political balances, emerging areas of mutual interest between the major powers, technical advances in the detection of nuclear blasts, and the development of new weapons systems encourage constant conferences on the various phases of disarmament and arms control. However, any agreement reached must include safeguards for U.S. national security and domestic economy. It is generally held that disarmament is a step-by-step process and that any measure to reduce the risk of war is a step of value, not only in itself, but also in creating an atmosphere of mutual confidence in which a disarmed world is possible.

"(4) *Maintaining the principle of one vote for each member nation.* Leagues, after considerable evaluation, have concluded that in spite of the changed composition of the United Nations, the original Charter requirement that each nation be allowed one vote in the General Assembly, regardless of the nation's size, wealth, or military power, is at present wise. A deliberative body discussing the concerns of all mankind must mirror these concerns and act with a sense of responsibility toward all mankind.

"(5) *Preserving the integrity of the office of the Secretary-General.* The Secretary-General is the executive officer of the United Nations. Important responsibilities are given to him by the Charter and further tasks are continually assigned to him by the General Assembly and the Security Council. He must have the power and the freedom to carry out his vast duties free from the pressure of national interests or from a veto imposed by any hydra-headed executive arrangement. Too much emphasis cannot be placed on the importance of developing a truly international civil service which will act in the interest of all nations.

"(6) *Making greater use of the World Court to settle international disputes.* Since the 1920s the League has pressed for the settlement of international disputes through adjudication. We believe strongly that no self-judging clause such as the Connally Amendment should restrict U.S. access to the World Court. World peace must rest in part on the body of law which will develop through treaties, covenants, agreements, and the judgments of international courts."

One of the most controversial episodes in the history of the LWV revolved around the question of the so-called Bricker Amendment. At the time of the LWV's 1952 national convention, U.S. Senator John Bricker (R.-Ohio) had just introduced a constitutional amendment designed to prevent the President of the United States from concluding a treaty that would be in violation of the Constitution. At that time, Bricker and others were disturbed that there were Americans who believed that the entire Charter of the United Nations – a treaty – was automatically the supreme law of the land. These disturbed Americans believed that the social and economic life of the American people were and should remain within the province of domestic law and not in the realm of treaties between the United States and any foreign power or group of powers. In its essence, the debate over the acceptance of the Bricker Amendment was between those who wished to retain American sovereignty and those who were willing to relinquish it to the care of an international organization – in this case the United Nations – in which the United States was only one of scores of members.

The Bricker Amendment had been introduced into the Congress too late for the National Board of the LWV to go through its ritual of a "concentrated study" and consensus. But it did initiate the ritual. The study material was sent out to the local league with the intention that a position would be announced in the 1954 Convention.

On January 13, 1954, Mrs. John G. Lee, president of the LWV, wrote to President Dwight Eisenhower: "The League of Women Voters of the United States is opposed to the Bricker Amendment. During the past year Leagues throughout the country have studied the issues involved and the weight of opinion expressed is clearly against the Bricker Amendment as not only unnecessary but as dangerous for the future security of our country."

Mrs. Lee, in a completely arbitrary fashion, had presumed to speak for every member of the LWV. No vote or poll had ever been taken as to how the members felt about the Bricker Amendment. Mrs. Lee mentioned that members had studied the issues, but there was no excuse for her hasty action. Constitutional amendments are ordinarily not ratified overnight — the process is generally lengthy. And there was every indication that the Bricker Amendment was going to be hotly debated in the Senate and in the state legislatures. There can be little doubt that the action of the LWV's hierarchy was taken because the Bricker Amendment would deny to the United Nations the opportunity to interfere in the domestic life of the United States.

Oddly enough, Mrs. Lee and her fellow board members could partially justify her arbitrary action on the Bricker Amendment issue because the National Board has authority "to make timely decisions" on behalf of the League. When the National Board feels that there is an emergency, it may decide it is "Time for Action" and call upon all members to support the LWV's official position by the use of radio, TV, newspapers, letters to Congressmen, or other communicative means. The National Board issues instructions to local leagues: "A league shall respond to a Time for Action sent by a national or state Board. If a local League does not agree with the position of the state or national League on an issue, or if it feels its membership is not prepared on the subject, it may choose not to take legislative action. However, it shall inform its members of the Time for Action so that they can act as individuals if they wish to do so. A report as to why no action was taken shall be sent by the [local] Board to the state or national Board for its information. A local League shall not take official action contrary to a state or national stand . . . ."

Of course, no "Time for Action" had been issued before Mrs. Lee opposed the Bricker Amendment. She didn't attempt to poll the members, but this is explained away by the LWV's rules: "Polling the membership, particularly by mail or phone, to arrive at an agreement, is not sound. It tends to force crystallization of opinion without benefit of deliberation. Moreover, it does not allow for variation of opinion." Mrs. Lee did not wait for a consensus, and if she had it really wouldn't have mattered. Nothing could be more flexible than LWV's standards for consensus: "Determining consensus should be an interpretive process. The Board should take into account areas of agreement expressed in general membership meetings, in unit meetings, and in Conventions and the annual meeting when the Program was selected. The Board should give continuous attention to the development of membership thinking throughout the year as each Program item is discussed. In this way the Board is in touch with membership thinking as it develops and does not need to seek it when an emergency arises . . . ."

In line with the LWV's stand against the Bricker Amendment has been its long-time campaign for repeal of the Connally Reservation. The Reservation consists of six words ("as determined by the United States") in the Senate Resolution which consented to the United States acceptance of the compulsory jurisdiction of the World Court, the principal judicial organ of the United Nations. The Reservation and Resolution exclude: "Disputes with regard to matters which are essentially within the domestic jurisdiction of the United States as determined by the United States." By seeking repeal of the Connally Reservation, the LWV indicated its desire that the United States relinquish its inherent right to decide what disputes with any other nations are within American jurisdiction and not within the jurisdiction of the World Court.

Over the decades, the LWV has developed a set of working principles which have not varied in recent years. The principles are so loosely worded and so devoid of definitions that the most obnoxious legislation, executive actions, and judicial decisions could be justified by a partisan interpretation of the principles. The principles read: "1. The principles of representative government and individual liberty established in the Constitution of the United States. 2. A system of government which is responsive to the will of the people and which enables the voter to carry out his obligations as a citizen. 3. A system of government in which responsibility is clearly fixed. 4. A system of government which promotes coordination of the operations of federal, state, and local governments. 5. Governmental organization and administration which contribute to economy and efficiency. 6. A merit system for the selection, retention, and promotion of government personnel. 7. Legal protection of citizens in their right to vote. 8. A system of free public education which provides equal opportunity for all. 9. Protection of minority groups against discrimination. 10. Removal of legal and administrative discriminations against women. 11. A system of federal, state, and local taxation which is flexible and equitable. 12. Fiscal and monetary policies which promote a stable and expanding economy. 13. Responsibility of government to share in the solution of social and economic problems which affect the general welfare. 14. Adequate financing of government functions and services. 15. Conservation and development of natural resources in the public interest. 16. Domestic policies which facilitate the solution of international problems. 17. Cooperation with other nations in solving international problems and promoting world peace. 18. Development of international organization and international law to achieve permanent means of cooperation."

The LWV cannot be faulted if it claims that its continuing responsibilities and its positions on issues square with its principles, but there can be no denying that in carrying out these principles the LWV — invariably on the national level and generally on the state and local levels — follows a left-of-center liberal, and internationalist line.

As one of the LWV's "continuing responsibilities," there is: "*Loyalty-Security:* Support of standardized procedures, 'common sense' judgment, and greatest possible protection for the individual under the federal loyalty-security programs; opposition to extension of such programs to nonsensitive positions." In living up to this particular responsibility, the LWV has been extremely critical of congressional investigations, governmental loyalty programs, and anti-subversion legislation. If the LWV accomplished its "loyalty-security" program, Communists and other subversives would have complete freedom to work in non-sensitive [the LWV never defines "sensitive"] positions in the executive branch and in any position in the legislative and judicial branches of government, or in industries working on defense contracts. The LWV's "loyalty-security" posture has all the major elements of an anti-anti-Communist counterattack against reasonable measures to protect United States integrity and security from destruction from within the ranks of taxpayer-supported public servants. (Mrs. Lucy Benson, who was elected president of LWV in 1968, has said: "What got me active in the League of Women Voters was the era of the McCarthy investigations." Mrs. Benson has proven to be left-of-center, following the tradition of preceding LWV presidents.)

The LWV has an unblemished record of supporting every U.S. foreign giveaway program (so-called foreign aid), back to the Lend-Lease and Marshall Plan programs of the 1940's. The LWV lobbied for the Food, Drug and Cosmetic Acts, the Social Security System, the Tennessee Valley Authority, civil rights acts, the U.S.-Soviet Union consular treaty and nuclear testing treaty, and all war-on-poverty legislation. It has also lobbied for reform of the electoral college along liberal lines; for expansion of trade with the Communist bloc; for racially integrated schools; and for home rule in Washington, D.C. The LWV has always taken a strong stand against a ceiling on federal income tax rates.

One of the most successful campaigns waged by the LWV began in 1966 when United States-Red China relations became a major part of the LWV's foreign policy program. By 1969, after a three-year period of "study," the League emerged with a call to the United States government to take the initiative to normalize relations with the People's Republic of [Red] China. Every feature that had ever been mentioned by Red China lobbyists was included in the recommendations offered by the League through its foreign policy committee chairman, Mrs. David G. Bradley: "The League of Women Voters has persistently searched for policy formulations and governmental programs which can reduce the risk of war and assure non-violent resolution of conflict between nations. This is the common theme of our foreign policy positions, and this concern has guided the League's review of U.S. policy toward the People's Republic of China. An overwhelming number of nearly 1000 Leagues reporting to date hold that the United States should take 'initiatives which would facilitate participation by the People's Republic of China in the world community and relax tensions between the United States and mainland China.' The key words used over and over again are communication, coexistence, cooperation. The Leagues want a U.S. policy designed to invite a

106

peaceful response from the People's Republic, welcoming her participation in the family of nations.

"One of the most striking impressions which remains after reading through the consensus reports is the sense of agreement on this basic philosophy which prevails in the Leagues in every section of the country. Support for existing policies is negligible, confined to a small number of Leagues.

"In 1966 when the convention adopted the China study it identified U.S. relations with mainland China as being of critical importance. Now, in 1969, this organization has taken a long look at political reality and the consensus which has emerged defines essential specific policy changes. Furthermore, the Leagues recognize the complexities of the China puzzle. They are aware of the effect of the war in Vietnam on the possibility of immediate action. They see the necessity for careful international diplomacy in seeking a resolution to the Taiwan problem. They acknowledge the difficulties inherent in the tangled relationships between Washington, Moscow and Peking. They know that the passage of time will be necessary to some forms of progress. They accept the need for political astuteness and proper timing.

"In spite of the fact that there were no queries on specific policies in the consensus questions, the Leagues spontaneously chose six basic areas in which to recommend new approaches.

"In advocating policies 'which would encourage normalization of U.S. relations with the Chinese mainland' the League holds that U.S. policies toward China should be the same as those for any country, regardless of ideological or political differences. The first step should be to open the channels for trade in non-strategic goods. This country should also seek opportunities for travel for American and Chinese citizens in both countries. We should furthermore seek contacts through cultural exchange, including international meetings ranging from scientific confabs to disarmament conferences. Such moves would build a favorable climate for further diplomatic initiatives. And the League wants the government to take the initiative.

"Beyond trade, travel and cultural exchange, League members urge that this country should 'withdraw its opposition to representation of the Chinese People's Republic in the United Nations.' They admit the difficulties: the possibility of a need for change in the U.N. itself, perhaps in the Security Council; the sensitivity of both mainland China and Taiwan to the question; the international aspects of the problem.

"Each League sees it a little differently and we have no blueprint to offer on Taiwan. However, this approach may prove to be a realistic one. Solutions to political problems seldom fit preconceived patterns. If the United States does cease opposing representation for mainland China, the door might be opened for the United Nations to find a resolution of the problem of Taiwan's future status in the United Nations.

"Finally, we should 'move toward establishing diplomatic relations.' Some want to do it at once, some as soon as practicable. Some emphasize de facto recognition now. But the overall agreement is clear — the People's Republic is the legitimate government of the mainland and the United States should move in the direction of recognizing that government.

"The League is now in a position to urge changes in basic U.S. policies which have cut this nation off from communication or cooperation with the People's Republic. We have stated our objectives and determined specific policy directions. In the future we can measure policy proposals against the objectives and take action."

There were many things remarkable about the LWV's 800-word position statement. Somehow the composers of the statement managed to avoid a single mention of Communism or Communists. There was no mention of the fact that Red China was deeply involved in the Vietnam War against the United States, nor was there any allusion to the unresolved Korean War — another instance of Red China opposed to the United States. There wasn't the slightest reference to the fact that though Ambassadors from Red China and the United States had met in Warsaw for a series of about 150 talks since 1955, there had never been any report that anything had been accomplished through these meetings at the highest diplomatic level. There was no indication as to what, if any, advantages would accrue to the United States from exchanges of scientific data. The statement provided no hint that the LWV had even considered the risks to United States national security that were obviously inherent in any invitation allowing Red Chinese to wander around this country at will. There was no explanation as to how the LWV had arrived at the conclusion that Red China "is the legitimate government of the mainland." The LWV could not have been any cruder in its dismissal of Free China, a charter member of the

LWV's beloved United Nations. Perhaps the most remarkable feature of the LWV's position statement on Red China is that it preceded by two years, in every detail, the Nixon Administration's surrender to the Red China lobby. (As early as January 1966, the LWV's pro-Red China posture was easily predictable at the time the very active Massachusetts LWV sponsored a panel for a discussion of Red China. The panelists included John K. Fairbank, Roger Hilsman, Harold R. Isaacs, and Ezra F. Vogel. The wonder is that the Massachusetts group did not invite Chou En-lai and Mao Tse-tung to plead their case. But they did the next best thing by inviting the aforementioned Red China lobbyists plus Felix Greene, a most accomplished apologist and propagandist for Mao Tse-tung.)

In recent years, the LWV has been most concerned in its support for the socialistic and phony war on poverty — especially the programs of the Office of Economic Opportunity. In early 1971, when President Lucy Benson of the LWV heard that the Nixon Administration might reduce funds for the OEO, she called a closed-door conference in Washington, D.C., to which she invited leaders of left-of-center groups. From that meeting, Miss Benson sent a telegram to President Nixon: "We were shaken by the recent report that the 1972 OEO budget is being cut by 23 per cent and that its major volunteer program, VISTA, is being eliminated. We have continually pressed for adequate funding for OEO and for administrative leadership to gain and hold the confidence of the poor and other Americans who are anxious for this abundant nation to keep its promises."

Mrs. Benson was joined in this telegram, which pleaded for more welfare statism, by leaders of the Rural Housing Coalition, the National Council of Jewish Women, the National Urban Coalition, the National Council for Negro Women, the National Tenants Organization, the United Automobile Workers Union, the National Welfare Rights Organization, the American Institute of Architects, the American Institute of Planners, the Center for Community Change, the Americans for Democratic Action, the National Jewish Welfare Board, the National Association for Community Development, the National Assembly for Social Policy and Developments, the Americans for Indian Opportunity Action Council, the National VISTA Alliance, the National Council of OEO Union Locals, Local 2677, and the Federal Employees Union (AFL-CIO).

During the several months following Mrs. Benson's closed-door conference of leftwingers, the LWV continued to build up its coalition of leftist agitators. On April 20, 1971, Cynthia Hannum, LWV's action chairman, announced that the coalition had six recommendations to make to the Congress. Notwithstanding the fact that OEO had been a colossal boondoggle and that much of OEO's funds and personnel had contributed to the promotion of ultra-leftist projects, the coalition recommended: "Strengthen and expand OEO by extending the EOA Act for at least two years. OEO should receive increased funding. The legal services program should be strengthened and expanded. The VISTA program should be preserved and maintained in OEO. The local share for community action and other OEO programs should not be raised to 25 percent."

By mid-April 1971, the coalition started by Mrs. Benson had grown to eleven organizations, including some of the most outrageously leftist groups in the country — the Americans for Democratic Action, the Anti-Defamation League, Common Cause, the National Association for the Advancement of Colored People, the National Farmer's Union, the National Urban Coalition, the National Sharecroppers Fund, the National Student Association, the National Welfare Rights Organization, Planned Parenthood-World Population, and the Unitarian-Universalist Association.

In 1969, the LWV made preparations for its fiftieth anniversary year — 1970. President Nixon was prevailed upon to issue a routine, meaningless proclamation: "Now, therefore, I, Richard Nixon, President of the United States of America, call upon all our citizens to join with the League of Women Voters of the United States in the observance of its fiftieth anniversary in 1970. I urge all businesses, industries, foundations, and civic organizations to give the full measure of their support to the League and its activities."

Editorial writers in the liberal press throughout the country reacted in puppet-like fashion as they lavished encomiums upon the fifty-year-old League. In conjunction with the fiftieth anniversary, the LWV began an $11 million campaign "to prepare for even more significant responsibilities in citizen participation in government." To lend prestige to its fund-raising campaign, the League compiled a list of sponsors "who endorse its past accomplishments and future plans." The list included an impressive cross-section of leftist-liberal Americans: I.W.

Abel, Morris Abram, Eugenie Anderson, Joseph A. Beirne, Daniel Bell, Barry Bingham, Eugene Carson Blake, Ralph J. Bunche, Erwin D. Canham, Harlan Cleveland, James B. Conant, Andrew W. Cordier, Norman Cousins, David Dubinsky, Arthur S. Flemming, John W. Gardner, Paul G. Hoffman, Joseph E. Johnson, Edward M. Kennedy, Arthur Larson, Sol Linowitz, Benjamin E. Mays, George Meany, Charles H. Percy, Jacob Potofsky, Walter Reuther, Bayard Rustin, Sargent Shriver, Marietta Tree, George Wald, James Warburg, Jerome Wiesner, Roy Wilkins, and Willard Wirtz.

In conjunction with the anniversary celebration, the LWV promulgated a campaign statement to go along with its fund-raising drive. The statement was entitled "An Assignment from Society." With its customary presumptuousness, the LWV somehow discovered "the challenge of an all-out attack on citizen bewilderment and frustration." The LWV accepted the challenge and actively sought an assignment from society: "To help resolve the growing problems of our cities; to increase the political effectiveness of the citizens in the ghetto and to remove the ghetto itself. To make citizens of this country aware of our responsibilities for international cooperation and to share with citizens of other countries the processes and techniques for strengthening an open society. To increase citizens' ability to work for the improved management of our water, land, and air resources in the interests of an attractive, healthy environment. To direct itself to the task of revitalizing and strengthening state and local governments. To expand its Voters Service in clarifying issues and supplying non-partisan information on candidates, in increasing the numbers registered and voting, and in encouraging active party participation."

The campaign statement gave every indication that its collective leadership had been brainwashed by problem-seeking, problem-solving social science elitists who simply cannot allow individuals to act and think for themselves. How else explain: "Who knows what it will take to be a citizen — an effective citizen — in a continuously changing society? The challenges of the immediate future and the projected needs of the long-range view are staggering in their enormity, complexity, and intensity. Many citizens today are feeling increasingly powerless to influence their own destinies, and as a result, are detaching themselves from citizen responsibility. Others, with rising expectations,

111

are feeling more and more intensely that they must be given the full rights of citizenship now."

In 1954, the LWV, as might be expected, was titillated by the Supreme Court's incredible decision in favor of desegregation of schools. Since that time, the LWV has slavishly followed the authoritarian agitators who have caused so much turmoil and racial trouble in the school systems. (Nothing better demonstrates the commitment of the LWV to racial agitation than the hysterical reaction of Mrs. Robert J. Stewart, president of the LWV, at the time of Martin L. King's death: "All white America stands guilty for what happened to Dr. Martin Luther King last night in Memphis. The League of Women Voters shares the feelings of outrage and frustration that grips the nation . . . . If each of us takes on the same kind of personal commitment that characterized Dr. King's life, his goals can be achieved. They must be achieved.")

In March 1972, when the Congress had under consideration a constitutional amendment which would ban bussing to achieve racial balance in schools, LWV President Lucy Benson said: "To act favorably [on the Amendment] could only imply withdrawal of Congressional support, under emotional pressure, for efforts undertaken already to integrate our schools. The League urges this committee and the entire Congress not to be a party to such a disaster." Mrs. Benson charged that the Administration and the Congress had responded to "hysteria with an equivalent emotion rather than responsible leadership."

In February 1972, the LWV cast aside any vestiges of nonpartisanship that might have remained after its long and persistent history of liberalism. For the first time, the LWV honored members of the Congress for their voting records. Based on their 1971 votes, a perfect rating was bestowed by the LWV upon: Senator Edmund S. Muskie of Maine, Senator Hubert H. Humphrey of Minnesota, Senator Henry M. Jackson of Washington, Senator Edward M. Kennedy of Massachusetts, and Representative Wilbur Mills of Arkansas – all Democrats; and Representative Paul N. McCloskey of California, who has difficulty deciding whether he's a Republican or a Democrat.

NATIONAL COORDINATING COMMITTEE TO END THE WAR IN VIETNAM
NOVEMBER 8 MOBILIZATION COMMITTEE

*SPRING MOBILIZATION COMMITTEE TO END
    THE WAR IN VIETNAM
STUDENT MOBILIZATION COMMITTEE TO END
    THE WAR IN VIETNAM
NATIONAL MOBILIZATION COMMITTEE TO END
    THE WAR IN VIETNAM
NEW MOBILIZATION COMMITTEE TO END
    THE WAR IN VIETNAM
NATIONAL PEACE ACTION COALITION
NATIONAL COALITION AGAINST WAR, RACISM
    AND REPRESSION
PEOPLE'S COALITION FOR PEACE AND JUSTICE
PEOPLE'S PEACE TREATY*

In August 1965, the National Coordinating Committee to End the War in Vietnam [NCCEW] was formed. The NCCEW was a coalition of Communist and non-Communist organizations. The activities of the NCCEW were directed by leaders of anti-Vietnam War groups that had been formed by the Socialist Workers Party and the Young Socialist Alliance. The most prominent individuals in the NCCEW were Arnold Johnson, the publicity director of the Communist Party; David Dellinger, a self-admitted Communist, but who denied formal membership in the Communist Party or any other party; Irving Beinin, who worked for the Communist weekly *National Guardian*; Jerry Rubin of California's Vietnam Day Committee; and Trotskyites Larry Seigle and Robin Maisel. The director of NCCEW was Frank Emspak, who had been closely associated with Communist-organized youth organizations; his father was the late Frank Emspak, a Communist Party official.

In March 1966, the NCCEW conducted the two-day International Days of Protest demonstrations, which were saturated with Communists. In New York, the demonstrations were led by the Fifth Avenue Vietnam Peace Parade Committee, which included leaders of the Communist Party, the Socialist Workers Party, and the Progressive Labor Party. Among the participants in the New York demonstration were large numbers of Communists, Trotskyites, and members of the Workers World Party and its offshoot, Youth Against War and Fascism. In Chicago, LeRoy Wolins of the Communist Party led the demonstration as head of Veterans for Peace in Vietnam. At the University of Wisconsin, Communist Party official Herbert Aptheker was the best-known demonstrator. In Los Angeles, the regional chairman of the Communist Party, Dorothy Healey, headed the demonstration.

After the International Days of Protest, the NCCEW was plagued with dissension. The Communist Party leaders insisted that demonstrations had to focus on all aspects of foreign and domestic policy, in order to adhere completely to the Communist line laid down by Moscow. The other major group in the NCCEW, the Socialist Workers Party, desired a concentration of energies upon the demand for immediate and total withdrawal of United States forces from Vietnam.

In September 1966, at Cleveland, a National Leadership Conference was organized by the University Circle Teach-In Committee and led by Sidney Peck, whose membership in the Communist Party has been certified on many occasions by congressional investigative committees. The Cleveland get-together was attended by leaders of extreme leftist and radical pacifist groups, including the Communist Party, the Socialist Workers Party, the American Friends Service Committee, the Fellowship of Reconciliation, the Fifth Avenue Vietnam Peace Parade Committee, the W.E.B. DuBois Clubs, Youth Against War and Fascism, Clergy and Laymen Concerned About Vietnam, the Young Socialist Alliance, the Chicago Peace Council, Women Strike for Peace, and Students for a Democratic Society. Among the better known radical leaders at Cleveland were Stewart Meacham, Sidney Lens, A.J. Muste, Jack Spiegel, Rev. Richard Fernandez, Hugh Fowler, Edward Keating of *Ramparts* magazine, Barbara Bick, Frank Emspak, and Carl Oglesby.

At the September meeting, the November 8 Mobilization Committee was established as an ad hoc united-front coalition in an attempt to get Communists and Trotskyites to work together under the "peace" banner. The key leaders of the ad hoc group were Fred Halstead and Sylvia Krushner. Halstead, a veteran leader of the Trotskyite Socialist Workers Party, was most anxious to concentrate the activities of the "peace" movement on US-get-out-of-Vietnam agitation. Krushner, a Communist leader of the well-organized Chicago Peace Council, was cooperating in the ad hoc group to insure the Communist Party's influence in the "peace" movement on the singular issue of Vietnam. Other Communists would continue to promote the Party's multi-faceted interest in foreign and domestic issues.

The November 8 Mobilization Committee emerged from its September meeting with a list of officials that included Barbara Bick, a

Communist and a leader of Women Strike for Peace; Robert Greenblatt, an apologist and propagandist for the Viet Cong; Sidney Peck; Edward Keating; Communist Otto Nathan; Carl Oglesby, former president of Students for a Democratic Society; Communist Jack Spiegel, a leader of the Communist-operated Chicago Peace Council; Communist Party theoretician Herbert Aptheker; Sidney Lens; Communist Franklin Alexander, chairman of the Communist Party's W.E.B. DuBois Clubs; Lew Jones and Gus Horowitz of the Socialist Workers Party; Rev. Philip Berrigan, who had been convicted and imprisoned for destroying draft files; Staughton Lynd of the W.E.B. DuBois Clubs, who had visited Hanoi; and Deidre Griswold of Youth Against War and Fascism.

In November 1966, the November 8 Mobilization Committee conducted 3-day mass demonstrations throughout the country against the Vietnam War. The demonstrations were moderately successful, especially in New York, where the chief participants were Communist Herbert Aptheker, Judy White of the Socialist Workers Party, Sue Eanet of Students for a Democratic Society, Communist Grace Newman, and Pauline Rosen of Women Strike for Peace. David Dellinger sent his and his hosts' greetings to the New York demonstrators from North Vietnam.

After the demonstrations, the November 8 Mobilization Committee met in Cleveland for its second and last conference. Over half of the conferees were from the Socialist Workers Party or its offshoot, the Young Socialist Alliance. The Communist Party was represented by Arnold Johnson, James West, Frank Emspak, Hugh Fowler (executive secretary of the DuBois Clubs), and others. Benjamin Spock and A.J. Muste spoke at the conference, as did David Dellinger, who regaled his audience with an account of his recent trip to North Vietnam, where he and his Communist hosts had deplored United States aggression, but had solaced themselves by reflecting upon the "heroic resistance" of the North Vietnamese people.

On November 27, 1966, the November 8 Mobilization Committee decided to reorganize as the Spring Mobilization Committee to End the War in Vietnam [Spring Mobe]. The reorganization was a major effort to bring under the umbrella of a united front a wider variety of groups than the customary Communist and Trotskyite ones. The Cleveland meeting produced a resolution by which Spring Mobe was created: "In view of the opposing need for new initiatives and nationwide coordination of activity to achieve peace, the November 5-8 Mobilization Committee hereby [*sic*] constitutes itself on a more formal basis as the Spring Mobilization Committee to End the War in Vietnam.

"The Mobilization Committee shall consist of those members and officers who are currently sponsors of the November 5-8 Mobilization Committee and those who designate their willingness to continue in that role, as well as such others as the Committee itself shall add to its ranks under procedures established in September. In addition to the present leadership there shall be designated by this meeting four Vice-Chairmen (Dave Dellinger, Sidney Peck, Robert Greenblatt, and Ed Keating), to assist in guidance and leadership, under the direction of the current Chairman, A.J. Muste . . . .

"The Mobilization Committee shall be charged with organizing a national action April 15, 1967 in San Francisco and New York, with the details to be worked out by the committee at its executive meetings.

"The Mobilization Committee shall be charged with suggesting, stimulating and/or organizing such actions of a more limited and more localized nature as may be feasible, with the aim of broadening the influence of the peace movement as much as possible, as long as these actions clearly fall within the consensus reached by the diverse viewpoints of this conference . . . .

"The Mobilization Committee will seek to make the April 15 action an international one. The Mobilization Committee shall also seek to widen the movement into such localities and professional milieux, including, but not limited to, labor, literacy, military, civil rights, traditional peace groups, religious, electoral, as are now presently organized or which need our organizational assistance."

The resolution received the complete approval of signatories from the Communist Party (Arnold Johnson, Jack Spiegel, Sidney Peck, Barbara Bick, Frank Emspak, and Otto Nathan), Students for a Democratic Society (Paul Booth and Carl Oglesby), the DuBois Clubs (Hugh Fowler and Staughton Lynd), the Socialist Workers Party (Fred Halstead, Lew Jones, Kipp Dawson, Peter Buch, and Gus Horowitz), Youth Against War and Fascism (Deidre Griswold), and the Student Nonviolent Coordinating Committee (Stokely Carmichael).

The first chairman of Spring Mobe was A.J. Muste, one of America's all-time influential radical leaders, who was always insistent that a united front was useless unless it included Communists and all others of the extreme left. Other officials of Spring Mobe were David Dellinger, Robert Greenblatt, Edward Keating, Sidney Peck, and Dagmar Wilson, the founder and leader of Women Strike for Peace, and a determined apologist for North Vietnam, which she had visited.

For the April 15, 1967, Spring Mobe demonstrations, preparations were arranged in the west by Socialist Workers Party leaders Kipp Dawson, Asher Harer, Kathie Harer, and Robert Himmel, and Communist Party official Donald Hamerquist; in the midwest, by Communist leaders Sidney Peck and Sylvia Krushner. In New York, two black groups were very active in the preparations: the Black United Action Front and Blacks Against Negative Dying.

The Spring Mobe was probably the most successful united front operation since the 1930's. The April 1967 demonstrations were supported by the top leadership of the Communist Party; the Socialist Workers Party and its Young Socialist Alliance; the pro-Peking Progressive Labor Party; Students for a Democratic Society; the National Lawyers Guild; the International Longshoremen's and Warehousemen's Union; Women Strike for Peace; the Communist-created Veterans for Peace in Vietnam; the DuBois Clubs; the Los Angeles Committee for Defense of the Bill of Rights; the Trade Unionists for Peace; the Fort Hood Three Defense Committee; the Peace Action Council of Southern California; the Trotskyite Freedom Socialist Party of Washington, the Baltimore Spartacist League, and the Los Angeles Committee to End the War in Vietnam; the pro-Viet Cong Revolutionary Contingent of New York and Americans for a National Liberation Front Victory of California; David Dellinger's Fifth Avenue Peace Parade Committee; Youth Against War and Fascism; and the Student Mobilization Committee to End the War in Vietnam. (Student Mobe was organized in December 1966 at the suggestion of Bettina Aptheker, a Communist and the daughter of Herbert Aptheker, the Communist Party's theoretician. Communists and Trotskyites formed Student Mobe but eventually the group became completely controlled by the Trotskyite Young Socialist Alliance.)

An impressive list of radicals supported Spring Mobe, including Communist Party members Bettina Aptheker, Benjamin Dreyfus, Hunter Pitts O'Dell, Martin Hall, Terence Hallinan, Albert J. "Mickey" Lima, James R. Lindsay, Leon Wofsy, Ben Dobbs, Arnold Johnson,

Robert Treuhaft, Donald Rothenberg, Morris Watson, Malvina Renyolds, Jesse Gray, Al Richmond, Jack Spiegel, Rev. William H. Melish, Irving Sarnoff, Eli Katz, Jessica Mitford, Corliss Lamont, Lester Cole, Aubrey Grossman, Carl Braden, and Rev. John W. Darr; Socialist Workers Party members Fred Halstead, Brian Shannon, Ove Ospoy, Jaimey Allen, Lew Jones, Gus Horowitz, Kipp Dawson, and Peter Camejo; DuBois Clubs leaders Hugh Fowler, Robert Cugini, and Marian Gordon; Beverly Axelrod of the National Lawyers Guild; Young Socialist Alliance members Robert Davis, Nelson Blackstock, and Dan Rosenshine; west coast radicals Donald Kalish and Linus Pauling; Black Panther leader Eldridge Cleaver; Anne Braden and Rev. Fred Shuttlesworth of the Southern Conference Educational Fund; Mae Mallory of the Workers World Party; Abe Weisburd of Trade Unionists for Peace; Carlton Goodlett of the Soviet-controlled World Peace Council; Students for a Democratic Society leaders Paul Booth, Nick Egleson, and Sue Eanet; and veteran radicals Rev. Stephen Fritchman, Sidney Lens, and Al Evanoff.

The Spring Mobe's planned demonstrations received strong encouragement from North Vietnam. North Vietnamese Premier Pham van Dong praised the movement "to demand [the] United States Government stop [its] war of aggression in Vietnam and bring American troops home." The Hanoi regime's official newspaper, *Nhan Dan*, "hailed the mounting struggle of the entire people of the United States of America against Johnson's aggressive war in Vietnam."

On April 15, 1967, more than 100,000 participated in Spring Mobe's march and rally in New York City. Chairmen of the rally were David Dellinger and Benjamin Spock. Speakers at the rally included Stokely Carmichael, Nick Egelson, William F. Pepper of the National Conference for New Politics, and Juan Roa of the Movement for Puerto Rican Independence, a leading pro-Communist organization and an ally of Stokely Carmichael's Student Nonviolent Coordinating Committee. The Communist Party's favorite entertainer, Pete Seeger, sang at the rally. The Communist Party's general secretary, Gus Hall, and publicity director, Arnold Johnson, led the Party's contingent in the march.

The Spring Mobe rally in San Francisco featured as speakers Communist Malvina Reynolds, Socialist Workers Party member Kipp Dawson, Communist Grace Newman, and Black Panther leader Eldridge Cleaver.

On May 20 and 21, 1967, Spring Mobe held a National Anti-War Conference in Washington, D.C. A week earlier, Student Mobe held a conference in Chicago and proposed a massive demonstration in Washington, D.C., for October 21, 1967. At the Washington meeting of Spring Mobe, the Student Mobe proposal was adopted by the more than 700 delegates who were in attendance.

Again a change in name occurred. After the Washington meeting, Spring Mobe became the National Mobilization Committee to End the War in Vietnam. The National Mobe roster of officials contained the customary names with a few additions. David Dellinger was chairman. Co-chairmen included Robert Greenblatt, Al Evanoff, Donald Kalish, Sidney Lens, Sidney Peck, Dagmar Wilson, John Wilson, an officer of the Student Nonviolent Coordinating Committee, and Lincoln Lynch, an officer of the Congress of Racial Equality. Greenblatt was named national coordinator. Project directors were John Wilson and Jerry Rubin, a leader of California's Vietnam Day Committee. Medical preparations for planned demonstrations were assigned to the Medical Committee for Human Rights which had as one of its top leaders Dr. Quentin Young of Chicago, a Fifth Amendment pleader. Legal arrangements were under the care of members of the Law Center for Constitutional Rights, the National Lawyers Guild, and the Emergency Civil Liberties Committee, including attorneys Morton Stavis, a Communist, and the well-known radicals Arthur Kinoy and William Kunstler.

On October 21, 1967, the National Mobe held a demonstration in Washington. The organization had received widespread encouragement from abroad through news that simultaneous demonstrations of support would be held in Moscow, Budapest, Tokyo, Stockholm, Munich, Paris, and in various Canadian cities. The Soviet-controlled Stockholm World Conference on Vietnam directed "peace" groups throughout the world to observe October 21 with demonstrations sympathetic to National Mobe's efforts. Hanoi Radio broadcast: "We highly value the American people's movement against the U.S. war in Vietnam and regard this movement as a just and valiant action. May the October 21 struggle mark a new development in the American people's movement for an end of the United States war in Vietnam. We wish you brilliant success." North Vietnamese Premier Pham van Dong sent his greetings to National Mobe: "The Vietnamese people thank their friends in America and wish them great success in their mounting movement."

The October 21, 1967 activities of National Mobe in Washington included a march, a rally at the Lincoln Memorial, and a violent attempt to enter the Pentagon "to confront the warmakers" and "disrupt the war machine." The marchers included Communist Party officials Arnold Johnson, Mike Zagarell, and James Jackson, and members and officials of the Socialist Workers Party, the Young Socialist Alliance, the DuBois Clubs, Youth Against War and Fascism, Students for a Democratic Society, Student Mobe, the Student Nonviolent Coordinating Committee, the Black Panthers, Women Strike for Peace, the Progressive Labor Party, Veterans of the Abraham Lincoln Brigade, Trade Unionists for Peace, the Trotskyite Spartacist League, Veterans for Peace in Vietnam, the National Conference for New Politics, the Fifth Avenue Vietnam Peace Parade Committee, the United States Committee to Aid the National Liberation Front of South Vietnam, and the Chicago Area Draft Resisters.

At the Lincoln Memorial rally, more than 50,000 listened to speeches delivered by David Dellinger, actor Ossie Davis, Lincoln Lynch, Benjamin Spock, Dagmar Wilson, Fred Davis of Students for a Democratic Society, John Wilson, and Linda Morse of Student Mobe. Black demonstrators were treated to a separate rally, where they were harangued by leaders from the black nationalist Mau Maus, the pro-Peking Revolutionary Action Movement, and the Student Nonviolent Coordinating Committee.

The demonstrations at the Pentagon resulted in almost 700 arrests, injuries to a number of demonstrators, marshals, and soldiers, and widespread coverage by the nation's television networks. The spectacle pleased National Mobe's leaders, who estimated that their future efforts would become increasingly militant. Of great significance was the fact that members of the Communist hierarchy were openly participating in National Mobe's demonstrations and marches.

In the wake of the October 21, 1967 demonstrations, the National Mobe held a series of meetings in Washington, D.C., New York City, and the Chicago area. In the course of these meetings, it was decided to plan for disruptive demonstrations at the 1968 Democratic National Convention, and the planning continued right up until the eve of the convention. The Communist Party was not only well represented at all the planning sessions, but also volunteered financial help to establish a headquarters in Chicago and to furnish traveling expenses to blacks so that they might attend planning sessions, especially in Chicago.

On December 27, 1967, the National Mobe's administrative committee met in New York City. In attendance were representatives of the Communist Party, the Socialist Workers Party, Students for a Democratic Society, Workers World Party, the DuBois Clubs, Veterans and Reservists for Peace in Vietnam, Student Mobe, and the Young Socialist Alliance. The theme of the meeting was concentration on plans for militant disruption of the Democratic National Convention. Rennie Davis, a project director for the convention protests, informed the group that a full-time staff of fifteen in Chicago was already preparing the logistics of the demonstrations.

On January 26, 1968, at the National Lawyers Guild's offices in New York City, a National Mobe group met "to discuss the establishment of a nationwide legal defense apparatus to deal with the projected legal problems" that could be anticipated as a result of the demonstrations at the convention. At this meeting, Rennie Davis and Tom Hayden, project directors for the convention protests, and Bernardine Dohrn, who would later be the chief rabble rouser for the Weatherman faction of SDS, played major roles in the discussions. Even from the sketchy minutes of the meeting, it is quite obvious that the National Mobe leaders were planning demonstrations violent enough to result in wholesale arrests on charges so serious as to warrant a great deal of stand-by legal talent.

On February 11, 1968, a planning session was held and again there was stress on militant demonstrations. At the meeting were David Dellinger, Fred Halstead, Sidney Lens, Tom Hayden, Sidney Peck, Dagmar Wilson, Earl Durham and Charlene Mitchell of the Communist Party's national committee, and Communist Party members Kendra Alexander, Jack Spiegel, Carolyn Black, and Donald Hamerquist. Jack Spiegel told the group: "We can't call 200,000 people to Chicago and then disassociate ourselves from violence. Disruption and violence will occur. It's going to happen and we'll have to deal with that fact." Donald Hamerquist advised: "What we must do is make concrete demands on the Convention which the Convention cannot respond to."

At Camp Ravenswood, near Chicago, the National Mobe held a three-day conference, during which there was a definite decision to demonstrate at the Democratic National Convention. Significantly, the National Mobe was going beyond its ritualistic "anti-Vietnam War" activities by emphasizing its concern for blacks. In the conference's statement of program and purpose for the convention demonstrations, it was stated: "The strategy developed by the Conference will be to underscore through action organization the real issues this country must face. Those issues are the immediate withdrawal of American troops from Vietnam, the right of the Vietnamese people to national independence and self-determination, the end of American attempts to control and direct the future of the underdeveloped areas of the world for its own economic and political interests, an immediate end to the draft and the virtual military occupation of Black Communities and the recognition of the right of Black People to control their own lives and determine their own future in this country."

The months of detailed preparation by National Mobe were rewarded when approximately 10,000 demonstrators took part in the tumultuous riots that plagued the Democratic National Convention in August 1968. FBI Director J. Edgar Hoover summarized the events: "Demonstrations held during the convention period included taunting of the police: they were referred to as 'pigs,' they were spat upon, obscenities were shouted at them and they were the targets of all kinds of unbelievable abuse; on several occasions undisciplined mobs intent on marching to the convention site without legal authority had to be repulsed by the police and National Guard. Reportedly many of the hippies used drugs regularly.

"The demonstrations resulted in mass arrests. Also, there were numerous police and demonstrators injured. Approximately 650 arrests were made by local authorities and nearly 200 police officers were injured during the confrontations with the demonstrators. It has been estimated that more than 900 persons obtained emergency treatment for injuries received during the disorder."

The Chicago demonstrations were appreciated in Hanoi. On September 14, 1968, the North Vietnamese government announced that its "South Vietnamese People's Committee for Solidarity with the American People" had sent a letter to National Mobe "thanking the progressive American people of all strata for their seething, resolute, and courageous struggle conducted last month when the convention of the Democratic Party was meeting . . . . Despite the huge, barbarous repression machinery unleashed by Johnson, Humphrey, and their ilk, you have come down into the streets for demonstrations and shouted slogans demanding an end to the U.S. war of aggression in Vietnam, cessation of the bombing on the whole territory of the DRV [Democratic Republic of Vietnam], and withdrawal of troops of the United States and of its allied countries in the Vietnam war. By your activities you have raised the just voice of the United States, a country with a traditional love for freedom and justice.

"We express to you our deep sympathy and ask you to convey to the American people our heartfelt thanks for their participation in or support of the recent action in Chicago . . . . You have shed your blood for the honor of the United States and . . . in defense of the Vietnamese people's right to self-determination, which is being flouted by the American aggressors, and of the peace in Southeast Asia and in the world now being trampled underfoot by the U.S. warmongers . . . . We are daily and hourly following with great enthusiasm your persistent and valiant struggle.

"Your recent actions in Chicago, as well as throughout the United States, against the U.S. policy of aggression in Vietnam have strongly stimulated our people in South Vietnam who are conducting the powerful general offensive . . . . We wish you to convey our best wishes to our American friends who were wounded or arrested during the recent demonstrations."

In the aftermath of the Chicago riots, National Mobe's chairman David Dellinger and seven of his cohorts were indicted for violating the anti-riot provisions of the 1968 Civil Rights Act by crossing state lines with the intent to incite a riot. (Convictions for seven of the group, known as The Conspiracy, were arrived at on February 18, 1970.)

On September 14, 1968, Dellinger conducted an administrative committee meeting of National Mobe in Washington, D.C. He was joined by other National Mobe leaders Tom Hayden and Rennie Davis, Arnold Johnson of the Communist Party, and representatives of Young Socialist Alliance, Women Strike for Peace, Student Nonviolent Coordinating Committee, Socialist Workers Party, and Students for a Democratic Society. At this and subsequent meetings, plans were made to conduct "counter-inaugural" demonstrations on January 18, 19, and 20, 1969.

The coordinator for National Mobe's "counter-inaugural" was

Rennie Davis. He was aided by Stewart Meacham of the American Friends Service Committee, Rev. Richard Fernandez of Clergy and Laymen Concerned About Vietnam, Barbara Bick of Women Strike for Peace, Dennis Mora of the DuBois Clubs, Norma Becker of the Fifth Avenue Vietnam Peace Parade Committee, and his National Mobe cohorts David Dellinger and John Wilson. Davis received complete cooperation from such participating organizations as the Communist Party, the Socialist Workers Party, the Young Socialist Alliance, various local groups of Students for a Democratic Society, several fronts of Youth Against War and Fascism, the Freedom and Peace Party (a Communist front), the Southern Student Organizing Committee, and Veterans for Peace in Vietnam.

The "counter-inaugural" was not a huge success for National Mobe. The crowds of demonstrators were not as large in numbers as had been anticipated. FBI Director J. Edgar Hoover presented this summary: "The demonstration activity at Washington, D.C., over the inaugural weekend began on January 18, 1969, with 600 to 1,000 individuals participating in workshops and conferences which were described as completely disorganized and chaotic. Among other activities on January 19 were a march by approximately 4,000 individuals and demonstrations including one at the Smithsonian Institute where a reception was held for Vice President Agnew and his wife. Some of the demonstrators threw clods of dirt and other items and, as a result, it was necessary for police to break up the demonstration. During the meetings on January 19, 1969, several of the demonstrators called for a confrontation with the police on January 20, 1969. The counter-inaugural ball, which was held by the demonstrators on the evening of January 19, 1969, was poorly attended and disorganized.

"On January 20, 1969, 600 to 800 of the demonstrators positioned themselves along the inaugural parade route, particularly from 12th to 15th Street on Pennsylvania Avenue. They attempted to disrupt the parade by throwing objects, including a few smoke bombs, but were unsuccessful in their attempts. However, their actions made it necessary for police to disperse them.

"During the three days of demonstrations, 119 individuals were arrested, the majority on charges of disorderly conduct. During the three days, six of those arrested were charged with mutilation, burning, or desecration of the U.S. flag. Of those arrested, 10 were juveniles."

After the January 1969 demonstrations at President Nixon's inauguration, National Mobe, as a central rallying point, became rather quiet. Its leaders, for the most part, conducted their activities through the medium of other anti-war groups, such as the Chicago Peace Council, the Fifth Avenue Vietnam Peace Parade Committee, Students for a Democratic Society, and the Young Socialist Alliance.

In May 1969, a large group of Americans attended the Emergency Action Conference of the Soviet-controlled Stockholm Conference on Vietnam in Stockholm, Sweden. The American delegation included John Wilson and Sherman Adams of the Student Nonviolent Coordinating Committee; Amy Swerdlow, Serita Crown, and Althea Alexander of Women Strike for Peace; Noam Chomsky of Resist; Bob Eaton and Bronson Clark of the American Friends Service Committee; Joseph Crown, Richard Falk, and Stanley Swerdlow of the Lawyers Committee on American Policy Towards Vietnam; Doris Roberson of the National Lawyers Guild; Carlton Goodlett of National Mobe; George Carrano and Donald McDonough of the American Deserters Committee; and Rev. Thomas Leo Hayes of Clergy and Laymen Concerned About Vietnam. All the organizations represented by the Americans had at some time been deeply involved in National Mobe's activities. And many of the individuals had served in positions of leadership with National Mobe.

The Stockholm Conference, which was merely another step in the Soviet Union's long-time "peace" campaign, was a showplace where the North Vietnamese could conduct their anti-U.S. propaganda. In their literature, the Stockholm Conference officials said that there was a need for an international perspective for the anti-Vietnam War movement, and "That is why it is so imperative to come together, to make a thorough analysis of the situation and to find ways and means of action which perhaps could be used all over the world. Action coordinated and supported on this scale has a much bigger chance to lead to results than separate action, different methods and different dates or doing nothing while feeling exhausted . . . .

"The basic idea of the Stockholm Conference on Vietnam is from the beginning that the Vietnam question is the first one to be solved if we want a liveable world. As long as the U.S. war machine is maiming Vietnamese children with napalm and destroying crops by herbicides, none of the other big problems of the world will be solved. This was the reason why we called the first Conference in July 1967 and invited everybody to unite to help ending the war in Vietnam, without consideration of differences of opinion in other questions."

The Stockholm conferees were especially anxious to encourage American draft dodgers and deserters. The Conference recommended "increased international support for resistance in America and by Americans abroad in refusing the draft, in defecting from the US armed forces, for carrying on propaganda within the army and for militant action against the Selective Service Systems."

In June 1969, a three-day session of the Soviet-controlled World Assembly for Peace was held in East Germany. A large number of Americans were in attendance, including actor Dick Gregory; Stanley Faulkner of the National Lawyers Guild; Susan Bornstein and Karen Ackerman of the DuBois Clubs; Communist Party leader Herbert Aptheker; May Clarke and Barbara Bick of Women Strike for Peace; Communist Party members Mary-Angie Dickerson, Martin Hall, Jarvis Tyner, and Irving Sarnoff; Carlton Goodlett of National Mobe; and Harlan Weitzel of Clergy and Laymen Concerned About Vietnam. The individuals and the organizations represented by them in the American delegation were all closely affiliated with National Mobe.

In East Berlin, the Americans issued an "official statement" in which they alleged that the "U.S. has demonstrated since its founding days a systematic policy of exploitation, imperialism and genocide. We are constantly threatened by increasing repression of the voices of dissent. Since foreign policy is the mirrored image of domestic policy, a nation which employs racism, violence and repression on the domestic scene will resort in kind to racism, violence and repression in its international affairs. The war in Vietnam, above all else, is a racist war. The horrible crimes committed against the Vietnamese people reflect the arrogance, yet deadly sickness of a racist society which has not yet dared to inflict such inhumanity on a white nation . . . ."

The "official statement" declared that the forces for peace in the United States must mobilize and exert pressure to end the Vietnam War and "make new initiatives involving power confrontations against both the political and military-industrial establishments of the nation." In its conclusion, the "official statement" read: "We cannot close without paying deep tribute to the courage and remarkable heroism of our Vietnamese friends who in this day, through incalculable sacrifices, are manning humanity's front line in the defense, first, of their own country and, second, of the cause of human freedom. Vietnam's example should lead us all to make, in this hall, a covenant that no sacrifice is too great — even the threat to life itself — to deter man in his quest to be free . . . . The peace forces of the U.S. and the world, through our sacrifices, can become a beacon light . . . ."

Irving Sarnoff, an active Communist in National Mobe's affairs, addressed the World Assembly of Peace. His speech remains a classic of anti-American venom: "It is with both shame and honour that I speak as a member of the American delegation. Shame because it is my country that is responsible for so much of the evil being perpetrated in the world today. I speak with the knowledge of the reality that for years the people of my country have permitted the warmakers to use the most modern, horrendous weapons of war to kill and repress the peoples of Vietnam as they struggle to determine their own destiny. I speak with a broken heart — as a father and a worker — when I think of the thousands of lives of children and workers we have destroyed so that the rich in America can rob and plunder the lands belonging to other peoples in Vietnam and throughout the world.

"This policy is rooted in our history as a racist society, a nation that has destroyed the lives and dignity of millions of Indians and blacks, and today keeps millions in economic and political slavery throughout the world. As the rich get richer in America, 33 million of our people live in grinding poverty, the Blacks, Browns, Indians, youth and old people among the worst of the oppressed and exploited.

"As if this were not enough, rulers of America have used all the modern means of psychological warfare to destroy the conscience and humanity of our people, to condition our people to be insensitive to the needs of other people, and through racism to justify the robbing and killing in our own country and throughout the world.

"But I speak here today also with pride for that section of America that is now involved in a life and death struggle to change the policies and system of our country. Our new Nixon administration's answer to the crying needs of the people has been to propose a new missile system that will cost billions. The answer of the Nixons has been to use the experience of Vietnam to spread tear gas from helicopters on our youth, as they demonstrate for a better America. From one end of America to the other Black Panthers, fighting against white supremacy

127

at home and in Vietnam, are being killed, jailed and harassed. New forms of repression are now being prepared to investigate and jail those that would oppose the policies of war, racism and poverty. The struggle against these policies is involving ever larger numbers — students on almost every campus protesting the war in Vietnam and militarism — even high school and junior high school youth. Black and Brown students and ghetto dwellers are in constant struggle against the oppression and racism that is intensified because of the war.

"On Army bases across America, G.I.'s are organizing and speaking out against the war — the stockades are full, but this historic movement continues to grow. There are over 25 underground anti-war newspapers being published by soldiers in the Armed Forces.

"There are literally thousands of young people also who are resisting the draft, refusing to allow themselves to be used by the government to kill and plunder. And, as their ancestors did many years ago, thousands of our youth are going into exile to escape from a violent, racist society that is daily finding new ways to repress the people.

"There are people involved in sacrificing themselves for human dignity from almost every section of the clergy — destroying draft files and the property of Dow chemical, producers of napalm. There is even the beginning of motion against the war and militarism in some important areas of our labour movement, as they oppose the Nixon administration's ABM proposals and the extra-taxation for war.

"Our task, more evident than ever before, is to broaden and unify the anti-war movement in America so that it becomes impossible for Nixon to continue his new-colonialist, aggressive aims.

"Our task is to broaden the base and understanding of our movement to include the many organized groups who are in motion around specific issues — wages, welfare, prices, taxes, racism, repression, housing, and to make them understand that there can be no improvement until the war in Vietnam is ended and the national priorities are re-ordered.

"Our task is to bring to our people an understanding that the nature of the neo-colonialist policy is not only to exploit and oppress the rest of the world, but to exploit and oppress the American people.

"That is why our country is moving toward repression and violence and the increased exploitation of the American people. The increased role of the military and the billions spent to satisfy their appetites and those of the industrialists are what is oppressing the people world-wide as well as our people.

"It is our responsibility to show that Vietnam is not just a mistake made by a previous administration, but part of the nature of a system that requires a cheap source of raw materials and a market to drop its surplus goods and capital.

"We know full well the immensity of the struggle that faces us, but we also know the responsibility that lies on our shoulders for the killing and destruction that we have caused in Vietnam and throughout the world. We will continue to organize, to go to jail, and, if necessary, die so that mankind can be freed from a system that robs and kills to keep a few rich. Long live the heroic Vietnamese people as they struggle for their national independence and sovereignty. Long live the unity of the exploited and oppressed in America and throughout the world as we struggle against a common enemy. Power to the people!"

In the spring of 1969, twenty-seven leaders of the anti-Vietnam War Movement endorsed a call to a National Anti-War Conference to be held in Cleveland on July 4 and 5 "to broaden and unify the anti-war forces in this country and to plan co-ordinated national anti-war actions for the fall." The idea for the Cleveland conference originated with Sidney Peck, a National Mobe official and a one-time officer of the Communist Party in Wisconsin. Peck used National Mobe's mailing list to issue his "call," which was endorsed by Norma Becker, Charles Cairns of the Socialist Workers Party, David Dellinger, Douglas Dowd, Al Evanoff, Jerry Gordon, Robert Greenblatt, Donald Kalish, Sidney Lens, Carol Lipman, Arthur Kinoy, Stewart Meacham, Max Primack of the Socialist Workers Party, Irving Sarnoff, Benjamin Spock, Cora Weiss, and Dagmar Wilson. The participating national organizations included the Black Panther Party, the Communist Party, the Socialist Workers Party, the Progressive Labor Party, Workers World Party, the DuBois Clubs, Clergy and Laymen Concerned About Vietnam, the Lawyers Committee on American Policy Towards Vietnam, the National Lawyers Guild, the Southern Conference Educational Fund, the Student Nonviolent Coordinating Committee, Students for a Democratic Society, Women Strike for Peace, Veterans for Peace in Vietnam, and the Young Socialist Alliance. Local and regional "peace" groups were in attendance, as were the newly organized "GI groups" — the American Servicemen's Union, the GIs United Against the War in Vietnam, and the GI Civil Liberties Defense Committee — all of which were organized and controlled by extreme leftists.

The proceedings at the Cleveland conference indicated that there were critical differences in the potpourri of organizations that had regularly cooperated in the projects of National Mobe. Every organization was against the Vietnam War and for the withdrawal of American forces. Some organizational leaders felt that the entire left should concentrate on that war issue. Others believed that the war, poverty, and racism should be equal issues of concern. There were some leaders who criticized National Mobe for concentrating too much on the war issue, while others were critical because they believed National Mobe had drifted into a shotgun approach.

Violence *vis-à-vis* nonviolence was a major point of difference. Some leaders believed that violence was absolutely necessary if the "peace" movement were to succeed. Others believed that violence caused a bad public reaction — enough to antagonize the "peace" movement supporters and to cause "repression" against the peaceniks.

Many of the conferees at Cleveland were critical of National Mobe on the ground that it had not conducted large-scale actions. Such criticism may have been inspired in part by the counter-inaugural demonstrations in January which had proven unsuccessful.

In the two-day conference, the major differences that existed among the major organizational leaders were not resolved. And they resorted to a tactic that had been employed previously. They scrapped National Mobe and created the New Mobilization Committee to End the War in Vietnam. The same old leaders were in control. The same cooperating organizations were willing to work under New Mobe's umbrella.

Shortly after New Mobe was organized, its leaders announced "the most intense anti-war campaign ever undertaken in the United States — the Fall Offensive." The so-called Fall Offensive was, in reality, an afterthought of New Mobe's leaders. One part of the offensive was a Vietnam Moratorium, organized by the Vietnam Moratorium Committee [VMC], led by David Hawk. The VMC scheduled its moratorium for October 15, 1969. Stewart Meacham of the American Friends Service Committee, while at the Cleveland Conference, proposed a "reading of the dead," whereby individuals would congregate and march in Washington, each person wearing the name of a dead American soldier around his neck. New Mobe adopted the Moratorium and the "reading of the dead" as its own and added a November 15 March on Washington to comprise the Fall Offensive.

Out of the Cleveland conference, New Mobe emerged with a steering committee that was unmistakably under the control of Communists. Its members included Marc Beallor and Terence Hallinan, members of the Communist Party and the DuBois Clubs; Marjorie Colvin, Fred Halstead, Gus Horowitz, Allen Myers, and Carol Lipman, members of the Trotskyite Socialist Workers Party; Joe Miles, Larry Seigle, Larry Swingle, and Peer Vinther of the Trotskyite Young Socialist Alliance; David Dellinger, an admitted "non-Soviet" Communist; Sidney Lens, former leader of the Communist Revolutionary Workers League; Jerry Gordon, a former leader of the Communist Party's Labor Youth League; and Sidney Peck, Arnold Johnson, Sylvia Krushner, and Irving Sarnoff, current or past members of the Communist Party.

For the Fall Offensive, the three major organizations were New Mobe, the Vietnam Moratorium Committee, and Student Mobe. New Mobe's leaders explained the relationship in a press release: "The leadership of the three groups sees the activities of the others as complimentary [sic] to its own. In other words, the activities of one organization is [sic] in no way seen as contradictory to the others, neither are the activities 'competitive.' Clearly, there is a need for viable anti-war activity moving forward on various levels and under various operating procedures. Thus, the Vietnam Moratorium Committee organizes on the local level for strictly local activity; the New Mobilization Committee organizes to bring people to Washington on specific days; and the Student Mobilization Committee organizes students on campuses for activities there and for the Washington March."

Throughout the summer and fall of 1969, many meetings were held around the country as the leaders of the Fall Offensive raised money and drafted their strategy for the October and November demonstrations. In all the meetings, there was a strong presence of Communists.

On October 15, 1969, Vietnam Moratorium Committees managed massive protests throughout the country. The VMC received complete support from the Communist Party, the Socialist Workers Party, the Young Socialist Alliance, and the lesser organizations within the structure of New Mobe. In major cities and on campuses, VMC demonstrators held anti-war rallies and listened to such speakers as

131

Communists Angela Davis, Jesse Gray, and Rasheed Storey; U.S. Senator George McGovern; Socialist Workers Party members Paul Bontelle, Don Gurewitz, and Peter Camejo ("The fighters of the National Liberation Front are the most beautiful people in the world"); Herman Ferguson of the Revolutionary Action Movement; actor Ossie Davis; Howard Zinn; Student Mobe leader Carl Lipman; Hosea Williams of the Southern Christian Leadership Conference; and Donald Kalish.

On November 13, the New Mobe conducted its March Against Death in Washington, D.C. From Arlington National Cemetery to the White House, about 45,000 marchers carried individual placards, each bearing the name of an American killed in Vietnam.

On November 15, demonstrations were held principally in Washington, D.C., and San Francisco. More than a quarter of a million attended the Washington activities. They marched. They listened to speeches by Benjamin Spock, Ossie Davis, David Dellinger, David Hawk, Carol Lipman, and others. They were entertained by Pete Seeger and other favorite Communist Party entertainers. In San Francisco, about 100,000 demonstrators heard Rennie Davis, Black Panther leader David Hilliard, and other speakers.

The November 15 march in Washington was unquestionably New Mobe's greatest success. In the parade were delegations from the Communist Party, the Black Panther Party, the Socialist Workers Party, the Freedom and Peace Party, the New Party, the Progressive Labor Party, the Youth International Party (Yippies), the DuBois Clubs, Clergy and Laymen Concerned About Vietnam, the Southern Conference Educational Fund, the Young Socialist Alliance, Women Strike for Peace, the American Friends Service Committee, the Workers League, the War Resisters League, the Spartacist League, Veterans for Peace in Vietnam, Youth Against War and Fascism, and lesser groups.

The Fall Offensive of New Mobe received great acclaim from the international Communist scene. North Vietnamese Premier Pham van Dong sent New Mobe a message: "Progressive people in the U.S. have so far struggled against the war of aggression in Vietnam this fall. The broad masses of the American people, encouraged and supported by many peace and justice-loving American personalities, have again started a broad and powerful drive in the whole country to demand that the Nixon administration stop its war of aggression in Vietnam and immediately bring home all U.S. troops. Your drive eloquently reflects the legitimate and pressing demand of your people to save the honor of the United States and to prevent the useless death of their sons in Vietnam. This is also a very fitting and timely response to U.S. authorities who stubbornly persist in intensifying and prolonging the war of aggression in Vietnam in defiance of massive protests and American and world public opinion. The Vietnamese people demand that the U.S. government completely and unconditionally pull out of Vietnam all U.S. troops and those of foreign countries belonging to its camp and let the Vietnamese people decide themselves their own destiny. The Vietnamese people deeply cherish peace, but a peace in independence and freedom. So long as the U.S. government has not stopped its aggression in Vietnam, the Vietnamese people will tenaciously fight on to defend their fundamental national rights. The patriotic fight of our people is also a fight for the objectives of peace and justice you are pursuing. We are firmly confident that with the solidarity and courage of our two peoples, with sympathy and support of the peace-loving peoples in world [sic], the struggle of Vietnamese people and of progressive people in the United States against U.S. aggressions will end in total victory. I wish your 'Fall Offensive' a brilliant success."

The Stockholm Conference on Vietnam endorsed the November 15 New Mobe demonstrations and urged that similar programs be carried on throughout the world: "This 'Fall Offensive' is the most encouraging development in the US since a long time. It is organized by the 'New Mobilization Committee to End the War in Vietnam,' which groups and unites the most active and significant US Peace Groups and other organizations opposed to Nixon's war policy.

"We urge all organizations to support this campaign as it signifies the biggest move so far to oppose the war in Vietnam and to call for the immediate withdrawal of all US forces from Vietnam. It should be echoed in all countries with demonstrations and all sorts of suitable action on and around November 15, so as to show president Nixon that the peoples of the world want him to stop the US aggression in Vietnam.

"The New Mobe constitutes the crucial work of mobilizing the American people against the war of aggression and counter-revolution in Vietnam. What is so important about the 'New Mobe' is that it is a coalition which now is said to reflect a majority movement and to that extent it encompasses within its midst the widest spectrum of forces yet to unite in opposition and resistance to the war."

On October 11 and 12, 1969, the International Liaison Committee of the Stockholm Conference on Vietnam adopted a resolution in favor of New Mobe's activities: "The Stockholm Conference on Vietnam welcomes the formation of the broadest coalition of US anti-war forces yet known which have joined together in the New Mobilization Committee to End the War in Vietnam to mount a series of massive demonstrations. The Fall Offensive began with demonstrations in Chicago on September 24 in support of the 8 Anti-War leaders on trial for conspiracy. The campaign will continue with the Vietnam Moratorium on October 15 and will culminate in mass national demonstrations in Washington and San Francisco from November 13 to 15. The New Mobilization Committee is committed to the total and immediate withdrawal of US forces and war material from South Vietnam.

"The Stockholm Conference wholeheartedly supports the Fall Offensive and calls for mass demonstrations and other activities throughout the world on November 15 to match the unparalleled outpouring of popular opposition to the war now spreading across the United States. All actions on this day of International Mobilization should be centered on the demand of the Vietnam Appeal calling for the immediate, total and unconditional withdrawal of US and allied troops from South Vietnam. This is the only basis for bringing the war to a rapid conclusion. In those countries linked to the US war effort, there should be demonstrations demanding an end to these pacts of complicity.

"Together with the New Mobilization Committee we call for a campaign which will not end on November 15 but will rise in intensity until US aggression in Vietnam is ended and the Vietnamese have won the independence and peace for which they have fought so long."

It was not surprising that New Mobe attracted such a response from international Communists. Leaders of New Mobe had placed themselves squarely on the side of the Hanoi regime. Many had visited Hanoi and sang the praises of the North Vietnamese over Hanoi radio broadcasts and through the American news media. Several New Mobe leaders, in their public statements, went all-out for the Communist side of the Vietnam War. Said New Mobe co-chairman Sidney Peck: "We want an end to the war, a war that is a war of intervention and aggression and we want the complete and total withdrawal of American forces from Vietnam and if that results in a victory for the National Liberation Front or the Democratic Republic of Vietnam [North Vietnam], we are pleased with that result because that would in effect be the wishes of the Vietnamese people."

Stewart Meacham of the American Friends Service Committee, who is a New Mobe co-chairman, said: "It's quite likely, if we get out, that the government that would come into power in South Vietnam would be a communist government of some [sort] .... I would much prefer to see that government emerge if that is the government that the political forces in Vietnam would end up with than to see the present situation continue."

Douglas Dowd, a New Mobe co-chairman, said: "One of the tensions that we've had to work out within the National Mobilization [Committee] and consequently the New Mobilization [Committee] is that the people who are doing the organizing for this kind of thing, almost all of them, really feel that not only the war should end but if there had to be a side in that war I think most of us feel we would be on the other side."

On December 13 and 14, 1969, the New Mobe held a steering committee meeting in Cleveland. Most of New Mobe's leaders were in attendance and they decided to institute a six-month campaign to end the Vietnam War. In a press release, New Mobe explained its planned campaign as a three-pronged thrust: "A variety of actions to oppose repression is a necessary aspect of opposing the war. The Mobilization will help to organize activities to support Black Panther demands for a UN investigation of the systematic pattern by government and police against the Panthers. Mobilization spokesmen announced that plans were being made for decentralized demonstrations to support the eight anti-war leaders on trial in Chicago as the Conspiracy trial comes to an end in January ....

"Anti-inflation picketing and boycotts at groceries, etc.; group tax protests or refusal, visits to IRS offices, tax payments to the poor, etc.; support for strikers resisting efforts of business and government to put the burden of the war on workers; demonstrations, sit-downs, etc. at offices and stockholders meetings of major war corporations; savings bond returns (GI's); demonstrations, etc., protesting perpetuation of poverty, low level of welfare and medical payments, etc., caused by the war. These efforts will reach a peak on or around April 15, the time when Americans return tax payments . . . .

"New Mobe announced that it will actively support GI's and draft age youth in exercising their right to refuse to serve the government's war against Vietnam. The spring campaign may culminate in massive GI support demonstrations for peace on May 30, Memorial Day."

As part of their "six-month campaign," New Mobe leaders increased their contacts with international Communists. John McAuliff of the New Mobe steering committee wrote of a mission he made for the organization: "Over the weekend of January 17-18, I traveled to Sweden on behalf of the Coordinating Council of the New Mobilization Committee. The occasion was a meeting of the International Liaison Committee of the Stockholm Conference, an association of anti-war organizations from different countries. The formal purpose of the gathering was to plan major world conference on the war [sic]. We agreed on March 28-30 as the best dates and Stockholm as the location.

"This Easter weekend conference is open to all organizations which support the total, immediate, unconditioned withdrawal of US and allied troops from South Vietnam. It is anticipated that many countries will be represented. Delegations from the Democratic Republic of Vietnam (North Vietnam), the National Liberation Front and the Provisional Revolutionary Government (South Vietnam) will take part . . . .

"The meeting last month in Stockholm also called for the mass circulation of total and immediate withdrawal petitions between now and the world conference. In support of the plans of the New Mobe the meeting declared April 15 an international 'U.S. Out of Vietnam' day.

"Interest was expressed by some of the delegates present to develop supporting actions to the Mobe's late April campaign against US war-profiteering and imperialist corporations. (A real opportunity exists here since the aggressive presence of US corporations is a sensitive issue in many European and third world countries. The Mobe delegation to the Easter conference should do some energetic organizing to help bring off anti-US corporations actions world wide.)

"They talked also of the importance for the US antiwar movement to make concrete practical demands on our government, for example that the US should agree in Paris to negotiate directly with the

136

Provisional Revolutionary Government on the basis of the NLF's overall 10 point solution."

On January 30 and 31, 1970, New Mobe leaders met in Quebec, Canada, with representatives of the Hanoi regime and of the Soviet-controlled World Peace Council. Arnold Johnson, Stewart Meacham, and Katharine Camp of New Mobe, Masai Hewitt of the Black Panther Party, Stanley Faulkner of the National Lawyers Guild, Joseph Crown of the Lawyers Committee on American Policy toward Vietnam, and several other Americans took part in the Quebec meeting where New Mobe's "six-month campaign" was discussed and approved.

On February 7 and 8, 1970, New Mobe leaders attended a World Peace Council meeting they had arranged in Vancouver, British Columbia. An account of the get-together appeared in a New Mobe newsletter: "About 100 Americans from the West Coast, representing about 70 organizations, and a delegation of Canadian peace people met at a conference February 7 and 8 in Vancouver, B.C. [British Columbia], called by the World Peace Council to discuss international co-operation to end the war in Vietnam [sic]. New Mobe arranged the United States participation. In fact, the meeting was initiated by Carlton Goodlett and Irving Sarnoff (both New Mobe steering committee members) at a WPC meeting in Africa last month.

"WPC delegates were: Tran Cong Tuong, one of the chief DRV (Democratic Republic of Vietnam) negotiators at the Paris sessions; Ha Huy Oanh, DRV negotiating team; Krishna Menon, India, Pastor Martin Niemoller, Germany, Romesh Chandra, Sec-General of the WPC; and A. Ratsifehera, Madagascar.

"The conference endorsed and called for international support to the work stoppage being called on April 15 to protest the war. A statement unanimously adopted by the Conference declared that the most urgent need of all people is immediate withdrawal from Vietnam, but placed priority on overcoming the related evils of racism, poverty and repression.

"The conference recommended that an international meeting on racism be held in 1970; endorsed selection of Montreal as site for a Commission of Inquiry into war crimes on Vietnam, projected for summer 1970. The Vietnam delegates addressed the assemblage, answered questions, and participated in workshops. The conference was historic in that it was the first time representatives of the DRV

137

government have met with US citizens and the first time in the WPC [*sic*] has sponsored so broadly represented a meeting in the Western Hemisphere.

"New Mobe office has copies of the statement adopted by the conference; we will soon have tapes of talks by the Vietnamese and printed reports of what they said . . . ."

From March 28 until March 30, 1970, New Mobe leaders were at the fifth Stockholm Conference on Vietnam. The American delegates included such New Mobe stalwarts as William Davidon, Douglas Dowd, Carlton Goodlett, Robert Greenblatt, Sylvia Krushner, and Irving Sarnoff. They joined with other delegates in approving a resolution to support the National Liberation Front: "The U.S. war against the Vietnamese people is continuing and growing in intensity. United States troops, who are surrounded in their bases, continue their 'search and clear' operations, massacres, torture, bombing with its attendant violence, and the use of poisonous chemical products has increased considerably. Despite the gigantic means they have used, the aggressors have been stopped by the heroism of the Vietnamese people and they are now seeking new ways to maintain their domination and prolong the war by using Vietnamese to fight Vietnamese.

"This so-called Vietnamization is nothing but a mystification, destined to fail. Nixon, so far from fulfilling the promises of withdrawal that he was forced to make, is trying to keep U.S. troops indefinitely in South Vietnam. At the Paris Conference, the U.S. government has demonstrated quite clearly its determination to avoid any real negotiations.

"Through more overt intervention in Laos, the U.S. government has recently escalated the aggressive war in that country. It has perpetrated a *coup d' état* in Cambodia, following a tactical CIA pattern in order to carry out its manoeuvres to extend the war. As a result the whole of Indochina risks becoming a war theatre that would threaten the peace and security of all the countries in Southeast Asia.

"Events of the last weeks show even more clearly the dangers that ruling U.S. circles have created for the peoples of the world by their policy of aggression, which is a direct result of the expansionist political military and economic policies of the U.S. throughout the world and a part of a vast general strategy.

"Each people must recognize its own responsibility in this struggle which concerns it directly, and each inhabitant of the world must become aware that his or her action can help to force the aggressor to withdraw.

"Nixon's intensification of the war in Vietnam has been accompanied by increased governmental repression against the U.S. peace forces, young and old, male and female, white and black. In order to continue their war of genocide against the Vietnamese people the U.S. ruling circles have intensified the use of racism as an ideological weapon at home and abroad. But in spite of governmental oppression the peace movement in the United States is increasing its fight for true peace in Southeast Asia, and for freedom and justice at home.

"The Conference is convinced that in order to reach a correct solution of the problem of real peace in Vietnam, the United States government must satisfy the legitimate demands of the Vietnamese people as contained in the ten-point overall solution of the NLF and the PRG of the Republic of South Vietnam, which are based on the total, immediate and unconditional withdrawal of the U.S. and allied forces and establishment of a provisional coalition government which would organize free, democratic elections.

"In order to prevent the extension of the war in Indochina, the United States must be required to cease immediately and unconditionally its war of aggression in Vietnam and the bombing of Laos, it must put an end to the intervention in Cambodia and respect its independence, neutrality and territorial integrity.

"The Stockholm Conference calls upon all national and international organizations, in countries throughout the world, to demand the withdrawal of U.S. troops from South Vietnam by giving massive circulation to its Appeal, by vigorously condemning United States crimes in Vietnam, by developing actions of political support and material aid for the just struggle of the Vietnamese people for independence, freedom and genuine peace.

"To achieve this, the Conference recommends that there should be set up in each country an action programme in cooperation with the antiwar movement in the United States. In this way powerful pressure will be created throughout the world, that will oblige the US government to respect the peace, independence and the right to self-determination of the Vietnamese, Laotian and Cambodian peoples. It recommends the organization of broadly-based, continuing actions that will be coordinated and developed in each region, each country, each sector, according to their conditions and to the concrete problems posed. In this way, the desired results will be achieved and peace will win."

The New Mobe and its "six-month campaign" were the center of attention at the Stockholm Conference, especially New Mobe's newly devised "Outnow Project," which was enthusiastically adopted by the conferees and was described in a conference document: "Responding to the call of the Stockholm Conference on Vietnam, the New Mobilization Committee in the USA has proposed a world-wide campaign to collect signatures of millions of people everywhere on appeals embodying the demand of the total, immediate, unconditional withdrawal of U.S. and allied troops and weapons from South Vietnam.

"The campaign is to be known as the Outnow Project. The campaign will take different forms in different countries. In the USA cables are being sent to President Nixon with the one word Stop.

"All international and national organizations are invited to follow this method or obtain signatures to the Vietnam Appeal, which embodies the key Outnow demand. In countries whose governments support, directly or indirectly, the U.S. aggression in Vietnam, the campaign will be linked to the demands to break with these war policies.

"The 5th Stockholm Conference on Vietnam fully supports this campaign, will assist on the collection of signatures, and will make the best possible use of these."

At Stockholm, the North Vietnamese expressed their appreciation to New Mobe through a spokesman, Xuan Thuy, who told the conferees: "Particularly, with regard to the American people's anti-war movement, we are delighted to note that in spite of the Nixon Administration's policy of repression and maneuvers of concealing the truth, the American people, throughout last year, did not sit quiet and let the U.S. Government commit in their name acts of intervention and aggression and crimes in Vietnam and in many other places, impairing the honour and fine traditions of the American nation.

"Last year, the American people's movement against the Vietnam war was marked by important events so far unknown in American history. The 'Moratorium Day' (October 15, 1969), the demonstrations on November 13, 14, 15, 1969, the opposition to the Chicago trial, the denunciation, of U.S. troops' crimes in South Vietnam, the anti-draft movement, the opposition to the war budget, the statements made inside and outside the Congress against the Nixon Administration's policy, and innumerable other actions of support to the Vietnamese people were warmly hailed and responded to by the Vietnamese people and the World people.

"The Stockholm Conference expresses the firm determination of the various and massive forces of the world people, national and international organizations, of personalities embodying the desire for peace and genuine friendship among peoples. It constitutes once again a great source of encouragement for our people.

"It is necessary to make pressure on the U.S. government by concrete acts, demanding that it rapidly, totally withdraw from South Vietnam U.S. troops and those of the other foreign countries in the U.S. camp, without posing any condition, that it let the Vietnamese people settle themselves their own affairs without foreign interference.

". . . Reality shows that the Nixon Administration . . . cannot be blind to the reaction of public opinion, in the first place American public opinion. What the United States has had to accept so far, for instance the cessation of bombardments against the Democratic Republic of Vietnam [North Vietnam], etc. is precisely prompted by its defeats on the battlefield and the pressure of public opinion . . . .

"That is why, the coordination between our people's struggle and the world people's support is one of the most important questions. This co-ordination will surely compel the Nixon Administration to renounce its scheme of aggression and colonialism, to engage in serious negotiations so as to bring the Paris Conference to results as we wish. As to the forms of struggle experience shows that they are increasingly multiple and varied. We have had an example: the movement in the United States has so far imagined highly rich and effective forms of struggle.

"The Vietnamese people welcome and deeply thank the Stockholm Conference, all national and international organizations, and personalities that have been working in the aforesaid spirit.

"Every expression of support, political or material, great or small, every word spoken, every concrete act from your part and from the world people constitutes a contribution that the Vietnamese people will remember for ever."

In March 1970, New Mobe began its "six-month campaign" with Anti-Draft Week. From March 15 until March 22, selective service offices in sixteen states and Washington, D.C., were the objects of demonstrations, including violence. There were instances of bomb threats, sabotage, robbing, and vandalism.

On April 15, 1970, New Mobe demonstrations were conducted at more than forty internal revenue offices throughout the country. On the same day, there were other anti-war demonstrations, including a Student Mobe-led strike of junior and senior high school students in New York City.

On April 28, 1970, demonstrators disrupted stockholders' meetings of the Gulf Oil Corporation and the Honeywell Corporation as part of New Mobe's second thrust of its "six-month campaign" ("Who Pays for the War and Who Profits from the War?").

From May 8 until May 10, 1970, Washington, D.C., was the scene of New Mobe's last major activity, which brought an abrupt and premature end to the "six-month campaign." A hastily organized demonstration was called by New Mobe leaders to protest the Vietnam War, the invasion of Cambodia, and the deaths of students at Kent State University. At least 80,000 took part in the demonstrations, of which the major one was a rally at the Ellipse. Speakers at the rally included Benjamin Spock, Coretta King, actress Jane Fonda, Fred Halstead, Dave Dellinger, and Robert Scheer. The usual Communist and Trotskyite Communist groups supported the demonstrations: the Communist Party, the Socialist Workers Party, the Black Panther Party, the Spartacist League, the Workers League, the Young Socialist Alliance, Youth Against War and Fascism, and Student Mobe.

The three days of demonstrations were marked by extreme violence. The Federal Bureau of Investigation reported that the federal government incurred losses in damages and other expenses to the amount of $1,147,416. Damages to private property and expenses incurred by the Washington, D.C., police amounted to approximately two million dollars.

Before, during, and after the May 1970 demonstrations, New Mobe was having internal difficulties. The Trotskyites, no matter how much they cooperated in New Mobe's projects, persisted in their belief that nothing would be accomplished unless the Left concentrated its energies upon the one issue of the Vietnam War. On the other hand, the

142

Communist Party of the United States — mindful of its allegiance to international Communism — insisted that, along with protests against the Vietnam War, there were war-related issues that should be given as much attention as the war: poverty, racism, and repression. The Communists believed that, unless many issues were presented as targets for protest, it would be impossible to attract non-Communist groups into a united front.

In June 1970, the split in New Mobe between the Trotskyites and the Communists became so serious that each group held its own conference to decide on future action. From June 19 until June 21, the Cleveland Area Peace Action Council was host to the National Emergency Conference against the Cambodia-Laos-Vietnam War — a Trotskyite meeting.

The "Call" to the Cleveland conference said: "President Nixon has expanded the war in Southeast Asia against the will of the majority of the American people. His latest reckless move in Cambodia dooms thousands of additional GIs, Cambodians and Vietnamese to death and threatens a confrontation with China. The frenzy and recklessness which now characterize U.S. foreign policy do not preclude the end result of nuclear holocaust.

"Nixon has acted against the clearly expressed desires of the American people who want to get out of the war. His order to invade Cambodia was issued without the consent of Congress. It is now perfectly clear that Nixon's real policy is not to withdraw from Southeast Asia but to 'win' the illegal, immoral Indochina war.

"In this historic crisis for humanity it is imperative that the American antiwar movement be a beacon light for the tens of millions of Americans who will join the struggle to end the war if given leadership. The movement must provide a focus and a form for the expression of the broadest opposition to Nixon's course and for the immediate withdrawal of all U.S. forces from Southeast Asia. That is the only way to spare the lives involved; to save humanity from the horrors to which Nixon is leading it; to protect the living standards of American workers which are being destroyed by war-inspired inflation; and to achieve a reordering of national priorities away from a war economy. It is imperative — and at this time it is possible — that the movement expand to embrace the millions of Americans who have not previously protested. It is imperative and it is also possible that significant elements of such powerful social forces as organized labor be involved and integrated in the antiwar struggle. This is the time for those opponents of the war who understand the importance of immense masses in action, for those who understand the importance of giving form to the majority sentiment against the war, to unify for that task and launch a program of action on which such broad forces can agree.

"For these reasons the undersigned issue this call for a National Emergency Conference against the Cambodia-Laos-Vietnam War to be held in Cleveland June 19-20, 1970. The Cleveland Area Peace Action Council, which hosted the conferences which gave birth to the largest antiwar demonstrations in American History — including April 15, 1967 and November 13-15, 1969 — has agreed to host this conference.

"June 20 is the date when Vice President Agnew is speaking in Cleveland at a $250-a-plate Republican fund-raising dinner. CAPAC is organizing a massive, peaceful demonstration to confront Agnew on this occasion. The conference itself will be an effective answer to Agnew and all participants in the conference will be urged to join the demonstration.

"The purpose of the emergency conference is simple and to the point: to plan antiwar demonstrations and other antiwar activities of the most massive kind centering on the crucial issue of withdrawal from the war and conducted in a peaceful and orderly fashion. This is the way to involve immense masses of ordinary people, trade unionists, GIs and their families, students, moderates, liberals and radicals, young and old, and all those who oppose the war regardless of their differences on various other matters.

"This conference is not intended to solve or even necessarily discuss all the problems of our crisis-ridden society. It is not a conference to hammer out the strategy or tactics of social revolution or to found a new political party or movement. It is not a conference in competition with any tendency or movement for social change. It is a conference to organize massive opposition to the war. All those who want to see such opposition organized are welcome to participate regardless of their political ideas or affiliation."

The "Call" was issued by the Cleveland Area Peace Action Council and its chairman Jerry Gordon; the Socialist Workers Party and its leaders Fred Halstead and Gus Horowitz; the Berkeley Faculty-Student

Ad Hoc Peace Committee; the Berkeley Strike Coordinating Committee; Kay Camp, national chairman of Women's International League for Peace and Freedom; Noam Chomsky of the Massachusetts Institute of Technology; Dick Gregory; Student Mobe and its leaders Carol Lipman and Don Gurewitz; Herb Magidson of Individuals Against the Crime of Silence; and state and regional groups of radicals.

The seriousness of the split between Trotskyites and Communists was evident in a directive "to all organizers and anti-war directors" sent by Gus Horowitz, the national anti-war director of the Socialist Workers Party. In his directive, Horowitz called for a major effort to publicize and build up the Cleveland conference. He said: "This antiwar conference is particularly important. It will be the first major national antiwar conference since the student strike upsurge of May, and the conference discussions will take place in the context of greatly enhanced opportunities for mass antiwar mobilizations. Not only has there been a qualitative leap forward in the political consciousness of the mass of students, but the expansion of the war and the mass student upsurge has also affected other sectors of the population. We should note in particular the signs of a greater labor involvement in the antiwar struggle. This is reflected in the conference call, which includes more labor sponsorship than for any previous antiwar conference. The recent issues of the *Militant* give a general roundup of developments in this area.

"This conference, as the call specifically states, is called for the purpose of organizing mass antiwar demonstrations, and not for action of a civil disobedience or confrontationist nature.

"The New Mobilization Committee is continuing along the anti-mass-action course that it has been based around after the November 15 march on Washington. The line that the NMC apparatus has projected is that of civil disobedience. Accordingly, the NMC has taken a hostile attitude toward the Cleveland antiwar conference, and at this time is trying to call an antiwar gathering of its own for the purpose of organizing civil disobedience. The breadth of support for this NMC line is very narrow. Whether this projected NMC meeting gets off the ground or not, the Cleveland conference is proceeding as scheduled.

"In some areas the CP has been intervening in antiwar organizations to a greater extent than previously. The CP's goal is to divert the antiwar movement away from independent mass action and into support for capitalist candidates in the 1970 elections. In so doing they also attempt to weaken support for our mass action line within the antiwar movement by whatever means they can. In some cases (the NMC and the New York Parade Committee, for example) the CP has been functioning in a temporary bloc with civil disobedience and pacifist forces, and ultra-lefts around the issue of anti-Trotskyism and anti-mass-action. We should be alert to increased intervention by the CP in the antiwar movement. Please send in any information on this to the national office.

"The key to the continued projection of mass antiwar action in the immediate period is the success of the Cleveland antiwar conference. Not much time remains to build it. From now until the conference we should go on a campaign basis to ensure its success."

Chairman Jerry Gordon of the Cleveland Area Peace Action Council, who was instrumental in organizing the Trotskyite conference, indicated that the May demonstrations in Washington were the immediate reasons for the Trotskyites' decision to go their own way. Gordon quoted Arthur Waskow's criticism of the May protests: "If even just 15,000 (let alone 75,000) had nonviolently sat down in the D.C. streets as they were prepared to do, and waited (in shifts, etc.) until the Monday 50-governors' meeting or until mass-arrested or until gassed, I think there would have been numerous massive imitations of that action all over the country by Tuesday or Wednesday. New York City and San Francisco would have shut down, the national crisis would have been intensified, and the war might well have been ended within six weeks."

Gordon was in total agreement with Waskow. He believed that prolonged massive demonstrations could be conducted if the leadership avoided violence that could disrupt the demonstrations before they had accomplished their purpose. He felt that New Mobe leaders had taken unnecessary risks at the Washington demonstration and that only the good sense of Fred Halstead and Brad Lyttle prevented David Dellinger, New Mobe's leader, from leading the demonstrations into a violent confrontation that could have had disastrous consequences for the demonstators. Wrote Gordon: "Typical of the thinking of these New Mobe leaders were the plans they made for the Washington May 9 demonstration. Over 100,000 people went to Washington on a few days notice to register their profound opposition to the Cambodia invasion.

The demonstration dramatized for millions of Americans the depth and breadth of opposition to the invasion in a way few other anti-war demonstrations ever have. The anti-war movement gained wide public support as a result of this demonstration in no small part because it was conducted in a peaceful and orderly fashion. But credit for this goes to the good sense of the thousands of demonstrators and to the skill of the marshals — over 4,000 students — who frustrated the high risk confrontation plans of the New Mobe coordinating committee. Heading up the marshals together with Fred Halstead was Brad Lyttle, who has himself advocated and practiced civil disobedience for years. Yet Lyttle opposed the plans of action advanced by New Mobe leaders and he explained why in a memorandum: 'We calculated that it would take more than an hour to move 100,000 people out of the H Street area. A gas attack or a police charge with clubbing in a situation like that could result in hundreds of people being trampled to death. Victims would be those who had come just to attend a peaceful rally as well as people who were prepared for the dangers of a sit-down. The idea that the enormous crowd should surround the White House posed many of the same problems.'

"Dave Dellinger, a key spokesman for the New Mobe, wrote an article in the June 4, 1970 *Village Voice* which reveals how some of the New Mobe leadership views the historic May 9 demonstration and the dangerous possibilities described by Lyttle above. Dellinger begins his article by explaining what he considers the need for 'open, disciplined, carefully focused non-violent resistance' and he cautions against mass marches and demonstrations that 'fail to prepare people for more militant forms of resistance.' He then explains that 'non-violent direct action' was 'the de facto tactic called for by the New Mobe when it invited people to protest in Washington on May 9 not only without government permits but in an area near the White House which, as the Mobe clearly pointed out, had been declared "off limits" to protestors.' 'Because the Mobe clearly called for massive protest without permits in a banned area,' he says, 'thousands of persons came conscious of the fact that they might be arrested, gassed, or otherwise assaulted.' He then laments 'the mistake . . . of asking for the Ellipse' and explains that 'if there was a "failure of nerve" and a "betrayal" that weekend, it occurred when this decision [to ask for the Ellipse] was made.' "

In the Cleveland meeting, the Socialist Workers Party and the Young

Socialist Alliance controlled about two-thirds of the votes held by the 1,500 in attendance. The conference resulted in the formation of the National Peace Action Coalition. The Trotskyite NPAC decided to hold three major demonstrations in 1970: in Cleveland (August 6-9), to commemorate the 1945 bombings of Hiroshima and Nagasaki; in Los Angeles (August 29), to demonstrate against the Vietnam War in collaboration with a Chicano [Mexican-American] Moratorium group; and on October 31, a nationwide anti-war demonstration.

The Communist Party-controlled wing of New Mobe convened its own Strategy Action Conference in Milwaukee. The "Call" for the June 27-28 conference was issued from New Mobe's Washington, D.C. headquarters. The Communists received their instruction through an editorial in the June 1970 issue of the Party's *Political Affairs*: "Struggles are growing in scope and intensity, against the war, against the mounting repression and racist oppression. But far more is required. Above all, if success is to be won, these struggles must all be linked together. This means that masses of white Americans must link the fight against the war with that against the brutal oppression of the Black, Puerto Rican and Chicano peoples. The police killings of Black Americans in the South have brought forth a strong protest in the form of the March Against Repression through the state of Georgia, culminating in the mass demonstration in Augusta. What is needed, however, is a massive outpouring of protest by the trade union movement and by white working people generally against these and other murders, against the growing violence and terror and all other forms of oppression. Only thus can that unity be achieved which will assure the defeat of the reactionary Nixon policies.

"What is called for, in the words of the statement of the Communist Party, USA, is 'the creation of a militant people front whose scope and power surpasses anything history has ever seen . . . .'

"Such a front, headed by the working class and the Black people, can compel the withholding of funds for military operations in Indochina and the withdrawal of all U.S. troops. It can compel the ending of racist terror and oppression at home. It can force an end to mammoth war budgets and to the war-induced inflation and high taxes which are wrecking living standards. It can enforce the sanctity of Constitutional rights and bring about the freeing of all political prisoners, such as the Black Panthers and the draft resisters . . . .

"This is the need of the day, a need which transcends all others. To this task Communists above all are called on to dedicate themselves to the fullest. On the successful building of such a people's front depends the future of our people, our country and the world."

The formal "Call" to the Strategy Action Conference read: "Killings in Jackson, Mississippi . . . Augusta, Georgia . . . Kent, Ohio . . . Expanding police attacks on the Black Panther Party . . . Rising unemployment . . . Continuing inflation . . . a dramatic escalation of the war throughout S.E. Asia . . . America is in a crisis.

"Squandering our limited resources on war has created a torrent of dissent. The government has been forced into a sharp choice. Either withdraw from S.E. Asia immediately and redirect vast sums of money into reparations and economic assistance payments at home and abroad. Or clamp down on unrest and gamble on a rapid and devastating military assault in Indo-China.

"At the present time, it seems all too clear which course the government is pursuing. The probable consequences in Indo-China are intensified bombing of North Vietnam, including Hanoi and Haiphong, and possible use of nuclear weapons. The inevitable consequences at home will be a deepening economic crisis taking its heaviest toll on Blacks, the poor, and through inflation on all working people. We will face an escalation of repression and further usurpation of legislative authority.

"This sense of crisis has struck home across the country. In hundreds of communities new coalitions have sprung into action – developing tactics of massive, disciplined, non-violent resistance, confronting the draft, forcing ROTC and military contracts off campus, reaching out to middle America at the factory gates and the front door. Now we must learn from these actions and build a national response strong enough to stop the war and repression.

"Compelled by this sense of urgency and a desire for unity among many groups, we are calling an emergency Strategy Action Conference in Milwaukee on June 27-28. We will bring together community activists and regional/national organizers. We will share experiences in small, informal workshops. We will explore the new potential for joint actions by Blacks, students, labor, women, clergy, Chicanos, GIs, and anti-war forces.

"We will be meeting in close liaison with the national conference of

149

students from schools on strike. We support the student strike's three demands, that the U.S. end repression of dissent and release all political prisoners, such as Bobby Seale and other Black Panthers; that the U.S. cease expansion of the Vietnam War and immediately withdraw all forces from S.E. Asia; that universities end complicity in the war machine by ending defense research, ROTC, counter-insurgency research and other such programs.

"Delegations for this working conference will be chosen jointly by community groups working on problems of racism, welfare organizing, ending the war, GI rights, campus complicity, labor organizing, sexism, political action, etc."

The "Call" was sponsored by New Mobe veterans David Dellinger, Benjamin Spock, Rennie Davis, and Sidney Peck; Ralph Abernathy and Dorothy Cotton of the Southern Christian Leadership Conference; David Hawk and John Zinner of the Vietnam Moratorium Committee; Stewart Meacham of the American Friends Service Committee; George Wiley, Johnnie Tilman, and Beulah Sanders of the National Welfare Rights Organization; Jesse Jackson of Chicago's Operation Breadbasket; Black Panther leader David Hilliard and the Black Panther Party's attorney, Charles Garry; Roberto Elias, Rosa Lio Munoz, and Guadalupe de Savedra of the Chicano Moratorium; Rev. A. Cecil Williams and Carlton Goodlett of the Soviet-controlled World Peace Council; Trudi Young of Women Strike for Peace; Ronald Dellums of Berkeley's City Council; Episcopal Bishop C. Edward Crowther of Santa Barbara; Rev. John J. Reiger of the National Council of Churches; Ron Young of the Fellowship of Reconciliation; and labor officials Pat Gorman, Frank Rosenblum, David Livingston, Paul Schrade, and Bill Tate.

Among the better known delegates to the Strategy Action Conference were Norma Becker, Barbara Bick, Allan Brick, Ken Cloke, Ruth Gage-Colby, Ralph DiGia, Douglas Dowd, John Froines, Gil Green, Robert Greenblatt, Don Gurewitz, Arnold Johnson, Sidney Lens, John McAuliff, Jarvis Tyner, and Cora Weiss. The Communist Party was well represented, as were the Young Worker's Liberation League, the National Council to Repeal the Draft, the Vietnam Peace Parade Committee, various Welfare groups, various Resistance groups, the Committee for Nonviolent Action, the War Resisters League, the Women's International League for Peace and Freedom, Federal Employees for Peace, and Women's Liberation groups.

The 800 delegates to the Milwaukee Strategy Action Conference did not accomplish much in June except to agree that regional conferences should be held. The agreement was explained in a thank-you letter from Kathy Sophos of Strategy Action to contributors who made the Milwaukee meeting possible: "With your assistance we were able to launch regional conferences around the issues of poverty, racism, repression of all kinds, and the war. People from the entire spectrum of the Movement are getting together to plan regionally targetted and coordinated actions as well as mass national actions focused on these issues. The need for 'grass roots' organizing is being emphasized. Your continuing support is both needed and appreciated; if we're ever going to form a broad-based coalition to combat the repressive forces evident in America today, now is the time! Power to the People!"

The most important of the regional Strategy Action Conferences was held in Milwaukee from September 11 to 13. The 80 delegates at this conference represented the Communist Party, the Black Panther Party, Women Strike for Peace, Women's International League for Peace and Freedom, and the Young Workers Liberation League. The delegates tolled the death knell for New Mobe and created the National Coalition Against War, Racism and Repression [NCAWRR].

In the September 20 issue of the NCAWRR's *Midwest Regional Newsletter*, there was a summary of the proceedings of the September 11-13 conference at Milwaukee and a description of NCAWRR and its program: "Why it was formed: There has been a growing realization for some time amongst people active in 'the movement' that the individual issues on which we have all been fighting are in fact integrated, and that it would be helpful if some means could be found by which those of us who have been working to end the war, racism, repression, poverty, and sexism, could collaborate in a common effort.

"To implement this idea, a conference of 750 people was called in Milwaukee in June. Present were representatives of the New Mobe, various anti-war coalitions, some of the leaders of the Southern Christian Leadership Conference, some of the leaders of the National Welfare Rights Organization, Chicano Moratorium groups, Womens' Liberation, a number of collectives (the Seattle Liberation Front, and collectives from Indianapolis and Baltimore), and a number of trade unionists. The idea of a broad coalition was unanimously endorsed, and a staff formed to implement it. In order to build a firm leadership from the bottom up and to stimulate local and regional activity, the next step was to hold a dozen or more regional conferences — mostly in August. And the third step was a meeting September 11-13 in Milwaukee of delegates from these regional conferences, as well as from national organizations, to formulate a program of action and select an interim committee. That meeting — of some 85 representatives — took the official name of National Coalition Against War, Racism and Repression, and is now in business trying to stimulate and coordinate activity on a wide variety of fronts.

"What has worried most of us in recent times is that we engage in a dramatic demonstration two or three times a year, but do little in between; that each of our organizations is forced to act on its own, because there is little communication, contact, or coordination between us. The new coalition makes it possible to remedy these defects.

"The program of action this fall: The coalition has no desire to tell any group what it should or should not do, nor is it suggesting that any group give up any of the activities it is normally engaged in. It is hoped, however, that we can cooperate on a program of action for this fall that will take place in many cities simultaneously. That program includes the following: (1) A demonstration of support to the Black Panther Party members on trial in Milwaukee, September 26th-27th . . . . (2) Local demonstrations in front of welfare offices on Friday, September 25th in behalf of the Welfare Rights Organization program of 'Fifty-five Hundred or Fight' . . . . (3) October 3rd. Washington demonstration against the visit of General Ky to the United States . . . . (4) The regional conference at Wheeling [West Virginia] decided to call and promote two weeks of city mobilization prior to the election November 3rd . . . . Some groups will want to coordinate this with their electoral work, and will strive to be legal and work 'within the system.' Others will want to do it outside the electoral process and may decide on nonviolent acts of civil disobedience, such as holding a meeting in a bank, in a department store, the Standard Oil offices, draft boards, etc. (5) On October 30th, a Friday, it is planned to hold demonstrations at the welfare offices, at induction centers, and if possible, at factories, to dramatize the related issues of war, the draft, poverty, and unemployment . . . . (6) On October 31st there will be mass vigils or marches in each city and town, to dramatize our opposition to the war, and related issues. (7) During the week of November 15th there will be a massive national action in New York, at the United Nations build-

ing, in opposition to American genocide at home and abroad . . . .
Copies of the Genocide Petitions are available at your regional office, to
be circulated. (8) Finally, a gigantic action is planned for early in May,
1971, if the war is still on, which will include nonviolent civil disobedience and other nonviolent mass action.

"Ongoing activities: One of the major dividends we hope will come
out of the National Coalition Against War, Racism and Repression is
continued, ceaseless, steady, ongoing activity on the local level, and on a
dozen fronts. We hope that teams – or 'collectives' – will form as widely
as possible to give such ongoing actions full scope . . . [and] here are a few
suggestions: (1) Leafletting factories on a regular basis to rap with the
workers about the issues we are interested in, especially the war, as it
causes inflation and unemployment. (2) Soliciting speaking engagements
to unions, churches, schools, womens' organizations, etc. (3) Distribution of leaflets and guerrilla theatre in front of churches and other institutions. (4) Opening of coffee houses, especially near military installations
and at universities, where Movement people can congregate and plan action. (5) Draft counselling. (6) Leafletting military installations and
USO offices. (7) Leafletting at unemployment offices and welfare offices. (8) House to house leafletting, especially in black and brown areas.
(9) Formation of teams that will work together on a constant basis and
will figure out their own specific activities. These collectives should focus
on problems of their own communities. (10) Holding of vigils in the center of town on a regular basis, with signs and leaflets. (11) Formation of a
media committee to solicit appearances on radio and television; as well as
to secure newspaper coverage and, perhaps arrange debates.

"The following are six resolutions strongly supported at the coalition conference in Milwaukee September 11-13, 1970: (1) *UAW strike*:
Because the UAW strike is made necessary by the combination of war-
induced inflation and recession, and the normal exploitative policies of
the giant auto corporations, we urge regional and national organizations
to work together in support of striking UAW workers. Our support for
the workers' needs, and for the efforts of the rank and file movements
to democratize the union to realize those needs, does not imply uncritical support for the present union leadership. Suggested techniques include: a) help in picketing; b) distributing leaflets in public places calling for a boycott of GM and Chrysler cars, and showing the relationship
between the strike and the pressing problems in our country; c) hold-

ing meetings in support of the strike; d) bringing coffee and donuts to the strikers, raising support funds, helping in the publication of strike bulletins where useful; e) calling demonstrations for the strike and against the war, poverty, sexism and racism; f) bringing workers into contact with N.W.R.O., anti-war activists, Panthers, and leaders of the black struggle.

"(2) *Motion on fall actions*: That we go on record as supporting the efforts already under way to make the period of October 15, 1970, to November 15, 1970, one of intensive mass actions on war, racism, welfare rights, and repression, with local committees deciding whether these be single or multiple actions. That this month of action wind up in a national action at the United Nations on the issue of genocide. That we give fullest support and help to rally large numbers to any demonstration called in defense of Bobby Seale. That we issue a call for international protest during this period in solidarity with these actions.

"(3) *Motion on spring action*: We support in principle, a proposal for massive non-violent civil disobedience and other forms of non-violent mass actions in Washington, D.C., and other cities, in early May, 1971. That we commend the action to a variety of national organizations and groups and regional coalitions. That the timing of the call for the action be the earliest result of extensive consultation with these other national and regional forces. That a consultation committee be established for this purpose.

"(4) *Motion on national welfare rights organization*: We urge this Strategy-Action Coalition to start taking positive steps in relationship with dealing with the N.W.R.O. The attitude which has been projected, both at this conference and the first one, is one of verbal commitment only; we are asking for a more positive and relevant commitment. The following steps should be taken by this conference in order to move in a more positive manner: a) This Coalition in its long-range projections for actions and involvement, should maintain an involvement with N.W.R.O. actions on both a national and local level. N.W.R.O. has an action calendar and there is always some drive or problem which all of you attending this conference can relate to on the basis of ending the war being a major solution. b) Friends groups should be established by all Coalition groups. c) There should be an immediate policy of contacting the local N.W.R.O. chapter in the different regions, and the maximum input should be made. This is to take place at the end of this conference.

"(5) *Motion on Chicano Moratorium*: That we have solidarity with the September 16 Mexican Independence Day marches and rallies which will be sponsored by Chicanos across the country.

"(6) *Motion on Standard Oil boycott*: Because Standard Oil is one of the largest war contractors (591,000,000 in military contracts in 1969), and because Standard Oil urged the U.S. government into Vietnam in the first place (*Rockefeller Brothers Report*, 1958), and because S.O. has lobbied for a great build-up of the U.S. military, a National Boycott of Standard Oil is being organized. Other reasons for boycotting Standard Oil include its unfair labor practices, its exploitation of the people and resources of Latin America, its support of the racist apartheid government of South Africa, its racial and sexual discrimination in hiring, its disregard for ecology (oil slicks, poison chemical fertilizers, etc.), its opposition to subsidies for good, cheap public transportation — and many others. What is needed now is organizers on every level, everywhere. This is an action project that local organizations can adopt. We intend to distribute widely two educational pamphlets on Standard Oil. Also, we will issue a Standard Oil Discredit card. Certain demands will be made of Standard Oil. Everyone's help is needed."

The NCAWRR set up an elaborate organization with a national council and twenty-five regional councils, and an elaborate system of representation in the national council for representatives of regional councils, national organizations, student organizations, and special projects.

The new coalition invited an extraordinary collection of organizations to become members of its national council, including trade unions (American Federation of Teachers; United Automobile Workers; American Federation of State, County and Municipal Employees; United Farm Workers Union; Longshoremen's and Warehousemen's Union; Amalgamated Clothing Workers; Amalgamated Meat Cutters and Butcher Workmen; and various locals of other unions); religious groups (Episcopal Peace Fellowship; Fellowship of Reconciliation; Clergy and Laymen Concerned About Vietnam; National Council of Churches; National Council of Black Churches; and Union of American Hebrew Congregations); women's groups (National Organization of Women; Women Strike for Peace; Women's International League for Peace and Freedom; Women's Liberation Movement; National Council of Black Women; and Another Mother for Peace); student groups (National

Student Association and Association for Student Governments); and miscellaneous groups such as the Communist Party, the Black Panther Party, the White Panther Party, the New Party, the Southern Christian Leadership Conference, the Southern Conference Educational Fund, the Congress of Racial Equality, the Chicano Moratorium, Gay Liberation, National Lawyers Guild, Resist, Business Executives Move Against the War in Vietnam, National Welfare Rights Organization, National Urban Coalition, American Guild of Variety Artists, Young Lords, American Servicemen's Union, National Conference of Black Lawyers, Black Economic Development Conference, and Vietnam Veterans for Peace.

In November 1970, many of the NCAWRR leaders journeyed to Stockholm to participate in the Soviet-controlled World Conference on Vietnam, Laos, and Cambodia. (In May 1970, the Executive Committee of the Stockholm Conference had placed itself completely on the side of the Communists in Southeast Asia: "The Stockholm Conference on Vietnam stands with the peoples of Indo-China. We support the joint declaration of the recent summit conference of the Indo-Chinese peoples. We support their legitimate representatives: the Government of the Democratic Republic of Vietnam, the Provisional Revolutionary Government of the Republic of South Vietnam, the Lao Patriotic Front and the Royal Cambodian Government of National Unity.") The American delegates to the November conference joined major international Communist organizations in a three-day orgy of anti-United States denunciations. The delegation included William Douthard, coordinator of NCAWRR; Sidney Peck and David Dellinger of NCAWRR; Congressman-elect Ronald Dellums of California; Ron Young of the Fellowship of Reconciliation; Estelle Cypher and Eleanor Fowler of Women's International League for Peace and Freedom; Stanley Faulkner of the Lawyers Committee on American Policy Towards Vietnam; Carlton Goodlett of the World Peace Council; Gil Green of the Communist Party; Janey Hayes and Pauline Rosen of Women Strike for Peace; Rev. Thomas L. Hayes of Clergy and Laymen Concerned About Vietnam; and Sylvia Krushner of the Chicago Peace Council.

At the Stockholm Conference, the official representative of North Vietnam's Premier Pham van Dong said: "At this time when the lying propaganda and the demagogic actions and words of Nixon are attempting to confuse people and to create an illusion to cover the real intentions, the Delegation of the DRV proposes that our Conference: Organize a campaign of explanation to denounce and condemn the obstinate and perfidious policy of the Nixon administration in Vietnam, Laos and Cambodia. Support politically, morally and materially the struggle of the Indochinese peoples to attain their common aims and their particular aims as defined in the Joint Declaration of the Summit Conference of the Indochinese peoples and in other official documents of the various parties at this Conference. Support the anti-war movement in America, and establish a broad program of mass action in coordination with the activities of this movement in the Spring of 1971."

Nguyen van Hieu of the National Liberation Front directed his remarks "to the American representatives here, and through them to the various mass organizations in the anti-war movement in the United States." He said: "The Nixon administration is obliged to consider the condemnation of its policy by world opinion, including American opinion . . . . The union of forces of freedom and peace, in a world wide mass movement, fighting against American aggression in Indochina, has been shown to be of the utmost importance and greatly contributes to isolating the Nixon administration and its henchmen . . . . To the American people, struggling as we are against the policy of war and oppression of its administration, we convey our deep friendship. We are particularly pleased at the increasingly close cooperation between American antiwar movements and urban South Vietnamese which open the way to new kinds of solidarity between our two peoples."

The program adopted by the American and other delegates at Stockholm called for international support of American anti-war groups in demonstrations against American "aggression." It called for parliamentarians, scientists, and scholars in all nations to apply pressure against their American counterparts to work for the withdrawal of United States and allied forces from Vietnam. It called for the boycott of American products and/or American companies, especially those companies participating in the United States war effort. It called for support of American draft dodgers and resisters. It called for international support of Black Panthers and others in the United States subject to "the brutal repression taking place in the United States."

And on "genocide" and "repression," the program said: "We urge a special exposure of the racist policies of the U.S. government which find their genocidal expression in Indochina in the wanton murder of hundreds of thousands of men, women and children and, in the United States, in the oppressive treatment of black, brown, red, and yellow minorities.

"We call special attention to the grave threat confronting a number of Americans facing the death penalty for their heroic struggle against the war and against racist repression. These include Angela Davis, Erica Huggins and Bobby Seale, and John Sweeney who faces the death penalty on the charge of desertion from the field of battle. This is the first such charge against a deserter and shows the determination of the U.S. government to crush the anti-war movement in the U.S. armed forces. All movements and groups are urged to establish special committees to organize meetings and demonstrations and to promote parliamentary and other protests in defense of these and other American political victims."

From January 8 to January 10, 1971, the NCAWRR held a conference in Chicago to make plans for 1971 activities. More than 350 delegates, representing 119 organizations, approved three projects: (1) Nationwide demonstrations (April 2-4) in commemoration of Martin L. King's death, which would also include the usual anti-Vietnam War, anti-poverty, anti-racism, and anti-political repression protests; (2) A week of demonstrations, rallies, and other activities in Washington, D.C., and elsewhere in the Spring, with anti-war protests joined together with "the issues of racism, poverty, unemployment, repression, sexism, inflation, taxes" (Rennie Davis, a leader of NCAWRR, said: "In this situation we have to create an atmosphere of struggle in May that leads to an international crisis. I don't agree that the [North] Vietnamese are screaming for one big action on one day united under one big umbrella. We have to organize a militant protracted struggle that may divide us from certain constituencies." Davis was hopeful that simultaneously with the planned May demonstrations there would be "a dramatic collapse of the Saigon regime and a mutiny of U.S. troops in Vietnam"); and (3) Circulation of the Joint Treaty of Peace between the People of the United States, South Vietnam, and North Vietnam, popularly known as the "People's Peace Treaty."

The NCAWRR conferees at Chicago were in receipt of a letter from Nguyen thi Binh, the chief negotiator for the Viet Cong at the Paris "Peace Talks." Mrs. Binh wrote: "In this New Year letter, I wish first of all to extend my best wishes for happiness and good luck to you and your families. I appreciate this initiative of the American anti-war movement to sinign a joint declaration of peace with the Vietnamese youth, students, and people. This initiative very rightly springs from the feelings and thoughts that our two peoples have no enmity against each other. On the contrary, we wish only to live in peace and friendship. Over the past decade, not only have the Vietnamese people, but also the American people, undergone untold losses and sufferings because of the most savage war waged by the US government in our country.

"At present, President Nixon is always talking peace, but in fact, on his orders, the war has been intensified, the attacks against the Indochinese countries and the supplying of armaments, bombs and shells have increased; and the U.S. government has of late threatened to indulge in new military adventures in North Vietnam. As for the peace wanted by both the Vietnamese and American peoples it is a genuine peace, in conformity with justice and based upon the respect of the sovereignty, independence and inalienable right to self-determination of all peoples.

"In the face of continued war by the U.S. government, this initiative of signing a peace treaty between the American and Vietnamese peoples, meets our two peoples' urgent demands and earnest aspirations for peace.

"But to be effective, the Peace Treaty should point out the concrete measures to be taken to end the present war. The joint declaration between the three delegations from the United States, North Vietnam and South Vietnam has shown those right fundamental points: First of all, in order to put an end to the war and restore peace, the peoples of Vietnam and the United States should demand that the Nixon Administration withdraw all U.S. troops from South Vietnam within a rapid and reasonable time-limit. And why this could not be before June 30, 1971, as we and many people, right in the United States have proposed? If it can be so, the South Vietnamese people will be spared of rains of bombs and shells, they will no longer be poisoned by toxic chemicals and gases, nor will they longer be the victims of such massacres as Song My. And at the same time, young Americans drafted to Vietnam will no longer be exposed to a useless death and all U.S. servicemen in South Vietnam including the captured will be promptly reunited with their families.

"This is not the demand of a small number of people in South Vietnam or the South Vietnam National Front for Liberation or the Provisional Revolutionary Government of South Vietnam only, but it is one of all young people and students, as well as people of all walks of life in Saigon and other regions of South Vietnam still temporarily occupied by the U.S. and Saigon forces; it is one of every self-respecting Vietnamese, including those working in the Saigon puppet army and administration.

"The aspiration to live in independence and to decide oneself one's destiny is an elementary right and a legitimate aspiration, that is solemnly recognized in the Declaration of Independence and Constitution of the United States. Therefore, the Nixon Administration has no right at all to impose upon the South Vietnam people an administration it has itself set up, a dictatorial and bellicose administration which is killing the South Vietnamese people, jailing and savagely torturing honest people who only want peace and neutrality, and which is frenziedly opposing the reconciliation and union of people of the same nation.

"Would the American people accept that the U.S. government continue to squander the wealth and blood of the American people to foster that handful of traitors who are despised and hated by every South Vietnamese from the country-side to the towns, who firmly urge their overthrow?

"And what right has the Nixon Administration to prevent the South Vietnam people from setting up a government broadly representing the whole South Vietnam people and favouring peace, independence and neutrality, meeting the aspirations of all strata of people in South Vietnam? This government of coalition and national concord will organize free general elections over the whole territory of South Vietnam.

"To restore peace in Vietnam, we should also pay due attention to the situation of North Vietnam, Laos and Cambodia. No law, no ethical principle allows the Nixon Administration to send planes to make reconnaissance flights over, to bomb and to destroy another country. U.S. planes and warships must immediately stop all acts of war infringing upon the sovereignty and security of the Democratic Republic of Vietnam.

"The U.S. government has no reason at all to justify its policy of war against the peoples of Laos and Cambodia. To bring a solid peace in Vietnam and Indochina, and to extricate the United States from the bog of an issueless war, the U.S. government must also give up its policy of aggression against Laos and Cambodia, and really respect their independence, neutrality and territorial integrity.

"We support this initiative of the American anti-war movement to make a Peace Treaty and believe its content will be widely approved by all sectors of the American society, students, women, clergymen, intellectuals, trade-unionists, businessmen, servicemen, etc. . . . all those Americans who are courageously opposing the U.S. Criminal war in our country. I wish the best successes to your Spring activities and plans for mass demonstrations in May. May the joint efforts by millions of Vietnamese and Americans concerted with those of innumerable peace lovers the world over soon bring about the results that we all wish for: an end to the war in Vietnam."

After the January 8-10 conference the NCAWRR changed its name to Peoples Coalition for Peace and Justice [PCPJ]. The PCPJ's original coordinating committee included David Dellinger, Rennie Davis, William Douthard, Irving Beinin, Carlton Goodlett, Gil Green, Terence Hallinan, Sylvia Krushner, Sidney Lens, Sidney Peck, Irving Sarnoff, Jack Spiegel, and Jarvis Tyner – almost all of whom are or have been members of the Communist Party.

Sidney Peck explained the "politics" of the PCPJ and, in the course of his exposition, he stressed the continuing differences between the PCPJ and the Trotskyites who were operating under the name of National Peace Action Coalition. Wrote Peck:

"The politics of the Peoples Coalition for Peace and Justice had its early beginnings in the initial formation of a developing coalition against the war back in July, 1966. At that time representatives of a number of national peace, civil rights, and youth groups met in Cleveland and agreed to the following political ideas: (1) That U.S. involvement in Vietnam was not the result of 'mistakes' or 'errors,' but the calculated expression of neo-imperialist policies in the Far East. Therefore, we must demand the withdrawal of all U.S. military forces and hardware as the primary way to end this war of aggression and intervention. (2) That the war in Vietnam is directly related to policies of global militarism abroad and the systematic oppression of the poor, blacks, Chicanos, women, workers, etc., at home. Therefore, we must at all times point to the interrelationship of the struggle to end poverty, racism, and repression at home — with the struggle to end the war in Vietnam. (3) That the war abroad and the repression at home was typically justified by an anti-Communist mythology. Therefore, we must challenge that mythology head on by a non-exclusionary attitude to all forces on the radical left who respect the right of self-determination for the Vietnamese (and all who struggle for national independence).

"These three political principles have provided the basis for a working concensus among the most diverse forces in what has been termed the 'anti-war coalition': the violation of any one of these basic political ideas has usually led to significant internal division and political immobility.

"It should be clear from the above ideas that the coalition of forces moving against war, poverty, racism and repression for the past five years is not a revolutionary movement. Neither is it a socialist movement. Rather, it is a coalition of revolutionary and non-revolutionary groups, radicals and liberals, who are moving to change Establishment policies. The aim of the coalition is not to overthrow capitalism but to get the U.S. out of Southeast Asia, to secure $5500 adequate income for the poor, to free political prisoners and to attack blatant forms of racism and sexism. While there have been efforts on the part of forces in the Socialist Workers Party, the Young Socialist Alliance, the Student Mobilization Committee and certain liberal political elements around national SANE and the Moratorium to confine this movement to a single issue concerned with the war, the actual political events in the past half dozen years with respect to issues of racism, poverty, sexism, and repression have moved the anti-war forces into an organic multi-issue movement for peace and justice.

"As Dave McReynolds stated so well in his memorandum to the Chicago national meeting, January 8-10: '. . . our movement has become "multi-issue" not as an artificial way of building a coalition; not because the white peace movement is afraid of being "race-baited" if it doesn't give lip service to Third World demands; and not because the poor are so desperate for allies that they will settle for a coalition with white liberals and radicals in the peace movement, but because not one of our interests can be resolved without tackling a range of problems. What we have . . . is . . . a movement which is beginning to realize that America has to undergo radical social change if we are to cease, as a nation, terrorizing the world and oppressing our own people.'

"Those who have repeatedly urged a single issue struggle against the war have also put forward the idea of a rally-march mobilization as a single tactic for the movement. But the politics of a multi-issue coalition of forces necessitates a multi-tactical approach. This multi-tactical set is grounded on a firm adherence to the principle of non-violent mass action. Thus, the strategy of this movement combines the use of dissent and resistance tactics. It means that we not only advocate rallies and mobilizations and teach-ins and speak-outs – but we also urge all forms of non-violent resistance to illegitimate authority. In specific situations, this will involve massive civil disobedience, i.e., draft resistance, tax refusal, sit-ins, strikes, etc.

"One further point. The politics of a coalition of forces in this new multi-issue movement are held together by decision making based upon concensual agreement. Our politics do not issue from a single-minded ideological perspective. On the contrary, they flow from a recognition of profound differences of political ideology and opinion, which characterize the diversity of forces in this movement. Concensus is only attainable because there is a genuine respect for these obvious political differences firmly rooted in our adherence to the principle of political non-exclusion."

From February 5 to February 7, 1971, at the University of Michigan in Ann Arbor, about 2,000 attended the Student and Youth Conference on a People's Peace. The conference was called together by the National Student Association, and during the course of the three-day session, the spring demonstrations were approved and the "People's Peace Treaty" was endorsed. Among the leaders at the conference were Rennie Davis and Ron Young of the Peoples Coalition for Peace and Justice, and Don Gurewitz of the Trotskyite National Peace Action Coalition. Despite the widely publicized rift, the NPAC and the PCPJ were at least planning to cooperate on the spring demonstrations and the "People's Peace Treaty" project. The NPAC had received a directive in January from the International Executive Committee of the

Fourth [Trotskyite] International: "The antiwar movement in the United States has decided to organize marches on Washington and San Francisco on April 24 by way of denouncing the hypocritical attitude of the Nixon government, which, under guise of a 'progressive withdrawal' of the American troops and 'Vietnamization' of the war, has again intensified its aggressive actions against the Vietnamese people, resuming bombings and commando raids against the Democratic Republic of Vietnam.

"In face of the obvious incapacity of American imperialism to reduce the heroic resistance of the Vietnamese people against the aggression, and to undermine their resolution to win their national and social liberation, the high command in Washington is cooking up new adventures and barbarous acts to 'resolve' the war in Vietnam in accordance with their own purposes.

"Within this framework, the mobilization of the largest possible masses in the United States to compel the immediate and unconditional withdrawal of the American troops from Vietnam constitutes precious aid to the Vietnamese revolution. The fact that more and more trade union organizations are joining the antiwar movement exposes the lies of the Nixon Administration and the venal press about a 'silent majority' of the American people allegedly supporting the aggression in Vietnam while only a minority of students and intellectuals oppose it. The increased hostility of the Black masses and the Chicanos to the war is another indication of the growing cohesion among all the exploited layers in the United States in the struggle against the dirty imperialist war in Vietnam.

"Under these conditions, it is the duty of all the revolutionary organizations throughout the world to mount the broadest and most active aid possible to the antiwar movement in the United States, in this way aiding the Vietnamese revolution with concrete acts of solidarity.

"The Fourth International appeals to the workers, the students, poor farmers, and progressive intellectuals of all countries throughout the world to organize powerful demonstrations April 24 in solidarity with the Vietnamese revolution and with the antiwar movement in the United States, through effective anti-imperialist united fronts commensurate to the needs of each country.

"Let's make April 24, 1971, a day of active world solidarity with the heroic Vietnam revolution! Let's demonstrate everywhere April 24,

1971, showing our solidarity with the courageous antiwar movement in the United States! For the immediate and unconditional withdrawal of the American troops from Vietnam! For the victory of the Vietnamese revolution – everyone in the streets April 24, 1971!"

The so-called People's Peace Treaty which was of so much interest to the Viet Cong's Nguyen thi Binh, the Chicago conference of the PCPJ, and the National Student Association's Ann Arbor conference had its origins in the 1970 annual congress of the National Student Association. In sworn testimony on May 20, 1971 before the House Internal Security Committee, Charles Stephens and Neil Salonen of American Youth for a Just Peace described what they had discovered during a lengthy investigation of the People's Peace Treaty. In the course of his remarks, Stephens said: "There is a vast distinction between what the People's Peace Treaty is and what it claims to be. It claims to be, and this is the title of the treaty, 'A Joint Treaty of Peace between the people of the United States, South Vietnam and North Vietnam.' Now, it almost goes without saying that this is a preposterous presumption, as when the treaty was negotiated, neither the American people nor the South Vietnamese people nor, for that matter, the North Vietnamese people were even aware of its existence, and I daresay that the majority of the American and South Vietnamese people do know little, if anything, about it today . . . .

"The treaty was negotiated by a handful of students – of American students, of North Vietnamese students, and in South Vietnam perhaps only just one student. The students in the United States were members of the National Student Association, in North Vietnam members of the North Vietnamese National Student Union, which is a puppet organization of the Communist Party of North Vietnam, and in South Vietnam by the head of an organization called the Saigon Student Union. Now, the negotiating process for this Joint Treaty of Peace emanated from a conference which was held in August, an annual congress of the National Student Association, in 1970, and at that congress the NSA officers were mandated, and I quote, 'to engage in negotiations for a peace treaty between the students of North and South Vietnam and the students of the United States.' Now, following that mandate, a delegation of 15 members of the National Student Association, headed by a guy called David Ifshin, who is the ex-president, student body president of Syracuse University, led a group of 15 delegates to Hanoi, and in Hanoi, with representatives of the North Vietnamese Student Union there and other Communist Party [of North Vietnam] functionaries, they established a Declaration of Peace and signed a Declaration of Peace sometime in early December of 1971 . . . in Hanoi by their own admission . . . .

"There are many, many different versions of the People's Peace Treaty. In fact, all groups are encouraged to write their own preamble . . . . The treaty, as I have seen it, varies in terms of the preamble, but in terms of its nine basic points, they have been the same. The preamble varies . . . .

"I might add that one member of the National Student Association delegation got into Saigon, a Mr. Douglas Hostetter, and there he drew up and allegedly signed a declaration with the head of the Saigon Student Union. He then went on to Vientiane, Laos, and from Laos joined the rest of his friends in Hanoi. They remained in Hanoi a total of about 2 weeks, and then from Hanoi they went to Paris, where they had a press conference announcing their peace treaty, and subsequently a press conference was held in Washington, D.C. . . . . .

"I should say, at this point, that the People's Peace Treaty, as it was produced in Hanoi, as a result of the two treaties that were melded together, one from Saigon and in Hanoi, is almost a carbon copy of Madame Binh's negotiating points in Paris, Madame Binh being the principal Vietcong negotiator in Paris, and a carbon copy of Hanoi's negotiating points in Paris. So in the guise of a People's Peace Treaty, Hanoi's terms for a settlement in Vietnam have gotten a great range of exposure in the United States."

Neil Salonen testified about the results of his investigation in South Vietnam of the People's Peace Treaty. Said Salonen: "In this country, before I went to Vietnam, you may know that the principal supporter that has been listed by the NSA, and those who have been supporting the People's Peace Treaty for South Vietnamese support among the students has been Huynh Tan Mam, and his position is listed as president of the Vietnam National Student Union, and David Ifshin handed this particular piece of paper which has a banner, 'The Vietnam National Student Union.' It refers in the text to Huynh Tan Mam as the president of that group. However, the stamp in Vietnamese says 'The Saigon Student Union,' and the address is also the Saigon Student Union, which is only one of many universities in South Vietnam. So I traveled and I mét with various student groups in Saigon, in Dalat, and in Hue, and I asked them to document their feelings about the Vietnam National Student Union, the representative character of Huynh Tan Mam, the contents of the People's Peace Treaty, and even beyond that, we shared feelings about the war and the true path of peace.

"There is no such organization as the Vietnam National Student Union. There have been repeated attempts on the part of the student unions of the various South Vietnam universities to form a National Student Union, which have failed. All of the legitimate groups, such as the Catholic Students' Federation, representing 25 per cent of the students in South Vietnam, completely refuted any authority on the part of Huynh Tan Mam to speak for them on their views on the war. They rejected the People's Peace Treaty explicitly as being unenforceable, since the first point calls for the unilateral withdrawal of the U.S. troops, after which all other points would be unenforceable, including the promise to enter negotiations for the release of American POWs. Therefore, all the groups I met with, including the Labor Youth Association and several college executive committees . . . repudiated all three of those points."

On April 29, 1971, Representative Bella Abzug (D.-N.Y.) and seven of her colleagues (Herman Badillo, James Scheuer, and Shirley Chisholm [N.Y.] ; Parren Mitchell [Md.] ; John Conyers [Mich.] ; and Ronald Dellums [Calif.] — all Democrats) introduced a concurrent resolution expressing "the sense of the Congress that the People's Peace Treaty embodies the legitimate aspirations of the American and Vietnamese peoples for an enduring and just peace in Indochina." Mrs. Abzug, in explanation of the action taken by herself and her colleagues, said: "We do so because of the wide support the treaty has received among many Americans, especially the young. We believe the Congress has the power to end the war in Vietnam. We believe the Congress will and must do so by passing the Vietnam Disengagement Act calling for the withdrawal of our troops before the end of this year. This People's Peace Treaty is a very deeply moving expression of the yearning of people throughout this Nation and Indochina to see this war end by their own actions in the face of nonaction by this body.

"This treaty has been endorsed by tens of thousands of Americans from all walks of life. Prominent American labor leaders, clergymen, educators, and mayors, student bodies and college student governments, churches and community groups have ratified the treaty. The names of some of the organizations and individuals who have endorsed the treaty are listed below. The treaty has been introduced into the Vermont State Legislature and the Cambridge, Mass., City Council. On April 27, the Detroit City Council approved the treaty. In the coming weeks the City Councils of Pueblo, Colorado, Cleveland, Ohio, and Madison, Wisconsin, will be asked to ratify it.

"Because of the widespread support this treaty is receiving, we bring it to the attention of our colleagues in the Congress in the form of a supporting resolution. It is our belief that this treaty is being offered by the people to their Government as yet another testament of their will that we in Congress act immediately to end this war."

The preamble of the "People's Peace Treaty," as introduced by Congresswoman Abzug, read: "Be it known that the American and Vietnamese people are not enemies. The war is carried out in the name of the people of the United States, but without our consent. It destroys the land and the people of Viet Nam. It drains America of her resources, her youth and her honor.

"We hereby agree to end the war on the following terms, so that both peoples can live under the joy of independence and can devote themselves to building a society based on human equality and respect for the earth. In rejecting the war we also reject all forms of racism and discrimination against people based on color, class, sex, national origin and ethnic grouping which form a basis of the war policies, present and past, of the United States."

The nine principles of the "People's Peace Treaty" were:

"1. The Americans agree to immediate and total withdrawal from Vietnam, and publicly to set the date by which all U.S. military forces will be removed.

"2. The Vietnamese pledge that as soon as the U.S. government publicly sets a date for total withdrawal, they will enter discussions to secure the release of all American prisoners, including pilots captured while bombing North Vietnam.

"3. There will be an immediate cease-fire between U.S. forces and those led by the Provisional Revolutionary Government of South Vietnam.

"4. They will enter discussions on the procedures to guarantee the safety of all withdrawing troops.

"5. The Americans pledge to end the imposition of Thieu, Ky and Khiem on the people of South Vietnam in order to insure their right to self-determination, and so that all political prisoners can be released.

"6. The Vietnamese pledge to form a provisional coalition government to organize democratic elections. All parties agree to respect the results of elections in which all South Vietnamese can participate freely without the presence of any foreign troops.

"7. The South Vietnamese pledge to enter discussion of procedures to guarantee the safety and political freedom of those South Vietnamese who have collaborated with the U.S. or with the U.S.-supported regime.

"8. The Americans and Vienamese agree to respect the independence, peace and neutrality of Laos and Cambodia in accord with the 1954 and 1962 Geneva conventions, and not to interfere in the internal affairs of these two countries.

"9. Upon these points of agreement, we pledge to end the war and resolve all other questions in the spirit of self-determination and mutual respect for the independence and political freedom of the people of Vietnam and the United States."

At the time Mrs. Abzug introduced her concurrent resolution, student body presidents and campus newspaper editors at American colleges, seminaries, and universities had ratified the "People's Peace Treaty." Student senates, councils, governments, and congresses had also ratified it. The treaty was endorsed by the American Friends Service Committee, Clergy and Laymen Concerned About Vietnam, the National Lawyers Guild, the New University Conference, Women Strike for Peace, Women's International League for Peace and Freedom, and, of course, the People's Coalition for Peace and Justice, which made the "People's Peace Treaty" a focal point of newspaper advertisements. One such PCPJ advertisement carried endorsements by Physicians for Social Responsibility, the May Day Tribe, the Gay Liberation Front, the Harrisburg 8 Defense Committee, Resist, and the Medical Committee for Human Rights.

Organizational leaders who have endorsed the People's Peace Treaty include Ralph Abernathy of the Southern Christian Leadership Conference; Kay Camp of the Women's International League for Peace and Freedom; Gerhard Elston and David Hunter of the National Council of Churches; David Hawk and Marge Sklencar of the Vietnam Moratorium

Committee; Al Hubbard and John Kerry of Vietnam Veterans against the War; Erica Huggens and Bobby Seale of the Black Panther Party; Jesse Jackson of Operation Breadbasket; Stewart Meacham of American Friends Service Committee; Ben Peckin and Irwin Salk of Business Executives Move for Vietnam Peace; Amy Swerdlow, Trudi Young, and Cora Weiss of Women Strike for Peace; Sister Margaret Traxler of the National Coalition of American Nuns; George Wiley of the National Welfare Rights Organization; Melvin Wulf of the American Civil Liberties Union; Ron Young of the Fellowship of Reconciliation; Joseph Duffey of the Americans for Democratic Action; Marcus Raskin of the Institute for Policy Studies; Charles E. Magraw and Timothy E. Guiney of Physicians for Social Responsibility; Abbie Hoffman of Yippies; Cynthia Fredrick of the Committee of Concerned Asian Scholars; Richard N. West of the Unitarian-Universalist Association; and Richard Fernandez of Clergy and Laymen Concerned About Vietnam.

Other sponsors include authors and literary figures — Jules Feiffer, Betty Friedan, Mitchell Goodman, Francine du Plessex Gray, Denise Levertov, Kate Millett, Grace Paley, Erich Segal, Gloria Steinem, Paul M. Sweezy, Studs Terkel, Dalton Trumbo, and Karl Hess; U.S. Senators Charles E. Goodell (R.-N.Y.) and Eugene J. McCarthy (D.-Minn.); Congressmen Don Edwards (D.-Cal.), Michael Harrington (D.-Mass.), and William Fitts Ryan (D.-N.Y.); entertainers — Roscoe Lee Browne, Godfrey Cambridge, Judy Collins, Jane Fonda, Ben Gazzara, Dick Gregory, Julie Harris, Rock Hudson, Jennifer Jones, Janice Rule, Robert Ryan, and Joan Baez; clergymen - Rev. Daniel Berrigan, Rev. Philip Berrigan, Rev. Malcolm Boyd, Rabbi Balfour Brickner, Rev. William Sloane Coffin Jr., Bishop Daniel Corrigan, Bishop William Crittenden, Bishop C. Edward Crowther, Bishop William Davidson, Bishop Robert L. DeWitt, Rev. James Groppi, Bishop Thomas J. Gumbleton, Bishop Bernard Kelly, Rev. Richard McSorley, Bishop Paul J. Moore Jr., Rev. Peter Riga, Rabbi Arthur Lelyveld, Bishop John H. Burt, and Msgr. John J. Egan; academicians — George Wald, Franz Schurmann, Linus Pauling, Jonathan Mirsky, Charles E. Merrill, Daniel Ellsberg, Richard Falk, Robert Jay Lifton, Noam Chomsky, Robert MacAfee Brown, Salvador E. Luria, Harvey Cox, and Howard Zinn; labor organizers — Leon Davis, Abe Feinglass, Thomas Flavell, Henry Foner, Moe Foner, Patrick Gorman, Robert Z. Lewis, Sol Silverman, and Joseph Tarantola; attorneys William Kunstler, Arthur Kinoy, Allan

Brotsky, Charles P. Garry, Kenneth Cockerel, Leonard Boudin, and Mark Lane; and assorted radicals — Benjamin Spock, Coretta King, Stewart Mott, Bess Myerson Grant, Julian Bond, Arthur Waskow, and Mrs. Philip Hart.

While the PCPJ was planning its "spring offensive" and promoting the "People's Peace Treaty," the Trotskyites in the NPAC were making their own plans. They set the date April 24 for massive anti-war demonstrations in Washington, D.C., and San Francisco. They concentrated on two demands: an immediate end to the draft and an immediate, unconditional withdrawal of all American forces from Indochina.

The PCPJ and NPAC disagreed on the date for the Washington demonstrations, but the NPAC agreed to support the Martin L. King commemorative activities scheduled for the first four days in April. Disagreements came to a temporary halt, however, when Xuan Thuy, the Hanoi regime's ambassador to the Paris "peace talks," sent a message on February 27 to the American anti-war agitators: "Facing the serious situation as it's now presented, I call upon the progressive American people and all antiwar organizations in the United States to unite closely, to associate all forces and strata of the population irrespective of their skin color, religion and political trend, thus making a wide and strong movement so as to curb in time new military adventures by the U.S. Administration, to demand an end to their war of aggression in South Vietnam, Laos and Cambodia, to demand the withdrawal of all American troops from Indochina and let the Indochinese people settle their own internal affairs. Such is the way beneficial to the peoples of Vietnam and Indochina, beneficial to the American people, beneficial to peace in the world. I wish you every success in your coming activities."

The PCPJ and NPAC reacted to Xuan Thuy's message by agreeing to cooperate in one major anti-war demonstration on April 24. The agreement was made known on March 2 by the PCPJ at a news conference. A statement released at the conference was reprinted in newspaper advertisements: "We face two wars. A recent Gallup poll shows that 73 percent of the American people now want U.S. military forces out of Vietnam by the end of the year. But despite this clear mandate to end this barbaric war against the Indochinese people, the slaughter continues to escalate and Nixon continues to issue his hypocritical pronouncements that the war is winding down. The Laos invasion shows the hypocrisy of Nixon's statement that he is ending the war. And it demonstrates how easily the racism that plagues us at home becomes translated into a policy of cynical reliance on Vietnamese mercenaries. As the Laos invasion continues to go badly, threat of direct U.S. intervention in Laos, of an invasion of North Vietnam and, possibly, of the use of tactical nuclear weapons, increases.

"At home another war continues. It is the war of the corporate rich against the poor. While Congress continues to appropriate funds in record amounts for supersonic polluting transports, moon trips, and mass destruction weapons, the working and welfare poor face a different kind of death. It is a slow and agonizing death. Children die from eating the poisonous paint falling off tenement walls. Teenagers overdose from heroin. Others, robbed of their right to creative and secure employment, are psychologically destroyed, convinced they deserve no better. And the old die silently.

"Thus far the government's response to the nation's increasing cry for life has not been a change for the better, but brutal repression. Brilliant black leaders have been shot in their beds or put on trial for their lives; innocent students have been murdered as bystanders; priests, passionately committed to the cause of nonviolence, have been jailed; senators and congressmen have their phones tapped — all by the government. The governing administration has become the enemy of the people, both at home and abroad.

"The people must turn this country around. They must force an end to the war which is sucking the life from the country and begin in earnest the struggle against poverty, racism and repression at home.

"The Peoples Coalition for Peace and Justice announces our Spring Offensive of sustained, nonviolent struggle against the evils which are tearing our country apart. We are merging the struggle against our government's two wars: that against the Indochinese people and that against the poor at home. We are beginning our campaign in unity with the forces of the Southern Christian Leadership Conference and the National Welfare Rights Organization. We are lending support to the National Farmworker's Organizing Committee, the women's liberation movement and the Vietnam Veterans Against the War. We are moving together!"

In its customary shotgun approach, the PCPJ included in its spring offensive plans these demands: "Free all political prisoners, immediate

172

withdrawal of all air, land and sea forces from Indochina [and] set the date for completion of withdrawal." They scheduled protests against "welfare repression." They urged support of the lettuce boycott sponsored by Cesar Chavez and his United Farm Workers Organizing Committee. They urged boycotts of Standard Oil products and A & P supermarkets. They demanded the vote for 18-year-olds in all local, state, and federal elections. They demanded home rule for Washington, D.C.

The "spring offensive" of the PCPJ and the NPAC took place in Washington, D.C., beginning with a massive demonstration on April 24 — police estimated that between 175,000 and 185,000 participated. The demonstrators received wholehearted encouragement from leading Democrats, including former Attorney General Ramsey Clark; U.S. Senators Edmund Muskie of Maine, Mike Gravel of Alaska, Edward Kennedy of Massachusetts, Philip Hart of Michigan, Vance Hartke of Indiana, and George McGovern of South Dakota; and Congressmen Herman Badillo, Bella Abzug, John Dow, Charles Rangel, Edward Koch, Benjamin Rosenthal, Jonathan Bingham, and James Scheur of New York, Phillip Burton and Ronald Dellums of California, Robert Kastenmeier of Wisconsin, Parren Mitchell of Maryland, and Michael Harrington of Massachusetts.

Between April 22 and May 6, police in Washington, D.C., made 14,517 arrests, most of them for disorderly conduct, unlawful assembly, and unlawful entry. The cost to the Metropolitan Police was $3 million for the period May 1 to May 6. More than $100,000 in damages were inflicted on the Washington Monument grounds. In West Potomac Park, the campsite of the PCPJ, there was another $190,000 in damages. There were demonstrations in the Senate galleries, in various Senators' offices, at the Selective Service building, at the Health, Education and Welfare building, at the South Vietnamese embassy, and elsewhere. Marchers paraded under Communist Party and Viet Cong flags. American flags were torn down and destroyed. Obscenities were painted on walls, benches, and monuments. Private property also suffered extensive damage. Only the large-scale arrests by the police, which were bitterly protested by Senator Edward Kennedy and other bleeding hearts in Congress, eventually stopped the demonstration.

In May and June 1971, the House Internal Security Committee held hearings on the NPAC and PCPJ. When HISC announced what it was going to do, it attracted the condemnation of eleven Representatives from the far left, who issued a statement: "Only three weeks ago – during debate in the House over funds for the House Internal Security Committee (HISC) – we cautioned our colleagues that continued funding of this committee could only result in continued harassment of those individuals and groups involved in activities of which the committee does not approve. Our warnings were ignored, the committee received more money than ever before and this morning HISC – in what appears to be an attempt to discredit the peace movement in this country – is beginning hearings on organizations that have sponsored anti-war demonstrations here in Washington over the last month.

"Once again HISC has determined to ignore the First Amendment rights of every citizen of this country and will attempt to intimidate those who would exercise their rights to peacefully protest a policy of this government.

"However, if HISC is to disparage the entire anti-war movement, it will have to take on an overwhelming majority of the people in this country. Anti-war sentiment is not restricted to a few dissenting groups or individuals at this point in time; it is shared by over 73 percent of the public, a percentage that is constantly growing. HISC cannot attack or single out any individual anti-war group at this time without impugning the integrity of millions of Americans who are opposed to our involvement in Southeast Asia. By initiating another witch hunt HISC is actually questioning the integrity of a majority of Americans who desire peace, who abhor killing and senseless destruction, who long for the day when billions of dollars now spent on bullets and guns can be used to revitalize our decaying cities, to improve our schools, and to provide health care and a decent home for every American.

"In this context HISC is guilty of what we would term the ultimate un-American activity and we call on all Americans to join with us in expressing abhorrence of this latest and most outrageous action of this committee."

The signers of the statement were Phillip Burton and Don Edwards of California, John Conyers of Michigan, Donald Fraser of Minnesota, Michael Harrington of Massachusetts, Edward Koch, Benjamin Rosenthal, and William Fitts Ryan of New York, Henry Helstoski of New Jersey, and Abner Mikva of Illinois – all Democrats. Their sentiments were echoed by Jerry Gordon, co-ordinator for NPAC, who charged that HISC was engaging in a "red smear" and "desperately trying to revive the McCarthyism of the 1950's."

In 1972, the NPAC and the PCPJ announced plans for a new "peace offensive" to be conducted between April 1 and May 15, with massive demonstrations scheduled for April 22 in New York and Los Angeles. The planned April 22 demonstrations, according to the Trotskyites, received endorsements from New York Mayor John Lindsay, former U.S. Senator Eugene McCarthy of Minnesota, U.S. Senator Hubert Humphrey of Minnesota, and U.S. Senator Edmund Muskie of Maine.

Chairman Richard Ichord of the House Internal Security Committee warned his colleagues of the "peace offensive" in a speech delivered on March 13, 1972. He prefaced his warning by saying: "We need have no further illusion about who and what NPAC and PCPJ are today. The NPAC is totally controlled, in its every pulse beat, by the Trotskyite Communist Socialist Workers Party – SWP – and its youth arm, the Young Socialist Alliance. The presence of key officials of the Communist Party USA on the National Steering Committee of PCPJ evidences the commitment of CPUSA to the program and direction of PCPJ."

Ichord provided his colleagues with the background of the NPAC-PCPJ "peace offensive": "The proposed demonstrations this year were completely developed after lengthy deliberation by a conference called the World Assembly for Peace and Independence of the Peoples of Indochina. The conference was held in Versailles, France, on February 11-13, 1972, and was called by the Communist-directed Stockholm Conference on Vietnam and the Communist-run World Peace Council. Every single item on the agenda of demonstrations planned for the United States was debated, discussed, and approved – not by a group of Americans alone – but by 1,200 delegates from 84 nations including most of the countries controlled by Communist governments. There were also delegations representing the underground Communist guerrilla forces in South Vietnam, Cambodia, and Laos. The American delegation numbered between 140 and 150, just slightly more than 10 percent of the total number of delegates.

"Though the American delegation represented only a small portion of the delegates, the conference bestowed upon the American delegation a special position of importance. CPUSA's weekly publication *World* magazine accurately described the importance of the American

175

delegation as follows: 'Next to the four Indochinese delegate bodies – from the Democratic Republic of Vietnam (North Vietnam), the Provisional Revolutionary Government of South Vietnam (the Vietcong), the Patriotic Front of Laos (Pathet Lao) and the Royal Government of the National Union of Cambodia (Prince Sihanouk and the Cambodian Communists in exile in Communist China) – the U.S. delegation occupied a central position in the Assembly proceedings. It was the only delegation beside the Indochinese that was privileged to report formally in the plenary sessions, and it was rendered special greetings and honors by all. As the voice, the genuine voice, of the American people it was accepted as the symbol of mankind's condemnation and rejection of the Nixon war.'

"Continuing, the exultant Communist *World* magazine added: 'In other ways, too, the spotlight fell on the Americans present. The greatest standing ovation given at the Assembly, exceeding even that rendered to the Vietnamese, was for Angela Davis, presented as the epitome of resistance to the war and to the fascistic repressions that have accompanied it in the United States.' "

Ichord continued: "The *World* Assembly received encouragement from many of the world's Communist leaders. Soviet Party leader Leonid Brezhnev sent a message of praise to the delegates who, he declared, had gathered 'to express wrath and indignation over the barbarous aggression of American imperialism.' Cambodia's pro-Communist Prince-in-exile – Sihanouk – sent his greetings from his sanctuary in Red China. North Vietnam's Premier Pham Van Dong and the Pathet Lao Leader, Prince Souphanouvong, also extended messages of cheer and support. Throughout the conference, the 1,200 delegates laughed and cheered and applauded the constant denunciations of the United States – particularly the scurrilous jibes uttered by spokesmen of the American delegation."

At the Versailles conference, besides the NPAC and the PCPJ, other American organizations formally represented in the delegation were the American Friends Service Committee, Clergy and Laymen Concerned About Vietnam, the National Welfare Rights Organization, the National Committee for a Sane Nuclear Policy, Women Strike for Peace, Women's International League for Peace and Freedom, and Trade Union Action for Democracy. A number of the American delegates were identifiable by their affiliation with various organizations, including the Young Workers Liberation League, the War Resisters League, the Harrisburg 8 Defense Committee, the Angela Davis Defense Committee, the Peace Action Council of Southern California, the National Student Association, Fund for Peace Education, and the Catholic Peace Fellowship. Among the better known American radicals at Versailles were Bronson Clark, Jane Fonda, John Froines, Ruth Gage-Colby, Jerry Gordon, Rev. James Groppi, Fred Halstead, Al Hubbard, Gabriel Kolko, Bradford Lyttle, Sidney Peck, Beulah Sanders, Irving Sarnoff, Michael Zagarell, and Howard Zinn.

In his account of the Versailles conference, Representative Ichord said to his colleagues in the House: "Now let us look at this calendar of demonstrations which this world assembly worked out for the United States of America to take place within the United States of America. The calendar adopted was as follows:

"April 1: In Harrisburg, Pa., a demonstration opposing the so-called Berrigan conspiracy trial and, in San Jose, Calif., a demonstration opposing the criminal prosecution of Angela Davis on charges involving a Federal charge of unlawful flight to avoid prosecution and State charges of murder, kidnapping and conspiracy.

"April 15: Nationwide demonstrations against the payment of Federal income taxes which provide the revenue for financing our armed services in the war in Southeast Asia.

"April 22: Massive turnouts of demonstrators in New York City and Los Angeles demanding an end to U.S. involvement in Vietnam and a demand for an immediate, unconditional end of the war on Communist North Vietnam's terms.

"May 1 to 15: Local demonstrations against U.S. corporations dealing in the production of war material. These are to be supported by demonstrations overseas against U.S. embassies.

"These efforts are to be supplemented during 1972 by continuing efforts to persuade active-duty GI's to refuse to participate in the war in Southeast Asia and to develop militant protests against the Republican National Convention in San Diego."

The plans developed at Versailles for protests against the Republican Convention were quite comprehensive. The American delegation presented recommendations that were adopted by the World Assembly of Peace, and the language of the formal document was totally revolutionary in character. The hoary Marxist clichés directed against

America's alleged imperialism, capitalism, militarism, repression, and racism saturated the document. The outline of a "People's Platform" was drafted as a possible presentation to the Democratic and Republican National Conventions. The platform outline reflected the multi-issue strategy of the orthodox Communists and their PCPJ rather than the single-issue of the Trotskyites and their NPAC: "The People's Platform would have five points: (1) A specific plan for total withdrawal from Indochina; (2) a plan for rationalizing the economy; (3) a plank calling for the reversal of the Nixon policies of internal repression and control; (4) a plank on racism; and (5) a plank on sexism."

The American delegation at Versailles, with the approval of the Communist delegations from around the world, presented their political objectives in confronting the Republican Convention: "1) To make it clear that we want an immediate end to all aspects of the war in Indochina and that, if this urgent desire of the great majority of the people of the U.S. is not met, the elected government will have no legitimacy and stand no chance of being re-elected. (a) We will demand the U.S. government accept the 7-point peace plan of the P.R.C. (b) We are committed to exposing and stopping the escalating technological . . . air war in Southeast Asia.

"2) To expose and struggle against the move towards a domestic police state and the increasing repression and control over our lives. This control is exemplified by such things as: the use of grand juries, the murder of George Jackson and the slaughter at Attica, the cutbacks in Welfare and the wage controls, we will fiercely oppose the re-election of any President who continues repressive police and economic policies.

"3) To mobilize a massive array of Americans united in their opposition to the war and their determination to take control of their lives.

"4) To expose the true interests of the leadership of the Republican Party, and thereby strip them of their legitimacy as leaders.

"5) To accelerate the growth of a local movement in San Diego and contribute to the growth of the national movement.

"6) To give encouragement to revolutionary movements of oppressed people in other countries by demonstrating our solidarity with them and by showing the growing strength of our movement in the U.S. We have been inspired by the persistent struggle of the Vietnamese people against U.S. domination, and are interpretationalists.

"7) To fight the defeatism and sense of powerlessness of the people in the U.S. The movement we are building in San Diego must demonstrate the power people can have through organized united action, and serve to inspire people throughout the U.S. to take initiative in fighting for control of their own lives. We do not want to be just another anti-war group but wish to help construct a life-sustaining revolutionary movement."

The main speaker of the Versailles conference was Sidney Peck, a coordinator of the PCPJ and the PCPJ's head delegate at the conference. His speech was delivered on behalf of the entire American delegation. In the course of his address, Peck said: "The delegation from the United States represents the broadest and most diversified delegation ever to participate in an international conference on the Indochina question. And this is because we represent a majority movement that is composed of every major stratum of our people.

"Where did this majority movement in the U.S. come from? It was not all that long ago that the American people were immobilized. They were viewed as a silent generation in the mid-fifties.

"But in the struggle for civil rights, free speech, academic freedom, there emerged in the sixties the beginnings of a new awakening of the American people. And while our eyes were partially opened in the efforts to break down the walls of segregation and restore the right to dissent, it was our growing understanding about the war which brought us fully awake.

"The courageous struggle of resistance waged by the people of Indochina contributed immeasurably to this process of awakening. A process that had already been aided by the struggle for black liberation at home, by the struggle of the Chicano and Puerto Rican peoples, by the struggle of the Indian peoples in the U.S. And so the youth were awakened, as was the movement among women — a movement that has finally emerged from its slumber. And to this one must also add the awakened consciousness of a new veterans' and active-duty GI movement.

"We believe our majority movement expresses a strong potential to translate its great numbers and growing political awareness into real success in changing policy. Why? Because the people in the U.S. who suffer the most and carry the burden of the war are the poor — the poor who are still able to find employment — and those without jobs and income. Increasingly the working people in the U.S. have become aware that it was first of all their sons and brothers and husbands who were taken to the slaughter in Vietnam, and they were aroused to oppose the war. Now there is a new understanding that the very standard of living of the working poor, the ability to have enough money for food on the table, for meat, and clothes for the children is being crushed by the inflation of continued military spending.

"There is welfare money for Lockheed aircraft but not for hungry poor. If they do not have a job, they must suffer the indignities of poverty. If they are working their wages are frozen — while prices and profits continue to rise. And so, the working poor, the labor movement, the rank and file of trade unions are beginning to awake as a new giant of political opposition.

"The potential of our movement will be fully realized when our struggle around these issues of the war, inflation, unemployment, racism, poverty, repression and sexism . . . day in and day out . . . results in the growing organic unity of the American people joined in their opposition and resistance to those who rule our land. Then we will truly have a peoples movement in the U.S. worthy of its political potential.

"Dear Friends: The movement against the war in the U.S. needs your help in the struggle to end the Indochina war. We sincerely hope that this Assembly will not only engage in an exchange of views and resolutions — but that we must also decide to plan for coordinated international action. We hope this will not be a perfunctory program of action. Rather, we look forward to a decision of this Assembly that will establish some means by which to implement — by which to make sure, that actions on a world scale in solidarity with the cause for the peace and independence of the Indochinese does take place.

"For our part, we can consider the year 1972 as a year of sustained struggle to end the war. We have projected a whole series of actions in which we shall press the major issues of the war and its effect on the American people in this election year. But we are also suggesting that internationally we consider the period from April 1 through May 15, as a time of joint struggle around the world on the Indochina question . . . . We shall win, with the help and support of all that you represent here today. And in our mutual victory, true love and friendship between the peoples in Indochina and the United States will finally have an opportunity to express itself in the mutual respect for the right of peoples to self-determination without fear of foreign intervention and aggression."

At the conclusion of the Versailles conference, the American delegates joined their comrades in a march through the streets of Paris. They marched under Viet Cong, North Vietnamese, and French Communist Party flags. The marchers chanted: "Nixon — Fascist, Murderer" — "U.S. Go Home."

PUBLIC CITIZEN

In the fall of 1971, full-page advertisements in major newspapers announced the founding of Public Citizen. A coupon at the bottom of the advertisement read: "I *am* a Public Citizen. Here's my $15.00 (I enclose an additional contribution of $ ___). Please don't waste any of it sending me a thank-you letter, a membership card or literature. I know what's wrong. What I want is to see something done about it." The mailing address was given as a post office box in Washington, D.C.

The advertisement for Public Citizen had the format of a letter written to "dear fellow citizen" from Ralph Nader, the self-appointed consumers' advocate. His message was, in effect, a summary of what he has been preaching for the past several years: there is very little that is right in America — a land of persecuted people, including consumers, factory workers, miners, office workers, small businessmen, home-owners, and students. By Nader's estimate, Americans are being crushed by hunger, poverty, air pollution, water pollution, inadequate medical care, and whatever remains of the free enterprise system. He focuses his attention on a host of villains: corporations, the military establishment, private interests, private wealth, special interest groups, lobbyists, the medical profession, supermarkets, and automobile manufacturers. His heroes are his co-workers and would-be co-workers who, in his litany, are dedicated, determined, valiant, concerned, selfless, lean and hard-working, energetic, idealistic, sacrificial, and public-spirited.

In Nader's message, it is very clear that he is totally opposed to free enterprise, the free exchange in the market place of goods and services. He is against bigness in business, but he is very anxious to encourage more and more bigness in government by having government assume more and more regulatory and administrative control over the entire spectrum of American economic and social life. He is obviously displeased with representative government as it has evolved in the United States over the past two centuries. He is a leveller — an equalizer. He wants a "democratic system" — a socialist system.

Nader's letter to a "dear fellow citizen" is not so much a solicitation for funds as it is a manifesto for a radical revolution of American life to be undertaken by his messianic self and his youth force of recent college graduates: "Imagine that 25 or 30 years ago citizens concerned about the future quality of life in America had gotten together to do something about it. Suppose they had begun an effective citizen's campaign to make government agencies and industry management sensitive and responsive to the needs of the people. The real needs, of all the people. Think how much that was already wrong would have been corrected by now. Think how much that has gone wrong since then would never have been allowed to happen.

"We would long ago have rid ourselves of the inexcusable pockets of hunger and poverty in our land of plenty. Long before the 60s we would have begun to reduce the unspeakable massive suffering of the 'other America.' Our urban centers would not be choked with cars, or laced with concrete belts that strangle the polluted cities in ever-increasing slums, corruption, crime, noise and public waste.

"Our rivers, lakes, and oceans would still be producing untainted fish and would be safe for swimming. The air would not be as filled with vile and violent contaminants, and the land not ravaged by insensitive corporate and government forces wasting our resources faster than they are replenished. Consumers would not be exploited by shoddy goods and services, deceptive practices, and price-fixing that (according to Senator Philip Hart's studies) take at least 25% of every consumer dollar.

"Thousands of American workers would not be dying or sickened each year because of toxic-chemicals, gases and dust that pervade so many factories, foundries, and mines. Equal opportunity in education and employment and adequate medical care would have avoided the misery that cruelly affects many Americans. Factory and office workers would not be taxed 20% of their wages while countless men of great wealth are assessed 4% or less and many who have enormous incomes pay nothing.

"Small businessmen and homeowners would not be made to pay inequitably burdensome taxes because large corporate owners of land, real estate and minerals pay far less than their required fair share. The power and expenditures of our military establishment and their civilian superiors would have been scrutinized, and perhaps curtailed, many painful, costly years ago. Our people would not be disenchanted and disillusioned. And the prevailing mood in America would not have turned from confidence and pride and hope to growing feelings of frustration and outrage and hopelessness.

"In another 30 years our population will have doubled. What if our rampant economic 'growth' is allowed to continue indiscriminately – mindless of the public's hopes and indifferent to their problems? What if we continue to do nothing because we assume that others are taking care of these problems? Who *is* taking care of them?

"It is abundantly clear that our institutions, public and private, are not really performing their regulatory functions. They are allowing our resources to be wasted or poisoned. They tend not to control power democratically, but to concentrate it, and to serve special interest groups at the expense of voiceless citizens. Almost all the organized legal representation in our country is working to protect private interests and private wealth.

"Who represents the citizen? Who can? Only ourselves. And that is why I urge you, as a public citizen – a citizen concerned about your community and your country – to support Public Citizen. If we do not speak up in the public interest now, if we allow the problems to multiply, life in America could be intolerable. Perhaps impossible.

"We have seen how a few dedicated and determined citizens can overcome overwhelming odds to better their communities. If more valiant and concerned people were able to work similarly, continuously and on a broader scale, think how much more could be accomplished.

"That is why Public Citizen has been formed. Thousands of graduates of law, medical, science and engineering schools and other disciplines want to work full-time in the public interest. They know that our society cannot solve its problems if *all* our most highly trained professionals work for private industry or government agencies. They want to work as independent experts to advance the public interest uses of knowledge – to study, monitor, challenge our public and private institutions. And to reform them where necessary.

"Every day the mail brings applications from concerned young professionals eager to work long hours, at minimal wages, to represent the citizen-consumer interest before the regulatory agencies, the courts, the legislatures and the corporations that decide so much of what affects so many unrepresented people. If these selfless young people are willing to sacrifice conventional rewards to pioneer the future, other public spirited citizens will surely want to make it possible — through Public Citizen — for them to do so.

"Through Public Citizen, we ask you to contribute $15 to support a lean, hard-working group of these citizen-advocates. Their work, and your support, will exemplify citizenship focusing on accomplishment, citizenship applying daily the democratic ethic to public policy.

"You may be familiar with some of our work in air and water pollution, workmen's safety, food safety and nutrition, freedom of information, rural poverty, regulatory agency reform, automobile safety, corporate responsibility, pesticides, nursing homes for the aged, the medical profession and other areas of concern. What has been accomplished so far is not the work of one person. More than 30 young men and women — lawyers, other professionals and students — are working on these and other fronts.

"Through published studies and documentation, they have helped sharpen public awareness of these problems. That may be one of our major contributions. Public awareness leads to public action. There will soon be published studies of anti-trust enforcement; California land usage; the DuPont Company; the First National City Bank of New York; super-markets and food marketing to children; and a report on the National Institutes of Mental Health.

"Historically, and particularly in recent years in America, the idealism and energy of students has been a potent force for change. We hope to provide a dynamic vehicle and clear goals for those hopeful qualities by organizing student supported public interest groups throughout the country to work for lasting change through an orderly, democratic system. They will represent disadvantaged minority groups, including students, before the various legal agencies of state and federal governments. They will seek to temper the actions of large corporations that have acquired power far out of proportion to their contributions to society.

"In some important way, every major company touches on the lives of thousands of people — employees, consumers, retailers, taxpayers and whole communities. Shouldn't these people have a voice about policies that directly and adversely affect them? Must not a just legal system accord victims the ability to deter the forces that tend to victimize them?

"Unless the citizen is to remain powerless to protect himself, a way must be found for the individual to make a real impact on corporate boardrooms — and on the government agencies that often serve as protectors, even service arms, of the industries they are supposed to regulate. Bureaucrats cannot easily resist the overwhelming pressures brought by hundreds of special interest lobbies in Washington and state capitals. But there can be a far greater countervailing pressure — the pressure of citizens lobbying for the public interest.

"To create a *voice* for the individual citizen is one goal of Public Citizen. To point out avenues for citizenship *action* is another. Once a year, as a Public Citizen supporter, you will receive a report on significant new citizen involvements that have been effective in achieving reform or relief at the local, state, or national level. Hopefully, you will apply them in the areas of your own commitment to action, because citizenship skills must be continually sharpened and used if we are to succeed in preventing or diminishing injustice.

"There can be an end to mass injustice if enough private citizens become *public citizens*. Potentially, there are 200 million of us unable to work full-time for the public interest but with a full-time anxiety about it. Please mail the coupon and your check for $15 or more to help Public Citizen continue and expand the work that is already under way. Let it not be said by a future, forlorn generation that we wasted and lost our great potential because our despair was so deep we didn't even try, or because each of us thought someone else was worrying about our problems."

REPUBLIC OF NEW AFRICA

In 1928, Workers Library Publishers — an "official Communist Party, U.S.A. publishing house" — issued a ten-cent pamphlet, *American Negro Problems,* by John Pepper, born Joseph Pogany. In his pamphlet, Pogany-Pepper stated: "The southern states are stirred up by the political struggle of the communist speakers and organizers for the Negro masses . . . . The candidates of the Communist Party are everywhere putting up a courageous fight for the full social and political equality of the Negro race.

185

"The Workers (Communist) Party of America puts forward correctly as its central slogan: Abolition of the whole system of race discrimination. Full racial, social and political equality for the Negro people. But it is necessary to supplement the struggle for the full racial, social and political equality of the Negroes with a struggle for their right of national self-determination. Self-determination means the right to establish their own state, to erect their own government, if they choose to do so . . . .

"The Workers (Communist) Party of America must come out openly and unreservedly for the right of national self-determination for the Negroes, but at the same time the Communist Party must state sharply that the realization of this self-determination cannot be secured under the present relations of power under capitalism. National self-determination for the Negro is a bourgeois-democratic demand but it can be realized only in the course of the proletarian revolution. The abolition of the half-feudal, half-slave remnants in the south will also be only 'a by-product' (Lenin) of the general proletarian revolution. It would be a major mistake to believe that there can be any other revolution in imperialist America, in the country of the most powerful, most centralized and concentrated industry, than a proletarian revolution.

"The Communist Party of America must recognize the right of national self-determination for the Negroes and must respect their own decision about the form of the realization of this self-determination. The Negro Communists should emphasize in their propaganda the establishment of a Negro Soviet Republic."

In 1935, Workers Library Publishers issued a booklet, *The Negroes in a Soviet America*, by James W. Ford and James S. Allen (born Solomon Auerbach). Ford and Auerbach-Allen expanded on the 1928 ideas presented by Pogany-Pepper: "The special oppression of the Negro people in the United States is due to the firmly rooted remainders of chattel slavery. Every one knows that while chattel slavery was abolished as a result of the Civil War, freedom — such as even the white workers have under capitalism — did not take its place. Elements of the old chattel slave system remain to this very day . . . .

"To fully realize how much of chattel slavery still remains in the South one has only to know that the largest mass of Negroes still live in the territory of the old slave plantations. The plantations have remained and have imprisoned a large portion of the Negro population. On this territory − the Black Belt − the Negroes are in the majority of the population. Yet precisely here is the center of the enslavement of the Negro people. As long as the plantations and share-cropping remain, it will be impossible for Negroes to obtain equality. For in order to rise above the plantation level, it is first necessary to remove the plantation and divide the land among the tillers of the soil . . . .

"But the revolution will not stop with the seizure of the land. That will just be the beginning of a complete, really basic change in the homeland of lynch terror. For just consider where this land revolution will take place: precisely in the plantation country, where the Negroes are today the most oppressed section of the population and where they form the majority of the population. Let us imagine such a revolution taking place in the Mississippi River Delta . . . .

"The same will occur throughout the plantation area − from southeastern Virginia, down through the Carolinas and central Georgia, across Alabama, Mississippi and Louisiana, reaching even into Arkansas and parts of Tennessee and Texas. Now will be the opportunity to really establish the basis of Negro freedom. This land, on which the Negroes have been enslaved for generations, can then be made into a free land. It can be proclaimed as a new country, in which the land has been freed from the exploiters, where the majority − the Negro people − rule with the cooperation of the white masses in the territory . . . .

"The real test of freedom for the Negro people in the Black Belt lies in their right to self-determination. Unless they can chose freely for themselves what the relationship of this new government will be to the United States as a whole, they will not be free. If the capitalists are still in power in Washington we can rest assured that they will oppose and try to crush the rebellion of the Negro people. The Negro people need powerful allies to carry through and to defend this revolution for freedom. They will have such an ally in the working class, the leading force in the struggles of all oppressed sections of the population of the United States against capitalist exploitation.

"The Communists fight for the right of the Black Belt territory to self-determination. This means not only that the Negro people shall no longer be oppressed but shall come into their rightful position as the majority of the population in the Black Belt. It means equally the right of the Black Belt republic freely to determine its relations to the United States.

187

"One cannot tell in advance under what circumstances the question of the right of self-determination for the Negro people in the Black Belt will arise for definite solution. There are two distinct possibilities:

"First: The revolution in the plantation country might mature sooner than the proletarian revolution in the country as a whole. This is a possibility because of the fact that capitalism is weakest in the South and the enslaved Negro masses on the land are a revolutionary force of great power .... The working class, led by the Communist Party, would come to the aid of the masses in the South to prevent the capitalist ruling class of the North from suppressing the revolution in the Black Belt. Under these circumstances the Communists in the Black Belt would favor, and would do everything in their power to win the laboring people of the Black Belt to favor complete independence from the capitalist-ruled republic of the North. For complete independence of the Black Belt region would then mean greater freedom for the Negroes and a serious weakening of the power of capitalism in the country as a whole. All Communists would defend the right of the Negro people to make their choice.

"Second: The proletarian revolution may overthrow capitalism and establish a Soviet Government for the country as a whole before the revolution comes to a head in the Black Belt. However it must be kept in mind that the two phases of the revolution will not develop separately. Thus, while the workers are leading the onslaught against capitalism, the revolutionary seizure of the plantation land and large-scale farms may at the same time be proceeding in the South. But once the workers come to power in the United States the revolution for land and freedom will be hastened and completed. One of the first steps of the central Soviet government will be to grant the right of self-determination to the Negro people in the Black Belt ....

"We assume here that the new Negro Republic created as a result of the revolution for land and freedom is a Soviet Republic and that this Republic has settled the question of self-determination in favor of federation with the Soviet United States .... The actual extent of this new Republic ... would be certain to include such cities as Richmond and Norfolk, Va.; Columbia and Charleston, S.C.; Atlanta, Augusta, Savannah and Macon, Georgia; Montgomery, Alabama; New Orleans and Shreveport, Louisiana; Little Rock, Arkansas; and Memphis, Tennessee. In the actual determination of the boundaries of the new

188

Republic, other industrial cities may be included. The actual settlement of the question of boundaries will depend largely on the steps taken to assure well-rounded economic development to the Negro Republic."

On May 28, 1969, Richard B. Henry of Detroit entered a Department of State building in Washington, D.C. Mr. Henry was a technical writer, employed by the U.S. Army at the Automotive Tank Command at Warren, Michigan. He was met at State by two security officers, who introduced themselves as special assistants to Secretary of State Dean Rusk. Mr. Henry gave the two men a letter to Secretary Rusk. The letter originated at The Republic of New Africa and was signed by Richard B. Henry's brother, Milton R. Henry, First Vice President. The letter read: "Greetings: This note is to advise you of the willingness of the Republic of New Africa to enter immediately into negotiations with the United States of America for the purpose of settling the long-standing grievances between our two peoples and correcting long-standing wrongs.

"The wrongs to which we refer are those, of course, which attended the slavery of black people in this country and the oppression of black people, since slavery, which continues to our own day. The grievances relate to the failure of the United States to enter into any bilateral agreements with black people, either before or after the Civil War, which reflect free consent and true mutuality. Black people were never accorded the choices of free people once the United States had ceased, theoretically its enslavement of black people, and this constitutes a fatal defect in the attempt to impose U.S. citizenship upon blacks in America.

"The existence of the Republic of New Africa poses a realistic settlement for these grievances and wrongs. We offer new hope for your country as for ours. We wish to see an end to war in the streets. We wish to lift from your country, from your people, the poorest, most depressed segment of the population, and, with them, work out our own destiny, on what has been the poorest states in your union (Mississippi, Louisiana, Alabama, Georgia, and South Carolina), making a separate free, and independent black nation.

"Our discussions should involve land and all those questions connected with the prompt transfer of sovereignty in black areas from the United States to the Republic of New Africa. They must also involve reparations. We suggest that a settlement of not less than $10,000 per black person be accepted as a basis for discussion. We do assure you that the Republic of New Africa remains ready instantly to open good faith negotiations, at a time and under conditions to be mutually agreed. We urge your acceptance of this invitation for talks in the name of peace, justice, and decency."

On March 30 and 31, 1968, a National Black Government Conference was held in Detroit, Michigan, at the Shrine of the Black Madonna (Central United Church of Christ), where the ultra-leftist Rev. Albert Cleage is the pastor. The Conference was called together by Milton and Richard Henry and was held under the auspices of the Malcolm X Society. (Milton Henry, a graduate of Yale University and a former city councilman of Pontiac, Michigan, is a lawyer.)

About fifty delegates and one hundred observers attended the Conference at which the brothers Henry, in cooperation with the conferees, established the Republic of New Africa [RNA]. A Declaration of Independence was promulgated: "We, the Black People in America, in consequence of arriving at a knowledge of ourselves as a people with dignity, long deprived of that knowledge; as a consequence of revolting with every decimal of our collective and individual beings against the oppression that for three hundred years has destroyed and broken and warped the bodies and minds and spirits of our people in America, in consequence of our raging desire to be free of this oppression, to destroy this oppression wherever it assaults mankind in the world, and in consequence of our inextinguishable determination to go a different way, to build a new and better society in a new and better world, do hereby declare ourselves forever free and independent of the jurisdiction of the United States of America and the obligations which that country's unilateral decision to make our ancestors and ourselves paper-citizens placed upon us.

"We claim no rights from the United States of America other than those rights belonging to human beings anywhere in the world, and these include the right to damages, reparations, due us for the grievous injuries sustained by our ancestors and ourselves by reason of United States lawlessness . . . .

"To free black people in America from oppression; To support and wage the world revolution until all people everywhere are so free; To build a new Society that is better than what we now know and as perfect as man can make it; To assure all people in the New Society maximum opportunity and equal access to that maximum; To promote industriousness, responsibility, scholarship, and service; To create conditions in which freedom of religion abounds and man's pursuit of God and/or the destiny, place, and purpose of man in the Universe will be without hindrance; To build a black independent nation where no sect or religious creed subverts or impedes the building of the New Society, the New State Government, or the achievement of the aims of the Revolution as set forth in this Declaration; To end exploitation of man by man or his environment; To assure equality of rights for the sexes; To end color and class discrimination, while not abolishing salubrious diversity, and to promote self-respect and mutual respect among all people in the Society; To protect and promote the personal dignity and integrity of the individual, and his natural rights; To assure justice for all; To place the major means of production and trade in the trust of the State to assure the benefits of this earth and man's genius and labor to society and all its members, and; To encourage and reward the individual for hard work and initiative and insight and devotion to the revolution. And to support this Declaration and to assure the success of our revolution we pledge without reservation ourselves, our talents, and all our worldly goods."

Within a year of the founding conference, the RNA had an elaborate list of executive officers, cabinet officers, and other officials — most of whom had adopted allegedly Arabic names. Robert F. Williams was elected president-in-exile. (Williams, a militant black nationalist, was a fugitive from a kidnapping charge in North Carolina. In 1961, he fled to Communist Cuba. He moved to Peking, Red China, in 1966. From May 1968 until September 1968, he resided in Tanzania. From September 1968 until the summer of 1969, he was again in Peking. In September 1969, he flew from Tanzania to Detroit, by way of Cairo and London. Williams obviously relished the idea of being president, even in exile, of the RNA. From his base in Tanzania, he said: "I envisage a Democratic socialist economy wherein the exploitation of man by man will be abolished. Racial oppression will also be abolished. The concept of the Republic of New Africa is not a segregationist concept, but rather one of self-determination for an oppressed people. It represents a rallying point for progressive and constructive Black Nationalism. Some doubting Thomases and white-folks-loving Uncle Toms are loud and shrill in proclaiming the idea as fanatical and utopian. This is definitely not the case, and I feel as certain now of the ultimate acceptance of the

191

idea as I did when I advocated a policy of meeting violence with violence during the height of the era of nonviolence. America is at the crossroads. The black man is becoming consciously revolutionary. He has as much chance of succeeding as the American Revolutionaries in 1775. As people of conscience who are in sympathy with the oppressed peoples of the world, our self-respect and human dignity dictate that we separate from racist America. Our survival demands it and the concept of the Republic of New Africa is our point of rally.")

Other executive officers were listed as Milton R. Henry [Gaidi], first vice president, and Betty Shabazz [Bahiyah Betty Shabazz], widow of Malcolm X, second vice president. Cabinet members included Obaboa Brady [Obaboa Olowo], treasurer; Wilbur Grattan Sr., minister of state and foreign affairs; Imari Obadele, minister of interior; Walter Eugene King, alias Serge Kingh [Baba Oseijeman Adefunmi], minister of culture and education; LeRoi Jones and Ronald Everett [Maulani Ron Karenga], ministers of culture; Audley Moore [Queen Mother Moore], minister of health and welfare; Joan Franklin [John Franklin, Esq.], minister of justice; Richard Henry [Brother Imari], minister of information (Richard Henry had a security clearance for his work with the Army. A spokesman for the Automotive Tank Command said that his security clearance would be reviewed *if* he renounced his citizenship.); Charles W. Enoch, deputy minister of information; H. Rap Brown, minister of defense; Raymond E. Willis, minister of finance; and Maxwell Stanford, special ambassador. A few consuls were listed: Mae Mallory (New York), Lewis Robinson (Cleveland), Omar Bey (Chicago), Rev. Willie Thomas [Maulana Tuungani] (Cincinnati); and Hakim Jamal (Los Angeles). Lana Mitchel of Dayton was national council secretary. Other early activists in RNA were Anias Lugman, John Crawford, Camille Landry, Roy J. Lewis, James Harvey, Rev. Archie Hargraves, and Ishmael Flory (a Communist Party member) — all in Chicago; Dorothy Sanders [Sister Olewa] and Chuck Moore in New York City; Irv Joyner and Sonny Carson in Brooklyn; Henry Wells, Hazel Gibbs, Warren Galloway, and David Mundy in Detroit; and Leroy Boston [Alajo Adegbala] in Boston. (By the end of 1968, RNA leaders claimed that consulates had been established in New York, Baltimore, Pittsburgh, Philadelphia, Washington, D.C., Chicago, Cleveland, Los Angeles, and San Francisco.) Many of the RNA group were associated with the Revolutionary Action Movement, the Progressive Labor Party, the

Communist Party, and various Communist and black militant organizations.

On May 30 and June 1, 1968, the RNA held its first legislative meeting in Chicago, with about 100 men and women in attendance. Milton Henry promised the would-be citizens of RNA land, money, food, and jobs for everybody. He explained that there would be a 2 per cent voluntary tax and all citizens were expected to invest in RNA bonds. As well as taking over the States of Mississippi, Alabama, Georgia, Louisiana, and South Carolina as the homeland, black RNA enclaves would also be established in Harlem, Brooklyn, Chicago, Detroit, and Philadelphia, he said. Plans had been made to establish black unions and to take over black unions already established in Chicago and Detroit. Henry promised there would be diplomatic overtures made toward "friendly" nations and RNA would seek recognition from the United Nations. (A delegation from RNA did go to the UN on such a mission but was rebuffed.) Under strict security measures, the group was given a manual with instructions on the improvisation of explosives: how to make napalm, Molotov cocktails, thermite incendiaries, and grenades. Suggested targets for the explosives were banks, police stations, post offices, courthouses, and communication centers.

From the beginning, the RNA had two adjuncts: the Afro-American Liberation Party, the political arm of RNA, and the Black Legion. The Black Legion was an overt uniformed army to protect RNA property and an underground army to attack enemies of RNA. (In his syndicated column of April 12, 1969, Victor Riesel described a visit paid to the RNA president-in-exile in Tanzania. The visitors were the Henry brothers and Mae Mallory. Williams had flown from Red China to Tanzania on a mission for the "American desk" in Peking. His specific assignment was to meet with the RNA officials from America. According to Riesel: "He [Williams] flew in from Peking with promises and money . . . . Williams told his allies . . . that he could promise them considerable industrial equipment. Chairman Mao [Tse-tung] had pledged this. Furthermore, he could promise military advisors to help train the Republic of New Africa's own force, the Black Legion, which wears green military uniforms, leopard-head shoulder decorations, black berets and black boots. It would, of course, be difficult to use this equipment — machinery, tools, farm implements and Chinese military officers in the U.S. — until the Republic of New Africa actually holds political power in five southern states. But the friendly Tanzanian government was ready to grant the RNA sufficient land on which to build a commune until the new government could shift operations to America.")

In the November 1968 issue of the Communist Party's *Political Affairs*, Claude Lightfoot, a veteran national Party leader, gave his endorsement to the Republic of New Africa. In his article, "The Right of Black America to Create a Nation," Lightfoot did not commit the Party to an endorsement (evidently not enough was known by the Communists with respect to RNA's leaders and what they might do) and he insisted that the views expressed were his own. Said Lightfoot: "The Special National Convention of the CPUSA, held last July, deferred discussion of the question of self-determination for black America to the next regular convention, to be held in April 1969. In preparation for such a discussion, this article is presented . . . .

"In view of a long background of vacillation in the handling of the slogan of self-determination within the Party, it is imperative that we present this question today in a way that will stand the test of time. We must avoid dotting i's and crossing t's in respect to future development. Marxism-Leninism does not equip us to do that. At best it enables us to perceive what is new, what is aborning, and to indicate the direction in which things are moving. It also enables us to foresee the possibilities inherent in a given trend. But it does not enable us to blueprint the exact form that trend may take.

"In this discussion, therefore, we must combat a dogmatic, mechanical presentation of the matter. We must likewise strive to avoid being overwhelmed by the present state of affairs and acting as if it will prevail forever. With these yardsticks in focus, we shall discuss: (1) The historical background of the Communist Party's handling of the slogan of self-determination. (2) A more precise definition of the national character of the black people's movement, especially as it exists today. (3) Some proposals as to how this matter should be formulated in our draft program. (4) The main prerequisites for a black nation in the United States.

"In 1930 the Communist Party adopted a resolution on the Negro question· in the United States . . . . The 1930 resolution had three main features. First, we inscribed on our banner the goal of full economic, political and social equality for black America. We were the first political party to take this stand. A second feature was the characterization we made of the special forms of oppression peculiar to black people on the American scene. Third, we declared that these special features of black persecution, coupled with such historical developments as slavery, had resulted in the development of a black nation in the Black Belt of the South.

"The Party arrived at this conclusion on the basis of the Marxist criteria of nationhood. The essence of these is: A nation is a historically evolved, stable community of people having a common territory, a common language and a common economic life, reflected in a common psychological makeup or culture. Using these yardsticks, it was concluded that in the Black Belt black people had all the requisites of a nation, and therefore the right of self-determination applied to them. We called for equal rights for black people everywhere and self-determination in the Black Belt . . . .

"After declaring its position in 1930 the Communist Party proceeded to organize struggles based on the concept of equality and elaborated a series of special demands covering every aspect of oppression and superexploitation of black America . . . . It was during this period that it came to be known as the party of the Negro people . . . . There were many black forces who hailed the role of the Communist Party in fostering unity and raising the special demands of the Negro people. But they rejected the idea of nationhood in the Black Belt and the slogan of self-determination . . . .

"After several years of effort during which little or no consciousness of nationhood was manifested, and no significant response to the slogan of self-determination, the Party began to abandon it . . . . In 1946 the National Committee decided once again to raise the slogan of self-determination in the Black Belt . . . . Between 1946 and 1959, we witnessed an accelerated growth of struggles designed to establish first-class citizenship for black Americans. Simultaneously, there was a tremendous shift of population from the rural areas of the South into the urban regions of both the South and the North. The black population of the United States became widely dispersed and was no longer a substantial majority in any section of the country and the 1959 National Convention once again [decided] to withdraw the slogan of self-determination . . . .

"Paradoxically, after we reversed our position forces began to emerge which did reflect a consciousness of the necessity of nationhood. This was evident especially in a significant trend toward support of the policies of Elijah Muhammad and Malcolm X of the Black Muslim movement . . . .

"At the time [1959] we adopted the resolution discarding the slogan of self-determination it was realized by most comrades that the resolution left some matters unexplained. This was expressed in the following paragraph: 'To conclude that the Negro people in the United States are not a nation is not to say that the Negro question in our country is not a national question. It is indeed a national question. The question is, however, a national question of what type, with what distinguishing characteristics, calling for what strategic concept of its solution.'

"Those of us who authored this resolution definitely felt that the concept of nationhood had been undermined. Nevertheless, we were conscious of the fact that the Negro people as a national minority differed from other national groups in the United States, though we did not elaborate on these differences. In retrospect, it is my judgment that from the very beginning our Party made an error when it applied the right of self-determination to the Black Belt rather than to the black people as a people, for in doing so we reduced the matter of self-determination to an artificial geographical consideration . . . ."

Looking forward to the Communist Party's 1969 convention, Lightfoot recommended a draft program for the problem of the Negro people: "It should be formulated as follows: 'We stand for full economic, political and social equality for black America. Toward that end we call for changes in all American institutions and the creation of guarantees that will make the black minority equals in a majority white society.'

"This should be the central thrust of our Party. In addition, we should call for a plebiscite of all black Americans on whether they want to remain in the general commonwealth or to establish another nation within the continental United States. If this plebiscite should reveal that there is a significant number, even though a minority, who desire such a path, we Communists must say that we will have no hesitation in helping to establish such a nation, and that we will work to place at its disposal such resources and assistance as would make of it a prosperous community. Thus, the slogan of self-determination today means the struggle for the right of black America to form a nation if it elects to do so.

"In putting this position forward, we should make it clear that we Communists are internationalists and that our conception of the world of tomorrow envisions, not the breaking up of mankind into small units, but a world in which national distinction will pass into the abyss of time. We see a new world in which all people, be they black, white, red, brown or yellow, can walk this earth as brothers and sisters and as equals.

"However, since we have lived for several centuries under an exploitative system in which people of some nations and races have been subjugated by others, it is necessary to create a condition in which confidence among the peoples can be established. This is the rationale behind our use of the slogan of self-determination . . . . Whether or not self-determination is appropriate will be determined by black America itself. Regardless of the form in which the black people express this right, we Communists must be prepared to assist them in every possible way . . . .

"It follows that the advocates of a black nation must identify themselves with all that is required to set up a socialist America. This means understanding the class nature of capitalist society. Above all else, it means recognizing that black people alone could never destroy capitalism and usher in a new system which would permit a reorganization of our entire society, a condition basic to carving out a black nation in continental United States. This fact surfaces the necessity for allies. The advocates of a separate black nation for tomorrow must act in concert with other forces today. Most nationalist organizations do not comprehend this basic truth, and yet, unless it is grasped, the long range goal will remain empty — 'a sound and fury signifying nothing.' "

In the January 1969 issue of *Esquire* magazine, the Republic of New Africa received its largest single piece of publicity. (*Esquire's* circulation at the time exceeded one million.) Robert Sherrill, a radical leftwing writer, produced an exhaustive and friendly account of RNA and its leaders in an extraordinary interview with Milton Henry.

Sherrill asked Henry about his plans to move his RNA into the South and how he expected to establish RNA there. Henry said that he would begin with a relatively small number of people in predominantly black-populated counties. He expected to have enough people and enough guns to take over such counties one by one, peaceably at the polls if possible, and forcibly if necessary. Henry explained: "Nothing is really peaceful. We may have to use arms. We will take over Mississippi county by county. To do that, we must have the power to get our votes counted. This embraces two needs: the power to ward off economic pressure and the power to ward off physical pressure. The reason we are setting up a Black Legion is so we will get our votes counted. If you bring in enough voters to take over a county, that gives you a sheriff. If you are wise in selecting your county — particularly in the Mississippi delta — you will have a large number of blacks to build with. Then we will have a legitimate military force, legitimate under U.S. law, made up of people who can be deputized and armed. The influence we will then exercise over the whole area of Mississippi will immediately be disproportionate to the numbers under our command. If we had only four sheriffs down there, with all that can be done with deputizing, we could change the state of Mississippi."

Henry seemed confident that his RNA would not have any real difficulty with any forces sent against him by the United States government, but in a series of replies to Sherrill's questions he seemed to intersperse fantasy with his real convictions and ambitions in a deliberate attempt to forestall drastic legal action, which could conceivably embrace charges of conspiracy or subversion. In many instances, he was obviously playing the part of a braggadocio, but in other instances, his proposed tactics could certainly keep law enforcement authorities quite puzzled:

"Q. Will you feel you can take over the five states when you have five black governors? A. We may not have to wait until we control these governors' offices before we make our demands as a new nation. The real question is not whether we control the governors but whether we control the land, and we can do that by controlling the sheriffs. That's the important thing: having physical control of the land. In terms of real control of the land and real confrontation — there will be other things going on in this country. It could be burned to the ground while U.S. officials are playing games with us. They could be engaged in very costly guerrilla activities. The problems in the North aren't going to be settled. We say the U.S. government will talk to us, and they will talk seriously to us about separation prior to the time we control the governors.

198

"Q. If the government sees what you are up to and moves in to stop you, do you think you could whip the U.S. Army? A. With the aid of nuclear weapons from our allies, such as [Red] China, sure we could. China could never help us until we could show that we were capable of a separate, independent existence. But we could show it by the actual fact that we were there and had a majority of the people and were not subject to U.S. jurisdiction. Then China would back us with missiles. But we don't want to fight. It's better to have nice relations. We would only have to neutralize the U.S. Army, not fight it. We don't want another Vietnam, flames and napalm. Neutralizing the U.S. is the only way Castro could survive, and that's the way we would do it, too.

"Q. At this point China is only a tentative hope for you to rely on. What do you have in the way of retaliatory firepower to fall back on until you can be sure of China's help? A. We've got second-strike power right now in our guerrillas within the metropolitan areas — black men, armed. Say we started taking over Mississippi — which we are capable of doing right now — and the United States started to interfere. Well, our guerrillas all over the country would strike. Our second-strike capability would be to prevent the United States Armed Forces from working us over, not the local forces. The local forces couldn't compete with our forces. We can handle them. The second-strike capability already exists, and all the United States has to do to find out is to make the wrong move. The guerrillas will be operative until we take possession of the physical land. Ultimately, when we have the land, we will get the missiles from around the world.

"Q. What makes you think the U.S. will let you have the land when they wouldn't let the Confederacy secede? A. . . . There are a sizable number of people who want self-determination, separation, land. They want that more than life itself. They can't shoot all of us. They can't shoot enough to discourage others . . . . We can fight from within. How are they going to get us out of here? Where would they make the guns to shoot us — in the United States? Do you think we are just going to let them keep on making guns? How will they transport their guns and soldiers — on railroad trains? The United States can be destroyed.

"Q. Do you mean you would do all this by sabotage and guerrilla warfare? A. Obviously. We're within the country. This country will either talk to the separatists today or will talk to them later. At which time perhaps this country will have lost a great deal, in terms of lives and property."

Henry said that RNA would confiscate Southern industries and let the U.S. compensate the owners. He was willing to allow white technicians to enter RNA on visas to work in the industries, which would be government-operated.

When Sherrill seemed skeptical of Henry's claim that his followers were well armed, Henry replied: "The blacks have been arming along defense lines so far. We are now going through the period of holding action. But most astute people see that a different pattern is developing. Everywhere you can see a frustration, the willingness on the part of black people to say the hell with it. Some black people right now are so keyed up they just want to shoot it out. They want it all right now — right now. They don't want to wait. So far there has been sparing use of the gun and the Molotov cocktail. But we are urging that every black home have a gun for self-defence . . . ."

Henry outlined some of the features that he planned for RNA. Polygamy would be practiced. There would be no party politics and no elections for at least thirty years. There would be no labor unions. There would be compulsory military service for all men and women. Whites who wished to live and work in RNA would be rigorously screened, and if acceptable would receive resident visas. There would be no quota on white immigrants, but only those whose skills were needed would be allowed in RNA. Government propaganda would be transmitted through the arts, and the press would be censored.

Henry and his cohorts did not expect the U.S. government to capitulate immediately to RNA's demands for more than $400 billion. Until the payoffs began, Henry was going to rely on a fund-raising drive aimed at prospective citizens of RNA. For the drive, he sent out promotional literature which indicated that RNA was a reality. The literature's come-on said: "Come to the Land. Can you teach? Man a saw? Build a generator? Tend an infirmary? Drive a tractor? Finish concrete? Lay pipe? Run a press? Tailor a dashiki? Shoot a gun? You can help make black people's most important dream — our most important necessity — a reality by serving in Mississippi as we build a model community.

"We are establishing an independent black nation in the South, taking in Louisiana, Mississippi, Alabama, Georgia, and South Carolina.

We are doing this because independence — such as Canada has or Cuba has or Tanzania has — is the only way that we can once and for all solve the great problems that face us as a people. With independence we can have power, the respect of the world, wealth as a people, and a better life for all of us. The time to act is now. The first step is the model community, with modern housing, fine food, good schooling, excellent health facilities, industry owned by the people together, and an up-tight military defense. All built by our own effort, vision, and courage. You can help. The need is for capable people, willing to give of themselves sacrificially."

The new model community, according to RNA, was going to be a product of New African Ujamaa (Economics). It was all explained in a socialistic prospectus: "The minimum dollar cost for starting a New Community of 500 families (or, approximately, 2,500 people) is seven-and-a-half million dollars. This money provides the basic money for constructing the community's schools, medical center, government and economic offices, industry, radio-TV movie facilities, and utilities, and for acquiring agricultural equipment and structures.

"These key principles must always be remembered: (1) All industry and agriculture are owned by the people as a whole and administered by the government of the Republic of New Africa and various community trusts. (2) All economic activity is carefully planned out in advance and carefully watched as it develops. People are trained and assigned to work in accordance with their preference, their ability, and the needs of the Community and the Nation. All able-bodied persons train and work. (3) People work to build a strong, technologically excellent community and nation — not to earn pay, because everyone will have those things which in the United States people cannot have unless they have 'pay.' These things are housing, food, clothing, health services, and education. People will receive 'pay' out of the wealth which a Community creates by everyone working on community goals; after community needs are satisfied, wealth is divided equally among all workers (as 'pay' or, better, personal income). (4) A Community strives to produce all the food, housing, clothing, health services, education, and other goods which it needs for itself. It will specialize, however, in those goods and services which it best produces. All production will be in accordance with the National Economic Plan. (5) The New Community also strives to produce extra. This extra (or 'surplus') is sold outside of the Community. The 'profit' from such sales is divided equally among all workers. (6) One of the key things which every Community builds in the beginning is a pre-fab housing factory. The housing factory is designed to produce ten units per week. In a year it would produce a new house for every family in the community. Every family has a house as a matter of right (just as drinking water in your home is a right). No one pays mortgage or rent.

"(7) The $7,500,000 in 'start' money for a New Community of 500 families is to be used in this way: $800,000, housing plant; $140,000, land, roads, water, and sewage; $2,700,000, material cost for 500 dwellings; $500,000 health center; $350,000, schools; $135,000, recreation center; $200,000, nursery complex; $350,000, communications and visual arts center; $125,000, offices of bank, economic group, and government; $250,000, shopping center; $150,000 agricultural materials; and $1,300,000, industrial plant and 'start' materials: $7,000,000, total 'infra-structure' costs; plus $500,000, personal money ($1,000 per family to prime economy): $7,500,000, total start money for a new community (500 families). The $7,500,000 in start money is equal to $15,000 per family.

"The National Black Bank. Our most important source of start money is our own pockets. All of us, whether or not we intend to live in New Africa personally, must contribute to our black National Bank. Right now the formal name of this bank is The Society for the Development of New Communities. A membership-subcription is five dollars. We must have at least a million-and-a-half (1,500,000) such memberships. Each time these million-and-a-half members pay a five-dollar subscription we will have $7,500,000 – the cost of starting a New Community. We would hope that members would buy such subscriptions at least six times a year."

On March 29, 1969, the second national convention of the black separatist Republic of New Africa was being held in Detroit's New Bethel Baptist Church. A Detroit patrolman saw a group of armed men standing outside the church. (The men were later identified as members of the Black Legion, a paramilitary unit of the Republic of New Africa, serving as bodyguards for Milton Henry.) When the patrolman called out to the men, one of them shot and killed him instantly, and the killer and his companions fled in the direction of the church. The dead patrolman's partner, who was wounded in the shooting, radioed police headquarters for help. When police reinforcements arrived they were fired upon from the church. The police entered the building by force. They arrested 143 persons. They confiscated rifles, pistols, and ammunition. A few hours later — on a Sunday morning — Judge George Crockett Jr. began holding habeas corpus proceedings, and by early afternoon all but a few of those arrested had been released from police custody. (Some time later, FBI Director J. Edgar Hoover described Crockett's action as "releasing a gang of trigger-happy racial militants.") City officials, the Detroit Police Officers Association, and thousands of Detroit citizens protested Crockett's actions — but in vain. (On the other side of the coin, Crockett's bizarre conduct was hailed by the ultra-radical Americans for Democratic Action, the ultra-radical American Civil Liberties Union, and the National Lawyers Guild, a Communist front.) At a news conference, Crockett defended his actions by saying: "Can any of you imagine the Detroit police invading an all-white church and rounding up everyone in sight to be bused to a wholesale lockup in a garage? Can any of you imagine a (white) church group . . . being held in communicado for seven hours . . . without their constitutional rights to counsel? Can anyone explain in any other than racial terms the shooting by police inside a closed and surrounded church?" Crockett, of course, ignored the facts: (1) a policeman had been slain; (2) another policeman had been wounded; (3) the police had sighted an armed group of the paramilitary Black Legion, which fled into the church; and (4) the "church group" for which Crockett was so solicitous was a convention of the revolutionary Republic of New Africa, which had as its objective the establishment of an all-black republic located in the southern States. The group had pledged itself to wage guerrilla warfare in the North. It had attempted to plead its case for independence before the United Nations. It had already tried to establish diplomatic relations with Red China and Communist Cuba.

In the July 12, 1969 issue of *Human Events*, there was a report on a black symposium, in which Imari Obadele, RNA's minister of the interior, and Communist leader Claude Lightfoot played leading roles: "Does the U.S. Communist party still encourage the violent overthrow of American institutions? While liberals have been saying 'No,' a leading American Communist contradicted them last week. That was the import of the actions of Claude M. Lightfoot, chairman of the U.S.

Communist party commission, in giving his blessings to the revolutionary Republic of New Africa at a black symposium at Wisconsin's Beloit College June 27.

"In a high point of the meeting, Imari Obadele ... minister of interior for the Republic which claims black militants Ron Karenga, H. Rap Brown and exile Robert F. Williams as officers, outlined his plan for seizing the states of North and South Carolina, Georgia, Mississippi and Alabama to form a new black nation.

"Claiming to have the backing of Red China, Obadele stressed to the college students that the RNA was raising an army in groups of 1,000 to 5,000 men in major cities to conduct guerrilla warfare, primarily in Mississippi. The group, he maintained, is trying to find an area over which to claim sovereignty before beginning operations in Mississippi . . . .

"Obadele went on to say the cities and industrial potential of the United States would be held hostage to insure the safety of the organization. 'In all cities "brothers" are preparing to destroy the industrial production of the country as surely as a missile attack,' he emphasized.

"Lightfoot, who claimed that he was 'sentenced to five years in prison' many years ago for saying just what Obadele had said, felt that 'all of America's dispossessed people' — not just the blacks — should work for freedom, but he felt the program described by Obadele was 'a lot more sober and sound than others.' Lightfoot then added additional words of encouragement for RNA's goal. So much for the carefully groomed thesis that American Communists no longer believe in using force and violence against the United States."

Of course, the writer of the item in *Human Events* was perfectly correct in his evaluation of the Communist Party. It had not renounced force and violence. Yet, at the same time, Lightfoot's enthusiasm for the RNA was not shared by his fellow members of the Communist Party's hierarchy. In the March 1969 issue of *Political Affairs*, there appeared two criticisms of Lightfoot's article of November 1968, in which he endorsed RNA, even though he did not use its name. James E. Jackson, in his article, "Separatism — A Bourgeois-Nationalist Trap," insisted that Lightfoot had misinterpreted Marxist-Leninist-Stalinist writings and had thereby confused "separatism" with "self-determination." In this 14-page critique Jackson, who like Lightfoot is a Negro, smothered Lightfoot's thesis with citations from a host of

Communist documents. Wrote Jackson: "The article of Claude Light-foot in the November, 1968, issue of *Political Affairs* has evoked considerable interest. In my opinion the article adds no clarity to the discussion of the question under review but reflects a serious disorientation itself.

"The very title of the article contains a basic confusion of concept. The title is 'The Right of Black America to Create a Nation,' but the often cited and generally accepted definition of a nation which Comrade Lightfoot himself refers to, clearly implies that a nation is an objective phenomenon. It is a material community of people with very definite features. The classical definition, which Comrade Lightfoot cited, states: 'A nation is a historically constituted, stable community of people, formed on the basis of a common language, territory, economic life and psychological make-up manifested in a common culture.' (J. Stalin, *Marxism and the National Question,* p. 16.)

"A nation is in being only when a community of people have evolved a combination of such characteristic features. One feature or another may be stronger than others — this gives each nation its peculiar national identity — but every one of the above stated characteristics must be present or the community cannot be a nation. A nation being a historic phenomenon arises, develops and declines, undergoing constant change. A community of people may evolve into a nation by acquiring precisely those characteristic features listed in the given definition. But it is not something that can be willed or chosen. A nation exists as an objective fact, or it doesn't exist, because of certain mitigating historical circumstances which left it deprived of the requisite attributes . . . .

"There can be nothing wrong with 'tieing into' a certain popularity that the term self-determination has currently among circles of radicals of various hues, providing one makes clear that it is not intended to convey the Marxist meaning in political science . . . .

"What Comrade Lightfoot essays in his article is not to arrive at a popular usage for the now fashionable term of self-determination; rather it is to demand the revision of the Marxist-Leninist definition of both nation and self-determination. And he wants to qualify these scientific definitions and concepts to make it easier to replace the Party's main line with a confused accommodation to the revolution-ariness of the petty-bourgeois, revolutionary Black nationalists.

"But should the reader get lost in some fast semantical foot-work . . . Comrade Lightfoot leaves no doubt where he stands on the strategic concept for the black people's liberation movement. He comes out as an advocate of a separatist national solution. He declares: 'The slogan of self-determination today means the struggle for the right of black Americans to form a nation [a state — J.J.] if it elects to do so.' And he urges that 'We should call for a plebiscite of all black Americans on whether they want to remain in the general commonwealth or to establish another nation [state — J.J.] within continental United States.'

"As to this latter point, Communists cannot determine policies and make political decisions on the basis of the outcome of a plebiscite or a Gallup poll, but by the careful assembly of all relevant facts and submitting them to a thorough analysis, as illuminated by the guiding principles of Marxism-Leninism.

"As for Comrade Lightfoot's case for exhuming the corpse of a variant of the hapless old slogan of *self-determination for the oppressed black nation in America*, we think life has affirmed the correctness of our Party having retired that slogan a decade ago."

Ted Bassett in his article in *Political Affairs*, "Slogan of Self-Determination Unwarranted," also condemned Lightfoot's misinterpretation of the Communist creed. He did not bludgeon Lightfoot with documentation as did Jackson, but the effect was the same. Wrote Bassett: ". . . It seems to me that his call for the restoration of the slogan of self-determination and the holding of a plebiscite are unwarranted. For one thing, what he has advanced in asserting that 'self-determination must be applied to the people and not to a territorial unit' in reality represents the policy of national autonomy, which was rejected long ago as a Marxist-Leninist approach . . . .

"In actuality, what Lightfoot has done, is to confuse the Marxist-Leninist concept of self-determination with the popular connotation of the black nationalists . . . .

"With the advent of revolutionary working-class power and the socialist reconstruction of society, assuring a high degree of democracy and respect for the will of the Negro people — or even prior to that under favorable conditions — these trends could lead, dependent upon the desire of the black people, to a redrawing of political-administrative boundaries, even of the present state frontiers, to enable a wider region of autonomy and self-government in areas of the remaining Black Belt in the South.

"Given the unlikely desire of the black people, or a sector of them, to form a national state as a separate entity, either before or after the overthrow of capitalism, Communists would be bound to uphold such a right, but would agitate for or against secession, dependent upon the merits of the situation existing at the moment.

"The right to separate, and the act of separation, are not identical. Should reaction be riding high, the agitation would be of separation. In the advent of a people's anti-monopoly or socialist government, the agitation would certainly be against seccession.

"However, grounds for such a possibility are so unsubstantial, they do not warrant placing self-determination in the program today, or calling for a plebiscite . . . .

"It is in view of these factors, the dispersal of the black population rendering unrealistic a definite territorial area for the realization of statehood, the lack of national consciousness moving in that direction, that it seems to me the restoration of the slogan of self-determination and the calling of a plebiscite, as proposed by Lightfoot, is strategically not justified."

Lightfoot must obviously have been taken aback by the criticisms directed against him but, as a Party member since 1931, he must have appreciated the fact that Henry and his RNA were not in tune with the Party. At the Party's 1969 Convention, the RNA was dismissed with sympathy, but there was no endorsement of Henry's group. The Party's hierarchy concluded that black Americans did not constitute a nation according to the precepts of Lenin and Stalin. The pertinent resolution at the Convention did soften the blow somewhat, as it said that the Party unequivocally supported the black people in their right to determine their own destiny, including institutional and territorial arrangements. The resolution expressed the possibility of the black people developing into a nation, in which case Party support for their determination of their own destiny would express itself in the form of unqualified support for the right of self-determination.

There are several possible reasons for the refusal of the Communist Party to give Henry and RNA overt support. One factor must have been related to the youth of most of Henry's followers. The great majority were under thirty years of age and, for the most part, were inexperienced in radicalism. Henry's belligerency, his contant mention of violence and guns, and his overly paramilitary followers were probably unappreciated by veteran Communists, who preferred more devious means of promoting their cause. It was obvious that Henry would come under the closest type of surveillance by law enforcement authorities. And, lastly, Henry made no secret of his attachment to Red China and Mao Tse-tung. He apparently did not find reason to praise the Soviet Union or its leaders.

The Communists, in the months that followed their refusal to support Henry, must have been happy about their action. In November 1969, Robert Williams resigned the presidency of RNA and was succeeded by the minister of the interior, Imari Obadele. In January 1970, RNA was split in two when Milton Henry's brother, Richard [Imari], walked out of RNA, charging that Milton was trying to establish an idiotic dictatorship.

In the spring of 1971, a contingent of the RNA, accompanied by members of the Black Legion, dedicated land for their capital on a farm, near Bolton, Mississippi. (The farmer who owned the land claimed that the RNA reneged on a promise to pay him for his land.) While in Mississippi, members of the RNA were in constant trouble with local law enforcement authorities. President Imari Obadele was one of many RNA'ers arrested and held on murder charges related to the shooting death of a Jackson, Mississippi, policeman. In November 1971, three members of RNA hijacked a Trans World Airlines jet liner from Albuquerque to Cuba. The three were wanted for the murder of a New Mexico state policeman who was gunned down when he stopped them for a traffic violation.

In December 1971, Akin Shegun, who described himself as western regional vice president of RNA, announced: "After we gain the confidence of the [black] people, we want to hold a plebiscite where they would have a choice to go with the Republic of New Africa or the United States .... We intend to wage war after that vote, the kind of civil war the Vietnamese are waging. Civil rights is dead. The only way to gain dignity is through physical confrontation with the forces of evil."

SING-IN FOR PEACE COMMITTEE

Entertainers have played a major role in supporting the leftist

208

anti-Vietnam War agitation. The Sing-In for Peace Committee held a concert in Carnegie Hall, then used the proceeds from the concert to place an advertisement in the *New York Times*. In the advertisement, the entertainers and their friends emphasized the guilt complex which the left presumes to implant in all Americans, while at the same time remaining silent with regard to the barbaric aggression of North Vietnam. The Sing-In advertisement read: "American boys are dying today in Vietnam in a brutal, senseless war. Their deaths constitute a national tragedy.

"Vietnamese — soldiers and civilians alike — are dying by the thousands through acts of war conducted in our names. Their deaths constitute a blot of shame on our national honor.

"Love of our country and a decent respect for the opinion of mankind, together with the knowledge that our own government is the only one which we are mandated to influence, moves us, the undersigned folksingers and associates, to demand of our President and framers of our national policy: 'Stop the War in Vietnam Now!' "

Most of the signers had a long history as leftwing petitioners or front joiners. They included Joan Baez, Eric Bentley, Judy Collins, Barbara Dane, Ossie Davis, Ruby Dee, Nat Hentoff, Paul Krassner, Chad Mitchell, Tom Paxton, Malvina Reynolds, and Pete Seeger.

Biographical Dictionary Of The Left

BELLA ABZUG was born on July 24, 1920 in New York City, daughter of Esther and Emmanuel Savitsky. She married Martin Abzug. She is an alumna of Hunter College (A.B., 1942) and Columbia University (LL.B., 1947). In 1947, she was admitted to the New York bar.

Since 1947, Mrs. Abzug has maintained a law practice in New York City. Throughout her legal career, she has been active in the National Lawyers Guild. According to *Human Events*, May 15, 1971: "In 1948, for instance, she [Mrs. Abzug] was an official NLG representative in Prague at the Third Congress of the International Association of Democratic Lawyers, also a Communist front. At that gathering, Mrs. Abzug co-sponsored a resolution denouncing 'persecutions directed against the leaders of the American Communist Party by the government of the U.S.A.'" (The House Committee on Un-American Activities has cited the NLG as a Communist front which "is the foremost legal bulwark of the Communist Party, its front organizations, and controlled unions" and which "since its inception has never failed to rally to the legal defense of the Communist Party and individual members thereof, including known espionage agents." The Senate Internal Security Subcommittee has said: "To defend the cases of Communist lawbreakers, fronts have been devised making special appeals in behalf of civil liberties and reaching out far beyond the confines of the Communist Party itself. Among these organizations are the ... National Lawyers Guild. When the Communist Party itself is under fire these offer a bulwark of protection.")

Throughout her career, Mrs. Abzug has specialized in labor law, but this has not been her exclusive concern. She has served as attorney for the ultra-radical American Civil Liberties Union and the Civil Rights Congress. (The Subversive Activities Control Board said that the Civil Rights Congress "was created and established by the Communist Party as an organization which would utilize defense of civil rights for Party purposes and raise and maintain mass defense and bail funds for Party use ... [and succeed] to the role of the International Labor Defense as the Party's legal defense arm .... The CRC has raised and utilized in excess of one million dollars for legal defense and bail for Party leaders and members ... [and] has through mass campaigns aroused support for the Party and its policies. It is reasonable to conclude that this support would not have been realized in the same degree without the efforts of ... [the CRC] in its ostensible role as other than a Communist organization.") Mrs. Abzug also served as an attorney for Fifth Amendment pleaders who were testifying before the McCarthy committee, and she was the defense attorney for New York State teachers who were accused of leftist activities by the Rapp-Coudert state legislative committee.

As early as 1941, Mrs. Abzug achieved recognition for her leftist activities. On March 18, 1941, the *New York Post* noted that she had "generally followed the Communist Party line." Throughout the years, Mrs. Abzug acquired a deserved reputation as a left-wing activist. Among her affiliations were the Citizens Committee of the Upper West Side ("a subversive organization in New York City which is among the affiliates and committees of the Communist Party, U.S.A., and 'which seeks to alter the form of government of the United States by unconstitutional means' "); the National Council of the Arts, Sciences and Professions ("a Communist front used to appeal to special occupational groups"); the American Committee for the Protection of Foreign Born [Americans] ("subversive and Communist"); and the Veterans of the Abraham Lincoln Brigade ("subversive and Communist"). In 1961, she was a founder of Women Strike for Peace, an anti-war group which was soon heavily infiltrated by Communists. She served as WSP's lobbyist and led WSP demonstrations on behalf of the nuclear test ban, disarmament, and an end to the war in Vietnam. In the 1960's, in New York City, she was extremely active in supporting the political campaigns of so-called peace candidates. In 1967 and 1968, she was a leader of the leftist-pacifist forces in the "dump-Lyndon Johnson movement." In 1967 and 1968, she was a founder and leader of the leftist-pacifist Coalition for a Democratic Alternative, the backbone of Senator Eugene McCarthy's presidential campaign. In 1968, she was a founder – and remains a leader – of the ultra-leftist New Democratic Coalition. In 1969, she was a leading campaigner for the re-election of Mayor John V. Lindsay, and she has served as an advisor to Lindsay.

In 1970, Mrs. Abzug announced her candidacy for the Democratic nomination to Congress from New York's 19th district. The incumbent, Leonard Farbstein, had held the seat for fourteen years, but Mrs. Abzug waged a vigorous campaign and defeated him in the June primary. She was endorsed by the ultra-leftist Reform Democrats. She was endorsed by Mayor Lindsay, the Communist press, and a host of peacenik groups. She received strong support from the leftist-oriented Women's Liberation Forces, especially after she sponsored Women's Strike for Equality. The one major leftist group which did not support her was New York's Socialist Party, on grounds that she had shown a "general unwillingness to be outspokenly critical of Communist actions threatening peace and freedom in the world." The Socialists charged that during a convention of the ultra-leftist New Democratic Coalition, Mrs. Abzug had opposed offering American sanctuary to anti-Communists if the Communists achieved victory in Vietnam. Vietnamese anti-Communists, according to Mrs. Abzug, deserved the "punishment that awaits them." The Socialists also opposed Mrs. Abzug on grounds that she had supported Black Caucus resolutions, condemning Israel as an "imperialist aggressor," during proceedings of the ultra-leftist 1967 New Politics Conference. (Ironically, in her collegiate days Mrs. Abzug had achieved some fame as an active Zionist.)

After Mrs. Abzug scored an upset victory over Leonard Farbstein, she attracted enough formerly disgruntled Democrats to defeat Barry Farber, the Republican-Liberal candidate, in the November election.

Mrs. Abzug attracted a great deal of national attention on her first day in the Congress. She introduced a resolution calling for the withdrawal of all American troops from Southeast Asia by July 4, 1971. At the close of the House proceedings that day, she went to the steps of the Capitol with Shirley Chisholm, another ultra-leftist Congresswoman from New York. While 600 members of the Communist-infiltrated Women Strike for Peace looked on, Mrs. Chisholm administered a "special peace oath" to Mrs. Abzug.

Throughout her first year in the Congress, Mrs. Abzug waged a vigorous and vitriolic campaign against the military. She attempted to gain a seat on the House Armed Services Committee, but its chairman, F. Edward Hébert, was aware of her ultra-leftist background and was not willing to give her access to secret military material.

Along with Mrs. Abzug's attacks upon the U.S. involvement in the Vietnam War, she called for an end to the military draft and for the abolition of the entire Selective Service System. She also called for hearings on alleged war crimes in Vietnam. In May 1971, she took a very prominent part in the so-called May Day demonstrations. When militant May Day leaders brought thousands of their followers onto the Capitol grounds, she greeted them and informed the police that the demonstrators were her personal guests. While they paraded under the Viet Cong flags and chanted obscenities, she heaped praises upon them as peace-loving victims of government repression.

During her first session in Congress, Mrs. Abzug called for federal financing of 24-hour-a-day child care centers. She urged a Congressional probe of the Federal Bureau of Investigation, with special emphasis on the competency of Director J. Edgar Hoover. She initiated a move of the voters of New York City to petition Congress for statehood for their city. She voted against appropriations for the House Committee on Internal Security. (In 1966, she signed a statement that appeared in the Communist *Daily Worker,* which denied that Congressional committees had any right to investigate subversive activities.)

Mrs. Abzug has endorsed the Hanoi-inspired People's Peace Treaty. She is a member of the ultra-leftist National Peace Action Coalition. She has been a very strong supporter of the ultra-leftist Vietnam Veterans Against the War. She is a leader in the leftist-oriented Women's National Political Caucus.

ROBERT J. ALEXANDER was born on November 26, 1918 in Canton, Ohio, son of Ruth Jackson and Ralph Alexander. He married Joan Powell. He is an alumnus of Columbia University (B.A., 1940; M.A., 1941; Ph.D., 1950). He is the author of *The Peron Era* (1951); *Communism in Latin America* (1957); *The Bolivian National Revolution* (1958); *Prophets of the Revolution* (1962); *A Primer of Economic Development* (1962); *Latin America* (1964); *The Venezuelan Democratic Revolution* (1964); *Organized Labor in Latin America* (1965); and *Latin American Politics and Government* (1965). He is co-author of *The Struggle for Democracy in Latin America* (1961).

In 1942, Alexander was an economist with the Board of Economic Warfare. In 1945 and 1946, he was an economist with the Office of Inter-American Affairs. Since 1947, he has been on the economics faculty at Rutgers University as an instructor (1947-1950), assistant professor (1950-1956), associate professor (1956-1961), and professor (since 1961). He has been a visiting professor at Atlanta University, Columbia University, and the University of Puerto Rico. Since 1948, he has been a consultant to the American Federation of Labor and the AFL-CIO. In 1951 and 1952, he was a member of the Economic Cooperation Administration Mission to Spain. From 1953 until 1956, he was on the board of directors of the ultra-radical Rand School of Social Sciences. From 1955 until 1965, he was on the board of directors of the Socialist League for Industrial Democracy. From 1957 until 1966, he was a national committeeman of the Socialist Party-Social Democratic Federation. He is a long-time resident member of the Council on Foreign Relations, the unofficial foreign policy directorate of the United States.

WILLIAM SHERIDAN ALLEN was born on October 5, 1932 in Evanston, Illinois, son of Rose Brahm and William Allen. He married Luella Stinson. He is an alumnus of the University of Michigan (A.B., 1955); the University of Connecticut (M.A., 1956); and the University of Minnesota (Ph.D., 1962). He pursued graduate studies at the Free University of Berlin and the University of Goettingen. He is the author of *The Nazi Seizure of Power: The Experience of a Single German Town, 1930-35* (1965).

In 1958 and 1959, Allen was a history instructor at Bay City Junior College in Michigan. In 1960 and 1961, he was a humanities instructor at the Massachusetts Institute of Technology. From 1961 until 1967, he was on the history faculty at the University of Missouri as assistant professor (1961-1966) and associate professor (1966-1967). Since 1967, he has been a professor of history at Wayne State University.

Allen has been a long-time member of the Socialist Party. He has also been affiliated with the leftist-racist Congress of Racial Equality; the ultra-leftist American Civil Liberties Union; and the ultra-leftist Norman Thomas 80th Birthday Committee.

GAR ALPEROVITZ was born on May 5, 1936 in Racine, Wisconsin, son of Emily Bensman and Julius Alperovitz. His second wife is Guillemette Caron. He is an alumnus of the University of Wisconsin (B.S., 1958); the University of California at Berkeley (M.A., 1960); and the University of Cambridge in England (Ph.D., 1964). He is the author of *Atomic Diplomacy: Hiroshima and Potsdam* (1965) and *Cold War Essays* (1969).

In 1961 and 1962, Alperovitz was a legislative assistant to U.S. Representative Robert W. Kastenmeier (D.-Wisc.). In 1964 and 1965, he served successively as a research assistant for U.S. Senator William Proxmire (D.-Wisc.) and as legislative director for U.S. Senator Gaylord Nelson (D.-Wisc.). In 1965 and 1966, he was a foreign affairs officer with the Department of State. From 1964 until 1968, he was a fellow of King's College of Cambridge University in England. From 1965 until 1968, he was a fellow of the Institute for Politics at Harvard University. Since 1968, he has been a fellow of the Institute for Policy Studies, a leftist-propaganda agency for disarmament.

Alperovitz is a socialist. He has been affiliated with the leftist-oriented Science Action Coordinating Committee, which has demanded a moratorium on war research. He was a member of the ultra-leftist Committee to Defend the [Chicago] Conspiracy. He participated in "Vietnam Summer: A Nationwide Peace-In," a leftist-pacifist project. He has been affiliated with the *New England Free Press*, a leftist newsletter. He has been affiliated with the New University Conference, an ultra-radical project. He has been affiliated with the leftist-pacifist American Friends Service Committee.

JOSEPH G. ANTHONY was born on December 19, 1899 in Philadelphia, Pennsylvania, son of Rachel Humphreys and Charles Anthony. He married Dorothy McClaren. He is an alumnus of Swarthmore College (A.B., 1923) and Harvard University (LL.B., 1926). He was admitted to the Hawaiian bar in 1926. He is the author of *Hawaii Under Army Rule.*

Since 1926, Anthony has had a private law practice in Honolulu. In 1942 and 1943, he was the Attorney General of Hawaii. He is a long-time activist in the ultra-leftist American Civil Liberties Union. He was a member of the National Council for Civic Responsibility, an election-year's drive against anti-Communists by the Democrat Party in 1966.

HERBERT APTHEKER was born on July 31, 1915 in Brooklyn, son of Rebecca Komar and Benjamin Aptheker. He is married. He is an alumnus of Columbia University (B.S., 1936; A.M., 1937; Ph.D., 1943). He is the author of *The Negro in the Civil War* (1938); *Negro Slave Revolts in the United States: 1526-1860* (1939); *The Negro in the American Revolution* (1940); *The Negro in the Abolitionist Movement* (1941); *American Negro Slave Revolts* (1943 and 1963); *Essays in the History of the American Negro* (1945 and 1964); *The Negro People in America* (1946); *To Be Free: Studies in American Negro History* (1948); *A Documentary History of the Negro People in the United States* (1951); *Labor Movement in the South During Slavery* (1954); *Laureates of Imperialism* (1954); *Era of McCarthyism* (1955); *History and Reality* (1955); *Toward Negro Freedom* (1956); *The Truth*

About Hungary (1957); *History of American People: The Colonial Era* (1959); *History of American People: The American Revolution, 1763-1783* (1960); *American Civil War* (1961); *Dare We Be Free?* (1961); *And Why Not Every Man?* (1961); *The World of C. Wright Mills* (1961); *American Foreign Policy and the Cold War* (1962); *The Negro Today* (1962); *Soul of the Republic* (1964); *One Continual Cry: Walker's Appeal* (1965); *Mission to Hanoi* (1966); *Nat Turner's Slave Rebellion* (1966); *The Niagara Movement* (1967); and *The Nature of Democracy, Freedom and Revolution* (1967). He is the editor of *Disarmament and the American Economy* (1958); *Marxism and Democracy* (1965); *Marxism and Alienation* (1966); *Marxism and Christianity* (1968); and *Autobiography of W.E.B. DuBois* (1968).

On at least two occasions, in federal courts, Aptheker has testified under oath that he joined the Communist Party of the United States in 1939. From 1942 until 1946, he served in the U.S. Army. As a witness for the Communist Party before the Subversive Activities Control Board, he admitted that he retained his membership in the Communist Party during the time he was an intelligence officer in the U.S. Army and later an education and information officer for the Seventh Army in Europe. He left the Army with the rank of major.

Aptheker has had a long association with Communist publications. From 1948 until 1953, he was associate editor of *Masses and Mainstream.* From 1953 until 1963, he was editor of *Political Affairs.* Since 1955, he has been on the editorial board of *Mainstream.* He has contributed numerous articles to *Negro Quarterly, The Worker, Daily Worker, Daily World,* and *New World Review.*

Aptheker has had a long association with Communist schools. The association began in 1940 when he was an instructor at the School for Democracy, which was established by Communist teachers who had been ousted from New York City's public school system. From 1946 until 1953, he was an instructor at the Jefferson School of Social Science. He was a teacher at the California Labor School. Since 1960, he has been director of the New York School for Marxist Studies. He has lectured at Camp Midvale, New Jersey, a top secret training school for young Marxists. He has served on the faculty of the Free University of New York, an unaccredited institution dedicated to the achievement of revolutionary socialism. Since 1964, he has been director of the American Institute for Marxist Studies. On April 28, 1966, there was a dual celebration of Aptheker's fiftieth birthday and the second anniversary of his American Institute for Marxist Studies. A testimonial dinner was held at the New York Hilton. The sponsors of the affair included an extraordinary cross-section of Communists and fellow-travelers, including John J. Abt, James Aronson, Robert S. Cohen, Howard Da Silva, Ossie Davis, Shirley DuBois, Will Geer, Maxwell Geismar, Eugene Genovese, Carlton Goodlett, Gus Hall, Vincent Hallinan, Robert W. Kenny, Rockwell Kent, Clark Kissinger, Oliver Loud, Bishop Edgar Love, Staughton Lynd, Carl Marzani, Jessica Mitford, A.J. Muste, Karl Niebyl, Howard Parsons, Victor Rabinowitz, Anatol Rapoport, Norman Rudich, Frederick Schuman, Jessica Smith, Dirk Struik, Willard Uphaus, Henry Winston, Nathan Witt, and Howard Zinn.

On the political scene, Aptheker has customarily worked for the candidacy of Communists running on the Communist Party ticket. In 1948, however, he worked in the presidential campaign of Henry A. Wallace. In 1966, Aptheker was an unsuccessful Independent Peace candidate for Congress in Brooklyn's 12th district. In 1964, he supported the candidacy of Lyndon B. Johnson.

In the academic field, Aptheker was a Guggenheim fellow in 1946 and 1947. He has been a recipient of grants from the Social Science Research Council and the Rabinowitz Foundation. He has been a guest speaker at campuses throughout the United States, including Dickinson College, Skidmore College, the University of Massachusetts, West Virginia University, Western Washington State College, the University of California at Los Angeles, Hofstra University, Villanova University, Douglass College of Rutgers University, LaSalle College, Grinnell College, Marist College, the University of Vermont, Vanderbilt University, Fisk University, St. Vincent College, Brooklyn College, City College of New York, Clark University, Long Island University, Lawrence University, Franconia College, the University of Illinois, State University of New York at Buffalo, Oberlin College, San Francisco State College, Trinity College, State University College at Geneseo in New York, College of Wooster, Loyola University of Los Angeles, the University of Notre Dame, Ohio State University, the University of Pennsylvania, San Fernando Valley State College, the University of California at Santa Barbara, the University of Southern California, the University of California at Berkeley, Wayne State University, Michigan State University, Hunter College, Rutgers University, Duke University, the University of North Carolina, Queens College, Boston University, Brandeis University, St. Francis College of Maine, Bryn Mawr College, the University of

Wisconsin, Harpur College, New York University, the University of Miami, Harvard University, Northwestern University, the University of Chicago, Loyola University of Chicago, Indiana University, Briar Cliff College, Temple University, Kent State University, Earlham College, Pennsylvania State University, Amherst College, Union University, the University of Buffalo, Syracuse University, the University of Santa Clara, the University of Dayton, Assumption College, Denison University, Indiana State University, Valparaiso University, Marquette University, the University of Minnesota, the University of South Dakota, the University of Connecticut, the University of Kentucky, Williams College, and Purdue University.

Aptheker is generally described as the Communist Party's chief theoretician. He has served on the national committee of the Communist Party of the United States. He is recognized in the Soviet Union as a leading figure of the Communist Party, and in 1966, on the 45th anniversary of the CPUSA, he spoke in Moscow under the auspices of the Soviet Communist Party's Central Committee. At the Moscow funeral of Elizabeth Gurley Flynn, matriarch of the CPUSA, Aptheker served as a pallbearer, representing the CPUSA.

To supplement his official and formal duties with the Communist Party, Aptheker has lent his energy and prestige to a wide variety of front activities, including the Committee for a Democratic Far Eastern Policy ("Communist"); the American Continental Congress for Peace ("another phase in the Communist 'peace' campaign, aimed at consolidating anti-American forces throughout the Western Hemisphere"); the World Peace Congress ("Communist front"); the Scientific and Cultural Conference for

World Peace ("Communist front"); the Stockholm Peace Appeal ("Communist Party campaign"); the National Committee to Secure Justice in the Rosenberg Case ("Communist front"); the World Assembly of Peace of 1969, a get-together of world Communists in East Berlin; the Fort Hood Three Defense Committee, an ultra-leftist group working on behalf of three soldiers who sought to evade service in Vietnam; the Civil Rights Congress ("subversive and Communist"); the Progressive Citizens of America ("political Communist front"); the Tri-Continental Information Center, a mouthpiece for Latin American guerrillas, the Viet Cong, and the Havana-based Castroite Tri-Continental Organization; the American Society for the Study of the German Democratic Republic, an ultra-leftist group; the Citizens Committee for Robert Thompson and Benjamin J. Davis, two of America's leading Communists; the Spring Mobilization Committee to End the War in Vietnam, a major group of leftist agitators; the leftist-oriented Ad Hoc Committee for an Open Letter on Vietnam; the leftist-pacifist Ad Hoc Faculty Committee on Vietnam; the leftist-pacifist Ad Hoc Committee of Veterans for Peace in Vietnam; the leftist-oriented Committee for a Just Peace in the Mid-East; and the ultra-leftist American-Korean Friendship and Information Center, which he serves as director. He has been a prominent participant in the annual Socialist Scholars Conferences. As a featured speaker and panelist, he has utilized the conferences as a forum where he can bring his fellow Communists and their fellow-travelers up to date on the Communist line on a variety of issues.

In the summer of 1965, while in Helsinki, Aptheker received orders to visit Hanoi accompanied by one or two

Americans who had political viewpoints different from his own. Fully realizing that his orders were given in the Aesopian language so frequently used by Communists, Aptheker chose as his traveling companions Staughton Lynd, a self-admitted Marxist, and Thomas Hayden, a founder of the ultra-leftist Students for a Democratic Society. The trio traveled to North Vietnam in December 1965, and their trip proved to be a highly successful anti-American, pro-Communist propaganda coup. Although the trip was made in violation of State Department passport regulations, the trio encountered no difficulty upon their return to the United States, and immigration officials allowed them to retain their passports. Aptheker and his two companions not only reaped a vast amount of publicity at the time of their trip, but continued to do so in the ensuing months through their writings and public speeches extolling the North Vietnamese cause.

Aside from his widespread anti-Vietnam War activities, Aptheker in recent years has been an extremely important factor in the area of racial agitation. Probably no other Communist has done so much to perpetuate the myth of the Communist Party's concern for the welfare of American Negroes. For more than thirty years Aptheker, in the guise of a scholar, has produced a vast literature purporting to be the history of American Negroes. He has, however, offered his readers only what the Communist Party believes is useful as a means of recruiting Negroes and creating a hostile division between Negroes and non-Communist Americans. Beyond his writings, Aptheker has developed close ties with militant blacks, including those in the Communist-created W.E.B. DuBois Clubs and the Communist-oriented Black Panthers. He has encouraged Negroes to be extremely militant in their pursuit of a massive social revolution. And he once described the riot in the Watts area of Los Angeles as "glorious" but merely a step in the right direction. In his role as an agitator of American Negroes, he has added to his stature by becoming the custodian of all the letters and papers of W.E.B. DuBois, whose contributions to the Communist cause surpassed those of any other American Negro. Perhaps nothing Aptheker has ever written is more indicative of his devotion to Communist deceit than a passage in the *Daily World's Magazine* (April 25, 1970) wherein he wrote of Lenin's alleged "dedication to the anti-racist struggle." Said Aptheker: "The world-wide Communist movement, of which he [Lenin] was the chief architect, already has delivered massive blows against the infection [of racism]. The Union of Soviet Socialist Republics, of which Lenin was the founder, was the first State in history dedicated to the ending of all forms of elitism, including racism. That the Czar's prison house is now a united land of socialist republics, with men and women of scores of nationalities and of varying colors living together in solidarity and equality, is the greatest achievement in all history." Less than a year earlier, Aptheker, the author of this supreme idiocy, was appointed director of the Black Studies Program in the history department of Bryn Mawr College. In describing his appointment, which was requested by black students at Bryn Mawr, Aptheker said: "It is thrilling, with wide national significance for the Communist Party. It also reflects something of what this student movement is all about, which many people have failed to understand."

ROBERT E. ASHER was born on October 18, 1910 in Chicago, son of Alice Wormser and Louis Asher. He married Ethel Watson. He is an alumnus of the University of Chicago (Ph.B., 1932; M.A., 1934). He also studied at Dartmouth College and the University of Berlin. He is the author of *The UN and Promotion of the General Welfare* (1957); *The UN and Economic and Social Cooperation* (1957); *Grants, Loans and Local Currencies: Their Role in Foreign Aid* (1961); and *Development of the Emerging Countries: An Agenda for Research* (1962).

In 1934 and 1935, Asher was a researcher for the American Public Welfare Association in Chicago and the Federal Emergency Relief Administration in Washington, D.C. From 1935 until 1939, he was with the Works Progress Administration as a researcher (1935-1937) and chief of procedures and statistics (1937-1939). From 1939 until 1942, he was assistant to the deputy administrator of the National Youth Administration. In 1942 and 1943, he was chief of the clearance section in the office of civilian supply for the War Production Board. In 1943, he was an executive assistant with the Lend-Lease Administration. In 1944, he was a deputy chief on the planning and control staff for liberated areas in the Foreign Economic Administration. From 1944 until 1946, he held several civilian positions with UNRRA (United Nations Relief and Rehabilitation Administration) and at Supreme Headquarters of the Allied Expeditionary Forces. From 1946 until 1954, he was with the Department of State: assistant to the chief of the Mission for Economic Affairs in London (1946-1947); deputy chief and chief with the Economic Commission for Europe in Switzerland (1947-1950); adviser to the director of European Regional Affairs (1950-1951); and assistant secretary of state for economic affairs (1951-1954).

Since 1954, Asher has been a senior fellow on the foreign policy studies staff of the Brookings Institution in Washington, D.C. He has been a vice-president of international affairs for the leftist Americans for Democratic Action. He has served on the national council of the Foreign Policy Association, which has been a highly effective pro-Communist vehicle.

ROBERT A. AURTHUR was born on June 10, 1922 in New York City, son of Margaret Brock and William Aurthur. His second wife is Jane Wetherell. He is an alumnus of the University of Pennsylvania (B.A., 1946). He is the author of *The History of the Third Marine Division* (1947) and *The Glorification of Al Toolum* (1952). He is the author of Broadway plays, including *A Very Special Baby* (1956), *Kwamina* (1961), and *Carry Me Back to Morningside Heights* (1968). He is the author of screenplays, including *Grand Prix* (1967), *For Love of Ivy* (1968), and *The Lost Man* (1968). For his television work, he has received the Sylvania award (1954 and 1955) and the Emmy award (1955).

From 1948 until 1952, Aurthur wrote short stories for various magazines. From 1952 until 1956, he was a free-lance television writer. In 1955 and 1956, he was successively associate producer and producer of the Philco TV Playhouse. From 1957 until 1959, he was a film writer. In 1959 and 1960, he was producer of NBC Sunday Showcase. In 1961 and 1962, he was vice president of Talent Associates, Ltd. In 1963 and 1964, he was in charge of production for United Artists TV. Since 1965, he has been a film writer.

Aurthur is a member of the National

Association for the Advancement of Colored People, the fountainhead of Negro agitation for more than half a century, and the ultra-leftist American Civil Liberties Union. In 1971, he joined the ultra-leftist National Peace Action Coalition.

ROBERT B. AVAKIAN was born on March 7, 1943 in Washington, D.C. His father is Alameda County Superior Court Judge Spurgeon Avakian. He married Elizabeth Sucher. Between 1961 and 1965, he intermittently attended the University of California at Berkeley.

In 1964, while on the Berkeley campus, Avakian was arrested for his participation in the tumultuous Free Speech Movement demonstrations. In 1965, he was head of the leftist-oriented Vietnam Day Committee speakers bureau on the Berkeley campus. In 1966, he was head of the Campus Community for Robert Scheer, an ultra-leftist candidate for Congress. In 1967, Avakian ran for the Berkeley City Council as a candidate of the ultra-leftist Community for New Politics. At that same time, he was a staff writer for the ultra-leftist *Ramparts* magazine. As a sometime collegian, he was on the national council of the ultra-radical Students for a Democratic Society, and he was a leader of the SDS's Revolutionary Youth Movement.

Ideologically, Avakian is a combination Marxist-Stalinist-Maoist. In 1968, he established a Maoist group, the Revolutionary Union. He has also served as a major recruiter for the Revolutionary Union, directing much of his energy toward the already established groups of Students for a Democratic Society. On one occasion, he told his SDS audience that there was need for a "real Communist Party in the United

States, one that recognized the U.S. imperialist ruling class as the real enemy and one which would fight to create a dictatorship of the proletariat." He supplements such Marxist jargon with extensive quotations from Stalin, Mao Tse-tung, and Lin Piao. In late 1971, Avakian and other leaders of the Revolutionary Union spent six weeks in Red China, where they received the friendliest of receptions. Avakian had personal audiences with Chou En-lai and Mao Tse-tung. And Avakian has boasted that the Revolutionary Union is the favored pro-Red Chinese group in the United States.

For many years, Avakian has been deeply involved with black militants. In 1967, he participated in a meeting of the Bay Area Emergency Action Committee, at which he said to the audience: "If the Negroes want guns to protect themselves from the police we should help them by giving them guns." He distributed leaflets which read: "We have the responsibility . . . to make it possible for black people to have a fighting chance for defending themselves . . . . Among other things, this means that we could help raise funds and supply weapons for groups like the Black Panther Party for Self-Defense, which is arming and organizing black people for self-defense . . . . We must either come to the aid of the black revolution, or, through inaction, or misguided action, inadvertently aid the power structure."

In July 1969, Avakian attended the organizing meeting of the National Conference for a United Front Against Fascism. The conference was called by the Black Panthers and it was attacked by such Communist Party leaders as Herbert Aptheker, Roscoe Proctor and Archie Brown, and other leaders of the ultra-left community.

In 1969, Avakian founded the Young Partisans, a militant youth group devoted to the principles of Marx and Mao Tse-tung. From its beginning, the Young Partisans organization has worked closely with the Black Panthers. In 1970, Avakian was an organizer and participant in the Revolutionary People's Constitutional Convention, another Black Panther project. (Avakian, in his patronizing efforts toward the black militants, has said: "Black people are the vanguard and are inspiration. Watch us with a suspicious eye and see if we don't deliver.") He was formerly affiliated with the ultra-leftist Friends of the Panthers and the ultra-leftist Peace and Freedom Party.

HERMAN BADILLO was born on August 21, 1929 in Caguas, Puerto Rico, son of Carmen Rivera and Francisco Badillo. He was married to and divorced from Norma Lit. He is married to Irma Deutsch. He is an alumnus of the City College of New York (B.B.A., 1951) and Brooklyn Law School (LL.B., 1954). In 1955, he was admitted to the New York bar; since then, he has had a private law practice in New York City. In 1956, he became a Certified Public Accountant.

Since 1960, Badillo has been active in Democrat Party politics. In 1960, he was chairman of the East Harlem Kennedy-for-President Committee. In 1961, he founded the John F. Kennedy Democratic Club in New York City. In the same year, he supported the successful re-election campaign of Mayor Robert F. Wagner, who appointed Badillo as deputy real estate commissioner. In 1962, Wagner named Badillo as commissioner for the department of relocation, a position he held until 1965.

In 1965, Badillo began a five-year tenure as Bronx borough president. In 1968, as a Reform Democrat, he supported the presidential candidacy of Robert F. Kennedy and later the candidacy of Eugene McCarthy. In 1968, as a delegate to the Democratic National Convention, he achieved some national notoriety by supporting Julian Bond's attempt to seat an insurgent delegation from Georgia at the convention. (In 1968, Badillo also attracted attention by his participation in the Poor People's Campaign and his outspoken and dovish remarks against the Vietnam War.)

In 1969, Badillo, endorsed by such prominent leftists as Jacob Javits, Paul O'Dwyer, and Eugene McCarthy, ran in New York City's mayoralty primary as "the only liberal candidate." After losing in the primary, he joined with Paul O'Dwyer in forming the New Democratic Coalition. Badillo was vice-chairman of the new group, which was composed of Reform Democrats and Liberals, and which supported the successful re-election campaign of Mayor John Lindsay against Republican-Conservative John Marchi and Democrat Mario Procaccino. Badillo, although an unsuccessful mayoralty candidate in 1969, received considerable and impressive support from the Left. He had been endorsed by the *New York Post*, the *New York Times*, the *Amsterdam News*, the Columbia Broadcasting System's television editorialists, Arthur Schlesinger Jr., William van den Heuvel (from the Robert F. Kennedy campaign staff), and various leftwing union locals. He also received very favorable notice in the Communists' *Daily World*.

In 1970, Badillo was elected to the Congress of the United States as a Democrat from the newly-created 21st Congressional District in New York. He promised to represent not only the people of his own district, but also the people of Puerto Rico. (In 1970, Badillo once again received support from the left, including the Communists' *Daily World.*)

Badillo has been affiliated with the ultra-leftist National Peace Action Coalition and the People's Peace Treaty (a notorious leftist project in 1971). In the Congress, he has joined with the most extreme leftists of both parties. One of his earliest pro-left-moves in the Congress was his vote against appropriations for the House Committee on Internal Security. As a member of the Education and Labor Committee, he has promoted socialist legislation in the so-called anti-poverty war.

WILLIAM BAIRD, a minister of the United Church of Christ, has been in recent years executive director of North Californians Against Repressive Legislation. In the *Daily World* of November 7, 1970, as part of the "Free Angela Davis" drive, the Communists quoted Baird: "Given the present climate of repression in this country, the extradition of Angela Davis to California would be an injustice, not only to her but to all Black people. It was Judge George Crockett of Detroit who said a few months ago that it was impossible for a Black person to get a fair trial in this country. At the present time there is not a single shred of proof that would stand up in any court of law that Angela Davis engaged in the actions of which she is accused."

Throughout most of his ministerial career, Baird has worked in Chicago and for many years was minister of the Essex Community Church in that city.

During the past twenty-five years, Baird has been in the forefront of leftist American clergymen. He has been affiliated with the American Committee for Protection of Foreign Born [Americans]

("subversive and Communist" – "one of the oldest auxiliaries of the Communist Party in the United States"); the Chicago Ad Hoc Committee of Welcome for the [Red] Dean of Canterbury, paying honor to England's most notorious Red clergyman; the Chicago Committee to Secure Justice in the Rosenberg Case ("Communist front"); the Chicago Sobell Committee ("active in the Communist propaganda campaign exploiting atomic spies"); the ultra-leftist Committee of First Amendment Defendants; the Emergency Civil Liberties Committee ("Communist front"); the Illinois Committee for Peaceful Alternatives to the Atlantic Pact ("Communist front" – "part of Soviet psychological warfare against the United States"); the Jefferson School of Social Science ("adjunct of the Communist Party"); Lobby for Peace (sponsored by the American Peace Crusade – "Communist front"); the National Committee to Repeal the McCarran Act ("Communist front" – "subversive"); the National Committee to Secure Justice for Morton Sobell ("Communist campaign"); the National Committee to Win Amnesty for Smith Act Victims ("subversive" – "Communist Party project"); the National Conference to Study and Discuss United Socialist Action, a Communist project; the *New Christian,* a pro-Communist publication; *Protestant* ("Communist front"); Civil Rights Congress ("subversive and Communist"); American Youth for Democracy ("subversive and Communist"); World Peace Council ("heralded by the Moscow radio as 'the expression of the determination of the peoples to take into their own hands the struggle for peace' "); the American Peace Crusade ("Communist front"); the Castro-subsidized Fair Play for Cuba Committee; the leftist Committee to

Defend the [Chicago] Conspiracy; the Communist-operated World Youth Festival; the Aptheker Dinner Program, honoring both the Communist Party's chief theoretician and the second anniversary of the American Institute for Marxist Studies; the leftist G.I. Defense Committee; the ultra-leftist-pacifist World Fellowship; the ultra-leftist Committee to Aid the Monroe Defendants; the ultra-leftist Committee for the Defense of the Bill of Rights; the National Committee to Abolish the House Un-American Activities Committee ("to lead and direct the Communist Party's 'Operation Abolition' campaign"); the National Committee to Secure Justice in the Rosenberg Case ("Communist front"); the National Assembly for Democratic Rights ("created, dominated, and controlled by members and officials of the Communist Party"); Fidel Castro's Medical Aid to Cuba Committee; tribute to the Communist Party's *Daily World* ("deserves the support of all who cherish peace, democracy and social progress"); the ultra-leftist Committee for Independent Political Action; and the Southern California Peace Crusade ("Communist front").

Baird has signed open letters, *amicus curiae* briefs, and petitions on behalf of the Communist Party and individual Communists who were convicted under the Smith Act.

LEE BALL, a Methodist minister, has been executive secretary of the Methodist Federation for Social Action for about fifteen years. He has worked in parishes in Lake Mahopac, New Paltz, and Ardsley – all in New York.

On July 7, 1953, Benjamin Gitlow – a founder and former general secretary of the Communist Party in the United States – testified before the House Committee on Un-American Activities.

Mr. Gitlow was asked: "What kind of an organization was the Methodist Federation for Social Action, and how did it differ from a Communist-front organization?"

Mr. Gitlow replied: "The Methodist Federation for Social Action, originally called the Methodist Federation for Social Service, was first organized by a group of Socialist-Marxist clergymen of the Methodist Church, headed by Dr. Harry F. Ward. Dr. Ward was the organizer, for almost a lifetime its secretary and actual leader. He at all times set its ideological and political pattern. Its objective was to transform the Methodist Church and Christianity into an instrument for the achievement of socialism. It was established in 1907, twelve years before the organization of the Communist Party of the United States in 1919. The outbreak of the Bolshevik Revolution in Russia in November 1917 had a tremendous effect upon the Socialist ministers of this organization and especially upon Dr. Ward. When the Communist Party was organized in 1919, Dr. Ward was already a convinced Communist with a few insignificant minor reservations. By 1920 he was already, though not yet a member of the Communist Party, cooperating and collaborating with the Communist Party. This collaboration of Dr. Ward with the Communist Party was reflected in the expressions and activities of the Methodist Federation for Social Action.

"The Methodist Federation for Social Action is a membership organization made up entirely of Methodists. It does not affiliate other organizations with it. The Communist Party is not included as an affiliate. The organization is a Communist Party instrument controlled by the Communist Party through the Communist cell secretly operating as a Communist Party disciplined unit in the Federation."

Gitlow has also testified under oath that Lee Ball is one of "the principal individuals involved in the Communist conspiracy to subvert the Methodist Church."

As of 1970, the Methodist Federation for Social Action claimed that, in its ten chapters, it had a total of 3,500 members, and described itself as an "unofficial organization of ministers and laymen of the Methodist Church." In a talented display of Aesopian linguistics, the Federation described its current mission: "Seeks to deepen within the Church the sense of social obligation and the opportunity to study, from the Christian point of view, social problems and their solutions, and to promote social action in the spirit of Jesus; stands for the complete abolition of war; rejects the method of the struggle for profit as the economic base for society and seeks to replace it with social-economic planning to develop a society without class or group discriminations and privileges."

Ball has been affiliated with the American Committee for Protection of Foreign Born [Americans] ("subversive and Communist" – "one of the oldest auxiliaries of the Communist Party in the United States" – under "complete domination" of the Communist Party); the American Continental Congress for Peace ("another phase in the Communist 'peace' campaign, aimed at consolidating anti-American forces throughout the Western Hemisphere"), the American Peace Mobilization ("subversive and Communist"); the China Welfare Appeal ("subversive"); the Citizens' Victory Committee for Harry Bridges ("Communist front"); the Committee for Citizenship Rights ("to protect Communist subversion from any penalties under the law"); the Committee to End Sedition Laws ("complete domination by the Communist Party"); the Committee of One Thousand ("Communist created and controlled front organization"); the Committee for Peaceful Alternatives to the Atlantic Pact ("a Communist front" – "part of Soviet psychological warfare against the United Stastes"); the Conference for Legislation in the National Interest ("Communist front"); the Citizens Committee for Constitutional Liberties ("Communist front" – "created, dominated, and controlled by members and officials of the Communist Party"); the International Workers Order ("subversive and Communist"); the National Committee to Repeal the McCarran Act ("a Communist front" – "subversive"); the National Council of the Arts, Sciences and Professions ("a Communist front used to appeal to special occupational groups"); the National Emergency Conference for Democratic Rights ("Communist front" – "subversive and un-American"); the National Federation for Constitutional Liberties ("subversive and Communist" – "under [Communist] Party domination and headed by responsible Party functionaries"); the New York Conference for Inalienable Rights ("Communist front"); the *Protestant* ("Communist front"); the Schappes Defense Committee ("Communist"); the Schneiderman-Darcy Defense Committee ("Communist"); the ultra-leftist American-Korean Friendship and Information Center; the ultra-leftist American Society for the Study of the German Democratic Republic; the Student Mobilization Committee to End the War in Vietnam, dominated by Communists and fellow-travelers; the ultra-leftist-pacifist World Fellowship; the Aptheker Dinner Program, honoring both the Communist Party's chief theoretician and the second anniversary of the American Institute for Marxist Studies; the Tri-Continental Information Center, a mouthpiece for Latin American guerrillas, the Viet Cong, and the Havana-based Tri-Continental Organization; the National Assembly for Democratic Rights ("created, dominated, and controlled by members and officials of the Communist Party"); the Emergency Civil Liberties Committee ("Communist front" — "subversive"); the Stockholm Peace Appeal ("subversive" — "Communist Party campaign"); the leftist Spring Mobilization Committee; the Communist-operated World Youth Festival; and various "open letter" projects and petitions on behalf of the Communist Party and individual Communists.

Ball's and the Methodist Federation's complete adherence to the Communist-oriented traditions established by Harry F. Ward and his Moscow bosses has been best demonstrated on the occasion of Lenin's centenary. Ball, as executive secretary of the Methodist Federation, contributed a statement to the Communists' *Daily World* (April 23, 1970): "I have had the privilege of making two visits to the Soviet Union. When one looks upon Lenin, as he lies full length in his tomb in Red Square, one thinks that this small and seemingly frail man, with his almost delicate hands and fingers, has written his name indelibly in the books of world history. He devised and made effective a new way of living for 180 million people, wherein unemployment is no longer known, wherein all the children are in school and students are paid to go to college, wherein poverty is abolished, wherein apartments and housing are built for the people, wherein the sick are cared for without expense to themselves, wherein there is hunger no more, wherein the people are dedicated

to peace. He set in motion a new way of living for other millions of people beyond the Soviet Union, a new way of living that is testing all of mankind's older ways of living.

"There are many pictures of Lenin across the width of the Soviet Union, and many statues. An unforgettable statue stands before the Pioneer Palace in Tashkent — Lenin is seated, holding a child on his knee, looking upon her with affection. This statue commemorates Lenin's concern for education. In the bitter early days when 19 foreign countries were on Soviet soil trying to strangle this new way of life, Lenin was worrying because the children in faraway Tashkent could not read, and despite the war he sent a trainload of teachers to Tashkent. So disorganized was the country, it took them 63 days to arrive!"

BERNARD BARBER was born on January 29, 1918 in Boston, Massachusetts, son of Jennie Lieberman and Albert Barber. He married Elinor Gellert. He is an alumnus of Harvard University (A.B., 1939; A.M., 1942; Ph.D., 1949). He is the author of *Science and Social Order* (1951); *Social Stratification* (1957); and *Drugs and Society* (1967). He is co-editor of *Sociology of Science* (1962) and *European Social Class* (1965).

From 1946 until 1948, Barber was a tutor at Harvard University. From 1948 until 1952, he was at Smith College as an instructor (1948-1949) and assistant professor (1949-1952) of sociology. Since 1952, he has been at Barnard College as assistant professor (1952-1955), associate professor (1955-1961), and professor (1961 to the present) of sociology, and chairman of the sociology department (1962-1965 and 1968 to the present). In 1964 he was a member of the National

Council for Civic Responsibility, an election year's drive by the Democratic Party against anti-Communists.

JOSEPH BARBER was born on June 20, 1909 in Lowell, Massachusetts, son of Grace Harris and Joseph Barber. He married Eileen Paradis. He is an alumnus of Harvard University (A.B., 1931) and Columbia University (B.J., 1933). He also studied at the University of Munich. He is the author of *Hawaii: Restless Rampart* (1941); *Good Fences Make Good Neighbors* (1958); and *These Are The Committees* (1964). He is the co-author of *Political Handbook of the World* (1953). He is the editor of *American Policy toward Germany* (1947); *The Marshall Plan as American Policy* (1948); *Military Cooperation with Western Europe* (1949); *American Policy Toward China* (1950); *The Containment of Soviet Expansion* (1951); *Foreign Aid and the National Interest* (1952); *Foreign Trade and U.S. Tariff Policy* (1953); *Diplomacy and the Communist Challenge* (1954); *Alliances and American Security* (1960); *Red China and Our U.N. Policy* (1961); and *Atlantic Unity and the American Interest* (1963).

In 1933 and 1934, Barber was a correspondent in Berlin for the Hearst newspapers. In 1934 and 1935, he was director of publications for the Institute of Pacific Relations (an "instrument of Communist policy, propaganda and military intelligence"). He also contributed to the IPR's publications, *Far Eastern Survey* and *Pacific Affairs.* From 1935 until 1938, he was the managing editor of *Atlantic Monthly.* From 1938 until 1940, he was a public relations counsel in Honolulu. From 1941 until 1943, he was an associate editor of the leftwing *Washington Post.* From 1946 until 1963, he was employed by the Council on Foreign Relations, the most influential organization in the ruling leftist-liberal Establishment. He served the CFR as a director of affiliated Committees on Foreign Relations in thirty-three cities. In recent years, he has retained his resident membership in the CFR.

JONAS A. BARISH was born on March 22, 1922 in New York City, son of Mollie Schaffer and Philip Barish. He married Mildred Seaquist. He is an alumnus of Harvard University (A.B., 1942; M.A., 1947; Ph.D., 1952). He is the author of *Ben Jonson and the Language of Prose Comedy* (1960). He is the editor of Shakespeare's *All's Well That Ends Well* (1964) and Ben Jonson's *Sejanus* (1965).

In 1953 and 1954, Barish was an instructor at Yale University. Since 1954, he has been at the University of California in Berkeley as assistant professor (1954-1960), associate professor (1960-1966), and professor (since 1966) in the English department. In 1961 and 1962, he was a Fulbright research fellow in Paris. In 1961 and 1962, he was also a fellow of the American Council of Learned Societies.

Barish has been active in leftist agitation in the Bay Area against the Vietnam War. He has also contributed to the Huey Newton Defense Fund, an ultra-leftist project.

HARRY BARNARD was born on September 5, 1906 in Pueblo, Colorado, son of Pauline Halpern and David Kletzky. He was married to and divorced from Miriam Helstein. He is married to Ruth Eisenstat. He is an alumnus of the University of Chicago (Ph.B., 1928). He also studied at the University of Denver and the John Marshall Law School in Chicago. He is the author of *Eagle*

Forgotten: The Life of John Peter Alt-
geld (1938); Rutherford B. Hayes and
His America (1954); and Independent
Man: The Life of Senator James Couzens
(1958). He is the editor of Pope John's
Mater et Magistra (1962). He is the
co-editor of Along the Way (1962). He
has contributed articles to the Dictionary
of American Biography, Saturday Review, Nation, and the Encyclopedia
Americana.

From 1928 until 1934, Barnard was
on the editorial staff of the Chicago
Herald-Examiner. In 1934 and 1935, he
was on the research staff of the Illinois
Tax Commission. From 1935 until 1942,
he was director of research for the
Chicago Law Department. In 1943, he
was director of press relations for the
University of Chicago. In 1944, he was
chief editorial writer for the Chicago
Times. From 1945 until 1947, he was on
the staff of the Chicago Sun. From 1948
until 1958, he worked in the advertising
business and in public relations. From
1958 until 1961, his column, "Liberal at
Large," appeared in the Chicago Daily
News and in the Des Moines Register
syndicate. From 1964 until 1966, he
taught American politics at Columbia
College in Chicago. From 1966 until
1968, he worked in the public relations
department of Northwestern University.
Since 1968, he has been an instructor of
biography and journalism and a writer-
in-residence at Roosevelt University in
Chicago.

Barnard has had a number of leftwing
affiliations, including membership in the
National Committee for a Sane Nuclear
Policy, the Committee to Defend the Bill
of Rights, the Chicago Civil Liberties
Committee, the National Committee to
Abolish the House Un-American Activi-
ties Committee, and the Medical Aid to
[Castro's] Cuba Committee.

RICHARD J. BARNET was born on
May 7, 1929 in Massachusetts, son of
Margaret Block and Carl Barnet. He
married Ann Birnbaum. He is an alumnus of Harvard University (A.B., 1952;
LL.B., 1954). He is the author of Who
Wants Disarmament? (1961); Intervention and Revolution (1968); and Economics of Death (1969). He is a contributor to The New Left (1969) and Washington Plans an Aggressive War (1971).

In 1954, Barnet was admitted to the
Massachusetts bar. From 1958 until
1960 he practiced law in Boston. In
1960 and 1961, he was a research fellow
at Harvard University. From 1961 until
1963, he was a deputy director of
political research for the U.S. Arms
Control and Disarmament Agency and
he also served in a consulting capacity to
the Department of State and the Department of Defense.

In 1963, Barnet and Marcus Raskin
founded the Institute for Policy Studies
and completed a merger with the ultra-
leftist-pacifist Peace Research Institute.
From the beginning, the IPS – a tax-
exempt educational institution ("think
tank") – has been supported by foundations, universities, colleges, and individuals. Its annual budget of approximately $400,000 has been financed by
the Ford Foundation, the Edgar Stern
Family Fund, the Samuel Rubin Foundation, the Milbank Foundation, the
Field Foundation, the Edwin Janss
Foundation, the Cudahy Fund, the Institute for International Order, the Society for the Psychological Study of
Social Issues, the National Board of
Missions of the Presbyterian Church, and
individuals including James P. Warburg,
Michael Gellert, Walter E. Meyer, and
Jennifer Cafritz.

Since 1963, Barnet and his cohorts
have waged a massive and incessant

propaganda war against the so-called military-industrial complex. Their tactics have included a drive for unilateral disarmament of the United States; unilateral abandonment of all nuclear testing; total cooperation in scientific and other areas with the Soviet Union; diplomatic recognition by the United States of Red China, North Korea, North Vietnam, and East Germany; drastic reductions in the U.S. military and security budgets; surrender of American sovereignty matters to the United Nations; elimination of the Selective Service System; and an international police force.

In *Barron's Weekly* (October 6, 1969), Shirley Scheibla has described another main interest of Barnet's IPS: "The Institute actually has set up communes and neighborhood corporations with the ultimate aim of taking over important functions of municipal government, including the control of police, schools, housing for the poor and health services.

"According to at least one IPS book, 'Neighborhood Government,' the message of the riots is that the poor want such community control, and civil war will result unless they get it. Nothing less will suffice, it maintains. The ultimate aim is to establish such control through a network of federally funded ghetto corporations.

"At least two IPS associate fellows hold government posts in which they are able to apply such theories. Other fellows, once having held such posts, apparently continue to influence the executive and legislative branches of government."

Miss Scheibla also described the interest Barnet's IPS had in the race riots that plagued the nation in the 1960's: ". . . Black employees of the Library of Congress began receiving cards. One side

was headed, 'Committee for Emergency Support,' and bore the address of the Institute. It read: 'We are in sympathy with the despair of the black people in America. We share their sense of powerlessness to relieve repressive conditions by conventional political means. We are frustrated in our attempts to control the decisions which affect our lives in the capital city.

" 'We are all victims. We are ready in an emergency to assist the black community of Washington with food, housing, medical care and legal aid. We are committed to act to remove repressive military and political intervention.'

"The other side of the card advised calling the IPS phone number 'in a riot or rebellion to obtain information, for legal assistance, for medical aid, for food and housing, to report police brutality.' "

Over the years, Barnet and his co-director, Marcus Raskin, have been able to attract an impressive group of individuals to serve as IPS trustees. The names in the group unquestionably attract financial and other support for the IPS. They include Thurman Arnold, James Dixon, Michael Gellert, Edwin Janss Jr., Christopher Jencks, Milton Kotler, Arthur Larson, Hans Morgenthau, Gerard Piel, David Riesman, Philip Stern, James Warburg, and Peter Weiss.

The IPS has used a number of fellows and associate fellows to produce pamphlets, books, and articles, and to conduct seminars. Under IPS auspices about thirty books and thousands of articles have been published. Seminars and off-the-record briefings are conducted for groups of congressional assistants and for such leftist organizations as the Council for a Livable World, Members of Congress for Peace Through Law, the National Conference on Military Priorities, and the New Mobilization Committee to End the War in Vietnam.

The most important individual brought into IPS by Barnet and Raskin has been Arthur Waskow, who carries the title of senior fellow. Waskow has written that the IPS is committed to the view that, to develop social theory, one must be involved in social action and experimentation. It works for creative disorder, meaning "to simply keep experimenting and to discover at what point one is neither smashed nor ignored, but creates enough change to move the society."

In 1965, Waskow represented Barnet and Raskin in a meeting at the ultra-leftist Center for the Study of Democratic Institutions. The meeting resulted in a "Call to Convention," written by Waskow, who described the "tactics of creative disorder" in some detail: "We intend to build a different American future. We intend to end the destruction of Vietnam. We intend to end the destruction of scores of other countries by the economic and political pressures of the great powers to keep them poor and powerless. We intend to abolish the armies that consume the world's substance. We intend to begin the building of 'Mankind' — which we know our children will have to continue. We intend to end poverty, fear and despair at home. We intend to end the bribery and subversion of our private associations, unions and churches by the secret agencies of 'our' own government. We intend to make our government accountable to us. We intend to make our own workplaces accountable to us. We intend to make the election process meaningful again. We intend to make it available to those who have always been excluded from it. We intend to use other kinds of tactics of creative disorder: sit-ins and marches, rent strikes and labor strikes and school boycotts. We plan to invent our own institutions, to found neighborhood governments based on neighborhood power; to open new kinds of schools and grocery stores and medical centers, new sorts of law firms and social work agencies and research institutes and to transform the old ones. We will not be trapped inside the old parties; and we will not be trapped outside of them. And if we should build a party, it will be not merely a party, but a movement."

What Waskow described in his "Call" was nothing less than a synopsis of the work directed in IPS by Barnet and Raskin. The "Call" issued by Waskow was to the National Conference for New Politics, a united front dominated by Communists.

Barnet has never confined his energies to the directorship of IPS. He has been in the forefront of ultra-leftist protests against the Vietnam War. He has been an intellectual-in-residence for the ultra-leftist Business Executives Move for a Vietnam Peace. He has been a member of the ultra-leftist Committee of Liaison with Families of Servicemen Detained in North Vietnam, which has exploited the misery and sufferings of families of POW's. He has been a member of the New University Conference, an ultra-radical project. He has endorsed the Hanoi-inspired People's Peace Treaty.

Barnet has long been involved with the ultra-leftist Lawyers Committee on American Policy toward Vietnam. In 1967, he shared in drafting a lengthy document, issued by the Lawyers Committee, which purported to be a legal argument against U.S. involvement in the Vietnam War, but which was in reality a pro-Hanoi, anti-United States propaganda piece. The document was directed to President Johnson and his foreign policy advisers. It urged the Johnson Administration to take five immediate steps: "1. Unconditional termination of bombings in North Vietnam. 2. Cooperate in replacing U.S. military forces with personnel of the International Control Commission which is legally responsible for supervising the execution of the 1954 Geneva Accords. 3. De-escalation of military operations in South Vietnam starting with the cessation of offensive operations. 4. Recognition of the National Liberation Front as possessing belligerent status, and hence negotiating status, equal to that of the Saigon regime. 5. Commitment to negotiate on the basis of the 1954 Geneva accords, including the withdrawal of all foreign military forces and the elimination of all foreign bases in South and North Vietnam within a specified period of time."

The basic reasoning to justify the five steps was a five-point analysis of "the legality or illegality of our involvement in Vietnam: Point I — The unilateral military intervention of the United States in Vietnam violates the Charter of the United Nations. The Charter's exceptional authorization of individual and collective self-defense 'if an armed attack occurs against a member of the United Nations' does not apply in the case of Vietnam. 1. There has been no 'armed attack' upon South Vietnam within the meaning of Article 51 of the Charter. 2. The United States failed to fulfill its charter obligation to seek a peaceful solution in Vietnam. 3. The doctrine of 'collective self-defense' cannot justify the United States military intervention in the civil war in South Vietnam. 4. The 'request' of the 'Government' of South Vietnam does not provide a legal basis for 'collective self-defense.' 5. The Korean precedent does not justify the unilateral intervention of the United

States in Vietnam. Point II — the military presence of the United States in Vietnam violates the Geneva accords of 1954. Point III — The United States is not committed by the SEATO Treaty or otherwise to intervene in Vietnam. Point IV — the intensity and destructiveness of United States warfare in Vietnam is contrary to international law. Point V — United States actions in Vietnam violate treaties which are part of the supreme law of the land, and hence violate the United States Constitution."

In the verbose explanations of every point and sub-point there was not a single phrase or sentence either critical of the North Vietnamese or condemnatory of Communism. If the Analysis had been written in Hanoi, it could not have been substantially improved as a policy position for the Communist regime.

In the spring of 1969, Barnet and Raskin were the main writers of a report that the chief doves in the Senate and House endorsed as an opening salvo in a fight to have Congress "reassert control over the military bureaucracy and the policy decisions it has pre-empted." The report called for a radical and unilateral reduction of America's armed forces; a drastic reduction of the military budget; a unilateral postponement in the deployment of the anti-ballistic missile system; and an immediate reduction of American troops in Vietnam. The authors and endorsers of the report were anxious to force a Communist coalition government on South Vietnam. Every one of the measures called for in the report was something advocated previously by Barnet and/or his associates in the IPS.

In November 1969, Barnet went to Hanoi. He spoke at a rally sponsored by two of the Hanoi regime's 'peace' fronts, the Vietnam Peace Committee and the Vietnam Committee for Solidarity with the American People. Hanoi Radio quoted Barnet as voicing "the solidarity of the American people with the just struggle of the Vietnamese people" and urging "the immediate withdrawal of U.S. troops." He further said: "In the few days that we've been in Hanoi and in the provinces, we have good reason not to despair and the message that we would bring back with us is the message that the Vietnamese will continue to fight against the aggressors, the same aggressors that we will continue to fight in our own country . . . ."

From Hanoi, Barnet sent three long dispatches to the *St. Louis Post-Dispatch.* Not since Walter Duranty, Edgar Snow, and Herbert Matthews reported on Stalin's Russia, Mao Tse-tung's Red China, and Castro's Cuba, respectively, has any American sent home such unadulterated pro-enemy propaganda to a metropolitan newspaper.

Barnet interviewed leaders of North Vietnam and its National Liberation Front. He faithfully quoted their harsh criticisms of Presidents Nixon and Johnson, American military men and their strategy and tactics, America's diplomatic history, and the Saigon regime. He recorded the wisdom of the Communist leaders; the courage of the North Vietnamese regulars and the Viet Cong; the determination, the courage, and the resourcefulness of the North Vietnamese men, women, and children. He readily accepted Communist twistings of history. It was all presented in the guise of objective reporting but nowhere was there anything in the dispatches to indicate the slightest deviation from the pro-Hanoi line that has been standard fare for American television viewers and American readers of the liberal press. A careful study of Barnet's dispatches would lead to a reasonable assumption

that he need never have left his desk at IPS to write them. He could have produced substantially the same material by referring to the writings of himself and his associates, accounts in the *New York Times,* and commentaries on the American television networks. Furthermore, much of what Barnet wrote from Hanoi had already been said repeatedly by the doves in the United States Congress.

Quotations used by Barnet and paraphrases of remarks made to him constituted the major part of his dispatches. Although the material was presented in a journalistic style, the entire context appeared to be a poorly disguised press release written for American consumption. Much of what he wrote would have been rejected as ridiculous by North Vietnamese people. On the other hand, gullible Americans – ignorant of Barnet's background and accustomed to daily dosages of leftist-liberal misinformation on the Vietnam War – could accept Barnet's accounts as unbiased and reliable. He carefully avoided quoting or using hammer-and-tong Communist jargon. He seemed intent on proving that the United States war effort was an all-out attempt to crush North Vietnam militarily and that there was an honest intention on the part of the White House to prevent South Vietnam and the rest of Southeast Asia from going under Communist control.

A random sampling of Barnet's remarks provides intrinsic evidence that his sympathies are with North Vietnam and its National Liberation Front and Viet Cong: "The United States is not really interested in negotiations, and the Nixon policy is a direct continuation of the Lyndon B. Johnson policy with the objective of permanent American domination of South Vietnam politics." – "North Vietnam leaders are convinced that Mr. Nixon has no interest in the Paris talks." — "Mr. Nixon's political goal, Hanoi leaders believe, is to force them and the National Liberation Front to submit to an election organized by the Thieu regime." — "An election under Thieu's direction is seen by North Vietnamese leaders as an American-controlled election."

In one interesting passage, Barnet cleverly portrayed the U.S. forces as poised to drop bombs on children because the U.S. had lost the war of attrition: "North Vietnam officials say it is their troops who must now go looking for the enemy. The U.S. has curtailed its 'search and destroy' missions to minimize casualties, while stationing the bulk of its forces in defensive positions around Saigon, Hue and Da Nang.

"North Vietnamese believe that the 1968 Tet offensive was primarily responsible for Johnson's first move toward de-escalation. Although they say they are increasingly impressed by the American antiwar movement, they continue to put their primary faith in their own efforts on the battlefield.

"All the foregoing changes in U.S. strategy convinced Hanoi officials that the U.S. has lost the war of attrition — but they are under no illusions that they have yet won. They are preparing for a long war.

"Mr. Nixon's threat to take 'strong and effective measures' did not go unnoticed in Hanoi. They believe that the Vietnamization policy implies a distinct possibility of a re-escalation, including the resumption of the bombing of the North.

"Most of the children are back in Hanoi from the evacuation centers in the country; but the new Polytechnical Institute, the only really modern building in the city, stands empty. Factories are still dispersed in hundreds of caves and grottos throughout the countryside. The shelters one sees every few feet along each street of Hanoi are kept in readiness. Little has been done to repair the considerable damage to the residential areas of the capital. 'We are very much on the alert,' an elderly former mandarin, now a deputy in the National Assembly, told me."

In an analysis of the Nixon Administration's Vietnamization policy, Barnet managed to incorporate the idea that North Vietnamese are not intransigent negotiators, that South Vietnamese will not be subjected to mass reprisals in the event their country is conquered by Communists; and that the National Liberation Front has been pacing itself in battle: "Mr. Nixon must know, they reason, that if he really withdraws the U.S. combat units, the Saigon regime would fall. Therefore, they suspect that he is merely attempting to set an elaborate stage for some sort of re-escalation when the failure of the present strategy becomes evident. North Vietnam leaders see Mr. Nixon as attempting to gain public support for intensifying the war by cutting down the draft and moving toward a professional army, by emphasizing Hanoi's alleged intransigence at the negotiating table, and by fanning the flames of nationalism in the United States. This Mr. Nixon will do, Hanoi officials believe, by continuing to evoke the prospect of mass reprisals if the U.S. would leave Vietnam and by making emotional appeals to preserve the national honor.

"If Mr. Nixon's present strategy is premised on National Liberation Front restraint on the battlefield, it is bound to fail, these officials say. There is no lull on the battlefield even now, officials contend. Nor is there any understanding for a future lull. A Viet Cong leader explained, 'The battlefield has a rhythm of its own.'

"Reductions of military activity at one time or another are temporary. They have not renounced the initiative on the battlefield, nor do they lack the capacity, Pham Van Dong told me, to step up the war if necessary."

In the introduction to his second dispatch from Hanoi, Barnet made it quite evident that, in his opinion, South Vietnam did not really exist and that his hosts in Hanoi were the authentic spokesmen for all Vietnamese: "I went to North Vietnam sure that its leaders would seek to convince me of their unshakable determination to carry on the war if their minimum political objections were not met. The United States and all other foreigners must be out of Vietnam, bag and baggage. Not only must the troops go, but more important, the foreign political control which those troops represent must be ended.

"In the course of my recent talks with high officials in Hanoi, including Premier Pham Von Dong, these minimum objectives were emphasized again and again. North Vietnamese leaders told me that they were eager for a political settlement along these lines but were prepared to fight indefinitely if the United States would not agree. 'Our will is stronger than ever,' Dong stated with quiet assurance.

"The determination of Vietnamese leadership to resist American military pressure is, of course, their principal weapon. In a war of attrition, staying power makes the crucial difference. I therefore expected to hear expressions of self-confidence. What I was completely unprepared for was the depth and obvious sincerity of their conviction that they are winning.

" 'The United States defeat is already evident,' Dong declared in the course of an interview. They are certain that they will drive the foreigners from their land and they hold this belief with all the tenacity of a religious faith. No American can comprehend Vietnamese thinking on the war unless he tries to see their history and tradition as they do.

"Vietnamese officials gently remind American visitors that they have arrived in the middle of the play. Again and again the high officials to whom I talked spoke of the 2000-year history of Vietnam, its single culture, its one language . . . . The U.S. efforts that began in 1954 to create and maintain a separate state in South Vietnam is for them merely one more such effort. It is a brief interlude in the long history of a united Vietnam.

"North Vietnamese leaders are not prepared to let the United States dismiss the Geneva settlement as ancient history. The state created below the Seventeenth Parallel under Ngo Dinh Diem after the Geneva Conference of 1954 they see as nothing more than a U.S. political device for keeping a foothold in Southeast Asia.

"The meaning of the Geneva settlement, they say again and again, is that Vietnam is one country. It will take a long time, they admit, to achieve reunification, but the fundamental right of the Vietnamese themselves to bring this about by peaceful means must be recognized."

Of special interest was Barnet's extraordinary effort to prove the courage and long-suffering of North Vietnam vis-a-vis American atrocities: "What do they [the North Vietnamese] believe will enable them to carry on the fight against the world's strongest power 'for another twenty-five years or more, if necessary?'

"First, they know that in the severe trials to which they have been subject they have shown that they can take punishment and even thrive on it. One high official pointed out that North and South Vietnam had received the equivalent of one megaton hydrogen bomb apiece. More than 600 sections of dikes have been bombed, they say, and they have been able to contain the floods. (They showed me a number of pictures in corroboration.) The wide use of defoliants and toxic gases has caused some chemical change in the soil, but the rice crop is up. I saw entire towns where as many as 40,000 had lived with nothing left but a dozen fragments of charred wall, but the survivors do not appear intimidated. North Vietnamese officials concede that more horrors may lie ahead of them. Some fully expect it. But they feel that they have been tested and that they have emerged from the trial with greater strength than ever.

"Second, there is abundant evidence of economic growth in the years of escalation, they assert. There are 20,000 more university students this year than in 1965. The yield per acre in the rice crop, despite periodic setbacks, has almost doubled. Under the pressure of war, age-old public health problems have been solved. Malaria, plague, cholera and yellow fever have been virtually eliminated. Each year new dispensaries and hospitals are built in villages and districts. Since 1965, an entire new industrial network has been established. Hundreds of small workshops, machine tool factories and light industry have been built into the sides of mountains and in grottos. I saw one workshop inside an enlarged cave where men and women were huddled over simple lathes turning out pistons for trucks and other spare parts. Under pressure of war the Vietnamese have decentralized their education, medical services, agriculture, as well as industrial production. The administrative head of a province emphasized that the radical reforms the Vietnamese had carried out under the bombings should more accurately be characterized as 'divided responsibility' rather than 'decentralization.' Their economy, he pointed out, is still centrally managed. Whatever the term, there is no doubt that the changes are popular and have raised morale.

"The third source of strength is the increasing sense of unity of the people. For this, Vietnamese leaders give the U.S. Air Force much of the credit. 'When the first wave of planes came over the North,' one of the country's leading intellectuals told me, 'some Catholic priests openly applauded.' These long-time foes of North Vietnam's Communist government led their flocks into the local churches certain that they would be the last places the Americans would bomb. But Catholic churches have been bombed in great number. The official count is 465. (I counted more than 10 in a short visit to a single province.) The result has been to unite dissident elements in the society in the common struggle against the outside attacker . . . .

"But perhaps the crucial source of strength of the Vietnamese, as they see it, is their very backwardness. I was shown movies of the Viet Cong at work, navigating streams in rafts, obtaining food, shelter and protection from the forest. 'Look how little we need for fighting,' was the message contantly impressed upon me. It is clearly a message they believe themselves.

"Another point they make is symbolized by the giant bomb craters I saw scarring the countryside in Thanh Hoa province. They seemed irrelevant. At their edge new huts had been built or a new rice crop planted. Although province officials were concerned that the craters were becoming breeding grounds for mosquitos, the bombings had not disrupted the social system. Many had been killed and wounded, but life went on much as it always has. Vietnam appears to be one of the countries in the world least vulnerable to massive air bombardment.

"While conceding that the advanced Chinese and Soviet military equipment I saw on the highway had something to do with their survival, Vietnamese officials constantly repeated, 'We are a primitive country.' They said it triumphantly. 'Our people don't need much to eat. We can get along on rice, fish and a little meat, if it is available. Ten meters of cloth and one pair of shoes a year is more than enough.' The kind of house to which most of the population is accustomed can be put together in short order with a minimum of easily available materials. One of the most important exhibits in the Museum of the Revolution in Hanoi shows Ho Chi Minh's small straw suitcase with his sandals and tunic, the total possessions he carried with him in the long months of World War II. It is a pointed symbol of the national capacity for making do."

Barnet made a strong attempt to minimize morale and casualties as factors that could weaken the Communists' war effort: "I questioned the North Vietnamese and National Liberation Front officials closely on two factors which, according to United States military sources, are seriously weakening their capacity to continue the war: The supposedly serious decline in morale in the North, and the unacceptably high casualty rate in the South. When I asked Premier Pham Van Dong about morale, he replied, 'After the death of our president, Ho Chi Minh, we are closing ranks.' He was referring specifically to speculation about rivalry among the leadership, and he spoke with the authority of a man in charge.

"When I asked whether the bombing halt had not produced a psychological letdown in the North, another speculation popular in Washington, I received this answer: 'The country is still at war and the people still feel part of the struggle.' I understood these words better when I heard a class of kindergarten children singing songs about shooting down American planes.

"Wherever I turned, I saw small groups of Vietnamese preparing for the long war they see ahead. In the early morning, I walked alone in Hanoi's Unity Park and watched classes of young women assembling rifles among neatly planted flower beds. Several mornings at 4 o'clock I heard the clatter of militia marching in shouted cadence below my bedroom window.

"When I questioned National Liberation Front leaders about the crippling losses the U.S. Army claims to have inflicted on the Viet Cong, they said that after reading the U.S. figures they did not understand how they themselves could still be alive. They produced a complete list of the annual estimates of U.S. military leaders on the demise of the Viet Cong dated back to 1965, then noted their offensive operations that followed these premature death notices. The Viet Cong do not deny that they have suffered heavy casualties but, as a National Liberation Front official just back from the front told me: 'We are now operating far more effectively in the cities than ever before. The National Liberation Front has a major military headquarters operating within the city limits of Saigon itself.' "

In the concluding portion of his third

and last dispatch from Hanoi, Barnet managed to include a boost for the doves and a knock for the hawks in America: "Although the Hanoi leaders believe that they are more than holding their own on the battlefield, they see two favorable political trends. The rising opposition to the war in the United States has plainly surprised them, but they have a realistic estimate of its strength. Above all, they rely on their own will and strength. They believe that U.S. policy will eventually change enough to permit a negotiated settlement because the United States is willing to accept considerably fewer losses to protect a distant imperial outpost than they themselves are prepared to accept to rid Vietnam of foreign domination. 'Some day the United States must come to see its own interest,' said one Hanoi official.

"The second trend to which they attach considerable importance is the deterioration of political strength of the Saigon government .... Top Hanoi officials are convinced that the day is not too far off when the people in the South will demand a 'government of peace' to talk seriously with the National Liberation Front with a view to 'setting up a very broad coalition government.' The central question, as they see it, is: When will the United States permit this inevitable evolution to take place? When Washington is ready to accept such a development, North Vietnamese leaders indicate, the road to serious negotiation will be open."

Barnet, of course, had no legitimate reason for making his journey to Hanoi. He was under no compulsion to write his enemy-serving dispatches. He has never claimed that his dispatches were edited or censored or that they represented anything but his own beliefs. And, since his return from Hanoi, he has confirmed in many ways that he is completely committed to the destruction of any American military might that could be used anywhere to block the progress of Communism.

In 1970, at the time of the Cambodian invasion, Barnet raised the bogy of nuclear weapons. In an address to a meeting of Business Executives Move for Vietnam Peace, he held out the strong possibility of nuclear weapons being used in Vietnam. In a highly emotional exposition, he visualized the Nixon Administration launching a nuclear attack in Vietnam if the Cambodian invasion failed and the war were prolonged. He also seized the opportunity to plead his decade-old cause, disarmament: "The President's sudden decision to invade Cambodia dramatizes the dangers of permitting the war to drag on and exposes the American people to many risks. Specifically, the serious risk that nuclear weapons might be used in similar mistaken effort to achieve a decisive military victory must now be faced. There is a likelihood that if the war continues for many more months President Nixon will find himself in a position in which he may be strongly disposed to use tactical nuclear weapons in Indochina ....

"The most plausible evidence that there is a substantial risk is the lack of alternative military options given the character of the war and the 'Vietnamization' program. Let us assume that President Nixon does reduce the American force level in Vietnam to 200,000 or less and confines them to enclaves. Assume further that at such point the North Vietnamese and the NLF launch major offensives against South Vietnamese forces, a highly probable contingency unless they believe that the U.S. means to pull all its troops out in a reasonable time. It is equally likely that they will overrun the South Vietnamese army, thus leaving the U.S. with the options of executing a Dunkirk-like evacuation, sitting idly by in enclaves while the forces they are supposedly there to protect are slaughtered, or carrying out a sudden dramatic escalation. The possibilities of escalation are severely limited. Bringing massive numbers of U.S. troops back would be tactically and politically impossible. Bombing the North would be tactically irrelevant, since the enemy forces would already be in the South. Under these highly plausible circumstances the pressure would mount to explode a nuclear weapon as a demonstration of American will. It would be justified as the ultimate psychological pressure to convince Hanoi that they must negotiate on our terms. It should not be forgotten that the only time nuclear weapons have actually been used in war, the sole justification was 'to save lives.' . . .

"It is impossible to know how substantial these risks are, although it is clear from the structure of the military, military doctrine, the President's own past thinking, and the developing situation on the battlefield, that the risks are not trivial. Once such weapons are used, events will move very fast and it will be exceedingly difficult for public or Congressional protest to have any effect. The only effective Congressional role in such a world tragedy is to prevent it . . . .

"I raise the prospect of the use of nuclear weapons, horrible as it is, because although it is something apparently mad, people should confront it in a straightforward fashion. The lack of public protest and demonstration of real public anger will, by the momentum of events, allow the President to take the fateful chance. So I would ask all of you

to raise your voices, write, protest, and demand that these nuclear weapons not be used and that they be taken out of the area."

In the *New York Times* (June 19, 1971) there appeared an essay by Barnet – "Farewell to the Nation-State." He began his essay with the declaration: "The nation-state is obsolete." He never did define "nation-state" or say what, if anything, had replaced it, but he did indicate that the United States and Soviet Union were nation-states. However, the essay did afford Barnet an opportunity to reiterate his usual preachments for disarmament and his routine slanders against the United States: "In the nuclear age the crucial relationship between the citizen and the state is the suicide pact." – "Planetary survival will depend upon how quickly the power of the nation-state can be contained and a wider human identity can be established." – "As the frantic public relations campaign to sell the American flag and similar propaganda efforts in the Soviet Union suggest, spontaneous love of country is in short supply." – "The United States has tried to impose its vision of a stable world through military and economic power, but in a world in revolution the costs of those traditional imperial methods have proved prohibitive." – "The United States may succeed in devastating Vietnam but there is no evidence that it can successfully dominate it. The brutal methods the United States Government has used to establish its worldwide 'credibility' undermine its legitimacy. The strategy creates more revolutionaries than it destroys, at home as well as abroad." – "The United States has proclaimed the right to bomb countries at will."

In his contribution to *Washington Plans an Aggressive War*, published in late 1971, Barnet's emotions on the Vietnam War had run amok. He was ready to charge Americans responsible for involvement in the Vietnam War with crimes against the "civilized conscience." He wanted those guilty ones excluded from public office for a decade. He favored the enactment of a statute which would forbid officials to "preach or advocate" militarism or genocide, or to conduct militaristic, genocidal, or similar [!] policies.

ALLEN H. BARTON was born on October 7, 1924 in Greenwich, Connecticut, son of Elizabeth Hoisington and H. Allen Barton. He married Judith Schneider. He is an alumnus of Harvard University (B.A., 1947) and Columbia University (Ph.D., 1957). He is the author of *Studying the Effects of College Education* (1959); *Organizational Measurement* (1961); and *Communities in Disaster* (1969). He has contributed to *The Policy Sciences* (1951); *Complex Organizations* (1961); *Man and Society in Disaster* (1962); *Radical Sociology* (1971); and *Handbook of Social Problems* (1971).

In 1948 and 1949, Barton was a sociology lecturer at the University of Oslo in Norway. In 1953 and 1954, he was an instructor at Columbia University. From 1954 until 1957, he was an assistant professor of sociology at the University of Chicago's Law School. Since 1957, he has been at Columbia University as assistant professor (1957-1962) and associate professor of sociology and director of the Bureau of Applied Social Research (since 1962).

Barton was a member of the ultra-radical Americans for Democratic Action; the National Association for the Advancement of Colored People, the fountainhead of Negro agitation for more than half a century; and the ultra-leftist American Civil Liberties Union.

JAMES F. BECKER was born on November 3, 1921 in Cedar Rapids, Iowa. He is married. He is an alumnus of the University of Iowa (B.A., 1947; M.A., 1949) and Columbia University (Ph.D., 1957). In 1959, he was a Danforth fellow at Harvard University.

In 1947 and 1948, Becker was an instructor in journalism, and in 1949, an instructor in economics, at the University of Iowa. In 1949 and 1950, he was an instructor in economics at Iowa State Teachers College. Since 1953, he has been at New York University, serving successively as an assistant professor, associate professor, and professor of economics.

Becker has been an active participant in the annual Socialist Scholars Conferences, get-togethers of Marxian Socialists and their fellow-travelers. In 1966, he sponsored the Herbert Aptheker dinner program, a dual celebration commemorating the fiftieth birthday of America's best-known Communist Party theoretician and the second anniversary of Aptheker's American Institute for Marxist Studies.

SAMUEL BELKIN was born on December 12, 1911 in Swislicz, Poland, son of Mina Sattir and Solomon Belkin. He came to the United States in 1929 and was naturalized in 1941. His first wife was Selma Ehrlich. He is married to Abby Polesie. After studies at Radin Theological Seminary, he was ordained as a rabbi in 1928. He is an alumnus of Brown University (Ph.D., 1935). He also studied at Harvard University. He is the author of *The Alexandrian Halakah in Apologetic Literature of the First Cen-*

tury (1936); *Philo and the Oral Law* (1940); *Essays in Traditional Jewish Thought* (1956); and *In His Image* (1961).

In 1929 and 1930, Belkin lectured in the Talmud at the New Haven Rabbinical Seminary in Cleveland, Ohio. Since 1935, he has been at Yeshiva University as instructor in Greek (1935-1940), professor of Hellenistic literature (1940-1943), and president of the university (since 1943). Since 1936, Belkin has also been associated with the Rabbi Isaac Elchanan Theological Seminary in New York as instructor of the Talmud (1936-1940), dean of the seminary (1940-1943), and president of the seminary (since 1943).

Belkin has been a long-time official of the leftwing-internationalist United World Federalists. He was a member of the National Council for Civic Responsibility, an anti-anti-Communist hatchet crew in the 1964 presidential campaign.

[MARVIN] ROBERT BENDINER was born on December 15, 1909 in Pittsburgh, son of Lillian Schwartz and William Bendiner. He married Kathryn Rosenberg. He attended the City College of New York. He is the author of *The Riddle of the State Department* (1942); *White House Fever* (1960); *Obstacle Course on Capitol Hill* (1964); *Just Around the Corner* (1967); and *The Politics of Schools* (1969).

From 1937 until 1950, Bendiner was with the leftist *Nation* magazine as managing editor (1937-1944) and associate editor (1946-1950). From 1956 until 1960, he was a contributing editor to the leftist *Reporter* magazine. From 1959 until 1961, he was an American correspondent for *New Statesman*. From 1946 until 1953, he was a lecturer at Wellesley College's Summer Institute for Social

Progress. In 1956, he was a lecturer at the Salzburg [Austria] Seminar in American Studies. From 1961 until 1969, he was a free-lance writer, contributing to such periodicals as *Harper's, Horizon, Life, New York Times Magazine, Redbook,* and *Saturday Evening Post.* In 1962, he held a Guggenheim fellowship. Since 1969, he has been on the editorial board of the *New York Times.*

Bendiner was a long-time member of the ultra-leftist Union for Democratic Action. When the UDA disbanded, Bendiner became the founder of the ultra-radical Americans for Democratic Action and eventually a long-time member of ADA's national board. He has also been a long-time member and official of the socialist League for Industrial Democracy.

ROBERT S. BENJAMIN was born on May 14, 1909 in New York City. He married Jean Kortright. He is an alumnus of Fordham University (LL.B., 1931). He also attended the City College of New York. In 1931, he was admitted to the New York bar.

Since 1931, Benjamin has had a law practice in New York. In 1938, he became a general partner in the legal firm of Phillips & Nizer. Later, he became a partner in Phillips, Nizer, Benjamin & Krim & Ballon. From 1937 until 1941, he was vice-president of Pathé Film Corporation. From 1945 until 1967, he was president of J. Arthur Rank Organization, Incorporated. He has also served as vice-president and general counsel for Pathé Industries, Incorporated; Eagle-Lion Films, Incorporated; and United World Pictures, Incorporated. He has been chairman of the board of the United Artists Corporation. In 1960, he was finance chairman and a national director of the National Committee of Business and Professional Men and Women for Kennedy and Johnson. He has also been on the advisory council of the National Democratic Committee.

Benjamin is a long-time member of the Council on Foreign Relations, the informal supra-State Department of the United States. He has been a director of the leftist-oriented Urban League of Greater New York. From 1961 until 1964, he was national chairman of the United States Committee for the United Nations, a leftist-oriented pro-UN propaganda agency. From 1961 until 1964, he served successively as director and national chairman of the American Association for the United Nations, another leftist-oriented pro-UN propaganda agency. He is presently a member of the United Nations Association of the United States, which is now the main leftist propaganda arm for the UN. He has also been affiliated with other leftist-oriented groups such as the Eleanor Roosevelt Memorial Foundation, the Corporation for Public Broadcasting, and the Citizen's Committee for International Development.

LERONE BENNETT JR. was born on October 17, 1928 in Clarksdale, Mississippi, son of Alma Reed and Lerone Bennett. He married Gloria Sylvester. He is an alumnus of Morehouse College (B.A., 1949). He is the author of *Before the Mayflower: A History of the Negro in America, 1619-1964* (1964); *The Negro Mood* (1964); *What Manner of Man: A Biography of Martin Luther King Jr.* (1964); *Confrontation: Black and White* (1965); *Black Power U.S.A.* (1968); and *Pioneers in Protest* (1968).

From 1949 until 1953, Bennett was with the *Atlanta* [Ga.] *Daily World* as reporter (1949-1951) and city editor (1952-1953). Since 1953, he has been with *Ebony* magazine as associate editor (1953-1958) and senior editor (1958 to the present). In 1969, he was a visiting professor of history at Northwestern University.

Ebony magazine is the most influential publication in the country devoted almost exclusively to news and feature stories about American blacks. Through his editorial work at *Ebony*, Bennett has been a major force in the encouragement of separatism. He denies that he favors either violence or separatism as a solution for any problems involving white or black Americans. At the same time, he boasts that he coined the phrase "Black Power." He has urged blacks to form their own labor unions. To his fellow blacks, he has said: "Nobody gave us nothing. The question is not one of love and friendship, but of our own interests and power." On another occasion, speaking of the American scene, he said: "Black men are not free because white men are not free – the depth of the racism is a measure of the unfreedom of the whites." On still another occasion, speaking on black and white relations, he said: "It would help enormously in America if there were a ten-year moratorium on the word 'love.' It is not required, finally, that we love each other. What is required is something infinitely more difficult – for us to confront each other."

Despite his disavowals of violence, Bennett in his writings and public utterances has glorified and encouraged black militants. He has cooperated with leaders of such radical racist groups as the Congress of Racial Equality and the Student Nonviolent Coordinating Committee. He has been affiliated with the Committee of National Inquiry, a leftist black political group.

EMILE BENOIT was born on July 14, 1909 in New York City, son of Rosina Freeman and Isadore Benoit-Smullyan. His first wife was Mary Mincher. He is now married to Etta Fleming. He is an alumnus of Harvard University (B.A., 1932; M.A., 1933; Ph.D., 1938). He is the author of *Europe at Sixes and Sevens: The Common Market, the Free Trade Association and the United States* (1961). He is the co-author of *The Balance of Payments and Domestic Prosperity* (1963). He is the co-editor of *Disarmament and the Economy* (1963) and *Disarmament and World Economic Interdependence* (1967). He is a contributor to *Social Thought from Lore to Science* (1938); *United Nations or World Government* (1947); *An Introduction to the History of Sociology* (1948); *The Sterling Area: An American Analysis* (1951); *Echo der Welt* (1958); *Economics of Our Times* (1959); *Joint International Business Ventures* (1961); *The Liberal Papers* (1962); *Preventing World War III* (1962); and *The Crossroad Papers* (1965). He has contributed articles to *American Economic Review, Antioch Review, Challenge*, and *Current History*. Since 1962, he has been on the editorial board of *The International Executive*. Since 1963, he has been on the editorial board of *Disarmament and Arms Control*. In 1963 and 1964, he was on the editorial board of the *Journal of Arms Control*. Since 1964, he has been on the editorial board of the *Columbia Journal of World Business*. Since 1966, he has been on the editorial board of *Journal of Conflict Resolution*. Since 1968, he has been on the editorial board of the *American Review of East-West Trade*.

From 1934 until 1936, Benoit was a tutor at Harvard University and Radcliffe College. In 1938 and 1939, he was an economics instructor at the University of Illinois. From 1939 until 1942, he was an economics instructor at Wells College. From 1942 until 1947, he was an analyst and an economist with the War Production Board and the Department of Labor. From 1948 until 1953, he was an economic attaché, successively, at the United States embassies in London (1948-1951) and Vienna (1951-1953). From 1954 until 1956, he was an economist with the McGraw-Hill Publishing Company. Since 1956, he has been at Columbia University's Graduate School of Business and the School of International Affairs as a professor of international business. In 1960 and 1961, he was a visiting professor and director of a research program on economic adjustments to disarmament at the Brookings Institution. In 1961 and 1962, he was a consultant to the U.S. Arms Control and Disarmament Agency and to the United Nations Secretariat. He was the director of a research program on the economics of arms control for the ultra-radical Ford Foundation and the leftist-pacifist Carnegie Foundation.

Benoit has been a member of the foreign policy committee of the leftist-pacifist Friends Committee on National Legislation. He has been a member of the committee of church and economic life of the leftist-oriented National Council of Churches. He is a long-time member and official of the ultra-radical Americans for Democratic Action.

LUCY BENSON was born on August 25, 1927 in New York City, daughter of Helen Peters and Willard Wilson. She married Bruce Benson. She is an alumna of Smith College (B.A., 1949; M.A., 1955).

In 1949 and 1950, Mrs. Benson was an executive trainee in a New York City department store. From 1950 until 1953, she worked in public relations at

BENTLEY

Smith College. In 1955, she worked in public relations at Mount Holyoke College. In 1956 and 1957, she was a research assistant in the department of American studies at Amherst College.

Since 1957, Mrs. Benson has been an active official of the leftist-oriented League of Women Voters as chapter president (1957-1961), president of the Massachusetts League of Women Voters (1961-1965), and director of the national League of Women Voters (1965-1966). In 1968, she became president of the national League of Women Voters.

Mrs. Benson is a member of the ultra-leftist American Civil Liberties Union; the National Association for the Advancement of Colored People, the fountainhead of Negro agitation for more than half a century; the United Nations Association of the United States, the most prestigious leftwing propaganda agency for the UN in this country; the leftist-oriented Urban League; and the leftist-oriented Boston Human Rights Council. Since 1969, she has been a member of the steering committee of the leftist-oriented National Urban Coalition.

ERIC BENTLEY was born on September 14, 1916 in Bolton, England, son of Laura Eveleen and Fred Bentley. He was married to and divorced from Maja Tschernjakow. He is now married to Joanne Davis. He is an alumnus of Oxford University (B.A., 1938; Litt. B., 1939) and Yale University (Ph.D., 1941). He is the author of *A Century of Hero Worship* (1944 and 1957); *The Playwright as Thinker* (1946); *Bernard Shaw: A Reconsideration* (1947, 1957, and 1967); *In Search of Theater* (1953); *The Dramatic Event* (1954); *What is Theatre?* (1956); *The Life of the Drama*

(1964); *The Theatre of Commitment, and Other Essays on Drama in Our Society* (1967); and *Theory of the Modern Stage* (1968). He is the editor of *The Importance of Scrutiny* (1948); G.B. Shaw's *On Music* (1955); *From the Modern Repertoire* (1949, 1952, and 1956); *The Play* (1951); Luigi Pirandello's *Naked Masks* (1952); *The Modern Theatre* (1955-1960); *Let's Get a Divorce, and Other Plays* (1958); Anton Chekhov's *Brute, and Other Forces* (1958); *The Classic Theatre* (1958-1961); *The Storm Over "The Deputy"* (1964); *The Genius of the Italian Theatre* (1964); and Bertolt Brecht's *The Good Woman of Setzuan* (1966). He is co-editor of *Songs of Bertolt Brecht and Hanns Eisler* (1966). He has translated a number of Bertolt Brecht's writings, including *Private Life of the Master Race* (1944); *Parables for the Theater* (1948 and 1965); "In the Swamp" and "A Man's a Man," in *Seven Plays* (1961); *Baal*, in Sokel's *Anthology of German Expressionist Drama* (1963); *Mother Courage and Her Children* (1963); *The Jewish Wife, and Other Plays* (1965); *Manuel of Piety* (1966); and *Edward II* (1966). He has also translated Georges Courteline's *These Cornfields* (1957); Carl Sternheim's *The Underpants* (1960); and Luigi Pirandello's *The Emperor* (1952) and *Right You Are* (1954). He has contributed articles to *Harper's, Kenyon Review, Partisan Review,* and *Theater Arts.* Bentley has done a considerable amount of work for the leftist music house, Folkways Records. He is editor and commentator of "Brecht Before the House Un-American Activities Committee," a Folkways record published in 1963. He is adaptor, lyricist and narrator for the album of Brecht's "A Man's a Man," published by Spoken Arts Records. He sang Brecht's songs and accompanied himself on the organ on the recording "Bentley on Brecht," originally published by Riverside Records in 1963 and re-issued by Folkways Records in 1965. He sang the album "Songs of Hanns Eisler," published by Folkways Records in 1965. (Brecht and Eisler were notorious German Communists.)

From 1942 until 1944, Bentley taught history, literature and drama at Black Mountain College. From 1944 until 1948, he taught history, literature, and drama at the University of Minnesota. In 1948 and 1949, he was a Guggenheim fellow. In 1949 and 1950, he held a Rockefeller Foundation grant. From 1952 until 1956, he was drama critic for the leftist *New Republic* magazine. In 1953, he held a grant from the National Institute of Arts and Letters. Since 1954, he has been the Brander Matthews Professor of Dramatic Literature at Columbia University. In 1960 and 1961, he was the Norton Professor of Poetry at Harvard University. In 1964 and 1965, he was artist-in-residence in Berlin for the ultra-leftist Ford Foundation. In 1967 and 1968, he held a Guggenheim fellowship.

Bentley has been affiliated with the National Committee to Abolish the House Un-American Activities Committee ("to lead and direct the Communist Party's 'Operation Abolition' campaign"); the ultra-leftist Sing-In for Peace Committee; the ultra-leftist Fort Hood Three Defense Committee; and the ultra-leftist National Peace Action Coalition.

LEONARD BERNSTEIN was born on August 25, 1918 in Lawrence, Massachusetts, son of Jennie Resnick and Samuel Bernstein. He married Felicia Cohn. He is an alumnus of Harvard University (A.B., 1939). In 1941, he graduated from the Curtis Institute of Music. He studied piano under the tutelage of Helen Coates, Henrich Gebhard, and Isabella Vengerova. He studied conducting under Fritz Reiner and Serge Koussevitsky. He is the author of *The Joy of Music* (1959); *Leonard Bernstein's Young People's Concerts for Reading and Listening* (1962); and *The Infinite Variety of Music* (1966). He has composed scores for Broadway musicals and Hollywood films. He has also composed symphonies, instrumental works, and a one-act opera.

In 1942, Bernstein was an assistant to Serge Koussevitsky at the Berkshire Music Center in Massachusetts. In 1943 and 1944, he was assistant conductor of the New York Philharmonic Symphony. From 1945 until 1948, he was conductor of the New York City Symphony. In 1948 and 1949, he was a musical adviser to the Israel Philharmonic Orchestra. From 1948 until 1955, he was on the faculty of the Berkshire Music Center, where he was head of the conducting department from 1951 until 1955. From 1951 until 1956, he was a professor of music at Brandeis University. In 1957 and 1958, he was co-conductor of the New York Philharmonic. Since 1958, he has been music director of the New York Philharmonic, which appointed him laureate conductor for life in 1969. He has toured Europe, Asia, and Latin America with the New York Philharmonic and as a guest conductor of other great orchestras.

Since the 1940's, Bernstein has been especially devoted to a wide variety of leftwing causes and projects. His affiliations have included People's Songs ("subversive"); the National Negro Congress ("subversive and Communist"); the Joint Anti-Fascist Refugee Committee ("subversive and Communist"); the Progressive Citizens of America ("political Communist front"); the Civil Rights Congress ("Communist front" — "subversive and Communist"); the American Council for a Democratic Greece ("subversive and Communist"); the Committee for a Democratic Far Eastern Policy ("Communist"); American Youth for Democracy ("subversive and Communist"); the Southern Conference for Human Welfare ("Communist front"); the Voice of Freedom Committee ("to defend pro-Communist radio speakers"); the Scientific and Cultural Conference for World Peace ("Communist front"); the Committee for the Re-election of [Communist Party leader] Benjamin J. Davis; the World Federation of Democratic Youth ("a pressure group on behalf of Soviet foreign policy"); the Jefferson School of Social Science ("adjunct of the Communist Party"); the National Council of the Arts, Sciences and Professions ("a Communist front used to appeal to special occupational groups"); the Committee for the First Amendment ("purpose is to create favorable public opinion for the Communists who refused to testify before the House Committee on Un-American Activities"); Artists' Front to Win the War ("Communist front"); the American Committee for Spanish Freedom ("Communist"); the World Peace Council ("leftist"); the leftist-pacifist Women's International League for Peace and Freedom; the National Association for the Advancement of Colored People, the fountainhead of Negro agitation for more than half a century; the leftist-pacifist National Committee for a Sane Nuclear Policy; the leftist Committee to Defend the [Chicago] Conspiracy; the leftist-pacifist Congressional Campaign Peace Committee; the Committee for Public Justice, a leftwing group to conduct a "scholarly

and objective" inquiry into the work of the Federal Bureau of Investigation; the leftist American-Soviet Music Society; and the Communist-led protest against the deportation of the German Communist Hanns Eisler.

On January 14, 1970, Bernstein and his wife, Felicia, held a fund-raising party in their New York City apartment on behalf of twenty-one Black Panthers who had been charged with conspiracy to bomb department stores. A sum of more than $10,000 was raised. In May 1971, the Bernsteins used their apartment for a fund-raising party on behalf of Rev. Philip Berrigan, S.S.J., and his co-defendants, who were charged with conspiracy to kidnap presidential advisor Henry A. Kissinger, to blow up heating tunnels in Washington, D.C., and to destroy Selective Service files. With about 125 people in attendance, the Bernsteins raised $35,000 from their guests.

DANIEL BESSIE was born on August 28, 1932 in Land Grove, Vermont. His father, Alvah, was a well-known Communist and one of the top Reds in Hollywood during the 1940's.

On October 20, 1959, Daniel Bessie appeared before the House Committee on Un-American Activities. In response to all questions pertaining to his membership in the Communist Party, he invoked the Fifth Amendment. During the mid-1950's, he was chairman of various Labor Youth League clubs in the Santa Monica, California area. (The Subversive Activities Control Board reported: "Although purportedly an independent organization devoted to the so-called needs of the youth, and educating and stimulating the interest of the youth in the spirit of 'Socialism,' the Labor Youth League was never intended to be, and is not in actuality, independent of the Communist Party. It is operated and maintained in such a way as to be completely subservient to the Party and is used to promote and carry out important Party objectives . . . . To a controlling extent those who are active in the management, direction, or supervision of the League, whether or not holding office therein, are individuals who are either active in the management, direction, or supervision of, or are representatives of, the Communist Party. The Labor Youth League is the principal means whereby a segment of American youth is indoctrinated and trained for dedicated membership and future positions of leadership in the Party. It is also the means whereby these individuals are put into active service in support and in aid of Communist Party policies and objectives.")

In January 1951, Daniel Bessie was a delegate from the Santa Monica area to the Los Angeles County Communist Party Convention. At the same period, he attended meetings of the Youth Commission of the Communist Party's Southern California District. In November 1959 and January 1960, he was a delegate to the Second Convention of the Southern California District of the Communist Party. At the convention he was elected a delegate from the area to the 17th National Convention of the Communist Party. In 1961, he participated in demonstrations conducted by the Los Angeles Fair Play for Cuba Committee, a Communist group working on behalf of Castro's regime.

Daniel Bessie has been affiliated with the New Left School in California; the California Constitutional Liberties Information Center ("Communist front"); and the Youth Action Union, the Los Angeles counterpart to the Communist-created DuBois Clubs.

ROBERT BIERSTEDT was born on March 20, 1913 in Burlington, Iowa, son of Bertha Strauss and Henry Bierstedt. He married Betty MacIver. He is an alumnus of the University of Iowa (A.B., 1934) and Columbia University (M.A., 1935; Ph.D., 1950). He also studied at Harvard University. He is the author of *The Social Order* (1957 and 1963). He is the co-author of *Modern Social Science* (1964) and *Émile Durkheim* (1966). He is the editor of *The Making of Society* (1959) and *Florian Znaniecki* (1969).

From 1937 until 1939, Bierstedt was a lecturer in philosophy at Columbia University. In 1939 and 1940, he was a social studies instructor at Bennington College. From 1940 until 1943, he was a philosophy instructor at Bard College. In 1946 and 1947, he was an assistant professor of sociology at Wellesley College. From 1947 until 1953, he was at the University of Illinois as assistant professor (1947-1951) and associate professor (1951-1953) of sociology. From 1953 until 1959, he was professor of sociology and chairman of the sociology and anthropology department at the City College of New York. In 1959 and 1960, he was a Fulbright lecturer at Edinburgh University in Scotland. Since 1960, he has been at New York University as head of the sociology department (1960-1966) and professor of sociology (since 1960). He has also lectured at Oxford University, Stanford University, the University of Washington, and, as a Fulbright lecturer, at the London School of Economics. Since 1957, he has been an advisory editor for the publishing firm of Dodd, Mead and Co.

He has been an official of the leftist-oriented American Association of University Professors. He has been an official of the leftist-oriented American Sociological Association. He is a long-time member of the board of directors of the ultra-leftist American Civil Liberties Union. He has been a member of the National Committee to Abolish the House Un-American Activities Committee ("to lead and direct the Communist Party's 'Operation Abolition' campaign").

ARTHUR I. BLAUSTEIN was born on September 1, 1933 in New York City, son of Esther Schneider and Morris Blaustein. He is an alumnus of Bard College (B.A., 1957) and Columbia University (M.A., 1970). He is a doctoral candidate at the University of California at Berkeley. He is co-editor of *Man Against Poverty: World War III* (1968) and *Who Gives a Damn?* (1971). He is a contributing editor to the ultra-leftist *Ramparts* magazine.

From 1958 until 1961, Blaustein was president of Gesalt, Inc. From 1959 until 1961, he was executive director of the New York Metropolitan Committee of the ultra-leftist United World Federalists. From 1961 until 1963, he was associate editor of the leftist-pacifist *War/Peace Report*. From 1963 until 1965, he was program director for the Foreign Policy Association, a highly effective pro-Communist vehicle. From 1965 until 1968, he was employed in various capacities by the U.S. Office of Economic Opportunity. Since 1968, he has been employed by the Earl Warren Legal Institute of the University of California at Berkeley. In 1964, while on leave from the Foreign Policy Association, he was on the staff of Vice President Hubert H. Humphrey.

He has been a member of the Institute for American Democracy, an anti-anti-Communist witch-hunting offshoot of the defamatory Anti-Defamation League. He has been an official of the United Nations Association of the United States, the most prestigious left-wing propaganda agency for the UN in this country.

LINCOLN P. BLOOMFIELD was born on July 7, 1920 in Boston, Massachusetts, son of Sylvia Palmer and Meyer Bloomfield. He married Irirangi Coates. He is an alumnus of Harvard University (B.S., 1941; M.P.A., 1952; Ph.D., 1956). He is the author of *Evolution or Revolution?* (1957); *The United Nations and U.S. Foreign Policy* (1960 and 1967); *Outer Space: Prospects for Man and Society* (1962); *International Military Forces* (1964); and *Controlling Small Wars* (1968). He is co-author of *Khrushchev and the Arms Race* (1966).

In 1941 and 1942, Bloomfield worked for the U.S. Department of Agriculture in Portland, Oregon. From 1946 until 1957, he was with the U.S. Department of State as a special assistant to the Assistant Secretary of State (1946-1956) and a special assistant on policy planning (1956-1957). Since 1957, he has been at Massachusetts Institute of Technology as associate professor (1959-1963) and professor (1963 to the present) of political science; a member of the senior staff of the Center for International Studies, an adjunct of the Central Intelligence Agency (1957 to the present); director of the United Nations Project (1957-1961); and director of the Arms Control Project (1961 to the present). He has lectured at the Foreign Service Institute, the several United States war colleges, and the several Canadian war colleges. He is a consultant to the U.S. Department of State and the U.S. Arms Control and Disarmament Agency.

Bloomfield is a member of the Council on Foreign Relations, the informal supra-State Department of the United States, and the World Affairs Council, a pivotal agency in a complex of one-world, leftist, and pacifist groups. He is associated with the Hudson Institute and the Institute for Defense Analyses, two think factories employed by the ruling Establishment. He was a member of a study group which produced a dovish report for the leftist-pacifist Carnegie Endowment for International Peace.

KERMIT BLOOMGARDEN was born on December 15, 1904 in Brooklyn, son of Annie Groden and Zemad Bloomgarden. He was married to the late Hattie Richardson. He was married to and divorced from Virginia Kaye. He is an alumnus of New York University (B.C.S., 1926).

From 1926 until 1932, Bloomgarden worked as a certified public accountant. In 1932, he began his lifelong career in the theatrical business. He has been a producer of many Broadway plays, and has received most of the outstanding theatrical awards.

Away from the theatrical business, Bloomgarden has engaged in leftwing activities. He was affiliated with the Independent Citizens Committee of the Arts, Sciences and Professions ("subversive"); the Artists' Front to Win the War ("Communist front"); the World Peace Council (leftist); and the Henry A. Wallace presidential campaign of 1948, a leftist project. He was a supporter of the ultra-leftist Hollywood Ten. In 1971, he was associated with the ultra-leftist National Peace Action Coalition.

DWIGHT L. BOLINGER was born on August 18, 1907 in Topeka, Kansas, son of Gertrude Ott and Arthur Bolinger. He married Louise Schrynemakers. He is an alumnus of Washburn College of Topeka (A.B., 1930); the University of Kansas (M.A., 1932); and the University of Wisconsin (Ph.D., 1936). He is the author of *Intensive Spanish* (1948); *Spanish Review Grammar* (1956); *Interrogative Structures of American English* (1957); *A Theory of Pitch Accent in English* (1958); *Forms of English: Accent, Morpheme, Order* (1965); and *Aspects of Language* (1968). He is co-author of *Modern Spanish* (1960 and 1966).

In 1936, Bolinger was a Spanish instructor at the University of Wisconsin. In 1937, he was a Spanish instructor at the Junior College of Kansas City in Missouri. From 1937 until 1944, he was an associate professor of Spanish at Washburn University. From 1944 until 1960, he was at the University of Southern California in Los Angeles as assistant professor (1944-1946), associate professor (1947-1948), and professor (1949-1960). From 1960 until 1963, he was a professor of Spanish at the University of Colorado. Since 1963, he has been a professor of Romance languages and literatures. He has held fellowships at Yale University and the Haskins Laboratories in New York City.

Bolinger has been affiliated with the ultra-leftist American Civil Liberties Union; the National Committee to Abolish the House Un-American Activities Committee ("to lead and direct the Communist Party's 'Operation Abolition' campaign"); the leftist-pacifist Ad Hoc Faculty Committee on Vietnam; and the ultra-leftist Medical Aid to [Castro's] Cuba Committee.

[EDMUND] BLAIR BOLLES was born on February 26, 1911 in St. Louis, Missouri, son of Zoe Blair and Stephen Bolles. He married Mona Dugas. He attended Yale University. He is the author of *Oil: An Economic Key to*

Peace (1944); *Congress and Foreign Policy* (1945); *Pillars of the United Nations – International Economic and Social Agencies* (1945); *Roosevelt's Foreign Policy* (1945); *World Nutrition and Agrarian Stability* (1946); *Influence of Armed Forces on U.S. Foreign Policy* (1946); *Reorganization of the State Department* (1947); *Who Makes Our Foreign Policy?* (1947 and 1951); *Bipartisanship in American Foreign Policy* (1948); *Military Establishment of the United States* (1949); *United States Military Policy* (1950); and *Switzerland: Oasis of Free Enterprise* (1950). He is co-author of *Arctic Diplomacy* (1948); *North Atlantic Defense Pact* (1949); and *The Armed Road to Peace: An Analysis of NATO* (1952). He is a contributor to *Empire's End in Southeast Asia* (1949); *Man and Food: The Lost Equation?* (1949); and *Scandinavia Today* (1951). (All of the above writings were published by the Foreign Policy Association. The FPA has had a long and consistent record of pro-Communism and anti-anti-Communism. It has been a center for pro-Soviet apologists and United Nations propagandists. The FPA's publications were among the most effective pro-Communist vehicles during the reign of Vera Micheles Dean, who from 1931 until 1938 was research associate and editor of the FPA's research publications, and from 1938 until 1961 was research director and editor of all the FPA's publications. Bolles was co-author, with Vera Micheles Dean, of *North Atlantic Defense Pact.*)

Bolles is also the author of *Tyrant from Illinois: Uncle Joe Cannon's Experiment with Personal Power* (1951); *How to Get Rich in Washington* (1952); *The Big Change in Europe* (1958); *Men of Good Intentions: Crisis of the American Presidency* (1960); and *Corruption in Washington* (1961). He has contributed political articles to magazines and newspapers including the *New York Times*, the *Toronto Star Weekly*, the *St. Louis Post-Dispatch*, the North American Newspaper Alliance, *Harper's* and *Reader's Digest.*

From 1930 until 1932, Bolles was a school teacher and advertising writer. In 1933, he was a reporter for the *Washington* [D.C.] *Sun* and the *Washington* [D.C.] *Herald.* In 1934, he was a rewrite man for the *New York American.* In 1934 and 1935, he was a congressional correspondent for Universal Service. From 1935 until 1944, he was a reporter and diplomatic correspondent for the *Washington* [D.C.] *Star.* From 1944 until 1953, he was with the Foreign Policy Association as director of the FPA's Washington bureau (1944-1951) and as the FPA's Washington correspondent (1951-1953). In 1952 and 1953, he was United States editor for *France Actuelle.* From 1953 until 1959, he was with the *Toledo Blade* as European correspondent (1953-1957) and associate editor (1957-1959). From 1959 until 1964, he was with Fairbanks, Morse, and Company as vice president for marketing and for government relations. Since 1964, he has been with Colt Industries as vice president for government affairs and for international affairs.

DOROTHY BORG was born on September 4, 1902 in Elberon, New Jersey, daughter of Madeleine Beer and Sidney Borg. She has been married and divorced. She is an alumna of Wellesley College (B.A., 1923) and Columbia University (M.A., 1931; Ph.D., 1946). She is the author of *American Policy and the Chinese Revolution, 1925-1928* (1947) and *The United States and the Far*

Eastern Crisis, 1933-1938 (1964). She is the compiler of *Historians and American Far Eastern Policy* (1966).

From 1938 until 1959, Miss Borg was a research associate on American-Chinese relations for the Institute of Pacific Relations. She contributed to the IPR's publications, *Far Eastern Survey* and *Pacific Affairs.* She also contributed to *Amerasia* ("a 'Communist-controlled' magazine which was 'so closely linked into the IPR system that the IPR family ordinarily treated it as simply another of their own publications' ").

In 1951 and 1952, the Senate Internal Security Subcommittee conducted an exhaustive investigation and held extensive hearings on the character of the Institute of Pacific Relations, its staff, and its members. The SISS concluded: "The Institute of Pacific Relations has not maintained the character of an objective, scholarly, and research organization. The IPR has been considered by the American Communist Party and by Soviet officials as an instrument of Communist policy, propaganda and military intelligence. The IPR disseminated and sought to popularize false information including information originating from Soviet and Communist sources.

"A small core of officials and staff members carried the main burden of IPR activities and directed its administration and policies. Members of the small core of officials and staff members who controlled IPR were either Communist or pro-Communist.

"There is no evidence that the large majority of its members supported the IPR for any reason except to advance the professed research and scholarly purposes of the organization. Most members of the IPR, and most members of its Board of Trustees, were inactive and obviously without any influence over the policies of the organization and the conduct of its affairs.

"IPR activities were made possible largely through the financial support of American industrialists, corporations, and foundations, the majority of whom were not familiar with the inner workings of the organization. The effective leadership of the IPR often sought to deceive IPR contributors and supporters as to the true character and activities of the organization. Neither the IPR nor any substantial body of those associated with it as executive officers, trustees or major financial contributors, has ever made any serious and objective investigation of the charges that the IPR was infiltrated by Communists and was used for pro-Communist and pro-Soviet purposes. The names of eminent individuals were by design used as a respectable and impressive screen for the activities of the IPR inner core, and as a defense when such activities came under scrutiny . . . .

"The effective leadership of the IPR used IPR prestige to promote the interests of the Soviet Union in the United States. A group of persons operating within and about the Institute of Pacific Relations exerted a substantial influence on United States far eastern policy. The IPR was a vehicle used by the Communists to orientate American far eastern policies toward Communist objectives . . . .

"A chief function of the IPR has been to influence United States public opinion . . . . The net effect of IPR activities on United States public opinion has been such as to serve international Communist interests and to affect adversely the interests of the United States."

On at least two occasions, Miss Borg's pro-Red Chinese writings were simultaneously released by the IPR and the Federated Press ("Certain Communist fronts are organized for the purpose of promulgating Communist ideas and misinformation into the bloodstream of public opinion. Examples of such organizations are the . . . Federated Press . . . .").

From 1959 until 1961, Miss Borg was a research associate at Harvard University's East Asian Research Center. Since 1962, she has been at Columbia University as a lecturer in the department of public law and government, a lecturer in American Far Eastern policy, and a senior research associate at Columbia's East Asian Institute.

FRANK H. BOWLES was born on November 20, 1907 in Taihoku, Japan, son of American citizens Sarah Siceloff and Frank Bowles. He married Frances Porcher. He is an alumnus of Columbia University (A.B., 1928; M.A., 1930). He also studied at Central College. He is the author of *How to Get Into College* (1958); *Access to Higher Education* (1963 and 1965); and *Re-founding of the College Board* (1968).

From 1934 until 1948, Bowles was director of admissions at Columbia University. From 1948 until 1963, he was president of the College Entrance Examination Board in New York. From 1960 until 1962, while on leave from the CEEB, he was director of the International Study of University Admissions, a project of the Communist-dominated UNESCO. Since 1963, he has been an executive in the socialist-internationalist Ford Foundation complex: director of the education program of the Ford Foundation (1963-1966); adviser to the president of the Ford Foundation in International Education (1966 to the present); vice-president of the Fund for Advancement in Education (1964-1967); president of the Fund for Advancement in Education (1967 to the present); and

president of the Fund for Adult Education (1965 to the present). He was on the leftist-oriented Fulbright National Selection Committee (1949-1951). He was a trustee of the leftist-internationalist Institute of International Education (1962-1963). He is a long-time member of the Council on Foreign Relations, the informal supra-State Department of the United States.

MALCOLM BOYD was born on June 8, 1923 in New York City, son of Beatrice Lowrie and Melville Boyd. He is an alumnus of the University of Arizona (B.A., 1944); the Church Divinity School of the Pacific (B.D., 1954); and Union Theological Seminary (S.T.M., 1956). He also studied at Oxford University in England. He is the author of *Crisis in Communication* (1957); *Christ and Celebrity Gods: The Church in Mass Culture* (1958); *Focus: Rethinking the Meaning of Our Evangelism* (1960); *If I Go Down to Hell* (1962); *The Hunger, The Thirst* (1964); *Are You Running With Me, Jesus?* (1965); *Free to Live, Free to Die* (1967); *Malcolm Boyd's Book of Days* (1968); and *As I Live and Breathe: Stages of an Autobiography* (1969). He has written plays, including *The Job, They Aren't Real to Me, Study in Color, Boy,* and *The Community* (1961-1965). He is editor of *On the Battle Lines* (1964) and *The Underground Church* (1968). He is a contributor to *Witness to a Generation* (1967).

In 1945 and 1946, Boyd was a copywriter for an advertising agency in Hollywood. In 1946, he produced and directed a homemakers' hour on radio in Hollywood. From 1947 until 1949, he was employed in various capacities by Republic Pictures and Sam Goldwyn Productions. From 1949 until 1951, he was vice-president and general manager of Pickford, Rogers and Boyd, Inc., an agency that packaged programs for radio and television. In 1951, he began his study for the Episcopal ministry. In 1955, he was ordained an Episcopal priest. In 1956, he studied at Union Theological Seminary under the leftist minister Reinhold Niebuhr. In 1957, he engaged in a worker-priest project at a monastic agricultural society near Cluny, France. From 1957 until 1959, he was rector of St. George's Episcopal Church in Indianapolis. From 1959 until 1961, he was the Episcopal chaplain at Colorado State University. At Colorado State, he began a career of avant-garde evangelism. He heard confessions and conducted informal seminars in coffee houses off campus. He became known as the "espresso priest" and was denounced by his bishop. In 1961, he resigned from Colorado State and became the Episcopal chaplain at Wayne State University, where he remained until 1964. While at Wayne State, he began a career as a civil rights agitator, and participated in various "freedom rides" and sit-in demonstrations. In this period, he wrote several short plays with a civil rights theme and attracted criticism from Michigan's Protestant Episcopal Bishop Richard S. Emrich, who said that since Boyd "preaches and practices high and sensitive standards in race relations, it astounds me that his standards in language are so low. Rejecting the sin that divides man from man, it is astonishing that he is willing to offend men by accepting the vulgarity and profanity of the avant-garde stage."

In 1964, Boyd resigned as chaplain of Wayne State and went to Washington, D.C., where he came under the jurisdiction of the sympathetic Episcopal suffragan bishop of Washington, Paul Moore Jr., a very active leftist. Bishop Moore assigned Boyd as assistant pastor of the Church of the Atonement, but Boyd immediately took a leave of absence to become an unofficial Episcopal "chaplain-at-large" to American college and university campuses. From 1965 until 1968, he was the national field representative for the leftist-oriented Episcopal Society for Cultural and Racial Unity. In 1968, he began a resident fellowship at Calhoun College of Yale University.

As an avant-garde evangelist, Boyd made two record albums ("Are You Running With Me, Jesus?" and "Happening, Prayer for Now") that consisted of Boyd reading prayers, accompanied by a guitarist. In 1966, he inaugurated a nightclub act. His first appearance was at the "hungry i" cabaret in San Francisco. He appeared nightly for a month at $1,000 a week, which he said was contributed to the civil rights cause. He read excerpts from his books, gave impromptu sermons, and answered questions for the audience. In 1967, he made a similar appearance at the Village Theatre in New York. In 1968, he made his acting debut in the hippie film, *You Are What You Eat.*

Since 1964, Boyd has been a contributing editor of *The Episcopalian.* Since 1963, he has reviewed motion pictures for *Christian Century.* Since 1965, he has been a correspondent for *Renewal* magazine. He has also contributed to *Encounter, Ave Maria, United Church Herald, Motive, Youth, Church and Race, Christianity and Crisis, Religion in Life, Theology Today,* and *Intercollegian.* Since 1955, he has lectured periodically for the leftist-oriented World Council of Churches. From 1962 until 1965, he was a columnist for the *Pittsburgh Courier.*

Boyd has been affiliated with the ultra-leftist Clergy and Laymen Concerned About Vietnam; the leftist-racist

Congress of Racial Equality; the ultra-radical Student Nonviolent Coordinating Committee; the leftist-oriented Episcopal Peace Fellowship; the National Association for the Advancement of Colored People, the fountainhead of Negro agitation for more than half a century; the ultra-leftist National Mobilization Committee to End the War in Vietnam; and the Hanoi-inspired People's Peace Treaty.

KAY BOYLE was born on February 19, 1903 in St. Paul, Minnesota, daughter of Katherine Evans and Howard Boyle. She was married to and divorced from Richard Brault and Laurence Vail. Her third husband was the late Baron Joseph von Franckenstein. She studied at the Cincinnati Conservatory of Music and the Ohio Mechanics' Institute. She is the author of *Wedding Day, and Other Stories* (1930); *Plagued by the Nightingale* (1931); *Year Before Last* (1932); *Gentlemen, I Address You Privately* (1933); *The First Lover, and Other Stories* (1933); *My Next Bride* (1934); *Death of a Man* (1936); *The White Horses of Vienna, and Other Stories* (1936); *Monday Night* (1938); *The Crazy Hunter* (1940); *Primer for Combat* (1942); *Avalanche* (1944); *A Frenchman Must Die* (1946); *Thirty Stories* (1946); *1939* (1948); *His Human Majesty* (1949); *The Smoking Mountain* (1951); *The Seagull on the Step* (1955); *Three Short Novels* (1958); *Generation Without Farewell* (1960); *Breaking the Silence* (1962); *Nothing Ever Breaks Except the Heart* (1966); *Pinky, The Cat Who Liked to Sleep* (1967); *The Autobiography of Emanuel Carnevali* (1967); *Being Geniuses Together* (1968); *Pinky in Persia* (1968); *The Long Walk at San Francisco State* (1970); and several volumes of poetry, including *Testament for*

My Students and Other Poems (1970). She has also contributed to *Harper's, Saturday Evening Post, American Mercury, Nation, New Yorker, Reader's Digest, Harper's Bazaar*, and the ultra-leftist *Liberation*.

From 1941 until 1943, Miss Boyle taught a night school course in writing in Nyack, New York. In 1944 and 1945, she was a secretary to a fashion writer and also worked on the staff of *Broom* magazine. From 1946 until 1953, she was a foreign correspondent for *New Yorker* magazine. Since 1963, she has been on the English faculty of San Francisco State College. In 1962, she was a member of the short story workshop at the radical New School for Social Research. In 1964, she directed a writers' conference at Wagner College. In 1943 and 1961, she was a Guggenheim fellow; in 1963, a fellow at Wesleyan University in Connecticut; and in 1965, a fellow at Radcliffe College's Institute for Independent Study.

Miss Boyle has been affiliated with the American Continental Congress for Peace ("another phase in the Communist 'peace' campaign, aimed at consolidating anti-American forces throughout the Western Hemisphere"); the National Committee to Abolish the House Un-American Activities Committee ("to lead and direct the Communist Party's 'Operation Abolition' campaign"); *New Masses* ("Communist periodical"); the World Peace Council (leftist); the American Committee for Protection of Foreign Born [Americans] ("subversive and Communist"); the Student Mobilization Committee to End the War in Vietnam (a peacenik group dominated by Communists and fellow travelers); the Soledad Brothers Defense Committee (ultra-leftist); the Joint Anti-Fascist Refugee Committee ("subversive and Communist"); the Committee for Nonviolent Action (leftist-pacifist); the Massachusetts Citizens Committee on Vietnam (leftist-pacifist); and the Women's International League for Peace and Freedom (leftist-pacifist).

ANNE BRADEN was born on July 28, 1924 in Louisville, Kentucky, daughter of Anita Crabbe and Gambrell McCarty. She married Carl Braden. She is an alumna of Randolph-Macon College (A.B., 1945). She is the author of *The Wall Between* (1958); *HUAC: Bulwark of Segregation* (1964); and *Southern Freedom Movement in Perspective* (1965).

From 1943 until 1946, Mrs. Braden was a reporter for the *Anniston* [Alabama] *Star.* In 1946 and 1947, she was a reporter for the *Birmingham* [Alabama] *News and Age Herald.* In 1947 and 1948, she was a reporter for the *Louisville Times.* In 1948 and 1949, she was news editor for *Labor's Voice* in Louisville. From 1952 until 1954, she was vice-president of Editors, Incorporated, of Louisville. Since 1957, she has been with the Southern Conference Educational Fund as field secretary (1957-1966), associate director (1966-1970), and executive director (1970 to the present). She has also been editor of the *Southern Patriot*, the publication of the Southern Conference Educational Fund. (In 1965, the Joint Legislative Committee on Un-American Activities in the State of Louisiana, after extensive hearings, concluded: "The evidence presented to the Committee in this hearing forcefully confirms the prior findings of the Committee that [the] Southern Conference Educational Fund is in fact a Communist Front organization and is a subversive organization because it is aiding and abetting the Communist Conspiracy. We do again so find at this time, the SCEF is being managed by some 14 or 15 people, at least 5 of whom have been previously identified as Communists. Through the operation of the SCEF, the leadership and influence of these Communists is transmitted to several other organizations. This is done under the guise and cover-story of integration of the races and 'civil rights.' These issues furnish the emotional appeal to blind the unwary idealists to the facts about SCEF. ... The planned program of the Communist Party to use the racial issue to further its goal of revolution in the United States has been carried out to a substantial degree. The SCEF has been an obvious and effective part of that program. The main function of the SCEF has been that of a 'transmission belt' between the active Communist Party, represented by the leaders of the SCEF, and the so-called 'civil rights movement.' Through the SCEF, various 'civil rights' organizations such as the Student Nonviolent Coordinating Committee and the National Association for the Advancement of Colored People have been substantially infiltrated and influenced by fellow-travelers and dupes of the Communist Party. This will be hotly denied, but the facts brought out in this hearing speak for themselves .... The 26-year history of open operations by the SCEF and its predecessor, the Southern Conference for Human Welfare, demonstrates the ineffectiveness of Federal legislation and enforcement in the control of Communist Fronts. It appears to the Committee that the subversive functions of a Communist Front should be treated as crime and regulated by the States the same as practically all other kinds of crime.")

Mrs. Braden, since 1955, has been a

member of the national council of the Emergency Civil Liberties Committee ("Communist front" – "subversive"). From 1950 until 1952, she was a national committeewoman of the Progressive Party, which had been a pawn of the Communists during the 1948 presidential campaign of Henry A. Wallace. She is a member of the ultra-radical National Association for the Advancement of Colored People and of the leftist-pacifist Women's International League for Peace and Freedom.

DAVID BRAYBROOKE was born on October 18, 1924 in Hackettstown, New Jersey, son of Netta Foyle and Walter Braybrooke. He married Alice Noble. He is an alumnus of Harvard University (B.A., 1948) and Cornell University (M.A., 1951; Ph.D., 1953). As an undergraduate, he also attended Hobart College. He pursued postgraduate and postdoctoral studies at Oxford University. He is the author of *Three Tests for Democracy* (1968). He is editor of *Philosophical Problems of the Social Sciences* (1965). He is a contributor to *The Public Interest* (1962) and *Politics and Social Life* (1963). His articles and reviews have appeared in *Analysis, Ethics, Journal of Philosophy, Philosophical Review*, and *Review of Metaphysics.*

From 1948 until 1950, Braybrooke was an instructor in history and literature at Hobart College. In 1953 and 1954, he was an instructor in philosophy at the University of Michigan. From 1954 until 1956, he was an instructor in philosophy at Bowdoin College. From 1956 until 1963, he was an assistant professor of philosophy at Yale University. Since 1963, he has been at Dalhousie University in Nova Scotia as associate professor of philosophy and politics (1963-1965) and professor

(1965 to the present). In 1957 and 1958, he was a research assistant for the leftist-oriented Social Science Research Council. In 1959 and 1960, he studied legal and political philosophy at Oxford University on a Rockefeller Foundation grant. From 1961 until 1963, he was a part-time dean of liberal arts at Bridgeport Engineering Institute. From 1961 until 1964, he was external examiner for Wesleyan University's College of Social Studies. In 1962 and 1963, he held a Guggenheim fellowship. In 1965 and 1966, he was a visiting professor at the University of Pittsburgh. In 1966 and 1967, he was a visiting professor at the University of Toronto.

Braybrooke is affiliated with the leftist-oriented American Association of University Professors. He is a long-time member of the ultra-leftist-pacifist National Committee for a Sane Nuclear Policy.

JOHN A. BROSS was born on January 17, 1911 in Chicago, son of Isabel Adams and Mason Bross. He was married to and divorced from Priscilla Prince. He is married to Joanne Bass. He is an alumnus of Harvard University (A.B., 1933; LL.B., 1936). In 1938, he was admitted to the New York bar.

From 1936 until 1942, from 1946 until 1949, and intermittently since 1949, Bross has practiced law in New York City; he has been associated with the firm of Parker & Duryee. From 1949 until 1951, he was assistant general counsel to the U.S. High Commissioner to Germany. From 1951 until 1957, and intermittently since 1960, he has been a consultant on foreign affairs to the Department of State. From 1957 until 1963, he was an advisor and coordinator to the U.S. embassy at Bonn, Germany. Since 1963, he has been deputy to the director of the Central Intelligence Agency for program evaluation.

Bross is a long-time nonresident member of the Council on Foreign Relations, the informal supra-State Department of the United States. He is a long-time member and has served as an official of the Foreign Policy Association, a bulwark of leftist internationalism.

SAMUEL W. BROWN JR. was born on July 27, 1943 in Council Bluffs, Iowa. He is an alumnus of the University of Redlands (A.B., 1965) and Rutgers University (M.A., 1966). He also studied at Harvard Divinity School. He has been a fellow at the John F. Kennedy Institute of Politics at Harvard University.

In his *The Making of a President: 1968,* Theodore H. White presents a poignant portrait of Sam Brown when Brown was a leader in Eugene McCarthy's presidential campaign: "It is well to linger over Sam Brown, whom I was later to see grow to full executive responsibility over the year. Curly-haired, slim, pale-cheeked, brown-eyed, soft and gentle of voice, he was armored with unshakable righteousness; and from thousands of similar young people of his goodwill and his unconscious arrogance, his purity of spirit and his remarkable ability, stems much of the perplexity of future American politics.

"Such young people as Sam Brown are throwbacks – they come of a strain of American life that goes back probably to the Abolitionists, explosive with morality. Born in Council Bluffs, Iowa, twenty-three years earlier, Sam came of what anyone in Council Bluffs would consider a 'best family.' His father is not only a good businessman, owner of a local shoe-store chain, but a music-lover, a member of local hospital boards, chair-

man of the school board, a Republican and a Rotarian; his mother is a preacher's daughter, active in the Methodist church. Sam had gone to Redlands University in Southern California, where first he was president of the Young Republicans, then president of the student body. His first reflex of rebellion had come when the university had banned Communist speakers from the campus and Sam, protesting the ban, was branded a Communist himself by the trustees. That summer – 1964 – Sam became involved in the National Students Association, thus meeting Al[lard] Lowenstein and becoming alert to politics. The summer of 1964 was also the summer of the student crusade in Mississippi and Sam felt the Democratic convention at Atlantic City that year sold out the students' cause by its compromise on seating the Mississippi Freedom Democratic Party.

"In the fall of 1965 Sam enrolled at Rutgers University to take a master's degree in political science, and fell under the influence of a luminous teacher, the late Paul Tillett, socialist, atheist, humanitarian. A dedicated student and dedicated teacher find magic in each other, and the two – Tillett and Brown – talked and talked. One night-long session, at three in the morning, both found themselves in tears. Tillett cried because, after his intense career in law and history, he had not yet found a way to help other people; how, how, how – that was the essential question – could one really help other people? Sam 'learned' that government really did not know how to help people. 'I had to go back and think. It made me think about how is it we go about helping people, and that drove me to divinity school.'

"Sam went on to Harvard Divinity School, and for a year and three months studied what they teach of the ways of God at divinity school; he turned in his draft card, sent back his deferment, refused to participate in the war of the United States; yet his local Council Bluffs draft board still refused to challenge him. Thus, he decided he must challenge the war outright, and the McCarthy movement was the way to challenge it. War was evil. The United States was an imperialist aggressor. One must follow conscience. Thus to his persuasion of [Blair] Clark that the students could be mobilized, and to his arrival in New Hampshire on February 12th as a theologian who had left divinity school to become the director of the student *putsch* in New Hampshire and, ultimately, an executive of prime promise. Sam abhorred violence, loved knowledge. But, he said in the Pleasant Street headquarters that morning, 'Study in universities is irrelevant. The war is on our minds. The rhetoric of the government is outmoded — the problem is how you affect government.' "

In 1969, Brown concentrated his energies upon anti-Vietnam War activities. He had participated in the Vietnam Summer, a 1967 anti-war protest run by the ultra-left, and he had indicated his own extreme position when he said: "Think of what we've grown up with. We've recognized the true nature of the United States. We saw the United States attack Cuba, it attacked the Dominican Republic, it attacked South Vietnam. The Communists are now a fragmented force; the United States is now the great imperialist-aggressor nation of the world." (On November 22, 1969, *Human Events* reported that Brown told New York City's Metromedia television commentator Dr. Martin Abend that he favors a Viet Cong victory.)

In 1969, Brown assumed direction of the Vietnam Moratorium Committee. Working hand in hand with just about every major leftist group, Brown produced a massive national protest against the war on October 15, 1969. He promoted later protests, but the first was the most successful. And in April 1970, Brown announced that the Vietnam Moratorium Committee had decided to disband.

Brown's decision to close down the Vietnam Moratorium Committee came less than two months after he had talked to the enemy of the United States, a disillusioning experience. He wrote of it in the *Washington Monthly* (August 1970): "When I visited the North Vietnamese and NLF representatives in Paris last February, they made it clear that they had never counted on the American left to end the war. Madame Nguyen Thi Binh, the foreign minister of the Provisional Revolutionary Government (of the NLF), remarked that she found student radicals very sectarian and reluctant to touch political power. She continued that the confused assortment of political objectives on the left — from legalizing marijuana to overthrowing the government to providing free abortions — dilutes the political impact of the peace movement. The result, she suggested, is that the Vietnamese people and American soldiers carry the burden of America's social problems. Insofar as unrelated issues are tied to the peace movement, weakening it, Vietnamese people and American soldiers die every day because the peace movement has exported the costs of America's social problems to Asia.

"I found these Vietnamese revolutionaries far more thoughtful than most young American revolutionaries. Their private conversation was radically different from their strident, ideological press releases, and they seemed to bear little malice toward the American people. They didn't express hatred for Middle America, or even for the soldiers in Vietnam. The negotiators seem to be tough-minded realists, who expect a long war and don't believe that America is anywhere near collapse. In short, these communist leaders are very connected to reality, where political self-delusion can cost people their lives."

In this same article, Brown admitted that the Vietnam Moratorium Committee had been embarrassed by the participation of the militant left in their demonstrations. He admitted that he did not know how to negotiate a friendly divorce from the militants. Whereas he had great praise for campus peaceniks, he was disappointed in congressional doves and other adults who were, in his opinion, out-maneuvered by the Nixon Administration. It was with great frustration that Brown closed down the Vietnam Moratorium Committee. He said: "In fact, most of us who have worked to end the war for some time believe that any semblance of a military victory in Vietnam would be disastrous for the United States. It would convince many Americans that the war was right and that it could be successfully repeated elsewhere. Also, a military triumph would go a long way toward replacing the Jeffersonian-revolutionary image of America as a place of hope with a Roman image of this country as a conquering empire."

In another part of his article, Brown seemed almost fearful that the Vietnam War would come to an end: "But the 'system' should not be applauded even if the war were to end tomorrow . . . . If the war is now ended by political action, as I believe it can be, some will undoubtedly argue that the system has

vindicated itself. That argument, however, is self-deceiving; for in many crucial respects our system has already failed and requires radical reconstruction."

Since 1970, Brown has lost some of his national impact. He has not, however, lost his anti-Vietnam War fervor. In one of his most widely circulated statements ("The Same Old Gang Turns Up in Washington," *Life*, January 29, 1971), he seemed to be settling for a third-party solution of the problems of the nation – a solution with heavy Marxian undertones. Wrote Brown: "The task ahead is to build a constituency among widely different groups of people with but one overlapping characteristic: the desire to redistribute power and wealth in society and the willingness to begin by refusing to endorse government by special interest.

"It will require giving up the current practice of letting political harangues substitute for honest exploration of the issues before us. It will require moving away from election-only politics toward full-time activism and organization. It will also require an abiding respect for the opinions of others (of students for workers, of whites for blacks, of young for old, and vice versa), not only because there are many cultural and organizational bridges to be built in forming the new coalition, but also because the proposed solutions seem so partial and the vision so incomplete.

"There is a great deal of tough intellectual homework to be done beyond these diagnostic feelings. But I do think the building of a new political coalition is the first step toward replacing ethnic arithmetic and government by vested interests with real political leadership in the public interest."

JANE J. BUCHENHOLZ was born on October 28, 1918 in New York City, daughter of Sofia Frucht and Joseph Jacobs. She was married to and divorced from Bruce Buchenholz. She is an alumna of Hunter College (A.B., 1942). She also studied at the radical New School for Social Research.

From 1942 until 1946, Mrs. Buchenholz was a teacher of mathematics, a control chemist, and a plant pathologist. From 1946 until 1949, she was a remedial reading teacher and a special teacher of emotionally disturbed children. From 1955 until 1961, she was a piano accompanist for modern dance classes. From 1962 until 1964, she was executive director for the Call for Action program on radio station WMCA. From 1966 until 1968, she was a special consultant for systems and inventory control for Bangor Punta Corporation. Since 1968, she has been director of development for the radical New School for Social Research.

Since 1961, Mrs. Buchenholz has been an activist in politics and leftwing organizations. From 1961 until the present, she has been with the ultra-radical Americans for Democratic Action as director of the National Roosevelt Day Dinner (1961-1966), national secretary of the ADA (1963-1967), and member of the ADA's national board (1963 to the present). In 1968, she was coordinator for Broadway for Peace, a leftist project. From 1966 until 1968, she was a member of the national board of the pacifist and ultra-leftist National Committee for a Sane Nuclear Policy. Since 1968, she has been a member of the national board of the National Emergency Civil Liberties Committee ("Communist front" – "subversive"). In 1966 and 1967, she was a member of the national advisory council of the National Conference for New Politics, a typical united-front third-party movement largely controlled by the Communist Party. In recent years, she has been a delegate to the leftist-oriented New Democratic Coalition of New York. Since 1966, she has been secretary-treasurer and a member of the foreign policy council of the New York Democrats. In 1968, she was an alternate delegate to the Democratic National Convention.

JUSTUS BUCHLER was born on March 27, 1914 in New York City, son of Ida Frost and Samuel Buchler. He married Evelyn Shirk. He is an alumnus of the City College of New York (B.S.S., 1934) and Columbia University (M.A., 1935; Ph.D., 1939). He is the author of *Charles Pierce's Empiricism* (1939); *Toward a General Theory of Human Judgment* (1951); *Nature and Judgment* (1955); *The Concept of Method* (1961); and *Metaphysics of Natural Complexes* (1966). He is co-author of *Philosophy: An Introduction* (1942); *Readings in Philosophy* (1946 and 1950); and *Studies in the Philosophy of Charles Sanders Peirce* (1952). He is a contributor to *The Philosophy of Bertrand Russell* (1944). He is the editor of *The Philosophy of Peirce* (1940 and 1946); *Introduction to Contemporary Civilization in the West* (1946); and *Chapters in Western Civilization* (1948).

From 1938 until 1943, Buchler was a philosophy instructor at Brooklyn College. Since 1937, he has been at Columbia University: philosophy instructor (1937-1947); assistant professor of philosophy (1947-1950); associate professor of philosophy (1950-1956); professor of philosophy (1956-1959); Johnsonian Professor (1959 to the present); chairman of the philosophy department (1964-1967); and chairman of the Contemporary Civilization program (1950-1956).

BURDEN

Buchler has been affiliated with the National Committee to Abolish the House Un-American Activities Committee ("to lead and direct the Communist Party's 'Operation Abolition' campaign"); the leftist-oriented American Association of University Professors; and the ultra-leftist American Civil Liberties Union, which he has served as vice-chairman of the ACLU's national academic freedom committee.

VERN L. BULLOUGH was born on July 24, 1928 in Salt Lake City, son of Augusta Rueckert and David Bullough. He married Bonnie Uckerman. He is an alumnus of the University of Utah (B.A., 1951) and the University of Chicago (M.A., 1951; Ph.D., 1954). He is the author of *History of Prostitution* (1964); *Development of Medicine as a Profession* (1966 and 1967); and *Causes of Scientific Revolution* (1968). He is co-author of *The Emergence of Modern Nursing* (1964) and *Issues in Nursing* (1966). He has contributed to *Isis, Speculum, The Humanist, The Journal of the History of Medicine, The Bulletin of the History of Medicine, The Journal of the History of Behavioral Sciences*, and such leftist-oriented publications as *Nation, The Progressive, New Leader*, and *The Journal of Conflict Resolution.*

From 1954 until 1959, Bullough was an assistant professor of history at Youngstown University in Ohio. Since 1959, he has been at San Fernando Valley State College in California as assistant professor of history (1959-1962), associate professor of history (1962-1965), and professor of history (1965 to the present). He has lectured at the University of California in Irvine and at the California College of Medicine in Los Angeles. He has held a Newberry fellowship and a Huntington Library fellowship. He has received research grants from the National Science Foundation, the American Philosophical Society, and the U.S. Office of Education. In 1966 and 1967, he was a Fulbright lecturer in the United Arab Republic.

Bullough has been affiliated with the National Committee to Abolish the House Un-American Activities Committee ("to lead and direct the Communist Party's 'Operation Abolition' campaign"); the leftist-pacifist Los Angeles Citizens for an Honorable Nonviolent U.S. Vietnam Policy; the Inter-University Committee for Debate on Foreign Policy, which initiated the teach-ins that have plagued university and college campuses with pro-Communist, anti-American agitation against the Vietnam War; and the leftist-oriented American Association of University Professors.

WILLIAM A.M. BURDEN was born on April 8, 1906 in New York City, son of Florence Twombly and William Burden. He married Margaret Partridge. He is an alumnus of Harvard University (A.B., 1927). He is the author of *The Struggle for Airways in Latin America* (1943).

From 1928 until 1932, Burden was an analyst of aviation securities for Brown Brothers, Harriman & Co. From 1932 until 1939, he was in charge of aviation research for Scudder, Stevens & Clark From 1939 until 1941, he was vice-president of the National Aviation Corporation, an investment trust. In 1941 and 1942, he was vice-president of Defense Supplies Corporation, a subsidiary of the Reconstruction Finance Corporation. In 1942 and 1943, he was a special aviation assistant to Secretary of Commerce Jesse Jones. From 1943 until 1947, he was Assistant Secretary of Commerce for Air. From 1947 until 1949, he was an aviation

259

consultant to Smith Barney & Co. Since 1949, he has been a partner in William A.M. Burden & Co. From 1950 until 1952, he was a special assistant for research and development to Secretary of the Air Force Thomas K. Finletter. From 1959 until 1961, he was U.S. Ambassador to Belgium. He is a director of the Allied Chemical Corporation, the Columbia Broadcasting System, Lockheed Aircraft Corporation, and the American Metal Climax.

Burden has been affiliated with such internationalist and leftist-oriented organizations as the Atlantic Council of the United States, the Atlantic Institute, the U.S. Citizens Commission on NATO, and the School of Advanced International Studies of The Johns Hopkins University. He has been chairman of the board for the Institute for Defense Analyses, a "think factory" associated with the ruling Establishment. He is a long-time active member of the Council on Foreign Relations, the informal supra-State Department of the United States. In years past, he was associated with the Institute of Pacific Relations (an "instrument of Communist policy, propaganda, and military intelligence").

W. RANDOLPH BURGESS was born on May 7, 1889 in Newport, Rhode Island, son of Ellen Wilbur and Isaac Burgess. He was married to the late May Ayres. He is now married to Helen Woods. He is an alumnus of Brown University (A.B. and A.M., 1912) and Columbia University (Ph.D., 1920). He also studied at McGill University. He is the author of *Trends of School Costs* (1920) and *The Reserve Banks and the Money Market* (1927, 1936 and 1946). He is the editor of *Interpretations of Federal Reserve Policy* (1930).

In 1919 and 1920, Burgess was a statistician with the Russell Sage Foundation. From 1920 until 1938, he was with the Federal Reserve Bank of New York as chief of the reports division (1920-1923), assistant federal reserve agent (1923-1930), deputy governor (1930-1935), and vice-president (1935-1938). From 1938 until 1953, he was with the National City Bank as vice-chairman (1938-1948) and chairman of the executive committee (1948-1953). From 1948 until 1953, he was chairman of the board of the City Bank & Farmers Trust Company. From 1953 until 1957, he was with the U.S. Department of the Treasury as deputy to the Secretary of the Treasury (1953-1954) and Under Secretary of the Treasury (1954-1957). From 1957 until 1961, he was U.S. Ambassador to NATO and the Organization for Economic Cooperation and Development. In 1962 and 1963, he was regents' professor of economics at the University of California at Berkeley. Since 1967, Burgess has been chairman of the executive committee of the leftist-internationalist Atlantic Council of the United States. He was a trustee of the leftist-pacifist Carnegie Corporation (1940-1957). Recently, he has been affiliated with the leftist Republicans for Progress.

WILLIAM F. BUTLER was born on December 17, 1917 in Arcade, New York, son of Beulah Yule and Howard Butler. He married Jane Kohl. He is an alumnus of Cornell University (B.A., 1937) and the University of Virginia (Ph.D., 1942).

From 1940 until 1942, Butler was an economics instructor at the University of Virginia. From 1942 until 1945, he was principal economist with the War Production Board. From 1945 until 1951, he was a senior economist with McGraw-

Hill Publishing Company. Since 1951, he has been with the Chase Manhattan Bank of New York City as a consultant and economist (1951-1956), vice-president (1956 to the present), director of economic research (1962 to the present), and chief economist (1969 to the present).

Butler is a long-time member of the Council on Foreign Relations, the informal supra-State Department of the United States. He is a long-time member of the ultra-radical American Civil Liberties Union.

NINA BYERS was born on January 19, 1930 in Los Angeles, daughter of Eva Gertzoff and I.M. Byers. She is an alumna of the University of California at Berkeley (B.A., 1950) and the University of Chicago (M.S., 1953; Ph.D., 1956).

From 1956 until 1958, Miss Byers was a research fellow at the University of Birmingham in England. From 1958 until 1961, she was at Stanford University as research associate (1958-1959) and assistant professor (1959-1961). Since 1961, she has been at the University of California at Los Angeles as assistant professor of physics (1961-1962), associate professor (1962-1967), and professor (since 1967). In 1964 and 1965, she was a visiting member of the School of Mathematics in the Institute for Advanced Study at Princeton, New Jersey. In 1967 and 1968, she was a fellow of Somerville College and a faculty lecturer at Oxford University in England. In 1964 and 1965, she was a Guggenheim fellow. From 1969 until 1971, she was a Janet Watson visiting fellow.

Miss Byers has been affiliated with the leftist-oriented American Association of Univeristy Professors; the ultra-leftist American Civil Liberties Union; the National Committee to Abolish the House Un-American Activities Committee ("to lead and direct the Communist Party's 'Operation Abolition' campaign"); and the Federation of American Scientists, a group of bleeding-heart leftwing pacifists.

JOHN M. CAMMETT was born on July 8, 1927 in Minneapolis. He is married. He is an alumnus of Wayne State University (B.A., 1949) and Columbia University (Ph.D., 1959). In 1950 and 1951, he was a Fulbright scholar in Italy. In 1956, he held a fellowship from the Italian Government. He is the author of *Antonia Gramsei and the Origins of Italian Communism* (1967). He is contributor to *Bibliography of Soviet Foreign Affairs and World Communism* (1964). He has written articles for *Science and Society* ("a Communist publication").

In 1952, 1953, and 1955, Cammett was an instructor in history at Wayne State University. From 1957 until 1959, he was an instructor in contemporary civilization at Middlebury College. In 1959 and 1960, he was an instructor in history at Columbia University. From 1960 until 1962, he was an instructor in history at Hunter College. From 1962 until 1967, he was an assistant professor of history at Rutgers University. Since 1967, he has been an associate professor of history at the John Jay College of Criminal Justice at the City University of New York.

Cammett is a Socialist. In 1967 and 1968, he was president of the Socialist Scholars Conference, an annual get-together of Marxian Socialists and their fellow-travelers.

JOHN COERT CAMPBELL was born on October 8, 1911 in New York City, son of Gertrude DuBois and Allan Campbell. He married Mary Hillis. He is an alumnus of Harvard University (A.B., 1933; M.A., 1936; Ph.D., 1940). He is the author of *The United States in World Affairs: 1945-1947* (1947): *The United States in World Affairs: 1947-1948* (1948), *The United States in World Affairs: 1948-1949* (1949); *Defense of The Middle East: Problems of American Policy* (1958 and 1960); *American Policy Toward Communist Eastern Europe: The Choices Ahead* (1965); and *Tito's Separate Road: America and Yugoslavia in World Politics* (1967).

In 1940 and 1941, Campbell was an instructor at the University of Louisville. In 1941 and 1942, he was a Rockefeller fellow at the Council on Foreign Relations. From 1942 until 1955, he was with the Department of State: specialist on Eastern Europe (1942-1946); secretary of the U.S. delegation and political adviser to the Council of Foreign Ministers and to the Paris Peace Conference (1946); political adviser to the U.S. delegation at the Danube Conference (1948); and member of the policy planning staff and officer-in-charge of Balkan Affairs (1949-1955). In the meantime, he held his second Rockefeller fellowship at the Council on Foreign Relations (1946-1949). Since 1955, he has been a senior research fellow and the director of political studies in the Council on Foreign Relations, the informal supra-State Department of the United States.

ARLENE D. CARSTEN was born on December 5, 1937 in Paterson, New Jersey, daughter of Ann Greutert and Albert Desmet. She married Alfred Carsten. She studied at Alfred University. By profession, Mrs. Carsten is a piano teacher.

In recent years, Mrs. Carsten has been active in politics: vice-president and treasurer of the San Diego Democratic Club (1965-1969); district representative to the leftist-oriented California Democratic Council (1967-1969); chairman of the San Diego write-in campaign for Eugene McCarthy (1968); member of the San Diego McCarthy-for-President Campaign Committee (1968); and member of the California Democratic State Committee (1968 to the present).

Mrs. Carsten is a member of the ultra-leftist American Civil Liberties Union; the leftwing-pacifist Women's International League for Peace and Freedom; and the leftist-oriented Ad Hoc Citizens Committee Against the War in Vietnam.

MARK A. CHAMBERLIN is a Methodist minister in Gresham, Oregon. For the past twenty-five years, he has been in the forefront of leftist American clergymen. He has been a long-time secretary of the Oregon chapter of the Methodist Federation for Social Action. (On July 7, 1953, Benjamin Gitlow — a founder and former general secretary of the Communist Party in the United States — testified before the House Committee on Un-American Activities and said: "The Methodist Federation for Social Action is a membership organization made up entirely of Methodists. It does not affiliate other organizations with it. The Communist Party is not included as an affiliate. The organization is a Communist Party instrument controlled by the Communist Party through the Communist cell secretly operating as a Communist Party disciplined unit in the Federation.")

In the November 27, 1965 issue of the Communist Party's *People's World*, there was a letter from Chamberlin, written in his capacity as Oregon secretary of the MFSA. He expressed his thanks to *People's World* for "past courtesies" and for placing the MESA's *Social Questions Bulletin* on the *People's World* exchange list. He described *People's World* as "an invaluable source of information, a part of the national news media which has not succumbed to the Establishment. The fight to keep alive has been tremendous, I know. All honor to those who have had a part in the struggle and for those who continue to carry the torch."

Chamberlin has been affiliated with the Emergency Civil Liberties Committee ("Communist front"); the Conference for Peaceful Alternatives to the Atlantic Pact ("Communist front"); the Cultural and Scientific Conference for World Peace ("a propaganda front for Soviet foreign policy and Soviet culture"); the American Committee for Protection of Foreign Born [Americans] ("one of the oldest auxiliaries of the Communist Party in the United States"); the Committee to End Sedition Laws ("complete domination by the Communist Party"); the ultra-leftist Hiroshima Commemorative Committee; the International Workers Order ("subversive and Communist"); the Jefferson School of Social Science ("adjunct of the Communist Party"); the Mid-Century Conference for Peace ("aimed at assembling as many gullible persons as possible under Communist direction and turning them into a vast sounding board for Communist propaganda"); the National Committee to Repeal the McCarran Act ("Communist front" – "subversive"); the National Committee to Win Amnesty for Smith Act Victims ("subversive" – "Communist Party project"); the National Council of the Arts, Sciences and Professions ("Communist front"); the Religious Freedom Committee (to abol-

ish the House Committee on Un-American Activities); the ultra-leftist American-Korean Friendship and Information Center; the Citizens Committee for Constitutional Liberties ("created, dominated, and controlled by members and officials of the Communist Party"); the National Assembly for Democratic Rights ("created, dominated, and controlled by members and officials of the Communist Party"); the World Peace Congress ("organized under Communist initiative in various countries throughout the world as part of a campaign against the North Atlantic Defense Pact"); and the [California] Constitutional Liberties Information Center ("Communist front").

Chamberlin has signed petitions, *amicus curiae* briefs, and open letters on behalf of the Communist Party and individual Communists who have been convicted under the Smith Act. He has been an apologist for the Soviet Union and its leaders.

CESAR CHAVEZ was born on July 31, 1927 in Yuma, Arizona. He married Helen Fabula.

The history of Chavez prior to 1950 has been lost in a welter of confusion. It is known that for a brief time in 1944 and 1945 he served in the U.S. Navy. He has claimed experience as a farm laborer, but there is no evidence that such work occupied very much of his time.

In 1950 or 1952 (the exact date is unimportant), Chavez became associated with Saul Alinsky and his Industrial Areas Foundation. (Alinsky is a Marxist-Leninist revolutionary and a professional agitator. In the guise of a civil rights worker, he has disrupted communities throughout the United States with the support of dupes who have included clergy of all faiths, labor officials, academicians, and officials of foundations.) Chavez has recalled his introduction to the Alinsky organization in an article he wrote for the July 1966 issue of *Ramparts* magazine: "It really started for me 16 years ago (*c.* 1950) in San Jose, California, when I was working on an apricot farm. We figured he [Fred Ross] was just another social worker ... and I kept refusing to meet with him. But he was persistent. Finally I got together some of the rough element in San Jose. We were going to teach the *gringo* a little bit of how we felt. There were 30 of us in the house, young guys mostly. I was supposed to give them a signal ... and then we were going to give him a lot of hell. But he started talking, and the more he talked the more wide eyed I became and the less inclined to give the signal. This fellow was making a lot of sense and I wanted to hear what he had to say .... His name was Fred Ross and he was an organizer for the Community Service Organization (CSO) which was working with Mexican Americans in the cities. I became immediately involved ...."

For more than ten years, Chavez worked with the Community Service Organization. He was trained in Chicago at the Industrial Areas Foundation, became a field worker, and eventually a director in Los Angeles. In 1962, he resigned from the CSO. He has explained that his resignation came because the CSO rejected his proposal that the organization should create a farm workers union. A short time after he left the CSO, he organized the National Farm Workers Association with headquarters in Delano, California. (Delano, in the San Joaquin Valley, is in the center of California's grape industry. It was one of the most prosperous farm communities in the United States for farmers and

farm workers. Most of the farm workers lived year-round in the Delano area, and very few migrant workers were employed in the local vineyards.)

In November 1963, Chavez filed the Constitution of the National Farm Workers Assocation with the California Division of Corporations. At about the same time, he obtained a license from the Division of Corporations for a Farm Workers Credit Union. In the same period, he founded a bi-weekly newspaper, *El Malcriado,* which had a very small paid circulation, but a distribution of about 10,000 copies of each issue.

In February 1962, Al Green, an organizer for the AFL-CIO in the San Joaquin Valley, re-activated the dormant Agricultural Workers Organizing Committee. In 1965, the AWOC called a strike of its workers in the Delano area. Chavez and his NFWA joined in the strike. At the time, Chavez claimed that he had 17,000 members of the NFWA working in the grape fields. Somehow, he never registered more than 2,500 such workers with the California authorities, and in truth, his membership was only a handful. However, in his first strike, Chavez was able to provide pickets who made his demonstration at least appear to be a legitimate strike. The pickets were recruited from outside of Delano. They represented a number of ultra-leftist groups, including the Congress of Racial Equality, the Student Nonviolent Coordinating Committee, the Students for a Democratic Society, the DuBois Clubs, and the Free Speech Movement of the Berkeley campus. Although hundreds of pickets were in evidence, fewer than sixty grape workers were on strike at the time.

Less than three weeks after Chavez joined the strike, the Office of Economic Opportunity announced that a grant of

$267,887 had been made to Chavez' NFWA. On December 16, 1965, Walter Reuther of the United Auto Workers Union visited Delano and pledged $5,000 a month to the NFWA for as long as it might take to win the strike. Reuther participated in a parade with Chavez and photographs of the two men appeared in newspapers and magazines throughout the country. By the end of 1965, Chavez was receiving support from a multitude of organizations, including the International Longshoremen's and Warehousemen's Union, the American Friends Service Committee, various locals of the American Federation of Teachers, the American Civil Liberties Union, Americans for Democratic Action, the California Democratic Council, the Vietnam Day Committee, and a wide variety of small civil rights, political, labor, and religious groups.

Within a year or two from the time he called his first strike, Chavez managed to recruit support from across the entire spectrum of the left. He was joined by United States Senators Robert F. Kennedy, Edward M. Kennedy, Harrison Williams, Eugene McCarthy, Ralph Yarborough, and Walter Mondale; Mayors John Lindsay of New York City, Kevin White of Boston, Jerome Cavanagh of Detroit, Richard Daley of Chicago, and Carl Stokes of Cleveland; Roman Catholic Bishops Aloysius J. Willinger, Walter J. Schoenherr, Floyd Begin, Hugh Donahue, Joseph F. Donnelly, and Timothy Manning; the Catholic Bishops Conference of California; Roman Catholic priests Eugene Boyle, James Vizzard, Mark Day, George G. Higgins, and Roger Mahoney; Secretary of Labor Willard Wirtz; Harry Bridges, head of the International Longshoremen's and Warehousemen's Union; black agitators Martin L. King Jr., Ralph Abernathy, H. Rap

Brown, Whitney Young, and Stokely Carmichael; George Meany of the AFL-CIO; the Black Panthers; the Progressive Labor Party; the National Catholic Welfare Conference; Paul Hall, head of the Seafarers Union; Harry Van Arsdale, head of the New York City Central Labor Council; Gloria Steinem; actors Steve Allen and Rafer Johnson; Johnny Carson; Ethel Kennedy; the Brown Berets; newsmen Jimmy Breslin and James Wechsler; radical-chic personalities such as Heidi Vanderbilt, Charlotte Ford Niarchos, Anita Colby, Huntington Hartford, Mark Goodson, and Abe Schrade; U.S. Representative Phillip Burton; Averell Harriman; the National Catholic Welfare Conference; the Episcopal Migrant Ministry; various officials of the Teamsters Union; Vice President Hubert H. Humphrey; the Columbia Broadcasting System; and publications, including the *San Francisco Chronicle,* the *Washington Post,* the *New York Times,* the *Los Angeles Times, Newsweek, Saturday Review, Cleveland Plain Dealer, Time,* the Communist press, the *New York Review of Books,* and *New Republic.*

In 1967, the California Senate Fact-finding Subcommittee on Un-American Activities reported: "At this juncture, the evidence shows that the Delano grape strike was of exceptional interest to the Communist Party and the leftists who supported it. We have not said that the strike was directed by Communists, but it was turned into a civil rights 'movement' and operated as a cause, not a labor dispute. This view is amply supported by the activity of known members of the Communist Party who were on the scene and aiding the strike almost from its inception; by the favorable accounts that consistently appeared in the Communist press; by the participation in strike demonstrations of such organizations as the DuBois Clubs of America; Students for a Democratic Society; Progressive Labor Party; Vietnam Day Committee; Trotskyite groups and other organizations moved by similar objectives; by the reports of all law enforcement agencies connected with the subject."

The same Subcommittee also reported on some of the publications which lent their support to Chavez: "The publication *Spartacist West* was much concerned with the Delano grape strike. It is the organ of the East Bay Spartacist Committee, which is the West Coast branch of the Spartacist League. The League's publication, *Spartacist*, declares on its masthead that the organization is comprised of ' . . . supporters of the Revolutionary Tendency, expelled from the Socialist Workers Party.' This would place it at the very extreme of the radical Communist movement. The followers of Leon Trotsky formed the Socialist Workers Party, which we have discussed in previous reports. Briefly, these members split away from the old Communist Party that remained loyal to Stalin after Trotsky was expelled from that party and from the Soviet Union. It remained hard-core militant, never relenting from the theory of permanent world revolution, as opposed to Stalin's concept of first building up a powerful organization in Russia. A more militant stand is difficult to conceive.

"[The *Militant*] . . . is the official organ of the 'orthodox' Trotskyist group, the Socialist Workers Party. It is published at 873 Broadway, New York. Joseph Hansen is the editor and Mrs. Karolyn Kerry is business manager. She and her husband, Tom Kerry, were once active in California. Hal Verb, who was listed in the AWOC guest register for November 6, 1965, is a contributor. The issue of November 22, 1965, carried his story, 'California Grape Pickers Strike,' and was datelined 'Delano, November 6.'

"The *Catholic Worker*, 175 Chrystie Street, New York, organ of the Catholic Worker Movement and edited by Dorothy Day, carried several articles on the Delano grape strike, one in the December 1966 issue by Bill Esher, strike activist and propagandist to whom we have already referred. His article, 'New Front in Delano,' gave much credit to Dolores Huerta, second in command of NFWA, mother of seven, lobbyist, strike leader and intellectual. Dorothy Day, one-time friend of the chairman of the Communist Party, U.S.A., the late Elizabeth Gurley Flynn, has followed the Marxist line meticulously in this supposedly religious publication. About the only thing Catholic about it is the name. Miss Day has been an outspoken supporter of Fidel Castro, and connected with numerous Communist fronts and causes. The strongest link between the Delano strike and the *Catholic Worker* and the Catholic Worker Movement is through Mrs. Dorothy Kauffman, who supports both. She is a member of the Citizens for Farm Labor Advisory Board, and was at AWOC headquarters on December 11, 1965.

"[*Insurgent*] . . . is the organ of the W.E.B. DuBois Clubs of America, which was published in the Chicago headquarters of the clubs. It was by no means laggard in printing a story favorable to the grape strike. The January-February, 1966, issue carried an article, 'Delano: The General Strike in the Grapes,' by Al Howard, with photographs by Howard Harawitz. The article stated that the Welfare Rights Organization had sent people to Delano to 'teach local residents their rights under welfare laws.' One of these 'people' was the photographer, Howard Harawitz, whose wife, Elly, was principal founder of the Welfare Rights Organization.

"The May-June 1966 issue of *Insurgent* ran an entire section on the Delano strike, the first, pages 16 and 17, on the pilgrimage, and another, pages 18 and 19, on 'Profile of a Striker.' We quote from the first article, 'Delano: Bread and Justice': 'The strikers in the vineyards of Delano are writing a chapter in the second American Revolution, that revolution which will achieve true democracy for all our people . . . .' And later: 'The strikers called the march a Pilgrimage of Penance, a witness to the past sufferings of the Mexican-American workers and to the sufferings to come in the long fight for justice in the valley . . . .' It also quotes the Plan of Delano, and it rings in a number of '*Vivas*,' concluding with '*Viva Cesar Chavez!*'

"*[Spark-Chispa]* . . . is the West Coast organ of the Progressive Labor Party, the pro-Maoist Communist group that split away from the CPUSA during the Sino-Soviet split. As stated in our 1965 report: 'It is already apparent that the new Progressive Labor Party is not only the most militant and aggressive Communist organization in this country, but that it is drawing younger members of the old CPUSA out of the ranks and attracting large numbers of radical youth from all parts of the country . . . .' The presence of this organization among the supporters of the Delano strike is perhaps even more ominous than the presence of the 'orthodox' Communists. In the October 1965 issue of this publication is a front-page headlined article, 'Guerrilla War in Fields – Farm Workers Strike for Union, Wages,' by Luis Valdez, whom we mentioned earlier as head of the Farm Workers Theater. It

tells the story from the viewpoint of the militant left, analyzing the beginnings of the strike . . . . The issue for January-February 1967 carries an article on current boycott actions by the union. Editors listed in this number are: Chris Raisner for *Spark*; Santiago Coronel for *Chispa*; Margaret Driggs, circulation, and Claude Beagerie, photography. Mrs. Driggs had formerly been listed on the masthead of the *National Guardian*, and left it for the more militant publication of the Maoist-oriented Progressive Labor Party.

". . . An entire section, pages 37-50, entitled '*Huelga!* Tales of the Delano Revolution,' ran . . . [in the July 1966 issue of *Ramparts*]. The first article was written by Paul Jacobs, and praised Chavez highly; the next, pages 40-43, is by Luis Valdez, whom we met as author of an article in the Progressive Labor Party publication. His article is entitled, 'The Tale of the *Raza*,' and explains that *raza* means race. 'The race is the Mexican people,' and goes on to say that he is a Mexican. He states that Cesar Chavez 'is our first *Mexican-American* leader,' as opposed to Mexican leaders such as Benito Juarez and leaders of the 1910 Revolution . . . . He says about the march to Sacramento (p. 42): 'Our pilgrimage is the match that will light our cause for all farmworkers to see what is happening here, so that they may do as we have done. *Viva la causa! Viva la huelga!*'

"Valdez continues in a vein uncomplimentary to Delano: '. . . After years of isolation in the *barrios* (outlying towns) of Great Valley slum towns like Delano . . . the Mexican-American farmworker is developing his own ideas about living in the United States . . . ' And he concludes: 'Listen to these people, and you will hear the first murmerings of revolution.'... It is impossible to discuss here in any detail the expensively produced 'slick' monthly magazine, *Ramparts,* published in San Francisco. The editor and publisher is Warren Hinkle III, and the managing editor is Robert Scheer. Among the contributing editors are Paul Krassner, editor of *The Realist*; Jessica Mitford, wife of attorney Robert Treuhaft and an identified Communist."

Chavez attracted a great deal of financial support. The Roger Baldwin Memorial Foundation of the American Civil Liberties Union gave Chavez $85,000 in tax-free funds. In 1966, the Office of Economic Opportunity granted $1,276,000 to establish California Rural Legal Assistance, of whose board of directors Chavez was the most important member. The AFL-CIO gave Chavez $10,000-a-month and the United Auto Workers increased their support from $5,000-a-month to $7,500-a-month. The tax-free Rosenberg Foundation gave Chavez support when he first began his organizing activities.

Six months after he began his strike against the grape growers, Chavez demonstrated his talent for attracting nation-wide publicity. This occurred during what became known as the "long march." California's Factfinding Subcommittee reported on the event: "Cesar Chavez has proven himself to be a showman *par excellence* on numerous occasions, but perhaps his greatest production was the Lenten Pilgrimage from Delano to Sacramento which began on St. Patrick's Day, 1966, and ended in a fiesta on Easter Sunday (April 10) at the State Capitol. This affair was replete with pageantry – ragged, barefoot farmworkers, some with small children; black-garbed Catholic priests and nuns; socially aroused Protestant ministers;

arrays of brightly colored banners, together with crude, hand-lettered signs, and other lesser banners floated over the heads of the hundred or more marchers.

"There was a colorful and well-publicized fiesta at every stop; Mexican Americans in the 25 towns along the way where stops were made had been alerted by advance agents of the march to 'make copy.' Terry Cannon, field secretary for the Student Nonviolent Coordinating Committee (SNCC) and editor of its West Coast newspaper *The Movement*, acted as press secretary.

"The pilgrimage, which attempted to present a different face to each of the widely divergent groups it sought to exploit, apparently omitted one for unionism. Ben Gines, who at the time of the march was the vice president of AWOC, said in a sworn statement to our committee that both he and the AFL-CIO organizer, Al Green, disapproved of an amalgamation of unionism and the civil rights movement. 'I believe in civil rights,' Gines said, 'but in the right place.'

"Cannon proved himself to be a capable press agent *par excellence*. Also, the pilgrimage of poor Mexican-American farmworkers seeking 'bread and dignity,' to quote Sam Kushner, the high-ranking Communist Party functionary who wrote feature articles for the *People's World*, made excellent copy for newspapers and provided colorful pictures for TV. To use a publicist's phraseology, the pilgrimage made every issue of the metropolitan daily newspapers of California during the entire 25-day period, to say nothing of national weekly news magazines, national TV networks, wire services and special correspondent reports in out-of-state newspapers. *Time* (March 18, 1966, pp. 28, 29) predicted great things for Cesar

268

Chavez; overnight he became a national figure.

"By this time Schenley [a grape grower] had capitulated, and the second largest grower, DiGiorgio, had offered the NFWA a contract with a no-strike clause to cover the peak of the grape-picking season. This Chavez dramatically spurned, and announced that the boycott of DiGiorgio products, already begun on a nationwide basis by civil rights groups, would continue until he obtained the settlement he wanted.

"No opportunity was overlooked, insofar as we can see, to attract the press. There was a pretty nurse along to minister to those who faltered along the way and to bind sore and bleeding feet at each night's caravansary. She was, incidentally, Peggy McGivern, who had walked on the Delano picket lines. On Good Friday the Stations of the Cross were set up along the way so devout marchers might follow church ritual without leaving the pilgrimage.

"Entertainment and refreshments were provided. Skits, dances, songs and guitar music designed to plead the case of the marchers were provided along the way by the recently established *El Teatro Campesino*, or Farm Workers' Theater. This small group of versatile, Spanish-speaking actors and musicians had been trained by Luis Valdez, former drama student at San Jose State College who had been with the Mime Troupe of San Francisco for several months. Before joining the Mime Troupe, Valdez accompanied a group of students, mostly members of the Maoist Progressive Labor Party, to Cuba in the summer of 1964, where they remained for about a month as guests of the Castro government. Valdez returned with lavish praise for the Communist regime.

"Governor [Edmund "Pat"] Brown chose to spend Easter Sunday at Palm Springs with his family instead of remaining at the Capitol to meet the marchers, which provoked considerable anger and resentment to those who were emotionally identified with the Chavez cause. Citizens for Facts from Delano, an organization opposing the strike, collected and published on a clipsheet a number of articles dealing with criticism of the priests and ministers in the march on Sacramento. Bakersfield rabbis opposed mixing religion with strike politics, and a Delano Baptist minister at Delano spoke out against professional agitators.

"The involvement of the migrant ministry in the Delano grape strike was excoriated in a letter to Bishop Donald H. Tippett, resident bishop of the northern California area of the Methodist Church, from the board of the Exeter Methodist Church in Tulare County. In Santa Monica, ministers and laymen of the Los Angeles Presbytery voted 143-122 against supporting the grape strike, a resolution which had been introduced by Rev. Wayne C. Hartmire, one of the grape strike leaders.

"The above is but a small segment of the tide of protest against the Chavez pageant and the involvement of the men of the cloth. We have included it here to indicate that Chavez and his dwindling number of pilgrimage marchers had not totally swept the state into their camp. The march, however, received an enormous amount of publicity. The commercial communiations media, which boast of their objectivity and ability to handle complicated subjects in depth, were notoriously shallow and uncritical and seemed unprecedentedly willing to substitute verbiage for perception. And, of course, the march had the all-out support of the Communist press, through

CHAVEZ

the *People's World* and other media they could reach. The widespread publicity given the pilgrimage was by no means a 'Communist plot,' though the Communists — as attested to by the coverage given it in not only the *People's World,* but also in the pro-Communist publication *National Guardian* — contributed in no small degree.

"Leaders from the Teamsters Union were on hand at the Sacramento demonstration, and there were others from the ILWU in San Francisco. Prominent Mexican American leaders, students, civil rights workers, and office seekers were present to praise Chavez and his organization. Negro author Louis Lomax and James Forman, national secretary of SNCC, were scheduled speakers. Schenley Industries, which had just been brought to its knees by the NFWA nationwide boycott of its products, furnished free beer and liquor."

In July 1966, Chavez decided to merge his group with the Agricultural Workers Organizing Committee. When the merger took place, an AFL-CIO charter was granted to the new entity, which was called the United Farm Workers Organizing Committee. By the spring of 1968, the UFWOC had won contracts from eleven major wine grape growers, including Schenley Industries, the DiGiorgio Corporation, the Christian Brothers' Mont LaSalle Vineyards, the Los Gatos Novitiate Winery, and the Gallo Winery. Then Chavez set his sights upon the table grape growers in California. His first move was to call for a blanket boycott of California grapes throughout the country. He sent two hundred UFWOC agents throughout the United States and Canada to mobilize support for the boycott. Within a few months, the boycott had received total cooperation from the mayors of New

York City, St. Louis, Boston, Detroit, and Cleveland. Regional and national grocery chains cooperated with the boycott. In Illinois, the Illinois Council of Churches voted overwhelmingly to support Chavez. In Minnesota, the Democratic Farm Labor Party and the Archdiocese of Minneapolis, St. Paul, endorsed the boycott. The General Board of the National Council of Churches voted to support Chavez.

Religious trappings were an important feature of the image projected by Chavez. Much of the support he received from religious groups was obviously a result of his spectacular religious demonstrations. In February and March of 1968, a few months before he called for his total boycott on table grapes, he conducted a fast which brought him and his cause widespread sympathy. The "fast" was reported by the *Religious News Service* on March 8, 1968: "Union leader Cesar Chavez ended his 'penitential fast' in a special 'bread-breaking' ceremony after a Mass attended by thousands of his followers. Among those attending were national and state leaders of various labor unions of the AFL-CIO and Sen. Robert Kennedy. In ending his fast the leader of the United Farm Workers union in California reportedly surpassed the longest fast of the late Mahatma Gandhi, celebrated Indian leader . . . . Since the start of his fast, Mr. Chavez had sipped only water or chewed ice cubes. He stayed in a small room in the United Farm Workers organization committee's cooperative building at Forty Acres, site of the union headquarters west of here . . . .

"It was also learned the United Auto Workers union has donated $50,000 to Mr. Chavez's farm workers' group to finance a union headquarters building at the Forty Acre site. It was presented to

Mr. Chavez by Paul Schrade, West Coast leader of the United Auto Workers, on behalf of Walter Reuther, UAW president. An additional check for $4,500 will also be presented from the UAW to enable the union to establish an educational program. It was also revealed that Dr. Martin Luther King, president of the Southern Christian Leadership Conference, had sent a telegram March 5 praising Mr. Chavez and congratulating him on his dedication to the principle of non-violence in 'the Gandhian tradition.' "

In the *New York Times* magazine, there was a further description of the ceremony: "Senator Robert F. Kennedy was at Chavez's side as he slumped in a chair set up on a flatbed truck and nibbled feebly at a tiny bit of bread handed him by a priest. Senator Kennedy took a portion from the same home-baked loaf, then hailed Chavez as 'one of the heroic figures of our time' and congratulated those who were 'locked with Cesar in the struggle for justice for the farm worker and the struggle for justice for Spanish speaking Americans.' "

In September 1968, the religious theme of Chavez' activities was again in evidence. From San Francisco, the religious news service of September 12, 1968 reported: "More than 1,000 farm workers and their sympathizers – including many priests and nuns – commemorated the third anniversary of the Delano grape pickers strike here today with a Mass and march to City Hall. Sponsored by the S.F. Boycott Support Committee and the Local Catholic Council for the Spanish speaking, the day's program was marred by the absence of Cesar Chavez, director of the United Farm Workers Organizing Committee. Mr. Chavez, suffering from a painful back ailment, entered a San Jose hospital September 6 (1968) ....

"After the noontime Mass, celebrated at the foot of a statue of Father Miguel Hidalgo – a famous 19th century Mexican social revolutionary figure – in Mission Dolores Park, the crowd walked a mile and one-half to the city Civic Center Plaza. Among the speakers at the plaza were San Francisco Supervisor Jack Morrison, TV comedian Bill Dana, Rabbi Arthur Abraham, and chairman of the Archdiocese of San Francisco's Commission on Social Justice, Father Eugene J. Boyle.

"Mr. Morrison told the crowd: 'Abuses of the farm worker have been flagrant and long continued. It is the responsibility of government to come to the aid of the farm workers.' He urged support for his proposed ordinance to make the city an official supporter of the strike and boycott. Mr. Dana said he and a group of Hollywood entertainers plan a TV show to 'bring the boycott to millions of Americans' who are uninformed of the issues involved. Rabbi Abraham assured the audience that 'we as Jews know what it means to be oppressed and exploited and we of the Jewish community will not let you down.' Father Boyle said that the San Francisco archdiocese joined the California Migrant Ministry in calling for collective bargaining rights for farm workers ....

"Father Boyle called upon churchmen and churches to use their influence in these ways: 'To openly support the Delano strike and the boycott of all California table grapes harvested under unfair labor conditions and to call on our constituents in the churches to do the same; To privately and publicly urge agricultural employers who are confronted with a labor organization to bargain with their organized workers; To provide a new emphasis in leadership for rural churches, pointing them in the direction of a future which will involve social change including the presence of a strong organization of farm workers; To develop effective programs of education and action designed to bring about the extension of the National Labor Relations Act to the farm workers.' "

By the summer of 1970, the boycott of table grapes was so successful that Chavez was able to sign union agreements with twenty-six grape growers. The grape growers were unable to withstand the pressure of nation-wide picketing, the pro-Chavez propaganda that flooded the press media, vandalism against stores carrying California grapes, harassment of store managers by demonstrators, and most of all, the very real threat of bankruptcy. In the agreement Chavez signed with the grape growers, there was included a blacklisting clause which Chavez insisted had to be a part of every contract with his UFWOC. The clause read: "It is agreed between the Company and the Union that there are certain employees employed by the Company or who may be employed by the Company, the names of which are to be agreed upon by the Company and the Union, whom the Union claims have substantially impaired the Union's organizing efforts in the grape industry and who might disrupt the contractual relationship between Company and Union if their anti-Union activities are allowed to continue. Therefore, Company agrees to carefully explain to said employees that they can no longer engage in such activities and that, if they continue to do so, they will be immediately fired."

In addition to the blacklisting agreement, Chavez forced the grape growers to sign a highly secretive agreement which would be very lucrative for his union. The agreement read: "Company agrees to contribute to the Farm Worker Fund of the National Farm Workers Service Center, Inc., as follows: 1. Two cents ($.02) per box (or comparable unit) of table grapes, tree fruit, and other agricultural products picked and packed by the box (or comparable unit), plus 2. Five cents ($.05) per man hour for all workers (covered by the Collective Bargaining Agreement) engaged in harvesting grapes (other than table grapes) and other agricultural products not picked and packed by the box (or comparable unit). Such monies will be a direct contribution and not part of wages. Said contribution will be made on all agricultural products picked by workers covered by the Collective Bargaining Agreement . . . . Contributions will be remitted weekly . . . ."

Since Chavez was able to force compulsory unionism upon the California grape workers, he has attempted to do the same to grape and cantaloupe workers in Arizona and lettuce workers in California, and in 1972, he began a major drive to force compulsory unionism upon citrus fruit workers in Florida.

The contracts negotiated by Chavez with the California grape growers have had dramatic results. There are now fewer grape growers, fewer vineyards, and fewer grape workers. Productivity is lower. Industry-wide business is less. Individual grape workers are earning less. On the other hand, Chavez, who has never received the support of the grape workers, now has a multi-million-dollar union with which he hopes to eventually obtain a stranglehold on all American agricultural workers.

JOHN CIARDI was born on June 24, 1916 in Boston, Massachusetts, son of

Concetta di Benedictis and Carminantonio Ciardi. He married Myra Hostetter. He is an alumnus of Tufts College (A.B., 1938) and the University of Michigan (M.A., 1939). His volumes of poetry include *Homeward to America* (1940); *Other Skies* (1947); *Live Another Day* (1949); *From Time to Time* (1951); *As If* (1955); *I Marry You: A Sheaf of Love Poems* (1958); *Thirty-nine Poems* (1959); *In the Stoneworks* (1961); *In Fact* (1962); *Person to Person* (1964); *This Strangest Everything* (1966); *An Alphabestiary* (1967); and several volumes for juveniles. He is editor of *Mid-Century American Poets* (1950). He is the translator of Dante's *Inferno* (1954) and *Purgatorio* (1961). His works appear in William White's *John Ciardi: A Bibliography* (1959) and Miller Williams' *The Achievement of John Ciardi* (1968). His prose includes *How Does A Poem Mean?* (1960) and *Dialogue with an Audience* (1963).

From 1940 until 1942, Ciardi was an English instructor at the University of Kansas City. From 1946 until 1953, he was at Harvard University as the Briggs-Copland Instructor in English (1946-1948) and assistant professor of English (1948-1953). From 1953 until 1961, he was at Rutgers University as lecturer (1953-1954), associate professor (1954-1956), and professor (1956-1961) of English. In 1950 and 1951, while on leave from Harvard, Ciardi lectured in American poetry at the Salzburg [Austria] Seminar in American Studies. Since 1947, he has been with the Bread Loaf Writer's Conference at Middlebury College as lecturer (1947 to the present) and director (1956 to the present). Since 1956, he has been poetry editor of *Saturday Review*. In 1961 and 1962, he conducted a weekly educational television program, *Accent*, on CBS-TV. In 1952, he studied under a grant from the leftist-oriented Fund for the Advancement of Education.

In 1970, the House Internal Security Committee listed Ciardi as a radical who had earned large fees on the college lecture circuit. In the *Saturday Review* of November 7, 1970, Ciardi replied to the citation of HISC in "A Poet's Declaration of Faith." Ciardi denied that he was or ever had been a radical. He explained: "I have, to be sure, affronted HISC by opposing its methods, or rather by opposing those of the House Un-American Activities Committee before it, and those of the Dies Committee before that ... [and] I take all three of these committees to be sequentially one, and consistently in the pattern of McCarthyism. Within that pattern, HISC's charge against me is reckless, cynical, or so seriously misinformed as to constitute an abuse of official responsibility."

HISC had merely cited Ciardi for his membership in the National Committee to Abolish the House Un-American Activities Committee ("to lead and direct the Communist Party's 'Operation Abolition' campaign"). HISC did not mention that Ciardi had spoken on behalf of the American Committee for Protection of Foreign Born [Americans] ("subversive and Communist"). HISC did not mention that Ciardi had signed a statement issued by the National Council of American-Soviet Friendship ("subversive and Communist"). HISC did not mention that Ciardi had signed statements in behalf of indicted Communist leaders in 1948 and 1949. HISC did not mention that Ciardi had signed a statement on behalf of expelled Communist-dominated CIO unions in 1950. However, Ciardi, in his reply to HISC, wrote: "I believe that the American system will prove, as it has proved in the past, that it is responsive to its own ideals and that it is capable of adjusting within itself to the strains of changing times. I honor that system, honor its stated ideals without reservation and dissent from such institutions as HISC because I see them as agencies of distrust that work against the good of the nation. In the exercise of my dissent, I have from time to time signed petitions and allowed organizations to list me on their letterheads. Presented with a petition, I have not looked under the psychic or social bed of the man who offered it to me. I read it. If I agreed with what it said, I signed it. In signing it I have agreed only with what I have read and not necessarily with any other declared or hidden purposes of those who circulated the petition. I will not deny what I believe to be just. The fact that the devil can quote scripture is no reason for turning the faithful against it. True, some devious organization might use my name, for what little it is worth, to promote something other than its declared ends. As far as I am concerned, I have, in any given case, signed only to what was openly declared — exactly that much and no more. Such a position may be attacked as politically naive. So be it. I am not in any deep sense a political animal . . . . I am an American. I hope to be a good American. HISC's action in branding me a radical is a slander."

In 1962, good American Ciardi said that it would be a happy day for him if he could relinquish his U.S. citizenship and "take out citizenship in the human race."

BRONSON P. CLARK was born on October 6, 1918 in Cleveland Heights, Ohio, son of Hazel Baker and Sheldon Clark. He married Eleanor Meanor. He is an alumnus of Antioch College (A.B.,

1941). He is the co-author of *Peace in Vietnam: A New Approach in Southeast Asia* (1966).

In 1941 and 1942, Clark was New England secretary of the leftist-pacifist Fellowship of Reconciliation (FOR). In 1943 and 1944, he served terms in U.S. penitentiaries as a conscientious objector. From 1945 until 1950, he worked with the leftist-pacifist American Friends Service Committee. From 1951 until 1960, he was secretary-treasurer of Community Development, Inc. From 1958 until 1967, he was with the Gilford Instrument Laboratories as director (1958-1964) and vice-president (1964-1967). In 1961, he again became active with the American Friends Service Committee. From 1964 until 1967, he was a member of the national board of the AFSC. In 1967 and 1968, he was very active in the AFSC's ultra-pacifist "Special Vietnam Effort." Since 1968, he has been executive secretary of the AFSC. (Under the direction of Clark, the AFSC has been hysterical in its criticism of the U.S. presence in Vietnam. Through its publications, and in newspaper advertisements, the AFSC has given more than a little aid and comfort to the Hanoi regime.)

Clark has had, aside from his leftist-pacifist work with the AFSC over the years and his connection with FOR in the early forties, a number of leftwing affiliations: the ultra-leftist American Civil Liberties Union; the Conference for Peaceful Alternatives to the Atlantic Pact ("initiated by Communists"); and the leftist-pacifist National Council to Repeal the Draft. He is a charter member of the leftist-pacifist Business Executives Move for Vietnam Peace.

WILLIAM L. CLAY was born on April 30, 1931 in St. Louis, Missouri, son of Luella Hyatt and Irving Clay. He married Carol Johnson. He is an alumnus of St. Louis University (B.A., 1953).

From 1955 until 1959, Clay was a real estate broker. From 1959 until 1961, he was manager of a life insurance company. From 1961 until 1964, he was business representative for the State, County and Municipal Employees Union. In 1966 and 1967, he was race relations coordinator for the Steamfitters Union Local 562. From 1959 until 1964, he was a Democratic alderman in St. Louis. From 1964 until 1969, he was Democratic Committeeman of St. Louis' predominantly black 26th Ward. Since 1969, he has been in the U.S. House of Representatives, the first Negro ever elected to Congress from Missouri. (*Ebony* magazine said of his congressional campaign: "In a district where 55 per cent of the registered voters are black [10 per cent less than the district's black population] and mostly poor, Clay reaffirmed his reputation as a civil rights militant by waging a campaign that was oblivious to the conservative 'law and order' nature of the political season. His liberal-to-radical preoccupations included the elimination – where not relevant to the job – of testing procedures, arrest records, diploma requirements and periods of unemployment as barriers to getting a job. He spoke out against 'brutal and insulting practices that are endured by black people at the hands of the police.' And a plank in his platform called for the establishment, in all penal institutions, of facilities to permit men and women to live with their spouses.")

Long before Clay entered Congress, he was on the executive board of the ultra-radical National Association for the Advancement of Colored People in St. Louis. He was a member of the leftist-racist Congress of Racial Equality. Since joining the U.S. Congress, he has continued his leftist ways. He has endorsed the Red-saturated Vietnam Moratorium Committee. He endorsed the leftist-contrived Vietnam Disengagement Act of 1971. He voted against appropriations for the House Committee on Internal Security. He was a strong supporter of the Committee to Defend the [Chicago] Conspiracy. He joined 14 other ultra-leftist Democrats in refusing to support a resolution which praised the courage of U.S. military men who made the daring but unsuccessful attempt to rescue American prisoners from the Son Tay prison camp in North Vietnam. In 1971, he was one of 12 Negro Democrats in the House of Representatives who formed a Black Caucus. The group selected him as their director of research. The group is concerned with promoting pro-Negro legislation, encouraging more Negro candidates for Congress in the hope that the Negroes will vote as a bloc to accomplish victories, and, where circumstances appear to preclude victory for Negroes, encouraging Negroes to vote for sympathetic white candidates. It is a fact that Clay and all members of the Black Caucus have voting records that square with the standards of the ultra-radical Americans for Democratic Action and the ultra-radical AFL-CIO Committee on Political Education.

ALBERT J. CLEAGE JR. is a minister of the United Church of Christ. He attended Detroit public schools and Wayne State University. He has served United Church and Presbyterian congregations in Lexington, Kentucky; San Francisco; and Springfield, Massachusetts. In recent years, he has been pastor of the Shrine of the Black Madonna in Detroit, where he leads the congregation in worship of the Black Messiah. (He is an ex-Black Muslim.)

In the late 1940's and early 1950's, Cleage was associated with a number of Communist Party enterprises and fronts, including the Civil Rights Congress ("created and established by the Communist Party as an organization which would utilize defense of civil rights for Party purposes and raise and maintain mass defense and bail funds for Party use"); the World Peace Appeal ("an instance of the so-called 'peace' activities of the Communist Party"); the Mid-Century Conference for Peace ("aimed at assembling as many gullible persons as possible under Communist direction and turning them into a vast sounding board for Communist propaganda"); and various petition campaigns to repeal the Internal Security Act. He has also belonged to the leftist Committee of Black Americans for Truth About the Middle East.

Chester Smith, general counsel of the House Committee on Un-American Activities in 1968, said of Cleage: "In recent years he has been an open supporter of the Trotskyist Socialist Workers Party, speaking at affairs of the Militant Labor Forum and Friday Night Socialist Forum, both of which are fronts for the Socialist Workers Party, and also openly endorsing Socialist Workers Party candidates in the 1964 and 1966 elections.

"In addition, he wrote a preface to *The Black Ghetto*, a pamphlet by Robert Vernon, a writer for *The Militant*, official newspaper of the Socialist Workers Party. This pamphlet contained articles on riots originally published in *The Militant*. In the preface he wrote that through the eyes of Vernon 'We are participants [in the riots], and we share the emotions, the frustrations, and even

the will to violence.' Quoting again, 'Black freedom fighters everywhere will welcome this series of articles by Robert Vernon . . . .' Reverend Cleage's writings have also appeared in the Communist magazine *Monthly Review* and in *Liberator*, a magazine edited by the militant black nationalist, Daniel Watts."

In 1963, Cleage — along with Communist Party member Conrad Lynn and leftist journalist William Worthy — founded the Freedom Now Party. In 1964, Cleage, as chairman of the Freedom Now Party in Michigan, was an unsuccessful gubernatorial candidate.

Since 1967, Cleage has been the head of Federation for Self-Determination, which claims to be a unifying force and clearinghouse for Negro programs. In 1968, the ultra-leftist Ford Foundation gave Cleage's Federation grants amounting to $100,000, which Cleage said he accepted because "whites have tried to absorb blacks paternalistically and on terms set by whites."

On March 30 and 31, 1968, a National Black Government Conference was held at Cleage's Shrine of the Black Madonna. The Conference was called together by brothers Milton and Richard Henry, and held under the auspices of the Malcolm X Society. Out of the conference emerged the Republic of New Africa, a wildly militant para-military organization with the goal of establishing a black nation by taking over Mississippi, Louisiana, Alabama, Georgia, and South Carolina.

Cleage has been a very influential leader in the Interreligious Foundation for Community Organization [IFCO], founded in 1967, which has been a lucrative source of financing for militant groups. In 1969, IFCO convened the Black Economic Development Conference in Detroit. At the conference, the militant leftist James Forman introduced his Black Manifesto, in which he demanded $500,000,000 from Christian white churches and Jewish synagogues as "a beginning of the reparations due us [blacks] as people who have been exploited and degraded, brutalized, killed and persecuted." IFCO, in which Cleage had great influence, not only ratified Forman's goals but voted him $270,000 in "seed money" until he could start collecting the half-billion-dollar reparations he had assessed against white Christians and Jews.

In *Human Events* (June 28, 1969), John C. Watson wrote about Cleage: "Recognized as one of the militant 'Black Power' leaders of Detroit and a vociferous foe of the Detroit Police Department, he is an ex-Muslim and was a close associate of the late Malcolm X. He is active in the Republic of New Africa movement, which believes in a separate nation within the United States run by blacks.

"Cleage's church has been the scene of numerous 'Black Power' rallies with such speakers as H. Rap Brown and Revolutionary Action Movement (RAM) leader Milton Henry. A 'People's Tribunal,' a mock trial against law enforcement officers, was also conducted in Cleage's church. In December 1967 IFCO announced its first $85,000 no-strings-attached gift to the City-wide Citizens' Action Committee founded and directed by the Rev. Albert Cleage."

Five days before the birth of the Republic of New Africa in his Shrine of the Black Madonna, Cleage addressed a Detroit meeting of the Michigan Public Relations Society. The *Associated Press* reported on the speech: "The Rev. Albert J. Cleage Jr., a Detroit Black Power advocate, says that Negroes do not intend to invade any suburbs this summer

and that if the Negro community is invaded 'we will have little Vietnams all over America.'

"Taking cognizance of rumors circulating around Detroit in recent weeks, Cleage told the Michigan Public Relations Society: 'We have no design on Bloomfield Hills, Grosse Pointe, Dearborn or Warren or any other suburb around Detroit. We do not intend to invade this summer and rape women in the streets and shoot little babies. We have no intention of doing anything in the suburbs this summer.

" 'We would just appreciate it tremendously if people in the suburbs stay in the suburbs . . . . Let us develop our black communities . . . let us make our communities the way we want to them to be, beautiful black communities run by black people, with pride and dignity. That's all we ask.'

"Cleage also said that in advocating Black Power, he was thinking of 'a nation within a nation, not taking over any state or going to Africa.'

"The movement for integration 'is dead' in the Negro community, and 'you cannot resurrect the dream of integration for black people,' he said. He also said that the Negro has discarded nonviolence, adding, 'we now believe in self-defense' and that 'in this sense we're now just like the white people.' "

In the *United Church Herald* of February 1968, Cleage granted an interview with Douglas Gilbert. In the interview, Cleage expanded on the idea of "a nation within a nation" as he expounded separatist ideas that were, in a few weeks, a major part of the Republic of New Africa's program. In his answers to the questions posed by Gilbert (or planted by Cleage), Cleage proved to be one of the most militant of all black separatists:

CLEAGE

Gilbert: "What is the nature of Central Church [Cleage's Shrine of the Black Madonna]?" *Cleage*: "We have all kinds of people here – and they come on the basis of a commitment or a conviction about the kind of Christianity we preach.... That's why I preach about the black nation all the time. If you come into the nation you put all the rest aside. This is the same thing that Jesus said to the rich young ruler."

Gilbert: "Has your preaching about the nation increased in intensity recently?" *Cleage*: "I wouldn't say 'increased in intensity.' It has developed. You don't all of a sudden realize that most of the things you learned in the seminary about Christianity are false. It takes a little time. Your preaching develops. Gradually you find a form in which the concepts are clarified.... You can be a pretty good preacher but not know what to preach. As situations give you a message, you can make Christianity relevant. If you're able to grasp what the message is for your day, then your preaching takes on an entirely new significance."

Gilbert: "You seem to welcome black militants into your church. Is this part of the style of your ministry?" *Cleage*: "Yes, we welcome black militants. By militants I presume you mean black people who are tired of oppression and who have given up on the assumption that you can talk white people into changing. Those black militants who are committed to change and who want to do something about it – activists – we welcome them. And Central is about the only church in Detroit where respectable black militants can come without shame."

Gilbert: "Are these persons ready for violence if that is necessary?" *Cleage*: "I think any black person – militant or non-militant – except the extreme Uncle Tom (and there aren't many of them left) – is ready for violence if it is necessary. Just like any white person is ready for violence if it is necessary."

Gilbert: "Under what conditions would violence be necessary?" *Cleage*: "You take the situation here at the present time. We know very well that in the peripheral sections of the city which are predominantly white, and in the suburbs, mass meetings are being held – weekly – to arouse white people to the danger of the black inner core of the city.

"Every kind of provocation and lies are given. Extremist groups speak of Communism fomenting riots in the inner city. All this is going on and gun clubs are organized. Thousands and thousands of guns are going into the suburbs, and these are not just rifles and shot guns. These are carbines – rapid fire carbines – machine guns, and hand grenades. All being accumulated in the outer city, largely through the deliberate manipulation of white extremists. They are utilizing the fear of white people about black power, which they don't understand. These extremists know there is no threat from the black inner city – except in terms of black people wanting to control their own destiny.

"How close would black militants be to violence? If the outer suburbs for any reason would try to invade the inner city, there would be wide-spread violence. In '43 white people invaded the black community. They tried to march into it by hundreds. If they did it today everyone would be slaughtered. In that situation there would be violence."

Gilbert: "Have guns been coming into the black community too?" *Cleage*: "Not in the way they've gone into the white community, because black people don't have access to arms the way white

278

persons do. A white person can get a permit for a hand gun in 24 hours. A black person would be lucky to get it in 12 months. You try to get a National Rifle Association gun club charter in the black community! It would take you 100 years."

Gilbert: "Do you suspect that some of our suburban laymen are active in these gun clubs?" *Cleage*: "I would suspect so. I don't see any reason why our churches would be different from others." '

Gilbert: "Have you had contact with local and suburban pastors over this threat of violence?" *Cleage*: "I have contact. I talk with them. I don't spend too much time, though, because I don't think they can do too much about it. I don't think they could make speeches about the number of guns coming into their communities. They would just destroy themselves. The fear and panic and paranoia in the suburban communities is astonishing."

Of course, Cleage did not offer a shred of evidence that whites in the suburbs of Detroit or anywhere else were arming themselves with "rapid fire carbines, machine guns, and hand grenades." He did not offer a single name of the alleged white extremists. And at no time did the alleged Christian minister even hint that legal authorities should be informed if anything he said were true, rather than have the black community prepare for an all-out shooting war. Cleage almost seemed to forget that the five-day Negro riot in July 1967 literally gutted Detroit, estimates of property damage ranging as high as $1 billion. More than 5,000 were left homeless, forty-three lives were lost, more than 2,000 were injured, and one of the major aims of looters was accomplished as they ransacked every store in the riot area

where guns and ammunition were sold.

Cleage insisted that the whites in the suburbs were paranoiac without reason: "Suburban folk feel threatened today just when there is less reason for fear than at any time in the history of the black struggle for freedom. Today we don't want anything they have. We don't want to move out there. We don't want to go to their schools. We don't want bussing. We don't care anything about open occupancy. We want our own community. We want everything in it equal. Only through outright lies can black power be interpreted as a direct threat to white people in the suburbs."

To Cleage, "black power" was a changed attitude – a change in the heads of a lot of black people – 25 million black people "with a gradual awareness that white people despise us."

The hatred that Cleage has for whites came out in his responses to a series of Gilbert's questions: "They [whites] don't fit into the nation . . . . I don't have to work for separation. The white man has done too good a job. I was separated from the day I was born. Every area of my life has been separate. Church? I always went to a black church. They were acting white but it was a black church. Schools? Predominantly black. Essentially all the people I know are black. You can't ask me if I'm advocating separation. I don't know anything else. I know all about separation. But I didn't do it. I just inherited it . . . .

"I say this separation exists and you won't end it with conversation. You may make some token steps. But we're not going to end the separation – which white men have made – by conversation. We're only going to end it when black people escape from powerlessness.

"If there is some transferral of power to black people, then black people will be able to negotiate and deal with white people upon some basis of equality. That's the only basis upon which separation can be ended.

"No one wants to integrate with an inferior. The white man would be sick if he wanted to integrate with someone he holds in contempt. If, in the long run, we want a world in which blacks and whites can live together in dignity and equality, we will first take steps to develop power in the black community.

"The black man must get over his sickness. He's got to stop being filled with self-contempt. He's got to get over his feeling of inferiority. That's got to happen before the white man will look at the black man as an equal. We've got to go through the stage by which the black man escapes from powerlessness . . . . Black consciousness. Black pride. The search for black identity. This is a people seeking mental health. We've been sick a long time. We lost our identity when we were brought to this country as slaves. We were told we were inferior. They cut us off from each other and from our African traditions.

"The white man has always asserted that black is ugly. It's written into the language. Anything distasteful is black. It was a black day. You're blackballed in a fraternity. Everything black is vicious. So there must be a candid acceptance, if you're going to have black and white co-existing, that black is just as beautiful as white. And as good. But it is even more important for black people to go through this process. The black man can't wait for the white man to decide that black is beautiful. He's got to decide for himself that black is beautiful. He's got to honestly and sincerely believe it. And this may take many forms. African dress. Afro hair styles. Self-respect. These assert that black is beautiful and

that I have as much right to my heritage as you have to yours . . . . Psychologically it is absolutely necessary for the black man. The effort to learn about Africa, to study Swahili . . . this kind of thing is happening everywhere."

Cleage, who had rubbed elbows with Communists or Trotskyist-Communists in their enterprises for more than twenty years, denied vigorously that Communists had any influence on the civil rights movement or in the black urban communities: "There have been no inroads made into any black community in the past 10 years. Communism is defunct in the black community. They couldn't even hold a meeting. A black Communist today would be considered an Uncle Tom because he is still talking about black and white unite and fight. Communists are completely lost in the ghetto. No influence, nothing to do with anything in the freedom movement from coast to coast."

PAT COCHRANE was born on July 27, 1916 in Melville, Montana, daughter of Eleanor Armstrong and John Hart. She married Gordon Cochrane. She is an alumna of Montana State College (B.S., 1939) and Boston University (M.A., 1940).

From 1937 until 1939, Mrs. Cochrane was a laboratory instructor at Montana State College. In 1940, she was a chemistry teacher at Boston Medical Junior College. From 1941 until 1943, she was a saleswoman. From 1949 until 1954, she owned and operated a bookstore in Richland, Washington. From 1957 until 1966, she was executive director of the Camp Fire Girls.

Since 1954, Mrs. Cochrane has been a political activist: president of the Richland Women's Democratic Club (1954-1956); member of the executive board (1954-1960), legislative chairman (1954-1956), and chairman (1956-1960) of the Washington State Federation of Democratic Women's Clubs; member of the executive board of the Washington Democratic State Central Committee (1954-1958); state committeewoman from Benton County, Washington (1954-1960); precinct committeewoman from Benton County, Washington (1954-1962); Washington State Fund Chairman for Adlai E. Stevenson (1956); alternate delegate to the Democratic National Convention (1956 and 1964); state chairman of Dollars-for-Democrats (1956-1960); and finance coordinator of the Washington Democratic Council (1969 to the present). She has also been a delegate to the Washington State Conference on Children and Youth (1959); a delegate to the White House Conference on Children and Youth (1960); a member of the Governor's Committee on Youth Employment, the Governor's Committee on Employed Women, and the Governor's Commission on the Status of Women in Washington (1963-1964); a delegate to the White House Conference on the International Cooperation Year (1965); a delegate to the U.S. Commission for UNESCO Conference (1965); and a member of the Head Start Advisory Committee in Washington (1965).

Mrs. Cochrane has been affiliated with the United Nations Association of the United States, the most prestigious leftwing propaganda agency for the UN in this country; the leftist-internationalist-pacifist World Peace through World Law Center; the leftist-oriented Adlai Stevenson Institute of International Affairs; the leftist-oriented American Association of University Women; the leftist-oriented League of Women Voters; the ultra-leftist American Civil Liberties Union; the National Association for the Advancement of Colored People, the fountainhead of Negro agitation for more than half a century; and the leftist-racist Congress of Racial Equality.

TRISTRAM COFFIN was born on June 25, 1912 in Hood River, Oregon, son of Lenora Smith and Clarence Coffin. He married Margaret Avery. He is an alumnus of DePauw University (A.B., 1933). He is the author of *Missouri Compromise* (1947); *Your Washington* (1954); *Not to the Swift* (1961); *The Passion of the Hawks: Militarism in Modern America* (1964); *Mine Eyes Have Seen the Glory* (1964); *The Sex Kick: Eroticism in Modern America* (1966); and *Senator Fulbright: Portrait of a Public Philosopher* (1966).

From 1933 until 1937, Coffin was a reporter for the *Indianapolis Times*. From 1937 until 1941, he was an assistant to the Governor of Indiana. From 1941 until 1944, he worked in the Office of Facts and Figures in Elmer Davis' Red-lined Office of War Information. From 1945 until 1947, he was a White House correspondent for Columbia Broadcasting System. From 1948 until 1951, he was a newspaper columnist. Since 1951, he has been a free-lance writer and broadcaster. Many of his articles have appeared in such leftist publications as *Progressive* magazine and *New Leader* magazine.

Over the past twenty-five years, Coffin has moved steadily leftward. Perhaps the turning point was his *The Passion of the Hawks*, which his publisher described as "a daring satirical critique of the American military establishment and the American spirit." In truth, Coffin's work was far from satire. It was a venomous and defamatory attack upon the highly elusive military-industrial complex – a sprawling conglomerate, according to Coffin: "The complex is a crew of military contractors, generals, public-relations scalawags, military associations, professors and scientists, congressmen, lobbyists, unions, and a general riffraff of local chamber of commerce secretaries, lawyers, and the like." Herbert Mitgang, reviewing the book in the *New York Times*, said that Coffin "pulls out the pins and flips hand grenades down the corridors of the Pentagon and other corners of American militarism . . . . Although some of his charges fail to go off, many are explosive."

Coffin's publisher said that he epitomizes the American military mind "in a biting portrait of 'King Mac – General Douglas MacArthur.' " In her syndicated column, Alice Widener astutely observed: "This Tristram Coffin seeks to drive nails through General MacArthur's impenetrably good reputation with much worse tools than biting criticism. Coffin doesn't bite, he spits. And his spittle smears almost seventeen pages of print about General MacArthur . . . . In my opinion, it is a sick symptom of our times that such a respectable firm as The Macmillan Company would publish such a book. Here is a typical Coffin comment: 'Korea is a key to Asia . . . . MacArthur was inattentive to Korea in a way that a lovely lady in the midst of a passionate love affair is inattentive to the thievery of her cook. The General was the occupation commander for Japan and the overseer of American forces in the Far East. But he was much more enamored of his role as lord paramount of the Orient and Son of Heaven.' The truth, as set forth in every intellectually honest historical document, is that until the outbreak of the Korean War, Korea was specifically excluded from Mac-Arthur's Far Eastern command."

Coffin's diatribe against the military did not go unrewarded. On September 16, 1964, the *New Times* of Moscow devoted two pages to a laudatory review of *The Passion of the Hawks* – a most unusual tribute by the Soviets to a book written by an American.

Next to the "military-industrial complex," Coffin's most worrisome writings have concerned anti-Communists. He does not like the far right, which by his standards includes just about everyone to the right of his special favorite, J. William Fulbright. The far right, according to Coffin, is composed of Yahoos who are the ideological descendants of Coffin's bête noire, Joseph R. McCarthy. If Coffin were to be taken seriously, any American who actively opposes socialistic (or any totalitarian) individuals, institutions, or programs must bear the appellation "Yahoo."

Since 1968, Coffin· has been the author of a newsletter, *The Washington Watch*. The newsletter is written and distributed under the auspices of Business Executives Move for Vietnam Peace, an extreme leftist group of doves and perhaps one of the best financed organizations of its kind. Coffin's commitment to the doves of Business Executives Move is not an isolated action. On August 22, 1968, the Communists' *Daily World* carried an article about "534 Authors In Anti-War Plea." Signatories to the plea included the usual roster of Communists and fellow-travelers from the literary world, and Coffin's name was among them.

ROBERT S. COHEN was born on February 18, 1923 in New York City, son of Mabel Reinschreiber and Mordecai Cohen. He married Robin Hirshhorn. He is an alumnus of Wesleyan

University (B.A., 1943) and Yale University (M.S., 1943; Ph.D., 1948).

In 1943 and 1944, Cohen was a physics instructor at Yale University. From 1944 until 1946, he was on the science staff in the division of war research at Columbia University. From 1949 until 1951, he was a philosophy instructor at Yale University. From 1949 until 1957, he was an assistant professor of physics and philosophy at Wesleyan University. Since 1957, he has been at Boston University as associate professor of physics (1957-1959) and professor and chairman of the department of physics (1959 to the present). He has been chairman of the Boston Colloquium of Philosophy of Science. In 1958-1959 and 1961-1962, he was a visiting lecturer in the humanities and the philosophy of science at the Massachusetts Institute of Technology. In 1959-1960, he was visiting professor of the history of ideas at Brandeis University. In summer sessions, from 1958 to 1965, he was a history instructor and a lecturer in philosophy and science at American University. In 1963, he was a visiting professor at the Yugoslav Academy of Science. In 1964, he was a visiting professor at the Hungarian Academy of Science. In 1969, he was a visiting professor at the University of California in San Diego. In 1948-1949, he held a fellowship in philosophy and science from the American Council of Learned Societies. In 1955-1956, he was a Ford Foundation faculty fellow at Cambridge in England. In 1962, he was an instructor in philosophy and sociology; and a visiting fellow at the Polish Academy of Science.

Since 1962, Cohen has been on the executive committee of the Emergency Civil Liberties Committee ("Communist front" — "subversive"). Since 1960, he has been a member of the Federation of American Scientists, a group of bleeding-heart, leftwing pacifists. He is the chairman of the American Institute for Marxist Studies. He was an initiating sponsor of the Aptheker Dinner Program, in celebration of the 50th birthday of the Communist Party's most celebrated theoretician. His other affiliations include the Jefferson School of Social Science ("adjunct of the Communist Party"); the Socialist Scholars Conference; the leftist-oriented Ad Hoc Committee for an Open Letter on Vietnam; the leftist-oriented Ad Hoc Committee on the Vietnam War; the leftist-pacifist Educational Committee to Halt Atomic Weapons; the leftwing-pacifist National Committee for a Sane Nuclear Policy; the National Committee to Abolish the House Un-American Activities Committee ("to lead and direct the Communist Party's 'Operation Abolition' campaign"); the ultra-leftist Fort Hood Three Defense Committee; the ultra-leftist American-Korean Friendship and Information Center; the leftist-pacifist American Friends Service Committee; the leftist Civil Defense Letter Committee; the ultra-leftist American Society for the Study of the German Democratic Republic; the leftist-oriented Greater Boston Faculty Statement of 1965, which defended the right of students to protest the draft and the war in Vietnam; the ultra-leftist American Civil Liberties Union; and the National Association for the Advancement of Colored People, the fountainhead of Negro agitation for more than half a century.

JAMES S. COLES was born on June 3, 1913 in Mansfield, Pennsylvania, son of Emavieve Rose and Edwin Coles. He married Martha Reed. He is an alumnus of Mansfield State College (B.S., 1934) and Columbia University (A.B., 1936; Ph.D., 1941). He is co-author of *Physical Principles of Chemistry* (1965).

From 1936 until 1941, Coles was a chemistry instructor at the City College of New York. From 1941 until 1943, he was an assistant professor of chemistry at Middlebury College. From 1943 until 1946, he was a research group leader and supervisor of the Underwater Explosives Research Laboratory at the Woods Hole Oceanographic Institution. From 1946 until 1952, he was at Brown University as assistant professor of chemistry (1946-1949), associate professor of chemistry (1949-1952), acting dean of the college (1951-1952), and executive officer of the chemistry department (1947-1952). From 1952 until 1967, he was president of Bowdoin College in Maine. Since 1968, he has been president of the Research Corporation of New York.

Coles is a long-time member of the Council on Foreign Relations, the informal supra-State Department of the United States; and the National Council for Civic Responsibility, an election year's drive in 1964 by the Democrat Party against anti-Communists.

JUDY COLLINS was born on May 1, 1939 in Seattle, daughter of Marjorie Byrd and Charles Collins. She was married to and divorced from Peter Taylor. She attended MacMurray College in Illinois and the University of Colorado.

In 1959, Miss Collins began a professional career as a folksinger. For about two years, she worked almost exclusively in nightclubs. In 1961 and 1962, she made record albums which consisted for the most part of Anglo-American folk ballads. In 1963, she joined the growing horde of folksingers whose recordings and concerts were composed almost ex-clusively of songs written by Communists, including Pete Seeger and Woody Guthrie. By the mid-1960's, she was in great demand to appear on television, on campuses, and at folk festivals.

Peter Benchley, writing for the Newsweek Service syndicate, said of Miss Collins in 1969: "She has led every trend and accompanied every political movement since the end of the flat '50's – giving new meaning to traditional songs, boosting new tunes to the top of the charts and, in recent years, writing her own sweet and melancholy melodies."

As an activist, Miss Collins has participated in civil rights demonstrations in Mississippi. She has supported the ultra-leftist Students for a Democratic Society. She has supported Joan Baez' ultra-leftist Institute for the Study of Non-violence. She was a producer and singer of a record album made for the leftist-pacifist Women Strike for Peace. She has supported the leftist-revolutionary Youth International Party (Yippies). She has been affiliated with the leftist Sing-In for Peace Committee; the leftist Committee to Defend the [Chicago] Conspiracy; and the leftist Spring Mobilization Committee. She has taken part in numerous leftist-dominated protests against the Vietnam War. She has sung at benefit performances to encourage resistance to the draft, and as a leader of the New Left, she endorsed the Hanoi-inspired People's Peace Treaty.

ROBERT G. COLODNY was born on August 5, 1915 in Phoenix, Arizona. He is an alumnus of the University of California at Berkeley (B.A., 1945; M.A., 1948; Ph.D., 1950). He is the author of *The Struggle for Madrid* (1959) and *Spain: The Glory and the Tragedy* (1971). He is the co-author of *The Battle of the Aleutians* (1944). He is a contributor to *The Warped Vision* (1965). He is the editor of *Frontiers of Science and Philosophy* (1962) and *Beyond the Edge of Certainty* (1965).

In 1956 and 1957, Colodny was an assistant professor of history at San Francisco State College. From 1957 until 1959, he was an assistant professor of history at the University of Kansas. Since 1959, he has been at the University of Pittsburgh as an associate professor (1959-1967) and professor (1967 to the present).

In the 1930's, Colodny fought with the Abraham Lincoln Brigade in the Spanish Civil War. The brigade was recruited and led by Soviet agents. (Frank Meyer, an editor of *National Review*, stated in 1961: " ... When I was in the leadership of the Illinois-Indiana district of the Communist Party, I had known Robert Colodny, then just returned wounded from the Spanish Civil War, as an organized and disciplined Communist.")

Colodny has been affiliated with the Joint Anti-Fascist Refugee Committee ("subversive and Communist"); the American Peace Crusade ("Communist front"); the American-Russian Institute ("subversive" – "Communist" – "specializing in pro-Soviet propaganda"); American Veterans for Peace ("another specialized 'peace' front of the Communist Party"); the Spanish Refugee Committee ("Communist front"); the American Student Union ("Communist front"); the Fair Play for Cuba Committee (Castro-subsidized); the Socialist Scholars Conferences; and the Veterans of the Abraham Lincoln Brigade ("subversive and Communist").

In 1961, the Chancellor of the University of Pittsburgh, Edward H. Litchfield, appointed a fact-finding committee to investigate Colodny's association with

international Communism. The question of Colodny's background had been raised in the Pennsylvania State Legislature and the public press. The fact-finding committee employed six professional people who spent four months investigating Colodny. Litchfield claimed that the fact-finding committee utilized every outside resource available to them and produced a thorough examination of his record. The committee concluded that Colodny was a loyal American and that he had never been a Communist. The committee described Colodny as an exceptionally gifted scholar and an inspiring professor who did not teach doctrines subversive to our government. The committee said that Colodny exhibited exceptional independence of thought and action, according to his own conscience, in both his scholarly and societal pursuits.

The fact-finding committee found that Colodny had in the past knowingly associated with Communists and had affiliated with Communist-front organizations. The committee explained Colodny's associations and affiliations as having been made solely in order to promote causes in which he believed deeply – especially the fight against Fascism and the establishment of a world peace. The committee further found that Colodny, in common with many other young men during the depression, had maintained hope for some of the promises of the Soviet Union, but that by 1961, that feeling had given way to disillusionment and criticism of Russia's oppression. By 1961, the committee said, Colodny branded Marxist doctrines as fallacious and believed that Communism had no place in American society. In the most dramatic part of the committee's whitewash, it was explained that Colodny risked death and suffered serious wounds fighting with the Abraham Lincoln Brigade in the Spanish Civil War because of his hatred of Fascism. And for the same reason – hatred of Hitler and Hitlerism – he volunteered in the U.S. Army before Pearl Harbor, despite severe physical disability.

Colodny's pro-Castro extremism and his membership in the Fair Play for Cuba Committee were dismissed rather abruptly by the committee when it said: "Dr. Colodny believes that the Cuban revolution gained its impetus through the peasants' hopes for agrarian reform, but that the Castro government now has slipped into the Soviet orbit. He believes this to be a calamity for the people of Cuba, of the United States, and of the entire Western Hemisphere."

Chancellor Litchfield joined in the whitewash wholeheartedly when he stated: "From all the evidence at hand, I have determined to my satisfaction that these findings of the committee are valid. I therefore wish specifically to say that to the very best of our knowledge, after most careful investigation, Dr. Colodny is a loyal American, is not a Communist or subversive person as defined by the Pennsylvania Loyalty Act of 1951, is an able and objective scholar, and is an inspiring teacher who does not teach doctrines subversive to our way of life." Less than five years after Litchfield and his fact-finding committee exonerated Colodny, he was in attendance – along with at least five Communists – at the Socialist Scholars Conference in New York City, where subversive doctrines were the order of the day.

CARL W. CONDIT was born on September 29, 1914 in Cincinnati, son of Gertrude Pletz and Arthur Condit. He married Isabel Campbell. He is an alumnus of Purdue University (B.S., 1936)

and the University of Cincinnati (M.A., 1939; Ph.D., 1941). He is the author of *The Rise of the Skyscraper* (1952); *American Building Art: The 19th Century* (1960); *American Building Art: The 20th Century* (1961); and *American Building: Materials and Techniques* (1968). He is co-author of *Technology in Western Civilization* (1967). Since 1962, he has been co-editor of *Technology and Culture*. He has contributed to the *Encyclopaedia Britannica, Collier's Encyclopedia of Science,* the *Harper Encyclopedia of Science,*the *Dictionary of American Biography,* and publications produced by the U.S. Department of State and the U.S. Information Service.

From 1939 until 1941, Condit was an English instructor at the University of Cincinnati. From 1941 until 1944, he was employed by the U.S. Army as a civilian instructor in mathematics and mechanics. In 1944 and 1945, he was an assistant design engineer in the building department of the New York Central Railroad. In 1945 and 1946, he was an English instructor at Northwestern University. In 1946 and 1947, he was an assistant professor of humanities and social sciences at Carnegie Institute of Technology. Since 1947, he has been on the faculty of Northwestern University as associate professor of English and the humanities (1947-1961), professor of English and the humanities (1961-1966), and professor of art and the history of science (1966 to the present). In 1966 and 1967, he was a research associate at the Smithsonian Institution.

Condit has been affiliated with the National Committee to Abolish the House Un-American Activities Committee ("to lead and direct the Communist Party's 'Operation Abolition' campaign"); the ultra-leftist American Society for the Study of the German Democratic Republic; the leftist-pacifist Ad Hoc Faculty Committee on Vietnam; the leftist-pacifist International Committee of Conscience on Vietnam; the Bill of Rights Conference ("subversive"); the Chicago Committee to Secure Justice in the Rosenberg Case ("Communist front"); the Communist-dominated World Youth Festival of 1962; the leftist-oriented American Association of University Professors; and the ultra-leftist American Civil Liberties Union.

PHILIP E. CONVERSE was born on November 17, 1928 in Concord, New Hampshire, son of Evelyn Eaton and Ernest Converse. He married Jean McDonnell. He is an alumnus of Denison University (B.A., 1949); the University of Iowa (M.A., 1950); and the University of Michigan (M.A., 1956; Ph.D., 1958). He also pursued graduate studies at the University of Paris (1953-1954). He is the co-author of *The American Voter* (1960); *Social Psychology: The Study of Human Interaction* (1965); *Elections and the Political Order* (1966); and *Vietnam and the Silent Majority* (1971).

In 1959 and 1960, Converse was a Fulbright research fellow in France. Since 1956, he has been with the University of Michigan's Survey Research Center as assistant study director of political behavior (1956-1958), study director (1958-1961), senior study director (1961-1965), and program director (1965 to the present). Since 1960, he has been on the faculty of the University of Michigan as assistant professor of sociology (1960-1964), associate professor of sociology (1964-1965), associate professor of political science (1963-1965), and professor of sociology and political science (1965 to the present). Since 1962, he has been associate director of the Inter-University Consor-

tium of Political Research. In 1961 and 1962, he held a research grant from the Social Science Research Council. In 1967 and 1968, he was a senior fellow of the National Science Foundation. From 1964 until 1967, he was a member of the committee on government and legal processes of the Social Science Research Council. Since 1967, he has been a member of the committee on comparative politics of the Social Science Research Council. Since 1965, he has been on the committee of information on the behavioral sciences of the National Academy of Science. He has lectured in France, Norway, and Sweden. He taught at the first UNESCO (Communist-dominated) European Seminar in Cologne (1964). He has been affiliated with the leftist-oriented Ad Hoc Committee of Veterans for Peace in Vietnam.

HOWARD A. COOK was born on April 4, 1915 in New Rochelle, New York, son of Blanche Gibbs and Howard Cook. He was married to and divorced from Diana Pattison. He is married to Diane Bissell. He is an alumnus of Harvard University (B.S., 1937) and Stanford University (M.A., 1947).

From 1937 until 1940, Cook was assistant head of the financial department in the Haskins & Sells firm of certified public accountants. In 1946 and 1947, he was assistant director of the leftist-internationalist Cleveland Council on World Affairs. From 1948 until 1952, he was an assistant director of the leftist-internationalist World Affairs Council of Northern California. From 1952 until 1955, he was with the Department of State as chief of the public services division. Since 1955, he has been president of International House in New York City. He is a long-time member of the Council on

Foreign Relations, the informal supra-State Department of the United States; and the Foreign Policy Association, a highly-effective pro-Communist vehicle.

PHILIP H. COOMBS was born on August 15, 1915 in Holyoke, Massachusetts, son of Nellie Hall and Charles Coombs. He married Helena Brooks. He is an alumnus of Amherst College (B.A., 1937). He pursued graduate studies at the University of Chicago (1937-1939) and at the Brookings Institution (1939-1940). He is the author of *The Fourth Dimension of Foreign Policy – Educational and Cultural Affairs* (1964); *Education and Foreign Aid* (1965); and *New Media: Memo to Educational Planners* (1967).

In 1939 and 1940-1941, Coombs was an economics instructor at Williams College. In 1941 and 1942, he was an economist with the Office of Price Administration. From 1943 until 1945, he served with the Office of Strategic Services. In 1945 and 1946, he was an economic adviser to the Office of Economic Stabilization. From 1947 until 1949, he was a professor of economics at Amherst College. From 1950 until 1952, he was the executive director of the President's Materials Policy Commission (Paley Commission). From 1952 until 1960, he was employed by the Socialist-oriented Ford Foundation as program director for education and director of research for the Fund for the Advancement of Education. In 1961 and 1962, he was with the U.S. Department of State as assistant secretary of state for international educational and cultural affairs. From 1963 until 1968, he was the director of the leftist-oriented International Institute for Educational Planning in Paris, France, and since 1969, he has been the Institute's director

of research. He has been a consultant on education and economic planning to the governments of India (1953 and 1955), Turkey (1957), and Spain (1969). He was chairman of the U.S. delegation to the leftist-dominated UNESCO conferences on economic growth and educational development in Addis Ababa (1961) and Santiago (1962). In 1962, he was chairman of the Organization for Economic Cooperation and Development Conference on Educational Investment and Economic Growth. In 1969, he was a visiting lecturer at Harvard University's Graduate School of Education. In 1962 and 1963, he held a Council on Foreign Relations fellowship. In 1963, he was a guest fellow at the Brookings Institution.

Coombs is a long-time member of the Council on Foreign Relations, the informal supra-State Department of the United States. He has also been affiliated with the ultra-radical Americans for Democratic Action.

PETER P. COOPER was born on June 26, 1925 in Frederick Hall, Virginia. He is married. He is an alumnus of Catawba College (B.A., 1949) and the University of North Carolina (M.A., 1950).

From 1950 until 1952, Cooper was director of the department of education of the Rowan County Alcoholic Beverage Control Board. From 1952 until 1955, he was executive director of the Tri-State United World Federalists, the most prestigious group of fellow-travelers and dupes working for world government at the expense of American sovereignty. Since 1955, he has been at Catawba College as director of public relations and communications (1955-1959); successively as instructor, assistant professor, associate professor, and professor of social science and anthropology (1959 to the present); chairman of the department of sociology and political science (1960-1964); and chairman of the department of political science (1964 to the present). From 1965 until 1968, he held research grants to study archaeology. He has held fellowships at the University of Colorado and the University of North Carolina.

Cooper is a member of the leftwing-internationalist United World Federalists. He is affiliated with the leftist-pacifist American Friends Service Committee and the leftist-pacifist American Freedom Association.

GIOVANNI COSTIGAN was born on February 15, 1905 in Kingston, England, son of Helen Warren and John Costigan. He married Anne Johnson. He is an alumnus of Oxford University (B.A., 1926; M.A. and B. Litt., 1930) and the University of Wisconsin (M.A., 1928; Ph.D., 1930). He is the author of *Sir Robert Wilson: A Soldier of Fortune in the Napoleonic Wars* (1932); *Sigmund Freud: A Short Biography* (1965); *Makers of Modern England* (1967); and *A History of Modern Ireland* (1969).

From 1930 until 1934, Costigan was an associate professor of history at the University of Idaho. Since 1934, he has been at the University of Washington as an assistant professor (1934-1942), associate professor (1942-1948), and professor (1948 to the present) of history.

Costigan has been affiliated with the Abraham Lincoln Brigade ("under the domination and control of the Comintern; its members were subject to, and the recipients of, Communist discipline for political dissidence"); the National Federation for Constitutional Liberties ("under [Communist] Party domination and headed by responsible Party func-

tionaries"); the Washington Commonwealth Federation ("a broad federation of progressive forces in the State of Washington, controlled by a Communist Party faction in it"); the National Lawyers Guild ("the foremost legal bulwark of the Communist Party, its front organizations, and controlled unions"); the ultra-leftist Fort Hood Three Defense Committee; the leftist-pacifist Teachers Committee for Peace in Vietnam; the Seattle Labor School ("a Communist-controlled institution"); the ultra-leftist American Civil Liberties Union; the Educators Appeal to the American People, a leftist effort against the war in Vietnam; and the leftist-pacifist Ad Hoc Committee of Veterans for Peace in Vietnam.

LOUIS G. COWAN was born on December 12, 1909 in Chicago, son of Hetty Smitz and Jacob Cowan. He married Pauline Spiegel. He is an alumnus of the University of Chicago (Ph.B., 1931).

From 1931 until 1941, Cowan had his own public relations firm, the Louis G. Cowan Company. From 1941 until 1943, he was a consultant in the radio section of the War Department's Bureau of Public Relations. From 1943 until 1945, he was chief of the New York City office for the overseas branch of the Red-lined Office of War Information. From 1946 until 1955, he was president of Louis G. Cowan, Inc., which produced radio and television programs. From 1955 until 1958, he was vice-president for creative services of the Columbia Broadcasting System, Inc. In 1958 and 1959, he was president of CBS Television Network. From 1961 until 1965, he was director of the Morse Communication Research Center at Brandeis University. Since 1962, he has been president and editor of Chilmark Press, Inc. Since 1965, he has been director of special programs at Columbia University's Graduate School of Journalism. He is chairman of publications and chairman of the advisory board of the ultra-leftist *Partisan Review*.

Cowan is a long-time member of the Council on Foreign Relations, the informal supra-State Department of the United States. He is a director of the leftist-oriented African-American Institute.

DANA S. CREEL was born on May 24, 1912 in College Park, Georgia, son of Mary Shannon and Dana Creel. He married Jane Haislip. He is an alumnus of Emory University (LL.B., 1934) and Harvard University (M.B.A., 1936). In 1934, he was admitted to the Georgia bar. In 1939, he was admitted to the New York bar.

From 1936 until 1939, Creel was employed by the Irving Trust Company. In 1939 and 1940, he was employed by Prentice-Hall Company. Since 1940, he has been associated with the philanthropical work of the late John D. Rockefeller Jr. Since 1947, he has been with the leftist-oriented Rockefeller Brothers Fund as secretary (1947-1951), director (1951-1968), and trustee and president (1968 to the present).

Creel is a long-time member of the Council on Foreign Relations, the informal supra-State Department of the United States. Since 1958, he has been trustee and vice-president of the leftist-oriented Interchurch Center. Since 1957, he has been on the board of trustees of the leftist-oriented African-American Institute.

RICHARD CRILEY was identified under oath as a member of the Communist Party by four former Communists who testified before the House Committee on Un-American Activities: Lee

Lundgren (September 2, 1952), Louis Rosser (December 1, 1953), Anzelm Czarnowski (December 4, 1956), and Carl Nelson (May 5, 1959).

On July 6, 1954, Criley testified before the Senate Internal Security Subcommittee. He told the Subcommittee that he attended grade school in Carmel, California, and high school in Monterey, California; that he attended Stanford University for two years; and that he received a B.A. degree from the University of California at Berkeley in 1934. After graduating from UC, he said, he worked about a year as a supervisor on a Works Project Administration project in northern California. He pleaded the Fifth Amendment when asked what employment he had following the WPA job. He did admit that he was drafted into the U.S. Army in 1942, was commissioned a second lieutenant in the military police in 1943, served overseas in North Africa, Italy, Sicily, England, and France, and attained the rank of captain before separating from the service in December 1945.

As of the day he testified, Criley said that he was a hod carrier employed in Wheaton, Illinois. He pleaded the Fifth Amendment when asked if he had been president of the League for Industrial Democracy at Berkeley; if, in 1936 at Berkeley, he had led a peace strike sponsored by the American League Against War and Fascism ["subversive and Communist" – "established in the United States in an effort to create public sentiment on behalf of a foreign policy adapted to the interests of the Soviet Union"]; if he had been, in 1936, executive secretary of the Young Communist League of California; if, in 1938, he had been a registered member of the Communist Party; if he had been a member of the Communist Party prior to entering the U.S. Army, after he left the service, or as of the moment; and if he had been expelled from Local 28 of the United Packinghouse Workers Union of Chicago because of his Communist activities. He denied being a Communist Party member while he was in the U.S. Army.

In May 1959, Criley appeared before the House Committee on Un-American Activities when the Committee was investigating Communist infiltration of vital industries and current techniques in the Chicago area. Richard Arens, staff director of HCUA, began his interrogation by asking Criley his occupation. Criley replied: "My ancestor, Childs Corey, died in Salem, Massachusetts, in the year 1692, a victim of the Salem witch hunt. Mr. Arens, I think you can understand if my family has a long aversion to witch hunts of any kind and also if it is an article of faith in my family to believe in the Bill of Rights. I cannot in conscience encourage a further erosion of the Bill of Rights by answering your question."

Criley made a number of speeches when asked if he was the executive secretary of the Chicago Committee to Defend Democratic Rights and if he had prepared a legislative bulletin, issued by that Committee, which read: "The Un-Americans are at it again! Two groups of Chicago unionists have been subpoenaed to appear before it on May 5 and 6. They include members and former members of the United Packinghouse Workers of America and of Local 113 (Tool and Die) of the International Association of Machinists. Additional unionists may still be called at a later date.

"It is clear that the House Un-American Activities Committee hearing is a direct intervention into the internal affairs of labor. The House Committee (whose general mandate to function was questioned by the U.S. Supreme Court) has no specific authorization from Congress to conduct such a hearing as that scheduled here. It is evident, also, that there can be no legitimate legislative purpose for this hearing. On both counts, the entire hearing is patently illegal, on the basis of the Supreme Court decision in the Watkins case which stated that the Committee had no right to expose 'for sake of exposure.'

"Chairman Walter's public statement that the hearing is for the purpose of 'investigating subversive infiltration' into defense industries is camouflage for a flagrant attack on unions and the constitutional rights of American workers. It will be recalled that the last 'labor investigation' of the Committee in this area was in 1952 when it was timed to disrupt the strike of International Harvester workers and the negotiations for a new contract in the meat packing industry.

"The House Committee has just completed a witch-hunt against labor in the Pittsburgh area. In February in Los Angeles under guise of investigating 'legal subversion,' it unfolded an attack on defense attorneys in civil liberties cases, and on the constitutional right to be represented by counsel. In Atlanta, Georgia, last year, the Committee was denounced by over 200 prominent Negro leaders in the South for 'trying to attach the "subversive" label to any liberal white Southerner who dares to raise his voice in support of our democratic ideals.'

"The recent actions of the House Un-American Activities Committee are the most potent argument for its abolition, and the cutting off of all further appropriations. (For 1959, it has already been voted $327,000 by the House of Representatives.)"

Criley pleaded the Fifth Amendment when asked if he was a member of the Communist Party, and if he knew Louis Rosser, who had identified Criley as a Communist. In response to all other questions, Rosen refused answers and argued with his interrogators.

Criley's next appearance before an investigative committee was in July 1961, when the Senate Internal Security Subcommittee was investigating Castro's network in the United States, specifically the Fair Play for Cuba Committee. Criley pleaded the Fifth Amendment when asked if he was married; if he had ever lived in California; if he spoke any language other than English; who were the officers of and how many members were in the Chicago chapter of the Fair Play for Cuba Committee and if he was a member; if he had established a chapter of the Fair Play for Cuba Committee at the University of Chicago; if he and his wife [Florence Atkinson, a Communist] had travelled to Cuba on a trip arranged by FPCC; if he knew Claude Lightfoot, a member of the Communist Party's hierarchy; if he and/or his wife were Communist Party members; if he knew Carl Nelson, who identified Criley as a Communist Party member from 1934 through 1949; and if he had attended FPCC and/or Communist Party meetings. In the course of his testimony Criley did deny that he ever engaged in espionage. He testified that his occupation was that of a secretary and that he had lost his job as a hod carrier in 1954 because he was called to testify before the Senate Internal Security Subcommittee.

In 1961, Criley testified for the second and last time before HCUA when it was investigating the manipulation of public opinion by organizations under concealed control of the Communist Party, with particular emphasis upon the National Assembly of Democratic Rights and the Citizens Committee for Constitutional Liberties. Criley pleaded the Fifth Amendment to all questions concerning his knowledge of and activities on behalf of the National Assembly for Democratic Rights and the Citizens Committee for Constitutional Liberties; when asked about his Communist Party activities between 1935 and 1961; and when asked to affirm or deny his identification as a Communist Party member by four former Communists.

At the conclusion of the 1961 hearings, HCUA reported: "On the basis of its investigations and hearings to date, the committee concludes that the National Assembly for Democratic Rights and a coordinating and organizing group in support thereof, titled the 'Citizens Committee for Constitutional Liberties,' are Communist fronts ["created, dominated, and controlled by members and officials of the Communist Party"]. The National Assembly for Democratic Rights and the Citizens Committee for Constitutional Liberties were organized as propaganda devices for the conduct of 'mass activity' in support of the avowed objective of 'reversal or nonapplication' of the Supreme Court decisions of June 5, 1961, which upheld the constitutionality of the registration and disclosure provisions of the Internal Security Act of 1950 as applied to the Communist Party, and the Smith Act membership clause making punishable active and purposive membership in the Communist Party."

Various congressional investigative committees have provided further information on Criley. He has been affiliated with the Emergency Civil Liberties Committee. ("The Emergency Civil Liberties Committee is an organization . . . whose

292

avowed purpose is to abolish the House Committee on Un-American Activities and discredit the FBI .... To defend the cases of Communist lawbreakers, fronts have been devised making special appeals in behalf of civil liberties and reaching out far beyond the confines of the Communist Party itself. Among these organizations [is] the ... Emergency Civil Liberties Committee. When the Communist Party is under fire these fronts offer a bulwark of protection.") He has been affiliated with the National Committee to Abolish the Un-American Activities Committee ("to lead and direct the Communist Party's 'Operation Abolition' campaign"). He has attended various Communist Party conventions. He once served as leader of the Communist Party's youth commission in Illinois. He was affiliated with the American Student Union ("the Young Communist League took credit for the creation of the organization"). In 1966, he was on the executive committee of the Committee for Independent Political Action, which had as its objective the formation of a new political party. The Committee was composed of radical pacifists, violent racists, representatives of New Left groups, and known members of the Communist Party. In 1967, he was a member of the National Conference for New Politics, a classical united-front third-party movement largely controlled by Communists.

In the March 5, 1966 issue of *Human Events*, it was reported: "The Lawndale Urban Progress Center in Chicago, Ill., which has received over $350,000 in federal funds since January 1965, has, under pressure from Mayor Daley, recently removed an accused Communist, Richard Criley, from its advisory council. Criley, identified as a Communist by an FBI informant, has refused to deny the charge. Executive secretary of the Chicago Committee to Defend the Bill of Rights, Criley was expelled from a United Packing Workers' Chicago local in 1947 on charges of Communist activities.

"Far more interesting than his removal, however, is the opposition to his removal put up by the federally financed center. The center's advisory council, by 23 to 15, actually voted against recommending Criley's ouster.

"Clarence Cash, director of the center, said he was not concerned with the charges against Criley and had removed him because he became a 'center of controversy' and because he had 'refused' to tell the council whether he was or was not a Communist.

"Cash actually indicated he might reconsider putting Criley back on the council even if he admits he is a Communist. Asked what he would do if Criley freely confessed to it, Cash said, 'Anyone can sit on the council if he doesn't cause a problem.'

"The question many concerned lawmakers want answered is: Why do Sargent Shriver's anti-poverty bureaucrats allow taxpayers' money to be channeled into such irresponsible groups?"

In 1970, Criley was one of 36 national sponsors of the Continuations Committee of the Chicago Emergency Conference to End Repression. The group petitioned the United Nations to indict the United States on charges of genocide because allegedly savage police (federal, state, and municipal) had carried out a program of genocide against "red, brown, yellow and particularly black Americans." With Criley as national sponsors were at least seven well-known Communists: Herbert Aptheker, William L. Patterson, Irving Sarnoff, Anne Braden, Charlene Mitchell, Aubrey Grossman, and Charles Garry.

Criley has been a sponsor of the ultra-leftist Emergency Conference to Defend the Right of the Black Panther Party to Exist. In the *National Laymen's Digest* (November 15, 1971), it was reported: "Hugh Hefner's lucrative sex-oriented magazine is not always wholly devoted to sex. The strange phenomenon which has gripped the left-wing forces within the United States – that of tying anything-goes type of sexual activity in with hatred of anti-Communism – was worked in reverse order in the pages of *Playboy.*

"In the November 1971 issue of *Playboy*, pages 78 and 79, there is a feature called 'Forum Newsfront,' which consists of short summary news items pertaining to sexual subjects for the most part. Sandwiched in with these is a slanted story about the Subversive Activities Control Board which holds hearings on Communist and Communist-oriented groups at the Federal government level. After referring to the type of hearings held by the SACB as 'similar to those held by Senator Joe McCarthy in the Fifties,' the writer of the article then refers the reader to a letter titled 'Burying the Bill of Rights' in this month's 'Playboy Forum.'

"The letter starts on page 84 and ends on page 86. It is a vicious attack on the SACB, running two full columns, and is signed by one Richard L. Criley, Midwest Director of an outfit calling itself National Committee Against Repressive Legislation, Chicago, Illinois." (The Criley committee is nothing less than the old National Committee to Abolish the Un-American Activities Committee under a new name.)

WILLIAM CRITTENDEN was born on June 28, 1908 in New Boston, Pennsylvania, son of Sue Cook and Ernest Crittenden. He married Eleanor Setchel. He is an alumnus of Lafayette College (B.S., 1929; D.D., 1954) and the Episcopal Theological School in Cambridge, Massachusetts (B.D., 1936). He also studied at Harvard University (1935-1936).

From 1934 until 1942, Crittenden did parish work: curate at St. Paul's Church in Brookline, Massachusetts (1934-1935); vicar of Grace Church in Dalton, Massachusetts, and St. Luke's Church in Lanesboro, Massachusetts (1936-1939); and rector of St. John's Church in North Adams, Massachusetts (1939-1942). From 1942 until 1945, he was a student pastor, an assistant professor of religion, and assistant to the president at Lafayette College. From 1945 until 1949, he was executive secretary of the youth division of the National Council of the Protestant Episcopal Church. From 1943 until 1953, he was chaplain of the Chautauqua Institute. From 1948 until 1952, he was a member of the board of the Ecumenical Institute in Geneva, Switzerland. From 1949 until 1952, he was archdeacon of the Southern Ohio Diocese. In 1952, he was consecrated bishop of the Episcopal Diocese of Erie, Pennsylvania, and has served that diocese to the present time. From 1963 until 1965, he was president of the Province of Washington of the Episcopal Church. Since 1960, he has been an official of the leftist-oriented National Council of the Churches of Christ as vice-president (1963-1966) and member of the general board (1960 to the present).

Crittenden has been affiliated with the leftist-pacifist Fellowship of Reconciliation; the ultra-leftist Clergy and Laymen Concerned about Vietnam; and the People's Peace Treaty, an ultra-leftist project. Since at least 1966, Crittenden has joined with the far-left Amerian clergy in applying pressure upon the U.S. Government to abandon the people in South Vietnam and their government under the pressure of Communist aggression.

GEORGE W. CROCKETT JR. was born in 1910 in Jacksonville, Florida. He is married. He attended Morehouse College. He is an alumnus of the University of Michigan (LL.B., 1934). Between 1934 and 1947, he practiced law in West Virginia. He worked as an attorney with the Department of Labor, the U.S. Fair Employment Practices Commission, and the United Automobile Workers. In 1948, he returned to the private practice of law in a Detroit firm headed by Communist Maurice Sugar. In 1965, he was an unsuccessful candidate for Detroit's city council. In 1966, he was elected to a six-year term as a judge in Detroit's Recorders Court.

On March 29, 1969, the second national convention of the black separatist Republic of New Africa was being held in Detroit's New Bethel Baptist Church. A Detroit patrolman saw a group of armed men standing outside the church. (The men were later identified as members of the Black Legion, a paramilitary unit of the Republic of New Africa.) When the patrolman called out to the men, one of them shot and killed him instantly, and the killer and his companions fled in the direction of the church. The dead patrolman's partner, who was wounded in the shooting, radioed police headquarters for help. When police reinforcements arrived they were fired upon from the church. The police entered the building by force. They arrested 143 persons. They confiscated rifles, pistols, and ammunition. A few hours later — on a Sunday morning —

Crockett began holding habeas corpus proceedings, and by early afternoon all but a few of those arrested were released from police custody. (Some time later, FBI director J. Edgar Hoover described Crockett's action as "releasing a gang of trigger-happy racial militants.") City officials, the Detroit Police Officers Association, and thousands of Detroit citizens protested Crockett's actions — but in vain. (On the other side of the coin, Crockett's bizarre conduct was hailed by the ultra-radical Americans for Democratic Action, the ultra-radical American Civil Liberties Union, and the National Lawyers Guild, a Communist front.) At a news conference, Crockett defended his actions by saying: "Can any of you imagine the Detroit police invading an all-white church and rounding up everyone in sight to be bused to a wholesale lockup in a garage? Can any of you imagine a [white] church group . . . being held incommunicado for seven hours . . . without their constitutional rights to counsel? Can anyone explain in any other than racial terms the shooting by police inside a closed and surrounded church?" Crockett, of course, ignored the facts: (1) a policeman had been slain; (2) another policeman had been wounded; (3) the police had sighted an armed group of the paramilitary Black Legion, which fled into the church; and (4) the "church group" for whom Crockett was so solicitous was a convention of the revolutionary Republic of New Africa, which had as its avowed objective the establishment of an all-black republic located in the southern States. The group had pledged itself to wage guerrilla warfare in the North. It had attempted to plead its case for independence before the United Nations. It had tried to establish diplomatic relations with Red China and Communist Cuba.

CROCKETT

Crockett's role in the New Bethel episode attracted a great deal of publicity and focused attention upon his long history of leftist activities. In 1946, he was a sponsor of the Civil Rights Congress when it was originally formed in Detroit, and he took part in its activities for many years. Found to be a "Communist-front organization" within the meaning of the Internal Security Act of 1950 and ordered to register as such with the Attorney General, ". . . the CRC (an unincorporated association) was formally brought into being in Detroit, Michigan, in April 1946, and . . . there was a merger into respondent [the Civil Rights Congress] of certain other organizations such as International Labor Defense (ILD), the National Federation for Constitutional Liberties (NFCL) and the National Negro Congress (NNC). [The CRC] was created and established by the Communist Party as an organization which would utilize defense of civil rights for Party purposes and raise and maintain mass defense and bail funds for Party use . . . . The respondent [CRC] succeeded to the role of the International Labor Defense as the Party's legal defense arm.

"With increasing congressional and executive action in 1948, designed to meet the threat of Communist subversion, *e.g.*, the indictment of the Party's national board under the Smith Act, the Party immediately directed respondent to fulfill its primary function to defend against the threat to the Party . . . . Respondent's major activity became the defense of Party leaders, and the Party continued to assign functionaries and members as officers of or to work in CRC to insure that respondent would operate in accordance with the Party program . . . . In addition, it is found that such Party representatives consti-

tute an important medium through which the Party exercises continuous domination and control over the operation of CRC.

" . . . The respondent conducted picket lines, issued literature, distributed petitions, sponsored mass rallies and demonstrations, and propagandized other civil rights cases, principally those involving Negroes, in order to arouse and gain mass support for the Party and its various programs and to raise funds for the defense of the Party. In so functioning the CRC has, pursuant to the Party's united front technique, associated the Party's struggle with the defense of civil liberties, Negro rights and protection of the foreign-born. It has, also pursuant to the Party strategy, recruited persons to join the CRC, for eventual recruitment into the Party.

"The CRC has raised and utilized in excess of one million dollars for legal defense and bail for Party leaders and members. [It] has through mass campaigns aroused support for the Party and its policies. It is reasonable to conclude that this support would not have been realized in the same degree without the efforts of respondent in its ostensible role as other than a Communist organization . . . . While ostensibly having a degree of autonomy, and being conducted by their own officials, . . . branches provided for by respondent's constitution . . . are, in effect, an integral part of respondent . . . . They were formed at the instance of the Party and have been dominated by Party members, as representatives of the Party who hold official positions in them." (Guide to Subversive Organizations and Publications.)

In 1949, Crockett was defense attorney for Jack Stachel, educational director for the Communist Party, and Carl Winter, Michigan organizer for the Communist Party. Stachel and Winter were two of 11 Communist Party leaders who were tried before Federal Judge Harold R. Medina and were convicted, under the Smith Act, for advocating the overthrow of the United States by force and violence. Judge Medina found Crockett in contempt of court and sentenced him to four months in federal prison for his disruptive activities during the course of the trial. (During the course of the trial, Crockett described the Communist Party as the "conscience of America." He also said: "So far as the Communist Party is concerned, it is probably more accurate to say that Negroes have used the Communist Party [rather than vice versa]. It is the one party in which they feel free to speak and to act like Americans. It is the only party that seemingly cares about the plight of the Negroes in this country." He had expressed similar sentiments when he was hired to defend Stachel and Winter: "The Communist Party, greatest champion of Negro rights, doesn't have to take their hats off to anyone when it comes to fighting on that issue, and, naturally, it would select a Negro attorney.")

In the aftermath of the trial, the Communist Party, using a newly contrived front (National Non-Partisan Committee to Defend the Rights of the 12 Communist Leaders), distributed in pamphlet form an abridged version of Crockett's summation to the jury. The pamphlet carried the title "Freedom Is Everybody's Job." It was a glowing tribute to the Communist Party and its leaders – especially its Negro leaders.

In 1950 and 1951, Crockett sponsored a petition submitted to the United Nations charging the United States with waging genocidal warfare against American Negroes. The petition was initiated by the Civil Rights Congress, which published the diatribe in the form of a booklet entitled "We Charge Genocide."

Since at least 1946, Crockett has been a member of the National Lawyers Guild. In 1964, he organized 66 attorneys to go to Mississippi in an NLG project designed to defend civil rights agitators. In 1968, he was vice-president of the NLG. (The National Lawyers Guild has been cited as a Communist front which "is the foremost legal bulwark of the Communist Party, its front organizations, and controlled unions" and which "since its inception has never failed to rally to the legal defense of the Communist Party and individual members thereof, including known espionage agents.") In 1963, Crockett was invited to the White House to discuss civil rights problems with President John F. Kennedy and Attorney General Robert F. Kennedy. In that same year, Crockett participated in the Selma-Montgomery march, led by the arch-agitator Martin L. King Jr.

Crockett has been affiliated with the American Committee for Protection of Foreign Born [Americans] ("subversive and Communist"); the National Assembly for Democratic Rights ("created, dominated and controlled by members of the Communist Party"); *Freedomways* ("a Communist publication"); and *Science and Society* ("a Communist publication"). He has served as defense attorney for scores of Communists and/ or Fifth Amendment pleaders in courts and before congressional investigating committees. He was active in the Communist-led demonstrations on behalf of the convicted atom spies, Ethel and Julius Rosenberg. He has emerged as a staunch supporter of Communist Angela Davis. (In 1971, Crockett was elected as head of the first formal organization of black judges during the annual conven-

CROSS

tion of the National Bar Association, a predominantly black organization of judges, lawyers, and law professors. During the course of the convention, the National Bar Association agreed to contribute money for Angela Davis' defense.) As recently as 1970, he visited the Soviet Union, where he expressed his admiration for the Soviet judicial system, the Soviet educational system, and, in general, the standard of living of the Soviet people.

EPHRAIM CROSS was born on March 6, 1893 in Boston, Massachusetts, son of Rose Vandenberg and Abraham Cross. He married Mary Hochlerner. He is an alumnus of the City College of New York (B.A., 1913); Columbia University (A.M., 1914; Ph.D., 1930); and New York University's School of Law (J.D., 1929). He is the author of *Change of Typology* (1967).

From 1914 until 1917, Cross was a high-school teacher in New York City. From 1917 until 1920, he was employed by the U.S. Government in various civilian capacities. In 1920 and 1921, he was an instructor in Romance languages at the New Jersey College for Women and Rutgers University. From 1922 until 1931, he was again a high-school teacher in New York City. Since 1931, he has been at the City College of New York as instructor (1931-1935), assistant professor (1936-1958), associate professor (1958-1963), and professor (since 1963). From 1965 until 1967, he was a visiting professor at Yeshiva College.

Cross has been affiliated with the American Committee for Democracy and Intellectual Freedom ("subversive and un-American" – "Communist front"); the American Committee for Protection of Foreign Born [Americans] ("subversive and Communist"); the

American Council on Soviet Relations ("established by the Communist Party"); American Peace Mobilization ("subversive"); the Artists' Front to Win the War ("Communist front"); the Citizens' Committee to Free Earl Browder ("Communist"); the Citizens Committee for Harry Bridges ("Communist"); the Citizens' Committee to Secure Bail for Martin Young ("Communist"); the Committee to End Sedition Laws ("complete domination by the Communist Party"); the Committee for Peaceful Alternatives to the Atlantic Pact ("Communist front – "part of Soviet psychological warfare against the United States"); the Committee to Secure Justice for Morton Sobell ("a Communist Party enterprise"); the National Committee to Secure Justice in the Rosenberg Case ("Communist front"); the Council on African Affairs ("subversive and Communist"); the Council for Pan-American Democracy ("subversive and Communist"); the National Committee to Repeal the McCarran Act ("Communist front" – "subversive"); the National Federation for Constitutional Liberties ("subversive and Communist"); the New York Council of the Arts, Sciences and Professions ("Communist front"); the World Peace Appeal ("subversive"); the [Morris] Schappes Defense Committee ("Communist"); the Civil Rights Congress ("subversive and Communist"); the School for Democracy ("a Communist Party-controlled institution"); the National Lawyers Guild ("the foremost legal bulwark of the Communist Party, its front organizations, and controlled unions"); Veterans of the Abraham Lincoln Brigade ("subversive and Communist"); the ultra-leftist American-Korean Friendship and Information Center; the ultra-leftist American Society for the Study of the German Democratic Republic; the Emergency Civil Liberties Committee ("Communist front" – "subversive"); the ultra-leftist Fort Hood Three Defense Committee; the Aptheker Dinner Program, celebrating the 50th birthday of the Communist Party's most celebrated theoretician; the leftist Conference for Legislation in the National Interest; the leftist Citizens Emergency Defense Conference; the ultra-leftist Medical Aid to [Castro's] Cuba Committee; the National Assembly for Democratic Rights ("created, dominated, and controlled by members and officials of the Communist Party"); the *Freedomways* tribute to DuBois, honoring one of the world's most prominent Communists; the Committee for GI Rights ("Communist front"); the Socialist Workers [Party] Campaign Committee ("subversive and Communist"); and the National Committee to Abolish the House Un-American Activities Committee ("to lead and direct the Communist Party's 'Operation Abolition' campaign"). He has often petitioned on behalf of Communist Party leaders. In 1965, he was counsel to the leftist-oriented Freedom Democratic Party in Mississippi. He is a veteran opponent of anti-subversive legislation and congressional investigating committees.

JAMES E. CROSS was born on October 8, 1921 in New York City, son of Martha McCook and Eliot Cross. He was married to and divorced from Mary Goelet. He is married to Meredith Morgan. He is an alumnus of the University of Virginia (LL.B., 1948). He is the author of *Conflict in the Shadows: The Nature and Politics of Guerrilla War* (1964).

From 1943 until 1945, Cross served with the Office of Strategic Services. From 1948 until 1951, he was with the Central Intelligence Agency. In 1951 and 1952, he was a research assistant 'at the Princeton Institute for Advanced Study, which since its inception has been a haven for leftwing academicians. From 1952 until 1957, he was a research associate at Massachusetts Institute of Technology's Center for International Studies, an adjunct of the Central Intelligence Agency. From 1957 until 1961, he was a special assistant to the Secretary of the Navy and a special assistant to the Assistant Secretary of the Navy for Research and Development. From 1961 until 1969, Cross was with the Institute for Defense Analyses as a member (1961-1964) and secretary (1964-1969). During Cross's association with the Institute, the think factory produced its controversial three-volume report, *Study Fair*. The document dealt with United States foreign policy and military strategy. It recommended that limitations be placed upon the acquisition of military intelligence and information. It recommended a no-win war strategy and unilateral restraint of arms development and arms control. The major feature of the entire report was a policy of appeasement toward the Communist powers. Since 1963, Cross has been a visiting professional lecturer at American University's School for International Service.

Cross is a long-time nonresident member of the Council on Foreign Relations, the informal supra-State Department of the United States, and long-time member of the leftist-oriented Washington Institute of Foreign Affairs.

NORMAN DAIN was born on October 5, 1925 in New York City, son of Bessie Gordon and Joseph Dain. He married Phyllis Segal. He is an alumnus of Brooklyn College (B.A., 1953) and

Columbia University (M.A., 1957; Ph.D., 1961). He is the author of *Concepts of Insanity in the United States, 1789-1865* (1964).

In 1958, Dain was an instructor in history and economics at the Polytechnic Institute of Brooklyn. From 1958 until 1961, he was a research assistant in psychiatry at Cornell University's Medical College. Since 1961, he has been at Rutgers University as instructor (1961-1962), assistant professor (1962-1964), associate professor (1964-1968), and professor (1968 to the present) of history.

Dain has been affiliated with the leftist-pacifist Ad Hoc Faculty Committee on Vietnam. He has participated in several annual ultra-leftist Socialist Scholars Conferences.

GEORGE B. DANGERFIELD was born on October 28, 1904 in Newbury, England, son of Ethel Tyrer and George Dangerfield. He came to the United States in 1930 and was naturalized in 1943. He was married to and divorced from Helen Spedding. He is married to Mary Schott. He is an alumnus of Hertford College of Oxford University (B.A., 1927). He is the author of *Bengal Mutiny* (1932); *The Strange Death of Liberal England* (1935); *Victoria's Heir* (1942); *The Era of Good Feeling* (1952); *Chancellor Robert R. Livingston of New York* (1960); and *The Awakening of American Nationalism, 1815-1828* (1965). He is the co-editor of the abridged edition of Henry Adams' *History of the United States of America* (1963).

In 1928 and 1929, Dangerfield taught at the English Institute in Prague, Czecho-Slovakia. In 1929 and 1930, he taught at the English College in Hamburg, Germany. From 1930 until 1932, he was a reader and assistant editor for the publishing house of Brewer, Warren, and Putnam in New York. From 1933 until 1935, he was the literary editor of *Vanity Fair* magazine. Since 1935, he has been a free-lance lecturer and writer. In 1957 and 1958, he was a Benjamin D. Shreve fellow at Princeton University. Since 1968, he has been a lecturer in history at the University of California in Santa Barbara. He has received the Pulitzer prize in history, Columbia University's Bancroft prize in American history, the California Literature Silver Medal Award, and the Marquis Biographical Award.

Dangerfield has been affiliated with the ultra-leftist American Civil Liberties Union; the ultra-leftist Americans for Democratic Action; and the National Committee to Abolish the House Un-American Activities Committee ("to lead and direct the Communist Party's 'Operation Abolition' campaign").

PETER P. DARROW was born on September 12, 1919 in Glen Cove, New York, son of Michelena and Vasili Darrow. He married Charlotte Noble. He is an alumnus of New York University (B.S., 1942) and the University of Michigan Law School (LL.B., 1948).

Since 1948, Darrow has had a law practice in Ann Arbor. Since 1964, he has been secretary and a member of the board of International Automated Machines, Inc. In 1965, he organized and founded Ann Arbor Community Development, Inc. Since 1946, he has been active in the Democratic Party in Michigan on all levels — precinct, ward, city, county, district, and state; and in 1964, he was a delegate to the Democratic National Convention. In 1965, he was finance chairman in Weston Vivian's successful campaign for a seat in the House of Representatives. In 1966, he was a member of the steering committee in G. Mennen Williams' unsuccessful campaign for a seat in the U.S. Senate.

Darrow is a life member of the ultra-radical National Association for the Advancement of Colored People. He has been a member of the ultra-leftist American Civil Liberties Union; the leftist-oriented Episcopal Society for Cultural and Racial Unity; and the leftist-racist Congress of Racial Equality. He has been a member and an official of the ultra-radical Americans for Democratic Action.

MARCIA DAVENPORT was born on June 9, 1903 in New York City, daughter of Alma Gluck and Efrem Zimbalist (stepfather). She was married to the late Russell Davenport. She attended Wellesley College and the University of Grenoble in France. She is the author of *Mozart* (1932 and 1936); *Of Lena Geyer* (1936); *The Valley of Decision* (1942); *East Side, West Side* (1947); *My Brother's Keeper* (1954); *Garibaldi* (1957); *The Constant Image* (1960); and *Too Strong for Fantasy* (1967). She has contributed to magazines including *Fortune, McCall's, New Yorker, Reader's Digest*, and *Saturday Evening Post*.

From 1928 until 1931, Mrs. Davenport was on the editorial staff of *New Yorker* magazine. From 1932 until 1934, she was a free-lance writer. From 1934 until 1939, she was music critic for *Stage* magazine. In 1936 and 1937, and since 1965, she has been a commentator on Metropolitan Opera Broadcasts.

Mrs. Davenport is affiliated with the National Federation for Constitutional Liberties ("subversive and Communist") and the National Council for Civic Responsibility, an election year's drive (in 1964) against anti-Communists by the Democrat Party.

DONALD K. DAVID was born on February 15, 1896 in Moscow, Idaho, son of Ella Jameson and Frank David. He married Elizabeth Souien. He is an alumnus of the University of Idaho (A.B., 1916). He is the author of *Retail Store Management Problems* (1922). He is co-author of *Problems in Retailing* (1926).

Between 1919 and 1955, David was at Harvard's Graduate School of Business Administration as instructor (1919-1921), assistant professor (1921-1926), associate professor (1926-1927) of marketing; and assistant dean (1920-1927), associate dean (1942), and dean (1942-1955). From 1927 until 1930, he was with the Royal Baking Powder Company as executive vice-president (1927-1929) and president (1929-1930). In 1929 and 1930, he was vice-president of Standard Brands, Inc. From 1930 until 1941, he was vice-president of Great Islands Corporation. From 1932 until 1941, he was president of American Maize Products Company. He has been a director of R.H. Macy & Company, Pan Am World Airways, Alcan Aluminum, Ltd., and the Great Atlantic & Pacific Company.

David is a long-time member and/or nonresident member of the Council on Foreign Relations, the informal supra-State Department of the United States. He has been a member of the Business Advisory Council, virtually the CFR's patronage link to the federal goverment. He has been a member of the Committee for Economic Development, the major propaganda arm of the Council on Foreign Relations, in the important work of socializing the American economy. He has been a trustee of the ultra-leftist Ford Foundation.

WILLIAM DAVIDSON was born on July 20, 1919 in Miles City, Montana, son of Catherine Gold and Thomas Davidson. He married Mary Shoemaker. He is an alumnus of Montana State University (B.S., 1940) and Berkeley Divinity School (S.T.B., 1946). In 1947, he was ordained to the ministry of the Episcopalian Church.

From 1946 until 1956, Davidson served as minister and rector at various parishes in Montana. From 1956 until 1962, he was associate secretary of the division of town and country in the home department of the general council of the Episcopal Church. From 1962 until 1965, he was rector of Grace Church in Jamestown, North Dakota. Since 1966, he has been Episcopal bishop of Western Kansas.

Davidson has been affiliated with the ultra-leftist-pacifist Fellowship of Reconciliation; the leftist-pacifist National Citizens Committee for the Amendment to End the War; and the ultra-leftist Clergy and Laymen Concerned about Vietnam. He endorsed the Hanoi-inspired People's Peace Treaty, the pet 1971 project of the ultra-left in America.

ANGELA DAVIS was born on January 26, 1944 in Birmingham, Alabama, daughter of Sallye and B. Frank Davis.

In 1959, when Miss Davis had completed the tenth grade of high school in Birmingham, she was recruited by the Southern Negro Student Committee of the American Friends Service Committee to attend a northern school. The ultra-leftist-pacifist AFSC was at that time paying tuition for promising black southern students. Miss Davis was sent to the Elisabeth Irwin High School in New York City. The high school was an adjunct of the Little Red School House, a leftist educational complex which includes on its board of trustees Doxey Wilkerson, a long-time national committeeman of the Communist Party.

During the two years Angela Davis spent at Elisabeth Irwin High, she lived at the home of Rev. William Howard Melish and his family. Throughout his adult life, Melish had compiled a monumental history of affiliations with Communist fronts and Communist projects. When Miss Davis was living with the Melish family, William Melish was eastern representative of the Southern Conference Educational Fund. Melish has recounted what he remembers of Angela Davis when she was completing her high-school education: "Angela knew about the [civil rights] movement but her family had not been any part of it. It was very clear to us – and Sally [Davis, Angela's mother] had repeated this – that they had tried to shield their children from the difficulties in Birmingham. We think of Birmingham as the Johannesburg of the United States. Angela was not active at this time. Angela's political interests came after she moved here. Some people talk about Angela being active from the very beginning. It just ain't so." Melish mentioned that at least twice a year he travelled throughout the South, talking to people in the civil rights movement and meeting with black leaders. When the black leaders went to New York, they stayed at the Melish home. Said Melish: "They were all coming through our house while Angela was here. The whole atmosphere was one of activism. There probably were very few homes in the country where she would have been exposed to the movement as she was here." A classmate, Amy Saltz, has a different impression of Angela as a high-school student: "The school encouraged the questioning of social mores, political mores, the bourgeois society in general. I couldn't figure what she was doing there. She was so middle class. I remember feeling that she didn't have anything to do with the problems of the South — that she had led a very protected existence down there."

As part of her social studies program at Elisabeth Irwin High, Angela was required to spend a few hours in each week in community work. She chose a teenage center in Brooklyn where Mrs. Melish was the director. Youths from all over the city of New York congregated at the teen-age center. William Melish observed: "She showed a remarkable capacity from the start to sit down and talk to these youngsters and they would talk to her. They would rap for hours. Here was demonstrated for the first time her remarkable ability to communicate — quite an amazing thing."

In 1961, Miss Davis graduated from Elisabeth Irwin High. She applied for admission to a number of colleges in the North. She was accepted at Mount Holyoke, Western Reserve, and Brandeis University. Miss Davis enrolled at Brandeis and her decision was evidently influenced by the $1,500-a-year scholarship given her by that institution. In her junior year, under a special program, she studied at the Sorbonne in Paris. In Paris, she became deeply involved with Algerian students, and she became quite sympathetic to the Communists' drive for an independent Algeria.

When Miss Davis completed her studies at the Sorbonne, she returned to Brandeis University for her senior year, during which she came under the influence of Herbert Marcuse. Marcuse, a German-born Marxist, is frequently and accurately described as the "Prophet of the New Left." Campus radicals in Europe and America have been attracted to his blend of Marxism, nihilism, and anarchism. Angela Davis came under his spell to the extent that she studied every course offered by Marcuse during her senior year at Brandeis. For his part, Marcuse describes Angela Davis as one of the best or one of the two or three best students he has had in his teaching career, which spans more than three decades.

In 1965, Angela Davis received her A.B. from Brandeis University. With strong encouragement and advice from Marcuse, she enrolled in the Institute of Social Research at the Johann Wolfgang von Goethe University in Frankfurt, Germany. At Goethe, she studied under Marcuse' fellow Marxist and close friend, Theodore W. Adorno. During her two years in Frankfurt, she associated with extreme leftwing radical students. (Miss Davis once wrote: "While at Brandeis I first met (Herbert) Marcuse, and enrolled in some of his philosophy courses. He had the greatest influence on me through his lectures, his books, and as a person. As a result of this I decided to do my graduate work in philosophy. It was with Marcuse's recommendation that I was accepted as a student with Theodore W. Adorno at the Institute of Social Research in Frankfurt. I spent two years there. This Institute is a center for Marxist study.")

In 1967, Miss Davis returned to the United States and began to study again under the tutelage of Herbert Marcuse, who had moved from Brandeis to the University of California in San Diego. In 1968, Miss Davis received her M.A. from the University and began her doctoral candidacy under Marcuse. While at San Diego, she became closely associated with black militants in the Los Angeles area, especially the Black Panthers and Ron Karenga and his US organization. On the San Diego campus, she was a leader of black militants who agitated and demonstrated for a third college at the University. Miss Davis and her cohorts presented non-negotiable demands to the University's administrators. The demands were met, with the result that a black studies college was created on the campus. At the time when Miss Davis was becoming involved with black militants, she also became closely associated with Dorothy Healey, a veteran Communist Party official in southern California. In 1968, Miss Davis became a member of the Communist Party. She also joined the Che-Lumumba Club, a black adjunct of the Communist Party, which serves to recruit young blacks as Communists. She was herself recruited into the Che-Lumumba Club by Franklin and Kendra Alexander, two very prominent black Communists on the California scene. (Miss Davis wrote of her enlistment in the Communist Party: "My decision to join the Communist party emanated from my belief that the only true path of liberation for Black people is the one that leads toward a complete overthrow of the capitalist class in this country . . . . Convinced of the need to employ Marxist-Leninist principles in the struggle for liberation, I joined the Che-Lumumba Club, which is a militant, all-Black collective of the Communist Party in Los Angeles committed to the task of rendering Marxism-Leninism relevant to Black people . . . ." On another occasion when Miss Davis was asked by reporters why she had become a Communist, she replied: "I am from Birmingham. I was introduced to Marxism at a very early age as a result of my involvement in the civil rights movement.")

In the summer of 1969, Miss Davis was hired as an acting assistant professor of philosophy with an annual salary of $10,260 at the University of California.

Donald Kalish, head of UCLA's philosophy department, was responsible for the hiring of Miss Davis. Kalish, who had described himself as to the left of the Communist Party, said: "I did not know Miss Davis was a member of the Communist Party when I recommended her appointment to the Chancellor. If I had known, it would not have affected my decision to hire her." On July 1, 1969, in the UCLA's campus newspaper, the *Daily Bruin*, there was an item alleging that a Communist was a member of the philosophy faculty. On July 3, 1969, Ed Montgomery in the *San Francisco Examiner* named Angela Davis as the Communist. On July 5, 1969, the regents of UCLA requested Chancellor Charles E. Young to find out if Miss Davis was a Communist. He asked her by letter. She replied: "At the outset let me say that I think the question posed is impermissible. This, on grounds of constitutional freedom, as well as academic policy. However, and without waiving my objections to the question posed, my answer is that I am now a member of the Communist Party." On September 19, 1969, the regents met to discuss the case of Miss Davis. California Governor Ronald Reagan led a faction of the regents demanding her ouster and a majority of the regents followed Reagan's leadership. Ed Pauley, one of those who voted against Miss Davis, said: "I'm not a Communist and I don't propose to be a member of a board of regents or trustees that employs Communists or lets them propound their propaganda for a party that advocates the overthrow of the government of the United States. I would not advocate the state giving the university money if we did such a thing."(Professor Davad Kaplan of UCLA, a leader of the Ad Hoc Committee to Coordinate the Defense of

Angela Davis, told reporters at a news conference of the UCLA faculty's "almost universal sense of outrage" at Miss Davis' dismissal. Said Kaplan: "Among the primary responsibilities is intellectual honesty – to seek and state the truth as one sees it, free from hypocrisy of compromise with external pressures. I believe that Prof. Davis gives every evidence of having the courage of her convictions.")

After the regents made their decision, Miss Davis sought relief in court. She was supported by a majority of UCLA's faculty. On October 20, 1969, Judge Jerry Pacht of the County Superior Court, a leftist in his own right, overruled the regents, declared their action unconstitutional, and restored Miss Davis to her position on the faculty. (Jack V. Fox of United Press International provided an anecdote relating to Miss Davis: "During the controversy over whether she should be allowed to teach at UCLA, multimillionaire industrialist Norton Simon invited her to lunch at a Los Angeles restaurant. Simon, who unsuccessfully opposed Ronald Reagan for the GOP gubernatorial nomination in 1970, was a member of the university board of regents. After some brief small talk, Simon leaned over to the poised, soft-spoken woman and said: 'Well, you certainly don't look like a Communist and you don't act like a Communist.' Angela put down her knife and fork and turned to him. 'Mr. Simon, I do not want you to misunderstand one thing for a moment,' she said. 'I am dedicated to the overthrow of your system of government and your society.' ")

On June 19, 1970, the UCLA regents voted against the renewal of Miss Davis' contract. They did not mention her membership in the Communist Party. They gave as their reason for voting against her employment, "Extra-university commitments and activities interfere with her duties as a member of the faculty." One regent, Frederick Dutton, defended Miss Davis by saying: "A 26-year-old bookish black girl surely is no threat to our state or our country or the traditional values that the overwhelming majority of us believe in."

During her one year as a faculty member, Miss Davis had become a well-publicized activist and agitator. In the spring of 1970, she went to Cuba with the Venceremos Brigade – a trip which had become a favorite project of the New Left. Later she recalled: "When I came back from Cuba in 1970, for instance, and was approached by people in the news media, one of the things they would ask me was, 'if you like it so much over in Cuba, why didn't you stay?' I said that I certainly liked it, but precisely because of the fact, I feel that we have to achieve in this country what the Cubans achieved in Cuba. I had to come back and work toward that and not take the easy way out – living in Cuba or living in Africa."

In February 1970, Miss Davis spoke on the campus of the University of California at Santa Barbara, where there had been a number of violent student demonstrations. The subject of her talk was a shooting in Los Angeles between the police and Black Panthers. Said Miss Davis: "That's what we have to start talking about, demonstrative actions which show pig forces what we can do – even though we don't do it then – but we can do. And those thousands of black people who showed up [after the arrest of Black Panthers] were ready to move, we were ready to move and then, in fact, a number of people went inside the jail and some people were even talking about freeing the political prisoners. The trouble was that we didn't have our necessary implements with us. But we have to conceive of such actions as being potentially destructive things, destructive in a constructive manner. And I have to admit that I really felt proud standing out there on Central Avenue early in the morning of December 8 and saw that my brothers and sisters were able to hold off 300 pigs. They were able to hold off 300 pigs! We have to begin to show that force in the hands of the people is going to be a liberating force, not a destructive force the way it is in the hands of the oppressors. When people start saying that we are out to subvert, that we are subversive, we should say, 'Hell, yes, we are subversive. Hell, yes, and we're going to continue to be subversive until we have subverted the whole damn system of oppression.' "

On another occasion, Miss Davis spoke about the controversy between the regents and militants over the occupation of the People's Park on the Berkeley campus of the University of California. Said Miss Davis of the regents: "They killed, they brutalized, they murdered human beings."

Sensational public statements became commonplace. In a speech at Berkeley, Miss Davis said: "Maybe the real criminals in this society are not all of the people who populate prisons across the state but those people who have stolen the wealth of the world from the people. Those are the criminals. And that means the Rockefellers, the Kennedys, you know the whole Kennedy family, and that means the state that is designed to protect their property because that's what Nixon's doing, that's what Reagan's doing, that's what they're all doing." To a group of students at San Diego State College, she said: "As a Communist I have to seek radical change

and as I see it capitalism does not contain the solution to our problems today. Capitalism can provide only a token way of solving problems. People are beginning to wake up to the fact that we have to talk about radical solutions." On another occasion, she said: "The first condition of freedom is the open act of resistance. Physical resistance. Violent resistance. The road toward freedom, the path of liberation, is marked by resistance at every crossroad." And just after the Soledad case: "We have to talk about going into the streets but this time we have to talk about going with the masses of people, with the millions of people, and demanding our rights. Because if we do not do this at this point . . . then I think we can very well talk about an era of fascism coming into being. It's up to us. It's our responsibility to prevent this from coming about. It's our responsibility to stand up and resist and fight right here and now."

In March 1970, Miss Davis became involved with the Soledad brothers. The brothers were three unrelated black inmates of the California State Correctional Institution at Soledad. In January 1970, during a period of unrest at Soledad, a white guard was killed. Three inmates – George L. Jackson, John Cluchette, and Fleeta Drumgo – were indicted for murdering the guard. The defense of the "Soledad brothers" became a major cause for black militants and leftists. Angela Davis became the Soledad brothers' most active champion. She and George Jackson, the oldest of the Soledad trio, exchanged a great many letters and Jackson's younger brother Jonathan became her constant companion and bodyguard.

On August 7, 1970, Jonathan Jackson entered the San Rafael courtroom of Judge Harold J. Haley. Jackson carried four guns into the courtroom. He held the courtroom at gunpoint. He freed James McClain, a San Quentin convict on trial for assaulting a guard, and Ruchell Magee, another convict waiting to testify. Jackson gave McClain and Magee guns. Magee freed another convict, William Christmas, who was also waiting to testify. Jackson and the three convicts seized Judge Haley, Assistant District Attorney Gary Thomas, and three women jurors as hostages. Jackson shouted he wanted the release of all three Soledad brothers. The kidnappers wired a shotgun around the neck of Judge Haley. They fled with their hostages outside the courthouse in an attempt to reach an escape vehicle. Once outside the courthouse, however, police officers opened fire. Jackson, Christmas, and McClain were killed. Judge Haley was killed by a blast from the shotgun around his neck. Kidnapper Magee, Assistant District Attorney Thomas, and one woman juror were wounded. A week after the shoot-out, District Attorney Bruce Bales charged that of the four guns brought into the courtroom by Jackson, three were purchased by Angela Davis in Los Angeles in January 1968, April 1969, and July 1970. The fourth gun, said Bales, was purchased by Miss Davis in San Francisco two days before the shoot-out. In the meantime, it was learned that within less than three hours of the shoot-out, Miss Davis had fled from San Francisco to Los Angeles by plane. Four days later the Federal Bureau of Investigation placed her on its "ten most wanted" fugitive list. Miss Davis remained a fugitive until October 13, 1970 when she was arrested by the FBI in New York City. She was found in a motel in company with David R. Poindexter of Chicago, who had a history of Communist Party affiliations.

Miss Davis was charged with unlawful interstate flight to avoid prosecution for murder and kidnapping.

On October 15, 1970, two days after Miss Davis was arrested, the Communist Party in Los Angeles called a press conference. Franklin Alexander, chairman of the Communist Party's Che-Lumumba Club, announced that the Communist Party was going to build the "largest, broadest, most all-encompassing people's movement the country has ever seen to free our comrade, Angela Davis − political prisoner." Shortly thereafter, Alexander announced the formation of the National United Committee to Free Angela Davis. On November 21, 1970, Gus Hall, the head of the Communist Party in the United States, said: "The defense of Comrade Angela Davis is the most urgent task and is of key importance ... [and] the initial reactions are already evidence of this. The reaction to her arrest has been explosive. We have never had such a response from the world Communist movement, overnight her defense has become a world movement of great significance."

The importance Gus Hall ascribed to the case of Angela Davis was emphasized in a report he made to the National Committee of the Communist Party. In the report, reprinted in the *Daily World,* December 9, 1970, Hall said: "As the forces of repression and racism grow, the need for a new look, the need for new initiatives in the field of the defense of people's rights has become more urgent and pressing .... The frame-up of Angela Davis, the indictment of Arnold Johnson, the continued trials of Black Panther leaders, the increased activities of the Subversive Activities Control Board, all emphasize the need for greater efforts in the defense field.

"In all of this, the defense of Angela

Davis is of key importance. There is no question the defense of Angela Davis can trigger a movement that can free Angela Davis; a movement against repression, against racism and for the democratic rights of all Americans that is without precedent in our memory. The initial reactions are evidence of this fact. The frame-up case against Angela Davis has become symbolic to millions of the continued racist frame-up of 25,000,000 black Americans. Her imprisonment is symbolic of the racist ghetto imprisonment of 25,000,000 black Americans.

"The frustrations of Angela Davis, even after winning her degrees in philosophy, and her academic brilliance, are symbolic of the frustrations of millions of youth – especially black youth. To tens of thousands of youth, her probing and seeking for solutions to the evils of capitalism are symbolic of their probings. They identify with her militancy and dedication. The probing by Angela Davis and her experiences led her to join the Communist Party. What the ruling class most worries about and tries to avoid is that her joining the Communist Party may become symbolic for thousands of others. Angela Davis has become known to millions, through her struggles against racism and especially through her struggle to have a right to teach and to do so as a Communist.

"Angela Davis is also identified with the movement for the rights of prisoners. This movement has grown, especially against the barbarism and brutalities practiced against black youth in prisons. Racism in prison is genocide at its worst. In prison racism has its victims in chains beyond the protection of the law or the public.

"Thousands identify with the struggles against the social causes – the racism, hunger, slums that create the conditions from which young men and women are placed into prison. Countless numbers – thousands – serving long prison sentences are also victims of police department frame-ups. This is also a feature of racism. Thousands identify with the struggle against the causes and against the brutalities, while correctly not condoning or identifying with specific acts that result in prison sentences.

"Thousands identify with the struggles against the prison brutalities. The Soledad Brothers' struggles are a part of this struggle. They are victims of this vicious endless cycle. Young Jonathan Jackson was a victim of this struggle. Thousands identify with the motives of young Jackson to do something about the endless imprisonment of black youth. But while identifying with the motives, they most correctly see the events in San Rafael as ill-considered acts of desperation that can only lead to tragedy.

"Thousands correctly admire the personal heroism of 17-year-old Jackson, but see the events in San Rafael as an act that does not advance the very cause he so desperately wanted to serve. The lesson of all history of the class struggle, the lesson of all struggle against reaction, against racism, the lesson of San Rafael – is that the only path to keep people from being sent to prison or to free them from prison, or to end the barbarism of the prison system, is the path of mass struggle.

"Jonathan Jackson in his 17 short years personally lived; and learned about the brutalities of the system of racism. He had emerged for only a few brief moments into the movement to end that racist brutality. But he had not yet had time to learn that in the struggle against oppression there are detours but there are no shortcuts. In memory of many young Jonathan Jacksons of the past, and for the benefit of thousands joining into the battle, we cannot and we must not play hide-and-seek with what is right and what is wrong — what are right and what are mistaken concepts of struggle. In these matters we must not speak from both sides of the mouth at the same time.

"On matters of freeing prisoners by the force of guns, in the context of our struggles, there is no 'tactical diversity.' We cannot accept such concepts even though they are not the 'primary' or the 'sole,' tactic. Once this door is opened — that such concepts are all right if they are not 'the primary tactic' — then it follows that one can say: 'The final significance of Jonathan's revolt was its clear connection with the mass movement — certainly a revolutionary act.' An act that does not advance the revolutionary cause is not revolutionary. On the contrary, it was a separate act of heroic desperation, but unrelated to the movement and its needs. It was an act leading to a withdrawal from the mass movements.

"The racist enemy works very hard to make the link between individual acts of terror and the mass movements that they try to suppress. Therefore, we should not play this game. This is the very meaning of the frame-up of Angela Davis. Any concept of 'tactical diversity' opens the doors to the work of the police agents. Let us not open those doors.

"We Communists must have the deepest compassion and understanding of the hopes, desires and frustrations of the thousands of young Jonathan Jacksons — victims of capitalist and racist oppression — who are moving into the struggle. The youth who are probing and seeking for solutions — they are and they

will, join the Communist Party and the Young Workers Liberation League in ever greater and greater numbers. They will join the Communist movement on many levels of their development. As new forces always do, they will bring in the benefit of good experiences as well as some not so good. They will have to acquire through learning and further experiences the science of revolution.

"Our party is not a ready-made vehicle. We have high standards but our party is also an organization reflecting this process. It is for this reason that our party is an organization of struggle but is also a school of the working class. In our party every member goes through a daily 'on-the-job' training. We must not close the doors because of mechanical standards.

"Thousands who are in the struggle, thousands who are drawn to the revolutionary process, thousands who do now, and thousands who will, identify with the defense of Angela Davis, will become Marxist-Leninists in the experiences of the struggle. We must meet our responsibilities in furthering this process. We must have compassion and understanding but we cannot fulfill this responsibility by playing with or going around mistaken ideas. We must always put our position forward honestly in a straightforward manner. We cannot win people to the Marxist-Leninist position or to the party in any other way.

"We can win Angela Davis' freedom. We can do so by building a movement of mass defense that will go a long way in freeing all victims of racism and of capitalism."

The worldwide campaign for the defense of Angela Davis became a reality immediately after her arrest in New York. Singer Aretha Franklin volunteered to post any bail necessary to secure the release of Miss Davis. Black leaders Ralph Abernathy and Coretta King were among the first to rally to her side. Julian Bond, a black agitator and State Representative of Georgia, said: "All blacks should rally to the legal support of Angela Davis, she comes from us." James Baldwin, the author and black agitator, published an open letter to Angela Davis in the British *Manchester Guardian*, stating: "The enormous revolution in black consciousness which has occurred in your generation, my dear sister, means the beginning of the end of America." The Black Muslims, the Black Panthers, the Urban League, and almost all other major black organizations, went to her defense.

In Italy, Communists circulated petitions in factories, shops, and schools demanding that the Italian Government formally protest the imprisonment of Angela Davis. In Ceylon, 2,500 women held a three-day vigil honoring Angela Davis in front of the U.S. Embassy. In Sydney, Australia, a similar march was conducted by 700 women. Dolores Ibarruri, leader of the Spanish Communists, expressed "the solidarity of the complete Spanish Communrist Party with Angela Davis, our outstanding comrade and the most valiant representative of progressive American women." The World Federation of Teachers Unions, representing teachers in Europe, Asia, Africa, and Latin America, called upon all teachers and their organizations to fight for the freedom of Angela Davis. Communist groups in East Germany and West Germany demonstrated on behalf of Miss Davis. The entire cast and crew working on the motion picture *Z* signed and published a telegram demanding freedom for Angela Davis. The signers included Yves Montand, Simone Signoret, Costa Gavras, director of the film,

and musical composer Mikis Theodorakis. Former boxing champion Cassius Clay, alias Muhammad Ali, and actor Sammy Davis Jr. pledged their support to Miss Davis.

From Moscow, Peter J. Shaw of United Press International wrote: "In the eyes of the Kremlin, Angela Davis is an angel of Communism who can do no wrong. The Soviet Union is rooting for dismissal of the kidnaping, murder and conspiracy charges against her. Seldom has the Kremlin had a better vehicle for anti-American comment. The Soviet propaganda mill has found in the case rich grist for criticism of the United States.

" 'It is no accident that the baiting and persecution of Angela Davis coincided with a period when . . . the country is entering a period of political repression,' the official TASS news agency said. 'The Davis case is being staged after the worst models of McCarthyism which flourished in the United States in the fifties.'

"TASS leads the 'Free Angela Davis' movement in the Soviet Union. It said the 'frame-up charge' was made to stage a political trial 'directed against the Communist Party of the United States, Negro organizations which fight for civil rights and against the entire progressive and antiwar movement in the country.'

"The U.S. 'ruling circles are combatting public opposition at home all down the line,' TASS said. 'The San Rafael trial is part of this onslaught by American reaction. More and more people in the United States and beyond it are coming out in defense of Angela Davis and demanding an end to arbitrary rule and persecution and the release of all political prisoners in the United States.'

"*Pravda,* the Communist Party newspaper, describes Miss Davis as a 'well-known Communist and fighter against the oppression of Negroes.' *Pravda* said America was guilty of 'the vicious hounding of Angela Davis.' Police 'fabricated' her case, it said.

" 'The case of Angela Davis and the Vietnam War are links of a single chain of crimes in the United States,' TASS said in attacking what it called 'the prepared trial of the courageous Communist.' TASS said some of the Soviet Union's leading artists wrote President Nixon asking him to 'use his influence' to release Miss Davis. The signers included composers Dmitry Shostakovich and Aram Khachaturian and Bolshoi Prima Ballerina Maya Plisetskaya, TASS said. 'There is no doubt that they [U.S. authorities] put Angela Davis on trial to silence all those who naively believe that "McCarthyism is long gone," ' TASS quoted the letter to Nixon as saying."

On November 4, 1970, the national board of the YWCA issued "A Statement of Concern," which the Communists in their *Daily World* reported with more than a little interest: "The National Board of the YWCA issued a 'statement of concern' for Angela Davis, and urged that the black revolutionary's constitutional rights be protected. It was the first time the YWCA has spoken out on an individual's behalf, a spokesman said.

"The YWCA 'statement of concern' about Angela Davis notes 'that racism continues to permeate all institutions of our society' and that the YWCA will 'thrust our collective power toward the elimination of racism, wherever it exists and by any means necessary.' "

On May 26, 1971, the Religious News Service reported: "The Council on Church and Race of the United Presbyterian Church was mildly censured by the denomination's General Assembly when it was disclosed here that $10,000 of the committee's $100,000 Emergency Fund for Legal Aid went to help the defense of black militant Angela Davis. The General Assembly defeated two attempts to issue a strong rebuke to the committee, but declared that it 'entertains serious questions on the propriety of the grant' to Miss Davis' defense." The chairman of the Council on Church and Race, Rev. Edler Hawkins — a long-time veteran of Communist fronts — explained: "We made the grant because we knew this black lady needed help in securing an adequate defense just because she was a black and a woman and because she, too, must be treated as innocent until proven guilty."

At Brandeis University, the Committee to Elect Angela circulated a petition describing Miss Davis as "one of a large and growing number of political prisoners whom the government is jailing in an attempt to intimidate those who would fight for real change." The petitioners conducted a campaign to elect Angela Davis as president of the Brandeis University alumni association. She was not elected, but she did receive almost one-quarter of the votes cast.

When Angela Davis was arrested a number of radical lawyers rallied to her side. They included Allen Brotsky, Dennis Roberts, and John Thorne, all of whom were activists in the National Lawyers Guild — "the foremost legal bulwark of the Communist Party." Michael Tigar joined the defense; although a young man, he had amassed an impressive list of affiliations with the Communist Party and its fronts. Howard Moore Jr. from Atlanta had achieved fame with his defense of black revolutionaries H. Rap Brown and Stokely Carmichael. Moore made no attempt to hide his racism: "I would hate to see

Angela, a beautiful black woman, having a white defense. She's going to get a black defense. Look, I have tried many cases before red-neck juries. When the jury knows you are committed and you are a true adversary, they respond in a positive manner. Especially when you deal openly and up front with the question of racism. White people know they are racists, and if you conduct yourself in a manner in which you try to hide the fact that you know it, they don't respect you. You can't deal honestly with the kind of jury we're going to get unless you deal frontally with the question of racism. And that's what we're going to do . . . . She is in the clutches of the law. A trial is inevitable. She is being tried for her life. Given the deep-seated racial hatred and the political nature of the trial, the only way she can be freed is to bring enough pressure to insure that she has a fair trial. The outside pressure forces them to be more scrupulous. It is salutary . . . . We are going to raise the question of the national status of blacks in the courtroom. When we say that Angela should be judged by her peers, we mean by other blacks . . . . If we can get Angela a jury of her peers, the question of the outcome of this trial doesn't even have to be guessed at."

Margaret Burnham, who had been a grade-school classmate of Miss Davis, was one of the first attorneys to join the defense. Miss Burnham followed the line that Miss Davis was the victim of a political-racist frame-up: "The [Communist] Party is playing a major role. Angela is a member and it is incumbent on the party to come to her defense. I say that because we want to be up front about it. There is no 'infiltration' in the case – they are here." Miss Burnham, when asked the meaning of the slogan

"Free Angela," replied: "Well, we mean it literally. It is a bogus prosecution. The prosecution is a fraud. If she didn't have the color or politics that Angela has, she would be free. Since she is going to be prosecuted, though, she should have a fair trial."

John J. Abt, general counsel of the Communist Party, was perhaps the best-known attorney to join the Davis defense. Abt portrayed the case as a struggle between a young black Communist and her racist-fascist enemies. However, Abt did stress the "political frame-up" line: "If this were an ordinary criminal case, one could say with some reasonable confidence that the indictment of Angela would have to be dismissed because the evidence adduced before the grand jury was insufficient even to charge her with the crimes for which she was indicted. But this is not an ordinary case. It is a political case. Tonight Nixon is escalating the war against the people of Southeast Asia, and the escalation of that war is being accompanied by his escalation of the war against the civil liberties of the people of the United States. So the fight to free Angela becomes a fight against both of these escalations.

"The prejudice, the hysteria that the ruling circles in this country have tried to whip up against Angela, must be countered by a vast people's movement. Never in my experience as a civil liberties lawyer have I known such broad support for any case as the support that has been demonstrated for Angela Davis here in this country and throughout the world. Support that ranges all the way from the Young Women's Christian Association to the extreme left."

The National Conference of Black Lawyers offered its help to Angela Davis by appointing a panel of 12 black law professors from 11 colleges to provide advice and counsel to Miss Davis' attorneys. Dean Paul E. Miller of Howard University's Law School was chairman of the panel. Miller went to great lengths denying that he and his fellow panel members were primarily interested in the defense of a Communist. He made it quite clear that his panel was most concerned about the defense of a black, and he presented the strong implication that a team of white lawyers would not be conscientious if it defended Angela Davis: "We cannot allow capricious and arbitrary acts by government officials to deprive any individual of his dignity — and as long as one human being, be it Angela Davis or anyone else, is deprived of the social justice that is guaranteed under our Constitution, no citizen is safe. The time is gone forever when middle class Blacks who have a certain expertise will sit back and allow their leadership to be destroyed by those who believe that a contrary opinion is a dangerous force.

"Jack Johnson, the first Black heavyweight champion of the world, and W.E.B. DuBois, one of the greatest scholars the world has ever known, and Paul Robeson, one of the greatest singers of all times, who because of his political beliefs was driven from the stage — these Black leaders were all effectively silenced — and thus the Black community was deprived of dignity and heroes. No longer will we stand by and allow our community to be deprived of the best of our brains or our political dissenters.

"We are saying no, never again will a Black man be persecuted simply because he disagrees with a majority political belief or engages in activities which are not in conformity with majority values.

"The sum total of our lives, individually and collectively, is determined by the kinds of laws that we have and the manner in which they are administered. The law can bring equality to one's life. It can assure life, liberty and the pursuit of happiness, but the kind of laws being passed today do not aid equality or assure life, liberty or pursuit of happiness.

"The Blacks of today as well as the youth, Chicanos and brown Americans are, indeed, making certain demands of government. They are in fact demanding power to deal with the various political and legislative forces that repress them.

"They are demanding the freedom to participate in the formulation and application of standards of responsibility. These groups have been dictated to for centuries, and their identities have been defined for them. And for centuries American lawyers have sat by and refused to champion them in these demands for improvement. A lawyer has a responsibility to see that citizens are treated fairly, equally and with justice. We hope by forming this panel we can demonstrate to others this aspect of the lawyers' role to assure us that no citizen will go unprotected or will go without the guarantees that all citizens and humans under our government should have."

One of the first of many organizations formed to support Miss Davis was the Angela Davis Legal Defense Fund. The chairman of the fund was actor Ossie Davis, who on many occasions had performed similar services for other Communists in trouble. Ossie Davis knew the Communist line to be taken on behalf of Miss Davis, as he said: "Personally I am fully convinced that Angela Davis is the victim of a monstrous frame-up. There are in high places those who would silence her, hoping thus to terrorize tens of thousands of youths,

Black Americans and progressives of every color and creed who are inspired by her dauntless courage and moved by some phase of her program. I can only say, 'Forward to the Freedom of Angela Davis!' "

One of the most vocal supporters of Angela Davis was Rev. Ralph Abernathy, head of the Southern Christian Leadership Conference. Abernathy was a featured speaker at a combined 1971 birthday celebration and fund-raising event for Miss Davis, held at the Manhattan Center in New York City. In his address to the 5,000 gathered in the audience, Abernathy presented a wildly hyperbolic frame of reference for the case of Angela Davis. Said Abernathy: "Angela Davis would be the first to remind us that she is not the only political prisoner in America. Ladies and gentlemen, brothers and sisters, there are thousands of political prisoners in America, and the only way to free them is to get out and struggle in a mass movement of the people. We need fund raising for Angela Davis, but we also need hell-raising for millions of others in this country.

"Let us work to teach the people these things about the case of Angela Davis: Number one, in a democratic society an accused person is supposed to be presumed innocent until proven guilty. Yet already, in my estimation, Angela Davis has been tried and found guilty in the news media. Number two, an accused person has a right to a fair trial in which the accused is entitled to be judged by a jury of his or her peers. But I raise this question with you – how can Angela Davis get a fair trial in Ronald Reagan's California? Number three, since the state itself has placed the political beliefs of Angela Davis in question, and since public officials and the mass media have unloosed a torrent of adverse publicity before Miss Davis has even been brought to trial, this in fact is no ordinary criminal case, but a political case that raises overwhelming questions about the possibility of a fair trial. In fact, I see it as a trial, not of Angela Davis, but of America.

"I see the American system charged with the kidnapping, the murder and the conspiracy. I charge the American system with the kidnapping of Black people from Africa."

For two months after her arrest, Angela Davis and her attorneys fought extradition proceedings in the state and federal courts. When extradition was granted, she was removed to California on December 22, 1970. Two weeks later, she was arraigned at San Rafael. On March 16, 1971, pre-trial hearings began in the Marin County Court. For the next eleven months, Miss Davis and her attorneys played a stalling game. They fought for bail, for a change of venue, and for delays in the trial date. They challenged jurors and judges.

In the meantime, the Communist Party in the United States and throughout the world was making the cause of Angela Davis similar in scope to the earlier cases of the Scottsboro Boys, Sacco and Vanzetti, and the Rosenbergs. On September 23, 1971, the Communists printed a special Angela Davis issue of *World Magazine* as a supplement to the *Daily World*. The Communists boasted that more than 200 local Free Angela Davis Committees were at work in the United States. They boasted of the cities in scores of countries on every continent "where either meetings or demonstrations were held, and where newspapers and magazines published articles on Angela's behalf." Joseph North of the *Daily World* staff, in a fanciful account, wrote: "How universal is the outcry is attested to by my own experiences. In my recent travels to the Mongolian People's Republic, I found Angela's picture in the round tents of the herdsmen who asked me many questions about the case, Angela's health, the attitude of the American people, etc."

The *World* reported on the individuals and groups who had demanded the release of Angela Davis on bail. They included the American Federation of Teachers at their national convention; the International Longshoremen's and Warehousemen's Union at their national convention; the United Farm Workers Organizing Committee of Cesar Chavez; the California Federation of Teachers; the California Democratic Council; the National Association for the Advancement of Colored People; the National Black Lay Catholic Caucus; the Peoples Coalition for Peace and Justice; the Southern Christian Leadership Conference; the Southern Conference Educational Fund; the Young Workers Liberation League; the Veterans of the Abraham Lincoln Brigade; U.S. Representatives Bella Abzug, Shirley Chisholm, Ron Dellums, and Augustus Hawkins; entertainers Roberta Flack, Jane Fonda, Dick Gregory, Paul Newman, and Joanne Woodward; black agitators Rev. Wyatt Tee Walker, Coretta Scott King, and Rev. Jesse Jackson; historians Staughton Lynd and Howard Zinn; Mayors Warren Widener of Berkeley, California, and Robert Blackwell of Highland Park, Michigan; and individual Communist leaders Herbert Aptheker and Henry Winston. Others who gave their support to Angela Davis included Kay Camp of the Women's International League for Peace and Freedom; U.S. Representative Charles Rangel, Democrat of New York; Pete Seeger, veteran favorite entertainer of the Communist Party; Beulah Sand-

ers, chairwoman of the National Welfare Rights Organization; Anne Braden of the Southern Conference Educational Fund; and labor leaders Frank Angell, Abe Feinglass, Charles Hayes, Paul Schrade, Harry Syverson, and Tom Turner.

Throughout 1971, aside from the Communist press, Angela Davis was a popular topic in letters-to-the-editor columns in American newspapers. Invariably, the letters reflected the identical views presented by the Communist Party in its pro-Davis propaganda drive. A typical letter was the one printed in the *Philadelphia Inquirer* on May 8, 1971. It was submitted by 61 members of the staff and faculty of Temple University. It read, in part: "Angela Davis now faces a possible death sentence on charges of murder, kidnapping, and conspiracy, in connection with the Marin County Courthouse 'shootout' at which she was not present and with which she denies any connection. These charges are not separate from, but are a continuation of, her persecution for her political activities and associations.

"Further indications of the political nature of this case are the attempts to create public hysteria against her and to deny her access to proper judicial procedures such as her listing on the FBI's most wanted list as 'armed and dangerous,' exposing her to being shot on sight; the denial of bail; her imprisonment in solitary confinement; and California's refusal to release the indictment to her attorneys (needed to fight extradition from New York).

"The attack upon Angela Davis is part of an attempt by the repressive forces in the country to move it in a reactionary direction. The focus of the attack at this moment is someone they believe is most vulnerable — a black, Communist woman. In making charges of this magnitude against her, these forces count upon the racism and anti-Communism of our society to inhibit people from coming to her defense, to deny her the presumption of innocence, and to convict her before trial. It is of vital concern to us all that they fail."

In the summer of 1971, the Angela Davis furor was complemented by two incidents: the Attica prison uprising in New York and the death of 'Soledad brother' George Jackson when he attempted to escape from the prison at San Quentin. On October 8, 1971, the *New York Times* provided an opportunity for Angela Davis to present her views on Attica, the death of Jackson, and what she called other "acts of repression." She did this in an article, "Lessons: From Attica to Soledad," written in the Marin County jail. She wrote, in part: "Prisons have recently witnessed an accelerated influx of militant political activists. In utter disregard of the institutions' totalitarian aspirations, the passions and theories of black revolution and Social revolution have penetrated the wall. Outstanding political leaders have sprung up to enlighten their captive companions and initiate them into struggle. Years before George Jackson achieved a public presence, he was loved, respected and acknowledged as a political leader throughout the California prison system.

"The combined effect has been a conscious thrust among many prison populations toward new and arduously wrought collective life. Political in its general contours, this collective life is organically bound up with the dynamics of the liberation struggle in America and across the globe. Prisoners have recognized that their immediate objective must be to challenge the oppression which finds concrete expression in the penal system.

"It was precisely this new thrust which determined the content of the Attica prison revolt. Pervading their demands — which articulated their determination to end the barbarous conditions of their surroundings — was an astute political grasp of their own status. Their collective consciousness as *political* prisoners emerged with indisputable clarity . . . .

"Many observers were incredulous at the impressive organization and remarkable ability of the prisoners to forge a highly effective unity in action. Indeed, the revolt furnished irrefutable evidence of the colossal failure of the prison system in its totalitarianism. The prisoners' spirits will not be defeated by physical repression and psychological abuse. They would not be insulated from the passions and aspirations animating their communities . . . .

"Attica before the massacre afforded us a sleeping but graphic glimpse of the monumental feats attainable by men and women moving along a revolutionary course. The brothers at Attica could not have carried out the revolt without first surmounting formidable obstacles. Racism, for example, had to be internally conquered. Moreover, all this unfolded where dehumanizing efforts and racist practices are most severely and most deliberately at work.

"For those of us who are committed revolutionaries, the days preceding the massacre offered gratifying and invigorating experience. In a figurative sense, it evoked visions of the Paris Communes, the liberated areas of pre-revolutionary Cuba, free territories of Mozambique. The revolt was particularly edifying in that it burst forth as if to demonstrate that the brutal killing of George Jackson fell dismally short of its repressive aim. It was a very real affirmation that George's example, his principles and his mission live on. But at the top of the hierarchy from New York to Washington, the revolt was an unambiguous affirmation of the potential powerlessness of ruling circles . . . .

"In the aftermath, officials would resort to equivocation, untruths and myriad efforts to shift the blame onto the prisoners. But these maneuvers of deception might have been considered prior to the assault as not entirely inconceivable. In any event, plans to suppress the real story must have gone awry somewhere.

"The damage has been done. Scores of men are dead; and unknown numbers of wounded. By now, it would seem, more people should realize that such explosive acts of repression are not minor aberrations in a society not terribly disturbing in other respects. We have witnessed Birmingham, Orangeburg, Jackson State, Kent State, Mylai, San Quentin, August 21, 1970 – the list is unending. None emerged *ex nihilo*; rather all crystallized and attested to profound and extensive social infirmity.

"Perhaps, though, the events at Attica finally awakened greater numbers of people from their socially inflicted slumber. If this be true, they must recognize that their duty is twofold: to subject governments and prison bureaucracies to unqualified criticism and to acknowledge the rational and human kernel of the struggles unfolding behind prison walls through forthright supportive action."

By November 1971, after more than a year of fund-raising by Communists and others throughout the world, the Angela Davis defense team was pleading poverty. Their condition was reminiscent of so many instances in the past when they had boasted of their capacity to raise funds for the defense of a comrade. Of course, there was no public accounting for whatever funds were raised and those who conjectured that the funds were channeled into Communist Party coffers could only wait until a future defector should reveal the truth. In November 1971, writing from the Marin County jail, Angela Davis sent out her own emergency appeal for funds. In her letter she said: "As my trial approaches, the need to insure judicial fairness and bail in order that I may better prepare my defense becomes increasingly urgent. Even if we disagree on some things, we are surely united in our affirmation of principles of due process and equality before the law.

"I am charged with three capital offenses – murder, kidnapping and conspiracy. My life is at stake, but as I have repeatedly said, not simply the life of a lone individual, but a life which belongs to Black people and all who are tired of poverty and racism and the unjust imprisonment of tens of thousands.

"To have an opportunity to repel what may be a legal lynching I need your support. In the final analysis, it is not so much I who am on trial as America itself. I am less afraid for myself than for millions of present and potential victims. Having been singled out myself, my defense must be directed against the arbitrary, ruthless use of legal procedures to perpetuate injustice. Willingly I accept the risks; hopefully I will illuminate the issues as I advance understanding.

"Millions of people throughout the world – of all political persuasions and national and racial origins have voiced their concern over my trial. The national convention of the NAACP and the National Board of the YWCA have called for a fair trial and bail. The Reverend

DAVIS

Ralph Abernathy has called for my immediate release and recently visited with me. Mrs. Martin Luther King, in a statement issued last June, said: 'It is difficult to reject the conclusion that the conduct toward her is a consequence of triple bigotry. Angela Davis is Black, she is a woman militant and finally an acknowledged Communist.' Her statement concludes by reminding us that 'this situation has carried us a long way back to the agonizing inquisitions of the early fifties.'

"Intent on maintaining and intensifying the racist hysteria which I believe is inherent in the prosecution itself, the authorities have created an atmosphere of military occupation in the Marin Civic Center . . . .

"Nearly fifty years ago America, in the grip of hysteria toward the foreign-born, permitted the execution of Sacco and Vanzetti. Their blood still stains the nation's conscience. If all those who want to end what Bartolomeo Vanzetti called the days 'when man is wolf to man,' will treat this case not as mine but as theirs, a democratic victory is possible.

"Your contribution is urgently needed for my legal defense. We have exhausted our funds and many bills remain unpaid. We must conduct extensive research into the backgrounds of Marin County judges to challenge the composition of the grand jury and we must anticipate numerous complicated and expensive motions and procedures which can become a staggering financial burden." Miss Davis urged would-be contributors to send money to the treasurer of the Emergency Appeal, Gloria Steinem, the notorious leader of the women's liberation movement.

A short time after Miss Davis instituted her emergency appeal, the site of her trial was changed to San Jose in Santa Clara County. On February 7, 1972, Miss Davis was allowed to be interviewed for television by her spiritual adviser, Rev. Cecil Williams. The interview was shown over KPIX in San Francisco. The United Press International, in dispatches on February 7 and 8, reported some of the remarks broadcast by Miss Davis: "Angela Davis said Monday night that racism could not be destroyed in the United States 'until we've destroyed the whole system.' Miss Davis said that in the history of the United States 'the impact of racism has been to attempt to contain black people, has been to attempt to stifle the desires toward liberation.'

"Miss Davis also said she was a Communist 'because I have a very strong love for oppressed people, for my people.' She added, 'I want to see them free and I want to see all oppressed people through the world free. And I realize that the only way that we can do this is by moving towards a revolutionary society where the needs and the interests and the wishes of all people can be respected.'

"Miss Davis also said that the nation's law enforcement agencies 'railroad' black persons to prison. 'This is just one of the many ways that the system, and it's not a contrived effort in the sense that it's done consciously by a few men up at the top, it's built into the system. It's built into the nature of the society. And . . . a black revolutionary realizes that we cannot begin to combat racism and we cannot begin to effectively destroy racism until we've destroyed the whole system.'

"Any change in American society, the black militant and former UCLA philosophy instructor said, must come from the overthrow of 'the economic

318

structure where you have a few individuals who are in possession of the vast majority of the wealth in this country.'

"Miss Davis also called justice in America 'empty.' She said 'it has no content.' 'Things have been festering under the surface of a prison system for a long time,' she said. ' . . . And you see, I think that we have to look at what's going on in the prisons today in that respect as being a signal of what might possibly come in the society as a whole. I think that it is probably a truism by now that in any given society what goes on in the prisons reflects very important elements of the society as a whole and you can learn something about the nature of the society by looking at what happens behind its walls, among its captives.'

"She said the system repressed black activists by jailing them on charges that don't 'have any water,' then acquitting them months or even years later. ' . . . What has happened is that the black revolutionary leaders have been effectively silenced, they have been separated from their people, isolated from the community, for one year, two years, three years.' "

On February 23, 1972, Angela Davis was released from jail when $102,500 bail was provided by a California farmer, Rodger L. McAfee. She was granted bail a· week after the California Supreme Court ruled that the death penalty was unconstitutional and there was no longer the concept of capital crimes in the state. Miss Davis took advantage of her release by holding a news conference wherein she said that "the legal apparatus can no longer hold political prisoners in prison for long months prior to trial and attempt by isolating them and in many other ways to break their will to fight. It is a victory all right, but a larger victory – even in my own case – is yet to be obtained. There are many, many thousands of sisters and brothers all over this country who are forced to live their lives behind concrete and steel. We have to free our brothers and sisters." She also said that "this has been a victory in the sense that the abolition of capital punishment is very closely related to all the struggles conducted around the prisons in the last two years, related to the murder of George Jackson and to the massacre at Attica."

Long before Miss Davis was released on bail, she had achieved the stature of a martyr in the eyes of Communists and black revolutionaries, and the dupes of both groups. Few American women in all history have ever received more publicity than Miss Davis. Since the day in 1969 when she announced that she was a Communist, her picture has appeared with the frequency of a major political figure. Stories about Miss Davis are found in the most prominent places in newspapers and magazines. From the accounts of her academic career, there is little indication that she spent only a portion of one academic year with a limited teaching schedule that evidently was enough to detract from her graduate studies. The descriptions of Miss Davis as presented in the news media could understandably be envied by any American woman: "brilliant intellectual" – "warm" – "easy to be around" – "shy" – "very methodical" – "not impulsive" – "analytical mind" – "bookish" – "sensitive" – "poised" – "a certain dignity" – "strikingly attractive" – "quiet yet agreeable" – "handsome" – "sense of humor" – "attractive" – "articulate" – "extremely talented" – "always reserved" – "very modest" – "intellectually sound" – "quick to become involved with the joys and problems of other people." Once Miss Davis was released on bail, the way was paved for her trial on charges of kidnapping, murder, and conspiracy.

HORACE BANCROFT DAVIS was born on August 10, 1898 in Newport, Rhode Island, son of Anna Hallowell and Horace Davis. He was married to the late Marian Rubins. He is an alumnus of Harvard University (A.B., 1921) and Columbia University (Ph.D., 1934). He is the author of *Labor and Steel* (1934); *NRA: Fascismo e Comunismo* (1934); *Shoes: The Workers and the Industry* (1940); and *Nationalism and Socialism: Marxist and Labor Theories of Nationalism to 1917* (1967).

From 1926 until 1929, Davis was a fellow at Amherst College. In 1929 and 1930, he was an instructor at Southwestern College in Tennessee. From 1930 until 1933, he was a free-lance writer in New York City. In 1933 and 1934, he was a contracted professor at the Free School of Sociology and Politics in São Paulo in Brazil. From 1934 until 1936, he was an instructor at Bradford Junior College in Massachusetts. From 1936 until 1941, he was an instructor and assistant professor of economics at Simmons College in Boston. From 1941 until 1947, he was employed by unions and civic organizations. From 1947 until 1953, he was an associate professor of economics at the University of Kansas City. From 1955 until 1957, he was professor of economics at Benedict College in South Carolina. From 1957 until 1963, he was a professor of social sciences and chairman of the department of economics and business at Shaw College in North Carolina. Since 1963, he has been professor of economics at the University of Guyana. In 1967 and 1968, he was a special professor of

economics at Hofstra University in New York.

Davis has been affiliated with the Abraham Lincoln School ("an adjunct of the Communist Party"); the American Committee for the Protection of Foreign Born [Americans] ("subversive and Communist" — "one of the oldest auxiliaries of the Communist Party in the United States"); American Friends of the Chinese People ("Communist front"); the American League Against War and Fascism ("subversive and Communist"); the Citizens Committee to Free Earl Browder ("Communist"); the Conference on Pan-American Democracy ("Communist front"); the Council for Pan-American Democracy ("subversive and Communist"); the Emergency Civil Liberties Committee ("Communist front" — "subversive"); *Fight* ("a Communist front publication"); Friends of the Soviet Union ("to propagandize for and defend Russia and its system of government" — "directed from Moscow"); the International Labor Defense ("legal arm of the Communist Party"); the Jefferson School of Social Science ("adjunct of the Communist Party"); *Monthly Review*, a pro-Communist publication; the National Committee to Aid the Victims of German Fascism ("Communist front"); the National Federation for Constitutional Liberties ("under [Communist] Party domination and headed by responsible Party functionaries"); *New Masses* ("weekly journal of the Communist Party"); the Prisoners Relief Fund ("Communist front"); the [Morris] Schappes Defense Committee ("Communist"); the School for Democracy ("Communist Party-controlled institution"); *Science and Society* ("Communist publication"); the Workers Alliance of America ("Communist front"); the Federated Press ("Communist-controlled news syndicate"); the ultra-leftist American-Korean Friendship and Information Center; the ultra-leftist Medical Aid to [Castro's] Cuba Committee; the ultra-leftist American Society for the Study of the German Democratic Republic; the National Committee to Abolish the House Un-American Activities Committee ("to lead and direct the Communist Party's 'Operation Abolition' campaign"); and the CIO's Political Action Committee ("Communist front").

In 1953, Davis testified before the Senate Internal Security Subcommittee. He was questioned about his affiliations with the Communist Party and its fronts. Under protection of the Fifth Amendment, Davis refused to answer all questions concerning any affiliations with the Communist Party and most questions concerning his teaching experience. He was subsequently dismissed from the faculty of the University of Kansas City. As early as 1938, Davis had been identified as a member of the Communist Party, under oath, by a witness testifying before the House Special Committee on Un-American Activities. In 1944, the House Special Committee on Un-American Activities reported that Davis was a "leading member of the Communist Party." If Davis has ever left the Communist Party, the matter has not become public knowledge.

RONALD V. DELLUMS was born on November 24, 1935 in Oakland, California. He married Leola Higgs. He is an alumnus of Oakland City College (A.A., 1958); San Francisco State College (B.A., 1960); and the University of California (M.S.W., 1962).

From 1962 until 1964, Dellums was a psychiatric social worker in the California Department of Mental Hygiene. In 1964 and 1965, he was program director for the Bay View Community Center in Berkeley. In 1965 and 1966, he was associate director and director of the Hunters Point Youth Opportunity Center. In 1966 and 1967, he was planning consultant for the Bay Area Social Planning Council. In 1967 and 1968, he was director of the Concentrated Employment Program of the San Francisco Economic Opportunity Council. From 1968 until 1970, he was senior consultant for Social Dynamics, Inc. From 1967 until 1971, he was a member of the Berkeley City Council. He has been a part-time lecturer at San Francisco State College, the University of California at Berkeley, and the Berkeley Graduate School of Social Welfare. In 1970, he was elected as a Democrat to the U.S. House of Representatives from California's 7th congressional district.

During his four years on the Berkeley City Council, Dellums acquired notoriety as a radical. He had been a close ally of the ultra-radical Black Panthers. In 1969, he spoke on many occasions in defense of the leftist-controlled students who had created chaos on the San Francisco State College campus. In the Democratic primary race in 1970, he presented himself as a candidate of the ultra-leftist New Politics. His primary campaign was supported by blacks, student rebels, university faculty troublemakers, and leftist-pacifist opponents of the Vietnam War. When his primary victory was assured, he greeted his supporters with the clenched-fist salute.

During his election campaign of 1970, Dellums held on to his regular supporters and also acquired new ones, including Communist Jessica Mitford, Robert Treuhaft, Sargent Shriver of the Kennedy dynasty, and the AFL-CIO's hatchet-crew, the Committee on Political

Education. In September 1970, in Washington, D.C., the Women's National Democratic Club held a fund-raising affair for Dellums. The affair was sponsored by former Attorney General Ramsey Clark; the ultra-leftist Georgia legislator, Julian Bond; Coretta King; and U.S. Senators Birch Bayh, Alan Cranston, Fred Harris, Harold Hughes, Edward Kennedy, George McGovern, and Walter Mondale. He received generous support from the Communist press.

Dellums achieved an easy victory over his Republican opponent, John Healy, on November 2, 1970. On November 28, the congressman-elect was in Stockholm, Sweden, attending the World Peace Council's Conference on Vietnam, Laos, and Cambodia. Other Americans at the Communist conclave in Stockholm included Communists Herbert Aptheker, Gil Green, and Sylvia Krushner; and fellow-travelers Carlton Goodlett, David Dellinger, and Sidney Peck. The Communist press boasted that the Stockholm conference was "the largest international meeting in recent months to discuss U.S. aggression." Of course the results of the conference were predictable. Those in attendance endorsed North Vietnam, the Viet Cong, the Pathet Lao, and Cambodia's Red leader, Prince Sihanouk.

In Stockholm, Dellums addressed the opening session of the conference and delivered a remarkable anti-American diatribe. He certainly told his Red audience what it wanted to hear: "I have listened with concerned attention to the representatives of the peoples of Indochina as they have described the behavior of the military and the government of my country in the prosecution of this damnable war. For more than five long years, persons dedicated to bringing peace and sanity to United States foreign relations have invested their time, energy and resources in an attempt to put an end to our involvement in Southeast Asia. We look upon the initial conflict in South Vietnam as a civil war and, true to the position of our Federal government during the days of the United States Civil War, we condemn outside intervention. We believe that the Vietnamese people have every right to settle their internal problems without foreign interference.

"I doubt that I could lend any additional information to what you already know of the terrible events over the past seven years in the Vietnam War. Suffice it to say, never before in recorded history have the people of such a small nation demonstrated such heroism, courage and fortitude as the people of Vietnam in their 25-year struggle against foreign domination and external oppression.

"In the United States, the war in Indochina influences our every act and thought and is having a devastating effect upon our every political, economic and social program. This war threatens not only the survival of a tiny country 10,000 miles away, but also the domestic tranquility and moral fibre of our people at home. There is a rising cry of outrage from our citizens, in increasing numbers, who view the war in Indochina as immoral, and the behavior of our country as America's great shame and humanity's extraordinary burden. Never have the intellectuals, the youth, the religious leaders, the educators, labor and racial minorities — yes, even some members of the armed forces and the U.S. Government — been so vocal in courageous opposition to a national military undertaking.

". . . During the 1970 Congressional elections, a national coalition was formed in opposition to the war in

Indochina, racism and oppression. This was a continuing drive by the U.S. peace forces to politicize the Indochina war by electing to the Congress of the United States men and women more concerned about their responsibility to articulate the unquenchable desire of their constituents for peace than to respond to pressures from the executive branch of the government in passive support of the war. The efforts of this national coalition for peace were singularly successful, in that several peace candidates were elected.

"I stand before you as a demonstration that the peace forces of my country are becoming increasingly effective in the political pursuit of their task – of electing to the Congress persons who will respond to the cry: Out of Southeast Asia Now.

"I consider the opportunity to participate in this International Conference on Indochina an important event in the metamorphosis of candidate and Congressman-Elect Ronald Dellums into a more informed representative of the 7th Congressional District of California – a district made up of the students, faculty and administrative personnel of the University of California in Berkeley – a district that is perhaps the most politically informed, politically activist and politically demanding Congressional district in the nation. This opportunity, through this forum, for me to hear representatives of the Provisional Revolutionary Government of South Vietnam, the Democratic Republic of Vietnam, and representatives from Laos and Cambodia is a very valuable experience for me, for three purposes: First, to hear with keen interest your statement on the war being waged in your lands; Second, to reaffirm to you the dedication of my supporters to the cause of ending this war with immediate and complete withdrawal of U.S. and allied military forces; Third, out of this mutual exposure, to gain greater knowledge and develop a wider appreciation of the role I may play in the growing Congressional coalition determined to make ending the war in Southeast Asia the issue of prime importance in the 92nd Congress. Therefore, my essential mission in Stockholm is a search for information. I know that the formal presentations, as well as informal opportunities for the sharing of views, will have incalculable value.

"I have been honored by election to the United States Congress on a broad people's coalition opposed to the war in Indochina, opposed to racism and opposed to oppression. In the days that lie ahead, through the conscientious pursuit of my task, through utilization of every opportunity to speak out against humanity's three scourges – war, racism and poverty – I hope to win the treasured accolade of being counted among the growing legions of good men who challenged evil, and whose behavior demonstrated their opposition to doing nothing."

Once Dellums was seated in the House of Representatives, he wasted little time in living up to his radical reputation. In January 1971, he announced that he would head a one-man crusade to expose so-called war crimes allegedly committed by American troops in Vietnam. *Human Events* (February 6, 1971) reported: "Dellums unveiled a gory 'war crimes' exhibit in his Longworth House Office Building annex – four large poster boards with pictures of 'atrocities' and splattered with red paint to simulate blood. One photo shows a Vietnamese boy deformed by napalm. Other pictures show bomb ruins, the 'tiger cages' at Con Son prison and captured Viet Cong being tortured by U.S. soldiers.

"There is, of course, not the slightest suggestion that Communist forces in Viet Nam engage in terror as a matter of policy.

"Opening the exhibit last week, Dellums called for Nuremberg-style trials of U.S. officers responsible for so-called war crimes. 'We were very aggressive in World War II in prosecuting war crimes,' Dellums said. 'We ought to be just as interested in prosecuting our own.'

"Dellums' 'war crimes' exhibit will be staffed by the Citizens Commission of Inquiry on U.S. War Crimes, a radical-left group that has been circulating hysterical attacks on U.S. 'genocide.' A national coordinator for the group, Jeremy Rifkind, told newsmen in Dellums' office that 'there's at least prima facie evidence that war crimes are widespread and that they are the result of U.S. tactical policy in Viet Nam.' "

In May 1971, Dellums was an active supporter of riotous anti-Vietnam War demonstrators in Washington, D.C., and he also began to hold what he called war crime hearings. These activities caused Clay Claiborne, national director of the Black Silent Majority Committee, to issue a statement: "Freshman Rep. Dellums, in Congress only five months, has managed to abuse and degrade his office in an incredible manner. Indeed, he has become the New Left's version of Adam Clayton Powell.

"Ranting through a demonstrator's bullhorn and shouting insults at policemen on the steps of the capitol, Congressman Dellums openly encouraged an unruly mob to create still further disorder, at a time when most legislators and citizens were seeking to reduce tensions. When Dellums locked his doors and put his staff 'on strike,' he sided with subversive elements that cynically exploit racial problems and war dissent to push the nation toward needless anarchy and violent revolution.

"The Black Silent Majority Committee condemns Dellums for taking unfair and disgraceful advantage of his position to advance the goals of radical forces seeking to undermine the efforts of black and white Americans to end political and racial polarization.

"Dellums has done an injurious disservice to the nation's 26 million black citizens. He is one of a mere handful of Negroes serving in Congress, but has destroyed his effectiveness as a legislator by his brazen disregard of established Congressional procedures in putting together an ill-contrived Ad Hoc Committee on alleged war crimes, despite disapproval from his own party's leadership.

"The BSMC deplores the fact that Dellums' so-called hearings were not designed to evoke any objective understanding of issues, but rather to be a paltry exercise in radical propagandizing and cheap headline-grabbing. As an illustration of the hearings' lack of impartiality, at least one Vietnam veteran complained in the news media that he was flatly denied the right to testify when Dellums and other hearing organizers learned that the veteran's views were pro-American. Nothing constructive was achieved by the hearings, and Dellums should be censured for conducting a kangaroo court under guise of legitimate congressional investigation.

"Our committee wants it clearly understood that black America is shocked and outraged by Dellums' Carnival in Congress — just as all citizens are angered by those who make a mockery of courtroom proceedings and other functionings of a free society.

"Dellums casts an injurious reflection

DELSON

on every other black office holder in the nation. America has been blessed with the election of thousands of outstanding black men and women, who serve with dignity as judges, attorney generals, sheriffs, state secretaries and in other high positions."

From within the House of Representatives, Dellums' war crimes spectacle drew harsh criticism from Representative F. Edward Hébert, chairman of the Armed Services Committee, who characterized Dellums' hearings as challenging the whole committee system of the House. Said Hébert: "The rules of the House provide that evidence or testimony which may tend to degrade or intimidate any person shall be received in executive session. That rule is firmly based on justice and fair play and does not in any way impede or obstruct an investigation by a duly authorized competent committee.

"Our rules have grown out of many years of experience and are designed to promote the most efficient and effective conduct of the business of the House. They properly establish lines and boundaries of jurisdiction and those who willfully ignore or disregard them do no service to the Congress or the country."

Dellums has been affiliated with the ultra-leftist Soledad Brothers Defense Committee; the ultra-leftist National Mobilization Committee to End the War in Vietnam; the ultra-leftist Community for New Politics in Berkeley; the ultra-leftist National Peace Action Coalition; and the ultra-leftist United Front Against Fascism. He endorsed the Hanoi-inspired People's Peace Treaty. And, above all, he endorsed the resolution approved by the Soviet-controlled Stockholm conference, which read: "The war of aggression against the people of Viet Nam has now extended to a point of extreme gravity because of the renewed bombing of North Viet Nam. The aggression against the peoples of South Viet Nam, Laos and Cambodia has been intensified. The Nixon Administration is committed to a military victory over the peoples of Indochina. Its so-called 'peace proposals' are intended only to deceive the people and to prolong the war. We demand from the U.S. government:

"The immediate end of the U.S. war of aggression against the peoples of Viet Nam, Laos and Cambodia and respect of their right to self-determination. The complete and unconditional withdrawal from South Viet Nam of U.S. and satellite troops from Laos and Cambodia. The cessation of bombings and other war crimes against the three peoples. Stop U.S. support for Thieu-Ky-Khiem and the Lon Nol-Sirik Matak administration. This is the road to peace in Indochina. We demand that the U.S. government respond seriously to the fair and reasonable proposals of the peoples of Viet Nam, Laos and Cambodia. We appeal to all the peoples of the world to intensify their actions in solidarity with the just cause of the peoples of Indochina."

ROBERT DELSON was born on July 8, 1905 in New York City, son of Ethel Naumoff and Louis Delson. He married Marjorie Feldman. He is an alumnus of Cornell University (A.B., 1926) and Columbia University (LL.B., 1928). He was admitted to the New York bar in 1929.

From 1929 until 1931, Delson was associated with the law firm of Wise & Seligsberg. From 1931 until 1937, he was associate general counsel for Consolidated Film Industries, Inc., and for Republic Pictures Corporation. Since 1937, he has been an associate and member of the Delson & Gordon law

DeWITT

firm. Since 1939, he has worked as a legal specialist in international public and private law, and in international economic development. He has served as counsel for various foreign governments.

Delson has been general counsel for the leftist-oriented International League for the Rights of Man and the leftist American Committee on Africa. He has served on the national board of the ultra-radical Americans for Democratic Action. He has been a member of the ultra-leftist American Civil Liberties Union; the Foreign Policy Association, a highly effective pro-Communist vehicle; and the leftist Inter-American Association for Democracy and Freedom.

ROBERT L. DeWITT JR. was born on March 12, 1916 in Boston, Massachusetts, son of Ethel Furness and William DeWitt. He married Barbara De Yoc. He is an alumnus of Amherst College (B.A., 1937) and Episcopal Theological School (B.D., 1940). In 1940, he was ordained to the ministry of the Episcopal Church.

Between 1940 and 1960, DeWitt was at Christ Church in Oranbroak, Michigan, as curate (1940-1944) and rector (1948-1960). From 1944 until 1948, he was rector at St. Luke's Church in Ypsilanti, Michigan. From 1960 until 1964, he was the Episcopal suffragan bishop of Michigan. From 1964 to the present, he has been Episcopal bishop of Pennsylvania.

In 1971, DeWitt endorsed the Hanoi-inspired People's Peace Treaty, a pet project of the ultra-left in America.

L. HAROLD DeWOLF was born on January 31, 1905 in Columbus, Nebraska, son of Elsie Cook and Lotan DeWolf. He was married to the late Martha Monkman. He is married to Madeleine Marsh. He is an alumnus of Nebraska

Wesleyan University (A.B., 1924; S.T.D., 1948) and Boston University (S.T.B., 1926; Ph.D., 1935). He also studied at York College and the University of Nebraska. He is the author of *Issues Concerning Immortality in Thirty Ingersoll Lectures, 1896-1935* (1935); *The Religious Revolt Against Reason* (1949); *A Theology of the Living Church* (1953, 1967, and 1969); *Trends and Frontiers of Religious Thought* (1955); *The Case for Theology in Liberal Perspective* (1959); *Present Trends in Christian Thought* (1960); *The Enduring Message of the Bible* (1960); *Teaching Our Faith in God* (1963); and *A Hard Rain and A Cross* (1966).

DeWolf was ordained to the ministry of the Methodist Church in 1926. From 1926 until 1931, he was a pastor in the Nebraska Conference. From 1931 until 1936, he was a pastor in Dracut, Massachusetts. From 1934 until 1944, he was on the faculty at Boston University, starting as lecturer and ending as professor of philosophy. From 1944 until 1965, he was a professor of systematic theology at Boston University School of Theology. Since 1965, he has been dean and professor of systematic theology at the Wesley Theological Seminary. He has been a visiting lecturer at the University of Southern California, Wellesley College, the Methodist Theological Institute of Lincoln College in England, Vanderbilt University, the College of the Pacific, DePauw University, and the Facultad Evangelica de Teologia in Buenos Aires.

DeWolf has been affiliated with the Mid-Century Conference for Peace ("aimed at assembling as many gullible persons as possible under Communist direction and turning them into a vast sounding board for Communist propaganda"); the Methodist Federation for Social Action ("Communist front"); the leftist-pacifist National Committee for a Sane Nuclear Policy; the leftist-pacifist Voters Peace Pledge; the leftist-pacifist American Friends Service Committee; the leftist-pacifist Ad Hoc Committee for an Open Letter on Vietnam; and the leftist-pacifist Ad Hoc Faculty Committee on Vietnam. He has been a vigorous opponent of anti-Communist legislation, has petitioned on behalf of convicted Communist leaders; and has joined with the most extreme left of the American clergy in giving aid and comfort to the Hanoi regime.

MARIO A. DiCESARE was born on August 21, 1928 in New York City, son of Virginia DiPleco and Donato DiCesare. He married Emily Bell. He is an alumnus of St. Mary's Seminary (B.A., 1952) and Columbia University (M.A., 1954; Ph.D., 1960). He also studied at Indiana University. In 1958 and 1959, he was a Samuel S. Fels fellow. He is the author of *Vida's Christiad and Vergilian Epic* (1964) and *A Critical Study Guide to Vergil's Aeneid* (1968). He is co-author and translator of *The Book of Good Love* by Juan Ruiz (1969). He is a contributor to *From Homer to Joyce* (1959) and *Language and Style in Milton* (1967). In 1962, 1963, 1965, and 1966, he held Research Foundation-State University of New York faculty fellowships. In 1963 and 1964, he was a Guggenheim fellow.

In 1953 and 1954, DiCesare was an associate in English at Indiana University. In 1954 and 1955, he was an instructor at Duquesne University. From 1955 until 1959, he was an instructor at Pratt Institute. Since 1959, he has been at Harpur College of the State University of New York as instructor (1959-1961), assistant professor (1961-1964), associate professor (1964-1968), and professor (1968 to the present) of English; since 1968 he has been chairman of the department of English and comparative literature. He has been a visiting lecturer at Rutgers University and Brooklyn College. He has been a visiting associate professor at New York University.

DiCesare has been affiliated with the leftist-oriented Consumers Union; the leftist-racist Congress of Racial Equality; and the ultra-radical American Civil Liberties Union.

JANE DICK was born on June 6, 1906 in Lake Forest, Illinois, daughter of Marion Hall and Ezra Warner. She married Edison Dick. She is an alumna of the University of Chicago (A.B., 1958).

Mrs. Dick has been a political activist as chairman of the women's division of the Stevenson-for-Governor Committee (1948), vice-chairman of the National Volunteers for Stevenson (1952), national co-chairman of the Volunteers for Stevenson-Kefauver (1956), and chairman of the advisory committee of the Illinois Kennedy-for-President Committee (1960). From 1961 until 1965, she was the United States representative on the Social Commission of the Communist-dominated UNESCO. She was a special adviser to the U.S. delegation at the 16th, 17th, and 19th General Assemblies of the United Nations. She was a United States representative to the 18th General Assembly of the United Nations. She was a member of the U.S. delegation to the Communist-dominated ECOSOC at Geneva in 1961.

Mrs. Dick has been affiliated with the leftist-internationalist Chicago Council on Foreign Relations, the leftist Institute of International Education, the leftist-internationalist United Nations Association of the United States, and the leftist League of Women Voters.

JOHN SLOAN DICKEY was born on November 4, 1907 in Lock Haven, Pennsylvania, son of Gretchen Sloan and John Dickey. He married Christina Gillespie. He is an alumnus of Dartmouth College, where he was a Rufus Choate scholar (A.B., 1929), and Harvard University (LL.B., 1932). He is the author of *The Secretary of State* (1965). He is the editor of *The United States and Canada* (1965). In 1932, he was admitted to the Massachusetts bar.

In 1932, and from 1936 until 1940, Dickey practiced law in Boston. In 1933, he was an assistant to the commissioner of the Massachusetts Department of Correction. From 1934 until 1936, he was with the Department of State as assistant to the assistant secretary of state and as assistant to the Department's legal adviser. In 1940, he was a special assistant to Secretary of State Cordell Hull. From 1940 until 1944, he was a special assistant to Nelson A. Rockefeller, the Coordinator of Inter-American Affairs. In this same period, he was chief of the Department of State's Division of World Trade Intelligence. In 1944 and 1945, he was director of the Office of Public Affairs in the Department of State. In 1945, he was public liaison officer for the United States delegation at the organizing conference of the United Nations. In 1944 and 1945, he lectured on American foreign policy at the School of Advanced International Studies of The Johns Hopkins University. From 1945 until 1970, he was president of Dartmouth College.

Dickey is a long-time nonresident member of the Council on Foreign Relations, the informal supra-State Department of the United States. He has served on the board of directors of the leftist-internationalist Atlantic Council of the United States. He has served on the Committee for Economic Development, the major propaganda arm of the Council on Foreign Relations, in the important work of socializing the American economy. He has been affiliated with the Rockefeller Foundation, a pillar of the Liberal Establishment; the Ford Foundation, which has been a horn of plenty for leftwingers and leftwing projects on every continent; and the World Peace Foundation, which exerts considerable influence upon the Department of State, the Department of Defense, and the Central Intelligence Agency in an overall program of appeasement toward the Soviet Union. He has served as an advisor to the federal government on civil rights and disarmament.

IRVING DILLIARD was born on November 27, 1904 in Collinsville, Illinois, son of Mary Look and James Dilliard. He married Dorothy Dorris. He is an alumnus of the University of Illinois (B.A., 1927). He pursued graduate studies at Harvard University (1928-1929), and later (1939) was a Nieman fellow at Harvard. He is the author of *Building the Constitution* (1937); *The Development of a Free Press in Germany: An Aspect of American Military Government* (1949); and *I'm From Missouri* (1951). He is the editor of *Mr. Justice Brandeis: Great American* (1941); *The Spirit of Liberty: Papers and Addresses of Learned Hand* (1952); and *One Man's Stand for Freedom: Mr. Justice Black and the Bill of Rights* (1964). He is a contributor to *Missouri: A Guide to the Show-Me State* (1941); *Old Cahokia* (1949); *Lincoln for the Ages* (1960); *Quarrels That Have Shaped the Constitution* (1964); *The Missouri Reader* (1964); *Reporting the News*

(1965); *The Responsibility of the Press* (1966); and *Hugo Black and the Supreme Court* (1967). He has also contributed to the *Dictionary of American Biography*, the *Dictionary of American History*, the *Dictionary of Political Science*, *Encyclopaedia Britannica*, the *Encyclopedia of the Social Sciences*, the *Home Encyclopedia*, *Collier's Encyclopedia*, *World Book Encyclopedia*, *Notable American Women*, *American Scholar*, *Atlantic Monthly*, *Harper's*, *Nation*, *Journal of Negro History*, *New Republic*, *Public Opinion Quarterly*, *Yale Law Review*, and *Saturday Review*.

From 1923 until 1960, Dilliard was with the *St. Louis Post-Dispatch* as a local correspondent (1923-1927), reporter (1927-1930), editorial writer (1930-1960), and editor of the editorial page (1949-1957). From 1928 until 1936, he was a correspondent for the *Christian Science Monitor*. From 1962 until 1965, he was an editorial columnist for the *Chicago American*. Since 1963, he has been the Ferris Professor of Journalism at Princeton University. He has lectured at the University of Illinois, Colby College, Brandeis University, the University of New Mexico, the University of Oregon, DePauw University, the University of Kansas, the University of Nevada, and the University of California. He has also lectured at the Salzburg [Austria] Seminar in American Studies.

Dilliard has been a member of the national board of the ultra-radical Americans for Democratic Action. He has been a national committeeman of the ultra-leftist American Civil Liberties Union. He has been affiliated with the National Committee to Abolish the House Un-American Activities Committee ("to lead and direct the Communist Party's 'Operation Abolition' campaign") and the ultra-leftist-pacifist World Fellowship, Inc.

BEN DOBBS was born on February 23, 1912 in New York City. He attended the University of California at Los Angeles.

On April 24, 1962, Dobbs testified before the House Committee on Un-American Activities. He invoked the Fifth Amendment in response to all questions relating to his affiliations with the Communist Party. He joined the Communist Party on November 14, 1933 and became active in the Young Communist League. In 1938, he was administrative secretary of the Young Communist League in California. In 1948, 1949, and 1950, he was labor secretary for the Communist Party in Los Angeles County. In 1951, he was arrested for violation of the Smith Act. In 1952, he was convicted for conspiring to teach and advocate the violent overthrow of the United States Government. He was fined $10,000 and sentenced to five years imprisonment. He appealed the fine and prison sentence. Eventually, the Supreme Court of the United States reversed the decision of the lower courts and directed that he be granted a new trial. Subsequently, his indictment was dismissed upon the recommendation of the United States Attorney.

In recent years, Dobbs has served as administrative secretary of the Southern California District of the Communist Party and as a member of the executive board of the Party's Southern California District Council. He has been affiliated with the Castro-subsidized Fair Play for Cuba Committee; the ultra-leftist National Mobilization Committee to End the War in Vietnam; the ultra-leftist Huey Newton-Eldridge Cleaver Defense Committee; the Constitutional Liberties

Information Center ("Communist front"); the American Student Union ("Communist front"); and the ultra-leftist Spring Mobilization. In 1968, he ran for political office on the Peace and Freedom ticket. He is a member of the National Committee of the Communist Party.

M. EUGENE DODGE was born on November 1, 1930 in Minneapolis, son of Genevieve Coursolle and Marshall Dodge. He married Joan Kedrowske. Since 1951, he has been an associate engineer with the Northern States Power Company.

Since 1964, Dodge has been active in the leftist Democrat-Farmer-Labor Party. In 1966, he was an unsuccessful candidate for the state senate on the Democrat-Farmer-Labor ticket. In 1968, he was an alternate delegate to the Democratic National Convention. He has been affiliated with the ultra-leftist American Civil Liberties Union; the ultra-leftist Americans for Democratic Action; the leftwing-internationalist United World Federalists; the leftwing-internationalist United Nations Association of Minnesota; the leftist-pacifist Twin Cities Draft Information Center; and the ultra-leftist New Democratic Coalition.

WILLIAM VON EGGERS DOERING was born on June 22, 1917 in Ft. Worth, Texas, son of Antoinette von Eggers and Carl Doering. He was married to and divorced from Ruth Haines. He is an alumnus of Harvard University (B.S., 1938; Ph.D., 1943).

In 1941 and 1942, Doering was a research chemist with the National Defense Research Council at Harvard University. In 1943, he was a research chemist for Polaroid Corporation. From 1943 until 1952, he was a member of the faculty of Columbia University. From 1952 until 1967, he was at Yale University as professor (1952-1967) and director of the science division (1962-1965). Since 1967, he has been a professor at Harvard University. In 1944 and 1945, he was a research chemist for the Office of Product Research and Development. From 1947 until 1959, he was a director of the Hickrill Chemical Research Foundation. Since 1956, he has been a consultant to the Upjohn Company, and since 1958, a consultant to the Procter & Gamble Company.

Since 1962, Doering has been chairman of the Council for a Livable World, an ultra-leftwing pacifist and political pressure group making a special appeal to the scientific community. The CLW lobbies for a ban on all underground nuclear tests; a drastic reduction in military spending; abolition of all restrictions on East-West trade; an end to travel bans that prevent Americans from visiting North Viet Nam, Red China, and Communist Cuba; and a "non-aligned" Viet Nam. The CLW also makes substantial financial contributions to so-called peace candidates.

HEDLEY DONOVAN was born on May 24, 1914 in Brainerd, Minnesota, son of Alice Dougan and Percy Donovan. He married Dorothy Hannon. He is an alumnus of the University of Minnesota (A.B., 1934) and Oxford University in England, where he was a Rhodes scholar (B.A., 1936).

From 1937 until 1942, Donovan was a reporter for the leftist *Washington Post*. From 1945 until 1959, he was with *Fortune* magazine as writer and editor (1945-1951), associate managing editor (1951-1953), and managing editor (1953-1959). Since 1959, he has been with *Time* magazine as editorial director (1959-1964) and editor-in-chief (1964 to the present). Since 1962, he has been a member of the board of directors of Time, Inc. Under Donovan's editorial supervision, *Time, Life,* and *Fortune* magazines have had their editorial positions moved steadily leftward on politics and on domestic and international issues.

Donovan is a trustee of the leftist-pacifist Carnegie Endowment for International Peace. He is a long-time member of the Council on Foreign Relations, the informal supra-State Department of the United States.

NORMAN DORSEN was born on September 4, 1930 in New York City. He is an alumnus of Columbia University (A.B., 1952) and Harvard University (LL.B., 1953). He is the author of *Frontiers of Civil Liberties* (1968). He is the co-author of *Political and Civil Rights in the United States* (1967).

From 1953 until 1955, Dorsen was an assistant to the general counsel to the Secretary of the Army. In 1955 and 1956, he was a Fulbright fellow at the leftist London School of Economics. From 1956 until 1958, he was a law clerk. Since 1961, he has been at New York University School of Law as assistant professor (1961), associate professor (1961-1965), and professor (1965 to the present) of law; director of the Law School's Civil Liberties Center (1961 to the present); and director of the Project on Social Welfare Law (1966 to the present).

Dorsen has been affiliated with the National Committee to Abolish the House Un-American Activities Committee ("to lead and direct the Communist Party's 'Operation Abolition' campaign"). He has been a long-time vice-chairman and member of the board of directors of the ultra-leftist American Civil Liberties Union.

MELVIN DOUGLAS was born on April 5, 1901 in Macon, Georgia, son of Lena Shackelford and Edouard Hesselberg. He married Helen Gahagan. He began his theatrical career in 1919 and has been an actor, director, and producer. He has worked on radio, television, the Broadway stage, and in Hollywood films.

Douglas has been affiliated with the American League for Peace and Democracy ("subversive and Communist"); the Progressive Citizens of America ("Communist front"); the Southern Conference for Human Welfare ("Communist front"); the National Committee to Abolish the House Un-American Activities Committee ("to lead and direct the Communist Party's 'Operation Abolition' campaign"); *Social Work Today* ("a Communist magazine"); the American Slav Congress ("subversive and Communist"); the red-lined Union for Democratic Action; and the [First] Congress of the Mexican and Spanish-American Peoples of the United States ("Communist front"). He was a founder, and has been a member, of the ultra-radical Americans for Democratic Action. He has petitioned against congressional investigating committees. He has been affiliated with the leftist-pacifist Publishers for Peace. He has been a long-time member and official of the ultra-leftist American Civil Liberties Union and, in recent years, the ACLU's most prominent pitchman.

WILLIAM H. DRAPER JR. was born on August 10, 1894 in New York City, son of Mary Carey and William Draper. He was married to the late Katharine Baum. He is married to Eunice Barzynski. He is an alumnus of New York University (B.A., 1916; M.A., 1917).

From 1919 until 1921, Draper was a bookkeeper at the National City Bank of New York City. From 1923 until 1927, he was assistant treasurer of the Bankers Trust Company. From 1927 until 1953, he was associated with the investment banking firm of Dillon, Read & Company. From 1954 until 1959, he was chairman of the board of the Mexican Light & Power Company. From 1959 until 1967, he was a partner in the firm of Draper, Gaither & Anderson. From 1940 until 1947, Draper was on active duty with the U.S. Army, and rose to the rank of major general. From 1947 until 1949, he was Under Secretary of the Army. In 1952 and 1953, he was the United States Permanent Representative, with the rank of Ambassador, to the North Atlantic Treaty Organization.

Draper has been affiliated with the Council on Foreign Relations, the informal supra-State Department of the United States; the leftist-internationalist Atlantic Council of the United States; the leftist-oriented Population Crisis Committee, of which he was chairman in 1968; and the First National Convocation on the Challenge of Building Peace, conducted by the leftist-internationalist Fund for Peace.

MELVYN DUBOFSKY was born on October 25, 1934 in Brooklyn. He is an alumnus of Brooklyn College (B.A., 1955) and the University of Rochester (Ph.D., 1960). He is the author of *When Workers Organize: New York City in the Progressive Era* (1968).

In 1958 and 1959, Dubofsky was a lecturer at Brooklyn College. From 1959 until 1967, he was an assistant professor of history at Northern Illinois University. Since 1967, he has been an assistant professor at the University of Massachusetts in Amherst.

Dubofsky has been a participant in the Socialist Scholars Conference, an activity which reflects accurately upon his preoccupation with radical labor and social history.

JOSEPH D. DUFFEY was born on July 1, 1932 in Huntington, West Virginia, son of Ruth Wilson and Joseph Duffey. He married Patricia Fortney. He is an alumnus of Marshall University (B.A., 1954); Andover Newton Theological School (B.D., 1957); Yale University (S.T.M., 1963); and Hartford Seminary (Ph.D., 1969). In 1964 and 1965, he held a doctoral fellowship from the Rockefeller Foundation. In 1957, he was ordained a minister of the Congregational Church.

In 1956 and 1957, Duffey was the university pastor and associate chaplain at Boston University. From 1957 until 1960, he was pastor of First Congregational Church in Danvers, Massachusetts. From 1960 until 1966, he was an assistant professor of urban studies at Hartford Seminary. Since 1966, he has been the director of Hartford Seminary's Center for Urban Ethics. From 1962 until 1966, he was a member of the Community Renewal Team in Hartford. From 1964 until 1966, he was director of the Center for Study of Religion and Social Issues at Woods Hole, Massachusetts.

In 1963, Duffey became a political activist, being arrested and jailed while protesting alleged racial segregation in a construction union in the Bedford-Stuyvesant section of Brooklyn, New York. In 1964, he joined the ultra-radical Americans for Democratic Action. In 1966, he became chairman of Connecticut's chapter of the ADA. In 1967, he became active in Negotiation Now!, an ad hoc committee led by leftwing luminaries for appeasement in Vietnam, including Martin Luther King Jr., Joseph L. Rauh Jr., Victor Reuther, Arthur Schlesinger Jr., Reinhold Niebuhr, and John Kenneth Galbraith. In 1968, he joined leftist Allard Lowenstein in the disgruntled Democrat's dump-Lyndon B. Johnson campaign. Duffey's contribution to Lowenstein's efforts was service as co-chairman in Connecticut of Eugene McCarthy's presidential campaign. When McCarthy's campaign failed, Duffey formed and became chairman of the Caucus of Connecticut Democrats, an ultra-liberal coalition of former supporters of Eugene McCarthy and Robert F. Kennedy. In 1969, he became a member of the steering committee of the leftist-oriented New Democratic Coalition.

In 1969, Duffey was elected as the national chairman of the ultra-liberal Americans for Democratic Action – the youngest man ever to hold the post – and he was re-elected in 1970. He said at the time: "I am most caught up with the question of whether there is a future for reason in politics. I have much greater sympathy for a 20-year-old SDS'er with a beard than with a 45-year-old saying the same simplistic things on a Connecticut lawn. I am skeptical about many things, but I believe in a man who talks about hope with tears rather than stars in his eyes." It was about the same time that Duffey also said: "I guess you could call me revisionist-Marxist, but I certainly had very little sympathy with the Maoists."

In January 1970, when National Chairman Duffey announced the ADA's 1970 program, he insisted that a "full domestic liberal agenda will not be acted on unless the war in Vietnam ends and all American troops are brought home."

The posture of Duffey and the ADA was a detailed combination of pacifism and socialism. It called for total withdrawal of American troops from Vietnam and repeal of the Gulf of Tonkin Resolution. It stressed "reallocating resources" by suggesting severe reductions in the budget of the defense department. It advocated a congressional watchdog committee with power to demand that the Defense Department justify its spending programs on an annual basis. As a corollary to their anti-defense attacks, Duffey and the ADA wanted the Federal Government empowered to require defense industries to set aside a portion of their operating funds for planned conversion to civilian needs.

The civilian needs of the nation envisioned by Duffey and the ADA were many: guaranteed employment, financed for the most part by the Federal Government in a multi-billion-dollar public works program; a federal food program for the alleged hungry and the alleged undernourished, including free food stamps, and free breakfasts and lunches in schools; a guaranteed annual income above the poverty level (a level decreed by bureaucrats), with a minimum wage of $2.75 per hour and income maintenance, for those who allegedly were unable to work, pegged to a level of $5,500 for a family of four; minimum Social Security payments of $100 a month per individual and $200 a month per couple, increasing the wage-base for funding the Social Security program to $15,000 a year, and financing at least one third of Social Security payments from the general revenues of the Federal Government; a crash federal housing program which would establish six million low- and moderate-income housing units within five years; a federally-subsidized program of low interest rates for socially

DUGGER

desirable purposes; a federally-financed mass transportation program similar to the $50-billion interstate highway network; an almost threefold increase of federal handouts to education; a completely socialistic national health insurance program; a $1-billion program — financed by the Federal Government, of course — to "fight crime without compromising individual liberty," the liberals' euphemistic way of coddling criminals and punishing victims; the creation of a consumers' ombudsman program to harass American businessmen under the pretense of protecting American buyers; and a reform of the Selective Service System that would include abolition of student exemptions and establishment of federally dictated standards for the operation of all local Selective Service boards.

In 1970, Duffey sought the Democratic nomination to the United States Senate in Connecticut. The liberal community rallied to his side, including United States Senators Abraham Ribicoff of Connecticut, Edmund Muskie of Maine, and Edward M. Kennedy of Massachusetts; Cleveland's Mayor Carl Stokes; the ultra-leftist Coretta King, widow of the racial demagogue Martin Luther King Jr.; and actor Paul Newman, Duffey's most vigorous campaigner. The campaign was managed by Anne Wexler — a veteran of the 1968 McCarthy-for-President campaign — who was able to recruit hordes of campus revolutionaries and black radicals from throughout the country. The result was that Duffey obtained the Democratic nomination; but he lost the election to the Republican nominee, Lowell Weicker. Duffey's platform for his unsuccessful race was for the most part the 1970 ADA program. It was Socialism across the board, with heavy emphasis on nationalized

health insurance, nationalization of the nation's railroads, a high-tariff program, radical tax reforms, federal boondoggles in housing and unemployment, and the current liberals' rage for federal financing of anti-pollution panaceas. The foreign policy planks of his platform concentrated upon the Vietnam War — a total commitment by Duffey to extreme pacifism. Understandably, Duffey's candidacy in the 1970 senatorial race was financed in part by the National Committee for an Effective Congress, a very powerful ultra-leftist pressure group.

Aside from his ADA activities, Duffey has been active in the ultra-leftist Vietnam Moratorium Committee, and has endorsed the pet 1971 project of the ultra-left, the People's Peace Treaty.

RONNIE DUGGER was born on April 16, 1930 in Chicago, son of Mary King and William Dugger. He married Jean Williams. He is an alumnus of the University of Texas (B.A., 1950). He pursued graduate studies at the University of Texas and at Oxford University in England. In 1969, he held a Rockefeller fellowship. In 1969 and 1970, he was a research fellow at the Institute of Industrial Relations. He is the author of *Dark Star: Hiroshima Reconsidered In the Life of Claude Eatherly of Lincoln Park, Texas* (1967). He is the editor of *Three Men In Texas; Bedichek, Webb, and Dobie* (1967).

From 1947 until 1952, he worked variously as a newscaster, sports announcer, and sports writer. During this period, he was employed by the *San Antonio Express*, the International News Service, and several Texas newspapers for whom he served as British correspondent. From 1952 until 1954, he was an assistant to the executive director for writing and research of the National

334

Security Training Commission in Washington, D.C. Except for a brief time in 1961 and 1962, he has been with the ultra-liberal *Texas Observer* as editor and general manager (1954-1961; 1963-1965) and editor-at-large and publisher (1965 to the present).

Dugger has served on the national committee of the ultra-leftist American Civil Liberties Union. He was affiliated with the National Conference for New Politics, a classical united-front third-party movement largely controlled by the Communist Party. In 1965, he was the leader of a Washington, D.C., conference which produced the Committee for Independent Political Action, organized to promote candidates in the congressional election of 1966.

Dugger's preoccupation with radical third-party movements has continued. In 1970, he was asked by the editors of *The New Democrat*: "Do you believe the Democratic party is still capable of aggressively reforming itself by the 1972 convention, or do you believe that a fourth party is the only conceivable means of effecting change in 1972?" Dugger replied: "We must have a serious challenge from a new political party, or an independent movement, or both, because nothing else has the catalytic power to push the national Democrats into serious consideration of our basic economic system." Dugger represented himself as speaking for the "radically humanist liberal Democrats" who would like to "nationalize" all corporations doing 75 percent or more of their business with the Defense Department.

WILLIAM D. EBERLE was born on June 5, 1923 in Boise, Idaho, son of Clare Holcomb and J. Louis Eberle. He married Jean Quick. He is an alumnus of Stanford University (B.A., 1945) and Harvard University (M.B.A., 1947; LL.B., 1949). In 1950, he was admitted to the Idaho bar.

From 1950 until 1960, Eberle was a partner in the firm of Richards, Haga & Eberle in Boise. From 1952 until 1966, he was with Boise Cascade Corporation as director (1952-1956), secretary (1960-1965), and vice-president (1961-1966). Since 1966, he has been president and director of American Standard, Incorporated.

From 1953 until 1963, Eberle was a member of the Idaho State House of Representatives, serving as majority leader in 1957, minority leader in 1959, and speaker in 1961. From 1961 until 1966, he was chairman of the Idaho Republican Finance Committee and a member of the National Republican Finance Committee.

Eberle is a trustee of the African-American Institute, a leftist-liberal Establishment group. He is a trustee of the Committee for Economic Development, the major propaganda arm of the Council on Foreign Relations, in the important work of socializing the American economy. He is a member of the Council on Foreign Relations, the informal supra-State Department of the United States. In 1971, he participated in the Runnymede Project, a leftist-oriented conference run by anti-war students from the Massachusetts Institute of Technology.

MARIAN EDELMAN was born on June 6, 1939 in Bennettsville, South Carolina, daughter of Maggie Bowen and Arthur Wright. She married Peter Edelman. She is an alumna of Spelman College (B.A., 1960) and Yale University (LL.B., 1963).

From 1963 until 1968, Mrs. Edelman was a staff member with the ultra-radical

NAACP Legal Defense and Educational Fund in New York City (1963-1964) and in Jackson, Mississippi (1964-1968). Since 1968, she has been director of the leftist-oriented Washington Research Project. From 1961 until 1963, she was a member of the executive committee of the ultra-radical Student Nonviolent Coordinating Committee. She has been involved with such radical projects as the Citizens Crusade Against Poverty, the National Office for Rights of the Indigent, the National Sharecroppers Fund, the Capitol Area Civil Liberties Union, and the International Self-Help Housing Association. She has been an active lay worker for the leftist-dominated National Council of Churches and World Council of Churches. She is a director of the ultra-radical Americans for Democratic Action.

JOHN T. EDSALL was born on November 3, 1902 in Philadelphia, Pennsylvania, son of Margaret Tileston and David Edsall. He married Margaret Dunham. He is an alumnus of Harvard University (A.B., 1923; M.D., 1928). He pursued graduate studies at Cambridge University in England. He held Guggenheim fellowships at the California Institute of Technology (1940-1941) and at Harvard University (1954-1956).

Since 1928, Edsall has been at Harvard University as a tutor in biology and chemistry (1928-1932), assistant professor (1932-1938). associate professor (1938-1951), and professor (1951 to the present). He was a Fulbright lecturer at Cambridge University in England (1952) and the University of Tokyo (1964). In 1955, he was a visiting professor at the College of France in Paris. From 1950 until 1956, he was a representative on the U.S. National Commission for the leftist-dominated UNESCO.

Edsall has been affiliated with the Federation of American Scientists, a group of bleeding-heart, leftwing pacifists; the leftwing-pacifist Civil Defense Letter Committee; and the leftist-oriented Ad Hoc Committee for an Open Letter on Vietnam.

[ALBERT] RANDLE ELLIOTT was born on January 10, 1914 in St. Louis County, Missouri, son of Olinda Hoevel and Thomas Elliott. He married Gwendolyn Crawford. He is an alumnus of Westminster College (A.B., 1935) and Harvard University (A.M., 1938; Ph.D., 1949). From 1939 until 1941, he held a fellowship from the Rockefeller Foundation. He is the author of *Spain After the Civil War* (1940); *The Resources and Trade of Central America* (1941); and *The Institute of International Education, 1919-1944* (1944). He is the co-author of *The United States at War* (1942).

From 1936 until 1939, Elliott was a teaching assistant in the departments of government at Harvard University and Radcliffe College. From 1939 until 1941, he was a research associate with the Foreign Policy Association, when the FPA and its publications were highly effective pro-Communist vehicles under the leadership of the ultra-leftist Vera Micheles Dean. From 1941 until 1943, he was an administrative associate with the leftwing Institute of International Education. From 1943 until 1945, he was director of the Counsel and Guidance Center for Foreign Students in the United States. In 1945, he was an economic analyst for the U.S. Strategic Bombing Survey in England and Germany. In 1945 and 1946, he was the chief reports officer for the Office of Military Government for Germany in Berlin. In 1946 and 1947, he was the administrator of the Washington bureau of the leftwing Institute of International Education. In 1947 and 1948, he was the London correspondent for the McGraw-Hill World News. From 1949 until 1961, he was the executive director of the Greer School in Dutchess County, New York. Since 1961, he has been president of Hood College in Maryland.

Elliott has been a long-time nonresident member of the Council on Foreign Relations, the informal supra-State Department of the United States. He has been a long-time active member of the World Affairs Council, a pivotal agency in a complex of one-world, leftist, and pacifist groups, which has become a major propaganda arm for the United Nations.

OSBORN ELLIOTT was born on October 25, 1924 in New York City, son of Audrey Osborn and John Elliott. He married Deirdre Spencer. He is an alumnus of Harvard University (A.B., 1946). He is the author of *Men at the Top* (1959). He is the editor of *The Negro Revolution in America* (1964).

From 1946 until 1949, Elliott was a reporter for the *New York Journal of Commerce.* From 1949 until 1955, he was, successively, a contributing editor and associate editor of *Time* magazine. Since 1955, he has been with *Newsweek* magazine as senior business editor and managing editor (1955-1961) and director and editor (1961 to the present). He is a director of the ultra-leftist Washington Post Company.

Elliott is a long-time member of the Council on Foreign Relations, the informal supra-State Department of the United States. He has been on the board of directors of the Atlantic Council, an organization which stresses the need for closer cooperation, especially economic, between the United States and the so-

cialist nations of Western Europe. In 1971, he participated in the Runnymede Project, a leftist-oriented conference run by anti-war students of the Massachusetts Institute of Technology.

DANIEL ELLSBERG was born on April 7, 1931 in Chicago. He was married to and divorced from Carol Cummings. He is married to Patricia Marx. He is an alumnus of Harvard University (B.A., 1952; M.A., 1954; Ph.D., 1963). As an undergraduate, he held a full scholarship granted by the Pepsi-Cola Company. In 1952 and 1953, he studied at King's College of Cambridge University in England. From April 1954 until February 1957, he was in the U.S. Marines. From 1957 until 1959, he was at Harvard University as a member of the Society of Fellows.

In 1959, Ellsberg went to work for the RAND Corporation in Santa Monica, California. During 1959 and 1960, his work at RAND was concerned with problems of general nuclear warfare. In notes he submitted for his Harvard class reunion in 1967, he described his activities after 1960: ". . . I had spent most of 1961 [in Washington, D.C.] at DOD [Department of Defense], State [Department] and the White House. I continued to consult in 1962-63, in particular working on policy statements on strategic systems and NATO. On October 22, 1962 (the night of the President's speech on the missiles in Cuba) I was called to Washington as a consultant, where I worked without much sleep for the next week as a member of DOD and State working groups on the crisis.

"I left with an intense interest in the analysis of high-level decision-making in international crises, and when I came to Washington in 1964 it was to undertake a study jointly sponsored by State/Defense/CIA/White House, with combined access, of just this problem. I spent the next nine months in various sub-basement documents saferooms, reading mainly about the Cuban crisis (Schlesinger and Sorensen, I note, don't know, or don't tell, the half of it).

"In September, with my findings completed but only partially reported (that lies ahead, but still classified, despite the Schlesinger-Sorensen questionable precedent), I entered the government as special assistant (GS-18) to John McNaughton, assistant secretary of Defense for International Security Affairs.

"After a year, day and night, reading and responding to cables and intelligence on Vietnam, I felt maddeningly (and correctly, as I now see) that neither I, nor the others around me, reading the same cables, knew, or could learn from all this traffic, any of the things that needed knowing about South Vietnam. I tried, representing the government in Teach-ins that spring at Antioch, NYU, Harvard and Washington, to communicate honestly some of the complexities, and my own uncertainties to audiences of critical students, earning the tribute, as much as I'd hoped for, from a number of them after my remarks: 'Now I'm confused . . . I thought I knew what we should do . . . .'

"That intellectual frustration, plus a sense of responsibility for having finally urged (however marginal my impact) U.S. troop commitment in the spring of 1965, led me to think of going to Vietnam to work. When I learned that Major General Edward Lansdale, whose background and thoughts I knew and respected, was finally being sent back to Vietnam, I volunteered to go with him. Rather quixotically he accepted me: as an 'apprentice' member of a small group of his old, experienced and trusted associates from the campaign against the Huks in the Philippines and from the 1954-56 period in Vietnam.

"Although I had offered to accept any rank in joining his team, I was transferred from DOD to State as an FSR-1. (In the government system, this ranks like GS-18, equivalent to lieutenant general; which considerably perplexes people who happen to discover my grade, since in this milieu my qualifications for such a pay-rate do not leap out at them.) However, as a true beginning in the operations we were attempting, my status has been properly menial for most of my time here: distinctly down in the engine-room rather than the bridge, and it soon turned out, in a small, lonely ship in the convoy.

"I'm proud to have served with Lansdale, and I've learned fully as much as I hoped; and learned to care deeply for this tortured country, Vietnam (whose countryside, I think, is the most beautiful in the world, a fact that rarely seems to be mentioned), its children, its people and their future. But much of the knowledge is painful; I don't seem to have the temperament of a pathologist.

"It has been, most of it, an intensely frustrating and sad year and a half, though with a good deal of excitement and moments of hope. (A letter I wrote giving my impressions after the first several weeks was reproduced under the title 'Vietman Diary,' anonymously, in *The Reporter*, about February, 1966, the proceeds going to the family of a friend, mentioned in the piece, who had just been killed.) I'm more convinced than I could have been before that Lansdale's basic thoughts on political development, on nationalistic and democratic rivalry with Communists for leadership of revolutionary forces, and on counterguerrilla tactics are sound, relevant to Vietnam, and desperately needed here; but none of them are being applied in any degree (until the elections of last September and the ensuing political developments, on which I am pinning my hopes).

"When Deputy Ambassador Porter was put in charge of the newly-created Office of Civil Operations (consolidating the field operations of AID, JUSPAO and CIA) last December, I accepted a loosely defined post, with Lansdale's approval, as Porter's special assistant, a job that has kept me largely in the field since then."

In 1967, when Ellsberg was writing his class notes, he was ill in a Bangkok nursing home. *Time* magazine (July 5, 1971) provides a sequel to Ellsberg's notes: "Hospitalized with hepatitis, Ellsberg began to read more books about the long history of warfare in Indochina. He recuperated back in California, where he rejoined Rand and turned to a livelier life: a succession of dazzling girls, a red sports car and a share in a ramshackle Malibu Beach house. He flooded the place with psychedelic lighting to the point where police raided what they thought was a noisy pot party, only to find a number of tipsy Rand analysts dancing to rock music. He lived with a Swedish secretary before marrying Patricia Marx, who had been regularly dating New York Theater Critic John Simon.

"Friends say Dan and Patricia dove happily into most everything California offers uninhibited couples, including group-encounter sessions, Yoga, Buddhist self-improvement sects and nudism. They backpacked into mountains, and Dan enjoyed climbing with his son Robert. Husband and wife so loved the sea that even when they were a continent apart Dan would hold the telephone outside his window so Patricia could hear the Malibu breakers. Dan, who neither smokes nor drinks, also underwent psychiatric analysis, later told friends it was a turning point of his life."

In 1967, Secretary of Defense Robert McNamara instituted a study of the Vietnam War. For more than a year, researchers from the RAND Corporation and the Pentagon worked on the assignment. The researchers were given access to Pentagon documents dating back to the Truman Administration. Ellsberg worked on that project.

On June 13, 1971, on page one of *The New York Times,* a headline read: "Vietnam Archive: Pentagon Study Traces 3 Decades of Growing U.S. Involvement." The headline was followed by six pages of official cables, memoranda, and position papers – all classified as secret, top secret, or top secret-sensitive – from the files of the Pentagon. The material published by the *New York Times* was extracted from a 47-volume, 7,000-page study stolen from the RAND Corporation.

In the "Press" section of *Time* magazine (June 28, 1971), there was an outline of how the *New York Times* became involved with the Pentagon Papers: " 'Neil Sheehan feels Viet Nam is his story,' says a friend of the New York *Times* reporter. Sheehan's first reporting job was in 1962 as U.P.I.'s Saigon bureau chief; he covered the war for three years. But it was never more his story than last week, when the *Times* began publishing the Pentagon's secret record of U.S. involvement in Viet Nam.

"Neither Sheehan nor the *Times* is talking about the source of the material. But the evidence is that Daniel Ellsberg, a former Defense Department analyst, is the man (see *The Nation*) who volunteered the files to Sheehan. The reporter wrote a long, controversial book-review essay in March, weighing the question of whether U.S. officials had been guilty of war crimes. Ellsberg told friends that he admired Sheehan's analysis. A short time after the essay appeared, Sheehan, normally based in Washington, was in New York City carrying a sample of the 47-volume report. He spread the papers on the desk of *Times* Managing Editor A.M. Rosenthal, whose eyes widened. 'The decision to publish,' said Rosenthal, 'was made almost the moment it came into our hands.'

"Rosenthal dispatched Assistant Foreign Editor Gerald Gold to Washington, where he set up headquarters with Sheehan in a hotel room. But it soon became obvious that the project was too big for two people. On April 22, Sheehan and Gold moved their crates of paper into a five-room suite on the eleventh floor of the New York Hilton. They were joined by a team of eight or nine *Times* men and women selected not only for their knowledge of Viet Nam but also their ability to keep a secret. Inquisitive colleagues were told that Hedrick Smith, a diplomatic reporter soon to be assigned to Moscow, was 'off studying Russian'; E. W. Kenworthy, who covers the environment beat, took an unscheduled 'vacation,' Fox Butterfield was called in from his New Jersey suburban assignment. The team also included two other editors from the foreign desk and two secretaries. All worked under the operational charge of Foreign Editor James Greenfield, who brought a special expertise to the project: he had been Deputy Assistant (1962-64) and Assistant (1964-66) Secretary of State for Public Affairs in the crucial years of the Viet Nam commitment.

"The security problem was extraordinary, but in the end it was solved better than at the Pentagon. A telephone tie line from the suite to Washington was used, but all local calls were made from phone booths. A special identity check was required of anyone entering the team's headquarters.... For seven weeks the team worked seven days a week, often past midnight; in all, some 30 *Times* staff members were eventually involved.

"At the *Times* plant, a small, trusted composing crew was walled off to get the story in type; many editors realized the hush-hush project was ready only when they were told that their normal Sunday news space had been cut.

"Writing the story was an even bigger job than keeping it a secret. The pages of the huge report were unnumbered and out of order; they had to be organized before they were read, judged and condensed. The writers absorbed 45 books, preparing themselves to compare official, public statements with private memorandums in the report."

On June 14, 1971, after the *New York Times* had published two installments of the Pentagon Papers, U.S. Attorney General John Mitchell sent a telegram to the *Times*, calling attention to a provision in the espionage law for a ten-year sentence or $10,000 fine for anyone convicted of willingly disclosing secret information that could jeopardize the nation's safety. Mitchell requested that officials of the *Times* refrain from printing any more installments and he asked that all material be returned to the government. The *Times* officials ignored his request and the Department of Justice sought a temporary restraining order in the U.S. District Court in Manhattan. The restraining order was issued. The Department of Justice then sought a permanent injunction. On June 18, a hearing began on the matter of the permanent injunction. Meanwhile, the

Washington Post had begun to publish its version of the Pentagon Papers. The version was sent to the 345 client newspapers subscribing to the *Los Angeles Times-Washington Post* news service. The Associated Press and United Press International were carrying the Pentagon Papers story on their wires. (Eventually, the Pentagon Papers story also appeared in the *Chicago Sun-Times*, the *St. Louis Post-Dispatch, Newsday*, the *Boston Globe*, the *Christian Science Monitor*, and eleven papers of the Knight chain. On July 1, 1971, Ellsberg took full credit for the selection of newspapers receiving the Pentagon Papers: "I must say that I exercised a certain personal taste. I was anxious to give it to the newspapers that I thought had told me the truth in the past, and I thought they ought to have the chance to make this decision now.") The Department of Justice sought in vain for a temporary injunction against the *Washington Post* in the U.S. District Court in Washington, D.C. But a temporary injunction was granted by a federal appeals court, pending a full hearing in which the government would be required to prove necessity for a permanent injunction. Eventually, the matter reached the Supreme Court of the United States, where on June 30, in a 6-3 decision, the Court ruled that the *New York Times* and the *Washington Post* could resume publishing articles based on the Pentagon Papers.

On the night of June 16, Sidney Zion, a former reporter for the *New York Times* and a friend of Daniel Ellsberg, called the Barry Gray program on radio station WMCA in New York City. In an interview with Mr. Gray, Zion identified Ellsberg as the individual who had given the Pentagon Papers to the *New York Times*. In the course of

the interview and in a press conference called by Zion the following day, he expanded on his identification of Ellsberg. Zion described Ellsberg as conscience-stricken because "he felt he had some guilt about it because he was involved in the origins of the decision-making on the Vietnam War way back in the early days of the Kennedy Administration." Zion said that Ellsberg rejected the idea of producing the Pentagon Papers at a press conference because he did not believe there would be enough attention paid to his action, and Zion elaborated: "If he just did it, it wouldn't be the *New York Times* doing it. It would have been a lot less of a story, I mean. If he got up and had a press conference and handed out this thing, I don't think it would have had any kind of impact. As it is right now, I think he was very wise to give it to the best newspaper in the world."

When the Pentagon Papers were published in the *New York Times* and elsewhere, Ellsberg was a senior research associate at Massachusetts Institute of Technology's Center for International Studies, a position he took after leaving the RAND Corporation in 1970. When Zion identified Ellsberg as the source of the Pentagon Papers, Ellsberg was living in Cambridge, Massachusetts. In the wake of Zion's identification, reporters and Federal Bureau of Investigation agents could not find either Ellsberg or his wife at their Cambridge home. However, within the next few days, Ellsberg's background was widely printed and broadcast throughout the news media.

On June 17, Representative Paul McCloskey, a Republican from California and one of the most prominent pacifists in the House, revealed that he had met Ellsberg at Princeton University on April 19. At the time, Ellsberg told

McCloskey he had "information relevant to Vietnam, in particular my concern over the deception of Congress by the executive branch with respect to Vietnam." McCloskey said that after their first meeting, he received a number of Xeroxed sheets from Ellsberg, and the two men discussed the content of the sheets during a round trip they made to California. Said McCloskey: "I made a number of notes on his comments and checked the specific identifying language with him before presenting my testimony to the Senate Foreign Relations Committee on May 27, in which I identified the existence of the Vietnam task force study and asked that Sen. (J. William) Fulbright request such study from the State Department." McCloskey told reporters that he did not know whether the documents given to him by Ellsberg were a part of the Pentagon Papers. He did say that the documents in his possession were not stamped secret. (In the August 1, 1971 issue of *Parade* magazine, Democratic Senator George McGovern of South Dakota assumed credit for suggesting that Ellsberg had leaked the Pentagon Papers to the press: "What happened is that Mr. Ellsberg came to me and told me that such papers existed. I told him that I felt as a lawmaker that I could not be in the business of breaking the law, but I did make clear to him that I thought it would serve the public interest if he made those documents available to a respectable newspaper. I think Mr. Ellsberg took the proper course when he went to the *New York Times.* If I had released them, people would have said, 'Well, that's McGovern and his bid for the Presidency trying to embarrass the executive branch.' ")

In the *Boston Globe* of June 18, 1971, Thomas Oliphant, writing about Ellsberg, recalled that in March 1971, during the course of an interview with a *Globe* reporter, Ellsberg had summed up his work for the government by saying: "I was participating in a criminal conspiracy to wage aggressive war. When I started, I viewed the war as a well-intentioned effort, reasonable, though in retrospect mistaken. But it soon became completely clear that American actions were really a series of desperate gambles actually perceived as such by those who made them at the time." Oliphant recalled that in 1969, while Ellsberg was still working for the RAND Corporation, he and five colleagues had written a letter urging unilateral withdrawal by the United States from Vietnam. The letter was printed in the *New York Times* and the *Washington Post* just prior to the leftwing Moratorium demonstration in October. Oliphant also recalled that: "Since the first of the year, Ellsberg has 'gone public' with his anti-war views, writing and speaking extensively. Last month, he went to Washington for the Mayday demonstrations. 'I tried to get arrested, but failed,' he later told the *Globe.* 'I didn't look young enough.'

"Ellsberg also participated in the sit-in on May 6 at the Federal building here. He was not arrested, but was struck by a police officer's club at one point during the day. After that demonstration, he said: 'I obviously think the government should stop what it's doing. But until it does, we must be willing to put our bodies on the line, if only symbolically, to try and make it stop. I'm sorry this is necessary, but it is.' "

On June 18, 1971, the *Boston Herald* reported on an interview with Mrs. Paula B. Cronin, a long-time friend of Ellsberg and his wife: "The woman said Ellsberg's current wife, the former Patricia Marx of New York City, a 1959 Radcliffe graduate, met Ellsberg about six years ago at a party in Washington where she had a radio discussion program on a local station. Mrs. Ellsberg is the daughter of millionaire toy manufacturer Louis Marx of New York City.

"Mrs. Cronin said Ellsberg had been 'wrapped up' in his work for the government and Rand Corporation in California on Southeast Asian policy. Ellsberg, she said, was a former U.S. Marine who re-enlisted once during the Suez Canal crisis because he wanted to be part of the excitement of military action.

" 'He loved the military,' Mrs. Cronin said, adding she was told by the couple that Ellsberg and his future wife became very close but she refused his proposal of marriage because of his support for the Vietnam War. 'She was adamant about it,' Mrs. Cronin said. The relationship continued over a number of years, she said, during which Miss Marx once visited Ellsberg in Vietnam for three months. The friend said Miss Marx left, however, because Ellsberg's views of the war remained unchanged.

"After his return to the United States in 1967 they continued to meet, Mrs. Cronin said, adding she was told Miss Marx was eventually able to change his views on the war. 'He's very quick to give her the credit for changing his views,' the friend said."

On June 18, a spokesman for the Massachusetts Institute of Technology announced that Ellsberg had made a call to a former colleague. Ellsberg wished to reassure the Institute's authorities that he and his wife were well and that there was no need for concern over their disappearance. Ellsberg requested that MIT authorities should suggest to anyone who wished to know about his views on Vietnam be referred to reprints of his numerous articles on the subject. He also requested MIT authorities to make reprints of those articles available to anyone who wanted them.

In subsequent days, newsmen were unable to unearth very many earlier Ellsberg references. But there were a few. Early in 1970, he told a conference that had been sponsored by a group of anti-war Congressmen: "I speak, not as a researcher, but as a former official of the Defense Department and the State Department in Vietnam – of experiences which make me a possible defendant in a future war crimes trial. Some 10 years ago, I read the transcripts of the Nuremberg trials and that left me with the sense of what an exhibit in a war crimes trial looks like. As I was working at the Department of Defense, I did, in some cases, have the feeling while reading documents late at night that I was looking at future exhibits. There even exist in locked safes in Washington right now documents that could very aptly be described as plans for escalatory genocide. Such alleged plans reflect decisions by civilian officials which, I suggest, should be subjected in the future to more conscientious review."

In September 1970, Ellsberg presented an article ("Escalating in a Quagmire") to the American Political Science Association. The article later appeared in the *Public Policy* quarterly of the Kennedy Institute. He gave a copy of his original article to U.S. Senator J.W. Fulbright, chairman of the Senate Foreign Relations Committee. There is intrinsic evidence that Ellsberg utilized esoteric knowledge gleaned from his work on the Pentagon Papers. Excerpts of his article were reprinted under the title, "Ellsberg: The Quagmire Myth," in the *New York Times* of June 26, 1971. In his writings, Ellsberg seemed fearful that some day a presidential administration would prosecute the Vietnam War so vigorously as to achieve a military victory over North Vietnam and to entrench a strong anti-Communist regime in Saigon. To forestall any such eventuality he desired that the United States forsake even its limited military effort and withdraw unilaterally from Vietnam. He advanced arguments, buttressed by a carefully selected group of documents, in an attempt to prove that the limited war effort was really genocidal warfare conducted by American war criminals against North and South Vietnam, Laos, and Cambodia.

In his "Quagmire" article, Ellsberg wrote: "Kennedy did not live either to win the election or to leave the war. Instead he willed the war to a President determined not to be the first to lose one, leaving an unchanged U.S. policy toward Vietnam to an insecure successor who had some reason to fear the political consequences – even at the hands of the dead President's heirs, officials and supporters – of publicly abandoning it.

"The risk that 'losing' Vietnam would pose some risk from a faction within the President's own party was one that Johnson in 1964 shared with Eisenhower in 1954. Even Richard Nixon has seen himself as facing comparable problems in 1969-1971, his special assistant, Henry A. Kissinger, has reported in numerous 'backgrounders': 'If we had done in our first year what our loudest critics called on us to do, the 13 per cent that voted for Wallace would have grown to 35 or 40 per cent; the first thing the President set out to do was to neutralize that faction.'

"In any case, it appears that an appropriate abstraction of elements of the initial 1950 decision to intervene – despite the lack of major prior commitment or involvement – fits very well all

the major subsequent decisions to escalate or to prolong the war, at least through 1968 and probably beyond.

"We have already seen one Presidential ruling at work both in 1950 and 1961: 'This is a bad year for me to lose Vietnam to Communism.' In brief: A decade before what Schlesinger calls Kennedy's 'low-level crisis' in South Vietnam, the right wing of the Republican party tattooed on the skins of politicians and bureaucrats alike some vivid impressions of what could happen to a liberal administration that chanced to be in office the day a red flag rose over Saigon.

"Starting in early 1950, the first Administration to learn painfully this 'lesson of China' began to undertake – as in a game of Old Maid – to pass that contingency on to its successor. And each Administration since has found itself caught in the same game. Rule 1 of that game is: 'Do not lose the rest of Vietnam to Communist control before the next election.'

"It is not, after all, only Presidents and Cabinet members who have a powerful need and reason to deny their responsibility for this war. And who succeed at it. Just as Presidents and their partisans find comfort and political safety in the quicksand image of the President-as-victim, so Americans at large are reassured in sudden moments of doubt by the same image drawn large, America-as-victim. It is no more real than the first, and neither national understanding nor extrication truly lie that way.

"To understand the process as it emerges in the documents behind public statements, the concerns never written that moved decisions, the history scratched on the minds of bureaucrats; to translate that understanding into images that can guide actions close-related to reality, one must begin by seeing that it is Americans, our leaders and ourselves, that build the bog, a trap much more for other victims: our policies, our politics the quagmire in which Indochina drowns."

In an article written in March 1971 for the *New York Review of Books,* Ellsberg said: "Enough Americans must look past options, briefings, pros and cons, to what is being done in their name and refuse to be accomplices. They must recognize, and force the Congress and the president to act upon, the moral proposition that the U.S. must stop killing in Indochina." Aside from these references, the *New York Times* reprinted portions of a letter-to-the-editor written to that journal in November 1970. Mr. Ellsberg charged that "Nixon's clearly announced and demonstrated strategy entails not only prolonging but vastly expanding this immoral, illegal and unconstitutional war." He concluded the letter by writing, "To refuse any longer, wishfully, to believe that Nixon really means what he says and does, or to fail to resist his policy, is to become an accomplice."

One other earlier Ellsberg article did not come into the public light until November 3, 1971. At that time it was revealed that the Federal Bureau of Investigation had subpoenaed and received a seminar paper ("Escalation as a Military Strategy in Limited War"), delivered by Ellsberg to a study group of the Council on Foreign Relations. When the FBI first requested a copy of the paper, CFR officials declined the request. John T. Swing, associate executive director, explained: "We did not turn it over to them then because we have a council rule on confidentiality which extends to the government and which we take very seriously." The contents of

Ellsberg's paper have not been published.

On June 23, 1971, Walter Cronkite of CBS-TV visited the Boston area with a camera crew. Cronkite and his crew met with Ellsberg in a private home where Ellsberg was interviewed in great secrecy. The film of the interview was processed and transmitted to CBS-TV in New York through the facilities of WHDH-TV in Boston. On that same evening, Cronkite's 6:30 program included eight minutes of the Ellsberg interview. At 10:30 P.M., an expanded version of the interview was shown as a "CBS Special — Daniel Ellsberg."

In his opening remarks on the earlier interview, Cronkite said: "Ellsberg was a Pentagon and State Department analyst during the Vietnam buildup. Later he worked on the now-controversial Pentagon study of the war. Perhaps because of his clearly delicate legal position, he will not talk right now of whatever part he played in the release of secret documents. But he talks freely of what he hopes their release will accomplish, and what turned him from hawk to dove. Such as what he believes was official cold-heartedness toward the civilian casualties of war."

Ellsberg reacted to Cronkite's statements with a rambling monologue: "The fact here is that in the seven to ten thousand pages of this study, I don't think there was a line in them that contains an estimate of the likely impact of our policy on the overall casualties among the Vietnamese, or the refugees to be caused, the effects of defoliation in an ecological sense. There is neither an estimate nor a calculation of past effects, ever. And the documents simply concern the internal concerns — reflect the internal concerns of our officials. That says nothing more nor less than our officials never did concern themselves, certainly in any formal way or in writing, and I think in no informal way either, with the effect of our policies on the Vietnamese.

"I'm so struck by the cover of *Newsweek* here, if I can refer to this. The secret history of Vietnam. Map of Vietnam. With the faces of the important people who perfected that secret history of Vietnam, and you'll notice they're all American. Every one of them. Now that reflects accurately the way the history of Vietnam emerges from those studies. That is from the internal documents of the United States. It reflects the way the Vietnam war is seen from Washington, as to who matters and who doesn't. And there's great realism to that, actually. As I say, I'm familiar. I was part of that system. I know how that's looked at. There's realism to that.

"The war has been an American war. And there's certainly realism to the way that it's reflecting the actual attitudes of the people making the decisions. Never in those cables or estimates, I think, outside of memos by a few people, General Lansdale being one, I think will the public find when they read these, a Vietnamese leader described with concern, friendship, respect, or evaluated in any terms other than as an instrument of American policy.

"The Vietnamese leaders with whom we've been dealing, unfortunately have the character that they tend to see themselves that way. And the other Vietnamese know it. As for Vietnamese who weren't leaders, they're not in the study at all. They're just not there, on either side. And that's a large part of what's been wrong.

"I came back then with a sense – an additional sense of concern, and about what we were doing to the people of Vietnam as well as what was happening in this country. A concern that many people shared by '67 and '68. By '68, I had read most of the study, written a draft for one volume of it. And, well, can you imagine yourself what you'd feel like to have read those 7000 pages, judging from the thousand or so you've seen summaries of so far? And reading the news to the public every night, not able to tell them the existence of the study or what it was you had read?

"Suddenly I've been reading about myself obviously, in these accounts, and it's – some of it is almost amusing. The inferences, as my being very tortured by guilt. Actually, I had to say I didn't feel guilty for the things I'd done in Vietnam. I felt very concerned. I felt that the knowledge gave me a kind of a responsibility that I otherwise didn't have. But the very simple explanation came to me as to the impression I apparently had been giving people over the last year, was that I'd read this history. I've read all of it. I've read it several times. I think it obviously led me to kinds of activity against the war, publicly. But it was simply very baffling to my colleagues, none of whom had read the study. Almost none of whom knew of its existence or the fact that I had read it.

"I think maybe they'll understand there are some strange things about my intensity that they described, a month from now. I hope we'll see some more intense involvement in ending this war. I'm sure this story is more painful for many people at this moment than for me because, of course, it is familiar to me, having read it several times. But it must be painful for the American people now to read these papers, and there's a lot more to come, and to discover that the men who they gave so much respect and trust, as well as power, regarded them as contemptuously as they regarded our Vietnamese allies."

Ellsberg was asked: "What would you expect to be revealed from the documents that might come out in future days or weeks? What's still back there that we can look forward to?" Ellsberg replied: "Well, I think that the real lessons to be drawn are yet to be seen by the public. And they're not from any one period or any one episode. They really come from seeing the whole sweep of the history. There has never been any year when there would have been a war in Indo-China without American money shoring it.

"The perception that I had, just like I think most people in the country, that this was in some sense an on-going war which we had joined for good or bad, screened out many of the moral aspects of the conflict. And to discover on the contrary, that in Indo-China, if we had not been supplying the money and the napalm, and buying soldiers, paying for equipment, and finally supplying our own soldiers, there would have been violence. There would have been violence among non-Communists, among sects. Political violence. There would have been assassinations, raids, some degree of guerrilla action. Communists against other Communists. The Trotskyists were wiped out by other Communists in Saigon in '45. There wouldn't have been anything that looked like a war, and to say that, is to say that Americans may bear the major responsibility, as I read this history, for every death in combat in Indo-China in the last 25 years. And that's one to two million people."

In the course of the CBS Special, the expanded version of the Cronkite-Ellsberg interview, Cronkite's multiple-point questions elicited from Ellsberg confusing replies in which he was often evasive, always righteous, prone to generalities,

and at times almost incoherent. When Cronkite asked Ellsberg what he considered the most important revelations in the published Pentagon Papers, Ellsberg talked about a lesson: "So far, I think both from the papers themselves, and the reaction to them in the public and from the Administration, I think the lesson is that the people of this country can't afford to let the President run the country by himself. Even foreign affairs any more than domestic affairs, without the help of the Congress, without the help of the public. Obviously the public needs more information than it's gotten from the past four presidents in the area of Vietnam, if they're to discharge their responsibilities, I think."

Somehow, Cronkite understood Ellsberg's reply and he pursued the matter of "public information," as he asked: "Isn't this correcting of this problem of public information more in the character of the leaders in Washington than it is in anything that can be legislated? If the leadership wishes to be candid with the American people, presumably it will be. If it does not wish to there's almost nothing that the press can do other than attempt to expose the truth. But getting to documents is another problem."

Ellsberg disagreed with Cronkite's point but never explained the area of disagreement and instead expounded some rather unique political science theories: "I would disagree with that. It seems to me that, again, the leaders, by whom I think you're referring to the executive officials, to the Executive Branch of government, have fostered an impression that I think the rest of us have been too willing to accept over the last generation. And that is that the Executive Branch is the government. And that indeed they are leaders in a sense that may not be entirely healthy if we're to still think of ourselves as a democracy.

"I was struck in fact by President Johnson's reaction to these revelations as close to treason. Because it reflected to me the sense of — that what was damaging to the reputation of the particular administration or particular individual, was in effect treason, which is in effect very close to saying, I am the state. And I think that quite sincerely many presidents, not only Lyndon Johnson, have come to feel that.

"What these studies tell me is we must remember this is a self-governing country. We are the government. And in terms of institutions, the Constitution provides for a separation of powers, for Congress, for the Courts, informally for the press, protected by the First Amendment. We're seeing all of those branches — if we call them branches of the government — alive and functioning, and I think very well this last week. It hasn't always been the case. I think we cannot at all let the officials of the Executive Branch determine for us what it is that the public needs to know about how well and how they are discharging their functions."

At no time during the course of the interview was Ellsberg asked if he had transmitted the Pentagon Papers to the *New York Times*. Cronkite, however, did ask a series of questions specifically related to the matter of morality with respect to those responsible for revealing and publishing the secret documents. Ellsberg believed that those who were involved with the exposure of the documents had an obligation to the American people to publish the Pentagon Papers even in violation of law.

Cronkite asked Ellsberg: "Could a government function however if there was not a loyalty to the system? Now

the system maybe should be changed. I think that's a comparatively good point to be made. But, if the system is not changed, then how does the government sort of protect its own operations if each man makes his own decision on security?"

In his reply, Ellsberg dwelled on the term "system" and evaded the term "security" as he fell back on some unsubstantiated reflections: "The system should be changed I think, to begin with. One way that it should be changed is to — and I think Congress has an interest in this as does the public, as does the press — is in some way to protect the honest man in that system. I know people who have spoken out. Individuals. Any official does. If that official stays silent it's because he has seen what happened to the ones who went before him who spoke out too frankly. It's very hard really, the way our system operates now, for a truly frank, honest man, to stay in that system indefinitely, without being weeded out, or fired, or made apathetic, or in fact, corrupted in the end.

"That has to change. And the government — you ask how can the government function. I have to say the government is not functioning well with the odds weighted as they are now towards concealment, toward fright, in effect, fear. Fear of the consequences of obeying the constitutional obligation to inform the people."

One of the most striking features of the Cronkite-Ellsberg interview was Ellsberg's apparent inability to defend the intrinsic value of the published Pentagon Papers. He admitted that the published documents were only a fragment of the Vietnam story. He admitted that presidential decisions and the background of those decisions could not be accurately appreciated from a study of the Pentagon Papers. At one point he admitted: "My impression is that presidential opinion on such matters is less committed to paper than that of almost any other official. More on the telephone, more in private conversation. It doesn't leave a documentary trail. So it would certainly be right from an historical point of view to say that conclusions about presidential motive are least accessible from this particular documentary record." Yet Ellsberg, despite his admissions that the Pentagon Papers were "very incomplete" and "only a beginning," took strong exception when Cronkite described the Pentagon Papers as "the thinking of lower echelons on the contingency planning basis primarily," and he insisted that the public had a need and right to know what was contained in the fragmentary collection: "For [this is] more than contingency planning. That is a quite deceptive description being given to this by former officials and current ones. We're talking in most cases about plans that were called for by the President because of the recommendation by a high official, one or another, that they might well be used in the future. They were done in most cases in the period you're talking about, with the expectation that one of several of a small group of plans would be used.

"In many cases we're talking about a plan that was used, or a plan that was recommended. The fact that it was recommended, the fact that it had the character that it did, and the kind of argument that it did, is information that I would say is very much needed to know by the public. The quality of thinking, the kinds of alternatives that are presented to the public' – to the President.

"I certainly agree that one of the limitations to this is that it would be a mistake to infer too much from it as to what the President's own thinking was. For example it's quite possible that he was not getting at all alternatives that he would have been very receptive to. But it seems absurd to say that the public had no need to know, let alone a right to know, the nature of the recommendations ultimately that have been made by the appointed officials. And as a matter of fact, the President's judgment in choosing his appointed officials, and in staying with him year after year of experience, is again an aspect of presidential decision making. How much the President can be judged only if we know the kind of service he was getting from those subordinates."

In the broad context of the CBS Special, Ellsberg was afforded an opportunity to portray himself on the highest levels of humanitarianism. He was able to show himself as living up to the highest moral responsibilities as he stole and transferred secrets entrusted to his care. His virtues included his deep concern for the South Vietnamese peoples (soldiers and civilians), Vietnamese refugees, and the ecology of Vietnam. He was able to enter a fervent plea for his pet theories, which if put into practice would upset the American constitutional system by increasing the power of the Congress and Judiciary at the expense of the Executive. He was also able to pass judgment on all those individuals who knew, as did he, the secrets of the Pentagon Papers. Cronkite asked him: "How would you describe the men who do not have the same emotional reaction to reading this, in knowing these – being privy to these secrets as you? Are they cold? Are they heartless? Are they villainous?" Ellsberg replied: "The usual assumption, of course, the usual description of them is, that they are among the

ELLSBERG

most decent and respectable and responsible men that our society has to offer.
That's a very plausible judgment in terms
of their background. And yet having
read the history, and I think others will
join this, I can't help but feel that their
decency, their humane feelings are to be
judged in part of the decisions they
brought themselves to make. The reasons
for which they did them and the consequences."

Ellsberg knew at the time of his
interview with Cronkite that he and
those who published the Pentagon
Papers had selected fragments of a fragmented history, surrounded the fragments with extremely biased analyses,
and used sensational headlines to promote and to justify their anti-Vietnam
War policies. Yet, Ellsberg characterized
the Pentagon Papers fraud as "the
truth." He said: "My father had a
favorite line from the Bible which I used
to hear a great deal when I was a kid.
'The truth shall make you free.' And I
hope that the truth that's out now, it's
out in the press, it's out in homes where
it should be, where voters can discuss it.
It's out of the safe and there is no way,
no way, to get it back into the safe. I
hope that truth will free us of this war. I
hope that we will put this war behind us.
And we will learn from it in such a way
that the history of the next 20 years will
read nothing like the history of the last
20 years."

At the very time Ellsberg appeared on
the CBS Special, a federal grand jury in
Los Angeles was investigating how the
Pentagon Papers reached the *New York
Times.* One of the first witnesses subpoenaed was Anthony J. Russo, a former
employee of the RAND Corporation and
a close friend of Ellsberg. Russo told the
grand jury his name and occupation,
then refused to testify any further, and

pleaded the protection of the Fifth
Amendment. At the request of the Department of Justice, Russo was taken
before a United States District Court,
where he was granted immunity from
prosecution if he testified. The immunity did not change Russo's attitude and
he continued his refusal to testify. He
was then held in contempt of court. He
eventually served a 47-day jail term.

On June 23, the grand jury heard
testimony from Lynda Sinay. Miss
Sinay, a friend of Ellsberg and Russo,
was granted immunity from prosecution,
and she told the grand jury that Ellsberg
paid her $150 for the use of a Xerox
machine in her office. She said that she
Xeroxed copies of documents for Ellsberg.

On June 25, Attorney General John
Mitchell announced that a warrant had
been issued for the arrest of Daniel
Ellsberg, charging him with "unauthor-
ized possession of top-secret documents." With the warrant, there were
two affidavits. One affidavit, signed by
security officers of the RAND Corporation, said that Ellsberg had access to a
47-volume set of the Pentagon Papers
and had actual custody of 27 volumes
"at various times between October 23,
1969 and April 7, 1970." The second
affidavit was signed by Ellsberg's former
wife, Carol Cummings. The *Washington
Post* (June 26, 1971) reported: "Mrs.
Ellsberg's affidavit said that in October,
1969, 'I learned that my former husband . . . had been engaged in making
Xerox copies of a large number of
documents, some of which bore the
classification "top secret." ' She said
that after Xeroxing the documents 'he
cut the classification off.'

"She said she spoke to Ellsberg about
it and 'told him that I was extremely
concerned since in my opinion this was a

criminal act and he could go to jail for it.' Her affidavit says he told her 'he had done nothing illegal and there was no official secrets act in this country . . . .' He further said that people did this sort of thing all the time in their memoirs and that they mentioned things in print that had been top secret.

" 'My former husband at that time told me that he was very concerned about the war in Vietnam and that there were things that had not been disclosed which should be known. He then said he would only give it to authorized people like Sens. Fulbright and Goodell.' "

On the same day that the warrant was issued for Ellsberg's arrest, two attorneys, Leonard B. Boudin and Charles R. Nesson, held a news conference in Boston, Massachusetts. They announced that they represented Daniel Ellsberg and they were ready to accompany him to the U.S. Attorney's Office in Boston. (Boudin has had a long history of defending Communists and Communist fronts. Nesson, a professor at Harvard Law School, was not only co-counsel with Boudin for Ellsberg, but later the two would be co-counsels for the "Harrisburg 8" in the Berrigan conspiracy trial.)

On June 28, in Boston, Ellsberg surrendered to federal authorities and he told reporters that he had distributed copies of the Pentagon Papers to the press. To the newsmen, Ellsberg said: "In the fall of 1969, I took the responsibility on my own initiative of delivering to the chairman of the Foreign Relations Committee of the U.S. Senate [Senator J. William Fulbright] the information contained in the so-called Pentagon papers, including several studies on negotiations which have not been given to any newspaper. Until that time, these studies had been accessible only to me

and few other individuals. By this spring, two invasions later, and after 9,000 more Americans and hundreds of thousands of Indochinese had died, I could only regret that I had not at that time released that information to the American public through the newspapers. I have now done so." He also said: "I did this clearly at my own jeopardy and I am prepared to answer to all the consequences of these decisions. That includes the personal consequences to me and my family, whatever these may be. Would not you go to prison to help end the war?" After arraignment, Ellsberg was released on $50,000 bail.

On July 1, at a news conference in Cambridge, Massachusetts, Ellsberg said that he had been the primary source of the Pentagon Papers for all the newspapers which published articles based on the documents. He admitted that other individuals helped in the distribution, but he declined to identify any of them. He said that he released the material "because concealment of this information for 25 years has now led to the death of 50,000 Americans, several hundred thousand Vietnamese in the last few years. A couple of million in over 20 years. Judgment at this point of whether the American public is to be trusted to make these decisions versus the executive branch can now be judged by you, by citizens, and by the courts and Congress in the light of where secrecy has led us the last 25 years."

Before nine television cameras and about 100 American and foreign newsmen at his press conference, Ellsberg said that he had decided "it was urgent for me to get this history out at whatever jeopardy" two years before, when it became apparent to him that the Nixon Administration was "subject to the same trap of arrogance and ignorance" as the

351

previous administration, in which he had served. He said that "the policy was essentially the same, tactically different in terms of reducing American manpower, but the same in terms of using military method to avoid "defeat or failure in Vietnam for the administration that happens at this moment to be in office."

Ellsberg said that President Johnson did not lack accurate intelligence estimates from the Central Intelligence Agency before escalating the war. "The decisions seem to have been made year after year in the light of what was adequate information to make better decisions," he said. "If the President had this information available, why did he ignore it, why did he listen to Walt Rostow and McGeorge Bundy as experts on Vietnam instead of people who had a very good track record of prediction? I do not have any conclusive answer to that."

On July 13, 1971, Ellsberg was a guest of the ABC-TV "Dick Cavett Show." He said on the program that a major reason for giving the Pentagon Papers to the press was his reaction in 1969 when murder charges against eight Green Berets were dropped by former Secretary of the Army Stanley Resor. The Green Berets had been charged with the murder of a Vietnamese double agent. Resor argued that the men could not get a fair trial because they were involved with the Central Intelligence Agency. The Commanding General in Vietnam, Creighton Abrams, had demanded and had been promised a thorough investigation of the case. But Resor, according to Ellsberg, acted on behalf of the Johnson Administration: "The White House had made the decision. It was the first time a commander had been overruled. Abrams was mad

because he was told a lie. Then I started thinking. This is the system I spent 15 years serving – one that would conceal murder by lying. I decided I can't be part of that any more. I was tired of those who tell me when I should lie and how I should lie. And very soon after that, I made my decision." Ellsberg told Cavett's audience that he took his report on the Pentagon Papers to presidential aide Henry Kissinger in September 1970 and asked Kissinger to study the document. According to Ellsberg, Kissinger said that he already had a copy. (Kissinger denied in June 1971 that he ever saw the Pentagon Papers until they appeared in the *New York Times*.)

Henry M. Kissinger and Daniel Ellsberg were long-time acquaintances but their friendship evidently came apart on January 29, 1971 at a meeting called Project Runnemede in Dedham, Massachusetts. The events that occurred at the meeting have been described by Derek Shearer in the *Nation* ("An Evening with Henry," March 8, 1971), Don Clark in the *Boston Herald-Traveler* (June 18, 1971), and Crocker Snow Jr. in the *Boston Globe* (July 4, 1971). The three accounts are in substantial agreement. Project Runnemede had been first organized in 1970 after students from Massachusetts Institute of Technology demonstrated at the premises of several firms that had defense contracts. Franklin Lindsay, president of Itek, and the MIT students agreed to convene a meeting of students, academicians, and businessmen to discuss U.S. foreign policy. Henry Kissinger agreed to meet with the group if his remarks could be considered to be off-the-record. In the course of the meeting, a man asked Kissinger about the widening of the air war in Vietnam. Kissinger was evasive in his answer. Derek Shearer described what ensued:

ELLSBERG

"Another man rose and pressed the issue. He was Daniel Ellsberg, a former Defense Department official who had served under Robert McNamara, worked in the United States Embassy in Saigon, studied policy at Rand, and who is now at MIT's Center for International Studies.

"Since leaving Rand about a year ago, Ellsberg had been actively opposing the war, testifying at trials of draft resisters, writing articles and giving speeches at anti-war rallies. He noted that Kissinger had avoided part of what . . . the previous questioner had been saying. He suggested that a person's values showed by what he didn't say, and by his actions, no matter what his words.

"Ellsberg said he knew that Kissinger's staff had figures on estimated American casualties over the next year, but had the staff estimated Asian dead and wounded, including civilians, that would result from Vietnamization? Could Dr. Kissinger give us those figures? Kissinger recognized Ellsberg and when he responded his voice sounded suddenly less certain, he hesitated, then called Ellsberg's question 'cleverly worded. I answer even if I don't answer,' he said.

"Ellsberg interrupted to say that he had no intention of being clever, that this was a basic question – were such estimates made? Kissinger started to say that one had to consider the options. 'I know the option game, Dr. Kissinger,' said Ellsberg, 'can't you just give us an answer or tell us that you don't have such estimates?' Kissinger again evaded the question; he said the question had racist overtones. Ellsberg pressed him again. For the first time the meeting took on the air of confrontation – then the student moderator stood up and . . . ended the questioning, saying that Dr.

Kissinger was tired, and thanked him for coming . . . ."

On August 5, 1971, in the U.S. District Court in Boston, Ellsberg was ordered to appear in Los Angeles on August 16 to face arraignment on charges of theft of government property and failure to return documents classified as "top-secret-sensitive." The warrant for his arrest was issued in Los Angeles because he had access to the Pentagon Papers while working for the RAND Corporation in Santa Monica. Ellsberg's lawyers had delayed the Court's order for three weeks when they contended that illegal wiretapping and eavesdropping might have been used to obtain the indictment. Their contention was rejected as irrelevant and immaterial. The justice in the District Court said: "Proof of wiretap would not invalidate the indictment and would not invalidate the warrant, which was based on the indictment." On August 16 in Los Angeles, Ellsberg pleaded not guilty to the charges. His plea was accepted and pretrial motions were scheduled for January 4, 1972.

On September 14, 1971, at the U.S. District Court in Los Angeles, the Federal Government submitted an affidavit in support of an attempt to subpoena the records of Daniel Ellsberg. The affidavit said that Ellsberg had begun hoarding classified documents 18 months previously. The affidavit said that the documents were in a warehouse and were contained in "several metal handcases, a footlocker, 18 book volumes, a large cardboard carton, and a large carton file." On December 30, in the U.S. District Court in Los Angeles, Ellsberg was re-indicted for stealing, distributing, and refusing to return classified Defense Department documents, and for illegally keeping national defense papers in viola-

353

tion of the Espionage Act of 1940. Ellsberg was also charged with conspiracy, and if convicted on all twelve counts in the indictment, could be sentenced to 115 years in prison and fined $120,000. Indicted with Ellsberg was Anthony J. Russo, who had already spent 47 days in jail for contempt, when he refused to testify before a federal grand jury. Named as co-conspirators were Lynda Sinay, who had admitted making Xerox copies of the Pentagon Papers, and Vu van Thai, a former South Vietnamese diplomat. (Vu has an interesting background. Before the partition of Vietnam, he had worked with Ho chi Minh for about five years. After partition, he administered and distributed U.S. aid in South Vietnam. In 1965, he was named South Vietnamese Ambassador to the United States. Since that time, he has not returned to South Vietnam and, since his retirement from the diplomatic corps in 1967, has been a bitter opponent of the Saigon regime. There is strong speculation that he has had contacts with the Hanoi regime and the National Liberation Front in recent years. Vu, in the period between 1967 and 1970, worked for the RAND Corporation, and became a close friend and an associate of Ellsberg. Ellsberg has been indicted for giving one volume of the Pentagon Papers to Vu. At the time when Vu was named as a co-conspirator, he was working for the United Nations in Senegal. His reaction to the indictment was: "I am a friend of Dan Ellsberg. As to this case, it is a political affair, and since at the present time I am an international civil servant, rules forbid me to comment on a Vietnamese political affair.")

On January 4, 1972, at the U.S. District Court in Los Angeles, Ellsberg pleaded not guilty to all twelve charges in his indictment. In court with Ellsberg was Attorney Charles Goodell, former Republican Senator from New York. Goodell, who once employed Ellsberg as a consultant on Vietnam, called the indictment "a crazy quilt," because "it charges Mr. Ellsberg and Mr. Russo with stealing the truth and telling it to Americans." (Goodell, chairman of the National Defense Committee for Ellsberg, had hoped to be a co-counsel in the Ellsberg case, but he is not a member of the California bar.)

After Ellsberg entered his plea, he talked to reporters and said that he had "decided to give the Pentagon Papers to the American people" more than two years before when Goodell, then in the U.S. Senate, introduced a bill to end United States involvement in the Vietnam War by December 1, 1970. Ellsberg noted that the bill did not pass and the war continued, and said: "This is what this trial is about. It is about the right of the American public to know the facts . . . so that they can act together to end this war before another half million tons of bombs have been dropped."

In all that has been written about Ellsberg, one of the strongest themes is that he made the drastic conversion from hawk to dove. His apologists explain that his intenseness as a dove caused him to steal and to reveal the highly secret Pentagon Papers. What cannot be found in the millions of words written about Ellsberg since June 1971 is the precise time when his alleged conversion was complete or the precise time when he arrived at the decision to reveal the secret documents.

J. Anthony Lukas in the *New York Times* magazine provided several versions. Lukas interviewed Patricia Ellsberg and asked her if her refusal of Ellsberg's marriage proposal in 1966 caused him to

354

change from hawk to dove. She replied: "Oh absolutely not! It was 10 different things of which I was perhaps one small part. Sure there were differences between us in Vietnam. But it was more the difference between men and women. I looked at those kids in the streets, the refugees, the poverty, and the thought of what was happening to those human lives was just intolerable, sickening. Dan at that time was much more caught up in ideologies and abstract principles. He wanted things to be more humane, too, but was trying to bring that about through memos, internal reforms.

"But what changed Dan wasn't me. It was seeing the war and the devastation month after month, sitting in on all those conferences, reading all those memos, and it was time and his own personal liberation. When I saw him again in California, in the spring of 1969, he was much looser, much easier with himself and with nature. It was just a kind of *joie de vivre* that hadn't been there before. He was his own man. He was a man who could finally love and whom I could love."

Lukas described what occurred when he asked Ellsberg about the influence of his wife upon his drastic change of views: "When I asked the same question of Dan, he mentions many of the things and people we have already talked about, but gradually we move toward a conference of the War Resisters' League which he attended at Haverford College in September, 1969 — just weeks before he decided to Xerox the Pentagon Papers.

" 'There was this one young guy there — a Harvard graduate named Randy Kehler. A very good-looking guy, very reflective, thoughtful, calm, into the California culture as I was. The last evening of the conference, Randy gave a

talk about the peace movement. He talked of all the people in the movement who were going to jail. Then, out of the blue, he said, "and I'm very proud that I'm soon going to be joining them." He was resisting the draft and, sure enough, he was soon in prison.

" 'Well, I remember thinking, you see — this is our best, our very best, and we're sending them to prison, more important, we're in a world where they feel they just had to go to prison.'

"Suddenly, he [Ellsberg] begins to weep openly, burying his head in his arms in the half light seeping in from the East River. After a few seconds, he wipes his eyes. 'I'm never able to tell anyone about this without crying. "The best we had, our very best." All of a sudden, it set new standards for me of what one could be expected, or asked, to do, in the way of resistance to the war. I realized that these young men were very much like my friends in the Marine Corps who had gone into combat for their country. I saw that what these draft resisters were doing was entirely in that spirit. That they were very patriotic. And suddenly I realized that I too would have to enter a kind of resistance to the war even if I too had to go to prison.' "

Lukas heard Ellsberg describe two other turning points in his ideological struggle. He described a meeting between Ellsberg and Eqbal Ahmad: "At one point, Dan and Ahmad start reminiscing about their first meeting — at an April, 1968 Princeton conference on 'Revolution in a Changing World.' There Dan also met Janaki Tschannerl, an Indian girl who had a profound influence on him (particularly when she said 'In my world, there are no enemies').

"Now, he recalls, 'she gave me a vision, as a Gandhian, of a different way of living and resistance, of exercising power nonviolently. And as I saw it at that time, Martin Luther King began to seem to me to be our last hope. And he was killed that weekend. You were with me then,' he says to Ahmad in a choked voice."

While Lukas traveled around the country with Ellsberg, the latter recalled another turning point. Lukas wrote: "We pass an airport parking lot and he recalls an incident there several years ago with Tran Ngoc Chau, a member of South Vietnam's National Assembly and Ellsberg's closest Vietnamese friend. 'We were coming into this lot and as I took a ticket from the slot and the barrier went up, this recorded voice came out of a loudspeaker saying, "This is your ticket. Do not lose this ticket. Do not leave it in your car. Thank you." When we got through, Chau said, "Im-poss-i-ble," slowly like that in four syllables, "Im-poss-i-ble, that America should lose the war in Vietnam." ' (Chau was arrested in 1969 and given a 10-year sentence for having maintained contact with his brother, a convicted Viet Cong intelligence agent. Chau acknowledged the contacts but said he had kept the American Embassy and the C.I.A. informed of them. Later, the Supreme Court annulled the sentence, but President Thieu refused to release Chau. Ellsberg says the Chau affair was one of the turning points in his attitude toward the war.)"

Two syndicated columnists, Joseph Kraft and John P. Roche, had similar recollections of Ellsberg between 1966 and 1971. Both men seem to be in substantial agreement that by the spring of 1968, Ellsberg was fully committed to the dovish position on Vietnam. On June 30, 1971, Joseph Kraft wrote: "But if I came to admire Ellsberg abundantly over a period of five years of intermittent meetings on Vietnam, I also came to

doubt his judgments profoundly. And the story of those encounters is worth telling for it says something about the present plight of both Ellsberg and the country.

"Our first meeting took place in the Pentagon when Ellsberg was working for the late John McNaughton, who was then assistant Secretary of Defense for International Security Affairs. I had recently seen something of the Vietnamese Communists. At that time not much was known of them and I went to the Defense Department to tell McNaughton and Ellsberg my impressions.

"Ellsberg in particular posed a series of hard questions. He wanted to know about Communist morale, about possible leadership rifts, about conflicts between North and South Vietnamese Communists, about their relations with China and Russia, about the origins and history of the Liberation Front, about its infrastructure and doctrinal notions. At the end I was asked what way I saw of ending the conflict.

"I replied that the key was fostering in Saigon a regime that would negotiate with the Communists. That idea McNaughton and Ellsberg flatly rejected. There was no possible way for negotiation in their view. Vietnam was a test of the American will to resist Communist aggression.

"A second meeting took place in Saigon when Ellsberg was working for Brig. Gen. Edwin Lansdale. The Lansdale idea, of which Ellsberg had become a violent partisan, was that a Saigon regime friendly to the United States could filch the Communist appeal to the countryside by a combination of social reform and vigorous police action. That notion seemed to me a pernicious fallacy and I had written as much.

"When I first called him in Saigon,

ELLSBERG

Ellsberg refused to see me. Then we arranged a clandestine meeting. He told me that in view of my doubts about the policy there was no point in our talking.

"I next ran into Ellsberg in the spring of 1968 at a lunch in the home of Sen. Edward Kennedy in McLean, Va. By that time Ellsberg had changed his views and to the considerable embarrassment of everybody at lunch he talked at great length of how wrong he had been.

"After lunch I drove him back to Washington. As we drove he kept glancing nervously over his shoulder. When we finally reached town he directed me first to one hotel, then to a second, then to a third, where he finally got out. He was taking precautions, he said, to avoid being followed by agents of the FBI or the Pentagon.

"A last meeting took place several months ago at my house in Washington. By this time Ellsberg had long since become convinced that the war was profoundly immoral. He talked obsessively of America's guilt and the need to cleanse the national soul.

"He recounted in every detail debates he had had with leading figures in the government. He kept casting about for things that might be done to expose the officials responsible for Vietnam. It must have been about that time that the Pentagon papers were turned over to the *New York Times.*"

On July 22, 1971, John P. Roche wrote: "My first encounter with Ellsberg was in Saigon in the spring of 1966. There had been a big fight within the administration on whether the United States should encourage the development of representative government in Vietnam. Some argued that establishing constitutional government would be destabilizing in the middle of a war; others

felt it would be a move towards stability. President Johnson decided in February that it was essential and I was sent to Saigon (as a 'consultant on public administration') to provide an independent reading of the situation.

"Shortly after I arrived, I was invited by Gen. Edwin Lansdale to visit his 'team' at Cong Ly. Ellsberg was among those present. Without going into details, they had a theory of counter-insurgency that involved training 57-man Vietnamese teams to go out into the countryside. These political action teams (PAT) were supposed to provide the South Vietnamese peasants with the same sort of political dedication that the Communists provided in the north. This assembly-line approach to political warfare struck me as absurd, but what impressed me most was the revivalistic mood of the gathering. When I asked politely what precisely the PAT were supposed to believe in, what would be their ideological motivation, a curious hush fell over the room. It was rather as though a cardinal had questioned the existence of God. And I was written off as simply incapable of comprehending the higher verities.

"I forgot about Ellsberg until he turned up at the White House in late February or early March, 1968. He was peddling a memo all over town to the effect that the Tet offensive proved the war was lost, and brought a copy for one of my colleagues. The latter gave it to me to read and then invited me in with Ellsberg to discuss it. I thought Ellsberg was dead wrong in his analysis (which, I'm told, misled John Kenneth Galbraith into predicting at the time that the Saigon government would collapse in two weeks), but again what struck me most vividly was his fervor. And his total refusal to argue the question on the

357

merits — again I was exiled from the company of the faithful.

"The Tet offensive, in my judgment, had been a brilliantly executed political warfare operation, rather than an effort to take over the south militarily. It was designed, in short, to influence American opinion; in Gen. Giap's view, 40,000 to 50,000 dead was a small price to pay for undermining the American commitment. (Note that he sent his South Vietnamese — the main force VC — out on this suicide mission and kept his Hanoi divisions in reserve.) Ellsberg's reaction was precisely what Giap had in mind.

"This is not to question Ellsberg's loyalty to the United States, but to suggest that his judgment was bad and, more important, that whatever bad judgment he had was invariably disguised as a message from God. Rightly or wrongly, and wherever it may lead us, in a democratic society the man sent from God has only one vote."

Since June 1971, when Ellsberg was identified as the one who leaked the Pentagon Papers, he has appeared determined to prove beyond a shadow of a doubt that he is a pacifist and a leftist. He had earlier leftist-pacifist affiliations. He had worked with U.S. Senators Charles Goodell, Robert F. Kennedy, and Edward M. Kennedy. He had close associations with U.S. Senators J. William Fulbright and George McGovern and U.S. Representative Paul McCloskey. He had been affiliated with the Carnegie Endowment for International Peace and the Council on Foreign Relations, and both of these groups were overwhelmingly on the dovish side of the Vietnam War. Three of his closest friends in the academic community of Boston-Cambridge were the notorious leftists Richard Falk, Noam Chomsky, and Howard Zinn.

When Ellsberg held his first press conference after being arrested, the meeting was moderated by David Hawk of the New Mobilization. Within the next few months, Ellsberg was associating with such ultra-leftists as Abbie Hoffman, Jerry Rubin, John Froines, David Dellinger, and Rennie Davis. On July 29, 1971, Ellsberg addressed a three-day conference held by 17 anti-war members of the House of Representatives. He called upon the Congressmen to risk their all ("No one in this room has been asked to give his life as your sons and brothers have been asked to do.") by seeking to cut off all appropriations to finance the war; to move toward impeachments in the executive branch; to file court suits; and to find other means to stop the war in Vietnam.

Human Events of September 18, 1971 reported on a meeting Ellsberg attended with about 25 "peace" leaders, including some of the "Harrisburg 8" defendants and three (Rennie Davis, David Dellinger, and John Froines) of those convicted for plotting to disrupt the 1968 Democratic National Convention. *Human Events* also reported: "Also attending that session was Anthony J. Russo, the former Rand Corp. analyst charged with contempt of court for declining to testify before a federal grand jury probing the Pentagon Papers theft.

" 'According to several participants in the meeting,' reported the Los Angeles *Times*, 'the group discussed holding "war crimes trials" in Harrisburg during the trial of the eight defendants and in Los Angeles during Ellsberg's trial.'

"The ex-Pentagon employe has also agreed to protest the decision to refuse parole to the Berrigan brothers — Daniel and Philip — who are currently in federal prison at Danbury, Conn., for destroying draft records."

In the same item, it was also said: "Daniel Ellsberg, the ex-Defense Department employe indicted on charges of stealing those famous Pentagon Papers, has been busily plotting anti-war strategy with various 'peace groups.' In Wellfleet, Mass., recently, Ellsberg spoke at a fund-raising affair for the 'Harrisburg 8,' who are alleged to have destroyed draft records and to have planned the kidnapping of presidential adviser Henry Kissinger. He helped raise $7,000 for the defendants."

In September 1971, Ellsberg was in Washington, D.C., where he received the Federal Employee of the Year award from the ultra-leftist Federal Employees for Peace. The award read: "To Daniel Ellsberg, for exemplifying the highest ideals of public service and in grateful recognition for distinguished public service to the American people."

On October 14, 1971, Ellsberg returned to Massachusetts Institute of Technology, where he addressed a Vietnam Moratorium audience of more than 1,000. He told the audience that he brought them "an anarchic and seditious message." He explained: "If there is one message I have gotten from the Pentagon Papers, it is to distrust authority, distrust the President, distrust the men in power, even Americans in power, because power does corrupt, even Americans."

In October 1971, Ellsberg went to Chicago, where he received an award from the leftist-pacifist Business Executives Move for Vietnam Peace. The presentation was made by the leftist-pacifist former U.S. Attorney General Ramsey Clark. Others receiving awards at the same ceremony included such renowned leftists as journalist David Schoenbrun, former U.S. Senator Wayne Morse, folk-singer Joan Baez, Harvard University professor George Wald, and John Kerry of Vietnam Veterans Against the War.

On October 8, 1971, J. Anthony Lukas of the *New York Times* visited Ellsberg's home in Cambridge. Lukas described his experience: "From a nearby bookshelf Dan plucks down several books which he says have influenced his recent development: *Conquest of Violence: the Gandhian Philosophy of Conflict* by Joan V. Bondurant; *We Have Been Invaded by the 21st Century* by Dave McReynolds; *The Politics of History* by Howard Zinn, and, particularly, *Revolution and Equilibrium* by Barbara Deming, whose title essay ends: 'May those who say they believe in nonviolence learn to challenge more boldly those institutions of violence that constrict and cripple our humanity. And may those who have questioned nonviolence come to see that one's rights to life and happiness can only be claimed as inalienable if one grants, in action, that they belong to all men.' "

On November 6, 1971, Ellsberg was in Boston, Massachusetts, at a leftwing demonstration. Lucinda Smith described his appearance: "Dr. Daniel Ellsberg called for the impeachment of President Nixon yesterday in an impromptu speech before an estimated 5000 antiwar and anti-Amchitka blast demonstrators on the Boston Common.

"Ellsberg, who released the famous Pentagon Papers in June, told the rally: 'I would like to see impeachment proceedings start right now – two sets of proceedings.' He explained, 'One set against President Nixon for his repeated lies and violence to the Constitution of this country and to his countrymen, and the other set against the next president of the United States, to be dated three months from when he takes office.'

ELLSBERG

"Ellsberg continued, 'I would like the next President to say he will resign from office if the war is not ended within three months of the time he takes over. Nixon is trying to tell us that war is peace. He was elected because he said he had a secret plan to end the war. The next president must have a specific plan. We must demand these plans and all the specifics from all the candidates for president.' "

Along the way in 1971, Ellsberg endorsed the Hanoi-inspired People's Peace Treaty, which had become the favorite project of the ultra-left. On February 4, 1972, syndicated columnist Jeffrey Hart presented some astute observations on Ellsberg and showed how far Ellsberg had entered into the far left circles: "At first Daniel Ellsberg was presented to us as a recognizable Defense Department type á la Robert McNamara. He had one of those precision-tooled minds that supposedly could deal in a flash with innumerable factors and variables, snapping out a correct solution.

"Harmonious with this was the graduate record at Harvard, the stint with Rand Corp.; and he was said to have been a rather hawky hawk on Vietnam.

"Only, so the story went, his very rationality at last convinced him that the Vietnamese War was a blunder. And, characteristically, the precision-tooled mind snapped out another solution. He would do what he could to end the war. He would leak the Pentagon Papers. And thus he suddenly became a prophet not at all without honor in his own country.

"That there is something decidedly wrong with that portrait has begun to emerge only gradually. The most recent indication, but only the most recent, is Ellsberg's espousal of the cause of H. Bruce Franklin. A professor of English at Stanford, but also a self-styled Maoist-

Leninist revolutionary, Franklin has repeatedly advocated violence on the Stanford campus.

"He is one of the leaders of an armed revolutionary organization called Venceremos ('We shall overcome'). He has figured prominently in disruptive activities − the shouting down of speakers, the occupation of buildings on the campus. He expresses himself in a jargon of mind-boggling meaninglessness: 'The heroic struggle of the revolutionary masses of Vietnam throws the lie into the rotten teeth of those who libel and degrade humanity.'

"Franklin clearly has no connection at all with the scholarly and educational purposes of a university, and Stanford, after interminable hearings, finally salvaged a minimum of intellectual self-respect and fired him. Whereupon Ellsberg, among others, expressed 'outrage.'

"What was going on? Franklin's behavior certainly does not fall within any conceivable definition of academic freedom. And, in its substance, his position seems nonsensical.

"This is only the latest bit of evidence, however, that Ellsberg is now entirely absorbed in the milieu of radical chic, the principal characteristic of which is that the positions one takes do not have rational justification but are wholly in the nature of gestures."

On February 19, 1972, *Human Events* printed a startling item: "Guess who showed up last week to honor Daniel Ellsberg, filcher of the Pentagon Papers? None other than Alger Hiss. The former Soviet spy headed a New York confab of the Lawyers' Committee on American Policy Towards Viet Nam, saying he wanted to pay tribute to Ellsberg's 'great courage and principle.' "

In 1971, Ellsberg presented the American reading public with a long list of heroic utterances: February 1971 – "If I could find the proper forum, I would be willing to risk 20 years in jail. I must expose the duplicity of the government." May 6, 1971 – "I obviously think the government should stop what it's doing. But until it does we must be willing to put our bodies on the line, if only symbolically, to try to make it stop." June 28, 1971 – "I did this clearly at my own jeopardy and I am prepared to answer to all the consequences. Would not you go to prison to end the war?" July 13, 1971 – "If I have broken the law, I'll go to prison for it. But there's been a lot of law-breaking over the last 25 years." December 30, 1971 – "This Christmas present to me [indictment] is nothing compared to the Christmas present the President [Nixon] has recently given American fliers recently shot down over North Vietnam." December 30, 1971 – "How can you measure the jeopardy I'm in to the penalty that has been paid by 50,000 American families and hundreds of thousands of Vietnamese?"

J. Anthony Lukas in the *New York Times* magazine afforded his readers two more of Ellsberg's heroic quotations: " 'I [Ellsberg] realized how many men had died because those pages [the Pentagon Papers] had been stamped top secret and because generations of bureaucrats like me kept them secret . . . I realized that I had to reveal this information even if I had to go to prison for the rest of my life . . . I needed some help. Fortunately I had a friend named Tony Russo. That morning, I went over to Tony's apartment and I said "Tony, do you know where we can get a Xerox machine?" and he said "Yes" and that night we stayed up all night. That was two years ago, today, the night of September 30 to October 1, 1969.' " – "His classmates [at

his 20th class reunion at Harvard] give Dan a resounding ovation. Then, in the question period, one asks him whether he is suffering much harassment from the F.B.I. and other Government agencies. 'Oh, a bit,' he says with a laugh. 'My phone is tapped and all that. But after all I'm giving them a bit of trouble, too. I hope I'm giving them more trouble than they're giving me. And I have more trouble I can give them. And I will.' "

On December 30, 1971, Ellsberg, as he was re-indicted in Los Angeles, seemed something less than heroic as he cried: "I stole nothing and I did not commit espionage. I violated no laws and I have not intended to harm my country."

RUPERT EMERSON was born on August 20, 1899 in Rye, New York, son of Maria Furman and William Emerson. He married Alla Grosjean. He is an alumnus of Harvard University (A.B., 1921) and the London School of Economics (Ph.D., 1927). He is the author of *State and Sovereignty in Modern Germany* (1928); *Malaysia* (1937); *The Netherlands Indies and the U.S.* (1942); *Representative Government in Southeast Asia* (1955); *From Empire to Nation: The Rise to Self Assertion of Asian and African People* (1960); *Malaysia: A Study in Direct and Indirect Rule* (1966); and *Africa and United States Policy* (1967). He was a contributor to *America's Pacific Dependencies* (1949). He is co-editor of *Africa and World Order* (1963) and *The Political Awakening of Africa* (1965).

In 1921 and 1922, Emerson was a reporter for the *New York Sun*. Since 1927, he has been at Harvard University in the department of government as instructor (1927-1931), assistant professor (1931-1938), associate professor (1938-1946), and professor (1946 to the present). He has been a visiting lecturer at Yale University. He has been a visiting professor at the University of California at Berkeley and the University of California at Los Angeles. In 1940 and 1941, he was director of the U.S. Department of the Interior's division of territories and island possessions. In 1941 and 1942, he worked in the Office of Coordinator of Inter-American Affairs. In 1942, he was regional administrator for territories and possessions in the Office of Price Administration. In 1943, he was an assistant administrator in the Lend-Lease program. In 1944 and 1945, he was director of the liberated areas branch of the Foreign Economic Administration.

Emerson has long been affiliated with the Council on Foreign Relations, the informal supra-State Department of the United States. He was affiliated with the Inter-University Committee for a Public Hearing on Vietnam, which the Communist propaganda apparatus exploited for purely Communist purposes. He was affiliated with the leftist-pacifist Ad Hoc Committee for an Open Letter on Vietnam and the leftist-pacifist Ad Hoc Faculty Committee on Vietnam. He was long associated, as a member and as a trustee, with the Institute of Pacific Relations, "a vehicle used by the Communists to orientate American far eastern policies toward Communist objectives." He contributed to the IPR's publications, *Far Eastern Survey* and *Pacific Affairs.* He also contributed to *Amerasia*, a Communist-controlled magazine.

EDWARD ENGBERG was born on March 5, 1928, son of Corrine Olson and Molts Engberg. He married Catherine Lilek. He is an alumnus of the University of Chicago (A.B., 1952). He is the author of *The Spy in the Corporate Structure and the Right to Privacy* (1967). He is the co-author of *Listing in the Entertainment Industry* (1956). He has contributed to such publications as *Fortune, New Republic, Commonweal, New Leader,* and the *Chicago Tribune* Magazine.

From 1951 until 1959, Engberg was managing editor of *Business International.* From 1952 until 1954, he was an associate editor of *Fortune* magazine. From 1959 until 1965, he was a senior editor for Cowles Communications. Since 1967, he has been a senior fellow at the ultra-leftist Center for the Study of Democratic Institutions.

Engberg's writings are his most impressive credentials as a leftist. He has avoided a career in front organizations, but he did make an exception when he served on the ultra-leftist Norman Thomas 80th Birthday Anniversary Committee in a tribute to the patriarch of the Socialist Party. Engberg made his most startling contribution to the left as an interviewer for John Cogley's "blacklisting" project, an anti-anti-Communist witch-hunt financed by the Fund for the Republic.

CHARLES W. ENGELHARD JR. was born on February 15, 1917 in New York City, son of Emy Canthal and Charles Engelhard. He married Jane Reis-Brian. He is an alumnus of Princeton University (B.A., 1939).

Engelhard is chairman of the board of Engelhard Industries, which was founded by his father and is a worldwide firm specializing in precious metals. The firm has more than a dozen operating divisions in the United States and has subsidiaries in Australia, Austria, Canada, Colombia, Denmark, England, France, Italy, Japan, and Switzerland. He is chairman of Engelhard Hanovia, and he is also chairman of four corporations and a director of six in South Africa.

Engelhard is a resident member of the Council on Foreign Relations, the informal supra-State Department of the United States. He has been a member of the Committee for Economic Development, the major propaganda arm of the Council on Foreign Relations, in the important work of socializing the American economy. He has been an official of the Foreign Policy Association, a bulwark of leftist internationalism and a highly effective vehicle for pro-Communist propaganda. He has been an official of the Atlantic Council, an organization which stresses the need for closer cooperation, especially economic, between the United States and the socialist nations of Western Europe.

ROBERT ENGLER was born on July 12, 1922 in New York City, son of Esther Haber and Isidore Engler. He was married to and divorced from Rosalind Elowitz. He is an alumnus of the City College of New York (B.S.S., 1942) and the University of Wisconsin (M.A., 1943; Ph.D., 1947). He is the author of *The Politics of Oil: A Study of Private Power and Democratic Directions* (1961). He is a contributor to *The Dissenting Academy* (1968).

In 1946 and 1947, Engler was a political science instructor at the University of Wisconsin. From 1947 until 1951, he was at Syracuse University as instructor (1947-1948) and assistant professor (1948-1951). In 1950 and 1951, he was a special assistant to the president of the National Farmers Union. Since 1951, he has been a professor of political science at Sarah Lawrence College. From 1959 until 1963, he was a visiting lecturer in sociology at Columbia University. From 1961 until 1964, he was on the faculty of the radical New School for Social Research. Since 1964, he has been a visiting professor of political science at Queens College in New York. Since 1969, he has been a visiting professor at Brooklyn College. He has also been a visiting professor at the University of Puerto Rico. In 1955, he was awarded the Sidney Hillman Foundation prize for political writing, a tribute reserved for leftists.

Engler has been affiliated with the leftist-oriented American Association of University Professors; the ultra-leftist American Civil Liberties Union; the Socialist League for Industrial Democracy; and the Writers and Artists Protest, a leftist-pacifist group. He has participated in the ultra-leftist Socialist Scholars Conferences.

ALEXANDER ERLICH was born on November 23, 1912 in St. Petersburg, Russia. He is a naturalized American. He is an alumnus of the radical New School for Social Research (Ph.D., 1953). He is the author of *The Soviet Industrialization Debate, 1924-1928* (1967).

In 1949 and 1950, Erlich was a consultant to the Rand Corporation. From 1950 until 1954, he was a fellow at Harvard University. In 1954 and 1955, he was a research associate with the National Bureau of Economic Research. Since 1955, he has been on the economics faculty at Columbia University as visiting lecturer (1955-1957), visiting associate professor (1957-1959), associate professor (1959-1966), and professor (1966 to the present).

Erlich has been on the board of directors of the Socialist League for Industrial Democracy. He has been affiliated with the leftist-pacifist Ad Hoc Faculty Committee on Vietnam. He has been a strong supporter of the ultra-radical Students for a Democratic Society. In 1968, he was one of the most prominent faculty members to support the riotous students at Columbia University. He achieved a great deal of national notoriety when he delivered an address to rebel students who refused to attend Columbia's commencement exercises in June 1968. Erlich has been a prominent participant in the ultra-radical Socialist Scholars Conferences.

AMITAI ETZIONI was born on January 4, 1929 in Cologne, Germany, son of Gertrude Falk and Willi Etzioni. His first wife was Eva Horowitz. He is married to Minerva Morales. He is an alumnus of Hebrew University in Jerusalem (B.A., 1954; M.A., 1956) and the University of California at Berkeley (Ph.D., 1958). In 1960-1961 and in 1967-1968, he was a faculty fellow of the Social Science Research Council. In 1965-1966, he was a fellow of the Center for Advanced Study in the Behavioral Sciences. In 1968, he held a Guggenheim fellowship. He is the author of *A Diary of a Commando Soldier* (1952); *A Comparative Analysis of Complex Organizations* (1961); *The Hard Way to Peace* (1962); *Winning Without War* (1964); *The Moon-Doggle: Domestic and International Implications of the Space Race* (1964); *Modern Organizations* (1964); *Political Unification: A Comparative Study of Leaders and Forces* (1965); *Studies in Social Change* (1966); and *The Active Society* (1968). He is the editor of *Complex Organizations: A Sociological Reader* (1961) and *Social Change: Sources, Patterns, and Consequences* (1964).

Since 1958, Etzioni has been on the sociology faculty of Columbia University as instructor (1958-1959), assistant professor (1959-1961), associate professor (1961-1967), and professor (1967 to the present). Since 1961, he has been a research associate of the radical-pacifist Institute of War and Peace Studies.

Etzioni's extreme leftist-pacifism is reflected in his writings, especially in his *Winning Without War*. He has served on the national board of the ultra-radical Americans for Democratic Action. He has been affiliated with the leftist-pacifist Ad Hoc Faculty Committee on Vietnam. He has been affiliated with the leftist-pacifist Scientists on Survival.

RONALD [RON KARENGA] EVERETT was born on July 14, 1941 in Parsonburg, Maryland. He is married, but in December 1971 he filed suit for divorce. He is an alumnus of the University of California at Los Angeles (B.S., 1963; M.A., 1965), and for a brief time was a candidate for a doctorate.

After the 1965 riots in the Watts area of Los Angeles, Everett founded a militant black nationalist group which he called US. He explained the name of the group as: "US is the black people" with the motto "Anywhere we are, US is." Everett adopted the Swahili name, Karenga, meaning "keeper of tradition." To complement his extremist group, he also founded a new religious sect, Kuwaida, and he advised all blacks to abjure Christianity: "The Christian is our worst enemy. Jesus said: 'My blood will wash you white as snow.' Who wants to be white but sick 'Negroes,' or worse yet — washed that way by the blood of a dead Jew. You know if Nadinola bleaching cream couldn't do it, no dead Jew's blood is going to do it." For the patron saint of his newly-founded religion, Karenga chose the late Malcolm X.

Early in the history of US, Karenga described himself and his followers: "We're not African, and we're not American. We're Afro-Americans. We've got our own history, culture and set of values. We got soul." The philosophy of US was pure black racism and was to be found in Karenga's own words: "Blacks must develop their own heroic images. To the white boy, [Marcus] Garvey was a failure — to us, he was perfect for his time and context. To the white boy, Malcolm X was a hate teacher — to us he was the highest form of Black Manhood in his generation . . . . The Seven-fold path of the Blackness [of US] is to Think Black, Talk Black, Act Black, Create Black, Buy Black, Vote Black, and Live Black."

Karenga was critical of efforts made by other black American militants: "The revolution being fought now is a revolution to win the minds of our people. If we fail to win this we cannot wage the violent one. Sometimes [black] brothers get so hung up in the myth of revolution that they talk about bringing America to her knees and can't even wipe out one police station. A revolt is an attempt to overthrow the system; while the revolution is the complete overthrow of that system. A lot of brothers play revolutionary; they read a little [Frantz] Fanon, a little Mao [Tse-tung], and some [Karl] Marx. Although this information is necessary it is not sufficient for we must develop a new plan of revolution for Black people here in America. You can't fight a revolution on a local level. It has to be fought through a national struggle . . . . We must believe in our cause and be willing to die for it and we should stop reading other people's literature and write our own and stop pretending revolution and make it. The only thing that will make us invinci-

ble is for us to fight — to fight for our freedom and not our personal selves — to fight to get back the freedom we lost in 1565 . . . . Blacks live right in the heart of America. That is why we are best able to cripple this [white] man. And once you understand your role, you won't talk revolution, but you'll make it . . . . When the word is given, we'll see how tough you are. When it's 'burn,' let's see how much you burn. When it's 'kill,' let's see how much you kill. When it's 'blow up,' let's see how much you blow up. And when it's 'take that white girl's head too,' we'll really see how tough you are . . . . You cannot have a revolution without direction, and that direction can only come through an ideology developed for your own situation . . . . You must have a cultural revolution before the violent revolution. The cultural revolution gives identity, purpose and direction. We must gear the money going from the church to the support of the revolution. Revolution cannot succeed without finance. No revolt is isolated. When Blacks revolt in any section of the country it is an expression of the entire nation [sic] of Afro-America . . . . I remember my mother used to tell me — if you're bad the devil will get you. I didn't know that until the cops came . . . . Talking general truisms is necessary but not sufficient. To say the white man is the devil is not enough. What are you going to do about it? . . . Violence in itself without consideration for time or circumstance is as inadequate as non-violence . . . . Black people need a revolutionary school where they can be educated rather than trained . . . . We need Black Power to offset white power . . . ."

Karenga never formally aligned US with any political party, but under the heading of "Politics," he had these observations: "It is an Afro-American proverb that the only time Blacks are citizens is during war time and tax time. . . . 'Negroes' have been trying to adapt to America since they got here. We say that now America will have to adapt to the Black man . . . . If Black people want to build a Black nation they have to have a will to do so. No nation can exist without a will to exist . . . . In terms of conflict and movement, all of it should be to obtain Black Power, which is the means to obtain three things: self-determination, self-respect and self-defense . . . . It is no longer a question of being an American but of being free – and legislation will never make us free . . . . The cultural nation provides self-determination, self-respect and self-defense. That is also the concern of Black Power."

Karenga's anti-white racism could not have been more extreme. In reply to a question from a member of a white audience, he said: "You are not a black man and can never be one. Our membership is for Negroes only. Whites and blacks must not mix in marriage or anywhere else. Each must stay in his own world but have equal social rights. We are here to educate the Negro first – as to his culture, his history, and his pride in race. Black is black. White is white. They cannot meet." He expanded on his anti-white theme when he addressed a Black Congress rally in Los Angeles, stating that "black power emanates from political office, community organization, coalition and alliance, and disruption." He explained disruption: "Bring up controversial issues like the war in Vietnam . . . and like all them other things they are doing. These things have to be brought up to undermine the white man as a very corrupt and vile thing . . . . Let's talk about how to get white people fighting each other . . . . Let them shoot each other; let them march and picket and confront each other, and after it's all finished, we will have a better world. Yes, we're against violence, but after sundown anything might happen."

Despite Karenga's personal flamboyance, his organization remained very small with most of its members located in the Los Angeles area. Furthermore, there arose a serious conflict between US and the militant Black Panther organization, culminating in the fatal shooting of two Panthers. Three members of US were convicted of the killing and sentenced to life imprisonment. Then, for all practical purposes, the collapse of US occurred when Karenga and three of his henchmen were arrested and charged with torturing two of his women followers with a hot soldering iron and a vise. He was convicted on the charge and is currently serving a prison term of one to ten years.

MYRLIE EVERS was born on March 17, 1933 in Vicksburg, Mississippi, daughter of Mildred Washington and James Beasley. She was married to the late Medgar Evers. She is an alumna of Pomona College (B.A., 1968). She also studied at Alcorn A. and M. College. She is the author of *For Us, The Living* (1967). Since 1968, she has been a contributing editor to *Ladies' Home Journal.*

From 1954 until 1957, Mrs. Evers was a secretary and an administrator of the ultra-radical National Association for the Advancement of Colored People in Jackson, Mississippi. Since 1967, she has been an assistant director for planning and development in the Center for Educational Opportunity, an affiliate of the five colleges in Claremont, California. In

1970, Mrs. Evers was an unsuccessful Democratic Candidate for Congress from California's 24th District.

Mrs. Evers' continuing work for the NAACP and her leftist-liberalism in other areas have brought her an astonishing amount of recognition. She has received the Freedom House award (1963); the Human Rights award from the National Association of Colored Women's Clubs (1964); the Authors award (1968); the Literary award from Sigma Gamma Rho (1968); the Freedom award from the NAACP Regional Conference (1964); the Woman of the Year award from the Utility Club of America (1964); and the Humanitarian award from the National Council of Christians and Jews (1969). She has also received the keys to the cities of Cleveland, Indianapolis, and San Francisco.

RICHARD M. FAGLEY was born on December 24, 1910 in Oberlin, Ohio, son of Hortense Martin and Frederick Fagley. He married Mary Jane Cobourn. He is an alumnus of Yale University (B.A., 1932; B.D., 1935) and Olivet College (D.D., 1951). He pursued graduate studies at the radical London School of Economics. In 1939, he was ordained to the ministry of the Congregational Christian Church. He is the author of *Proposed Roads to Peace* (1934) and *The Population Explosion and Christian Responsibility* (1960). From 1938 until 1945, he was editor of *World Alliance News Letter*. In recent years, he has been an editorial consultant to the *United Church Herald* and *Social Action*.

Throughout Fagley's entire career, he has been very active in the ranks of the most extreme pacifistic and leftist-liberal clergymen. In 1936 and 1937, he was a research assistant in the Council for Social Action of the Congregational Christian Churches. From 1938 until 1945, he was education secretary for the leftist-oriented Church Peace Union and American Council of the World Alliance for International Friendship through the Churches. From 1945 until 1950, he was with the red-laden Federal Council of Churches as secretary of the Commission on a Just and Durable Peace (1945-1947) and co-secretary of the Department of International Justice and Goodwill (1948-1950). In 1950 and 1951, he was with the leftist-oriented National Council of Churches as director of the Department of International Justice and Goodwill. Since 1951, he has been executive secretary to the Commission of the Churches on International Affairs and consultant to the Communist-dominated UNESCO.

In 1938, Fagley was a delegate to the World Youth Congress, a Communist congress. Since that time, he has avoided direct affiliations with fronts and has confined his leftist-pacifist activities to his writings and his work in the church-related positions he has held.

RICHARD A. FALK was born on November 13, 1930 in New York City, son of Helene Pollak and Edwin Falk. He was married to and divorced from Irene Piggott and Maria Gabler. His third wife is Florence Goldstein. He is an alumnus of the University of Pennsylvania (B.S., 1952); Yale University (LL.B., 1955); and Harvard University (J.S.D., 1962). He is the author of *Law, Morality, and War in the Contemporary World* (1963); *The Role of Domestic Courts in the International Legal Order* (1964); *Legal Order in a Violent World* (1968); and *Neutralization and World Politics* (1968). He is co-author of *Essays on International Jurisdiction* (1961) and *Essays on the International Law of*

Espionage (1962). He is co-editor of *Security Through Disarmament* (1965); *The Strategy of World Order* (1966); and *The Vietnam War and International Law* (1968 and 1969). Since 1962, he has been a member of the editorial board of *World Politics*. Since 1964, he has been on the editorial board of the *American Journal of International Law.*

From 1955 until 1962, Falk served, successively, as assistant and associate professor of law at the College of Law at Ohio State University. Since 1962, he has been the Albert G. Milbank Professor of international law and practice in the Woodrow Wilson School at Princeton University. He is attached to the University's department of politics and the Center of International Studies. In 1958 and 1959, he held a fellowship from the ultra-leftist Ford Foundation. From 1965 until 1969, he held a McCosh Faculty fellowship. In 1968 and 1969, he was a fellow of the Center for Advanced Study in Behavioral Sciences. He has been a consultant to the World Law Fund, the U.S. Arms Control and Disarmament Agency, the U.S. Senate Foreign Relations Committee, and the U.S. Naval War College. In 1967 and 1968, he was a member of the editorial policy board of the leftist-oriented Public Broadcast Laboratory. He has been a trustee of the leftist-oriented Fund for Education in World Order. In 1965, he served as counsel at the International Court of Justice on behalf of the governments of Ethiopia and Liberia in their unsuccessful effort to deprive South Africa of its mandate over South-West Africa — a pet project of the Communist powers.

Falk has been affiliated with the Council on Foreign Relations, the informal supra-State Department of the United States; the Emergency Civil Liberties Committee ("Communist front" — "subversive"); the ultra-leftist Committee for a New China Policy; the leftist-internationalist World Law Fund; the ultra-leftist Soledad Brothers Defense Committee; the leftist-internationalist Fund for Peace; the leftist Lawyers Committee on American Policy Toward Vietnam; the 1969 Stockholm Conference on Vietnam, held under the auspices of the Communist-dominated World Peace Council; the Committee of Liaison with Families of Servicemen Detained in North Vietnam, which is headed by pro-Communists David Dellinger and Cora Weiss; and the People's Peace Treaty, a Hanoi-inspired project. In 1963, Falk signed an advertisement defending Americans who traveled to Communist Cuba. In 1967, Falk joined with other leftist lawyers in a widely-publicized anti-Vietnam War protest. They urged the President of the United States to take immediate steps, including: "(1) unconditional termination of bombings in North Vietnam; (2) cooperation in replacing U.S. military forces with personnel of the International Control Commission which is legally responsible for supervising the execution of the 1954 Geneva Accords; (3) de-escalation of military operations in South Vietnam starting with the cessation of offensive operations; (4) recognition of the National Liberation Front as possessing belligerent status, and hence negotiating status, equal to that of the Saigon regime; and (5) commitment to negotiate on the basis of the 1954 Geneva Accords, including the withdrawal of all foreign military forces and the elimination of all foreign bases in South and North Vietnam within a specified period of time." Falk and his fellow leftists insisted that there had been no "armed attack" upon South Vietnam in violation of the UN Charter. They claimed that the United States had violated its obligations under the UN Charter to seek a peaceful solution in Vietnam. They said that the doctrine of "collective self-defense" did not justify United States intervention in what they alleged was a civil war in South Vietnam. They further claimed that South Vietnam's request for American assistance was not a legal basis for "collective self-defense."

In 1968, at a time when he was serving as a foreign policy adviser to presidential candidate Eugene McCarthy, Falk made a week-long visit to North Vietnam, where he conferred with North Vietnamese and National Liberation Front officials. Six weeks later Falk and three of his colleagues from Princeton's Center of International Studies circulated a plan for the neutralization of South Vietnam. They claimed that the plan had principles of compromise which would be acceptable to the United States, North Vietnam, and the Viet Cong. The compromise included the withdrawal of United States and North Vietnamese troops from South Vietnam, the temporary stationing in South Vietnam of an international peace-keeping force, and the formation of a new government in Saigon willing to accept a ban on political and military alliances. Falk reported that he had presented the plan to North Vietnam's Premier Pham Van Dong, who "thought it was an interesting proposal and saw nothing inconsistent between neutralization and what the North Vietnamese Government thought was a reasonable basis for a peace settlement."

Falk proved to be a very sympathetic carrier of Hanoi's line to the American public. The North Vietnamese, he said, "are very weary of the war. They say they will be realistic and reasonable and

what they mean is they are going to do more than they think they ought to." He claimed that the North Vietnamese and the National Liberation Front were apparently quite willing to make a concession by regarding South Vietnam as a separate state — at least temporarily. To make the concession a reality, Falk explained that North Vietnam merely wished to exclude President Nguyen Van Thieu and Vice President Nguyen Cao Ky from a "neutral" Saigon regime that would include a major role for the Viet Cong. Of course, Falk's presentation was not only unoriginal but completely contrary to the well-established policies of the United States and South Vietnamese governments. However, Falk insisted upon explaining the advantages of his impossible neutralization proposals, and his explanation was merely warmed-over Communist propaganda. Said Falk: "North Vietnam would achieve through neutralization an end to the war, and the withdrawal of the American forces from South Vietnam. They would have to give up for an indefinite or for an agreed period, however, their goal of reunifying the two Vietnams, and would be called upon to respect the outcome of the processes of self-determination and to recognize the continuing existence of a separate state in the South. The United States would achieve through neutralization the withdrawal of the armed forces of North Vietnam from the territory of South Vietnam and a basis for the self-determination and territorial integrity of the latter state. At the same time, it would be called upon to withdraw its own armed forces from the territory of South Vietnam and to accept the compromise political system within that state that may be formed under the conditions created by neutralization."

In June 1971, Falk journeyed to

FAULK

Paris where he conferred with the Communists who represented North Vietnam and the Viet Cong at the Paris Peace Talks. Once again, Falk carried the Hanoi line back to the American public. His faith in his Communist friends remained unshaken, but toward President Richard Nixon, he was quite bitter. Wrote Falk: "The basic concern that emerges from extended new discussions with the delegations to the Paris Peace Talks of North Vietnam and the Provisional Revolutionary Government of South Vietnam is their continuing belief that the prisoner issue is a smokescreen behind which President Nixon intends to go on with the war. Nothing that Mr. Nixon has done or said since he became President gives the Vietnamese reason for hope that Washington genuinely desires a rapid negotiated settlement of the war. On their part, [North Vietnam's] Ambassador Xuan Thuy reaffirmed the central importance of setting a reasonable date for total U.S. withdrawal as the only pre-condition for prisoner release. This means, Thuy emphasized, that discussions could begin at once thereafter on how, not whether, to release the prisoners — the rate and physical means of release. The North Vietnamese officials emphasized over and over again that they have neither reason nor desire to hold Americans captive once there is clear evidence that the United States intends to end its combat role in Vietnam and to commit itself to total withdrawal." (*Boston Globe*, June 30, 1971.)

Throughout his account of his Paris visit, Falk remained consistent. His total commitment to his Hanoi friends left absolutely no room for a single word of criticism of the Hanoi regime or the Viet Cong. He directed his barbs only at Americans, their government, and its allies.

JOHN HENRY FAULK was born on August 21, 1913 in Austin, Texas, son of Martha Miner and John Faulk. His second wife is Elizabeth Peake. He is an alumnus of the University of Texas (B.A., 1936; M.A., 1940). In 1941, he held a fellowship from the Julius Rosenwald Foundation. He is the author of *Fear on Trial* (1964).

In 1942, Faulk was a faculty member in the English department of the University of Texas. From 1942 until 1944, he was a field director for the American Red Cross in Cairo, Egypt. From 1946 until 1957, he was employed by the Columbia Broadasting System. He appeared on such radio programs as "Johnny's Front Porch," the "Walk a Mile for a Camel" show, the Daniel Boone adventure series, and, from 1951 until 1957, "The John Henry Faulk Show" — a one-hour, five-day-a-week presentation heard on radio station WCBS in New York City.

In 1956, Faulk became a plaintiff in a libel suit which became one of the most celebrated in the history of American jurisprudence. The suit had its inception in February 1956, when AWARE, Inc., an anti-Communist organization, issued a bulletin alleging that Faulk had engaged in pro-Communist activities. (AWARE was organized in 1953 "to combat the Communist conspiracy in entertainment-communications.") The AWARE bulletin was especially directed at the results of a December 1955 election of officers in the American Federation of Television and Radio Artists. Faulk had been a member of AFTRA since 1946. In 1955, he and some of his friends decided to run on a slate against the incumbent officials of AFTRA. Faulk and his co-candidates called themselves the Middle-of-the-Road slate, committed against

370

Communism and against blacklisting. In the election, the Middle-of-the-Road won twenty-seven out of thirty-five offices, including Charles Collingwood as president, Orson Bean as first vice-president, and Faulk as second vice-president. (AFTRA board officials who were opposed to the Middle-of-the-Road group included Bud Collyer, Alan Bunce, Rex Marshall, and Conrad Nagel.)

On February 10, 1956, AWARE issued a bulletin commenting on the AFTRA election. The bulletin alleged that AFTRA's Middle-of-the-Road candidates were chosen by two standards: "their opposition to AWARE, Inc., and also their opposition to 'blacklisting and Communism.' " The bulletin advised that "the term 'blacklisting' is losing its plain meaning and becoming a Communist jargon-term for hard opposition to the exposure of Communism." The bulletin charged that an "unqualifiedly anti-Communist slate was defeated for the first time in eight years" and suggested that the Middle-of-the-Road slate held an ambiguous position on the Communist issue. The bulletin asked: "Will the 'middlers' enforce AFTRA's constitution which bars from union membership those who maintain membership or knowingly aid the Communist Party or other officially designated subversive organizations? Will they enforce AFTRA's National Rule, which provides disciplinary measures against union members who refuse to answer when asked by a Congressional committee if they are or have been Communist Party members?"

The bulletin listed fifteen members of AFTRA's New York local who had refused to cooperate with the House Committee on Un-American Activities in August and October, 1955, and AWARE wondered if the Middle-of-the-Road officers would do anything about the uncooperative fifteen. The bulletin then centered its attention upon Faulk: "John Henry Faulk was ... quoted as saying that 'all (middlers) were chosen for their opposition to Communism as well as their opposition to AWARE.' In most cases, this may well be true. But how about Faulk himself? What is his public record?"

AWARE's bulletin produced seven allegations against Faulk: "(1) According to the *Daily Worker* of April 22, 1946, 'Jack Faulk' was to appear on Club 65, 13 Astor Place, N.Y.C. – a favorite site of pro-Communist affairs. (2) According to the *Daily Worker* of April 17, 1947, 'Johnny Faulk' was to appear as an entertainer at the opening of 'Headline Cabaret,' sponsored by Stage for Action (officially designated a Communist front). The late Philip Loeb was billed as emcee. (3) According to the *Daily Worker* of April 5, 1948, 'John Faulk' contributed cabaret material to 'Show-Time for Wallace,' revues staged by the Progressive Citizens of America (officially designated a Communist front) in support of Henry A. Wallace's candidacy for the presidency of the U.S. Although Wallace was the officially endorsed candidate of the CP, by no means all his supporters were Communists or pro-Communists. What is in question here is support of any candidate given through a Communist-front setup. (4) A program dated April 25, 1946, named 'John Faulk' as a scheduled entertainer (with identified Communist Earl Robinson and two non-Communists) under the auspices of the Independent Citizens Committee of the Arts, Sciences and Professions (officially designated a Communist front, and predecessor of the Progressive Citizens of America). (5) Vol. 3, Nos. 1 & 2, of the Bulletin of People's Songs (officially designated a

Communist front) named Faulk as one who had sent greetings to People's Songs on its second anniversary. (6) 'Johnny Faulk' was listed in a circular as an entertainer or speaker (with Paul Robeson and two others) to appear at 'Spotlight on Wallace' to be held in Room 200 of the Jefferson School of Social Science on February 16, 1948. The Jefferson School has been found by the Federal Government to be what it is, the official training school of the Communist conspiracy in New York. (7) 'John H. Faulk' was a U.S. Sponsor of the American Continental Congress for Peace, staged in Mexico City, September 5-10, 1949, as shown by the official 'call.' The Congress was later described by the HUAC as 'another phase in the Communist world "peace" campaign, aimed at consolidating anti-American forces throughout the Western Hemisphere.' "

On February 12, 1956, Faulk first heard about AWARE's bulletin directed against him. During the next two months, he discussed the content of the bulletin and its impact upon his career with several officials of the Columbia Broadcasting System. He gained the impression that the officials did not view the AWARE bulletin seriously, and had not lost confidence in Faulk's ability to withstand the allegations directed against him. But the situation was to change in April 1956.

On April 11, 1956, at an AFTRA meeting, there was a clash between the Middle-of-the-Road group and the minority conservative opposition. Faulk suspected that his support had weakened among high echelon CBS officials, especially Carl Ward, the general manager of CBS-Radio.

On April 12, 1956, Faulk wrote an affidavit that was photostated and distributed by Ward and other officials to commercial sponsors of Faulk's program. The affidavit read: "I have been employed by station WCBS for the past five years and by CBS Network for one year in 1946-1947. In the intervening four years, I was employed by WOV and WPAT, and under the auspices of Columbia Lecture Bureau, lectured nationally before various women's and patriotic and civic organizations. Prior to my coming to New York City in 1946, and after my graduation from college, I taught at the University of Texas, spent a year overseas with the American Red Cross with American forces, and two years in the United States Army as an enlisted man.

"During all of this time, I was continuously before the public eye. In addition to the many thousands of broadcasts on radio and television, local and national, I appeared at several thousand dinners, conventions and functions as an entertainer and M.C., many of them at the request of CBS and WCBS. Most of them were in furtherance of my professional career and my employers' public relations.

"There has been no criticism (aside from criticism of my shortcomings as a performer), from any source whatever, about anything that I have ever said or done at any of these functions, on the air, or anything I said or did elsewhere. On the contrary, as WCBS knows, both they and I have received many letters of commendation for such public services, and citations from such groups as the Daughters of the American Revolution, the National Press Club of Washington, D.C., and Jewish, Catholic and Protestant organizations, as well as many civic and educational institutions. Although I am primarily a humorist, the usual subject of my lectures has been Our American Heritage, in which I stress the enormous advantages an American citizen has over people of other countries.

"For the past ten years, I have been a member of AFRA, which, since 1952, has been known as AFTRA. Last December, I was elected a member of the Board of Directors of the New York Local of AFTRA and then elected second Vice President of the Local. That board, at a meeting on March 22, 1956, adopted a resolution as follows: 'Whereas, the membership of the New York Local of AFTRA endorsed the proposition ."that its local officers should oppose denial of employment by discriminatory and intimidating practices, especially by outside organizations," in the recent local elections; and, Whereas, Aware, Inc., has, in spite of a vote of censure by the local membership, continued to circulate allegations of a derogatory nature about members of the union; Be it resolved that the employers of AFTRA members be forthwith advised in writing by the Executive Secretary that any discrimination by any such employer against any member of AFTRA on the basis of charges made by Aware, Inc. or any person or group exercising similar functions, will be promptly investigated and made subject of appropriate action by the Local Board.'

"This resolution was in accordance with the platform on which I and twenty-six other members of the Board ran. We took office under a mandate from the membership to effectuate Plank #5 of what was denominated a 'Declaration of Independents,' in which we said: 'We solemnly pledge . . . to oppose denial of employment by discriminatory and intimidating practices, especially by outside organizations.'

"Prior to that campaign and my election to the Board, and the Board's beginning to effectuate its opposition to discriminatory employment practices, there had not been one single charge, insinuation or complaint concerning my Americanism and complete loyalty to my government. However, there are those who have decided to make AFTRA their victim and seemingly I have been chosen as one of the first three of the new Board members of AFTRA to be attacked as part of this plan to control our union.

"There has been on file for the past five years in the offices of CBS my signed statement, along with those of all other CBS employees, that I was not then, nor at any time a member of the Communist Party, nor of any Communist Front, nor of any of the long list of organizations whose names were imprinted on that CBS form. I repeat now, and under oath, that I am not now nor have I ever been a member of the Communist Party.

"Shortly after the new Board took office and began to put into effect the platform on which it ran, a business corporation, Aware, Inc., which in the past has tried to institute a blacklist of performers and has so been condemned by the membership of our union by a vote of nearly two to one, began to circulate scurrilous rumors concerning the newly elected Board. In Aware Bulletin #16 of February 1956, a series of innuendoes and falsifications were made concerning the three top officers of the Board, Charles Collingwood, Orson Bean and myself. Apparently the hodgepodge of allegations made in this bulletin is the reason for your inquiry. I do not believe for one minute that CBS has any intention of becoming a party to the effort of Aware to institute or continue a blacklist in this industry.

"Frankly, I do not consider the allegations made by Aware of any relevance or importance. I have worked at CBS for a number of years, and there are many executives, commentators, performers in this organization, well-known civic and religious leaders in New York and elsewhere, as well as members of the New York Local Board of AFTRA, who are perfectly willing and competent to advise CBS and anyone else whom it might concern, on my personal integrity and my attitudes. I have always believed in the American system of government, in due process and in Constitutional liberties, and I will be the last man to betray those principles upon which our government was founded. I was raised a member of the Methodist church, and still am. I grew up as a practicing democrat and I expect to continue that way.

"As a member of the New York Local Board of AFTRA, I am pledged to combat discriminatory practices in the industry and I will continue to fulfill that pledge whatever the consequences to me personally may be. Our union is approaching negotiations in a friendly but firm manner. I am confident that the efforts of Aware to destroy the effectiveness of the newly elected Local Board, through personal attacks on its officers or by singling out particular members of the Local Board will arouse nothing but direct resentment and will serve to alert the membership to what is in reality an effort to control our union."

A few days after Faulk had composed his affidavit, he decided to file a libel suit against AWARE; Vincent Hartnett, the author of AWARE's bulletin; and Laurence Johnson, who caused the distribution of the bulletin. (Johnson owned six supermarkets in Syracuse, New York. He used AWARE's publications to influence commercial sponsors of radio and television programs and on occasion threatened to remove products from his supermarket shelves if sponsors persisted in their support of programs which employed individuals with Communist Party or Communist front records. The AWARE bulletins were ordinarily distributed by Hartnett to the membership of AWARE [about three hundred] and to newspaper editors and columnists, radio and television stations, advertising agencies, sponsors, motion picture studios, law enforcement agencies, and patriotic organizations.)

On June 26, 1956, Louis Nizer of the legal firm Phillips, Nizer, Benjamin and Krim filed suit in the New York State Supreme Court (*Faulk* v. *AWARE, Laurence Johnson, and Vincent Hartnett*). The Court decided that AWARE's bulletin was libelous and that the defendants sought to raise a question of Faulk's patriotism by innuendo. Then, the defendants made an immediate appeal to the Appellate Division of the New York State Supreme Court. (In the early history of the libel suit, Nizer and his legal associates received support from the *New York Herald Tribune* because its legal staff had investigated AWARE when AWARE sued John Crosby, the newspaper's radio-television columnist. Nizer also utilized John Cogley's two-volume *Blacklisting* which had been written and published under the auspices of the ultra-leftist Fund for the Republic.)

In April 1957, the Appellate Division of the New York State Supreme Court upheld the earlier ruling against AWARE. In the meantime, Faulk had paid Nizer a $10,000 retainer, two-thirds of which was furnished by the leftist CBS commentator Edward R. Murrow. Radio station WCBS had renewed

Faulk's contract for five years, with an option to release him at the end of any thirteen-week cycle. Charles Collingwood and Faulk had been reelected to AFTRA's board.

In July 1957, radio station WCBS exercised its option to terminate Faulk's contract, effective September 13, 1957. He was told that his listening audience had dwindled and that a change of business policies within the station's operations were responsible for his dismissal.

From September 1957 until April 1958, Faulk was unemployed. In April 1958, he began broadcasting a program on WBAI-FM in New York City, but for the most part, he met living expenses for himself and his family by obtaining loans and, in some cases, gifts of money. In December 1958, his circumstances were so straitened that friends of Faulk, including actress Myrna Loy and Eleanor Roosevelt, ran a fund-raising party for his benefit. But in March 1959, Faulk decided to seek work in his hometown of Austin, Texas. He left New York City with his family and for more than two years he remained in Austin where he specialized in public relations and advertising work.

In June 1958, Nizer and his associates began an examination-before-trial of Vincent Hartnett. The examination would not be completed until late 1959. When the examination of Hartnett was concluded that of Laurence Johnson began. Faulk was examined by the defendants' attorneys in August 1961.

In April 1962, the trial of *Faulk* v. *AWARE, Vincent Hartnett, and Laurence Johnson* began. It lasted until the end of June. During the course of the trial, Faulk's case was supported by a host of witnesses from the entertainment industry: David Susskind, Tony Ran-

dall, Kenneth Roberts, Kim Hunter, Mark Goodson, Everett Sloan, Garry Moore, and Joseph Cotten. At the conclusion of the trial, the jury awarded Faulk compensatory damages of $1,000,000 against AWARE, Hartnett, and the estate of Laurence Johnson, who died after the case had gone to the jury. Punitive damages were assessed at $1,250,000 each against AWARE and Hartnett. The trial had been the longest libel action in New York's history. The damages assessed were the largest in the history of American libel trials. (During the course of the trial, Hartnett, who was obligated to prove the truth of the seven allegations he had written against Faulk, was totally inept in his own defense. Faulk denied five of the allegations and there was no rebuttal from Hartnett. Faulk admitted to the *partial* truth of the two remaining allegations and again there was no rebuttal from Hartnett.)

Once Faulk had won his libel suit, he found immediate employment. He worked on television programs produced by Mark Goodson and David Susskind. He appeared on the Jack Paar program. He began a daily radio program on Westinghouse's radio station WINS in New York. He appeared in at least two motion pictures: *All the Way Home* (1963) and *The Best Man* (1964).

In February 1963, it was learned that the estate of the late Laurence Johnson was worth less than a quarter of a million dollars. (Faulk eventually settled for $175,000 in damages from the Johnson estate.) In October 1963, AWARE and Vincent Hartnett appealed their case to the Appellate Division of the New York State Supreme Court. They lost their appeal, but the Court reduced the damages awarded to Faulk. Compensatory damages of $400,000 were assessed against AWARE and Hartnett. Punitive damages were assessed at $50,000 against AWARE and $100,000 against Hartnett. AWARE and Hartnett appealed to the New York State Court of Appeals but were rejected. The Supreme Court of the United States later denied an AWARE-Hartnett petition for a review of their case.

In the aftermath of the celebrated libel trial, Faulk wrote *Fear on Trial*. His publishers, Simon and Schuster, described the book: ". . . an important and inspiring personal document of our time. It is the story of a man who challenged the forces threatening the rights of the individual in America, and who won for himself — and thereby for his countrymen — a historic victory." — "It is a historical document in which many readers will discover for the first time exactly how the blacklisters established and used their power. It is more than the experience of one man. It is a chronicle of a not-so-distant time when the sowers of distrust nearly paralyzed their country. It is the story of a landmark in the return to sanity and the reaffirmation of the rights of the individual in America."

In the Communist weekly, *National Guardian*, of January 30, 1965, Alexander L. Crosby hailed Faulk's *Fear on Trial* in a lengthy review. The book editor of the *Los Angeles Times,* Robert R. Kirsch, wrote a two-part review of *Fear on Trial*: ". . . ought to be read by every American" — "a story of heroic proportions" — "a document of classic value." (The Faulk trial was one of four cases described in Louis Nizer's *The Jury Returns*, published in 1966. The Faulk segment of Nizer's book appeared as a condensation in *Reader's Digest* of March 1967 under the title "Blacklisted!: The Story of John Henry Faulk." On Faulk, Nizer enthused: "One

lone man had pitted his faith in American justice against the powerful forces of vigilantism. And he had won.")

In the *Nation* of July 14, 1962, David Court wrote "Blacklisting: the Faulk Decision," which was a typical liberal-leftist evaluation of the Faulk-AWARE episode. Said Court: "One day the bill falls due for the wicked, sometimes, it is true, a lifetime or a thousand years late, but all morality and hope disappear when people cease to expect that day. It came, for thousands of people ruined in the 1950s [?], in New York Supreme Court, when the libel case of John Henry Faulk against Vincent W. Hartnett, Laurence E. Johnson and AWARE, Inc., went to the jury on the evening of June 28 . . . . For Faulk, a man who was anything but a Communist, had been indelibly branded as one — and so ruined." (Faulk was not branded as a Communist, indelibly or otherwise.) Court described Faulk as "a rich personality of effortless Texas charm, a liberal humanism and a built-in affection for the whole American heritage . . . a good-hearted, reasonable man from the country, who thought he was in a decent, reasonable world." The defendants in the case were, according to Court, comparable to the Reign of Terror of the French Revolution, "one mean little group of men," a "savage little cabal of very small men without talent, distinction or courage." Of the defendants' attorney, Court wrote: "A neighborly lynching, he said, is right and proper. Blacklisting is simply splendid and purely patriotic." Such sentiments were not, of course, uttered by any attorney during the course of the trial.

In *Look* magazine of May 7, 1963, Joseph P. Blank wrote a highly emotional account of the Faulk-AWARE confrontation, "The Ordeal of John Henry

Faulk: Blacklisted, A Radio and TV Performer Battles to Clear His Name." Blank's emotionalism was matched by the editors of *Look* who, in an epilogue to Blank's story, said: "The John Henry Faulk story has a nightmarish quality. Yet it is sadly true, as related above, and there were dozens of other such stories that never came to public attention in the ugly days of McCarthyism and its aftermath. No American who lived through those days has any right to feel superior to those actually involved in these cases. The guilt for John Henry Faulk's ordeal is shared by all – magazines, newspapers, radio and television, advertising agencies and just plain citizens. He who made no protest at the time has no license for smugness now. Let us hope that we have all learned our lesson well."

In the Communist Party's *Worker* of May 10, 1963, Ben Levine in his TV Views column ("Breaking the Blacklist Barrier") was delighted that Faulk had been able to recount the story of his libel suit on the Jack Paar television program. Levine lamented the fact that Faulk would not be able to collect the $3,500,000 judgment originally voted by the jury, but he consoled himself by writing: "The important thing, however, is that bigots and blackmailers and redbaiters are reminded that their business may bring losses instead of profits."

There is no disputing the fact that whatever troubles beset Faulk and his career in entertainment between the years 1956 and 1962 were directly traceable to allegations that he was associated in print with leftists and their fronts. Since 1962, there has been a recurrence of the pattern. In February 1963, according to the *Worker* of February 10, 1963, he appeared on a Carnegie Hall program sponsored by the leftist-

racist Student Nonviolent Coordinating Committee, and a fellow performer was Pete Seeger, whose close relationship with the Communist Party is undeniable.

Faulk contributed a book review to the October-November 1964 issue of *Rights*, published by a Communist front – the Emergency Civil Liberties Committee. In December 1963, the ECLC advertised that Faulk was scheduled to speak at a "Bill of Rights Dinner" in New York City. It was also mentioned that other speakers would include Mrs. Cyrus Eaton, a certifiable leftist, and James Baldwin, the novelist and rather notorious racist agitator. In the *Worker* of February 10, 1964, it was announced that Faulk had appeared at a rally sponsored by the Student Nonviolent Coordinating Committee. In 1964, Faulk was listed on the sponsoring committee for the 80th Birthday Celebration for Norman Thomas, a tribute to the patriarch of the Socialist Party.

In the *Village Voice* (November 11, 1965) and *National Guardian* (October 23, 1965), Faulk was listed as a scheduled speaker for a "Banquet for Freedom for Morton Sobell," the imprisoned atom spy. The banquet was held under the auspices of the Sobell Committee, a Communist front, and Faulk's co-speaker was announced as Attorney William Kunstler, whose career of defending Reds and other radicals has given him international notoriety.

On March 17, 1965, Faulk was the subject of an anonymous news item, datelined Washington, D.C., in the *Boston Globe*. The article began: "American freedom is more endangered by vigilante organizations and hate groups than by any Communist conspiracy, a victim of the McCarthy era hysteria said today. The chief poison peddler, according to ex-radio and television personality John

Henry Faulk, is the House Un-American Activities Committee — 'The old sow that suckles the hate pigs.' " Said Faulk: "The superpatriots who claim their purpose is to expose the Communist conspiracy never say that John Doe is a dues-paying Communist who committed a certain act of subversion on such-and-such a date. They do it all by innuendos . . . . [and] they've driven professors from classrooms and librarians from libraries, and they've silenced a dialogue." Faulk called upon the nation's civil rights movement to help expose the Red-baiters as power-hungry thought controllers.

The June 11, 1968, issue of the *National Review Bulletin* carried an item linking Faulk to the leftist-racist Southern Conference Educational Fund: "SCEF remains active on other fronts. Its recent annual dinner honored Ella Baker of the Mississippi Freedom Democratic Party, and featured Stokely Carmichael and the omnipresent Prof. Howard Zinn of Boston University on the dais. Somehow, even moderate Roy Wilkins was persuaded to join the sponsors' list, along with such as Sally Belfrage, John Henry Faulk, Jules Feiffer, James Forman, Milton Galamison, Katya and Bert Gilden, Corliss Lamont, Carl Marzani, Alex Munsell, Russ Nixon, Anton Refregier, Nathan Schwerner (father of the slain civil rights worker), Pete Seeger, [and] Willard Uphaus."

VICTOR C. FERKISS was born on August 2, 1925 in New York City, son of Pauline Kiss and Joseph Ferkiss. He married Barbara Jouvenal. He is an alumnus of the University of California at Berkeley (A.B., 1948; A.M., 1949); Yale University (M.A., 1950); and the University of Chicago (Ph.D., 1954). He is the author of *Communism Today: Belief*

and Practice (1962); *Foreign Aid: Moral and Political Aspects* (1965); and *Africa's Search for Identity* (1966). He has contributed articles to such leftist publications as *Commonweal, Nation,* and *Ramparts.*

In 1954 and 1955, he was an assistant professor of political science at Montana State University. From 1955 until 1962, he was at St. Mary's College in California as assistant professor of political science (1955-1960) and associate professor (1960-1962). Since 1962, he has been at Georgetown University as visiting associate professor of government (1962-1966) and professor (1966 to the present). He has been a visiting professor at the University of California at Berkeley and at The Johns Hopkins University. In 1959 and 1960, he was a field director of the Africa Training Program for the International Cooperation Administration. In 1961, he was a consultant on Africa to the Peace Corps. In 1959 and 1960, he held a Rockefeller Foundation fellowship in political philosophy.

From 1962 until 1964, he was a member of the board of directors of the leftist-pacifist Catholic Association for International Peace. From 1962 until 1966, he was on the national board of the ultra-radical Americans for Democratic Action.

ELIZABETH FETTER was born on September 4, 1904 in Philadelphia, Pennsylvania, daughter of Annie Wilkinson and Joseph Head. She married Ferdinand Fetter. She is an alumna of the University of Colorado (A.B., 1927). She also studied at Vassar College. Under the pseudonym of Hannah Lees, she is the author of *Women Will Be Doctors* (1939); *Rx: Prescription for Murder* (1941); *Till the Boys Come Home*

(1944); *The Dark Device* (1947); *Help Your Husband Stay Alive* (1957); and *The Sweet Death of Candor* (1969). She is the co-author of *Death in the Doll's House* (1942). She has contributed stories and articles to *Saturday Evening Post, New Yorker, Atlantic, Reporter, Collier's, McCall's, Good Housekeeping, Redbook, Reader's Digest, Ladies' Home Journal,* and *Cosmopolitan.*

From 1928 until 1934, Mrs. Fetter was an advertising copywriter in Philadelphia. From 1953 until 1956, she was a lecturer in experimental writing at Bryn Mawr College. From 1952 until 1959, she was a member of the Philadelphia City Commission on Human Relations.

Mrs. Fetter has been an official of the ultra-leftwing United World Federalists. In 1952 and 1953, and from 1959 until 1963, she was on the national board of the ultra-radical Americans for Democratic Action. She has been an official of the leftist-oriented Planned Parenthood Federation of America and the Planned Parenthood-World Population Council. She has also been affiliated with the ultra-leftist American Civil Liberties Union; the leftist-oriented League of Women Voters; and the National Association for the Advancement of Colored People, the fountainhead of Negro agitation for more than half a century.

ROGER D. FISHER was born on May 28, 1922 in Winnetka, Illinois, son of Katharine Dummer and Walter Fisher. He married Caroline Speer. He is an alumnus of Harvard University (A.B., 1943; LL.B., 1948). He is the author of *International Conflict for Beginners* (1969). He is the editor and co-author of *International Conflict and Behavioral Science — The Craigville Papers* (1964). He is the associate editor of the leftist-oriented *Journal of Conflict Resolution.*

In 1948 and 1949, Fisher was an attorney with the Economic Cooperation Administration in Paris. From 1950 until 1956, he was associated with a law firm in Washington, D.C. From 1956 until 1958, he was an assistant to the Solicitor-General of the United States. Since 1958, he has been at the Harvard Law School as a lecturer in law (1958-1960) and professor of law (1960 to the present). In 1965 and 1966, he was a visiting professor of international relations at the leftist London School of Economics. He has been a consultant on international security affairs to the Department of Defense. He has been a trustee of the Hudson Institute, one of the Establishment's think factories. In 1965 and 1966, he held a Guggenheim fellowship.

Fisher has been affiliated with the Council on Foreign Relations, the informal supra-State Department of the United States; the ultra-leftwing United World Federalists; and the leftist-oriented Commission to Study the Organization of Peace.

HARRY F. FLEISCHMAN was born on October 3, 1914 in New York City, son of Rachel Cohn and Abraham Fleischman. He married Natalie Wiencek. He attended the City College of New York. He is the author of *Let's Be Human* (1960) and *Norman Thomas: A Biography* (1964). He is a contributor to *Legal Aspects of the Civil Rights Movement* (1965). He is a pamphleteer for the National Labor Service and his works include *Is Labor Color Blind?* (1960); *Labor and the Civil Rights Revolution* (1960); *Equality in the Unions* (1961); *Epitaph for Jim Crow* (1963); *Norman Thomas: Leader at Large* (1966); and *The Civil Rights Story: A Year's Review*

(1966). His syndicated column, "Let's Be Human," appears in more than a hundred religious, labor, and Negro publications.

From 1942 until 1950, Fleischman was national secretary of the Socialist Party. From 1951 until 1953, he was labor editor for the Department of State's Voice of America. Since 1953, he has been with the leftist-oriented American Jewish Committee as director (1953 to the present) and race relations coordinator (since 1963). Since 1962, he has been chairman of the executive committee of the Socialist League for Industrial Democracy. Since 1963, he has been vice-president of the Workers Defense League, a leftwing group which defends political undesirables who are subject to deportation. From 1939 until 1942, he was the regional director for the Socialist Party in Indiana and Illinois.

Fleischman has been affiliated with the leftist-oriented Adult Education Association; the leftist Workmen's Circle; the ultra-leftist American Civil Liberties Union; the National Association for the Advancement of Colored People, the fountainhead of Negro agitation for more than half a century; the leftist-racist Congress of Racial Equality; and the Norman Thomas 80th Birthday Committee, of which he was chairman.

STUART B. FLEXNER was born on March 22, 1928 in Jacksonville, Illinois, son of Gertrude Berg and David Flexner. He was married to and divorced from Mimi Bogan. He is an alumnus of the University of Louisville (A.B., 1948; M.A., 1949). He also pursued graduate studies at Cornell University. He is co-editor of *The Dictionary of American Slang* (1960).

From 1949 until 1952, he was an instructor at Cornell University. From 1954 until 1958, he was an editor for various publishers, including the Macmillan Company. From 1960 until 1964, he was a bookseller, editor, and publisher in Mexico City. Since 1964, he has been an editor with Random House.

Flexner has been affiliated with the leftist-racist Congress of Racial Equality; the ultra-radical Americans for Democratic Action; and the ultra-leftist American Civil Liberties Union.

CHARLES W. FORMAN was born on December 2, 1916 in Gwalior, India, son of American citizens Sarah Taylor and Henry Forman. He married Janice Mitchell. He is an alumnus of Ohio State University (B.A. and M.A., 1938); the University of Wisconsin (Ph.D., 1941); and Union Theological Seminary (B.D., 1944; S.T.M., 1947). He was ordained a Presbyterian minister in 1944. He is the author of *A Christian's Handbook on Communism* (1953); *A Faith for the Nations* (1958); *The Nation and the Kingdom* (1964); and *Christianity in the Non-Western World* (1967).

From 1945 until 1950, Forman was a teacher of church history at the North India United Theological College. From 1951 until 1953, he held an executive position with the National Council of Churches in New York City. Since 1953, he has been at Yale Univeristy's Divinity School, where he has been, since 1961, the D. Willis James professor of missions. Since 1963, he has been chairman of the theological education fund of the leftist-oriented World Council of Churches.

Forman has joined the Leftists on Yale's faculty to petition against nuclear testing by the U.S. Government. He petitioned for amnesty for convicted Communist Party leaders. He was a member of the anti-anti-Communist National Council for Civic Responsibility.

He was a member of the leftist-pacifist International Committee of Conscience on Vietnam.

JAMES FORMAN was born on October 4, 1928 in Chicago. In published accounts, there is considerable disagreement on the details of Forman's career prior to 1961. Most observers agree that he graduated from Roosevelt University in Chicago, studied African affairs at Boston University, spent some time in the U.S. Air Force, may have studied briefly at Middlebury College in Vermont, spent about fifteen months as a mental patient in two hospitals in 1953 and 1954, was married and divorced (most sources indicate that his wife was Anne Romilly, daughter of Jessica Mitford and Esmond Romilly – two Communists; Anne is white, but Forman denies that he married a white woman), and that he was a school teacher in Chicago.

In 1961, Forman went to work for the Student Nonviolent Coordinating Committee (Snick), which had been recently organized by the famous racist agitator, Martin L. King Jr. (Columnists Rowland Evans and Robert Novak wrote in their syndicated column [August 3, 1967] that by 1960 "Forman was already a hardened radical and an associate of Negro terrorist Robert Williams, who fled to Cuba to escape Federal prosecution.")

For most of the period between 1961 and 1966, Forman was executive secretary of Snick. In its early years the Snick organization devoted most of its energies to so-called freedom rides and freedom schools, and to voter registration drives. From 1961 until 1963, Forman and other Snick leaders paid lip-service to Gandhian nonviolence as a means of achieving racial integration in public,

semi-private, and private facilities of various sorts. This all changed, however, in the fall of 1963, when Snick's leadership announced that they were going to conduct a massive program of intimidation against the people and the government of the State of Alabama. But the program never really got off the ground. Snick's white liberal supporters became a bit squeamish. (When Martin L. King founded Snick in 1960, he attracted the support of the U.S. National Student Association [subsidized by the Central Intelligence Agency]; the New World Foundation [founded by Anita McCormick Blaine. One of New World's directors was Whitney North Seymour, then president of the American Bar Association, and formerly board chairman of Freedom House, board chairman of the trustees of the Carnegie Endowment for International Peace, and national board member of the American Civil Liberties Union.], Attorney General Robert F. Kennedy's Department of Justice; the National Association for the Advancement of Colored People; the Congress of Racial Equality; King's Southern Christian Leadership Conference; and the civil rights agitators of the Medical Committee for Human Rights.)

When Snick's leaders realized that too much militancy might cause a collapse of their finances, they decided to concentrate – at least for a little while – upon political activity. In Lowndes County, Alabama, Snick organized an independent political party with an appeal for nation-wide support. (The new political party had as its symbol a black panther – precursor of the symbol of the organization that would soon become a terroristic force from coast to coast.)

The "political" guise adopted by Snick thrust Forman into the national spotlight. He posed as a political leader seeking integration. An interview with Forman appeared in *U.S. News & World Report* (February 24, 1964). His answers to questions were presented in such muted language that he appeared to be nothing more than a legitimate political leader seeking gains in the civil rights areas through political action and other peaceable means. In his replies to his interrogators, Forman seemed intent upon presenting himself as a moderate:

"Q. Mr. Forman, what trend do you see ahead in the drive for equal rights in this election year of 1964? A. I think that there will be continued pressure for a federal law requiring the opening of all public accommodations to Negroes. This pressure will take the form of demonstrations in local areas. These demonstrations will not be designed, primarily, to dramatize the need for a federal public-accommodations law. But that will be one of their consequences. There will also, of course, be pressure for local public-accommodations laws and for local desegregation . . . . I think, also, that there will be a renewed effort to register voters or to point out the inadequacies of existing legislation in the field of voting. As a result of this, there will be emphasis on the need of a federal law dealing with voting — a law much stronger than the ones now on the books.

"Q. Besides public accommodations and voting, what will be your other major objectives this year? A. I think that you will see continued pressure for school integration — or, at least equally important, for better schools. The fact is that, while nationally many groups have been pushing for integration, there is also a tremendous problem with the quality of schools. This is true not only in the South but also in the North. We want to improve the quality of educa-

tion — eliminate the overcrowded schools, the triple shifts and the mobile schoolrooms, get better teachers.

"Q. What will be the direction of your school campaign in the North? A. The focus will be on eliminating the *de facto* segregation that exists in Northern cities. Chicago is a good example. There will be a multiplicity of boycotts.

"Q. Will this campaign be directed at the system of neighborhood schools? Do Negroes feel that this system must be abolished to achieve integration? A. Yes, if the neighborhood school helps to perpetuate segregation. And I know that, in Chicago where I used to teach, the neighborhood-school system works against the Negro students because the schools in Negro neighborhoods are very, very inferior.

"Q. Will Negroes this year stage another March on Washington — or perhaps a march on Congress? A. There very well may be a march on the political conventions. This is in the tentative planning stage. But it is most unlikely that we will see anything on the magnitude of last year's March on Washington. While that was certainly a historic occasion, it left many things to be desired.

"Q. As a result of the mass demonstrations, do you sense any increase in the resistance of white people to Negro demands? A. Not really. I think that what you have is an airing of the issues on a larger national scale. When that happens, many people become concerned about the issue being raised right in their home towns . . . . When such issues are raised right at home, white people in these localities begin to raise questions. Personally, I think this is very good, because there can be no solution of the problem unless it comes out into the public forum. I think that now Americans are beginning to take it for granted that Negroes are going to gain their rights. This was not so widely accepted a few years ago, because there was not as much public dialogue then and not as much acceptance of the fact that people have a right to protest.

"Q. Do you see any danger that bloc voting against Negroes may develop among whites – and that this will work to the disadvantage of Negroes because they are a minority? A. First of all, I don't think that you are going to have too much bloc voting. People, traditionally, have different political allegiances, you see, and I don't think that there's ever going to be unanimity among Negroes over whom they're going to vote for – just as I don't think you are going to have unanimity among the whites.

"Q. Do you feel that, on the whole, you have won more white friends than you have alienated by your strategy? A. That's right. I think there are whites, as well as Negroes, who have accommodated themselves to certain techniques, and when they see somebody out there demonstrating, they feel that this is going to alienate friends. One of the favorite expressions of whites is that demonstrating has destroyed the lines of communication between the races. This is usually a rationalization to stop demonstrations. Often there hasn't been much real communication in the first place. I think that, in any type of social movement, you're going to have a dislocation of normal patterns of behavior. And we may as well recognize that in this nonviolent direct action we're instituting – here I'm not just talking about SNCC but about other groups, too – we may as well recognize that there are going to be people who will be alienated, people who can't understand – both Negroes and whites. But, ultimately, we have faith that there will be a

greater healing in the community. I think that this has already been proven.

"Q. In the political campaign itself – beyond the voter registration – will the Negro organizations play a more active role this year than in the past? A. There are signs that this is going to be the case. The National Association for the Advancement of Colored People has said that it is going to suggest for whom people should vote – and against whom. And I suspect that the NAACP structurally is about the only organization which may be capable of implementing that decision. In our own organization, we have very few voters since we are basically an organization of college students. We are also active mainly in the Deep South, where Negroes are still working to achieve the vote.

"Q. 'Nonviolent' is one word of your organization's name. What do you think are the prospects for violence in the civil-rights campaign this year? A. That is a question I really don't like to speculate upon, because, first of all, one can never say for sure in advance. In our own demonstrations, every effort is going to be made to keep them nonviolent.

"Q. Do you have training courses to teach your people the techniques of nonviolence and self-restraint? A. That's true. There are always training sessions. And then before demonstrations there are usually workshops in which we talk about the philosophy of nonviolence, ways in which demonstrators can protect themselves, what should be their behavior in jail and so forth.

"Q. Do you put public accommodations very high on your list of goals? A. Well, I put the destruction of all symbols of segregation very high. The destruction of all myths which help to perpetuate segregated institutions is very, very high – the myth that Negroes are inferior intellectually, for example. That is very important. And out of this drive for public accommodations has come a new sense of dignity that has made it possible for Negro youth to move ahead in other areas.

"Q. How important do you consider new laws? A. I think this is very important. There used to be a school of thought – and segregationists still try to maintain this school of thought – that the race problem is a problem of attitudes, that people have to have an attitude of good will before there can be good will. I think that the sociologists have disproved this theory of attitudes. For instance, they have found in housing projects that people who had anti-Negro attitudes before Negroes moved in changed those attitudes after Negroes moved in. The same thing is true in the Army. I recall that, when I was in the Army, I served with white guys from Mississippi who said that until they were forced to think about this problem they just never thought about it. The same is true in the area of education. So, therefore, I think that laws are extremely important because most Americans, by and large, are law-abiding people, and, if the law says something, then that's the way they are going to respond. Working within the framework of law forces people to develop new attitudes.

"Q. There have been reports that some of the Negro leaders across the nation are not entirely happy with some of the newer movements and tactics. Is there a serious division among Negro leadership? A. Well, you know, there's no uniformity in leadership in any particular ethnic group or in any particular stratum of society – and Negroes are no different. People have different backgrounds and aspirations. Consequently we cannot expect to have uniformity in

Negro thought. It is natural that some older Negro leaders would not necessarily look with too much favor on what some of the younger people are doing. Many of these older people, you have to understand, grew up in a segregated system where they learned to survive by accommodating themselves to the system. On the other hand, I really don't think there is any serious division among the Negro leadership. I think that there is a basic agreement upon certain objectives. There were some tensions within the civil-rights movement last spring, but I think that these have been resolved."

In 1964, Snick – under Forman's leadership – was instrumental in founding the Mississippi Freedom Democratic Party, a group which caused a great deal of commotion at the Democratic National Convention of that year. Of great significance was the tremendous amount of publicity the Freedom Party's antics received on television and radio and in the nation's newspapers and magazines.

In 1965, Snick reached its high point of achievement when it was the major force in Martin L. King Jr.'s violence-ridden voter registration drive in Selma, Alabama. Earlier in the same year, the red complexion of Snick had become so obvious that liberal columnists Rowland Evans and Robert Novak commented: ". . . There is no doubt that SNCC is substantially infiltrated by beatnicks, left wing revolutionaries and – worst of all – Communists." (As early as 1964, Snick was using the mailing plates of the Communist weekly, *National Guardian*. And, on at least one occasion in 1965, an advertisement for a Snick celebration was placed in the same journal.)

The red hue in Snick was pretty well confirmed by Forman when he was interviewed by Paul Niven on the Columbia Broadcasting System's radio and television program, "Face the Nation," on March 28, 1965. Forman went round and round the mulberry bush as he evaded the matter of Communist involvement in the entire area of civil rights: "*Mr. Niven*: Mr. Forman, a number of civil rights leaders, when asked about the Communist problem, say, well, when people come along and they share our goals and they will work under our rules for our objectives, we accept them, no matter who they are. I would like to ask you this question: Do you think that disciplined American Communists really want to help the Negro attain freedom, are really interested in the stated goals of the civil rights groups, or do they merely want to exacerbate the problem and create chaos? *Mr. Forman*: Well, I would like to answer that question in another way, you see, because one of our – you know, we have had – I won't mention the various columnists who have been most adamant on this particular point – but I take it we do have to look into the whole history of what people are saying and not – well, it is very difficult for me to talk without naming some columnists. I am really thinking of Rowland Evans and Robert Novak, who have something in today's paper, and had something about three or four days ago, about SNCC was Communist-infiltrated. Now, I noticed that for instance, these are the same columnists who back in January said that we went to Guinea, on an African trip and refused and completely bypassed the State Department and then didn't tell them, you know, about the conversations that we had. Now, my position is, you know, I don't think that the State Department, you know, demands, or that any citizen should submit to immediately coming by the State Department and reporting to them, you know, what you did abroad. I

don't know if you understand what I am saying, maybe it is very confused. But my position is that these fellows, you know, are deliberately misrepresenting the movement.

"*Mr. Niven*: In line with the question, Mr. Forman – *Mr. Forman*: Well, I don't know, you see, I am – one of the things that I think – I have their article right in front of me, and after they make this charge, then they go on and talk about what we – handed Dr. King an ultimatum in Selma that if he didn't march we would lead the march. And that of course, is not true, I mean, because we didn't have any contact with Dr. King that day, we talked to him the night before, and we were very solid in the meeting, and it was a meeting between the staff primarily.

"*Mr. Niven*: Mr. Forman, may I repeat my question? Do you think Communists really want to solve civil rights problems or to aggravate and exacerbate them? *Mr. Forman*: The reason, you see – the reason I am not answering that question – and I am not refusing to answer the question – I have an opinion on it, but you see, I want to try to get at some, what I think is some good causes. You see, because what happens is that being involved in the protest movement, you know, and when you are really working for what you feel are some basic objectives and basic rightness of certain wrongs, then people begin to engage in a certain witch hunt, and they try to discredit what you do by raising these questions. You see, I am not at all accusing you of doing that, but I am saying by making these charges that the thing is Communist-dominated, it tends – it tries to discredit it, like this morning the Klan said that the killing of the Reverend Reeb and this lady was a Communist plot.

"*Mr. Niven*: Are these charges true? *Mr. Forman*: No, these charges are not true.

"*Mr. Niven*: They are false? *Mr. Forman*: The charges are false. But the point is, on the other hand — you see, that we cannot accede — you know, we cannot accede to answering these questions, because we know what they are intended to do. Do you understand what I am saying? Look, I am saying that if we took our time to answer all the questions that are raised about the Communists are doing this, and the Communists are doing that, even the Communists killing Mrs. Liuzzo and the Reverend Reeb, that we are going to slow down our movement, we know what the basic injustices are. The people in Mississippi know that they get $2 and $3 a day on Eastland's plantation, and they know that that's not right, we know about the police business over our head, we don't need anybody to tell us that, that comes out of our own experience, and we know that —

"*Mr. Niven*: Mr. Forman, I am sorry, that's all the time we have."

Forman was not always as inarticulate and evasive as he appeared to be on "Face the Nation." In the August 28, 1965 issue of *Saturday Evening Post*, Richard Armstrong, in "Will Snick Overcome?" quoted Forman: "We go beyond civil rights in a lot of things. We raise threats to the whole value system of our society, to the whole system of young people devoting their lives to money. Most people in S.N.C.C. feel that there has to be a reshaping of American institutions. The kind of votes and deals that go on in Congress have to be changed. The poor have to get a better break. If that's socialism, all right, but most people in S.N.C.C. would shun the word, because there's socialism and so-cialism. We don't have a rigid program. We are pragmatic, chipping away. I consider myself basically an agitator seeking a nonviolent revolution in this country."

As befitted an organization with such strong ties to the Communists, Snick could find no charges too extravagant to make against the United States government. A Snick memo of March 1965 said, in part: "The whole racist structure of the enormously complex U.S. government provides those who govern too many 'outs' — the constitutionalism and legalism which always has been used to explain why the U.S. government must condone lynching, mass murder, [and] systematic terrorism." Six months after issuing this thoroughly dishonest and inflammatory statement, Snick raised $50,000 at a Hollywood party. The donors included Marlon Brando, Richard Burton, Harry Belafonte, Sidney Poitier, James Garner, Paul Newman, Burt Lancaster, Elizabeth Taylor, Joanne Woodward, and Mike Nichols.

In 1966, Snick dropped all pretense of working for integration through nonviolent methods. Shunted aside or into the background were such Snick leaders as Robert Moses (Parris), Julian Bond, John Lewis, and Tom Hayden. Forman was kicked upstairs to become Snick's director for international affairs. In their stead, as the real leader and spokesman of Snick, was Stokely Carmichael who harangued his audiences with calls for "Black Power." (With the advent of Carmichael, one of the organization's most dedicated apologists, the ultra-liberal Ralph McGill of the *Atlanta Constitution*, was forced to admit that: "Snick today seeks conflict between races — not peace and an equality of opportunity and political power." And McGill was one of the few liberal columnists to admit that Snick had gone overboard with the Reds: "In early 1966, talk of 'Havana money' became current. SNCC, unable to meet payrolls, suddenly could form a front and purchase a $65,000 building. That a once honorable idealistic student action group should now be taken over by what amounts to a secret klan-type group which openly states its racial hatreds and its objectives to foment disorder and chaos in order to destroy Western civilization is one of the more melancholy stories of our time.")

As chairman of Snick, Carmichael traveled with his gospel of hatred for whites and cries for black power to Algeria, Britain, Cuba, Czecho-Slovakia, Egypt, France, Guinea, North Vietnam, Spain, Sweden, Syria, and Tanzania, and to college campuses throughout the United States. He threatened Mississippi, Washington, D.C., Cleveland, and other places with destruction. He ranted and raved against the United States government and its officials but lauded Cuba's Castro and Guevara. He made threats against the lives of President Johnson and his cabinet, but somehow Snick's chairman remained above and beyond legal punishment.

In May, 1967, Hubert Geroid (Rap) Brown succeeded Carmichael as Snick's chairman. (Within a month of his election, Brown was openly advocating wholesale murder of whites by Negroes: "How can you be nonviolent in America, the most violent country in the world .... You better shoot that [white] man to death; that's what he's been doing to you.")

With Brown's ascendancy, the policies and programs of Snick were outlined at a press conference: "SNCC is a Human Rights organization interested not only in Human Rights in the United States, but throughout the world; that,

in the field of International Relations, we assert that we encourage and support the liberation struggles of all people against racism, exploitation, and oppression. We see our struggle here in America as an integral part of the world-wide movement of all oppressed people, such as in Vietnam, Angola, Mozambique, South Africa, Zimbabwe, and Latin America. Furthermore, we support the efforts of our brothers in Puerto Rico who are presently engaged in a fight for independence and liberation there.

"We shall seek to build a strong nation-wide Black Anti-Draft Program and movement to include the high school students, along with college students and other black men of draft age. We see no reason for black men who are daily murdered physically and mentally in this country to go and kill yellow people abroad, who have done nothing to us, and are, in fact, victims of the same oppression that our brothers in Vietnam suffer.

"Our major thrust will be in the building of National Freedom Organizations which will deal with all aspects of the problems facing black people in America. The political objective will manifest itself in creation of a viable, independent political force. The economic objective will be (1) to expel the exploiters who presently control our community, (2) to gain economic control of our communities, and (3) to create an economic system which will be responsible to and benefit the black community, rather than a few individuals. Our cultural objective will be (1) to destroy the myths and lies propagated by white America concerning our history in Africa and in this country and (2) to develop an awareness and appreciation of the beauty of our thick lips, broad noses, kinky hair and soul. In obtaining these objectives, we will work with all other black groups who are fighting for the same goals."

Brown, as chairman of the self-defined Human Rights organization, advised Negroes in Washington, D.C.: "Get you some guns . . . burn this town down. You have to tell the [white] man if you come into my community you are going to come in with the intent of dying or you don't come in at all. I say there should be more shooting than looting, so if you loot, loot a gun store. You've got to decide for yourself if you kill your enemy because that is an individual decision. But the white man is your enemy. You got to destroy your enemy. If you give me a gun and tell me to shoot my enemy, I might shoot Lady Bird [Johnson]."

In July 1967, Brown was arrested by FBI agents and charged with inciting a riot in Cambridge, Maryland. But the arrest did not deter Brown's defiance, as he stated: "We stand on the eve of a Black revolution. Masses of our people are on the move, fighting the enemy, tick for tack, responding to counter-revolutionary violence with revolutionary violence, an eye for an eye, a tooth for a tooth, and a life for a life. These rebellions are but a dress rehearsal for the real revolution." Out on bail, Brown continued to travel the country, screaming "Black Power" and urging his black audiences to "stop looting and start shooting." He addressed Black Panther meetings and spoke at a dinner sponsored by the Communist weekly *National Guardian*. (As early as 1963, Forman had been a guest at a *National Guardian* dinner.)

At the 1967 Labor Day convention of the National Conference for New Politics, where the hierarchy of America's ultra-Left had gathered, Forman arrived on the scene with bodyguards and a retinue of followers. His harangue at the convention was quite a contrast to the moderation he affected a few years previously when he was promoting Snick as a nonviolent civil rights group. Said Forman to his convention audience: "We are not Americans, we are Africans. . . . Those of us who have been trained to fight in Vietnam, for example, and do not want to fight and live in this country, may very soon have to form a Black International and return to Africa to fight or die for the liberation of the Mother Country. Africa is our home! One Africa, One People! . . . We Blacks, and we alone, have the responsibility to wage our own war of liberation as we see fit. No one, absolutely no one in the world or the United States, has the right to dictate to us the forms of our struggle. We insist on our right to define the manner in which we will fight our aggressors. It is our right, our responsibility, and anyone who doesn't like it can go to hell . . . . The dispossessed must assume direction and give leadership to the New Politics. If you're not going to support, you go your merry way, and we're going to liberate you whether you want to be liberated or not . . . . Black Power is a threat to white power . . . . We are prepared to wage a struggle to take that power . . . . If Johnson is willing to use napalm in Vietnam, you know what he is prepared to do to us niggers in America."

Meanwhile, Stokely Carmichael, Brown's predecessor, had continued working for Snick — and Forman was not idle. FBI Director J. Edgar Hoover described Snick as having developed, under the leadership of Brown and Carmichael, "into a full-blown all-Negro revolutionary organization." Directing his attention to Forman, Hoover said:

"One dominant figure at this time in the organization is James Forman. At the national conference [of Snick] held in Atlanta, Ga., in early June 1968, Forman was responsible for a complete reorganization of SNCC patterned after the structure of another militant black nationalist organization, the Black Panther Party .... James Forman has many contacts with representatives of foreign countries and has made a number of trips abroad. In April 1968, he traveled to Sweden as part of a group which met with individuals representing the North Vietnamese and the National Liberation Front of South Vietnam."

In the October 5, 1968 issue of *Human Events*, it was reported: "FBI Director J. Edgar Hoover disclosed last week that the Student Nonviolent Coordinating Committee held a top-secret conference earlier this year at which plans were discussed for the 'elimination of Mau Mau tactics' of mayors, chiefs of police and other local officials. Hoover said the closed-door conference was held in mid-April. A majority of participants were armed.

"Among the tactics discussed was the preparation of maps showing the homes of local officials who could be wiped out Mau Mau style, Hoover said. The deployment of snipers along travel routes of National Guard units and police forces was also discussed.

"Participants were urged to recruit Viet Nam war veterans to train militant blacks in demolition and guerrilla warfare. Black college students were to instruct ghetto residents in the care and use of firearms, the preparation of Molotov cocktails, and the reloading of spent cartridges."

Forman was a very active promoter of violence within the framework of Snick. In February 1968, Forman, Car-

michael, and Brown formed an alliance of Snick with the Black Panthers and all three assumed official titles in the Black Panther organization. The alliance only lasted a few months, because Snick was stricken with a power struggle. Carmichael and Snick came to a parting of the ways. Forman, however, remained as Snick's director of international affairs.

In his syndicated column during the week of July 7, 1969, Paul Scott shed some light on Forman's activities on the international and national scenes: "Operating from SNCC's headquarters in New York City, Forman has established a number of SNCC branch offices overseas, including one in Tanzania. U.S. intelligence authorities say the Tanzania office is used as a contact point between SNCC members and top Soviet and Chinese Communist agents in Africa....

"Attorney General John Mitchell is being privately urged to make available to appropriate Congressional committees the alarming information the FBI has collected on James Forman, promoter of the Black Manifesto, demanding $500 million in 'reparations' from the nation's churches. Members of the Senate Permanent Investigations Subcommittee, probing black militant groups, want Mitchell to air Forman's close ties with Moscow so American church leaders will have a clear idea of what is behind his multi-million dollar shakedown campaign. Instead of following the Kennedy-Johnson administration policy of suppressing FBI information on the Communist ties of the late Dr. Martin Luther King, the Senate probers headed by Senator John McClellan (D.-Ark.) believe the Justice Department should 'tell it as it is' about Forman and his associates. While the McClellan subcommittee has obtained information on Forman from the Detroit and New York police departments, none so far has been made available by the Justice Department. Specifically, the McClellan subcommittee is seeking data the FBI gathered on Forman's 1967 trip to Russia and Tanzania, Africa, as the international representative of the misnamed Student Nonviolent Coordinating Committee (SNCC).

"Since returning from that trip, Forman has preached the straight Moscow line on everything from the Vietnam war to calling on American Negroes to be the vanguard of a revolution to destroy American institutions including the churches. FBI recordings of Forman's private and public statements show that the SNCC official's main objective is to pressure the churches into channeling money into black militant groups seeking the overthrow of the government. Forman, considered by the FBI as the most dangerous black militant in the country, consistently has echoed the Soviet line that 'the U.S. is the most barbaric country in the world' and that 'the present form of American government must be destroyed by any means available.'

"Surrounded by a number of known Communists . . . Forman since 1967 has made no bones about supporting armed revolution to build a socialistic form of government in the U.S. 'While we talk of revolution, which will be an armed confrontation and long years of sustained guerrilla warfare inside this country, we must also talk of the type of world we want to live in,' Forman told a meeting of Black Militants in Detroit recently. Forman then stated that 'we must commit ourselves to a society where the total means of production are taken from the rich people and placed into the hands of the state for the welfare of all the people. This is what we mean when we say total control.' "

Forman's devotion to Marxism was very much appreciated by the Communists in the United States. On November 23, 1967, Forman delivered a long address to the Western Regional Black Youth Conference at Los Angeles. Claude Lightfoot, head of the Communist Party's department of Negro affairs and secretary of the Party's national committee, caused more than two full pages of excerpts from Forman's address to be printed in the *Worker*. Lightfoot said that Forman's remarks "would stimulate thinking and discussion of the tactical and ideological problems facing the black liberation movement and its white allies." The prominence given to Forman's excerpts was an obvious indication that Forman and/or his ghostwriters were in complete command of the Communist line as it was pertinent to blacks and their organizations in this country.

Much of Forman's address consisted of badly distorted history. In his inimitable style he deplored racism while he preached it. In his remarks, he said: "The masses of Black people have never accommodated themselves to the United States. And it is among the masses that our youth must work. Only from the masses of Black people will there come revolutionary leadership, a leadership that will not accommodate itself, that will continue to resist as our ancestors resisted, a leadership that will not mind dying for independence and freedom not only of blacks but for all oppressed. For those of us who consider ourselves freedom fighters it is imperative that we view our history in this manner, a history of resistance, not of accommodation. It is imperative that we realize that our culture and our people have been able to resist to survive and to make it possible for us to deal more death blows to our oppressors . . . .

"Brothers and sisters, bold analysis of the last six or seven paragraphs of this paper places into sharp focus three ways of looking at the fundamental causes of our problems. One, we can take the position that says we are exploited solely because of our skin color. This I call the skin analysis. Two, we can take a second position that says our exploitation is solely due to our class position in this society. This I call the exclusive class analysis. We can take a third position that says that our exploitation results both from class positions as well as from our race. Given all I said, it is obvious that I hold to the third position.

"The absolute necessity for me to raise this as a discussion item arises from my own experience within the movement. Once during a discussion with one of my brothers, I used the word Marxian. He jumped up and pounded on the table and yelled: 'But Marx was not a black. He was not black, do you hear! He was a white writer.' "

Forman explained in unequivocal terms how Snick was prepared for a violent revolution to achieve Black Power: "Within Snick today, we are discussing revolutionary black power as opposed to reactionary black power; for we have seen instance after instance where conservative forces have tried to explain away or excuse the revolutionary aspect of Black Power. But an understanding of what is meant by revolutionary Black Power hinges on how one sees the fundamental causes of our condition today. Resulting from this analysis will flow many things and many decisions and many ways of solving our problem.

"Within the concept of the colonized we must begin to speak more of the dispossessed, those who do not have. This is important for it determines where alliances are made.

"The dispossessed unite with the dispossessed. It must be clearly understood that the nature of the colonial experience is that racism is inherent in all its manifestations, even though the dispossessed unite with the dispossessed or even if the exploiters who are responsible for the colonizing are kicked out, the legacy of racism and remnants of the colonial experience remain and must be uprooted. The Chinese are saying in part through their cultural revolution that even though one eliminates the structural forms of capitalism, there are capitalistic ideas and thoughts that still remain and must be combatted.

"As Chairman H. Rap Brown stated to the Black Caucus at the National Conference on New Politics, the dispossessed in the United States are the people of African descent, the Puerto Ricans, the Mexican Americans, and many poor whites. We are the vanguard of that group because of our historical oppression and the racism inherent in it. Whether we will live up to our historical rule and lead forward that revolution remains to be seen.

"It is our job to go forth from this conference using whatever means necessary to liberate ourselves and other oppressed people, not only in the United States but throughout the world. In order to do this we must wage an unrelenting struggle against racism and exploitation of man. We must work, not for ourselves but for the unborn generations that will carry humanity and our people to new heights, to a world without racism, to a world of no more resistance, but only a community of concern. For this world we must be prepared to fight and to die. And we must believe that we will win. We must believe that our fight and our deaths are not in vain."

In 1968, when Snick was torn with dissension, Forman evidently decided that the organization was not the best means for him to achieve his ambition to become the nation's top militant black leader. For a time, he became relatively quiet. He emerged from his self-imposed obscurity on April 26, 1969, in Detroit, at the Black Economic Development Conference which had been convened under the auspices of the Interreligious Foundation for Community Organizations [IFCO], the National Council of Churches, the Episcopal Church, and other institutions.

At the Detroit conference, Forman made a lengthy presentation that was adopted by the conferees and was directed against "the white Christian churches and the Jewish synagogues in the United States of America and all other racist institutions." The presentation had two parts: (1) The introduction: "Total Control as the Only Solution to the Economic Problems of Black People." (2) The Black Manifesto.

In his introduction, Forman said: "We have come from all over the country, burning with anger and despair not only with the miserable economic plight of our people, but fully aware that the racism on which the Western World was built dominates our lives. There can be no separation of the problems of racism from the problems of our economic, political, and cultural degradation. To any black man, this is clear.

"But there are still some of our people who are clinging to the rhetoric of the Negro and we must separate ourselves from those Negroes who go around the country promoting all types of schemes for Black Capitalism.

"Ironically, some of the most militant Black Nationalists, as they call themselves, have been the first to jump on the bandwagon of black capitalism. They are pimps; Black Power Pimps and fraudulent leaders and the people must be educated to understand that any black man or Negro who is advocating a perpetuation of capitalism inside the United States is in fact seeking not only his ultimate destruction and death, but is contributing to the continuous exploitation of black people all over the world. For it is the power of the United States Government, this racist, imperialist government that is choking the life of all people around the world.

"We are an African people. We sit back and watch the Jews in this country make Israel a powerful conservative state in the Middle East, but we are not concerned actively about the plight of our brothers in Africa. We are the most advanced technological group of black people in the world, and there are many skills that could be offered to Africa. At the same time, it must be publicly stated that many African leaders are in disarray themselves, having been duped into following the lines as laid out by the Western Imperialist governments.

"Africans themselves succumbed to and are victims of the power of the United States . . . .

"In Africa today, there is a great suspicion of black people in this country. This is a correct suspicion since most of the Negroes who have left the States for work in Africa usually work for the Central Intelligence Agency (CIA) or the State Department. But the respect for us as a people continues to mount and the day will come when we can return to our homeland as brothers and sisters. But we should not think of going back to Africa today, for we are located in a strategic position. We live inside the U.S. which is the most barbaric country in the world and we have a chance to help bring this government down.

"Time is short and we do not have much time and it is time we stop mincing words. Caution is fine, but no oppressed people ever gained their liberation until they were ready to fight, to use whatever means necessary, including the use of force and power of the gun to bring down the colonizer.

"We have heard the rhetoric, but we have not heard the rhetoric which says that black people in this country must understand that we are the Vanguard Force. We shall liberate all the people in the U.S. and we will be instrumental in the liberation of colored people in the world around. We must understand this point very clearly so that we are not trapped into diversionary and reactionary movements. Any class analysis of the U.S. shows very clearly that black people are the most oppressed group of people inside the United States. We have suffered the most from racism and exploitation, cultural degradation and lack of political power. It follows from the laws of revolution that the most oppressed will make the revolution, but we are not talking about just making the revolution. All the parties on the left who consider themselves revolutionary will say that blacks are the Vanguard, but we are saying that not only are we the Vanguard, but we must assume leadership, total control and we must exercise the humanity which is inherent in us. We are the most humane people within the U.S. We have suffered and we understand suffering. Our hearts go out to the Vietnamese for we know what it is to suffer under the domination of racist America. Our hearts, our soul and all the compassion we can mount goes out to our brothers in Africa, Santa Domingo [*sic*], Latin America and Asia who are being tricked by the power structure of the U.S. which is dominating the world today. These ruthless, barbaric men have systematically tried to kill all people and organizations opposed to its imperialism. We no longer can just get by with the use of the word capitalism to describe the U.S., for it is an imperial power, sending money, missionaries and the army throughout the world to protect this government and the few rich whites who control it. General Motors and all the major auto industries are operating in South Africa, yet the white dominated leadership of the United Auto Workers sees no relationship to the exploitation of black people in South Africa and the exploitation of black people in the U.S. If they understand it, they certainly do not put it into practice which is the actual test. We as black people must be concerned with the total conditions of all black people in the world.

"But while we talk of revolution which will be an armed confrontation and long years of sustained guerrilla warfare inside this country, we must also talk of the type of world we want to live in. We must commit ourselves to a society where the total means of production are taken from the rich and placed into the hands of the state for the welfare of all the people. This is what we mean when we say total control. And we mean that black people who have suffered the most from exploitation and racism must move to protect their black interest by assuming leadership inside of the United States of everything that exists. The time has passed when we are second in command and the white boy stands on top. This is especially true of the Welfare Agencies in this country, but it is not enough to say that a black man is on top. He must be committed to building the new society, to taking the wealth away from the rich people such as General Motors, Ford, Chrysler, the DuPonts, the Rockefellers, the Mellons, and all the other rich white exploiters and racists who run this world.

"Where do we begin? We have already started. We started the moment we were brought to this country. In fact, we started on the shores of Africa, for we have always resisted attempts to make us slaves and now we must resist the attempts to make us capitalists. It is the financial interest of the U.S. to make us capitalists, for this will be the same line as that of integration into the mainstream of American life. Therefore, brothers and sisters, there is no need to fall into the trap that we have to get an ideology. We have an ideology. Our fight is against racism, capitalism and imperialism and we are dedicated to building a socialist society inside the United States where the total means of production and distribution are in the hands of the State and that must be led by black people, by revolutionary blacks who are concerned about the total humanity of this world. And, therefore, we obviously are different from some of those who seek a black nation in the United States, for there is no way for that nation to be viable if in fact the United States remains in the hands of white racists. Then too, let us deal with some arguments that we should share power with whites. We say that there must be a revolutionary black Vanguard and that white people in this country must be willing to accept black leadership, for that is the only protection that black people have to protect ourselves from racism rising again in this country.

"Racism in the U.S. is so pervasive in the mentality of whites that only an armed, well-disciplined, black-controlled government can insure the stamping out of racism in this country. And that is why we plead with black people not to be talking about a few crumbs, a few thousand dollars for this cooperative, or a thousand dollars which splits black people into fighting over the dollar. That is the intention of the government. We say . . . think in terms of total control of the U.S. Prepare ourselves to seize state power. Do not hedge, for time is short and all around the world, the forces of liberation are directing their attacks against the U.S. It is a powerful country, but that power is not greater than that of black people. We work the chief industries in this country and we could cripple the economy while the brothers fought guerrilla warfare in the streets. This will take some long range planning, but whether it happens in a thousand years is of no consequence. It cannot happen unless we start. How then is all of this related to this conference?

"First of all, this conference is called by a set of religious people, Christians, who have been involved in the exploitation and rape of black people since the country was founded. The missionary goes hand in hand with the power of the states. We must begin seizing power wherever we are and we must say to the planners of this conference that you are no longer in charge. We the people who have assembled here thank you for getting us here, but we are going to assume power over the conference and determine from this moment on the direction in which we want it to go. We are not saying that the conference was planned badly. The staff of the conference has worked hard and have done a magnificent job in bringing all of us together and we must include them in the new membership which must surface from this point on. The conference is now the property of the people who are assembled here. This we proclaim as fact and not rhetoric and there are demands that we are going to make and we insist that the planners of this conference help us implement them.

"We maintain we have the revolutionary right to do this. We have the same rights, if you will, as the Christians had in going into Africa and raping our Motherland and bringing us away from our continent of peace and into this hostile and alien environment where we have been living in perpetual warfare since 1619."

Forman's "Black Manifesto" was undoubtedly the most outrageous issued since the promulgation of Karl Marx's kindred "Communist Manifesto" in 1848. It had a very simple object: the destruction of America's *white* Christian churches and Jewish synagogues.

The Manifesto read, in part: "We, the black people assembled in Detroit, Michigan for the National Black Economic Development Conference are fully aware that we have been forced to come together because racist white America has exploited our resources, our minds, our bodies, our labor. For centuries we have been forced to live as colonized people inside the United States, victimized by the most vicious, racist system in the world. We have helped to build the most industrial country in the world.

"We are therefore demanding of the white Christian churches and Jewish synagogues, which are part and parcel of the system of capitalism, that they begin to pay reparations to black people in this country. We are demanding $500,000,000 from the Christian white churches and the Jewish synagogues. This total comes to 15 dollars per

nigger . . . . Fifteen dollars for every black brother and sister in the United States is only a beginning of the reparations due us as people who have been exploited and degraded, brutalized, killed and persecuted. Underneath all of this exploitation, the racism of this country has produced a psychological effect upon us that we are beginning to shake off. We are no longer afraid to demand our full rights as a people in this decadent society. We are demanding $500,000,000 to be spent in the following way:

"1) We call for the establishment of a Southern land bank to help our brothers and sisters who have to leave their land because of racist pressure for people who want to establish cooperative farms, but who have no funds . . . . We call for $200,000,000 to implement this program.

"2) We call for the establishment of four major publishing and printing industries in the United States to be funded with ten million dollars each. These publishing houses are to be located in Detroit, Atlanta, Los Angeles and New York. They will help to generate capital for further cooperative investments in the black community, provide jobs and an alternative to the white-dominated and controlled printing field.

"3) We call for the establishment of four of the most advanced scientific and futuristic audio-visual networks to be located in Detroit, Chicago, Cleveland and Washington, D.C. These TV networks will provide an alternative to racist propaganda that fills the current television networks. Each of these TV networks will be funded by ten million dollars each.

"4) We call for a research skills center which will provide research on the problems of black people. This center must be funded with no less than 30 million dollars.

"5) We call for the establishment of a training center for the teaching of skills in community organization, photography, movie making, television making and repair, radio building and repair and all other skills needed in communication. This training center shall be funded with no less than ten million dollars.

"6) We recognize the role of the National Welfare Rights Organization and we intend to work with them. We call for ten million dollars to assist in the organization of welfare recipients. We want to organize the welfare workers in this country so that they may demand more money from the government and better administration of the welfare system of this country.

"7) We call for $20,000,000 to establish a National Black Labor Strike and Defense Fund. This is necessary for the protection of black workers and their families who are fighting racist working conditions in this country.

"8) We call for the establishment of the International Black Appeal (IBA). This International Black Appeal will be funded with no less than $20,000,000 . . . .The IBA is charged with three functions and shall be headed by James Forman: (a) Raising money for the program of the National Black Economic Development Conference; (b) The development of cooperatives in African countries and support of African Liberation movements; (c) Establishment of a Black Anti-Defamation League which will protect our African image.

"9) We call for the establishment of a Black University to be funded with $130,000,000 to be located in the South.

"10) We demand that IFCO allocate all unused funds in the planning budget to implement the demands of this conference.

"In order to win our demands we are aware that we will have to have massive support, therefore:

"1) We call upon all black people throughout the United States to consider themselves as members of the National Black Economic Development Conference and to act in unity to help force the racist white Christian churches and Jewish synagogues to implement these demands.

"2) We call upon all the concerned black people across the country to contact black workers, black women, black students and the black unemployed, community groups, welfare organizations, teacher organizations, church leaders and organizations explaining how these demands are vital to the black community of the U.S. Pressure by whatever means necessary should be applied to the white power structure of the racist white Christian churches and Jewish synagogues. All black people should act boldly in confronting our white oppressors and demanding this modest reparation of 15 dollars per black man.

"3) Delegates and members of the National Black Economic Development Conference are urged to call press conferences in the cities and to attempt to get as many black organizations as possible to support the demands of the conference. The quick use of the press in the local areas will heighten the tension and these demands must be attempted to be won in a short period of time, although we are prepared for protracted and long range struggle.

"4) We call for the total disruption of selected church sponsored agencies operating anywhere in the U.S. and the world. Black workers, black women, black students and the black unemployed are encouraged to seize the offices, telephones, and printing apparatus of all church sponsored agencies and to hold these in trusteeship until our demands are met.

"5) We call upon all delegates and members of the National Black Economic Development Conference to stage sit-in demonstrations at selected black and white churches. This is not to be interpreted as a continuation of the sit-in movement of the early sixties but we know that active confrontation inside white churches is possible and will strengthen the possibility of meeting our demands. Such confrontation can take the form of reading the Black Manifesto instead of a sermon or passing it out to church members. The principle of self-defense should be applied if attacked.

"6) On May 4, 1969 or a date thereafter, depending upon local conditions, we call upon black people to commence the disruption of the racist churches and synagogues throughout the United States.

"7) We call upon IFCO to serve as a central staff to coordinate the mandate of the conference and to reproduce and distribute en mass [sic] literature, leaflets, news items, press releases and other material.

"8) We call upon all delegates to find within the white community those forces which will work under the leadership of blacks to implement these demands by whatever means necessary. By taking such actions, white Americans will demonstrate concretely that they are willing to fight the white skin privilege and the white supremacy and racism which has forced us as black people to make these demands.

"9) We call upon all white Christians and Jews to practice patience, tolerance,

understanding and nonviolence as they have encouraged, advised and demanded that we as black people should do throughout our entire enforced slavery in the United States. The true test of their faith and belief in the Cross and the words of the prophets will certainly be put to a test as we seek legitimate and extremely modest reparations for our role in developing the industrial base of the Western world through our slave labor. But we are no longer slaves, we are men and women, proud of our African ·heritage, determined to have our dignity.

" 10) We are so proud of our African heritage and realize concretely that our struggle is not only to make revolution in the United States, but to protect our brothers and sisters in Africa and to help them rid themselves of racism, capitalism and imperialism by whatever means necessary, including armed struggle. We are and must be willing to fight the defamation of our African image wherever it rears its ugly head. We are therefore charging the Steering Committee to create a Black Anti-Defamation League to be funded by money raised from the International Black Appeal.

" 11) We fully recognize that revolution in the United States and Africa, our Motherland, is more than a one dimensional operation. It will require the total integration of the political, economic, and military components and therefore, we call upon all our brothers and sisters who have acquired training and expertise in the fields of engineering, electronics, research, community organization, physics, biology, chemistry, mathematics, medicine, military science and warfare to assist the National Black Economic Development Conference in the implementation of its program.

"12) To implement these demands

... we must have a leadership which is willing to battle the church establishment to implement these demands. To win our demands we will have to declare war on the white Christian churches and synagogues and this means we may have to fight the total government structure of this country. Let no one here think that these demands will be met by our mere stating them. For the sake of the churches and synagogues, we hope that they have the wisdom to understand that these demands are modest and reasonable. But if the white Christians and Jews are not willing to meet our demands through peace and good will, then we declare war and we are prepared to fight by whatever means necessary . . . .

"And we say to the white Christian churches and Jewish synagogues, to the government of this country and to all the white racist imperialists who compose it, there is only one thing left that you can do to further degrade black people and that is to kill us. But we have been dying too long for this country. We have died in every war. We are dying in Vietnam today fighting the wrong enemy.

"The new black man wants to live and to live means that we must not become static or merely believe in self-defense. We must boldly go out and attack the white Western world at its power centers. The white Christian churches are another form of government in this country and they are used by the government of this country to exploit the people of Latin America, Asia and Africa, but the day is soon coming to an end. Therefore, brothers and sisters, the demands we make upon the white Christian churches and the Jewish synagogues are small demands. They represent 15 dollars per black person in these United States. We can

legitimately demand this from the church power structure. We must demand more from the United States Government.

"But to win our demands from the church which is linked up with the United States Government, we must not forget that it will ultimately be by force and power that we will win.

"We are not threatening the churches. We are saying that we know the churches came with the military might of the colonizers and have been sustained by the military might of the colonizers. Hence, if the churches in colonial territories were established by military might, we know deep within our hearts that we must be prepared to use force to get our demands. We are not saying that this is the road we want to take. It is not, but let us be very clear that we are not opposed to force and we are not opposed to violence. We were captured in Africa by violence. We were kept in bondage and political servitude and forced to work as slaves by the military machinery and the Christian church working hand in hand.

"We recognize that in issuing this manifesto we must prepare for a long range educational campaign in all communities of this country, but we know that the Christian churches have contributed to our oppression in white America. We do not intend to abuse our black brothers and sisters in black churches who have uncritically accepted Christianity. We want them to understand how the racist white Christian church with its hypocritical declarations and doctrines of brotherhood has abused our trust and faith. An attack on the religious beliefs of black people is not our major objective, even though we know that we were not Christians when we were brought to this country, but that Christianity was

398

used to help enslave us. Our objective in issuing this Manifesto is to force the racist white Christian church to begin the payment of reparations which are due to all black people, not only by the Church but also by private business and the U.S. government. We see this focus on the Christian church as an effort around which all black people can unite.

"Our demands are negotiable, but they cannot be minimized, they can only be increased and the Church is asked to come up with larger sums of money than we are asking. Our slogans are: All Roads Must Lead to Revolution; Unite with Whomever You Can Unite; Neutralize Wherever Possible; Fight Our Enemies Relentlessly; Victory to the People; Life and Good Health to Mankind; Resistance to Domination by the White Christian Churches and the Jewish Synagogues; Revolutionary Black Power; and We Shall Win Without a Doubt."

The Interreligious Foundation for Community Organization, which was the major organization that convened and financed Forman's National Black Economic Conference, was founded in September 1967. The American Baptist *Crusader* provided information on IFCO, which is herein paraphrased. By May 1969, twenty-three religious and other agencies were members of IFCO. IFCO described itself as "a unique national coalition of Protestant, Jewish and Roman Catholic social agencies and local and regional development groups. It seeks to implement common programs and strategies of member organizations, give a local assistance in technical areas, conduct research in cooperation with indigenous community groups, and raise funds for the development of mass-based community organization." By May 1969, IFCO raised $1,495,510 and disbursed it to about fifty community-type

social-activist and/or training organizations.

Rev. Lucius Walker Jr., an American Baptist clergyman, is the executive director of IFCO. Walker was very enthusiastic in his praise of Forman's Manifesto: "In my judgment the introduction of the concept of reparations through the National Black Economic Development Conference occasioned a new level of awareness and an encouraging turn in developments within the movement of black liberation. In the years ahead our society will need to deal with the question of restitution for its maintenance of and participation in the slave economy and in a dual system that has deprived and denied black citizens equal rights in American society. The guilt of white America has never been expiated in any formal manner. The concept of reparations will allow an opportunity for formal restitution which will not only contribute to the economic development of the black community but the psychological relief of the white community that can potentially diffuse the rising tension between the races and put us on the road towards viable reform rather than the present tack that we seem to be following towards revolution and conflict in American society."

Walker went on the defensive when it was charged that IFCO had ties with the Black Panther Party and other revolutionary and subversive groups: ". . . I would also like to make it very clear that IFCO funds have not gone exclusively to militant groups. Our funds go to projects that are inclusive in their membership and promote people power so that poor minority groups can redress their grievances in society. The groups we fund represent diverse segments of community population ranging from conservative to militant . . . . The claim that we are connected with the Black Panther Party is utterly ridiculous."

In the *Chicago Tribune* (May 12, 1969), Ronald Koziol described some of the "militant groups" supported by IFCO: "Disclosures of the link between the militants and the church-supported I.F.C.O. are expected to be made tomorrow by Sgt. Robert Thoms of the Los Angeles police intelligence division at a meeting of the International Security conference at the Sherman House. The three days of seminars are being held for security personnel and are sponsored by Security World Publishing Company.

"Thoms said that what began as a routine investigation of a Los Angeles group in January has turned into a comprehensive report which has been turned over to two federal agencies for a more detailed inquiry.

"However, Thoms' investigation disclosed the names of many militant groups funded by I.F.C.O., including the Garfield organization in Chicago which received $20,000. The group has participated in militant civil rights action against businesses and in April, 1968, several of its officers were arrested and charged with conspiracy to commit burglary and arson. The arrests came in the aftermath of rioting and looting on the west side.

"According to Thoms, I.F.C.O. has disbursed $885,831 since it was founded on Nov. 11, 1966. He learned that $774,514, or about 83 percent of the total, was granted to community groups involved in military of disruptive activities.

"The I.F.C.O. was described by Thoms as a nonprofit tax-exempt interfaith coalition created to coordinate development of community groups and to provide funds. He explained that 'this is an example of tax-exempt monies being utilized for non-charitable organizations bent on destroying what Americans believe in.' "

One of the best known of IFCO's officers is Rev. Albert Cleage Jr. In *Human Events* (June 28, 1969), John C. Watson wrote: "The Rev. Albert Cleage Jr., pastor of Detroit's Central United Church of Christ, has been a member of IFCO's board of directors from its inception. Recognized as one of the militant 'Black Power' leaders of Detroit and a vociferous foe of the Detroit Police Department, he is an ex-Muslim and was a close associate of the late Malcolm X. He is active in the Republic of New Africa movement which believes in a separate nation within the United States run by blacks.

"Cleage's church has been the scene of numerous 'Black Power' rallies with such speakers as H. Rap Brown and Revolutionary Action Movement (RAM) leader Milton Henry. A 'People's Tribunal,' a mock trial against law enforcement officers, was also conducted in Cleage's church. In December 1967 IFCO announced its first $85,000 no-strings attached gift to the City-wide Citizen's Action Committee founded and directed by the Rev. Albert Cleage."

Watson also wrote about another IFCO director: "The National Welfare Rights Organization in Washington, D.C., received $137,212 from IFCO. This is the group responsible for organizing the welfare rights march in the Nation's Capital, and for numerous demonstrations and confrontations with welfare administrators in other cities.

"In Los Angeles they threatened to tie up the welfare administration with court litigation unless demands for additional welfare benefits were met.

"NWRO official George A. Wiley told

a Washington rally of dissatisfied welfare recipients last year that 'if this country does not listen to the poor people after what happened in Detroit and Newark and New Haven, you haven't seen nothing yet.' Mr. Wiley is a member of IFCO's Board of Directors!" (In Forman's Manifesto, there was a demand that the NWRO be given $10,000,000.)

Forman, during the course of his Manifesto, set up a Steering Committee to handle his "reparations" (blackmail) program. The Committee included Lucius Walker (the executive director of IFCO), Luke Samuel Tripp (a member of the Revolutionary Action Movement), Forman, John Watson (self-described "revolutionary" – a Marxist-Leninist sympathetic to the Chinese Communist Party), and two well-known Southern agitators, Fannie Lou Hamer of Mississippi and Julian Bond of Georgia.

On May 2, 1969, Forman read his Manifesto to the General Board of the National Council of Churches in New York City. The Board thanked Forman and agreed to send the Manifesto to the NCC's constituent denominations for their consideration. The NCC's general secretary was told to prepare recommendations that would be submitted to a June 23 meeting of the NCC's executive committee.

On May 4, 1969, Forman and a group of his henchmen interrupted a Sunday-morning service at Riverside Church in New York City. As the opening hymn was concluded, Forman stood at the altar and read a series of the Manifesto's demands. The religious service was not resumed.

On May 5, the NCC's General Board advised its members, thirty-three Protestant and Orthodox churches, to pay serious attention to Forman's Manifesto. Two days later, the Board of Directors

of IFCO voted its approval of the Manifesto. The IFCO meeting was described in *Newsweek* magazine (May 19, 1969): ". . . Forman's efforts last week were aimed at getting further recognition for his conference followers. At a tense meeting of IFCO's directors in Manhattan's Interchurch Center, he largely succeeded. The board promised $270,000 in seed money and – employing deliberately ambiguous language – ratified conference goals 'in their programmatic aspects.'

"With IFCO behind him, plus the endorsement of 35 representatives of the black caucuses within the nation's white churches he next flew to Atlanta. There he won the equally important endorsement of the National Committee of Black Churchmen, representing some 700 clergy. In a special salute, the NCBC praised Forman as 'a modern-day prophet' and warned the white churches that 'it is too late to call for propriety and moderation.' "

After Forman had caused the disturbance at Riverside Church, the trustees of the Church obtained a restraining order to forestall any future disruptions by Forman. Forman burned a copy of the order on the steps of the chancery of the Catholic Diocese of New York. He gave the Catholic authorities a copy of his Manifesto, which included a demand that the Catholics pay $200,000,000 in reparations. The demand was immediately rejected. On May 6, Forman attached a copy of his demands to the front of the New York City headquarters of the Lutheran Church in America. His demand of the Lutherans for $50,000,000 in reparations was rejected.

On Sunday, May 11, 1969, Forman paid his second visit to Riverside Church during morning services. The *New York*

Times (May 12, 1969) reported the episode: "James Forman, the black militant leader, stood silently during the 20-minute sermon yesterday at Riverside Church, except for the occasional whispered words of 'peace, peace.' His demeanor was in sharp contrast to last week's visit to the church, when he interrupted a communion service by demanding 'reparations' for Negroes for the deprivations he said they had suffered in the white capitalist system. Before entering the huge gothic edifice, Mr. Forman read a statement from the church steps in which he described the Riverside trustees as 'white racist businessmen.' Then with 15 of his aides, he marched down the center aisle and quietly occupied two pews up front. They remained seated as the more than 2,000 worshippers stood and joined in congregational singing . . . .

"Garbed in a robin's egg blue African gown and with his hands clasped over a black, white-handled cane, Mr. Forman barely moved . . . . [Forman's attire and personal grooming changed over the years according to his audience. As a Snick executive, he wore sharecropper-style denim overalls or a business suit. His hair was neatly trimmed and he was clean shaven. But, as he became an overt revolutionary, the overalls and business suits gave way to dashikis, bubas, and robes. He gradually affected an Afro-style hairdo, moustache, and goatee.] The bearded, 40-year-old militant . . . arrived at the church at 122nd Street and Riverside Drive shortly before the 10:45 a.m. service began. He immediately mounted the church steps and read to the assembled newsmen a 1,500-word statement. The document said the Black Conference, which is seeking the so-called 'reparations,' had no quarrel with Dr. [Ernest T.] Campbell (senior minister of Riverside Church) but was only trying to 'expose the board of trustees of the church as rich white racist businessmen who are manipulating the church for their financial interest.' It called upon 'all black people across this country, and especially our black brothers and sisters in the churches,' to arm themselves with shotguns 'to stop the violence of the racist white man . . . .'

"Yesterday, a church spokesman made it clear that Riverside had no intention of giving money to Mr. Forman. At a news conference held in the church's basement assembly hall following the worship service, Mr. Forman and Dr. Campbell engaged in a discussion on what would constitute a responsible black channel for the reception of funds. The result was something of a stand-off, with Mr. Forman recommending his Black Conference, working through the Interreligious Foundation for Community Organization, and Dr. Campbell professing inadequate knowledge of either body."

On May 15, Forman was in San Antonio, where he addressed the General Assembly of the Presbyterian Church. The moderator of the Assembly later explained why Forman was invited to speak: ". . . James Forman is at present the most disturbing critic of the churches from the extreme militant point of view. We needed to hear him, to listen thoughtfully to him, to try to understand what he represents. I have received telegrams and letters protesting the bringing of Mr. Forman to San Antonio. Many have objected to the use of church money for this purpose. Those who wrote may not have recognized that the Assembly heard him not because it approved of him but because it needed him. And it would be unprecedented for a speaker to be invited to come to address the Assembly at his own expense." The General Assembly did not agree to pay reparations to Forman but did authorize a $50,000,000 fund-raising program for the poor for 1970.

On May 17, Forman spoke to the American Baptist Convention. He demanded that all unused American Baptist Convention lands in the South be given to his National Black Economic Development Conference along with 60 per cent of the Convention's stocks, bonds, and investments. He also demanded a $60,000,000 contribution to IFCO. The executive committee rejected Forman's Manifesto because of its ideology and rhetoric, but said: "We ought to thank God for Mr. Forman's implied call to repentance, restoration and reconciliation." The executive committee then urged all American Baptist congregations to make greater efforts to "end the inequities of our society."

The United Methodist Board of Missions rejected the Manifesto, but voted $1,300,000 to a program for "economic empowerment of black people," to be administered by black Methodists. The General Synod of the United Church of Christ turned down the Manifesto, but established a $500,000 annual budget for a Commission of Racial Justice, controlled by blacks.

Forman's Manifesto was rejected by the General Board of the Christian Church, the Southern Baptist Convention, the Synagogue Council of America, and the · National Jewish Community Relations Advisory Council.

The strongest condemnation of Forman's Manifesto came from the largest Negro denomination in America, the National Baptist Convention, whose president, Rev. Joseph H. Jackson, said that the Manifesto is "merely an echo of the Communist Manifesto of Karl Marx and, in reality, it is the same old Red Manifesto now painted black."

Forman did find a friendly response in the National Council of Churches. On June 23, 1969, the executive committee of the NCC agreed to negotiate with Forman on his half-billion-dollar demand for reparations. The committee donned sackcloth and ashes as it said: "There must be penitence and a readiness to make recompense . . . . Cognizant of the great injustices done to the black men and the brown men by Christian white men throughout the entire history of our country, to this very day, we declare that we have no right under God to refuse to listen to any demand presented to us, whatever may be our initial reaction to the form it takes. It is imperative that whites open every possible door and make every attempt to listen. We confess that we have no right to appear before the altar of God so long as this priority has not taken possession of us. Remembering that if our brother has anything against us, nothing we do is acceptable before the altar of God until first we be reconciled to our brother."

On September 11, the 200-man general board of the NCC asked the member churches to raise not less than $500,000 immediately, to be spent through IFCO and the National Committee of Black Churchmen. The board members rejected the ideology of Forman's Manifesto, but said: "We, as Christians, have no right under God to refuse to listen to any demand presented to us, whatever may be our initial reaction to the form it takes." The president of NCC, Arthur S. Flemming, said that since the churches have failed "to respond to the needs of the ghetto, we are now being called upon to respond to the politics of confrontation. If we fail today, it will be another step toward two societies – black and white and separate and unequal."

Forman's campaign for reparations, from a financial perspective, was not a huge success. By 1971, a spokesman for his group complained that only $300,000 in cash had been forthcoming from white churches. On the other hand, Forman's Marxist message of hate had been delivered. It has received an enormous amout of publicity. His tactics of intimidation had caused white churchmen, laity and clergy, to wallow in abasement. They accepted his grossest charges without refutation. They admitted to a history of racism and exploitation. They accepted totally slanderous indictments of their fellow Americans.

When the reparations campaign tapered off, Forman contented himself with a sabbatical from publicity. In August 1971, however, he arrived in Red China for a conference with Communist officials. News dispatches described him and his aides as representatives of the "Black Workers Congress."

Forman has prepared a legacy. It was described in the Communists' *Guardian* by Julius Lester: "James Forman of the Student Nonviolent Coordinating Committee (SNCC) is asking white revolutionaries for the following in the event that he is assassinated: Ten war factories destroyed. Fifteen police stations blown up. Thirty power plants demolished. No flowers. One Southern governor, two mayors and 500 racist white cops dead. And for the assassination of Stokely and/or Rap, he is asking the above figures be doubled."

WILLIAM T.R. FOX was born on January 12, 1912 in Chicago, son of Myrtle Perrigo and John Fox. He married Annette Baker. He is an alumnus of Haverford College (B.S., 1932) and the University of Chicago (M.A., 1934; Ph.D., 1940). He is the author of *The Super-Powers* (1944) and *The American Study of International Relations* (1968). He is the editor and co-author of *Theoretical Aspects of International Relations* (1959). He is co-author of *NATO and the Range of American Choice* (1967). Since 1948, he has held editorial positions with *World Politics.*

From 1936 until 1941, he was a political science instructor at Temple University. From 1941 until 1943, he was an instructor and conference director at Princeton University's School of Public and International Affairs. From 1943 until 1951, he was at Yale University as a research associate in the Institute of International Studies (1943-1951), assistant director of the Institute of International Studies (1948-1950), and associate professor of political science (1946-1950). Since 1950, he has been at Columbia University as professor of international relations (1950-1968) and a James T. Shotwell professor of international relations (1968 to the present). Since 1951, he has been director of the leftist-pacifist-oriented Institute of War and Peace Studies at Columbia University. From 1953 until 1964, he was chairman of the national security policy research committee of the leftist Social Science Research Council. Since 1944, he has served for about twenty years as a consultant to the U.S. Department of State.

Fox has been affiliated with the Council on Foreign Relations, the informal supra-state Department of the United States. He has been affiliated with the Hudson Institute, one of the Establishment's think factories. He has joined leftist-pacifists on Columbia's faculty to petition for de-escalation of the Vietnam War.

ISAIAH FRANK was born on November 7, 1917 in New York City, son of Rose Isserles and Henry Frank. He is married to Ruth Hershfield. He is an alumnus of the City College of New York (B.S., 1936); the Seminary of the College for Jewish Studies (B.H.L., 1937); and Columbia University (M.A., 1938; Ph.D., 1960). He is the author of *The European Common Market: An Analysis of Commercial Policy* (1961).

From 1936 until 1939, Frank was a research associate in the Council for Research and Social Sciences at Columbia University. From 1939 until 1941, he was a teaching fellow and instructor at Amherst College. In 1941 and 1942, he was a Carnegie fellow at the National Bureau for Economic Research. In 1942, he was a consultant to the War Production Board. From 1942 until 1944, he was a senior economist with the Office of Strategic Services. From 1945 until 1963, he held a variety of positions with the U.S. Department of State. Since 1952, he has been on the faculty of the School of Advanced International Studies of The Johns Hopkins University as a lecturer in international economic problems (1952-1964) and as William L. Clayton professor of international economic relations (1964 to the present). From 1964 until 1967, he held a research grant from the leftist Ford Foundation. Since 1963, he has been a consultant to the Department of State, the Treasury Department, the U.S. Agency for International Development, and the International Bank for Reconstruction and Development. He has also been a member of U.S. delegations to many international conferences on economic matters.

Frank, one of the ruling Establishment's favorite economists, is an advisor to the Committee for Economic Development, the major propaganda arm of the Council on Foreign Relations, in the important work of socializing the American economy. He is a long-time nonresident member of the Council on Foreign Relations, the informal supra-State Department of the United States.

J. WAYNE FREDERICKS was born on February 26, 1917 in Wakarusa, Indiana, son of Flossa Walters and William Fredericks. He married Anne Curtis. He is an alumnus of Purdue University (B.S., 1938).

Between 1938 and 1956, Fredericks was with the Kellogg Company as assistant manager in the foreign manufacturing division (1938-1940, 1946-1951, and 1954-1956). In 1946, he was an analyst in the aircraft division of the U.S. Strategic Bombing Survey in Germany and Japan. From 1951 until 1954, he was employed by the Department of Defense. Between 1956 and the present time, he has been with the ultra-leftist Ford Foundation as program associate for public affairs (1956-1958), associate director for the overseas development program for Asia (1958-1961), and head of the Middle East and African programs (1967 to the present). From 1961 until 1967, he was with the Department of State as deputy assistant secretary of state for African Affairs. He is a long-time nonresident member of the Council on Foreign Relations, the informal supra-State Department of the United States.

ELEANOR FRENCH was born on June 29, 1908 in Philadelphia, Pennsylvania, daughter of Elizabeth Bent and Herbert Clark. She married John French.

She studied at the Sorbonne, Harvard University, and Columbia University.

From 1932 until 1943, Mrs. French was a teacher and supervisor in elementary schools in New York City. From 1943 until 1946, she worked in the Office of Inter-American Affairs. In 1946 and 1947, she worked for the France Unitarian Service Committee. From 1949 until 1955, she was women's editor of the *New York Times.* In 1956, she was an unsuccessful candidate for the New York State Senate. From 1957 until 1960, she was vice-chairman of the New York State Democratic Committee. From 1961 until 1969, she was a member of the New York City Commission on Human Rights. From 1962 until 1966, she was the New York City Commissioner to the United Nations. In 1964, she was a candidate for the U.S. Congress at the Democratic National Convention.

Mrs. French has been affiliated with the leftist-pacifist National Committee for a Sane Nuclear Policy and the ultra-radical Americans for Democratic Action. She has been an official of the Foreign Policy Association, a highly effective pro-Communist vehicle.

GERALD FREUND was born on October 14, 1930 in Berlin, Germany, son of Annelise Josephthal and Kurt Freund. He is a naturalized American. He married Jane Trask. He is an alumnus of Haverford College (B.A., 1952) and Oxford University (Ph.D., 1955). He is the author of *Unholy Alliance: German-Russian Relations, 1917-1926* (1957) and *Germany Between Two Worlds* (1961).

In 1955 and 1956, he was a research fellow in modern history at St. Antony's College of Oxford University. In 1956 and 1957, while holding a Rockefeller grant, he was a research associate in history at the Institute for Advanced Study in Princeton, New Jersey. In 1957 and 1958, he was a Carnegie Research fellow in contemporary affairs at the Council on Foreign Relations in New York City. From 1958 until 1960, he was an assistant professor of political science at Haverford College. Since 1960, he has been with the leftist-liberal Rockefeller Foundation as consultant in the social sciences (1960-1961), assistant director of the social sciences (1961-1964), associate director of the humanities and social sciences (1964 to the present), and associate director of the arts (1965 to the present). In 1959 and 1960, while holding a Rockefeller research grant, he was a consultant to the Washington Center of Foreign Policy Research, a part of the ruling Establishment's circle of influence. Since 1959, he has been a member of the Commission to Study the Organization of Peace, the research arm of the leftist-internationalist United Nations Association of the United States. He is a long-time member of the Council on Foreign Relations, the informal supra-State Department of the United States.

WILLIAM R. FRYE was born on December 15, 1918 in Detroit, son of Anna Ruggles and William Frye. He married Joan Ripperger. He is an alumnus of Harvard University (B.S., 1940). He is the author of *A United Nations Peace Force* (1957) and *In Whitest Africa* (1968). He is a contributor to *Arms Control: Disarmament and National Security* (1961).

Between 1941 and 1963, Frye was with the *Christian Science Monitor* as reporter (1941-1942), copy-reader and assistant to the foreign editor (1946-1950), and United Nations correspondent (1950-1963). Since 1957, he has been director and editor of *World In Focus*, a newspaper syndicate. Since 1963, he has been a diplomatic correspondent and has distributed his own syndicated column.

Frye is a long-time member of the Council on Foreign Relations, the informal supra-State Department of the United States. In his writings, he has been a chronic apologist for the United Nations. As late as 1964, he wrote about Castro as a fellow-traveler. He has always seemed to be an easy mark for Communist propaganda. He has a remarkable faculty for following the pro-Communist line on just about every international issue. And, as might be expected, he is periodically haunted by McCarthyism.

C. DALE FULLER was born on September 24, 1915 in Iroquois, South Dakota, son of Hattie Stoner and Clyde Fuller. He married Ethelyn Goldberg. He is an alumnus of the University of Denver (B.A., 1937; M.A., 1939). He is the author of *Training Specialists in International Relations* (1957).

In 1937 and 1938, Fuller was a high-school teacher in South Dakota. From 1938 until 1959, he was at the University of Denver as instructor in international relations (1938-1942), assistant professor (1946-1950), and chairman of the department of international relations and director of the social science foundation (1953-1959). Since 1959, he has been executive vice president of the Foreign Policy Association. (The Foreign Policy Association has had a long and consistent record of pro-Communism and anti-anti-Communism. It has been a center for pro-Soviet apologists and United Nations propagandists.) From 1950 until 1952, he was a lecturer at Barnard College at Columbia Univer-

sity. In 1951, he was the director of a Russian project for the leftist-oriented National Association of Education Broadcasters. In 1952, he was a researcher in the information and education department of Radio Free Europe. He has worked in radio and on television as an analyst for "Journeys Behind the News," a weekly radio series (1938-1942 and 1946); a moderator of "Focus," a weekly TV series (1953-1959); and a narrator of "20th Century Revolutions in World Affairs," a 1959 TV series.

Fuller is a long-time member of the Council on Foreign Relations, the informal supra-State Department of the United States. He is a member of the leftist-oriented Adult Education Association.

MILTON GALAMISON was born on January 25, 1923 in Philadelphia, Pennsylvania. He is married to Gladys Hunt. He is an alumnus of Lincoln University (B.A., 1945; B.D., 1947) and Princeton Theological Seminary (Th.M., 1949). He was ordained as a Presbyterian minister in 1949.

Since 1949, Galamison has been pastor of the Siloam Presbyterian Church in Brooklyn, New York. In 1956, he began a career as a leftist-racist agitator when he made an unsuccessful attempt to integrate an all-Negro high school in Brooklyn. In 1959, he organized and became chairman of the Parents' Workshop for Equality in New York City Schools. In 1964 and 1965, he organized and led two city-wide school boycotts, during which he demanded racial integration and community control of the schools. In 1964, he was the keynote speaker at the founding convention of the W.E.B. DuBois Clubs, and he urged the Communist-spawned group to work for more sit-ins, stall-ins, and mass demonstrations to hasten the passage of civil rights legislation. Throughout the 1960's, his activity as a racist agitator caused him to be arrested at least nine times during his school demonstrations. In that same period, he was the president of the Brooklyn chapter of the National Association for the Advancement of Colored People, the fountainhead of Negro agitation for more than half a century.

In May 1968, Galamison organized a militant boycott aimed at integrating New York City schools. He took this action as director of the School and Community Organized for Partnership in Education (SCOPE), a group which received $160,000 from the Ford Foundation to finance its racist activities. In July 1968, Galamison was appointed by Mayor John Lindsay to membership on New York City's Board of Education. In October 1968, Galamison was elected vice-president of the board, and from that position a few months later, he advised a group of college students that almost anything they perpetrated in the name of the student revolution was justified.

Galamison has been affiliated with the Southern Conference Educational Fund, the financial backbone of racial agitators, including the "black power" revolutionaries; the Castro-subsidized Fair Play for Cuba Committee; the International Committee to Defend Eldridge Cleaver, dominated by ultra-leftists; the Student Mobilization Committee to End the War in Vietnam, dominated by Communists and fellow-travelers; and the Stockholm Peace Appeal, a Communist campaign. Despite Galamison's notorious leftist-racist background, he was hired in 1969 by Harvard University to organize an urban studies program for the university's graduate school of education.

RAYMOND L. GARTHOFF was born on March 26, 1929 in Cairo, Egypt, son of Margaret Frank and Arnold Garthoff. He married Vera Vasilieva. He is an alumnus of Princeton University (A.B., 1948) and Yale University (M.A., 1949; Ph.D., 1951). He is the author of *Soviet Military Doctrine* (1953); *Soviet Strategy in the Nuclear Age* (1958 and 1962); *The Soviet Image of Future War* (1959); *Soviet Military Policy: An Historical Analysis* (1965); *Sino-Soviet Military Relations* (1966); and *The Military-Technical Revolution* (1966). He is a contributor to *The Red Army* (1956); *The Soviet Air and Rocket Forces* (1959); *The Impact of Air Power* (1959); *The Transformation of Russian Society Since 1881* (1960); *Total War and Cold War: Problems in Civilian Control of the Military* (1962); *Russian Foreign Policy: Essays in Historical Perspective* (1962); *Military Strategy* (1963); *Communism and Revolution* (1963); and *Foreign Policy in the Sixties* (1965). He has translated and edited *Science and Technology in Contemporary War* (1959). He has contributed articles to *Foreign Affairs, Saturday Review, Reporter, Russian Review, World Politics,* and *Encyclopaedia Britannica.*

From 1950 until 1957, Garthoff was a Soviet affairs analyst in the social science division of the RAND Corporation, one of the most important think factories in the ruling liberal-leftist Establishment. From 1957 until 1961, he was a foreign affairs adviser in the Department of the Army. From 1961 until 1968, he was a special assistant on Soviet bloc political-military affairs in the Department of State. Since 1968, he has been a counselor for political-military affairs with the U.S. Mission to NATO in Belgium. In 1962 and 1964, he was a member of the U.S. delegation to the perennial disarmament conference in Geneva. From 1962 until 1964, he was a professorial lecturer at George Washington University's Institute of Sino-Soviet studies. He has lectured at the U.S. National War College, the U.S. Army War College, the U.S. Air Force College, the Foreign Service Institute, the Canadian National Defense College, and The Johns Hopkins University's School of Advanced International Studies. He is a long-time nonresident member of the Council on Foreign Relations.

JOHN GERASSI was born on July 12, 1931 in Paris, France, son of Stepha Awdykowicz and Fernando Gerassi. He married Marysa Navarro. He is an alumnus of Lycée Francais de New York (Baccalauréat ès Lettres, 1949; Baccalauréat ès Philosophie, 1950) and Columbia University (B.A., 1952; M.A., 1954). He is the author of *The Great Fear* (1963), reissued as *The Great Fear in Latin America* (1965); *The Boys of Boise: Furor, Vice, and Folly in an American City* (1966); and *North Vietnam: A Documentary* (1968). He is the editor of Che' Guevara's *Venceremos!* (1968). He has written for the Communist weekly, *National Guardian*. He has contributed articles to the leftist *New Republic*. He has been a contributing editor on Latin American affairs for the ultra-leftist *Ramparts* magazine. He has written for the pro-Communist *Monthly Review*.

From 1956 until 1961, Gerassi was an art critic for *Time* magazine, but he was dismissed from the staff because of his pro-Castro sentiments. In 1961 and 1962, he was a Latin American correspondent for the *New York Times*. In 1963, he taught French philosophy at Windham College in Vermont. From 1964 until 1966, he was a Latin Ameri-

can editor for *Newsweek* magazine. In 1966 and 1967, he taught journalism at New York University. In this same period, he taught a course ("Latin America – the Next Vietnam") at the leftist Free School of New York. While associated with the Free School, he sponsored the Spring Mobilization Committee, which waged a massive leftist demonstration against the war in Vietnam. In 1967 and 1968, he was at San Francisco State College teaching the course, "Nationalism and Revolution in the Third World." In December 1967, he led a chaotic and militant student demonstration at San Francisco State College. As a consequence, he was suspended from his teaching duties. During the course of his suspension, he spent some time in Puerto Rico at a Peace Corps training center where he encouraged the trainees to resign and return home to aid the student revolution.

In 1968, when Gerassi's edition of *Venceremos!* was published, the weekly *Human Events* commented: "The reputable Macmillan publishing company has come under heavy fire from veteran anti-Communists in the Nation's Capital. What has aroused their wrath is the way in which the company has given a sort of 'moral glow' to Communist revolutionary 'Che' Guevara in a new book, *Venceremos!,* edited by John Gerassi.

"In discussing Che', the book jacket claims that he 'stands alone . . . as a revolutionary, for his prime concern was non-nationalistic. He was for the oppressed everywhere.'

"The book jacket never once states that Guevara was a Communist, that he devoted his life to terroristic tactics or that his ideology has helped to enslave rather than liberate millions of people. On the contrary, this leading advocate of murder on an international scale is only described in romantic terms.

"The back of the jacket is also misleading regarding editor Gerassi. Termed an 'expert on Latin American affairs' who 'teaches Nationalism and Revolution in the Third World' at San Francisco State College, Gerassi, according to Macmillan, has edited an 'authoritative and moving book.'

"Gerassi, however, is more than just an interested observer of Che' Guevara. He is part of a guerrilla warfare-oriented group called Revolutionary Contingent, an openly Communist organization with headquarters in New York City. The contingent, according to the House Committee on Un-American Activities, 'calls for "guerrilla action" in the United States and for volunteers to serve with Communist guerrillas in other nations.'

"Gerassi is also an adviser to the Radical Education Project of the Students for a Democratic Society; served as director of the U.S. branch of the Bertrand Russell International War Crimes Tribunal which accused the U.S. of genocide in Viet Nam; and is a sponsor of the draft resistance movement.

"No one faults Macmillan for bringing out some of the writings of Che' Guevara, a leading revolutionary figure of the times. But there is much condemnation of the company for camouflaging the true character of both Guevara and editor Gerassi."

Gerassi has spoken under the auspices of the Militant Labor Forum, which is run by the Socialist Workers Party, a Trotskyist-Communist organization. He has been affiliated with the leftist-pacifist American Friends Service Committee; the leftist-pacifist Ad Hoc Committee of Veterans for Peace in Vietnam; the leftist Committee to Aid Activists;

the ultra-leftist National Mobilization Committee to End the War in Vietnam; the North American Congress on Latin America, a radical research group; and the radical New School for Social Research. He participated in the leftist-oriented 1967 teach-ins at the University of Michigan. He has been affiliated with Tri-Continental Information Center, which is a mouth-piece for Latin American guerrillas, the Viet Cong, and the Havana-based Tri-Continental Organization.

KENNETH GIBSON was born on May 15, 1932 in Enterprise, Alabama. He has been married and divorced. He has a second wife at the present time. He is an alumnus of the Newark College of Engineering (B.S., 1963).

After graduating from high school, Gibson worked in factories, spent two years in the Army, worked for the New Jersey State Highway Department, and studied for his degree in civil engineering at night. In 1963, he went to work for the Newark Housing Authority as a licensed engineer. He was active in the ultra-radical National Association for the Advancement of Colored People.

In 1966, Gibson was an unsuccessful candidate for Mayor of Newark. In 1970, he ran again and this time was elected as an independent to a four-year term as Newark's Mayor. In the 1970 campaign, he was supported by the militant-racist Black and Puerto Rican Convention. He was also supported by the New Ark Fund, a group led by the racist-militant playwright Le-Roi Jones, who now calls himself Imamu Amiri Baraki. When Gibson became the first-elected black mayor of a major Eastern city, the event was hailed by the Communists in the *Daily World*. Gibson, however, has described himself as a liberal, only a "nominal" Democrat, and a supporter of the late U.S. Senator Robert F. Kennedy. He was also a follower of the arch agitator Martin Luther King Jr.

In Gibson's first year as mayor, his administration was plagued by an 11-week teachers' strike. During the course of the strike, Gibson found himself opposed by his erstwhile supporter, LeRoi Jones. Jones, who has amassed a following of militant racists, exploited the racial differences which became most evident during the course of the strike. As a result, Jones vis-à-vis Gibson gained control of Newark's Board of Education at the expense of Newark's Teachers Union. Jones has advised his fellow blacks: "We must make it our world, man, and we cannot do this unless the white man is dead."

Gibson has suffered further defeats at the hands of Jones, who has gained virtual control of the Newark Housing Authority and of Newark's anti-poverty program, which is financed by the federal government. While the "liberal" Gibson has steadily compromised and retreated in the face of Jones's militant opposition, whites have fled from Newark to the suburbs.

WILLIAM J. GOODE was born on August 30, 1917 in Houston, Texas, son of Lillian Bare and William Goode. He was married to and divorced from Josephine Cannizzo. He is married to Ruth Siegel. He is an alumnus of the University of Texas (B.A., 1938; M.A., 1939) and Pennsylvania State University (Ph.D., 1946). He is the author of *Religion Among the Primitives* (1951); *Methods In Social Research* (1952); *After Divorce* (1956); *World Revolution and Family Patterns* (1963); *The Family* (1964); *Family and Society* (1965); and *Dynamics of Modern Society* (1966).

From 1941 until 1943, Goode was a sociology instructor at Pennsylvania State College. In 1943 and 1944, he was a social science analyst at the Inter-American Statistical Institute. From 1946 until 1950, he was an assistant professor of sociology at Wayne State University. Since 1950, he has been at Columbia University as associate research director (1950-1952), associate professor (1952-1956), and professor (1956 to the present). In 1954, he was a visiting professor at the Free University of Berlin. In 1965 and 1966, he was a Guggenheim fellow. In 1963, he was a U.S. delegate to the United Nations Conference on Aid to Technically Underdeveloped Nations.

Goode has been an official of the leftist-oriented Social Science Research Council, the Bureau of Applied Social Research, and the Sociological Research Association. He has been affiliated with the National Committee to Abolish the House Un-American Activities Committee ("to lead and direct the Communist Party's 'Operation Abolition' campaign"). He is a member of the ultra-leftist American Civil Liberties Union.

CARLTON B. GOODLETT is a Negro physician and surgeon in San Francisco. He has been a director of the ultra-leftist magazine, *Ramparts.* He is publisher of the *Sun-Reporter,* a daily newspaper which reports on the Negro community in the San Francisco area. (The *Sun-Reporter* regularly prints pronouncements of Communist Party leaders and press releases of Communist fronts.)

For more than twenty-five years, Goodlett, who holds M.D. and Ph.D. degrees, has been one of the most vocal and active leftists in the San Francisco area. He has been affiliated with the Committee for Peaceful Alternatives to the Atlantic Pact ("Communist front" – "part of Soviet psychological warfare against the United States"); the Civil Rights Congress ("subversive and Communist"); the National Council of the Arts, Sciences and Professions ("Communist front used to appeal to special occupational groups"); the Independent Progressive Party ("one of the largest and most successful fronts ever created by the Communists"); the National Negro Labor Council ("a Communist front" - "formed to provoke racial friction"); California Labor School ("a subversive and Communist organization"); the Southern Negro Youth Congress ("subversive" – "Communist front"); American Peace Crusade ("Communist front"); the Council on African Affairs ("subversive and Communist"); Fidel Castro's Fair Play for Cuba Committee; the American Russian Institute ("Communist organization"); the Mid-Century Conference for Peace ("aimed at assembling as many gullible persons as possible under Communist direction and turning them into a vast sounding board for Communist propaganda"); the Emergency Conference Committee, an ultra-leftist call to .the United Nations to impose sanctions against the United States until the United States ratifies the Genocide Treaty; the ultra-leftist Socialist Youth Conference of 1964; the National Committee to Abolish the Un-American Activities Committee ("to lead and direct the Communist Party's 'Operation Abolition' campaign"); the Tri-Continental Information Center, a mouthpiece for Latin American guerrillas, the Viet Cong, and the Havana-based Tri-Continental Organization; the ultra-radical National Association for the Advancement of Colored People; the ultra-leftist American-Korean Friendship and Information Center; the American Committee for Protection of Foreign Born [Americans] ("one of the oldest auxiliaries of the Communist Party in the United States"); the leftist American Committee on Africa; the Aptheker Dinner Program, honoring the chief theoretician of the Communist Party and the second anniversary of the American Institute for Marxist Studies; the American People's Congress and Exposition for Peace ("Communist front"); the leftist Bay Area Committee for the Vietnam Advertisement; the ultra-leftist National Mobilization Committee to End the War in Vietnam; the Sidney Roger Radio Fund, sponsoring a Communist Party radio commentator; the ultra-leftist United Front against Fascism; the United States Festival Committee for the Communist-operated World Youth Festival; Fidel Castro's Medical Aid to Cuba Committee; the ultra-leftist Community for New Politics in Berkeley, California; the ultra-leftist Soledad Brothers Defense Committee; the Hemispheric Conference to End the Vietnam War of 1968, run by the Communist Party; the ultra-leftist Freedom Now Committee; the National Conference for New Politics, a classic united-front third-party movement largely controlled by the Communist Party; the ultra-leftist Friends of the Panthers; the ultra-leftist Peace and Freedom Party; the National Assembly for Democratic Rights ("created, dominated, and controlled by members and officials of the Communist Party"); the Civil Rights Congress ("subversive and Communist"); the People's Peace Treaty, a Hanoi-inspired project carried out by the extreme left in America; the ultra-leftist Huey Newton Defense Fund; and the National Committee to Secure Justice in the Rosenberg Case ("Communist front").

Goodlett is a long-time official of the World Council of Peace, a Communist-financed and directed operation based in Vienna and Helsinki. He has attended conferences of the World Council of Peace in Moscow, Prague, East Berlin, Bucharest, Cyprus, Stockholm, Africa, British Columbia, and Budapest. The gatherings are generally devoted to all-out attacks upon the United States and, in recent years, especially United States involvement in the Vietnam War. When the Soviet invasion of Czecho-Slovakia took place, the WCP issued an apologia, explaining that the invasion was necessary because anti-socialist forces were growing strong in Czecho-Slovakia and there was a resurgence of neo-Nazism in West Germany. Goodlett was one of the few Americans to endorse the apologia. (In 1968, Goodlett was deported from England as undesirable because of his work with the World Council of Peace.)

In 1968 and 1969, Goodlett was a major instigator of the student riots at San Francisco State College. He denied at the time that he was interested in becoming president of the College: "It would be impossible for a militant man of my radical background to work under a college board of trustees dominated by Ronald Reagan and Max Rafferty." While the riots were in progress, he warned: "If police continue to beat people unmercifully, we'll be forced to go to the Negro community and we will bring guns on campus to protect ourselves."

In 1971, while en route to a World Council of Peace meeting in Budapest, Goodlett was in a small American delegation that met in Paris with officials of North Vietnam to plot and discuss anti-Vietnam war activities in the United States.

In recent years, Goodlett has been very close to the militant Black Panthers in the San Francisco area. He was one of the most influential and prominent participants in the organizing conference of the Panthers' United Front Against Fascism.

In 1971, Goodlett emerged as a leader in the ultra-leftist drive against Gulf Oil Corporation. The pretext for the drive is "to combat prejudice and racism" and to expose Gulf Oil's "covert and insensitive role" in supporting "fascist regimes such as Portugal and South Africa" in their "oppression of the indigenous people who form the national liberation movements of Angola, Mozambique, and South Africa."

Goodlett purchased five shares of stock in Gulf Oil. He attended a stockholders meeting on April 27, 1971 in Atlanta, Georgia. He was ejected from the meeting, but not before delivering a racist diatribe that hewed to the Communist line throughout: "Mr. Chairman, it is apropos to paraphrase the statement of a young black army inductee headed for the hell-hole of Vietnam who said, 'Why should black people and chicanos sacrifice their lives ten thousand miles from home, foolishly killing yellow men with whom they have no quarrel, for racist white America, when America, to which I'll be returning, will remain the same old hell-hole with business as usual and racism as usual?'

"The United States of America continues to be a polarized country composed of two nations, one white and one black, both separate and becoming daily more unequal. The black population ranges between 23 and 25 million persons, with an estimated gross product of $45 billion per year, 4.5 per cent of the nation's total $1 trillion. In many metropolitan areas where a number of our stations are located, blacks comprise from 80 to 90 per cent of the population; and upon a cursory survey, contribute substantially to the gross revenues of our corporation.

"Despite the fact that blacks have perennially patronized Gulf service stations, the policy of Gulf Oil Corporation has not been one of reciprocal response to the needs of the black community for jobs and advertising in its community newspapers, so as to reflect our corporation's appreciation of its responsibility in a free economy to observe, on one hand, fair and equitable employment policies and, on the other, fair and equitable expenditure of advertising dollars.

"The insensitivity of corporate enterprise to its responsibility to obey fair employment laws is amazing and in many instances distressing. We readily condemn the felon who violates the law; however, is a corporation which violates fair employment statutes less guilty and is not the violence which the corporation inflicts upon the hopes and aspirations of non-whites as grave to society as the deeds of the felon who robs and steals? Racism is a disease which will destroy the human personality; and similarly, institutional racism will destroy a great nation.

"We are demanding full equity in the employment of women and racial minorities, with no differential in salary or opportunities for upgrading because of covert forms of discrimination.

"It is regrettable that Gulf Oil Corporation is one of America's 50 largest corporations with in excess of 2,500 top executive positions, none of which are filled by a single black person.

"The fair employment practices statutes demand that there shall be no discrimination in employment based upon race, color, creed, sex or age: racial minorities, especially blacks, chicanos and oriental Americans, and also women, be integrated in all job categories of Gulf Oil Corporation, from the Board of Directors room all the way down to the janitor's closet. This, we believe, Gulf Oil Corporation has failed to do. Moreover, the conditions cited for the black population reflect similar forms of covert institutionalized racism practiced against chicano and oriental Americans.

"For the past quarter of a century, blacks have patronized our service stations; the response of Gulf Oil has not been reciprocal to the black community's needs, by providing sustained advertising in the black community newspaper so as to reflect our awareness of the responsibility to allocate an equitable expenditure of our advertising dollars to the community which contributes to our profits. The black community cannot develop a viable press as long as corporations such as Gulf continue to practice a policy of discrimination and insensitivity to the black community's demands for a proportionate share of Gulf Oil Corporation's advertising dollars.

"It is the right of every black purchaser to demand that promotional money derived from black customers be returned to the black community, so that the black nation may maintain a black-owned communications media which reflects its $45 billion purchasing power.

"No person in this meeting will accept personal responsibility for the discrimination which Gulf Oil Corporation practices upon black Americans in job opportunities and allocation of advertising dollars. However our continued silence and inaction on these problems represent a silent conspiracy against the constitutional mandate of freedom, equality and justice.

"To rectify these wrongs three recommendations are made in the form of motions: 1. That management be instructed to issue within the next 6 months a full report to our stockholders of its distribution of employees based upon race and sex, delineating policies of promotion in the main job categories. 2. That stockholders be given a report on the expenditure of advertising dollars in both the white and the black press. 3. That a stockholders' fair employment and fair advertising committee be appointed to assess the data and recommend to management a remedial program in fair employment and fair advertising, which will allow our corporation to lead the oil industry in meeting the serious challenges of the crisis-threatening '70's.

"One of the important purposes of this annual meeting of stockholders is the election of 10 directors. Inspection of the roster of officers and directors of our company reveals that those who have selected the 10 nominees to serve as directors until the next annual meeting of stockholders remain either uninformed or unconcerned about two of the most important and controversial issues now threatening the corporate tranquility: (1) the lack of women in the management and direction of private enterprise, and (2) the lack of opportunities provided members of racial minorities; notably black Americans, Chicano Americans and Oriental Americans, to participate meaningfully in the process of distillation so necessary for the development of the new directional thrust required of corporate enterprise in a nation polarized by social revolution.

"First, let us consider the question of participation by women in our operation and management. One of the most discriminated-against groups in our society happens to be women. The majority of stockholders in all U.S. business enterprises are female, and I doubt that Gulf Oil Corporation differs from the national pattern. Male chauvinism is the cause of Gulf's failure to utilize more women in operation and management.

"Now let us consider the matter of racial minority participation in operation and management, a question which daily becomes more crucial. We live in a society which is being destroyed by racism, and our company is a microcosm reflecting that society. We must begin, at the highest level of operation and management, by deeds and not words alone, to end discrimination based upon both sex and race. One of the great obstacles to racial harmony in the Nation is the refusal on the part of private enterprise to recognize the genius and skills of the racial minorities. Black Americans have a unique contribution to make in the thrust that private enterprise must create if peace and tranquility are to be restored in the revolutionary social upheaval now threatening the Nation.

" . . . A grave question disturbs many stockholders of our company: namely, the covert and insensitive role it plays in supporting Fascist regimes such as Portugal and South Africa, particularly the former, in their oppression of the indigenous people who form the national liberation movements of Angola, Mozambique and South Africa. If racial minorities and women were members of the policy-making boards of our company, we believe that Gulf would more adequately recognize its international responsibilities, and refrain from being a party, overtly or covertly, to the support of racists who build and maintain colonial empires and thwart the will of millions of people of color throughout the world to throw off the yoke of white U.S. imperialism.

"As an initial effort to correct the inequities of representation on our boards of directors, which reflect male chauvinism and racism, I nominate two additional persons as directors of our company.

"Mrs. Aileen Hernandez, the female nominee, is a free-lance business consultant and lecturer on urban affairs. Mrs. Hernandez is the new president of the National Organization of Women, a civil rights group formed in October, 1966, to bring women into the mainstream of American life 'in truly equal partnership with men.' Professionally, Mrs. Hernandez has advised business, labor, government and private groups on programs for utilizing the talents of minority groups and women, and assuring these groups full access to education, housing and employment opportunities. She has served as deputy director, California fair employment practices commission, and as commissioner, U.S. equal employment opportunity commission. Among many civic and political affiliations, she serves in the Urban League, the American Civil Liberties Union, steering committee of the National Urban Coalition, and Board of Directors of San Francisco Mount Zion Hospital.

"Willie L. Brown, Jr., Esq., attorney at law, state assemblyman 18th district, San Francisco, is the second nominee. Mr. Brown is a distinguished Californian who is a member of the San Francisco black community, a graduate of San Francisco State College, 1956, and the Hastings College of Law, 1958. He presently serves as chairman of the Ways and Means Committee in the California Assembly. His legislative interests include employment opportunities, civil rights and liberties, conservation and ecological issues, consumer protection and criminal law reform.

"Mr. Chairman, in the belief that the election of these two distinguished Americans to such positions of importance will be beneficial to our company, these two names: Mrs. Aileen Hernandez and Willie L. Brown, Jr., Esq., are submitted as nominees for the board of directors. We are being judged, by both women and blacks, not for our platitudinous statements but for our deeds."

LELAND GOODRICH was born on September 1, 1899 in Lewiston, Maine, son of Alice Tibbetts and Fred Goodrich. He is married to Eleanor Allen. He is an alumnus of Bowdoin College (A.B., 1920) and Harvard University (A.M., 1921; Ph.D., 1925). He also studied at the University of Brussels. He is author of *Korea: A Study of United States Policy in the United Nations* (1956) and *The United Nations* (1959). He is co-author of *Charter of the United Nations: Commentary and Documents* (1949); *The United Nations and the Maintenance of International Peace and Security* (1955); and *The United Nations in the Balance* (1965). He is the co-editor of *Documents on American Foreign Relations* (1942-1947).

In 1922 and 1923, Goodrich was an instructor in political science at Brown University. In 1925 and 1926, he was an instructor in government and law at Lafayette College. From 1926 until 1950, he was at Brown University as assistant professor of political science (1926-1931), associate professor (1931-1946), and professor (1946-1950). Since 1950, he has been at Columbia University as professor of international organization and administration (1950-1967), acting chairman of the department of public law and government (1965-1966), and a James T. Shotwell professor of international relations

(1967 to the present). In 1949 and 1950, he was a visiting lecturer in government at Harvard University. From 1943 until 1950, he held the rank of professor of international organization and administration in the Fletcher School of Law and Diplomacy. In 1948 and 1949, he was a visiting professor in the School of International Affairs at Columbia University.

Goodrich has been director and trustee of the World Peace Foundation, which exerts considerable influence upon the Department of State, the Department of Defense, and the Central Intelligence Agency in an over-all program of appeasement toward the Soviet Union. He has been affiliated with the Foreign Policy Association, a highly effective pro-Communist vehicle. He is a long-time member of the Council on Foreign Relations, the informal supra-State Department of the United States. He is a member of the United Nations Association of the United States, the most prestigious leftwing propaganda agency for the UN in this country.

KERMIT GORDON was born on July 3, 1916 in Philadelphia, Pennsylvania, son of Ida Robinson and H.B. Gordon. He married Mary Grinnell. He is an alumnus of Swarthmore College (B.A., 1938). In 1938 and 1939, he was a Rhodes scholar at Oxford University.

In 1939 and 1940, Gordon was a research associate in economics at Swarthmore College. In 1940 and 1941, he was an administration fellow at Harvard University. From 1941 until 1943, he was an economist with the Office of Price Administration. In 1945 and 1946, he was a special assistant to the Assistant Secretary of State for Economic Affairs. From 1946 until 1962, he was on the faculty at Williams College as assistant

professor and associate professor (1946-1955), professor of economics (1955-1962), and the David A. Wells professor of political economy (1961-1962). From 1962 until 1965, he was director of the Bureau of the Budget in the Kennedy-Johnson Administration. Since 1965, he has been with the Brookings Institution as vice-president (1965-1967) and president (1967 to the present). (Brookings Institution is a unique "think factory" which has influenced international trends in the federal government for the past fifty years.)

Gordon has long been affiliated with the ultra-leftist Ford Foundation as an executive associate (1956-1957), as director of the program for economic development and administration (1960-1961), and as a trustee (1967 to the present). Since 1967, he has been a nonresident member of the Council on Foreign Relations, the informal supra-State Department of the United States. He is a trustee of the Committee for Economic Development, the major propaganda arm of the Council on Foreign Relations, in the important work of socializing the American economy. He is a member of the ultra-leftist American Civil Liberties Union.

MARILYN GORLIN was born on March 27, 1925 in New York City, daughter of Henrietta Nathanson and Milton Alpern. She married Robert Gorlin. She is an alumna of Adelphi College (B.A., 1945). She also studied at the Ethical Culture School and the State University of Iowa.

In 1945 and 1946, Mrs. Gorlin was an editorial assistant in the education department of the National Foundation for Infantile Paralysis. From 1946 until 1952, she was an assistant story editor for Warner Brothers Pictures. She was a delegate to the 1964 Democratic National Convention. From 1962 until 1968, she was vice-chairwoman of the leftist-oriented Democrat-Farmer-Labor Party of Minnesota.

Mrs. Gorlin is a member of the ultra-leftist American Civil Liberties Union; the ultra-radical Americans for Democratic Action; and the National Association for the Advancement of Colored People, the fountainhead of Negro agitation for more than half a century.

ALEX GOTTFRIED was born on October 23, 1919 in Also-Zsolca, Hungary, son of Charlotte Braun and David Gottfried. He is a naturalized American. He married Sue Davidson. He is an alumnus of Chicago Teachers College (Ed.B., 1941) and the University of Chicago (A.M., 1948; Ph.D., 1952). He also studied at Central College in Chicago, Northwestern University, and the University of California. In 1947 and 1948, he was a Morton scholar. In 1949 and 1950, he was a Walgreen fellow. In 1951 and 1952, he was a Ford Foundation fellow. He received scholarship grants from the University of Washington (1953-1954; 1954-1955; 1961), Agnes Anderson (1959), the Citizenship Clearing House (1956-1959), the Eagleton Foundation (1960), and the Ford Foundation (1961). He is the author of *Boss Cermak of Chicago: A Study in Political Leadership* (1962). He is a contributor to *Political Behavior* (1956).

In 1948 and 1949, Gottfried was a lecturer in political science at the University of Chicago. From 1950 until 1960, he was an assistant professor at the University of Washington. In 1960 and 1961, he was an assistant professor at Stanford University. Since 1961, he has been an associate professor in political science at the University of Washington.

Gottfried has participated in the Educators Appeal to the American People, a leftist effort against the war in Vietnam. He has been a member of the leftist-pacifist Teachers Committee for Peace in Vietnam. He has been a member of the leftist-pacifist Ad Hoc Faculty Committee on Vietnam. He has been affiliated with the leftist-oriented American Association of University Professors. He has been a sponsor of the National Committee to Abolish the House Un-American Activities Committee ("to lead and direct the Communist Party's 'Operation Abolition' campaign"). He has been an official of the ultra-radical American Civil Liberties Union of Washington.

SANFORD GOTTLIEB was born on September 17, 1926 in Brooklyn. He married Gladys Blumenthal. He is an alumnus of Dartmouth College (B.A., 1946) and the University of Paris (D. Soc., 1952).

From 1955 until 1960, Gottlieb was a labor organizer and editor of labor publications. He worked in New York, West Virginia, Iowa, and Washington, D.C. In 1957, he was an original sponsor of the newspaper advertisement which led to the formation of the ultra-leftist-pacifist National Committee for a Sane Nuclear Policy. Since 1960, he has been SANE's political action director. (He has said: "I wouldn't call myself a pacifist. I've made no moral or religious commitment to avoid violence. But I do believe in peace as the only rational sort of existence. And I think of it as a positive, concrete state of affairs which must be constructed deliberately and thoughtfully, and deliberately maintained.")

On November 23, 1965, Fulton Lewis Jr. said on his "Top of the News" radio program: "Security officials report that he [Gottlieb] has, on a number of occasions since 1959, been in contact with officials of the Soviet embassy and with officials of various other Soviet bloc countries. He toured the Soviet Union during the summer of 1964 . . . ." In 1965, he went to Paris where he met and exchanged views with representatives of the North Vietnamese Government and the Viet Cong. In March 1966, he made similar exchanges in Paris and Algiers. After each visit with the enemy, he shared with the State Department his impressions of Communist viewpoints, and in public he became an abject apologist for the Hanoi regime and the Viet Cong. He was ever quick to criticize the United States as the unilateral barrier to peace.

In 1965, Gottlieb organized the "March on Washington for Peace in Vietnam." In his recruiting pitch for marches Gottlieb said: "We see no gain coming from the war in Vietnam. We see only the growing victimization of the Vietnamese people, the erosion of a better society at home and the clear possibility of a world conflict. Caught between terror, torture and the senseless use of force, the Vietnamese people have seen their land turned into a bloody testing ground by the Viet Cong, the Saigon Government, by the North Vietnamese and the United States.

"Caught between a commitment to eradicate racial injustice and poverty at home and a growing involvement in an Asian land war, the Johnson Administration will inevitably turn its resources and energies toward the military conflict.

"Caught in a competition for the loyalties of the poorest nations, the Soviet Union and China will seek to prove their militancy by aiding North Vietnam, thus increasing the chances of a direct clash with the United States.

"We seek to end this war. We affirm that no party to the conflict, the U.S. included, has done all it can to bring about negotiations and since the war will ultimately end at the conference table, we ask new actions to speed that day. We affirm our support for all the efforts including those of the United Nations Secretary General U Thant and Pope Paul to bring the dispute to the conference table, and we welcome a wider role for the United Nations in bringing about negotiations and in implementing any agreement. We recognize that the U.S. cannot negotiate an end to the war by itself, but we believe there are things our government could do, which it has left undone, that could lead more quickly to negotiations. And we believe we can help build the public understanding through which our government can vigorously pursue the path of peace.

"Toward the goal of a negotiated settlement in Vietnam we ask that our government call for a cease-fire, and to this end: halt the bombing of North Vietnam; halt the introduction of additional men and materiel, and ask the other side to do the same. We ask that our government state the conditions under which it will accept peace in Vietnam, and to this end: reiterate U.S. support for the principles of the 1954 Geneva accords, the eventual withdrawal of all foreign military forces, a prohibition against military alliances, the peaceful reunification of Vietnam and self-determination for the Vietnamese people; declare U.S. acceptance of negotiations with all concerned parties including the Viet Cong, a primary combatant; declare U.S. agreement to constitution of a representative new government in South Vietnam as part of the settlement; declare U.S. support for U.N. or other international machinery and guarantees to supervise the cease-fire, provide for peaceful establishment of a new government in South Vietnam, protect the rights of minority groups, and protect the neutrality of North and South Vietnam."

Gottlieb managed to recruit an impressive number of leftist, pacifist and/or radical organizations for his march, including the Congress of Racial Equality, the Student Nonviolent Coordinating Committee, the Women's International League for Peace and Freedom, Women Strike for Peace, the Committee to Aid the National Liberation Front of South Vietnam, Students for a Democratic Society, the W.E.B. DuBois Clubs, and the May 2nd Movement. The nation's most notable leftists joined Gottlieb's march. They included Coretta King, Benjamin Spock, Dana Greeley, Norman Thomas, James Farmer, Edwin Dahlberg, Carl Oglesby, Dagmar Wilson, Dorothy Hutchinson, and W.H. (Ping) Ferry. More than 20,000 marchers participated in Gottlieb's spectacle. There were many inflammatory placards and Viet Cong flags in evidence.

Gottlieb has not confined his activist interests to SANE. He has been affiliated with the leftist-pacifist National Council to Repeal the Draft; the leftist-pacifist Voters Peace Pledge; the leftist-pacifist Turn Toward Peace; the leftist-pacifist National Coalition for a Responsible Congress; the ultra-leftist National Mobilization Committee to End the War in Vietnam; the leftist-dominated Poor People's Campaign; and the Norman Thomas 80th Birthday Committee in a tribute to the patriarch of the Socialist Party. In 1967 and 1968, he supported the candidacy of the leftist-pacifist Eugene McCarthy. After McCarthy's unsuccessful campaign, Gottlieb joined the New Democratic Coalition within the Democratic Party, working to achieve leftist goals.

JESSE GRAY was born on May 14, 1923 in Tunica, Louisiana. He married Rosa Lee Brown. He attended Xavier College in New Orleans and Southern University in Baton Rouge.

In 1960, Albert Gaillard testified before the House Committee on Un-American Activities. Gaillard said that in 1957, he had been recruited into the Communist Party by Jesse Gray, whom he knew as the Communist Party's regional organizer for Harlem. He testified further that Gray had collected his party dues and had taught him Marxism-Leninism. He said that on the morning of his testimony he encountered Gray, who threatened: "If you don't take the Fifth, you will be in pretty bad shape in the Harlem community." Gray was called to testify and he invoked the Fifth Amendment twenty times when questioned about his Communist Party activities.

In 1952, Gray joined the Harlem Tenants Council. In 1956, he organized the Lower Harlem Tenants Council, which was later renamed the Community Council for Housing. It was Gray's ambition to organize every tenant building in Harlem. Each building would have a tenants' committee and the committee was expected to call a rent strike whenever it deemed that housing laws were being flagrantly ignored by the landlord. The committee would collect the rents of the tenants during the course of the strike and place the rents in an escrow account in a bank until the strike ended. Gray hoped that tenant-strikes would force the city government to seize tenement buildings under receivership, with the result that massive programs of federal, state, and municipal financing would rehabilitate Harlem.

In the 1950's, when Gray entered upon this "humanitarian" project, he was merely exploiting Harlemites for his chief purpose – recruitment for the Communist Party. In 1951, he was a delegate to the Communist-operated World Peace Congress. In 1952, he was vice-chairman of the Communist Party's United May Day Committee. In 1952, he was campaign manager for Benjamin Davis, a Communist leader who was seeking election to the New York State Assembly, and in 1958, he served again as campaign manager for Benjamin Davis.

In 1963, Gray led a massive rent strike in Harlem. The strike, although unsuccessful, brought Gray a great deal of national publicity. In 1964, Gray played a major part in the Harlem race riots. During the course of the riots he was a featured speaker at a rally in Harlem, where he called for a hundred men willing to fight and die in a crusade against "police brutality." He told his audience: "There is only one thing that can correct the situation, and that is guerrilla warfare." In December 1964, Gray was the keynote speaker at the Federation for Independent Political Action's first conference on "The Black Revolution – A Struggle for Political Power." Said Gray: "We should not confuse our being all black with the whole concept that if every time we meet we do not have someone white present, we are therefore anti-white. I think we have to make this very clear. Every ethnic group in this country meets together; there is the American Jewish Congress, and there is no question that all Jews meet; there is no question that all Italians meet .... If we need to discuss politics with [the Mayor] we therefore speak from the point of view of the bloc of the black people of the ghetto. Just as the Italians do when they meet in their Italian-American organiza-

tions, or the Irish in their Irish-American organizations, or the Jews in the American Jewish Congress. They to some degree examine what is needed by their groups and as a joint body or power body meet and put forward their demands."

Gray reminded his audience: "The lack of unified, organized black political power is one reason we are not yet a revolutionary movement. Another is that we require revolutionaries. Real revolutionaries are out in the streets organizing people around their day-to-day problems."

In 1964, when Gray was making his inflammatory remarks to the Federation for Independent Political Action, he was associated with ACT, a civil rights agitation group. In 1965, he became the chairman of the Organization for Black Power, the political arm of ACT, and there was little doubt that Gray had achieved recognition as one of the leading spokesmen of the black agitators in Harlem. When Malcolm X, the black nationalist leader, was slain, Gray caused merchants all along Harlem's main thoroughfare – 125th Street – to close their stores for two days in a show of respect for Malcolm X. Gray warned the storekeepers that they would face a boycott unless they obeyed his suggestion. Gray publicly stated that the murder of Malcolm X could be rightfully blamed upon the white power structure and the Central Intelligence Agency. Gray caused leaflets to be distributed which said: "We know this killing was ordered by the white power structure. The assassination of brother Malcolm X comes as one more violent act of terror and intimidation against militant and uncompromising black leaders."

In 1966, Gray made the headlines again when he was arrested during the course of a tumultuous sit-down demonstration at New York City's city hall. At the very time he was instigating the demonstrations, he was on the payroll of the federally financed Mobilization for Youth as an expert consultant. In September 1966, Gray was a prominent delegate to a black power meeting held under the direction of Representative Adam Clayton Powell from Harlem. The meeting was a prelude to a National Conference on Black Power, a get-together which was to include leaders of all the black militant groups.

In 1967, when Powell was being threatened with the loss of his congressional seat, Gray was the main speaker at a Hands-Off-Powell rally and said: "This is a conspiracy by the racists. They better not try to unseat Adam. I'm not advocating violence, but I'm not a nonviolent man . . . . If they keep Adam out of the country, we'll make him our black president-in-exile." (Less than three years later, Gray announced that he was entering the Democratic primary against Adam Clayton Powell. This was not Gray's only venture as a political candidate. In 1968, he filed nominating petitions in New Jersey's Democratic presidential primary, but one half the signatures he collected were ruled invalid. In 1969, he ran for the New York City Council as the Democratic nominee from Harlem, but he received only 34 per cent of the vote.)

In August 1967, Gray led a demonstration in the visitors' gallery of the House of Representatives. The demonstration was a violent one and was made in opposition to anti-riot legislation then under discussion in the Congress. At that time, Gray was a $50-a-day consultant to Harlem Backstreet Youth, a project funded by the federal government's Office of Economic Opportunity. (The di-

rector of OEO, Sargent Shriver, said that he had tried without success to prevent Gray from receiving anti-poverty funds and he preferred not to participate in programs with Gray, but he did not have the power to dismiss Gray.)

Gray has been affiliated with the ultra-leftist Monroe Defense Committee; the ultra-leftist Student Mobilization Committee to End the War in Vietnam; and the pro-Peking Revolutionary Action Movement. He has consistently received favorable notices in the Communist press down to the present time.

DICK GREGORY was born Richard Claxton Gregory in 1932 in St. Louis, Missouri. He is married. He attended Southern Illinois University. He is the author of *From the Back of the Bus* (1964); *nigger!* (1964) [which has the following dedication: "To Momma, wherever you are − if ever you hear the word nigger again, remember, they're advertising my book."] ; *What's Happening* (1965); *The Shadow That Scares Me* (1968); and *Write Me In* (1968).

Since 1958, Gregory has been a comedian, working nightclubs and appearing on television. He has made record albums and, in recent years, has written a weekly syndicated column.

Since 1962, Gregory has been a civil rights agitator. He has taken part in "freedom rides," sit-ins, stall-ins, boycotts, and marches. He has undertaken frequent fasts. He has been arrested at least twenty times, but has served very little time in jail.

Gregory has been affiliated with the leftist-racist Congress of Racial Equality; the ultra-radical Student Nonviolent Coordinating Committee; the leftist-racist Southern Conference Educational Fund; the leftist-oriented Hollywood March Committee; the ultra-leftist National

Peace Action Coalition; the March Against the War, an ultra-leftist project; the leftist Committee to Defend the [Chicago] Conspiracy; the ultra-leftist Committee to Defend the Panthers; the ultra-leftist Committee for Independent Political Action; the ultra-leftist National Conference for New Politics; the ultra-leftist Emergency Conference Committee; and the leftist-pacifist National Council to Repeal the Draft.

In 1966, Gregory was an unsuccessful candidate for mayor of Chicago. In 1968, he was a presidential candidate on the Freedom and Peace Party ticket. (On March 6, 1969, in a mock ceremony in Washington, D.C., he took an oath of office as president-in-exile.)

In June 1969, Gregory attended the Communist-operated World Assembly of Peace in East Berlin. He explained that he made his visit "to emphasize racism as the prime cause of war."

On campuses, street corners, political platforms, nightclub stages, and television, and in his writings, Gregory attracts a great deal of attention with his inflammatory remarks. In 1970, during one of his fasts, he wrote a widely-publicized letter to President Nixon charging that twenty million Americans went to bed hungry every night because of the war in Vietnam. In the aftermath of the racial riots in Detroit and the Watts area of Los Angeles, he stated that the riots were sanctioned by the Declaration of Independence. He also stated on the Watts riots: "If Watts was wrong, we'd better go burn all the American history books." In 1966, at a White House conference ("To Fulfill These Rights"), he said to his audience: "How can this white man's government arrange free elections in Vietnam . . . when you people can't get the vote here in Washington. It looks as if you're going to have to go downtown

and take it." In 1968, as a presidential candidate of the Freedom and Peace Party, he said: "America was so sick that it had no choice but to turn to ending racism and militarism at home in order to save itself from its own destruction." On the same theme, he said: "America is the most racist country in the world. Her citizens had better search and find her racism . . . realize it exists . . . because as long as you don't realize it you just keep on insulting me. Black people are tired of all the insults, all the injustice. We do not hate white folks per se, we hate his system, and that's what we're going to destroy."

In January 1968, Gregory was the featured speaker at the annual dinner for Yale University's graduating class. Said Gregory: "Let me tell you something tonight: we will burn your house down to the ground (and we mean that), if you think you are going to keep talking this insane and think you going to keep on insulting us like this we'll burn it down to the ground, man. This is what we're trying to say. We are sick and tired of your insults and we're not going to take them anymore, whether you like it or not.

"Let me ask you to raise your hands. How many of you read when Henry Ford, three and a half weeks ago, hired 6,000 Negroes? Any of you read that in the paper? Did you also read that they didn't have to take the tests when they hired them?

"Henry Ford, one of the largest corporations in the world, hired 6,000 niggers in two days. Why do you think they hired them? Because of non-violence? You **** right know it wasn't that! The fire got too close to the Ford plant, baby. Don't scorch the Mustangs, Baby. You-all, running around talking about how riots hurt, do you realize how long it would have taken us through peaceful channels to get 6,000 black folks hired and through those tests?

"Let me speak briefly on the insanity of that war in Viet Nam, and the insane country that you coming out into, the laws that we pass, and this flag sitting right here. We just got an insane law to say you can't burn an American flag. I say, What in the hell is the American flag but a **** rag like all the other flags all over the world. I'm not interested in rags . . . ."

"America is a cigarette machine to us. We didn't put forty cents in it to get something that was going to make us sick, we put 400 years of our lives in that machine, baby, to get something that was going to make us well, and we didn't get nothing, man . . . . So in the form of Detroit, Watts and Chicago we kicked that machine . . . . Now we gonna break this machine up in little, bitty pieces; that's what we say!"

Gregory has insisted on many occasions that he is not a racist. For example, he was asked if he felt bitter or prejudiced toward white people. He answered: "Am I prejudiced against white people? No. But before I got involved on the front line of this revolution, there could have been room for prejudice." He insists that "the revolution is not black against white, it's right against wrong." And, for himself and his fellow blacks, he has proclaimed: "We don't need liberals anymore. We need white radicals."

Despite his denials of racism, Gregory has been a strong defender of the undeniably racist Black Panthers. He has been a fund raiser for the undeniably racist Black Caucus members of the House of Representatives. And he has attended undeniably racist Black Power conferences.

In recent years, Gregory has dwelt a great deal upon the Vietnam War. In 1968, he met in Paris with members of the North Vietnam delegation to the perennial peace talks. In 1971, with Jane Fonda and Dalton Trumbo, he organized "Entertainment Industry for Peace and Justice," which sponsors Jane Fonda's anti-military roadshow designed to bring the leftist-pacifist message to members of the armed forces.

EUNICE GRIER was born on July 19, 1927 in Stamford, Connecticut, daughter of Velma Viles and Charles Sheridan. She married George Grier. She is an alumna of the University of Pennsylvania (B.S., 1948). She is co-author of *Privately Developed Inter-Racial Housing* (1960) and *Equality and Beyond* (1966).

From 1950 until 1952, Mrs. Grier was a writer for the leftist-pacifist American Friends Service Committee. In 1954 and 1955, she was a consultant to the ultra-leftist Fund for the Republic. From 1957 until 1960, she was a researcher for the New York State Commission Against Discrimination. From 1961 until 1965, she was employed by the Washington Center for Metropolitan Studies. Since 1965, she has been research director for the U.S. Commission on Civil Rights. She has been a consultant to the defamatory Anti-Defamation League. Since 1963, she has been on the national advisory committee for community relations of the leftist-pacifist American Friends Service Committee.

HELMUT GRUBER was born on July 20, 1928 in Austria. He is a naturalized American. He is an alumnus of the City College of New York (B.S.S., 1950) and Columbia University (M.A., 1951; Ph.D., 1962). He is the author of

International Communism in the Era of Lenin (1967).

Since 1957, Gruber has been at the Polytechnic Institute of Brooklyn as a history instructor (1957-1959), assistant professor (1959-1963), associate professor (1963-1965), and professor and head of the social science department (1965 to the present).

Gruber has participated in the Educators Appeal to the American People, a leftist effort against the War in Vietnam. He was a member of the leftist-oriented Ad Hoc Committee for an Open Letter on Vietnam. He has been a prominent participant in the Socialist Scholars Conferences, annual get-togethers of Marxian-Socialists and fellow-travelers.

LEO GRULIOW was born on May 27, 1913 in Bayonne, New Jersey, son of Rebecca Kagan and George Gruliow. He married Agnes Forrest. He is the editor of *Current Soviet Policies* (1953, 1957, 1960, 1962). He contributed to *The Press in Authoritarian Countries* (1959). Since 1966, he 'has been editor and publisher of *Counterpart.* He has contributed to the *Journal of International Affairs*, the *Columbia University Forum*, the *Boston Globe*, the *Washington Post*, and the *International Press Institute Report.*

In 1929, Gruliow was a reporter with the *Elizabeth* [N.J.] *Evening Times.* From 1930 until 1933, he was with the *New York Democrat* as reporter (1930) and managing editor (1931-1933). From 1933 until 1938, he was in the Soviet Union as a technical consultant with the *Moscow Daily News.* In 1939 and 1940, he was a Washington correspondent for Transradio Press Service. From 1941 until 1946, he worked for Russian War Relief, Inc., as research director (1941-1942), representative in the Soviet

Union (1943-1945), and public lecturer in America (1946). In 1946 and 1947, he was employed by the leftist American Friends Service Committee to lecture at seminars on international affairs. In 1947, he was a guest lecturer at Grinnell College in Iowa. In 1947 and 1948, he was a guest lecturer at the radical New School for Social Research. In 1948, he was a translator for a Russian book project of the American Council of Learned Societies. Since 1948, he has been founder and editor of *Current Digest of the Soviet Press,* published under the auspices of the American Council of Learned Societies and the Social Science Research Council. From 1952 until 1955, he was a lecturer at Columbia University. In 1954 and 1955, he was a television commentator for the American Broadcasting Company network. From 1955 until 1959, he was a commentator for the Canadian Broadcasting Corporation. In 1959 and 1960, he lectured at the Institut Universitaire de Hautes Études Internationales in Geneva, Switzerland. From 1960 until 1964, he was a guest lecturer at various colleges and universities. In 1961 and 1962, he was a research consultant at American University. From 1961 until 1965, he was a consultant to various radio and television networks. From 1961 until 1963, he worked with the leftist-pacifist American Friends Service Committee, for which he was a chairman of international seminars. In recent years, he has been president of Diorama Publications, Inc., of New York City.

EDMUND A. GULLION was born on March 2, 1913 in Lexington, Kentucky, son of Ruth Matthews and Allen Gullion. He married Patricia Palmer. He is an alumnus of Princeton University (A.B., 1935).

From 1937 until 1964, Gullion was with the Department of State as vice consul in Marseilles (1937); vice consul in Salonika (1939); third secretary in London (1942); temporary foreign service officer in Algiers (1942); third secretary in London (1943); chargé d'affaires in Helsinki (1943); second secretary in Stockholm (1944); foreign service officer in Washington, D.C. (1945-1950); counselor of the legation in Saigon (1950-1957); foreign service inspector (1957-1960); acting deputy director (1960) and deputy director (1961) of the U.S. Disarmament Administration; U.S. Ambassador to the Republic of the Congo (1961); and career minister (1962-1964). In recent years, he has been dean of the Fletcher School of Law and Diplomacy at Tufts University.

Gullion is a long-time member of the Council on Foreign Relations, the informal supra-State Department of the United States. He has been a director of the World Affairs Council of Boston, a major propaganda agency for the United Nations and one-worldism. He has been a director of the leftist-pacifist World Peace Foundation, which exerts considerable influence upon the Department of State, the Department of Defense, and the Central Intelligence Agency in an over-all program of appeasement toward the Soviet Union. He has been affiliated with the leftist International Movement for Atlantic Union, which works toward a political merger of Western Europe and the United States, as a major step toward world government.

RALPH H. GUNDLACH was born on June 17, 1902 in Kansas City, Missouri. He has been married twice. He is an alumnus of the University of Washington (B.A., 1924; M.A., 1925) and the University of Illinois (Ph.D., 1928).

From 1925 until 1927, Gundlach was a teaching assistant at the University of Illinois. From 1927 until 1949, he was at the University of Washington as instructor in psychology (1927-1930), assistant professor (1930-1937), and associate professor (1937-1949). Since 1953, he has been associated with New York Medical College and Metropolitan Hospital as senior psychologist in the postgraduate center for psychotherapy (1953-1967), associate director (1959 to the present), and psychologist in the mental health center (1967 to the present). Since 1953, he has also engaged in private practice. He has been a visiting lecturer at the University of California, the University of Southern California, the University of British Columbia, the University of Iowa, and New York University.

In 1948, Gundlach was identified as a member of the Communist Party by Sarah M. Eldredge, Isabel H. Costigan, H.C. Armstrong, Ward F. Warren, Nat Honig, and George Hewitt when they testified before the Washington State Joint Legislative Fact-Finding Committee on Un-American Activities. In 1949, Gundlach was named as one of the "contacts" of Gregori Kheifets, Soviet vice-consul at San Francisco around whom "West-Coast Communist espionage centered." This information was given by Larry Kerley, under oath, before the U.S. Senate Judiciary Subcommittee on Immigration and Naturalization. In 1954, Gundlach was identified as a member of the Communist Party by Harold W. Sunoo, who testified under oath before the House Committee on Un-American Activities. In 1948, when testifying before the Washington State Joint Legislative Fact-Finding Committee on Un-American Activities, Gundlach refused to answer the question whether he was or ever had been a member of the Communist Party.

Gundlach was an instructor at the Pacific Northwest Labor School ("a Communist-controlled institution") and the Tom Mooney Lake School ("a Communist Party school"). Gundlach has been affiliated with the American Committee for Protection of Foreign Born [Americans] ("subversive and Communist"); the Citizens Committee for Harry Bridges ("Communist"); the Committee for Citizenship Rights ("to protect Communist subversion from any penalties under the law"); the Committee for a Democratic Far Eastern Policy ("Communist"); Consumers Union ("subversive and un-American"); the Coordinating Committee to Lift the [Spanish] Embargo ("Communist front"); the National Emergency Conference ("Communist front"); the National Federation for Constitutional Liberties ("under [Communist] Party domination and headed by responsible Party functionaries"); *Science and Society* ("a Communist publication"); the Spanish Refugee Appeal ("subversive" − "Communist front"); the United American Spanish Aid Committee ("Communist"); Veterans of the Abraham Lincoln Brigade ("subversive and Communist"); the Joint Anti-Fascist Refugee Committee ("subversive and Communist"); the National Council of the Arts, Sciences and Professions ("Communist front"); the National Council of American-Soviet Friendship ("subversive and Communist" − "specializing in pro-Soviet propaganda"); the Conference for Peaceful Alternatives to the Atlantic Pact ("initiated by Communists"); the Bill of Rights Conference ("subversive"); the California Labor School ("a subversive and Communist organization"); the Civil Rights Congress ("subversive and Communist"); the In-

ternational Workers Order ("subversive and Communist"); the Jefferson School of Social Science ("adjunct of the Communist Party"); the National Committee to Repeal the McCarran Act ("subversive" − "Communist front"); the World Peace Appeal ("subversive"); the Emergency Civil Liberties Committee ("subversive" − "Communist front"); the Medical Bureau to Aid Spanish Democracy ("Communist enterprise"); the American Peace Mobilization ("subversive and Communist"); the Council for Pan-American Democracy ("subversive and Communist"); the North American Spanish Aid Committee ("Communist"); the Progressive Citizens of America ("Communist front"); the American Continental Congress for World Peace ("another phase in the Communist 'peace' campaign, aimed at consolidating anti-American forces throughout the Western hemisphere"); the ultra-leftist American-Korean Friendship and Information Center; the Conference for Legislation in the National Interest ("Communist front"); the National Committee to Win Amnesty for Smith Act Victims ("subversive" − "a Communist Party project"); the National Assembly for Democratic Rights ("created, dominated, and controlled by members and officials of the Communist Party"); the Committee of Welcome for the Very Reverend Hewlett Johnson, a tribute to England's leading Red clergyman; and the Continuations Committee of the Conference for Peaceful Alternatives to the Atlantic Pact ("Communist front"). He has petitioned in defense of Communist schools and on behalf of convicted Communists.

BRIJEN GUPTA was born on September 17, 1929 in Firozpur, India. He is a naturalized American. He is an alumnus of Dayanand College in India (B.A., 1952); Yale University (M.A., 1954); and the University of Chicago (Ph.D., 1958). In 1954, he was an Overbrook fellow. From 1955 until 1957, he held an Asian Foundation fellowship. From 1955 until 1958, he was a fellow at the University of Chicago. He is the author of *Sirajuddaullah and the East India Company, 1756-1757* (1962). He is co-author of *Indian and American Labor Legislations and Practices: A Comparative Analysis* (1966).

From 1958 until 1960, Gupta was a lecturer in history and government at Southern Illinois University. From 1960 until 1963, he was a lecturer in Asian studies at Victoria University in New Zealand. Since 1963, he has been at Brooklyn College as assistant professor of history (1963-1967) and associate professor (1967 to the present). In 1961 and 1962, he was a visiting fellow at the institute for advanced study at the Australian National University. In 1961 and 1962, he was in New Zealand on a grant from the Carnegie Social Science Research Fund. In 1965, he was a visiting professor at the University of Cincinnati. In 1967, he was a visiting professor at the University of Hawaii. In 1967 and 1968, he held a grant-in-aid from the American Philosophical Society. In 1968, he was a visiting professor at Columbia University.

Gupta has been a participant in the Socialist Scholars Conferences, annual get-togethers of Marxian-Socialists and fellow-travelers.

ALLEN GUTTMANN was born on October 13, 1932 in Chicago, son of Jeanette Krulewich and Emile Guttmann. He married Martha Ellis. He is an alumnus of the University of Florida (B.A., 1953); Columbia University (M.A., 1956); and the University of Minnesota (Ph.D., 1961). He is the author of *The Wound in the Heart: America and the Spanish Civil War* (1962) and *The Conservative Tradition in America* (1967). He is the co-editor of *The Removal of the Cherokee Nation* (1962) and *Communism, the Constitution, and the Courts* (1964). He is editor of *American Neutrality and the Spanish Civil War* (1963) and *Korea and the Theory of Limited War* (1967).

Since 1959, Guttmann has been at Amherst College as instructor (1959-1962), assistant professor (1962-1966), and associate professor (1966 to the present).

Guttmann has been affiliated with the leftist-oriented American Association of University Professors. He has been a participant in the Socialist Scholars Conferences, annual get-togethers of Marxian-Socialists and other extreme leftists.

DAVID L. GUYER was born on September 24, 1925 in Pasadena, California, son of Emily Shuford and Leigh Guyer. He married Carol Penney. He is an alumnus of Stanford University (B.A., 1948).

From 1950 until 1965, Guyer was with the United Nations as deputy resident representative to the Technical Assistance Board in India (1955-1958), chief of the Technical Assistance Recruitment Office for North America (1959-1960), and adviser on political and security council affairs to the U.S. Mission to the UN (1960-1965). Since 1965, he has been vice-president for development and public affairs for the leftist-oriented Institute of International Education.

Guyer has been a long-time official with the Foreign Policy Association, a highly effective pro-Communist vehicle, and he is a long-time trustee of Freedom House, a center for anti-anti-Communism.

WILLIAM F. HADDAD was born on July 25, 1928 in Charlotte, North Carolina, son of Esther Nowark and Charles Haddad. He married Kate Roosevelt. He is an alumnus of Columbia University (B.A., 1954). He pursued graduate studies at Georgetown University.

In 1955, Haddad was on the staff of the U.S. Senate Subcommittee on Juvenile Delinquency headed by Senator Estes Kefauver. In 1955, he accompanied Kefauver on a trip to the Soviet Union and other parts of the Communist bloc. In 1955 and 1956, he was the chief administrative officer in charge of Kefauver's vice-presidential campaign. In 1957, he worked as a systems engineer at RCA's Creative Electronics Division. From 1957 until 1961, he was a reporter for the leftist *New York Post*. In 1960, he was a special assistant to Robert F. Kennedy, who was managing John F. Kennedy's presidential campaign. From 1961 until 1963, he was with the Peace Corps as director of planning, coordination, and evaluation, and as associate director. From 1963 until 1965, he was an inspector-general with the Office of Economic Opportunity. In 1966, he was a major figure in Detroit Mayor Jerome Cavanagh's campaign for the Democratic nomination to the U.S. Senate against G. Mennen Williams. The Haddad-Cavanagh team campaigned on an extreme dovish position vis-á-vis the war in Vietnam.

Since 1966, he has been president of the U.S. Research and Development Corporation, which conducts training programs for the so-called hard-core unemployed. Since 1966, he has been co-publisher, with Roy Innis, the director of the Congress of Racial Equality, of the *Manhattan Tribune*, a community paper that purports to work for better relationships between blacks and whites on New York City's West Side.

Haddad has been on the governing board of the leftist-oriented American Jewish Congress. He has been on the board of directors of the leftist-oriented New York Urban Coalition. In 1964, he was an unsuccessful candidate for Congress, running as a Reform Democrat, i.e., with a far leftist position. In recent years, he has served on New York City's board of education, and he remains a power in New York City's Democratic Party.

MARTIN HALL was born *c.* 1900 in Germany. Until 1938, his name was Carl Adolph Rudolph Herman Jacobs. He has testified under oath that he changed his name legally at the Cook County Court in Chicago in 1938. He explained the change of name: "I was coming to this country as a refugee from Hitler Germany as a result of my opposition to the policies of Hitler. When I arrived here I still had some close relatives living in Germany. Of course, I was very eager to protect them from the kind of persecution that was going on at the time. My parents were living there, and the family of my wife. My wife was Jewish. The whole family was wiped out, but I at least saved my parents. This is the reason I changed my name legally, in order to protect these people who were close to me." Hall came to the United States in 1937. He was naturalized as an American citizen in 1945.

On July 7, 1953, Benjamin Gitlow — General Secretary of the Communist Party of the United States in the 1920's — testified before the House Committee on Un-American Activities: "Martin Hall is also known by the name of Herman Jacobs. He is a Communist of long standing, a well-known figure in the Communist Party of Germany. He has sponsored Communist-front movements in the country which gave him asylum [and] citizenship. He was vice-president of the German-American League for Culture, a Communist organization. He was also editor of the German Communist newspaper printed in the United States, *Volksecho.* He was a contributor to the monthly magazine of the Communist Party, *New Masses.* He contributed numerous articles to the official publication of the Communist International, *International Press Correspondence [Inprecorr]*, in 1935, 1936, and 1937. None but accredited Communist Party leaders wrote for *International Press Correspondence.* In order to get his United States citizenship he had to swear falsely and deny that he was a Communist, that he entertained Communist beliefs, and was affiliated with Communist organizations."

In 1954, Hall testified before the California Senate Fact-Finding Committee on Un-American Activities. He invoked the Fifth Amendment when asked if he had been in Germany in 1923; when asked if he had been a member of the national executive board of an organization operated by the Communist Party of Germany known as Kostufra; when asked if he had been a member of the Young Communist League in Germany; when asked if he had contributed articles to *International Press Correspondence;* when asked if he had taught at the People's Educational Center in Los Angeles and at the California Labor School; when asked if he had written speeches to be delivered by the Medical Division of the Arts, Sciences and Profes-

sions Council, when asked if he had been a speaker in a series of forums arranged by the Joint Anti-Fascist Refugee Committee; when asked if he sponsored the Conference for Peace presented at the Arts, Sciences and Professions Council in Los Angeles; when asked if he had been a member of the Civil Rights Congress; when asked if he had ever resided in Phoenix; when asked if he had ever been a delegate to the American Continental Congress for Peace in Mexico City; when asked if he had ever spoken in the interests of the Committee for Peaceful Alternatives to the Atlantic Pact; when asked if he had ever been affiliated with the International Workers Order; when asked if he had been associated with the American-Russian Institute; and when asked if he was a member of the Communist Party of the United States. He did admit that he was a free-lance writer on national and international affairs. He added: "My political opinions, therefore, are a question of public record. I have written for the *Nation,* the *Christian Century*, the *Christian Register*, the *Churchman*, and the *Frontier Magazine.* I am speaking at public meetings three or four times a week. Everyone who would like to know what I think about politics could ascertain that very easily because it is all of record."

In 1962, the House Committee on Un-American Activities reported: "Martin Hall, the chairman of LAFPCC [Los Angeles Fair Play for Cuba Commitee], has been a continuous supporter of front organizations, of the orthodox Communist Party, USA, ever since his arrival in the United States from Germany twenty-five years ago .... In 1936 and 1937, Martin Hall contributed articles to *International Press Correspondence,* official organ of the Communist International .... Since his arrival in this country,

Mr. Hall has received publicity for activities in behalf of the following organizations and publications . . . : *New Masses* ["Communist periodical"], contributor of articles, 1937; League of American Writers ["subversive and Communist"] and American Student Union ["Communist front"], scheduled speaker, 1937; Joint Anti-Fascist Refugee Committee ["subversive and Communist"], scheduled speaker, 1944; World Federation of Democratic Youth ["international Communist front"] and International Union of Students ["international Communist front"], attended their World Youth Festival held behind the Iron Curtain in 1947; Civil Rights Congress ["subversive and Communist"], signer of public statement, 1948; Conference for Peaceful Alternatives to the Atlantic Pact ["initiated by Communists"], signer of public statement, 1949; Southern California Chapter of the National Council of the Arts, Sciences and Professions ["a Communist front used to appeal to special occupational groups"], executive board member, 1949, subdivision chairman, 1951; National Council of American-Soviet Friendship ["subversive and Communist" – "specializing in pro-Soviet propaganda"], panel leader at conference, 1950; Independent Progressive Party ["one of the largest and most successful fronts ever created by the Communists"], scheduled speeches, 1950, 1951, and 1954; Jewish Peoples Fraternal Order ["Communist"], speaker, 1951; Los Angeles Committee to Secure Justice in the Rosenberg Case ["Communist front"], scheduled speaker and sponsor, 1952; California Labor School ["a subversive and Communist organization"], scheduled speaker, 1952; American-Russian Institute ["Communist"], scheduled speaker, 1954; Citizens Committee to Preserve American Freedoms ["Communist front"], speaker, 1954; Los Angeles Committee for Protection of Foreign Born [Americans] ["one of the oldest and most active Communist front organizations in California"], scheduled lecturer, 1955; People's World ["Communist daily"] Forum, scheduled speaker, 1959 and 1961; New World Review ["Communist publication"], author of article, 1961; [and] National Guardian ["Communist weekly"], author of article, 1962. Hall, a writer and lecturer by occupation, visited Cuba in August 1960 (*People's World*, August 6, 1960). His most recent trip abroad was as a delegate from the United States to the World Congress for General Disarmament and Peace, held in Moscow July 9-14, 1962, under the auspices of the international Communist front, the World Peace Council. His speech at a meeting of the Economic Commission of the Moscow Congress, in which he attacked the European Common Market as a cold-war weapon, was publicized in Moscow radio broadcasts, as well as in *The Worker*, the Communist Party's official newspaper in the United States. The committee has obtained information that, within a month after the public appearance of the Los Angeles Fair Play for Cuba Committee, members of the Southern California District of the Communist Party received instructions to turn out in force at LAFPCC meetings and to move into dominating positions in the pro-Castro propaganda organization."

Hall has also been affiliated with the Communist-dominated Peace Action Council; the Spring Mobilization Committee to End the War in Vietnam, a peacenik group dominated by Communists and fellow-travelers; the Constitutional Liberties Information Center, a Communist front; the Methodist Federation for Social Action ("Communist front"); the World Assembly of Peace in East Berlin in 1969, an international Communist get-together; the leftist Southland Jewish Organization of California; the leftist-pacifist Women's International League for Peace and Freedom; the Bill of Rights Conference ("subversive"); and the Emergency Civil Liberties Committee ("Communist front" – "subversive").

In 1968, the Communist weekly *National Guardian* carried an advertisement of a travel agency – the United States Travel Bureau of North Hollywood. The advertisement, under the heading "Study War No More," read: "Join this fortunate group under the leadership of Martin Hall, well-known lecturer and writer, who will offer a once-in-a-lifetime opportunity for dialogue with men and women who keep the peace in Europe. Visit Holland, both Germanys, Poland, Hungary, Bulgaria, and International Institute for Peace in Vienna."

MORTON H. HALPERIN was born on June 13, 1933 in Brooklyn, New York, son of Lillian Neubart and Harry Halperin. He married Ina Weinstein. He is an alumnus of Columbia University (B.A., 1958) and Yale University (M.A., 1959; Ph.D., 1961). He is the author of *Limited War in the Nuclear Age* (1963) and *China and the Bomb* (1965). He is co-author of *Strategy and Arms Control* (1961).

From 1961 until 1966, Halperin was at Harvard University in the Center for International Affairs as instructor (1961-1963), research associate (1961-1966) and assistant professor (1964-1966) of government. From 1966 until 1969, he was with the Department of Defense as a special assistant on planning to the assistant secretary of defense for internal

security affairs (1966-1967) and deputy assistant secretary of defense on policy planning and arms control (1967-1969). In 1969, he was a senior assistant to Henry A. Kissinger, the President's assistant for national security affairs. Since 1970, he has been a senior fellow at Brookings Institution. He has been a consultant to some of the more prestigious think factories: RAND Corporation (1960-1966), Hudson Institute (1961-1966), and the Institute for Defense Analyses (1961-1966). From 1961 until 1965, he was a consultant to the Raytheon Company. In the Nixon Administration, he was a consultant to the National Security Council, but he resigned the position in 1970 in protest against the President's decision to move American troops into Cambodia and to increase bombing raids against anti-aircraft installations in North Vietnam.

Since 1961, Halperin has been one of America's most prolific pleaders for disarmament and a policy of "limited" warfare. Writing in *Advance* (April 1961), he said: "American policy on the use of nuclear weapons in limited war is, or should be, closely related to its arms-control policy. I believe that the United States should adopt a conventional limited war strategy. It appears in fact that the Kennedy Administration is reversing the trend toward the dependence by American forces on nuclear weapons in limited war and may intend to rely increasingly on conventional forces. If the United States does adopt such a strategy, it should use arms-control negotiations and agreements to enhance the likelihood that a limited war would remain conventional."

Throughout the Kennedy and Johnson Administrations, Halperin was generally uncritical of the U.S. Government's decisions concerning disarmament and military strategy. He was especially pleased by the continuing negotiations between the United States and the Soviet Union and, as so many of the think-factory habitues preach, was convinced that within the Soviet hierarchy there were sincere and trustworthy negotiators.

During the Johnson Administration, Halperin was quite content with the Administration's no-win policy in Vietnam. He was under the illusion that as long as such a policy was followed, Communist China would not intervene militarily in Vietnam. In March 1966, while testifying before the Senate Foreign Relations Committee, Halperin urged that the United States extend diplomatic recognition to Red China and work for Red China's admission into the United Nations. Shortly thereafter, Halperin was appointed to a position in the Defense Department.

Halperin was retained in the Defense Department by the Nixon Administration. Even though the new administration followed the same no-win policy in Vietnam, displayed an even greater inclination to trust the Soviets at the bargaining table, and went further than any previous administration with appeasement gestures toward the Red Chinese, Halperin turned upon the Administration over Nixon's Cambodian venture. In view of the fact that Halperin had worked closely with Henry Kissinger, his charges of hawkism lacked even an iota of sincerity. In a letter dated May 13, 1970, appearing in the *New York Times* May 25, 1970, Halperin joined with four other doves in writing: "Probably no action by a President in the last half-century has been so generally condemned as President Nixon's incursion into Cambodia. We, the undersigned, have spent our professional lives in the study of strategy

and American foreign policy. We have had experience in Government service, and have acted as consultants or staff members of defense research organizations. Yet we strongly oppose this latest expansion of the war in Indochina. In our judgment, it procures no gain abroad, while imperiling the unity of this country at home.

"For a year, President Nixon has been telling us that he would withdraw American combat forces from Vietnam. Until last week he at no time suggested that the elimination of North Vietnamese sanctuaries in Cambodia would be essential to this purpose. The move into Cambodia to eliminate these sanctuaries is not likely to be successful unless we, or the South Vietnamese with our support, are ready to repeat it six months from now.

"The expansion of the war has caused a drastic disabling of domestic support for the President as foreign policy initiator. If the war in Indochina is not brought to a halt soon, America's position in world affairs will soon become paralyzed in a welter of domestic dissent. But, entirely aside from this, the move into Cambodia simply does not make sense. We urge the President to terminate it, and to reaffirm previous commitments in behalf of United States withdrawal."

Since Halperin has been a consultant to the National Security Council right up until the time of the Cambodian incursion, his expressed dismay and shock would seem to have been feigned rather than real. At any rate, Halperin had placed himself squarely in the midst of the doves.

Halperin has been affiliated with the internationalist-pacifist International Movement for Atlantic Union; Freedom House, a center for anti-anti-Commu-

433

nism; the American Friends of Vietnam, which was nothing less than a propaganda front for the late Ngo dinh Diem; and the leftist-oriented National Committee on United States-[Red] China Relations. He is a member of the ultraradical American Civil Liberties Union.

FREĐ W. HALSTEAD was born on April 21, 1927 in Los Angeles, son of Bloomah Buckholtz and Frank Halstead. He married Virginia Garza. He attended the University of California at Los Angeles for two years. He is the author of *Harlem Stirs* (1966); *If This Be Revolution* (1967), and *Interviews With Anti-War GIs* (1969).

From 1950 until 1966, Halstead was a garment cutter in Los Angeles, Detroit, and New York City. From 1955 until 1966, he was a staff writer for *The Militant*, a weekly newspaper published by the Socialist Workers Party. (The Socialist Workers Party is "a dissident Communist group not affiliated with the Communist International nor officially recognized by either the Communist hierarchy in Moscow or the Communist Party, U.S.A. Essentially, however, both the official and unofficial groups base themselves upon the teachings of Marx, Engels, and Lenin. The Socialist Workers Party are followers of Leon Trotsky, who was expelled from the Russian Communist Party.") In 1968, he was the presidential candidate of the Socialist Workers Party.

Since 1966, Halstead has been one of the major organizers of ultra-leftist demonstrations against the war in Vietnam. He has been affiliated with the Fifth Avenue Vietnam Peace Parade Committee, the GI Civil Liberties Defense Committee, the New Mobilization Committee to End the War in Vietnam, and Veterans for Peace — all of which are coali-

tions of the most extreme elements in far-left parties.

LOIS HAMER was born on March 10, 1916 in Waterloo, Iowa, daughter of Lydia Shafford and Orville Hamer. She is an alumna of the University of North Iowa (B.A., 1937) and Northwestern University (M.A., 1941). She is a deaconess of the Congregational Church.

From 1937 until 1939, Miss Hamer was a teacher and principal at Baldwin (Iowa) High School. From 1940 until 1943, she was principal of Carson High School. In 1943 and 1944, she worked at the Umatilla (Oregon) Ordnance Depot in the personnel department. In 1944 and 1945, she was program director at radio station KODI and dean of girls at Dalles (Oregon) High School. From 1945 until 1949, she was director of Christian education and youth work at the First Congregational Church in Salem, Oregon. In 1949 and 1950, she was a parish director in Klamath Falls, Oregon. From 1950 until 1954, she was employed by the Congregational Conference in Southern California in church and school work.

In 1954 and 1955, Miss Hamer was minister of Christian education at the First Congregational Church in Albuquerque. From 1955 until 1959, she was director of Christian education for the Montana Congregational Conference and the Congregational Christian Conference of North Dakota. From 1959 until 1962, she was executive secretary and director of the leftist-pacifist Fellowship of Reconciliation in Los Angeles. From 1962 until 1964, she was employed by the U.S. Peace Corps in Thailand. In 1964 and 1965, she was employed as a lecturer throughout the United States by the United Church of Christ. In 1966, she was a curriculum coordinator at the

Community Skill Center of the West Coast Trade Schools in Los Angeles. In 1966 and 1967, she was a special counselor at the Seven Seas Division of Chapman College in Orange, California. Since 1966, she has been a consultant for the Protestant Community Services of the Los Angeles Council of Churches. Since 1968, she has been director of the Program for Retired Citizens in Los Angeles. Since 1965, she has been very active in the leftist-pacifist Women's International League for Peace and Freedom as a member of the board of directors, as president of the Los Angeles branch, and as a national director. She is also affiliated with the leftist-oriented American Association of University Women and the United Nations Association of the United States, the most prestigious leftwing propaganda agency for the UN in this country.

PETE HAMILL was born on June 24, 1935, son of Anne Devlin and William Hamill. He has been married and divorced. He studied at Pratt Institute (1955-1956; 1957-1958) and Mexico City College (1956-1957). He is the author of *A Killing for Christ* (1968), the subject of a very favorable review in the Communists' *Daily World*. He has written "Doc," a screenplay for United Artists, and "Casualties of War," a screenplay for Warner Brothers. He has contributed to such publications as *Cosmopolitan, Life, New York,* the *New York Times Magazine, Playboy, Holiday, Sport, Men's Bazaar,* and the leftist *Ramparts* and *Village Voice.* In 1963, he edited the television series "East Side, West Side."

In 1951 and 1952, Hamill was a sheetmetal worker in Brooklyn. From 1957 until 1960, he was an advertising designer in New York City. Since 1960, with some intermittency, he has been with the leftist *New York Post* as reporter (1960-1963), political columnist (1965-1967; 1969 to the present), and war correspondent in South Vietnam (1966). In 1964 and 1965, he was a contributing editor to *Saturday Evening Post.* In 1968, he did free-lance writing.

Hamill's writings, especially in the *New York Post,* have brought him to the forefront of the New Left. He was one of the most radical members of the late Robert F. Kennedy's entourage. The hysteria of his radicalism was quite evident in the aftermath of the Kent State episode when he wrote: "When you call campus dissenters 'bums,' as Nixon did the other day, you should not be surprised when they are shot through the head and the chest by National Guardsmen. Nixon is as responsible for the Kent State slaughter as he and the rest of his bloodless gang of corporation men were for the anti-integration violence in Lamar, and for the pillage and murder that is taking place in the name of democracy in Cambodia . . . . At Kent State, two boys and two girls were shot to death by men unleashed by a President's slovenly rhetoric. If that's the brave new America, to hell with it." In the circumstances of the Calley trial, resulting from the My Lai episode, Hamill wanted harsh sentences pronounced upon "Lyndon Johnson, Hubert Humphrey, Walt Rostow, the Bundys and all the rest" in a trial to be held in "a town called Nuremberg." Few journalists can equal Hamill's mastery of the leftist-liberal jargon as he pleads the case for a completely socialized America.

Hamill has not been a joiner, but in 1971 he did become affiliated with the ultra-leftist National Peace Action Coalition.

CHARLES V. HAMILTON was born on October 19, 1929 in Muskogee, Oklahoma, son of Viola Haynes and Owen Hamilton. He married Dona Cooper. He is an alumnus of Roosevelt University (B.A., 1951); Loyola University of Chicago (J.D., 1954); and the University of Chicago (M.A., 1957; Ph.D., 1964). He is the author of *Minority Politics in Black Belt Alabama* (1962). He is co-author, with Stokely Carmichael, of *Black Power: The Politics of Liberation in America* (1967), which was recommended in the Communists' *Daily World* as a reading on Afro-American history.

In 1957 and 1958, Hamilton was an instructor at Albany State College in Georgia. From 1958 until 1960, he was an assistant professor of political science at Tuskegee Institute. In 1961 and 1962, he was a ·Charles Merriam fellow at the University of Chicago. In 1962 and 1963, he was a John Hay Whitney fellow at the University of Chicago. In 1963 and 1964, he was an instructor at Rutgers University. From 1964 until 1967, he was a professor at Lincoln University in Pennsylvania. From 1967 until 1969, he was chairman of the department and professor of political science at Roosevelt University. Since 1969, he has been a professor of political science and urban studies at Columbia University. In 1964 and 1967, he was a visiting professor at the University of California in Los Angeles.

In the fashion of the late Martin L. King, Hamilton projects himself as an advocate of nonviolence to achieve black power. He has often been described as a black power theorist. He has said that black power means the formation of political organizations by Negroes, independent of the white power structure. He has claimed that through such political organizations, Negroes can do for themselves by local majority rule at all levels what white leadership has never done satisfactorily in such areas as employment, housing, and education. It is his theory that Negroes might need to form independent political parties, their own unions of parents to control and improve schools, their own unions of tenants, their own unions of welfare recipients, and similar black organizations.

Hamilton, despite his professions of nonviolence, has not been adamant against violence on principle. He has explained: "Armed revolution is not feasible and will not become so. Blacks would lose a race war and it would break their spirit." He insisted that none of the riots by blacks throughout the country were planned or organized and that none were preludes to revolution. Rioting, he explained, stems from suppressed rage, induced by long oppression and the lack of political power to improve the conditions that fan the anger. He further explained that summer rioting is healthy for individual rioters because it gives them a psychological lift to confront the oppressive system.

As late as 1968, Hamilton insisted that American Negroes were righteously enraged because they were so demeaned that they were required to beg for rights and privileges from the white power structure. On another occasion, he offered a veiled ultimatum when he said, "And it must be clear that whites will have to bargain with blacks or continue to fight them in the streets of the Detroits and Newarks."

Hamilton is not above the rhetoric of the demagogue. In 1966, at the annual dinner of the *National Guardian*, a weekly Communist publication, he talked about his teaching experiences with Negro collegians: "I think the legitimate function of those of us fortunate enough to be exposed to these young people is to help them pick through to solutions, to help them clearly understand that a System, simply because it is a system, need not necessarily be right. I think it is our function to help strip away the bark of hypocrisy – bit by bit – and to pose the hard questions – questions indeed that challenge established mores. How legitimate is a political party system that can muster political power to *spend* men and money to kill Vietnamese children, but cannot quite order itself to solve the murder of four black American children in a bombed-out Birmingham church? How legitimate is a system that can quickly guarantee to Negroes safe passage *to* Vietnam but not to a home of their choice in Cicero, Illinois? How ludicrous and short-sighted can a society be that – according to the Secretary of Defense – must include within its poverty program increased military conscription?" A similar strain of demagoguery was evident when Hamilton reviewed his own experiences: "I graduated from Roosevelt, I got a law-degree from Loyola University, and I got a Ph.D. from the University of Chicago. And I'm going to tell you very clearly that my education over that twelve-to-fifteen-year period was geared toward making me a middle-class black Sambo. Nothing devious in that, and I'm not blaming my professors. It's just that that was their orientation. They were saying to me in no uncertain terms that in order to succeed I would have to orient myself to a Western Anglo-Saxon culture."

Hamilton has been affiliated with the National Association for the Advancement of Colored People, the fountain-head of Negro agitation for more than half a century; the ultra-radical Student Nonviolent Coordinating Committee; the Emergency Civil Liberties Committee ("Communist front" – "subversive"); the leftist-racist Congress of Racial Equality; and the leftist-pacifist National Coalition for a Responsible Congress. He was an ardent supporter of Black Panther leader Bobby Seale. In 1970, Hamilton was appointed as a consultant to the Presidential Commission on Campus Unrest.

FOWLER HAMILTON was born on May 7, 1911 in Kansas City, Missouri, son of Emily Fowler and Eugene Hamilton. He married Helen Miller. He is an alumnus of the University of Missouri (B.A., 1931) and Oxford University (B.A., B.C.L., M.A., 1934), where he was a Rhodes scholar. He was admitted to the Missouri bar in 1935, the Washington, D.C., bar in 1945, and the New York bar in 1947.

From 1935 until 1938, Hamilton practiced law in Missouri. From 1938 until 1942, he was a special assistant to the Attorney General of the United States. In 1942, he was director of the war frauds unit in the Department of Justice. In 1943, he was an attorney with the economic warfare division at the U.S. Embassy in London. In 1942 and 1943, he was chief of the enemy branch of the Foreign Economic Administration. In 1945, he was the chief legal consultant to the Department of Justice. Since 1946, he has practiced law in New York City. In 1961 and 1962, he was the New York administrator for the Agency for International Development. He is a long-time member of the Council on Foreign Relations, the informal supra-State Department of the United States. He is a long-time member of the Foreign Policy Association, which has had a long and consistent record of pro-Communism and anti-anti-Communism. It has been a center for pro-Soviet apologists and United Nations propagandists.

PAUL Y. HAMMOND was born on February 24, 1929 in Salt Lake City, son of Hortense Young and James Hammond. He married Merylyn Simmons. He is an alumnus of the University of Utah (B.A., 1949) and Harvard University (M.A., 1951; Ph.D., 1953). He is the author of *Organizing for Defense: The Administration of the American Military Establishment* (1961); *Directives for the Occupation of Germany: The Washington Story* (1962); and *Super-Carriers and B-36 Bombers: Appropriations, Strategy, and Politics* (1963). He is a co-author of *Strategies, Budgets, and Defense Politics: Three Studies in the Making of National Security Policy* (1962). He is a contributor to *National Defense in the Nuclear Age* (1960) and *The United States in a Disarmed World* (1966).

In 1951 and 1952, Hammond was a teaching fellow at Harvard University. In 1952 and 1953, he was a Fulbright scholar at the leftist London School of Economics. From 1953 until 1955, he was an instructor at Harvard University. In 1955, he was an academic consultant on international relations at the Naval War College. In 1956, he was a Forrestal fellow in Naval History at the U.S. Naval Academy. In 1956 and 1957, he was a lecturer and instructor at Columbia University. From 1954 until 1958, he was a research assistant at the leftist-oriented Twentieth Century Fund, working on a study of civil-military relations. From 1957 until 1962, he was an assistant professor at Yale University. From 1962 until 1964, he was a research associate at the leftist-oriented Washington Center of Foreign Policy Research of The Johns Hopkins University. In 1962 and 1963, he held a Rockefeller Founda-

tion fellowship. He was a consultant to the Institute for Defense Analyses (1961-1963), the Hudson Institute (1961-1964), and the Systems Development Corporation (1962-1964) — three of the ruling Establishment's think factories. From 1962 until 1964, he was a consultant to the Congressional Joint Committee on Atomic Energy. In 1963 and 1964, he was a consultant to the Department of Defense. Since 1964, he has been a senior staff member of the RAND Corporation — the most influential of the ruling Establishment's think factories.

EDGAR Y. HARBURG was born on April 8, 1898 in New York City, son of Mary Ricing and Lewis Harburg. His first wife was Alice Richmond. He is married to Edelaine Roden. He is an alumnus of the City College of New York (B.S., 1918).

From 1916 until 1929, Harburg contributed light verse to various newspapers and magazines. From 1921 until 1929, he was the proprietor of an electrical appliance company. Since 1929, he has been a lyricist and librettist, associated with the Broadway Stage and Hollywood films.

Harburg has been affiliated with the National Committee to Abolish the House Un-American Activities Committee ("to lead and direct the Communist Party 'Operation Abolition' campaign"); the Bill of Rights Conference ("subversive"); People's Songs ("subversive"); the Progressive Citizens of America ("Communist front"); the Joint Anti-Fascist Refugee Committee ("subversive and Communist"); the Independent Citizens Committee of the Arts, Sciences and Professions ("Communist front"); the National Citizens Political Action Committee ("Communist front"); the World

Peace Council ("Communist-dominated"); the National Council of the Arts, Sciences and Professions ("a Communist front used to appeal to special occupational groups"); the American Committee for Spanish Freedom ("Communist"); *People's World* ("Communist daily"); the National Federation for Constitutional Liberties ("under Communist Party domination and headed by responsible Party functionaries"); Stage for Action ("subversive"); the Civil Rights Congress ("subversive and Communist"); the Voice of Freedom Committee ("subversive"); the League of American Writers ("subversive and Communist"); the Hollywood Democratic Committee ("Communist front"); the Hollywood Independent Citizens Committee of the Arts, Sciences, and Professions ("political Communist front"); the Hollywood Writers Mobilization for Defense ("subversive and Communist"); the Methodist Federation for Social Action ("Communist front"); and the ultra-leftist National Peace Action Coalition of 1971.

NATHAN HARE was born on April 9, 1934 in Slick, Oklahoma. He is an alumnus of Langston University (A.B., 1954) and the University of Chicago (M.A., 1957; Ph.D., 1962). He is the author of *The Black Anglo-Saxons* (1965). He is a contributor to *The Black Power Revolt* (1968).

In 1957 and 1958, Hare was a sociology instructor at Virginia State College. From 1961 until 1967, he was at Howard University as instructor (1961-1963) and assistant professor (1963-1967). In 1968 and 1969, he was director of the black studies curriculum of San Francisco State College. In 1966 and 1967, he was a consultant to Columbia University's Teachers College.

While at Howard University, Hare described himself as the theorist of the black power movement which was being led by Stokely Carmichael. Because of his militancy, Hare was dismissed from Howard's faculty. He was constantly talking about guerrilla warfare between blacks and whites, and he predicted that militant activists would force university officials to bow to their demands. He said, "People will have to take over Howard and run it themselves to get a decent administration. The university might have to be brought to a halt, closed, wiped out, eliminated." To the militants at Howard, he gave this warning: "Unless every Howard student comes armed with a shotgun and a Molotov cocktail, they are defenseless against an oppressive 'Amos 'n' Andy' administration."

At San Francisco State College, Hare once again displayed his talent for trouble-making. He became a focal point of a riotous student strike conducted by the Black Student Union and the Third World Liberation Front. Among the demands by the striking students was the promotion of Hare to a full professorship. It was Hare's thesis that black studies had to be organized and taught by blacks who were committed to the ideals of black nationalism.

While the strike was in progress at San Francisco State, Hare's general attitude was expressed in "The Case for Separatism: 'Black Perspective,'" which appeared in *Newsweek* magazine. Said Hare: "Our cries for more black professors and black students have padded white colleges with more blacks in two years than decades of whimpering for 'integration' ever did. We blacks at white colleges remain associated with racists physically, although we seek social and psychological independence from their

HARE

oppression. The Amos 'n' Andy administrators at Negro colleges, by contrast, are
physically separated but accommodated
to their dependence on white racism as
well as the establishment's remote control of their black destiny.

"Blacks who teach at white colleges
have argued long and bitterly over course
content and instructor assignments with
white departmental chairmen of various
shades of racist persuasions. They would
rather have a white moderate professor
with a Ph.D. teaching a history sequence
starkly barren of blackness than a black
man without a degree who has spent
long hours in research on the
subject . . . . With regard to course content, the white aim is mainly to black
out the black perspective. White professors at universities such as Yale will dust
off old courses in race relations and
African tribalism for what might be
called a polka-dot studies program, while
Negro professors will trot out their old
courses in Negro history and Negro
music for Negro-studies courses which
they cynically call black. If all a black-
studies program needs is a professor with
a black skin to prattle about Negro
subject matter, then our Negro schools
would never have failed so painfully as
they have.

"In the search for educational relevance, black today is revolutionary and
nationalistic. A black-studies program
which is not revolutionary and nationalistic is, accordingly, quite profoundly
irrelevant. The black revolutionary nationalist, aware and proud of his blackness, demands the right to exist as a
distinct category, to be elevated as such
by any means necessary. The Negro,
contrarily, would just as soon be white.
He longs to escape his blackness and in
the search for integration achieves disin-
tegration.

"Thus, the key to the difference
between a black-studies program and a
Negro-studies program is a black perspective. Black students are descendants
of a people cut off from their attachment to land, culture and nation (or
peoplehood). This condition is aggra-
vated further by a whitewashed education. The expressive phase of the
black-studies program is designed to re-
generate the mortified ego of the black
child. For instance, a proud black history can restore and construct a sense of
pastness, of collective destiny, as a
springboard to the quest for a new
collective future. For black children crippled by defeatist attitudes, hardened by
generations of exclusion, this is potentially therapeutic.

"At the same time, we must resist the
white perspective which seeks to restrict
black studies to the stereotyped study of
art and religion predominantly. Black
studies should comprise a comprehensive, integrated body of interdisciplinary
courses just as in the case of long-estab-
lished departments of social science and
American studies."

In *Human Events* of January 25,
1969, Robert Bailey in his article, "Behind the Protests at San Francisco
State," commented on Hare's relationship to the revolutionary upheaval that
was attracting world-wide attention:
"The massive effort to dramatize the
Black Studies program and legitimate its
every facet, the pressures to force increased, but non-existent, appropriations
into its machinery, and the demand that
it be given stature disproportionate to its
relationship to the campus in general are
specifically designed to make this department an organizational tool and recruitment facility for the black militants to
institutionalize the black movement in
the Bay Area and provide for an 'aca-

demic' base for their 'community action.'

"In the Fall 1968 issue of *The Public Interest,* published by National Affairs, Inc., some of this concept is described and attributed to Dr. Nathan Hare. The article states: 'Central to Hare's whole proposal for a Department of Black Studies is the component of community involvement. To bring about this development it is necessary "to inspire and sustain a sense of collective destiny as a people and a consciousness of the value of education in a technological society . . . . " Students and other interested parties "will be organized into Black Cultural Councils which will sponsor cultural affairs in the Black community and establish Black holidays, festivities and celebrations." For example, a Black Winter Break could begin on February 21, the day they shot Malcolm X, run past George Washington's birthday and end with February 23, the birthday of the late Black Scholar, W.E.B. DuBois. "This," Hare says, "could approximate the Jewish Yom Kippur." There are many other suggestions: Black Information Centers "to increase communication, interpersonal contact, knowledge and socio-political awareness"; a Black Community Press, put together by "members of Black Current Events clubs and students taking courses in Black journalism"; a Bureau of Black Education "to provide Black scholars mutual aid and stimulation, and to organize Black textbook and syllabi writing corps." ' "

At the time when San Francisco State's campus was in total disorder, Hare carried his militancy to Stanford University, where he told an audience: "They say we are too few to fight. We should vote. But I can kill twenty [white] men. I can cut one's throat,

shoot another, drop a hand grenade in the middle of a whole bunch. I get only a single vote, and that's the lesser of two evils." Hare then took up the question of black historians. He said, "Black people must declare void what the white slave masters have written and must begin to write their own history and direct their destiny." He spoke about the draft and stated: "I was asked if I am an American first or a Negro first. I said I'm a black man first and not an American at all . . . . I couldn't fight for them [Americans], and if I did I would shoot as much as possible at the whites around me."

Because of his leadership of the campus demonstrations, Hare was fired from the faculty by President S.I. Hayakawa. This, however, did not deter Hare from his militant activities. In the fall of 1969, he joined other militants in presenting a "Declaration of Revolution" to the Central Committee of the World Council of Churches which was meeting at Canterbury, England. The declaration charged that white Christians had enslaved and killed hundreds of millions of blacks. Consequently, Hare and his colleagues demanded reparations of $144 million "as an immediate attempt to alter existing relations of power."

Hare has been affiliated with the National Committee to Abolish the House Un-American Activities Committee ("to lead and direct the Communist Party's 'Operation Abolition' campaign") and the ultra-leftist Friends of the Panthers. He has been active in the ultra-leftist Socialist Scholars Conferences. In 1971, he joined the ultra-leftist National Peace Action Coalition.

FRED H. HARRINGTON was born on June 24, 1942 in Watertown, New York, son of Elsie Sutton and Arthur

Harrington. He married Nancy Howes. He is an alumnus of Cornell University (A.B., 1933) and New York University (A.M., 1934; Ph.D., 1937). He held a Penfield fellowship (1933-1936); a Guggenheim fellowship (1943-1944); and a Ford faculty fellowship (1955-1956). He is the author of *God, Mammon and the Japanese: Dr. Horace N. Allen and Korean-American Relations, 1884-1905* (1944); *Fighting Politician: Major General N.P. Banks* (1948); and *Hanging Judge* (1951). He is a co-author of *An American History* (1950) and *History of American Civilization* (1953).

In 1936 and 1937, Harrington was a history instructor at New York University. From 1937 until 1940, he was at the University of Wisconsin as a history instructor (1937-1939) and assistant professor (1939-1940). From 1940 until 1944, he was head of the department and professor of history and political science at the University of Arkansas. Since 1944, he has been at the University of Wisconsin as associate professor (1944-1947), professor (1947 to the present), chairman of the history department (1952-1955), special assistant to the president (1956-1958), vice-president for academic affairs (1958-1962), vice-president of the university (1962), and president (1962 to the present). He has been a visiting professor at the University of West Virginia, Cornell University, the University of Pennsylvania, and Oxford University.

Harrington was director of the Carnegie Study of the Role of the University in Adult Education, a leftist-oriented project. Since 1962, he has been with the leftist-oriented American Council on Education as chairman of the academic affairs committee (1962-1965) and director (1966 to the present). Since 1966, he has been a director of the leftist-oriented National Association of Educational Broadcasters. He is a long-time member and has been a director of the Foreign Policy Association, a highly effective pro-Communist vehicle.

LOUIS HARRIS was born on January 6, 1921 in New Haven, Connecticut, son of Frances Smith and Harry Harris. He married Florence Yard. He is an alumnus of the University of North Carolina (A.B., 1942). He is the author of *Is There a Republican Majority? Political Trends, 1952-1956* (1954). He is the co-author of *The Negro Revolution in America* (1964) and *Black and White* (1967). He has contributed articles to *Collier's, New York Times Magazine, Public Opinion Quarterly,* and *Saturday Review.* His syndicated writings have appeared under the auspices of the *Washington Post-Los Angeles Times* (1963-1968) and the *Chicago Tribune-New York Daily News* (1969 to the present). From 1963 until 1968, he was a columnist for *Newsweek* magazine.

In 1946 and 1947, Harris was the national program and research director for the leftist American Veterans Committee. From 1947 until 1956, he was with Elmo Roper and Associates as columnist and script writer (1947-1954) and partner in the firm (1954-1956). In 1956, he founded and became proprietor of Louis Harris and Associates, a marketing and public opinion research firm. From 1962 until 1968, he was a consultant to CBS News, the leftist giant of radio and television. From 1954 until 1964, he was a faculty associate at Columbia University. Since 1964, he has been an adjunct professor of political science at the University of North Carolina.

Although most of Harris' work is done for business and industrial clients, he has gained his greatest fame through his political research polls, in which he uses door-to-door interviewers who gather information in pre-selected neighborhoods throughout the country. The information thus obtained is fed into computors, analyzed by Harris and his associates, and becomes the basis for his widely syndicated columns. Harris has also developed the Voter Profile Analysis, whereby a minute number of votes are used to project final election results.

Harris, an early member of the ultra-radical Americans for Democratic Action, received his greatest notoriety as a pollster, television coach, and campaign strategist for John F. Kennedy in the 1960 presidential campaign. Harris' advice to Senator Kennedy was to adopt a completely liberal posture – and the advice was followed. Because of his success in the Kennedy campaign, Harris has since become the pollster and adviser to hundreds of Republicans and Democrats in their campaigns for local, state or national office. Harris, the ultra-liberal, advises his clients as to how their constituents are thinking and which issues should be emphasized.

PATRICIA ROBERTS HARRIS was born on May 31, 1924 in Mattoon, Illinois, daughter of Hildren Johnson and Bert Roberts. She married William Harris. She is an alumnus of Howard University (A.B., 1945) and George Washington University (J.D., 1960). She also studied at the University of Chicago and American University.

From 1946 until 1949, Mrs. Harris was program director for the YWCA in Chicago. From 1949 until 1953, she was assistant director of the American Council on Human Rights. From 1953 until 1959, she was executive director of Delta Sigma Theta, a Negro sorority. In

1959 and 1960, she was a research associate at George Washington University's School of Law. In 1960, she was admitted to the bar in Washington, D.C. In 1960 and 1961, she was a trial attorney for the Department of Justice. From 1961 until 1969, she was at Howard University as associate dean of students and lecturer in law (1961-1963), associate professor of law (1963-1967), professor of law (1967-1969), and, for one month in 1969, dean of the Law School. (A student protest caused Mrs. Harris to resign her deanship.)

In 1964, Mrs. Harris was a delegate to the Democratic National Convention, and she seconded the nomination of Lyndon B. Johnson. In 1965, President Johnson appointed her as U.S. Ambassador to Luxembourg, in which position she served for two years. In 1966 and 1967, she served as an alternate delegate on the U.S. Mission to the United Nations General Assemblies. In 1968 and 1969, she served on the Presidential Commission on the Causes and Prevention of Violence.

Mrs. Harris has been an official of the ultra-leftist American Civil Liberties Union; the National Association for the Advancement of Colored People, the fountainhead of Negro agitation for more than half a century; and the United Nations Association of the United States, the most prestigious leftwing propaganda agency for the UN in this country. She has also been affiliated with the leftist-oriented Twentieth Century Fund; the leftist-oriented Atlantic Institute; the leftist-oriented Carnegie Commission on Future Higher Education; and the leftist-oriented Urban Coalition.

CARYL P. HASKINS was born on August 12, 1908 in Schenectady, New

HAUGHTON

York, son of Frances Parker and Caryl Haskins. He married Edna Ferrell. He is an alumnus of Yale University (Ph.B., 1930) and Harvard University (Ph.D., 1935). He is the author of *Of Ants and Men* (1939); *The Amazon: The Life History of a Mighty River* (1943); *Of Societies and Men* (1950); and *The Scientific Revolution and World Politics* (1964). He is the editor of *The Search for Understanding* (1967).

From 1931 until 1935, Haskins was a research chemist for the General Electric Company in Schenectady. From 1935 until 1945, he was a research associate at Massachusetts Institute of Technology. From 1937 until 1955, he was a research professor in biophysics at Union College in New York. From 1935 until 1955, he was president and research director of Haskins Laboratories, Inc. Since 1956, he has been president of the Carnegie Institution of Washington. From 1941 until 1943, he was with the Office of Scientific Research and Development as assistant liaison officer (1941-1942) and senior liaison officer (1942-1943). From 1943 until 1945, he was with the National Defense Research Committee as executive assistant to the chairman (1943-1944) and deputy executive officer (1944-1945). He has served as a consultant to the National Research and Development Board (1947-1951), to the Secretary of Defense (1950-1960), and to the Secretary of State (1950 to the present). Since 1955, he has been with the President's Science Advisory Committee as a member (1955-1958) and a consultant (1959 to the present).

Since 1955, Haskins has been a trustee of the leftist-oriented Carnegie Corporation. Since 1961, he has been on the board of directors of the Council on Foreign Relations, the informal supra-State Department of the United States.

Since 1955, he has been a trustee of the RAND Corporation, the most influential of the ruling Establishment's think factories.

ELEANOR LEACOCK HAUGHTON

was born on July 2, 1922 in Weehawken, New Jersey, daughter of Lily Batterham and Kenneth Burke. She was married to and divorced from Richard Leacock. She is married to James Haughton. She is the author of *Teaching and Learning in City Schools* (1968). She is the co-author of *Toward Integration in Suburban Housing* (1965). She is the editor of Lewis Henry Morgan's *Ancient Society* (1963) and *Culture of Poverty: A Critique* (1971). She is co-editor of *North American Indians in Historical Perspective* (1971).

From 1952 until 1955, Mrs. Haughton was a research assistant at the Cornell University Medical College and a staff member of the Yorkville Mental Health Project. In 1955 and 1956, she was a lecturer in anthropology and sociology at Queens College. From 1956 until 1960, she was a lecturer in anthropology and sociology at the City College of New York. From 1958 until 1965, she was a research associate at the Bank Street College of Education in New York City. Since 1963, she has been at the Polytechnic Institute in Brooklyn as associate professor (1963-1967) and professor (1967 to the present) of anthropology. She has been a faculty member at the Center for Marxist Education.

Mrs. Haughton has been affiliated with the leftist-pacifist Scientists on Survival; the leftist GI Civil Liberties Defense Committee; the leftist-pacifist Teachers Committee for Peace in Vietnam; the leftist-oriented Ad Hoc Committee for an Open Letter on Vietnam; the leftist-pacifist Ad Hoc Faculty Committee on Vietnam; and the leftist-oriented Ad Hoc Committee on the Vietnam War. She has been a participant in the annual ultra-leftist Socialist Scholars Conferences. She is a vigorous promoter of Socialist goals in education.

AUGUSTUS HAWKINS was born on August 31, 1907 in Shreveport, Louisiana, son of Hattie Freeman and Nyanza Hawkins. He was married to the late Pegga Smith. He is an alumnus of the University of California at Los Angeles (B.A., 1931).

From 1935 until 1962, Hawkins was in the California House of Representatives from Los Angeles County. Since 1963, he has been in the U.S. House of Representatives from the 21st congressional district of California. Since 1945, he has engaged in real estate, insurance, and retail businesses.

Hawkins is unquestionably one of the most extreme leftists ever to sit in the Congress of the United States. He has been identified under oath as a member of the Communist Party, but he has not admitted such membership. He has been affiliated with the People's Educational Center ("a Communist Party school"); Mobilization for Democracy ("a Communist-inspired and dominated organization, carefully window-dressed and directed" and "engaged in inciting riots, racial hatred, and disrespect for law and order"); the Sleepy Lagoon Defense Committee ("Communist front"); the American League for Peace and Democracy ("subversive and Communist"); the Progressive Citizens of America ("political Communist front"); the Tom Mooney Labor School ("Communist Party school"); the California Legislative Conference ("complete subservience to the twists and turns of the Communist Party line"); the National Negro Congress ("subversive and Communist"); and the United Negro and Allied Veterans of America ("subversive and among the affiliates and committees of the Communist Party U.S.A.").

As a member of Congress, Hawkins has compiled one of the most perfect Liberal voting records, by the standards of the ultra-radical Americans for Democratic Action. He has always voted against appropriations for the House Committee on Un-American Activities and its successor, the House Internal Security Committee. He has been a racist leader in the Congress. In 1969, he was a member of the all-black Congressional Ad Hoc Committee to investigate clashes between police and Black Panthers. As a member of the leftist-militant Black Caucus group in the House, and as a member of the House Education and Labor Committee, he has worked to increase the powers of the Equal Employment Opportunity Commission to give the EEOC virtual dictatorial powers in the area of civil rights. If Hawkins had his way, the EEOC would be highly discriminatory in favor of blacks. He has been a leader in the Citizens Committee for Equal Justice for Public Employees, and as such he favors compulsory unionism for all state and local government employees.

Hawkins has joined the far left in its opposition to U.S. involvement in Vietnam. He has been a supporter of the Communist-dominated Vietnam Moratorium Committee. He supported the Vietnam Disengagement Act of 1971.

When Communist Angela Davis was arrested for murder, kidnapping, and criminal conspiracy, Hawkins rushed to her defense, saying: "Current revelations indicate the government's case is based more on a dislike for her personal beliefs and associations than on legal evidence." He also said that "the persecution and official hysteria surrounding the Angela

Davis case are shocking examples of this nation's sickness in dealing with racial inequality and racial injustice." Of Miss Davis' position on the faculty of the University of California, Hawkins said he "defended Miss Davis' right of academic freedom while she taught at the University of California, of which he is an alumnus." From his warped viewpoint, Hawkins considered that Angela Davis, who flaunted her membership in the Communist Party, was working for "the opportunity to seek constructive change in a nation and world which badly needs persons with insight and moral convictions."

'WILLIAM HENDERSON was born on October 9, 1922 in New York City, son of Charlotte Fischer and James Henderson. He married Maxine Book. He is an alumnus of Hamilton College (B.A., 1942) and Columbia University (M.A., 1948). He pursued graduate studies at the University of Colorado. He is the author of *Pacific Settlement of Disputes: The Indonesian Question, 1946-1949* (1954) and *New Nations of Southeast Asia* (1955). He is a contributor to *Viet-Nam: The First Five Years* (1959) and *Problems of Freedom: South Vietnam Since Independence* (1962). He is editor of and a contributor to *Southeast Asia: Problems of United States Policy* (1964). Since 1966, he has been editor of *Vietnam Perspectives*, a quarterly journal published by the American Friends of Vietnam.

In 1942 and 1943, and in 1946, Henderson was an economist with the U.S. Office of the Alien Property Custodian. In 1948 and 1949, he was an instructor in history and government at Adelphi College. From 1949 until 1953, he was on the government faculty of Barnard College. From 1952 until 1962,

he held various positions, including associate director, with the Council on Foreign Relations, the informal supra-State Department of the United States. Since 1962, he has been with Mobil Oil Corporation, and since 1965, he has been Mobil's manager of international government relations. He has long been chairman of the executive committee of American Friends of Vietnam, a front of the Socialist-lined International Rescue Committee.

WILLIAM R. HEROD was born on February 13, 1898 in Indianapolis, son of Mary Applegate and William Herod. He married Caroline Fries. He is an alumnus of Yale University (Ph.B., 1918).

From 1919 until 1929, Herod worked in the construction engineering department of the General Electric Company. From 1929 until 1934, he was an assistant to the president of the International General Electric Company in New York City. From 1934 until 1937, he was assistant to the managing director of Associated Electrical Industries, Ltd., in London. From 1937 until 1960, he was with the International General Electric Company as vice-president (1937-1942), executive vice-president (1945), and president (1945-1960). From 1952 until 1960, he was vice-president of General Electric Company.

From 1938 until 1951, Herod was affiliated in various capacities with the Institute of Pacific Relations, "a vehicle used by the Communists to orientate American far eastern policies toward Communist objectives." As early as 1949, he was urging the United States Government to prepare for diplomatic recognition of Red China, and at that same early date, he was very much in favor of U.S. trade with Red China. He has long been affiliated with the Council on Foreign Relations, the informal supra-State Department of the United States; the leftist-oriented Atlantic Council; the leftist-oriented Institute of International Education; and the Foreign Policy Association, a highly effective vehicle for pro-Communist propaganda.

STEPHEN HESS was born on April 20, 1933 in New York City, son of Florence Morse and Charles Hess. He married Elena Shayne. He is an alumnus of The Johns Hopkins University (B.A., 1953). He also studied at the University of Chicago. He is the author of *America's Political Dynasties* (1966). He is co-author of *Hats in the Ring: The Making of Presidential Candidates* (1960); *The Republican Establishment* (1967); *The Ungentlemanly Art: A History of American Political Cartoons* (1968); and *Nixon: A Political Portrait* (1968).

From 1953 until 1955, Hess was an instructor in political science at The Johns Hopkins University. In 1956, he was an administrative assistant to the field director of the Republican Congressional Committee. In 1958, he was a member of the public relations staff of the Republican National Committee. From 1959 until 1961, he was on the White House staff working as a speech writer under the direction of the ultraliberal Malcolm Moos. In 1961, he was an assistant to the Republican whip in the U.S. Senate. In 1962, he was a speech writer in the California gubernatorial campaign of Richard M. Nixon. In 1964 and 1965, he was an associate fellow at the Institute for Policy Studies, a leftist propaganda agency for disarmament. In 1967 and 1968, he was a fellow at the Institute of Politics in the John F. Kennedy School of Government at Harvard University. In 1968, he was a speech writer in Spiro Agnew's vice-presidential campaign. In 1969 and 1970, he was a deputy assistant to the President for Urban Affairs. In 1970 and 1971, he was in charge of the White House Conference on Children and Youth.

When Hess became national chairman of the White House Conference on Children and Youth, he loaded his staff with ultra-liberals from both Democratic and Republican Parties. Members of the staff and interns in the WHCCY program were especially conspicuous for their attacks upon the Nixon Administration. For his part, Hess made a deliberate effort to cater to the demands of militant blacks, militant whites, leftwing-pacifists, and other radicals.

In April 1971, the WHCCY held a four-day session at Estes Park, Colorado. Hess admitted that he had deliberately stacked the body of delegates with representatives of minority groups. In the Colorado meeting, the delegates passed resolutions favoring the legalization of marijuana; a complete withdrawal of all U.S. forces from Vietnam and an end of all U.S. support for its allies in Vietnam; an all-volunteer army; a national health-care program for every American; amnesty for all draft dodgers in the United States and those who fled into exile; legislation granting 18-year-olds the right to vote, marry, and make contracts without parental consent; nationalization of the coal industry; a guaranteed annual income; the allocation of at least 25 per cent of the 1972 national budget for education; an end to legal restrictions on abortions; the recognition and toleration of any sexual behavior between consenting adults; and the adoption of the Hanoi-inspired People's Peace Treaty. The delegates also called for the resignation of FBI Director J. Edgar

Hoover. And, as might have been expected, Hess had nothing but praise for the work of his leftist-radical conferees.

WILLIAM H. HINTON was born on February 2, 1919 in Chicago, son of Carmelita Chase and Sebastian Hinton. He was married to and divorced from Bertha Sneck. He is married to Joanne Raiford. He is an alumnus of Cornell University (B.S., 1941). He also studied at Harvard University. He is the author of *Fanshen: A Documentary of Revolution in a Chinese Village* (1967 and 1968) and *Iron Oxen: A Documentary of Revolution in Chinese Farming* (1970).

In 1941 and 1942, Hinton was a farm manager at the Putney School in Putney, Vermont. In 1942 and 1943, he was a farm manager in West Campton, New Hampshire. In 1943, he was drafted under the Selective Service System but was sent to a camp for conscientious objectors at Weston, New Hampshire, where he stayed for more than a year. In 1944, he applied for military service but was rejected. He then returned to the Putney School. In 1945 and 1946, he was a propaganda analyst in China for the Red-lined Office of War Information. In 1946 and 1947, he was an organizer for the northeastern division of the National Farmers Union, when that division had a Communist as president. From 1947 and 1953, he was a tractor technician in China where he worked successively for UNRRA, the Red Chinese Government in Shansi Province, and the Red Chinese Government in Peking. From 1956 until 1963, he was a truck mechanic in Philadelphia, Pennsylvania. Since 1963, he has been a grain farmer in Fleetwood, Pennsylvania.

In 1954, Hinton testified before the Senate Internal Security Subcommittee.

During the course of his testimony he had frequent recourse to the protection of the Fifth Amendment. On dozens of occasions, he refused to tell the Subcommittee anything concerning his Communist Party membership, his associations with Communists, or his activities with Communists. Senator William E. Jenner, then chairman of the Subcommittee, subsequently described Hinton as follows: "... Hinton is a former American newspaperman. He had been farm manager for the Putney School at Putney, Vermont. Toward the end of World War II, he was sent to China by the Office of War Information. He returned to the United States in the spring of 1945 and was organizer for the National Farmers Union. He went back to China as an official of the United Nations Relief and Rehabilitation Administration in 1947. When the Moscow-armed Chinese Communists took over the Chinese mainland in the fall of 1949, this man Hinton remained as an employee of the Communist Government.

"He returned to the United States in August 1953, after a stopover in Moscow. Since his arrival in this country, he has been propagandizing on behalf of the brainwashing, soul-killing Red Chinese, whose soldiers were torturing and slaying Hinton's fellow Americans at the very moment he was on Red China's payroll.

"... One sister, Jean, was a friend of the notorious Nathan Gregory Silvermaster and worked under him at the old Farm Security Administration. Another sister, Joan, was an atomic research assistant at the Los Alamos project where she had access to classified material. Like her brother William, Joan also went to China and stayed there after the Communist triumph. She got a job through another American, Gerald Tannenbaum, who was executive director of the China Welfare Fund headed by Mme. Sun Yat-sen . . . . In China, Joan married Erwin [Sidney] Engst, who was also an old UNRRA man. Today the Engsts are somewhere in the depths of Inner Mongolia, serving the Communist cause. Joan came out of obscurity long enough to make a bitterly anti-American speech at the Communist-inspired fraud known as the Asian and Pacific Peace Conference, regarding which the subcommittee also expects to reveal a great deal.

"The Putney school, which is run by William Hinton's mother and where he himself was employed, is a story in itself. One of its faculty members was Edwin S. Smith. Smith later became a registered propagandist for the Soviet Government. He distributed photographs attempting to prove that the United States practiced germ warfare in North Korea. Another person closely associated with Putney was Owen Lattimore. The subcommittee found, after a 15-month inquiry, that Lattimore was a 'conscious, articulate instrument in the Soviet Conspiracy.'

"Lattimore built the Pacific Operations Branch of OWI, for which Hinton later worked in Chungking. John K. Fairbank was at the top of OWI's Chinese organization. Benjamin Kizer ran the Chinese branch of UNRRA for which Hinton also worked.

"Lattimore, Fairbank, and Kizer all were key figures in the Institute of Pacific Relations. All three were named as Communists in sworn testimony before us. All three denied the charge, but when counsel for the subcommittee asked Hinton about his connections with Lattimore and Kizer, he said it might incriminate him to give a true answer to the question."

In 1953, when Hinton returned to the United States, his "notes, diaries, correspondence and background material

on China" were seized by United States customs officials. In its 1956 Report, the Senate Internal Security Subcommittee said: "For many months, the material was studied by members of the subcommittee's professional staff, as well as by experts from the Library of Congress and other Government agencies. Individuals who had personal knowledge of the Chinese Communist revolution were also consulted. Throughout the entire period in which the documents were being studied, Hinton made persistent attempts to regain possession of them." Chairman Jenner summarized the story which unfolded in Hinton's material: "The documents were written by one who began as an observer. Then he joined a 'work group' and learned how to 'purify the party,' 'purify' being a Marxist synonym for 'purge.' His zealousness, his passionate, repeated, fully-expressed determination to wipe out all anti-Communist thought elevated him finally to the post of 'upper cadre.' As Hinton himself makes clear, this means that he occupied a place in the Communist command.

" 'We organized,' he says in the 'notes, diaries, correspondence, and background material,' which were seized from him by United States customs. 'We purified. We sent directives. We treated different cases differently. We upper cadres must take the blame.'

"The Hinton papers are also a compendium of Communist doctrine, of Communist official propaganda in both English and Chinese. There are nearly 400 photographs, some of them from official propaganda sources, and some which seem to be the work of amateur photographers. They include pictures of many Americans whose activities the subcommittee is scrutinizing, in our current study of 'The Scope of Soviet Activity.'

HINTON

".... William Hinton's picture... we found among the 'background material' he told us about. He is dressed in Chinese garb, standing on a platform in front of the Communist hammer and sickle, the flag of Communist China, and a picture of China's Communist dictator, Mao Tse-tung. He is making a speech to his fellow Communists.

"Here are some of William Hinton's own words, which we found among the 'notes, diaries, and correspondence' that he swore were his. First are selections from a letter he wrote to his two sisters, Jean and Joan. Before Joan's flight to China, she and Jean had a letter from their brother in far-off Tientsin. He did not like the news from home. 'That great beast, America,' he told his sisters, 'looks down upon the world and licks its lips.' And then, this: 'So far I have seen no evidence of the anti-American feeling that is supposed to be rampant here. This worries me a little since it indicates the people have not yet learned who their enemies are. The soldiers are a little more conscious of the facts of life and always look astounded when you tell them you are an American.' "

When he testified, Hinton pointedly remarked to the Subcommittee that the original of his "travelog, Yenan to Mongolia" was in the material seized by the U.S. customs officials. On May 10, 1956, on the floor of the Senate, the new chairman of the Subcommittee, James Eastland, reviewed Hinton's travelog: "It is clear from this document that the Communist Hinton had full freedom to come and go throughout Red China at a time when other Americans were being brainwashed, starved, and tortured in Communist prisons. There is no difficulty in understanding why, once we examine this cheerful little 'travelog.' Let me read a few passages.

"He visits a fort, and reports joyfully that 'life is moving ahead here with a swing .... The walls of the forts are plastered with slogans,' he writes. 'Carry out the new marriage law, Raise production, Join in the great land reform rechecking movement, Oppose America and aid Korea, Study the thought of Chairman Mao.'

"He meets a doctor, and complains because the latter seems to still have a little 'Chung Mey' (worship America) attitude. But, says Hinton, the doctor 'is learning fast and putting into practice many Soviet techniques ....'

"And then, in a railroad station, he looks upon 'a long crowded platform of People's Volunteers dancing and singing, as they waited for their train .... When this or that group got tired of dancing they stopped, lined up, and burst into song, singing "Leap Across the Yalu" and other popular tunes of the day .... The whole scene was one of collective gaiety and good spirits. I could not help thinking what the American soldiers must be like as they leave for the front. Do they dance and sing, laugh and joke, study reading and writing, push health and exercise? '

" '... Everyone,' Hinton reports, 'Everyone is putting renewed effort into aid for Korea to see to it that the imperialists never again dare poke their pigs snout into liberated China.'

"He taught in a North China 'university,' where boys and girls were trained for every kind of Communist revolutionary task. He took those boys and girls to a 'struggle meeting' in a former Catholic church, and gloated while one shivering human was shrieked at by a Red mob for 11 solid hours, for indulging in the crime of 'landlord thought.'

"He conferred and banqueted with a commissar of the Central Committee of

China's Communist Party. He taxed, purged, classified, and brought wholesale Communist discipline to terrified peasants in Chinese villages. He made a speech in a town square, urging his listeners not to yield to 'tolerance.' He surveyed a Red propaganda display and complained because it did not inflame the peasants to 'a broader scope of accusation.' He went to a meeting of foreign writers at a Red army school. He conferred with the Red army's chief of staff on the very eve of the great offensive of 1948. He danced in the streets to celebrate Soviet holidays and the victories of China's Red army. He met with Communist 'cadres' to discuss 'recruiting,' 'militia,' 'preferential treatment for soldiers families' and 'training with rifles, grenades, mines, etc.' He wept at the memorial service where Red China officially commemorated Agnes Smedley's 20 years service in the Communist underground, and to which it sent Red army soldiers to lay flowers on her grave. He rejoiced at the spectacle of 'People's Volunteers' on the way to North Korea to kill American boys. He brainwashed himself and others, time and time again, to wipe the last vestiges of Americanism from his mind and soul.

"His papers tell the story of that brainwashing. Here are a few passages, which show his gradual progression from an 'agricultural technician' to an 'upper cadre' of China's Communist legions. When he was still an UNRRA worker in the Nationalist territory, he wrote this to his then wife, Bertha, who was in the United States: 'There is a move on here to get me into the job of supplying Communist areas and if I can get it, I will take it . . . . I would be on salary and doing something that I have no qualms about.' Shortly thereafter, he begged her to 'come to China right away . . . . I have

burned certain bridges behind me,' he said. His wife burned bridges, too, in response to that plea, and her bridges remained burned. One of the first things Hinton did on returning to the United States was to get a Reno divorce and cast his wife and child adrift behind the Bronze curtain.

"Here is an example of self-brainwashing, of that Communist passion to believe everything good about the Soviets and everything bad about the United States: 'I suppose you have enough sense not to credit any of the stories about Russian artillery, Russian shells, Russian officers, Japanese troops, etc., etc., etc., that are pouring out of Mukden. There is no doubt that these are all fabrications . . . . No Russian arms, equipment, men, or anything else have ever been seen in Manchuria since the Russians withdrew. The American Government and the American press know this full well. (After all, we have a whole corps of men on the spot whose main task is just that, to prove that the Russians are helping the Reds. So far they have been grossly disappointed.) Yet they continue their insinuations, innuendoes, and outright lies . . . .'

". . . The story develops in many documents, including letters to Sidney Engst, another former UNRRA worker and renegade who married Hinton's sister, Joan, in China. Note it, against the background of Hinton's sworn statement at the American Consulate in Prague, to the effect that he had simply been an agricultural technician at a single state farm. 'I was just settling down to a quiet period of teaching and study when the land reform began in this Hsien,' he writes to Engst. 'Many students went out to join in the work and I got ants in my pants and rushed around until I, too, got permission to go . . . . We are in no way a high-powered group, so we made some bad mistakes and wandered all over the lot. After 2 months we still haven't organized the Peasants League, but we have organized the basic groups and purified the party.'

" 'Purified the party?' He means purged, does he not? This American, this so-called 'agricultural technician' is beginning to practice Soviet-discipline upon Chinese peasants on their own Chinese soil. A little later the 'agricultural technician' lays down his tools. 'As for the tools,' he says, 'I have been so busy with this land reform that I have neglected them quite a bit . . . .' Listen, as he becomes more and more enraptured. 'Everyone who calls himself a revolutionary or wants to work for the Chinese people must now examine himself, prepare himself for mass work, for handing leadership to poor peasants and hired laborers, to give up one's own land, perhaps even struggle against one's own parents . . . .

" 'Well, when you are going to treat different classes differently you must have some idea of who is in what class and that was one of the most interesting parts of the work. Standards were set by the Central Committee (based by the way on standards drawn up by Lenin back in 1919) and everyone including the most backward and illiterate peasants studied them. You have never seen such a mass education movement as this was. Millions of peasants learned how to distinguish a rich farmer from a middle farmer (this is the key point since the former are struggled and the latter protected) and a poor farmer from a middle one. They learned it by applying these standards to all the families in their village. The whole village was classified three times so that there would be no mistake. Each time everyone appeared before the people of his part of the village, reported his land and property and his opinion of his class. Then all discussed and decided what he was. After the whole village was finished the list was posted . . . .

" 'My work mainly consists of going from farm to farm, looking into the way things are done, helping to solve problems, criticizing and encouraging . . . .To arrive at any of the state farms is like a homecoming for me, for almost all of the drivers are my students, old friends, and comrades . . . . Every day, no matter how busy the work is, there is at least an hour or two of political study, and if it can't be carried out in an organized way during the heaviest rush of work it is done individually through reading the paper whenever there is a spare moment.

" 'It was while we were assembling the combines for the 10,000-mou wheat harvest that the Stockholm peace appeal reached the Chi-Heng State Farm. It was discussed for several days and was signed by everyone. [The Stockholm peace appeal, of course, was a routine Moscow fraud.]

" '. . . Of all the things I have seen in this last year and a half the most striking has been the development of the cadres and workers through the political education led by the Communist Party . . . . Through countless work review meetings and meetings for self and mutual criticism the people are gradually being united and steeled.'

"The people were united in other ways than in 'work review meetings.' They were united in death. *Time* magazine reported a few weeks ago that 'at least 20 million Chinese have been deprived of existence since the Communists took over.' *Time* adds, 'In no previous war, revolution, or human holocaust, either in the days of Tamerlane or in the time of Hitler, have so many people been destroyed in so short a period.'

"There is no charity, no grief, no horror at this 'human holocaust' in William Hinton's heart. In all the thousands of pages in the footlocker he brought home, we found only a paragraph or two to express disapproval. It is not the disapproval of Christian outrage. It is the ideological disapproval of the Communist 'upper cadre.' Here it is: 'The leftist errors really began to be serious in May 1947. Correction in our area began after Chairman Mao's Christmas report in about the middle of January. Beginning at that time we sent three directives from the Taihang subregion to the Diwey party committee . . . . The peasants must be under proletarian leadership. Without proletarian thought to guide them they commit just such errors and destroy the revolution. It has been our experience that whenever the peasants are mobilized to struggle they push on toward extreme equalitarianism and the cadres invariably follow along. In this case we upper cadres must take the blame for not having given the lower cadres full explanation and education about this point.' "

In 1967, when Hinton's *Fanshen* was published, it was hailed by Edgar Snow and Felix Greene, two of the most notorious mouthpieces for Mao Tsetung. For his own part, Hinton promoted *Fanshen* by fulfilling a speaking schedule under the auspices of the *National Guardian*, a Communist weekly. As might be expected, Hinton was a strong opponent of U.S. involvement in the Vietnam War. In 1967, he visited Hanoi where he received a welcome reserved exclusively for anti-American propagandists. He has been active in the ultra-leftist Committee of Concerned Asian Scholars. He is a member of the Berks County [Pennsylvania] Committee of Peace in Vietnam. And to round out his leftist credentials, he is a member of the ultra-leftist American Civil Liberties Union.

MAHLON B. HOAGLAND was born on October 5, 1921 in Boston, Massachusetts, son of Anna Plummer and Hudson Hoagland. His second wife is Olley Jones. He is an alumnus of Harvard University (M.D., 1948). He also studied at Williams College.

From 1948 until 1960, Hoagland served, successively, as research fellow and assistant professor of medicine on the Harvard Medical School faculty at Massachusetts General Hospital. From 1960 until 1967, he was an associate professor of bacteriology and immunology at Harvard Medical School. Since 1967, he has been a professor of biochemistry and chairman of the biochemistry department at Dartmouth Medical School. He was a research associate at the Carlsberg Laboratories in Copenhagen (1951-1952) and the Cavendish Laboratories in Cambridge, England (1957-1958). From 1954 until 1957, he was the executive secretary of the committee on research at Massachusetts General Hospital. He was a consultant to the National Institute of Health (1961-1964) and the American Cancer Society (1965-1968).

Hoagland has been affiliated with the leftist-oriented Ad Hoc Committee for an Open Letter on Vietnam; the leftist-pacifist Ad Hoc Faculty Committee on Vietnam; the leftist-pacifist Civil Defense Letter Committee; and the Federation of American Scientists, a bleeding heart group, members of which are generally affiliated with a variety of radical one-world and/or pacifist organizations.

JULIUS W. HOBSON was born in 1922 in Birmingham, Alabama. His second wife is Tina Lower. He is an alumnus of Tuskegee Institute.

From 1953 until 1970, Hobson was an economist with the Department of Health, Education, and Welfare. In the 1960's, he came into national prominence as a racist agitator in Washington, D.C. In 1964, he was so militant that the leftist-racist Congress of Racial Equality expelled him as head of its Washington, D.C., chapter. By that time, Hobson was a leader of ACT, which had been organized in 1964. Hobson stated that the group was "not a civil rights organization in the classical sense, but a revolutionary one in the American tradition." He was also a leader of ACT's political arm, the Organization for Black Power, whose aim was to win political control of major U.S. cities through mobilization and control of the Negro residents. According to its literature, OBP "is part of the revolutionary struggle of people all over the world to liberate themselves from the determination of the United States to impose its way of life on the whole world and to build a new world free from exploitation." (The chairman of the OBP, since its beginning in 1965, has been Jesse Gray, a former Communist Party organizer in Harlem.)

In March 1966, Hobson as head of ACT was cooperating in "The Free D.C. Movement," a pressure group of civil rights agitators who were attempting to intimidate the Congress into passing home-rule legislation that would put the agitators in complete control of the nation's capital city. The Movement's leaders, in order to build up a $100,000 slush fund to promote their home-rule program, decided to institute a boycott-blackmail operation by which merchants throughout Washington would be assessed for a contribution to the Movement or else have their businesses boycotted. The scheme attracted very unfavorable publicity and caused some of the leaders to abandon it. Hobson was quite disappointed. In vain he argued: "The Movement is trying to seek out its friends and enemies to identify them. We intend to punish those who are against us. There's nothing too bad to do to the merchants downtown, even burning their stores." His rallying cry was: "Violence is the order of the day."

Hobson was continuously in the limelight in 1966. He boycotted a White House Conference on Civil Rights, claiming that it was too mild in tone. Instead, he used his time to confer with Jesse Gray. In September 1966, he was a leading participant in a Black Power conference, held under the leadership of Representative Adam Clayton Powell. In the same period, he was also agitating in the courts on the matter of school segregation. He was at that time a member of the District's school board and by his side in the courts were Arthur Kinoy and William Kunstler – two who were long accustomed to representing far-leftists. (In June 1967, a U.S. Circuit Court judge ruled that the Washington, D.C., board of education had to adopt a school busing program. The ruling came on a suit filed by Hobson.)

There was no doubt about Hobson's leftism. In 1967, the *Washington Evening Star* quoted him: "You can't make Socialist promises within the capitalist system. It won't work. I'm a Marxist-Socialist, not a Communist, but I don't have any illusions that I can change the system, although I think I can improve it." As part of his improvement program, he advised poor people to file bankruptcy proceedings whenever they were burdened with instalment payments. He also urged Negroes to buy guns in order to protect themselves, because, he alleged, the Washington, D.C., police had declared war upon the Negro population. (In 1968, Hobson endorsed the Trotskyite-Communist Socialist Workers Party's national ticket.)

Throughout 1968 and 1969, Hobson continued to advocate violence in the district. He led marches on schools and police stations. He even called upon students to take over the schools physically. In April 1969, he spoke during a Black Awareness Week program at Georgetown University. *Human Events* (April 16, 1969) reported on his fiery speech: "Stressing his self-admitted 'Marxist-Socialist' philosophy, Hobson declared that the American free-enterprise system 'must be overthrown by force and violence' before the gap can be bridged between the nation's haves and have-nots. The black community, Hobson bellowed, 'is going to have to get angry and take over the schools, physically.' They have 'nothing to lose by raising hell . . . .[even if] they take over, control, occupy the schools . . . .'

"Hobson emphasized that he believes in 'force and violence' because 'it is not possible to solve the social problems under the present economic and social system.'

" 'I'm personally a Socialist,' Hobson asserted, and then he reiterated for disbelieving students that he felt the 'struggle is international, worldwide and we should make use of resources outside the United States . . . including Cuba and China' in the fight against capitalism. 'The destruction of capitalism is essential to ending poverty,' he declared."

As a result of Hobson's Georgetown speech, several members of the Congress insisted that he be fired from his position in the Department of Health, Education, and Welfare. Finally, on April 1, 1970, Hobson saw the handwriting on the wall and submitted his resignation. At almost the same time, he suffered a defeat when he sought a seat as the District of Columbia's non-voting delegate to the House of Representatives. Since that time, he has been somewhat less effective as a civil rights agitator.

DONALD C. HODGES was born on October 22, 1923 in Ft. Worth, Texas. He is married. He is an alumnus of New York University (B.A., 1947) and Columbia University (M.A., 1948; Ph.D., 1954). He is the author of *Socialist Humanism: The Outcome of Classical European Morality* (1969).

From 1949 until 1952, Hodges was at Hobart College and William Smith College as an instructor in humanities (1949-1950) and in philosophy (1950-1952). From 1952 until 1963, he was at the University of Missouri as instructor (1952-1954), assistant professor (1954-1957), associate professor (1957-1963), and chairman of the department of humanities (1956-1961). In 1963, he was a professor of philosophy at the University of Nebraska. In 1963 and 1964, he was a professor of philosophy at the University of Southern Florida. Since 1964, he has been at Florida State University as chairman of the department and professor of philosophy. He has been a resident fellow at the University of Missouri and Florida State University. He has been a visiting professor at the University of Hawaii.

Hodges has been affiliated with the ultra-leftist American-Korean Friendship and Information Center and the ultra-leftist American Society for the Study of the German Democratic Republic.

HOLLAND

WILLIAM L. HOLLAND was born on December 28, 1907 in South Malvern, New Zealand, son of Ada Jewell and Frederick Holland. He came to the United States in 1929. He was married to and divorced from Doreen McGarry. He is an alumnus of the University of New Zealand (B.A., 1928; M.A., 1930). In 1932 and 1933, he held a Rockefeller fellowship as a research student at Caius College at Cambridge University in England. He is the author of *China's Economic Development* (1931) and *Migrations in the Pacific* (1931). He is co-author of *Next Step in Asia* (1949). He is editor of *Commodity Control in the Pacific* (1935); *Problems of Economic Reconstruction in the Far East* (1949); and *Asian Nationalism and the West* (1953). He is co-editor of *Problems of the Pacific: War and Peace in the Pacific* (1943).

From 1928 until 1960, Holland was with the Institute of Pacific Relations: research assistant in Honolulu (1928-1932); research secretary in New York City, Tokyo, Shanghai, and Berkeley, California (1933-1943); and secretary-general and research director (1946-1960). He attended IPR conferences in Kyoto, Japan (1929), Shanghai (1931), Banff, Canada (1933), Yosemite, California (1936), Virginia Beach, Virginia (1939), Mont Tremblant, Quebec (1942), Hot Springs, Virginia (1945), Stratford-on-Avon (1947), Lucknow (1950), Kyoto (1954), and Lahore, Pakistan (1958). From 1953 until 1960, he was co-editor of the IPR's *Far Eastern Survey*. In 1943, and since 1953, he has been editor of the IPR's *Pacific Affairs*. In 1944, he lectured at the U.S. Navy's School of Military Government at Columbia University. In 1945 and 1946, he was director of the U.S. Office of War Information's China division in Chung-king. Since 1961, he has been chairman of the department and professor of Asian studies at the University of British Columbia. He has been a long-time non-resident member of the Council on Foreign Relations, the informal supra-State Department of the United States.

In Holland's more than four decades with the Institute of Pacific Relations, he has been one of that organization's most active and influential officials. In 1951, after five months of preliminary investigation, the Senate Internal Security Subcommittee held hearings on the IPR. Between July 25, 1951, and June 20, 1952, the SISS heard sixty-six witnesses in one of the most extensive congressional hearings ever held. The SISS sought to determine: "(a) Whether or to what extent the Institute of Pacific Relations was infiltrated and influenced or controlled by agents of the communist world conspiracy; (b) Whether or to what extent these agents and their dupes worked through the Institute into the United States Government to the point where they exerted an influence on United States far eastern policy; and if so, whether and to what extent they still exert such influence; (c) Whether or to what extent these agents and their dupes led or misled American public opinion, particularly with respect to far eastern policy."

During the course of the hearings, the SISS heard sworn testimony in which many IPRers were identified as Communists. They included: Solomon Adler; James S. Allen (Sol Auerbach); Asiaticus (Heinz Moeller, Hans Mueller, or M.G. Shippe); Hilda Austern; Joseph F. and Kathleen Barnes; T.A. Bisson; Evans Carlson; Abraham Chapman (John Arnold); Chen Han-seng (Geoffrey or Raymond D. Brooke); Chi Ch'ao-ting (Hansu Chan or T.B. Lowe); Harriet Levine Chi;

456

Frank Coe; Len De Caux; Israel Epstein; John K. Fairbank; Frederick Vanderbilt Field; Julian Friedman; Talitha Gerlach; Kumar Goshal; Alger Hiss; Philip Jaffe (James W. Phillips); Anthony Jenkinson; Benjamin H. Kizer; Corliss Lamont; Olga Lang; Owen Lattimore; William M. Mandel; Kate Mitchell; Harriet L. Moore; E. Herbert Norman; Hotsumi Ozaki; Mildred Price; Lee Pressman; Lawrence K. Rosinger; Helen Schneider; Agnes Smedley; Nym Wales (Mrs. Edgar Snow); Andrew Steiger; Maxwell Stewart; Anna Louise Strong; Ilona Ralf Sues; Daniel Thorner; Mary Van Kleeck; John Carter Vincent; and Ella Winter. (Of those identified, John K. Fairbank, Julian Friedman, Benjamin Kizer, Corliss Lamont, Owen Lattimore, Kate Mitchell, Maxwell Stewart, and John Carter Vincent denied under oath their alleged membership in the Communist Party.)

Many of the IPRers were identified as collaborators of the Soviet Union's intelligence apparatus (including Solomon Adler, Frank Coe, Lauchlin Currie, Laurence Duggan, Israel Epstein, Frederick V. Field, Michael Greenberg, Alger Hiss, Owen Lattimore, Hotsumi Ozaki, Fred Poland, Lee Pressman, Kimikazu Saionji, Agnes Smedley, Guenther Stein, Anna Louise Strong, Victor Vakhontoff, and Harry Dexter White; only Owen Lattimore, under oath, denied the alleged collaboration). Many IPRers were identified as writers for Communist Party publications, while others were the subjects of action by an agency of the U.S. Government or a foreign non-Communist government on grounds involving loyalty or national security.

The Senate Internal Security Subcommittee found: "The Institute of Pacific Relations has not maintained the character of an objective, scholarly and research organization. The IPR has been considered by the American Communist Party and by Soviet officials as an instrument of Communist policy, propaganda and military intelligence. The IPR disseminated and sought to popularize false information including information originating from Soviet and Communist sources. A small core of officials and staff members carried the main burden of IPR activities and directed its administration and policies. Members of the small core of officials and staff members who controlled IPR were either Communist or pro-Communist. There is no evidence that the large majority of its members supported the IPR for any reason except to advance the professed research and scholarly purposes of the organization. Most members of the IPR, and most members of its board of trustees, were inactive and obviously without any influence over the policies of the organization and the conduct of its affairs. IPR activities were made possible largely through the financial support of American industrialists, corporations, and foundations, the majority of whom were not familiar with the inner workings of the organization. The effective leadership of the IPR often sought to deceive IPR contributors and supporters as to the true character and activities of the organization. Neither the IPR nor any substantial body of those associated with it as executive officers, trustees or major financial contributors, has ever made any serious and objective investigation of the charges that the IPR was infiltrated by Communists and was used for pro-Communist and pro-Soviet purposes. The names of eminent individuals were by design used as a respectable and impressive screen for the activities of the IPR inner core, and as a defense when such activities came under scrutiny . . . . The effective leadership of

IPR worked consistently to set up actively cooperative and confidential relationships with persons in Government involved in the determination of foreign policy . . . . It was the continued practice of IPR to seek to place in Government posts both persons associated with IPR and other persons selected by the effective leadership of IPR. The IPR possessed close organic relations with the State Department through interchange of personnel, attendance of State Department officials at IPR conferences, constant exchange of information and social contacts . . . . The effective leadership of the IPR used IPR prestige to promote the interests of the Soviet Union in the United States. A group of persons operating within and about the Institute of Pacific Relations exerted a substantial influence on United States far eastern policy. The IPR was a vehicle used by the Communists to orientate American far eastern policies toward Communist objectives . . . . The net effect of IPR activities on United States public opinion has been such as to serve international Communist interests and to affect adversely the interests of the United States."

The IPR did not collapse once the SISS had made its findings known. As late as 1960, the IPR was advertising itself as "a non-partisan, unofficial organization devoted to the study of contemporary Asian problems. It has no axe to grind, and takes no stand on issues of public policy." But, after the SISS hearings, the IPR – as a viable institution – was an embarrassment to those who had been caught red-handed in the midst of international Communist conspirators. Finally, in 1961, the death of the IPR in the United States occurred when it was announced that, as of March 1961, IPR publications would be distributed from the University of British Columbia. And of course, Holland, as editor of the IPR's *Pacific Affairs*, was on the scene in the department of Asian studies at the University.

ROY HOOPES was born on May 17, 1922 in Salt Lake City, son of Lydia and Roy Hoopes. He is married. He is an alumnus of George Washington University (A.B., 1946; M.A., 1949). He is the author of *The Complete Peace Corps Guide* (1961 and 1968); *The Steel Crisis: 72 Hours That Shook the Nation* (1962); *What the President Does All Day* (1962); *A Report on Fallout in Your Food* (1962); and *Getting With Politics: A Young Person's Guide to Political Action* (1968). He is the editor of *Wit from Overseas* (1953); *Building Your Record Library* (1958); *The "High Fidelity" Reader* (1958); *State Colleges and Universities* (1962); and *The Peace Corps Experience* (1968).

From 1946 until 1948, Hoopes was a research analyst with the Department of State. From 1949 until 1952, he was an assistant world editor of *Pathfinder* magazine. In 1952 and 1953, he was general promotion manager of Time-Life International. From 1953 until 1956, he was managing editor of *High Fidelity* magazine. From 1956 until 1961, he was managing editor of *Democratic Digest*. From 1963 until 1965, he was an editor and writer for *National Geographic*. In 1965 and 1966, he was an associate editor of *Washingtonian*, a leftist-liberal magazine. Since 1966, he has been a free-lance writer and his contributions have appeared in *Esquire, Seventeen, Better Living,* the *Washington Star,* the leftist *Washington Post,* the leftist *Nation,* and the leftist *New Republic.*

Hoopes, as a writer and editor, has been involved in leftist-liberal Democratic circles, and he was especially favored by the Kennedy dynasty.

IRVING HOWE was born on June 11, 1920 in New York City, son of Netti Goldman and David Howe. He married Arien Hausknecht. He is an alumnus of the City College of New York (B.S., 1940). He is the author of *Sherwood Anderson: A Critical Biography* (1952); *William Faulkner: A Critical Study* (1952 and 1962); *Politics and the Novel* (1957); and *A World More Attractive: A View of Modern Literature and Politics* (1963). He is co-author of *U.A.W. and Walter Reuther* (1949); *The American Communist Party: A Critical History* (1958); and *Steady Work* (1966). He is editor of *Modern Literary Criticism* (1958); *Edith Wharton: A Collection of Critical Essays* (1962); George Gissing's *New Grub Street* (1962); Leon Trotsky's *Basic Writings* (1963); and George Orwell's *Nineteen Eighty-Four* (1963). He is co-editor of *Treasury of Yiddish Stories* (1954). He is editor of and contributor to *The Radical Papers* (1966). Since 1953, he has been editor of the Socialist quarterly, *Dissent.* He has contributed articles to *Commentary* and such leftist publications as *New Republic, New York Review of Books,* and *Partisan Review.*

From 1953 until 1961, Howe served successively as an associate professor and professor of English at Brandeis University. From 1961 until 1963, he was a professor of English at Stanford University. Since 1963, he has been a professor of English at Hunter College. He has been a visiting professor at the University of Vermont and the University of Washington. In 1954, he held the professorial chair of the Gauss Seminar of Princeton University. He has been a fellow at the University of Indiana's School of Letters. He has held a *Kenyon*

Review fellowship. In 1959 and 1960, he was a Bollingen Foundation fellow. In 1964 and 1965, he was a Guggenheim Foundation fellow.

In 1962, Howe sponsored the leftist-loaded conference on "The Impact of the Radical Right," held in San Francisco. In 1964, he sponsored the ultra-radical Ad Hoc Committee on the Triple Revolution. He was on the Norman Thomas 80th Birthday Committee, a tribute to the patriarch of the Socialist Party. He was affiliated with the Inter-University Committee for Debate on Foreign Policy, which in 1965 plagued university and college campuses with pro-Communist, anti-American agitation against the Vietnam War. He was also affiliated with the ultra-leftist Writers and Artists Protest; the ultra-leftist-pacifist National Committee for a Sane Nuclear Policy; and the Socialist League for Industrial Democracy. He is a self-admitted Socialist.

DOLLENA J. HUMES was born on April 22, 1921 in Buffalo, New York, daughter of Cecile Bonner and Harold Humes. She is an alumna of the University of California at Berkeley (A.B., 1950); the University of Nebraska (M.A., 1951); and Syracuse University (Ph.D., 1956). From 1951 until 1954, she was a Maxwell scholar and fellow at Syracuse. She is the author of *Oswald Garrison Villard: Liberal of the 1920's* (1960).

In 1953 and 1954, Miss Humes was an assistant instructor in political science at Syracuse University. From 1954 until 1957, she was an instructor in government at Connecticut College. Since 1957, she has been at Wells College in New York as assistant professor in history and government (1957-1962), associate professor (1962-1966), and professor of government (1966 to the present).

Miss Humes has been affiliated with the leftist-oriented American Association of University Professors and the ultra-leftist American Civil Liberties Union. Her reviews in scholarly journals reflect a strong leftist-liberal bias.

DAVID R. HUNTER was born on September 25, 1910 in Pittsburgh, son of Mabelle Fife and John Hunter. He was married to and divorced from Jewell Peterson. He is married to Carman Wolff. He is an alumnus of Westminster College of Pennsylvania (A.B., 1932); Union Theological Seminary (B.D., 1935); Harvard University (Ed. D., 1952); and St. Paul's University of Tokyo (D.D., 1958). In 1935, he was ordained to the ministry of the Congregational Church. In 1940, he was ordained as a deacon and priest of the Protestant Episcopal Church. He is the author of *Christian Education as Engagement* (1963).

From 1935 until 1938, Hunter was a chaplain at the State Infirmary in Tewksbury, Massachusetts. From 1938 until 1942, he was a chaplain at Massachusetts General Hospital. From 1936 until 1942, and from 1948 until 1952, he was a lecturer at the Episcopal Theological School in Cambridge, Massachusetts. From 1939 until 1941, he was rector of Trinity Episcopal Church in Bridgewater, Massachusetts. From 1941 until 1945, he was rector of the Church of the Holy Spirit in Boston. From 1945 until 1952, he was executive secretary for the department of Christian education for the Diocese of Massachusetts. From 1952 until 1963, he was director of the department of Christian education for the Protestant Episcopal Church. Since 1963, he has been deputy general secretary of the National Council of Churches. He has held high offices in the World Council of Churches, the World

Council of Christian Education, the National Training Laboratories, the Religious Education Association, and the World Council of Christian Education.

Hunter has been an active petitioner on behalf of individual Communists and the Communist Party. He was a leader in the National Committee on United States-China Relations. That leftist-dominated organization promoted travel by Americans to Red China, the sale of food and other items to Red China, and cultural and student exchanges between the United States and Red China. Hunter was also a leader in the Committee for a New China Policy, which urged withdrawal of all U.S. support from the Nationalist Chinese, favored Red Chinese control of Taiwan, advocated total social, cultural, and diplomatic relations between the U.S. and Red China, and demanded a complete withdrawal of all U.S. forces from Vietnam.

Hunter has long been affiliated with Clergy and Laymen Concerned about Vietnam, an ultra-leftist group which has given considerable aid and comfort to the Hanoi regime. For his part, Hunter proved himself to be an ideal member of the CLCV when he said, in 1966, "I don't want to live under Communism in the United States, but if I were in Viet Nam, I don't know if I would feel the same way. I doubt I would. Maybe the Vietnamese can better use Communism than anything else available as a way to move to democratization." Hunter was very critical of what he called "a stereotype conception of Communism that has dominated American thinking since World War II." The stereotype, said Hunter, "has caused us to think Communism is the worst thing that could happen to any people anywhere. That view has to be re-examined."

In 1969, Hunter joined with some of

the nation's most notorious leftists to lead a massive wave of demonstrations against U.S. participation in the Vietnam War. He placed the prestige of the National Council of Churches in the camp of David Dellinger, Sidney Peck, Stuart Meacham, Cora Weiss, Sanford Gottlieb, and other veteran leaders of ultra-leftist-pacifist groups.

In 1969, Hunter joined the National Religious Committee Opposing ABM, a group of well-known leftists who ranted against the anti-ballistic missile in the name of their misguided pacifism. In 1969, Hunter was an enthusiastic supporter of James Forman and his National Black Economic Development Conference. Forman and his paper organization at that time were making ridiculous but effective financial demands upon Protestant churches under the pretense that monies thus obtained would be expended on community organization projects among minority groups.

Hunter is a member of the Institute for American Democracy, an anti-anti-Communist witch-hunting offshoot of the defamatory Anti-Defamation League. In 1971, he became an adherent of the People's Peace Treaty, a Hanoi-inspired project.

SAMUEL P. HUNTINGTON was born on April 18, 1927 in New York City, son of Dorothy Phillips and Richard Huntington. He married Nancy Arkelyan. He is an alumnus of Yale University (B.A., 1946), the University of Chicago (M.A., 1948), and Harvard University (Ph.D., 1951). He is the author of *The Soldier and the State: The Theory and Politics of Civil-Military Relations* (1957); *The Common Defense: Strategic Programs in National Politics* (1961); and *Political Order in Changing Societies* (1968). He is the

co-author of *Political Power: The USA-USSR* (1964). He is the editor of *Changing Patterns of Military Politics* (1962).

From 1950 until 1958, Huntington was at Harvard University as instructor in government (1950-1953) and assistant professor (1953-1958). In 1952 and 1953, he was a research associate at Brookings Institution. From 1959 until 1962, he was at Columbia University as an associate professor of government and an associate director of the Institute of War and Peace Studies. Since 1963, he has been at Harvard University as research associate in Harvard's Center for International Affairs (1963-1964), professor at the Center (1963-1967), and chairman of the department and Frank G. Thomson professor of government (1967 to the present). He has been a visiting lecturer at the University of Michigan, Yale University, the University of California, Dartmouth College, Ohio State University, Carnegie Institute of Technology, the Air War College, the Naval War College, and the Industrial College of the Armed Forces. From 1960 until 1962, he was a Ford research professor at Columbia University. From 1954 until 1957, he was a research fellow of the Social Science Research Council. He has been a consultant to the Secretary of Defense and the U.S. Air Force Academy.

Huntington is a long-time nonresident member of the Council on Foreign Relations, the informal supra-State Department of the United States. His role in the ranks of the ruling internationalists is indicated by his position as consultant to the Institute for Defense Analysis, the Hudson Institute, the U.S. Agency for International Development, and the policy planning council of the U.S. Department of State.

DOROTHY H. HUTCHINSON was born on October 16, 1905 in Middletown, Connecticut, daughter of Evelyn Clark and Joseph Hewitt. She married R. Cranford Hutchinson. She is an alumna of Mt. Holyoke College (B.A., 1927) and Yale University (Ph.D., 1932). She is a contributor to *Peace in Vietnam: A New Approach in Southeast Asia* (1966).

In 1932 and 1933, Mrs. Hutchinson was a zoology instructor at Albertus Magnus College. From 1939 until 1959, she was editor of the Index Advance Abstract Service of the Wistar Institute Press publications. Since 1954, Mrs. Hutchinson has been on the speakers bureaus of the leftist-internationalist World Affairs Council and the leftist-internationalist United World Federalists. From 1961 until 1968, she was with the leftist-pacifist Women's International League for Peace and Freedom as president of the U.S. section (1961-1965) and international chairman (1965-1968).

Mrs. Hutchinson has been affiliated with the leftist-pacifist Friends Peace Committee; the ultra-leftist Clergy and Laymen Concerned About Vietnam; and the leftist-pacifist American Friends Service Committee. She was a leader in the 1965 March on Washington for Peace in Vietnam, a Red-laden demonstration.

ROY INNIS was born on June 6, 1934 in St. Croix, Virgin Islands, son of Georgianna Thomas and Alexander Innis. His second wife is Doris Funnye. He studied at the City College of New York.

From 1961 until 1963, Innis was a chemical technician for Vicks Chemical Company. From 1963 until 1967, he was a research assistant in the cardio-vascular research laboratories at Montefiore Hospital in New York City. Since 1963, Innis has been with the leftist-racist Congress of Racial Equality (CORE) as a member (1963 to the present); as educational chairman (1964) and chairman (1965-1967) of the Harlem chapter of CORE; and as second vice-chairman (1967-1968), associate director (1968), and director (1968 to the present) of the national CORE organization.

When Innis joined CORE, he was opposed to the nonviolent philosophy espoused by the organization's leaders. Through his activity in the Harlem chapter of CORE, he was influential in having CORE adopt a policy of self-defense. Since assuming the national directorship of CORE, he has converted the organization to his philosophy of black nationalism. He has defined black nationalism on several occasions. To *Ebony* magazine he said: "Under segregation, black people live together but their institutions are controlled by whites. Under integration, black people are dispersed and the institutions, goods and services are still controlled by whites. In effect, the two are the same. But under separatism, black people will control their own turf." To a Boston audience, Innis said: "We no longer want or seek integration. Integration ends up being almost as obnoxious to both blacks and whites as segregation. In areas where whites predominate, they should be in control. Where we predominate, we should be in control. This is the only arrangement possible for coexistence. This is the only way we can have our own police department to give us protection rather than oppression; cleaner streets since someone living on the other side of town won't be responsible for cleaning them; better health since we will have our own health department." To *Life* magazine Innis said: "Black nationalism is the philosophy of self-determination, the philosophy of an oppressed people. Oppression can occur in one's homeland or in the homeland of the oppressor. And the latter has been suffered by only two great peoples – the Jews and the American blacks. One solution to such oppression is assimilation – in essence, the loss of one's self. Moses tried the other solution – with his flight from Egypt. That won't work for us. We have to devise a philosophy applicable to our own dilemma. We must rehabilitate blacks as people. We must control the institutions in our areas. Integration is a total failure. We must continue as a separate entity." To *U.S. News & World Report* Innis said: "We want the transfer of institutions within the black community . . . into our hands so that we can maximize their effect on the stability of the community . . . . We want the return of our tax monies to institutions that belong to us so they can function for us . . . . We want a new social contract between whites and blacks – in short, a new Constitution . . . that gives black people, as a people, a per capita share of representation, to be selected and removed by our rules and responsive to our own interests . . . . Segregation is a very obnoxious relationship between two groups in society wherein one group dominates the other and controls its vital institutions, as in America right now. Separation, however, suggests that we both control our vital institutions and that neither of us dominates the other." He warned that unless separatism became a reality in the United States, there would develop "an unfortunate confrontation in which both races must lose – a dangerous social crisis – that could only lead to massive destruction on both sides."

In the summer of 1971, Innis accompanied a group of CORE officials to Africa, where they visited Kenya, Tanzania, Liberia, Guinea, Ethiopia, Ghana, Sierra Leone, and Senegal. When he returned to the United States, Innis announced that CORE would encourage black American support for black African interests. He said that black Americans were "the most prosperous and technologically and economically advanced blacks" in the world and that they had an obligation to the "rest of the family in Africa" to support and create programs that would help the African nations to rid themselves of the economic controls of "their former colonial masters."

For his African-American program, Innis suggested that black Americans invest money in Africa and open direct trade between themselves and black Africans; that black Americans organize so that they can respond immediately to the problems in black Africa and influence the American Government to react for the best interests of black African nations; that black Americans be allowed to hold dual citizenship as Americans and as citizens of African nations; that black professionals and technicians go to black African nations to live with the people, help them, and teach them; that American blacks respond to military threats against the African motherland; that black veterans of the Korean and Vietnam Wars be used in Guinea against the Portuguese, in the Sudan against Arabs, and in other "black liberation struggles" throughout the African continent; and that blacks influence the American Government to increase financial aid to black Africans commensurate with the aid that was given to European countries following World War II. It behooved CORE, said Innis, to promote the African-American program because it was vital for all blacks to see themselves as one family and to pool their strengths and interests.

At the 1971 convention of CORE,

Innis launched one of his strongest attacks against integration. Said Innis: "There must be two contracts negotiated between the black people of America and white America – one for the nationalists and another for the integrationists." Innis said that all black people had had to accept the goals of the integrationists even though they did not share those goals. "Integrationists have an entirely different goal," he said. "It is well known. It is recognized. It may be right for them but it should not be foisted upon us. Both groups must be permitted to pursue their own programs and must be accorded the dignity of equal recognition."

On the day before he spoke to the 1971 CORE convention, Innis explained his quarrel with the integrationists. "In America today," he said, "there are two kinds of black people – the field-hand blacks and the 'house niggers.' We of CORE – the nationalists – are the field-hand blacks. The integrationists of the National Association for the Advancement of Colored People are 'house niggers.' There is plenty of room in this vast country for both ideologies – the black nationalists and the integrationists. Thus far, however, America has only negotiated with one group – the integrationists." Innis said that leaders of integrationist groups had traditionally been "the Afro-European, the mixed-blood." He said that the integrationists had traditionally been lighter-complexioned blacks, who, having originally come from descendants of those having blood ties with whites, had sought assimilation into the white community. "These black people," Innis concluded, "are the only people in history who fight the oppressor to get into his bosom." Innis suggested that black nationals and integrationists agree to a non-aggression pact.

In late 1971, Innis was planning future visits to the Soviet Union and Red China in search of "viable alternatives to integration."

HAROLD R. ISAACS was born on September 13, 1910 in New York City, son of Sophie Berlin and Robert Isaacs. He married Viola Robinson. He is an alumnus of Columbia College (B.A., 1930). He is the author of *The Tragedy of the Chinese Revolution* (1938 and 1961); *No Peace for Asia* (1947); *Two-Thirds of the World* (1950); *Africa: New Crises in the Making* (1952); *Scratches on Our Minds: American Images of China and India* (1958); *Emergent Americans: A Report on Crossroads Africa* (1961); *The New World of Negro Americans* (1963); *India's Ex-Untouchables* (1965); and *American Jews in Israel* (1967).

From 1928 until 1930, Isaacs was a reporter and correspondent for the *New York Times*. In 1930, he was a reporter for the *Honolulu Advertiser*. In 1931, he was a reporter for the *China Press* of Shanghai. From 1931 until 1933, he was a reporter and editor of the *China Forum* of Shanghai, an English-language Communist periodical. From 1931 until 1940, he was with the Havas News Agency in Shanghai (1931-1934) and in New York (1935-1940). From 1940 until 1943, he was a writer and editor for the Columbia Broadcasting Company in New York City and Washington, D.C. From 1943 until 1950, he was an associate editor and correspondent for *Newsweek* magazine in New York City, Washington, D.C., China, India, and Southeast Asia. In 1951 and 1952, he was a lecturer at the radical New School for Social Research. In 1951, he was a visiting lecturer at Harvard University. Since 1953, he has been at the Massachusetts Institute of Technology's Center for International Studies as a research associate (1953-1965) and professor of political science (1965 to the present).

Isaacs' affiliations with the extreme left have been deep-rooted. He contributed articles to the Communist-controlled *Amerasia* magazine and to *Pacific Affairs,* a publication of the Communist-dominated Institute of Pacific Relations. His first book, *The Tragedy of the Chinese Revolution,* had a preface by Leon Trotsky, and the Trotskyite viewpoint was quite evident in that and other writings of Isaacs, especially throughout the 1930's. During his early years in China, Isaacs was a close associate of Comintern agent Agnes Smedley. The two were members of the Friends of the USSR, a Communist-front group, directed by the Comintern through agents in Shanghai.

ELMORE JACKSON was born on April 9, 1910 in Marengo, Ohio, son of Cora Osborn and John Jackson. He married Elisabeth Averill. He is an alumnus of Pacific College of Oregon (B.A., 1931) and Yale University (B.D., 1934). He is the author of *The United States and the Soviet Union* (1949) and *Meeting of Minds* (1952).

In 1935 and 1936, Jackson was a fellow at Yale University. From 1936 until 1961, he was with the leftist-pacifist American Friends Service Committee as assistant secretary in the social-industrial section (1936-1940), personnel director (1940-1946), assistant executive secretary (1946-1948), and director of the Quaker Program at the United Nations (1948-1961). From 1951 until 1954, he was a lecturer in international relations at Haverford College. In 1952 and 1953, he was a personal assistant to the United Nations Representative for India and Pakistan. From 1961 until 1966, he was with the Department of State as a special assistant on policy planning (1961-1964) and a special assistant (1964-1966) to the Assistant Secretary of State for International Organization Affairs. Since 1966, he has been vice-president of policy studies for the United Nations Association of the United States, the most prestigious left-wing propaganda agency for the UN in this country. He is a long-time member of the Council on Foreign Relations, the informal supra-State Department of the United States.

GLENNA JOHNSON was born on February 23, 1905 in Bristol Center, New York, daughter of Estella Warfield and Stephen Beach. She married Axel Johnson. She is an alumna of Syracuse University (B.A., 1926) and the University of Buffalo (M.S., 1938).

From 1928 until 1933, Mrs. Johnson was with the Family Service Association in Cleveland as a caseworker and student supervisor (1928-1930) and district secretary (1931-1933). In 1933 and 1934, she was district secretary for the Cuyahoga County Relief Administration. From 1934 until 1941, she was a casework supervisor for the Family Service Society of Buffalo. In 1941 and 1942, she was a caseworker for the Family Service Society of Cleveland and a case consultant for the Children's Bureau of Cleveland. From 1942 until 1945, she was director of social work for emergency child care for the Welfare Federation of Cleveland. In 1945 and 1946, she was director of social work for the Summit County Child Welfare Board in Akron. From 1946 until 1953, she was supervisor of child care for the Family Service Society in Akron. From 1953 until 1956, and in 1957 and 1958, she had a private practice in psychiatric social work in Akron. In 1956 and 1957, she was director of social services for the Summit County Mental Hygiene Clinic in Akron. From 1958 until 1961, she was executive secretary of the Travelers Aid Society in Akron. Since 1961, she has been director of casework for the Family Service Travelers Aid and has had a private practice in counseling in Des Moines.

Since 1968, Mrs. Johnson has been executive director of the leftist-pacifist Women's International League for Peace and Freedom. She is a member of the ultra-leftist American Civil Liberties Union; the National Association for the Advancement of Colored People, the fountainhead of Negro agitation for more than half a century; and the leftist-racist Congress of Racial Equality.

WILLIAM A. JOHNSON was born on August 20, 1932 in Brooklyn, New York, son of Ruth Anderson and Charles Johnson. He married Carol Lundquist. He is an alumnus of Queens College (B.A., 1953); Drew Theological Seminary (B.D., 1946); Columbia University (M.A., 1958); Union Theological Seminary and Columbia University (Ph.D., 1959); and the University of Lund, Sweden (Teol. Dr., 1962). In 1956, he was a Fulbright scholar. He has held an American-Scandinavian fellowship, two Rockefeller fellowships, a National Council for Religious Higher Education fellowship, and a Danforth fellowship. He is the author of *The Philosophy of Religion of Anders Nygren* (1958); *Christopher Polhem: The Father of Swedish Technology* (1962); *On Religion: Study of Theological Method* (1963); and *Nature and the Supernatural in the Theology of Horace Bushnell* (1963). He is co-author of *Swedish*

Contributions to Modern Theology (1967).

From 1953 until 1959, Johnson held Methodist pastorates in New York, New Jersey, and Connecticut. From 1957 until 1959, he was assistant professor of philosophy at Columbia University. From 1959 until 1963, he was an assistant professor of religion at Trinity College in Connecticut. From 1963 until 1967, he was chairman of the department and professor of religion at Drew University in New Jersey. In 1966, he was a research professor of religion at New York University. Since 1967, he has been a visiting professor at Princeton University and a professor of religion at Manhattanville College.

Johnson is a member of the National Association for the Advancement of Colored People, the fountainhead of Negro agitation for more than half a century; and the leftist-racist Congress of Racial Equality.

WINIFRED JOHNSTON was born in Topeka, Kansas, daughter of Sophia Doonan and John Johnston. She married Charles Perry. She is an alumna of the University of Oklahoma (B.A., 1924). She pursued graduate studies at the University of Oklahoma. She also studied at the University of Chicago and the New York Institute of Photography. She is the author of *Memo on the Movies* (1939) and *Visual Education* (1941). She is co-editor of *Readings in English Prose* (1931) and *New Hesperides, A Book of English Poetry* (1932).

From 1924 until 1927, Miss Johnston was an assistant instructor of English at the University of Oklahoma. In 1932, 1934, and 1935, she was a lecturer at the radical New School for Social Research. From 1932 until 1945, she lectured on motion picture history and aesthetics at the University of Oklahoma. From 1939 until 1942, she was an editor of Co-operative Books in Norman, Oklahoma. In 1945, she was a technical editor at the U.S. Naval Ordnance Laboratory in Washington. Since 1951, she has been director of the Open-Door Idea Agency in Norman, Oklahoma.

Miss Johnston has been affiliated with the leftist-oriented American Association of University Women; the leftist-oriented League of Women Voters; the ultra-leftist American Civil Liberties Union; the Workers Defense League, a leftwing group defending political undesirables who are subject to deportation; the Southern Conference for Human Welfare ("Communist front"); the ultra-radical Americans for Democratic Action; and the Foreign Policy Association, a highly effective pro-Communist vehicle.

WILLIAM H. JOSEPHSON was born on March 22, 1934 in Newark, New Jersey, son of Gertrude Brooks and Maurice Josephson. He is an alumnus of the University of Chicago (A.B., 1952) and Columbia University (LL.B., 1955). He pursued graduate studies at St. Antony's College of Oxford University. He was admitted to the New York bar (1956) and the District of Columbia bar (1966).

From 1955 until 1958, Josephson practiced law in New York City. In 1959, he was associated with Joseph L. Rauh Jr., the ultra-radical leader of Americans for Democratic Action, in Washington, D.C. From 1959 until 1961, he was the Far East regional counsel for the International Cooperation Administration. From 1961 until 1966, he was with the Peace Corps as special assistant to the director (1961-1962), deputy general counsel (1961-1963), and general

counsel (1963-1966). Since 1966, he has practiced law in New York City. He is a member of the ultra-leftist American Civil Liberties Union. He is a member of the Council on Foreign Relations, the informal supra-State Department of the United States.

DONALD KALISH was born on December 4, 1919 in Chicago, son of Mildred Pareira and Lionel Kalish. He has been married and divorced. He is an alumnus of the University of California at Berkeley (B.A., 1943; M.A., 1945; Ph.D., 1949). He is co-author of *Logic: The Techniques of Formal Reasoning* (1964).

In 1946 and 1947, Kalish was an instructor in philosophy at Swarthmore College. In 1947 and 1948, he was a lecturer in philosophy at the University of California at Berkeley. Since 1949, he has been at the University of California at Los Angeles as instructor (1949-1951), assistant professor (1951-1957), associate professor (1957-1964), and professor of philosophy (1964 to the present), and chairman of the philosophy department (1964 to the present).

In 1967, Kalish said: "I am far to the left of the Communist Party. Lots of people belong to Progressive Labor, Trotskyites, Dorothy Healey Communists, and some of us, as I say, are much more extreme than them, and I'm one of them, in our political views." In 1967 and 1968, he was national co-chairman and member of the steering committee of the New Mobilization Committee to End the War in Vietnam, a coalition of the most extreme elements in far-left parties. Since 1967, he has been on the steering committee of Resist, which organizes sit-ins, strikes and demonstrations at schools and universities in order to

KENNEDY

end alleged racist practices and direct complicity with militarism. Resist serves as a clearinghouse for information about anti-war and anti-draft groups, and grants funds to these groups. Kalish is the co-chairman of the Communist-dominated Peace Action Council of California. He sponsored the Communist-operated Hemispheric Conference to End the War in Vietnam. He is a member of the Committee of Liaison with Families of Servicemen detained in North Vietnam, an ultra-left group headed by David Dellinger and Cora Weiss. In 1969, he participated in the ultra-leftist National Anti-War Conference in Cleveland. He was a sponsor of the ultra-leftist Student Strike for Peace. He has been affiliated with the National Committee to Abolish the House Un-American Activities Committee ("to lead and direct the Communist Party's 'Operation Abolition' campaign); the leftist Committee to Defend the [Chicago] Conspiracy; the leftist GI Civil Liberties Defense Committee; the ultra-leftist Community for New Politics in Berkeley; the ultra-leftist Huey Newton-Eldridge Cleaver Defense Committee; the Emergency Conference Committee, an ultra-leftist group which called upon the United Nations to impose sanctions against the United States until the United States ratified the Genocide Treaty; the ultra-leftist Spring Mobilization project; the leftist-pacifist Committee of Responsibility; the leftist-pacifist Ad Hoc Faculty Committee on Vietnam; the Educators Appeal to the American People, a leftist effort against the war in Vietnam; the ultra-leftist Vietnam Moratorium demonstrations; Individuals Against the Crime of Silence, a leftist effort against the Vietnam War; the ultra-leftist Peace and Freedom Party; the leftist Committee to Aid the Bloomington Students; the leftist Committee

to Defend the Rights of Pfc. Howard Petrick, an operation of the Socialist Workers Party; and the National GI-Civilian Anti-War Action Conference, a project of the Young Socialist Alliance.

Kalish was responsible for placing Angela Davis on the faculty of the University of California at Los Angeles. Kalish said: "I did not know Miss Davis was a member of the Communist Party when I recommended her appointment to the Chancellor. If I had known, it would not have affected my decision to hire her." In 1970, Angela Davis was arrested and charged with murder, kidnapping, and criminal conspiracy in connection with a shoot-out in a San Rafael, California, courtroom. While she was awaiting trial, Kalish announced that he and other faculty members pledged themselves to campaign for her reinstatement on the faculty. Said Kalish: "We are determined that the moment Angela Davis is again free, a position is available to her. It is due her, and this campus needs Angela Davis."

RICHARD S. KENNEDY was born on October 13, 1920 in St. Paul, Minnesota, son of Nellie Foley and William Kennedy. He married Ella Dickinson. He is an alumnus of the University of California at Los Angeles (B.A., 1942); the University of Chicago (M.A., 1947); and Harvard University (Ph.D., 1953). He also studied at the University of Southern California. He is the author of *The Window of Memory: The Literary Career of Thomas Wolfe* (1962).

From 1948 until 1950, Kennedy was a teaching fellow at Harvard University. From 1950 until 1957, he was at the University of Rochester as instructor (1950-1955) and assistant professor (1955-1957). From 1957 until 1964, he was at the University of Wichita as associate professor (1957-1963) and professor (1963-1964). Since 1964, he has been a professor of English at Temple University.

Kennedy is a member of the National Association for the Advancement of Colored People, the fountainhead of Negro agitation for more than half a century; and the ultra-leftist American Civil Liberties Union.

STETSON KENNEDY was born on October 5, 1916 in Jacksonville, Florida, son of Wilkye Stetson and George Kennedy. He was married to and divorced from Edith Ogden, Kay Kerby, Marika Hellstrom, and Aniko Veres. He is married to Mary Bruce. He attended the University of Florida, the University of Paris, and the radical New School for Social Research. He is the author of *Palmetto County* (1942); *Southern Exposure* (1946); *I Rode With the Ku Klux Klan* (1954); and *Jim Crow Guide to the USA* (1959). He has contributed articles to the *New York Times, Saturday Review, New Masses* ("weekly journal of the Communist Party"), and such leftist publications as *Nation, New Republic, New York Post,* and *Southern Patriot.* From 1937 until 1950, he wrote a column, "Inside Out," for the Federated Press (a "Communist-controlled news syndicate").

Since the 1930's, Kennedy has been a writer and spokesman for various civil rights and peace groups. He has worked for Sidney Hillman's Political Action Committee ("Communist front") and the defamatory Anti-Defamation League. He has been a speaker at colleges and universities throughout the United States. He was an active campaigner for the Progressive Party in 1948. In 1950, he was an independent candidate for the U.S. Senate from Florida. He has spent more than three years living in various Communist countries.

Kennedy has been affiliated with the Civil Rights Congress ("created and established by the Communist Party"); the American Committee for the Protection of Foreign Born [Americans] ("subversive and Communist" – "one of the oldest auxiliaries of the Communist Party in the United States" – under the "complete domination" of the Communist Party); the World Peace Congress ("organized under Communist initiative"); the Southern Conference for Human Welfare ("Communist front"); the National Non-Partisan Committee to Defend the Rights of the 12 Communist Leaders, a Communist Party enterprise; the leftist-oriented International League for the Rights of Man; the Progressive Citizens of America ("political Communist front"); and the Scientific and Cultural Conference for World Peace ("Communist front").

JOHN F. KERRY was born on December 11, 1943 in Denver, Colorado, son of Rosemary Forbes and Richard Kerry. He married Julia Thorne. He is an alumnus of Yale University (B.A., 1966).

On April 22, 1971, Kerry became a national celebrity when he testified at televised hearings of the Senate Foreign Relations Committee. He appeared at the hearings as a spokesman for the Vietnam Veterans Against the War, whose officials claimed a membership ranging from about eight thousand to ten thousand. On the day following his televised appearance, a special dispatch in the *New York Times* revealed some of Kerry's background. He graduated from the U.S. Navy's Officer Candidate School early in 1968. He visited Vietnam for the first time when his ship stopped over at Danang after a brief tour in the

Gulf of Tonkin. Kerry recalled: "I went ashore and saw the barbed wire, the machine guns and a 'woodpile' of dead Viet Cong bodies, and it hit me all at once. This was my first contact with the land war, and at first it looked like something out of the movies. Then I reacted – I said 'my God, what is going on here – this is really a war.' " The first trip piqued his curiosity: "I wanted to go back and see for myself what was going on, but I didn't really want to get involved in the war." Late in 1968, he volunteered for duty in Vietnam on "swift boats." During his several months of Vietnam duty, he was wounded three times. He exercised his prerogative under Navy regulations as a three-time wounded veteran to return to the United States. His next duty was as an aide to an admiral in New York City. Of this period he said that "my opposition to the war was haunting me. The October moratorium came along and I did some work for it. It was just incredible, seeing all those people, and I said to myself, 'that's it.' " Kerry then asked for and received an early release from the Navy in order that he might run for Congress in Massachusetts on an anti-war platform. He campaigned for less than a month, then withdrew in favor of another Democratic candidate, Reverend Robert F. Drinan, S.J. Kerry campaigned for Drinan, who was elected to the Congress. During the course of his campaign work, Kerry appeared on the Dick Cavett television program and was seen by members of the newly-organized Vietnam Veterans Against the War. The group asked Kerry to become their full-time organizer, and he agreed to do so.

Kerry has related that during the course of his work as a VVAW organizer, he met Senator J. William Fulbright at a party and suggested that some veterans might testify before the Senate Foreign Relations Committee. Fulbright, chairman of the committee, agreed, and on the following day Kerry was called upon to make his appearance. In the preparation of the statement he would deliver to the Foreign Relations Committee, Kerry called upon the services of Adam Walinsky, a former speech-writer for Robert F. Kennedy.

When Kerry appeared to present his statement, the only members of the Foreign Relations Committee present were four bleeding-heart peaceniks: Senators Fulbright, Jacob Javits, Stuart Symington, and Claiborne Pell. They were later joined by another dove, George Aiken.

Kerry, in the course of his statement, presented a most outrageous indictment of American government officials, veterans of the armed forces, U.S. military leaders, South Vietnamese officials and the people of the United States and South Vietnam. In an extraordinary introduction to his statement, he recounted that the VVAW had a meeting in Detroit early in 1971 at which, he claimed, more than 150 honorably discharged, and many very highly decorated, veterans testified to war crimes committed in Southeast Asia. Said Kerry: "These were not isolated incidents but crimes committed on a day to day basis with the full awareness of officers at all levels of command. It is impossible to describe to you exactly what did happen in Detroit – the emotions in the room and the feelings of the men who were reliving their experiences in Vietnam. They relived the absolute horror of what this country, in a sense, made them do.

"They told stories that at times they had personally raped, cut off ears, cut

470

off heads, taped wires from portable telephones to human genitals and turned up the power, cut off limbs, blown up bodies, randomly shot at civilians, razed villages in fashion reminiscent of Genghis Khan, shot cattle and dogs for fun, poisoned food stocks, and generally ravaged the countryside of South Vietnam in addition to the normal ravage of war and the normal and very particular ravaging which is done by the applied bombing power of this country."

Kerry of course did not provide the names of the veterans who allegedly committed these atrocities. Instead, he resorted to the timeworn liberal ploy of placing the blame for the individuals' crimes upon society: "The country doesn't know it yet but it has created a monster, a monster in the form of millions of men who have been taught to deal and to trade in violence and who are given the chance to die for the biggest nothing in history; men who have returned with a sense of anger and a sense of betrayal which no one has yet grasped." In the same vein he said: "We saw Vietnam ravaged equally by American bombs and search and destroy missions, as well as by Viet Cong terrorism, and yet we listened while this country tried to blame all of the havoc on the Viet Cong. We rationalized destroying villages in order to save them. We saw America lose her sense of morality as she accepted very coolly a My Lai and refused to give up the image of American soldiers who hand out chocolate bars and chewing gum. We learned the meaning of free fire zones, shooting anything that moves, and we watched while America placed a cheapness on the lives of orientals."

Kerry centered much of his emotional fire on a personal attack upon President Nixon: "Each day to facilitate the process by which the United States washes her hands of Vietnam someone has to give up his life so that the United States doesn't have to admit something that the entire world already knows, so that we can't say that we have made a mistake. Someone has to die so that President Nixon won't be, and these are his words, 'the first President to lose a war.'

"We are asking Americans to think about that because how do you ask a man to be the last man to die in Vietnam? How do you ask a man to be the last man to die for a mistake? But we are trying to do that, and we are doing it with thousands of rationalizations, and if you read carefully the President's last speech to the people of this country, you can see that he says, and says clearly, 'but the issue, gentlemen, the issue, is communism, and the question is whether or not we will leave that country to the communists or whether or not we will try to give it hope to be a free people.' But the point is they are not a free people now under us. They are not a free people, and we cannot fight communism all over the world. I think we should have learned that lesson by now."

Kerry then launched into a wide-ranging attack upon Veterans Administration hospitals, unemployment, racism, the alleged violations of the Geneva Conventions by the United States, and the alleged lack of moral indignation among the American people. He saved his heaviest emotional barrage for his peroration, which soon became one of the most widely quoted passages in the liberals' repertoire: "We are also here to ask, and we are here to ask vehemently, where are the leaders of our country? Where is the leadership? We are here to ask where are McNamara, Rostow, Bundy, Gilpatric and so many others?

KERRY

Where are they now that we, the men whom they sent off to war, have returned? These are commanders who have deserted their troops, and there is no more serious crime in the law of war. The Army says they never leave their wounded. The Marines say they never leave even their dead. These men have left all the casualties and retreated behind a pious shield of public rectitude. They have left the real stuff of their reputations bleaching behind them in the sun in this country.

"Finally, this administration has done us the ultimate dishonor. They have attempted to disown us and the sacrifices we made for this country. In their blindness and fear they have tried to deny that we are veterans or that we served in Nam. We do not need their testimony. Our own scars and stumps of limbs are witness enough for others and for ourselves.

"We wish that a merciful God could wipe away our own memories of that service as easily as this administration has wiped away their memories of us. But all that they have done and all that they can do by this denial is to make more clear than ever our own determination to undertake one last mission — to search out and destroy the last vestige of this barbaric war, to pacify our own hearts, to conquer the hate and the fear that have driven this country these last ten years and more, so when 30 years from now our brothers go down the street without a leg, without an arm, or a face, and small boys ask why, we will be able to say 'Vietnam' and not mean a desert, not a filthy obscene memory, but mean instead the place where America finally turned and where soldiers like us helped it in the turning."

When Kerry had completed his statement, the members of the Senate For-eign Relations Committee afforded spectators a ridiculous spectacle as they sought from the 27-year-old Kerry his opinion on matters which by any reasonable standards were completely beyond his expertise. Senator Aiken asked Kerry if he thought either the North Vietnamese or the South Vietnamese would attempt to impede the complete withdrawal of American troops from Vietnam. Kerry replied that the South Vietnamese would be more prone to do so, and at the same time, he offered gratuitous remarks to the effect that the South Vietnamese under arms would lay down those arms in the event that the United States did withdraw its forces. He also said, in response to a question from Senator Aiken, that the United States had a very definite obligation to make extensive economic reparations to all the people of Indo-China — which of course meant that the North Vietnamese would be included. Senator Pell sought Kerry's opinion on Lt. William Calley and the My Lai episode. Senator Symington questioned Kerry on the possibility of the President and Congress receiving accurate and undistorted information through official military channels. The gist of Kerry's rambling answer was that there was no possibility. He provided the same sort of response to Senator Symington's inquiry about the press media. The most striking thing about Kerry's prepared statement and his responses to the Senators' questions was the total lack of hard-core, and the preponderance of hearsay, evidence.

The circumstances surrounding Kerry's famous appearance as spokesman for the Vietnam Veterans Against the War at the Senate Foreign Relations Committee hearings were rather hectic. *Human Events* had a reporter on the scene and he wrote (May 1, 1971): "Dressed mainly in combat boots and fatigues, the veterans descended on Washington to do battle with the 'Establishment.' They held services at Arlington National Cemetery; they camped out on the Mall, defying a Supreme Court order requiring them to move; they lobbied and badgered congressmen; they packed hearing rooms to provide support for their favorite lawmakers, and they got themselves arrested. Many of them chanted obscenities and puffed on pot while piously deploring our involvement in the war.

"Armed with toy machine guns and plastic M-16 rifles, others conducted guerrilla theater in public areas. Demonstration squads of veterans staged mock search-and-destroy missions at the Old Senate Office Building and on the east steps of the Capitol, astonishing scores of spring tourists.

"At the Capitol, three girls wearing straw coolie hats attempted to run away from a squad of 'infantrymen.' With a burst of simulated machinegun fire, the girls clutched their stomachs and popped plastic bags of red paint that splattered grotesquely over the Capitol steps.

"During the protests, several hundred veterans jammed a Senate Foreign Relations Committee hearing to cheer 'Right on, brother!' when Senator George McGovern accused the United States of barbarisms. The South Dakotan later received a standing ovation when he charged all American forces in Indochina with committing war crimes. Acknowledging the cheers, McGovern, the only declared 1972 presidential candidate, said: 'I have never been prouder of a group of Americans than I am of these combat veterans.' "

At the Washington, D.C., demonstrations, estimates of the VVAW participants ranged from nine hundred to twelve hundred. As the demonstrators became more and more talkative to members of the press, it became evident that many of the VVAW were not veterans, many of those who were veterans had never been in Vietnam, and many who had been in Vietnam had never spent a day in actual combat.

In the aftermath of the April-May 1971 demonstrations, Kerry became a familiar figure on television and radio talk-shows. He was lionized at radical-chic fund-raising affairs. The *New York Times* reported: ". . . a dozen of the city's wealthier men gathered at the apartment of Edgar Bronfman, president of Seagram's Distillers, to raise money for the Vietnam Veterans Against the War. After hearing John F. Kerry, the leader of the veterans, Mr. Bronfman asked how much each man was willing to give. Philip J. Levin, the president of Madison Square Garden, said $1,000. 'You can afford more than that, Phil,' called out Abraham Feinberg. 'If you give $5,000, I'll match it.' 'So will I,' said Mr. Bronfman, and the veterans had $15,000 of the $30,000 they needed for their trip to Washington."

On August 30, 1971, Enid Nemy, on the society page of the *New York Times*, wrote of a VVAW fund-raising affair held at the home of Mr. and Mrs. Burton Lane in East Hampton, Long Island. Kerry spoke to the gathering and showed a segment of a film and then solicited funds. Author and columnist Jimmy Breslin was present, as was Tom Paxton, the folksinger. Miss Nemy mentioned only a few of the 150 guests: Bruce J. Friedman, the author, and Mrs. Friedman; Alfred Crown, the film producer; William King, the sculptor; John Hubley, who has won three Academy Awards for his short films; Sheldon Harnick, the lyricist; Mr. and Mrs. Peter Maas, the writers; Donald Noonan, of the Nassau

Democratic party; Mr. Stein; Peter Davis, producer of the television documentary "The Selling of the Pentagon"; Mrs. Lula B. Bramwell, the ousted principal of the Joan of Arc Junior High School in New York; and Mrs. Patricia Kennedy Lawford.

By the fall of 1971, Kerry and the VVAW had obviously become fixtures in the New Left. There were insinuations from many quarters that Kerry was using the VVAW and the peace issue for his own political purposes. He denied that he had any immediate political plans, but at the same time he admitted: "I do know I'm going to work on all problems facing this country, not only Vietnam and the POW issue, but mass transportation, housing, welfare, and the like. I'm a lot freer to speak on issues than I would be as an elected official. What bothers me is that action must be taken now in the Paris peace talks. We need a date set now for total withdrawal from Vietnam." He also agitated about the alleged poor quality of Veterans Administration hospitals, the alleged lack of educational opportunities for veterans, and what he described as the drug problem of returning veterans.

CHARLOTTE KLEIN was born on June 20, 1923 in Detroit, daughter of Bessie Brown and Joseph Klein. She is an alumna of the University of California at Los Angeles (B.A., 1944). She pursued graduate studies at New York University.

In 1944 and 1945, Miss Klein was a staff correspondent for the United Press. In 1945, she was a staff writer for CBS Radio in Los Angeles. From 1946 until 1948, she was a publicist for Selznick Studios. From 1948 until 1950, she was New York director for Foladare Associates Publicity. From 1950 until 1962, she was with Edward Gottlieb & Associates as account executive (1950-1955), account supervisor (1956-1962), and vice-president (1955-1962). From 1962 until 1965, she was a vice-president and director of Flanley & Woodward, Inc. Since 1965, she has been with Harshe-Rotman & Druck, Inc., as vice-president (1965-1968) and senior vice-president (1968 to the present). In 1966, she was a guest lecturer at the radical New School for Social Research.

Miss Klein has been a member of the leftist-internationalist American Association for the United Nations; the ultra-leftist American Civil Liberties Union; and the National Association for the Advancement of Colored People, the fountainhead of Negro agitation for more than half a century.

EDWARD E. KLEIN was born on May 25, 1913 in Newark, New Jersey, son of Elsa Elkan and Benjamin Klein. He married Ruth Strauss. He is an alumnus of New York University (B.A., 1934) and Hebrew Union College-Jewish Institute of Religion (M.H.L., 1940; D.D., 1965). He also studied at Columbia University and Union Theological Seminary. In 1940, he was ordained a rabbi.

From 1940 until 1942, Klein was an assistant rabbi and the director of education at the Free Synagogue in New York. In 1942 and 1943, he was director of the B'nai B'rith Hillel Foundation at the University of California at Berkeley. Since 1943, he has been at the Free Synagogue as associate rabbi (1943-1949) and rabbi (1949 to the present). Since 1966, he has been a visiting lecturer in homiletics at Hebrew Union College-Jewish Institute of Religion.

Klein has been affiliated with the ultra-leftist-pacifist National Committee for a Sane Nuclear Policy; the National Association for the Advancement of Colored People, the fountainhead of Negro agitation for more than half a century; the National Committee to Abolish the House Un-American Activities Committee ("to lead and direct the Communist Party's 'Operation Abolition' campaign"); the leftist-pacifist Committee of Responsibility; the leftist-pacifist Voter's Pledge Campaign for Peace Candidates; the Mid-Century Conference for Peace ("aimed at assembling as many gullible persons as possible under Communist direction and turning them into a vast sounding board for Communist propaganda"); the Norman Thomas 80th Birthday Anniversary Committee, a tribute to the patriarch of the Socialist Party; and the National Religion and Labor Foundation ("Communist front"). He has been honorary vice-chairman of the ultra-leftist Liberal Party of New York.

HAROLD V. KNIGHT was born on March 16, 1907 in Cameron, Missouri, son of Hope Smith and George Knight. He married Ruth Gallup. He is an alumnus of Jamestown College of North Dakota (B.A., 1929). He is the author of *With Liberty and Justice for All* (1967).

From 1930 until 1936, Knight was a reporter for the *Stutsman County Record* in Jamestown, North Dakota. In 1936 and 1937, he attended the Brookwood Labor College, a Socialist training school for agitators. From 1938 until 1949, he was an editor for the leftist-oriented North Dakota Farmers Union. Since 1950, he has been a free-lance author and reporter. Since 1951, he has been a labor columnist for the *Colorado Scene*. Since 1952, his weekly column, "Statehouse Drama," has appeared in various publications. From 1954 until

1963, he was executive director of the ultra-leftist American Civil Liberties Union in Colorado.

Knight is a member of the ultra-leftist American Civil Liberties Union; the ultra-radical Americans for Democratic Action; the leftist-pacifist American Friends Service Committee; and the ultra-leftist-pacifist Fellowship of Reconciliation. He is a long-time foe of congressional committees investigating subversion.

GABRIEL KOLKO was born on August 17, 1932 in Paterson, New Jersey, son of Lillian Zadikow and Philip Kolko. He married Joyce Manning. He is an alumnus of Kent State University (B.A., 1954); the University of Wisconsin (M.S., 1955); and Harvard University (Ph.D., 1962). He held fellowships from the Social Science Research Council (1963-1964), the Guggenheim Foundation (1966-1967), and the Institute of Policy Studies (1967-1968). He is the author of *Wealth and Power in America* (1962); *The Triumph of Conservatism, 1900-1916* (1963); *Railroads and Regulation, 1877-1916* (1965); *The Politics of War, 1943-1945* (1969); and *The Roots of American Foreign Policy* (1969). He is a contributor to *The Critical Spirit: Essays in Honor of Herbert Marcuse* (1967).

In 1963 and 1964, Kolko was a research associate at Harvard University. From 1964 until 1968, he was an associate professor of history at the University of Pennsylvania. From 1968 until 1970, he was a professor at the State University of New York at Buffalo.

Kolko has been affiliated with the ultra-leftist-pacifist National Committee for a Sane Nuclear Policy; the Radical Education Project of the ultra-leftist Students for a Democratic Society; and the leftist-pacifist Ad Hoc Committee on the Vietnam War. He has been an active participant at the annual ultra-leftist Socialist Scholars Conferences. In 1967, he participated in the Communist-dominated "International Tribunal on War Crimes" at Stockholm. In 1970, the Communists' weekly *Guardian* reported: "Gabriel Kolko, a radical scholar active in the antiwar movement, was denied permanent residency in Canada after the U.S. government through the FBI reportedly pressured Canadian officials. Kolko, who formerly taught at the State University in Buffalo, was denied landed immigrant status and a temporary work permit. As a result, he will be unable to teach at York University in Toronto this fall. Kolko reported that Canadian officials as much as admitted that an FBI dossier was partly responsible for their decision."

AILEEN KRADITOR was born on April 12, 1928 in Brooklyn, New York, daughter of Henrietta and Abraham Kraditor. She is an alumna of Brooklyn College (B.A., 1950) and Columbia University (M.A., 1951; Ph.D., 1962). She also studied at Syracuse University. She is the author of *The Ideas of the Woman Suffrage Movement, 1890-1920* (1965) and *Means and Ends in American Abolitionism: Garrison and His Critics on Strategy and Tactics, 1834-1950* (1969). She is editor of and contributor to *Up from the Pedestal: Selected Writings in the History of American Feminism* (1968). She is a contributor to *Notable American Women* (1969).

Since 1962, Miss Kraditor has been at Rhode Island College as a history instructor (1962-1963), assistant professor (1963-1967), and associate professor (1967 to the present). Since 1968, she has been a visiting professor at Sir George Williams University in Montreal.

Miss Kraditor has participated in the annual ultra-leftist Socialist Scholars Conferences. She participated in the Educators Appeal to the American People, a leftist effort against the war in Vietnam. She has been a member of the leftist-oriented Teachers Committee for Peace in Vietnam.

IRVING KRISTOL was born on January 22, 1920 in New York City, son of Joseph Kristol. He married Gertrude Himmelfarb. He is an alumnus of the City College of New York (B.A., 1940). He is co-editor of *Encounters* (1963) and *Confrontation: The Student Rebellion and the Universities* (1969). He is a contributor to *Essays on Personal Knowledge* (1962) and *A Nation of Cities* (1968). His articles have appeared in *Atlantic, Harper's, Foreign Affairs, Fortune,* the *New York Times,* and *Yale Review.*

From 1947 until 1952, Kristol was managing editor of *Commentary.* From 1953 until 1959, he was co-founder and co-editor of the London-based *Encounter* magazine. (In 1968, Kristol denied that he had known that *Encounter* was subsidized by the Central Intelligence Agency.) In 1959 and 1960, he was an editor of the leftist-oriented *Reporter* magazine. Since 1960, he has been with Basic Books, Inc., as executive vice-president (1960-1969) and consulting editor (1969 to the present). Since 1965, he has been co-founder and co-editor of *Public Interest,* published quarterly by Freedom House, a prestigious center for anti-anti-Communism. In 1964, he was a regents lecturer at the University of California in Riverside. Since 1969, he has been the Henry R. Luce Professor of Urban Values at New York University. In 1967, he was associated with the

RAND Corporation in a study group on urban problems. He is a member of the Council on Foreign Relations, the informal supra-State Department of the United States.

MAYNARD C. KRUEGER was born on January 16, 1906 in Clark County, Missouri. He is married. He is an alumnus of the University of Missouri (A.B., 1926; A.M. 1927).

In 1927 and 1928, Krueger was a history instructor at Albion College. From 1928 until 1932, he was an economics instructor at the University of Pennsylvania's Wharton School of Finance and Commerce. Since 1932, he has been at the University of Chicago as an assistant professor (1932-1947), an associate professor (1947-1967), and professor (1967 to the present) of economics. He has been a Fulbright visiting professor in Vienna (1959-1960) and Athens (1963-1964).

Krueger has been affiliated with the Socialist League for Industrial Democracy; the leftist-oriented Students for Federal World Government; the American Youth Congress ("subversive and Communist"); the National Religion and Labor Foundation ("Communist front"); and the leftist Workers Defense League. In 1958, he was a member of the national board of the ultra-radical Americans for Democratic Action.

BETTINA APTHEKER KURZWEIL was born in 1944 in Brooklyn, daughter of Fay and Herbert Aptheker. She married Jack Kurzweil. She is an alumna of the University of California at Berkeley (B.S., 1967).

In an interview with Nicholas von Hoffman of the *Washington Post,* Bettina Aptheker reminisced about her childhood: "Mother came home early one evening. I don't know how old I was, but I couldn't have been more than a little girl because I'm only 21 now [1966], and it was toward the beginning of the McCarthy era. She said, 'I have something I want to tell you.' Mother made me sit on her lap and said something to the effect that things were going to be very difficult as a family. She said, 'Remember, Mommy and Daddy love you.' But I mustn't tell anybody what she was going to say. Then she told me that we were Communists.

"When Mother told me we were Communists, I felt proud that she had confidence in me and that I was being allowed to join the family circle of problems. It made me feel as though I were grown up, but also, in looking back, it makes me feel that I didn't have a childhood. I didn't really know what Mother meant when she told me. Of course, all during my childhood I knew my parents were different, but I didn't know why.

"I had some problems in school, but not too much, like sometimes parents not wanting me to play with their children. I cried a lot. Sometimes I didn't understand, like I remember going to a friend's house and seeing Daddy on the TV. He was appearing before the McCarthy committee. I didn't know what it meant. I thought, 'Gee, that's great. My Daddy's a celebrity on TV.' I remember another incident. During a trip our family – Mother, Daddy and me – was taking in the car. We did that a lot. I remember it was in a motel. I remember waking up because my father was screaming at McCarthy in his sleep."

Herbert Aptheker, Bettina's father, was not merely a run of the mill Communist when she was spending her childhood in Brooklyn. Aptheker, by the time he came to the attention of the McCarthy committee, was already celebrated as a high-ranking member of the Communist Party in the United States. Over the years he was generally characterized as the Communist Party's chief theoretician, but his activism was as real as his theoretical work.

In 1964, Bettina Aptheker achieved world-wide attention in her own right when she became leader of the Free Speech Movement on the Berkeley campus of the University of California. The FSM, under her leadership, instituted a series of riotous demonstrations on the Berkeley campus which were imitated on campuses throughout the United States and elsewhere.

By 1964, Bettina Aptheker had undergone a rather complete novitiate in agitation. In high school, she had participated in civil rights agitation. She had joined Advance, a Communist youth group. She had participated in marches against nuclear weapons and for passage of the nuclear test ban treaty. As a co-ed in California, she demonstrated against the Bay of Pigs fiasco and the war in Vietnam. She joined black militants in picket lines. She joined the Du-Bois Clubs, which had been organized under the auspices of the Communist Party.

In November 1965, Bettina Aptheker, then a junior at the Berkeley campus, wrote a letter to her fellow students in the campus newspaper, *The Daily Californian:* "It has been argued by some respectable and not so respectable people that I came to the University of California in the Fall of 1962 as part of an insidious Communist plot to corrupt the minds of my fellow students. Circumstantial evidence: I was the daughter of a very notorious Communist. Material evidence: I was on the steering commit-

tee hatching that nefarious plot – FSM.

"I am awed by the power I am alleged to have; but surely it must be clear that revolt is resultant from unjust and intolerable conditions. Revolts are not made by elite and manipulative conspiracies, they are made by People. And more specifically, the FSM revolt was made by the students on this campus. It would have occurred whether or not I was at Cal. FSM involved thousands of students. That was precisely what made it so powerful. Its power came from its Principle. And you made its Principle. Nothing anyone can ever say will change that very simple fact.

"There has been speculation for some time as to whether or not I am a Communist. Due to the attempt to outlaw the Communist Party it has been difficult to answer that question. I have, however, always affirmed that I am a Marxist and a socialist and have never hesitated to express my views. I wish, however, to take this occasion to go further. I have been for a number of years, I am now, and I propose to remain a member of the Communist Party of the United States.

"It will be argued that when I became a leader of the FSM I should have made it publicly known at that time that I was a Communist. My failure to do so may be considered by some deception. This was a problem with which I had to grapple. During the course of the FSM I told many of my co-workers that I was a Communist. But the weakness of the FSM in the early months of the struggle; the attack sustained by the FSM; and my own fears concerning personal repercussions caused me to refrain from making my affiliation publicly known. I have always stated my opinions candidly. Public acknowledgment of Party membership would have meant cooperation with a red-baiting attack on the FSM by helping to focus attention away from the issues raised by the FSM and onto the question of Communism. That is something I would not do. Whether or not I was a Communist was not the issue. The issue, if there was one, had to be what I thought, what positions I articulated, and why.

"As a student, as an American and as a Communist I have participated in common struggles for democratic liberties, for civil rights and for peace. I did so because I believed them to be virtuous struggles commensurate with socialist aspirations. I am a member of the Communist Party because, as I see it, that Party upholds principles which combine a particularly enlightened view of society, with a sense of humanity and peace not to be found elsewhere. As a Communist I believe in the fullest expansion of the democratic liberties of the American people. I believe in an end to poverty; an end to racism; an end to unemployment; an end to U.S. intervention in Vietnam and the Dominican Republic. The revolutionary Marxist outlook as developed in the Party's approach and program is profoundly relevant to the fundamental questions facing the American people today.

"The CPUSA is presently on trial in Washington because it has failed to register as an agent of the Soviet Union as required by the McCarran Internal Security Act. Forty-three persons have been ordered to register as members of the Communist Party, also under the McCarran Act. Their cases are pending. Failure to register carries a maximum penalty of five years in jail and a $10,000 fine for every day one does not register. According to the McCarran Act I owe the government $12,150,000 and 5,075 years in prison! But I will not

register under the McCarran Act, and thereby swear to Congress' definition of a Communist. I am not a foreign agent, and I will not sign away my principles. No Communist in this country has and no Communist will.

"It is time to challenge the assumption that there is an international Communist conspiracy; that Communists are agents of a foreign power; that Communists are traitors; that Communists are by definition 'evil' and must be exterminated. Anti-Communism has served as the fundamental objective of American domestic and foreign policy certainly since 1946. In the Holy name of Anti-Communism this government has conducted witchhunts and executed and imprisoned its victims. It has waged war, overthrown governments (by force and violence), intervened in the internal affairs of other nations; and is daily committing unspeakable atrocities in Vietnam.

"It is time to affirm the right to be a Communist; the right of Communists to speak and act; and the right of the American people to listen and think for themselves. It was difficult to make the decision to write this letter. Now that it is done I feel an immense sense of relief. Yes, I am a Communist. Now, let us go on together and do the best we can to build a better world."

At the time of her public confession, Bettina Aptheker was on the Communist Party's National Youth Commission. But two weeks after her letter was published in *The Daily Californian*, she was elected to the Campus Rules Committee which advises the University's administration on campus rules. A few months later Nicholas von Hoffman reported that Bettina "has kind blue eyes and almost everyone on the campus who knows her, students and faculty, seems extra fond of her. John Searle, special assistant to the Chancellor, says Tina 'is a fine person, very responsible. She's not one of the people around here urging reckless confrontations between the students and the administration.' "

As a young Communist celebrity, Bettina Aptheker has had the opportunity to bring the Communist line to collegiate and other groups across the country. She was especially active on California campuses, including the University of California at Riverside, the University of the Pacific, Raymond College, California State College, Stanislaus State College, Shasta Junior College, the College of Marin, the University of California at Los Angeles, California State College at Los Angeles, Pomona College, California State College at Long Beach, Pasadena State College, the University of Redlands, California State College at Hayward, and Santa Monica City College. She has also spoken at Queens College, Brooklyn College, and the University of Oregon.

GEORGE LAKEY was born on November 2, 1937 in Bangor, Pennsylvania, son of Dora Shook and Russell Lakey. He married Berit Mathiesen. He is an alumnus of Cheyney State College (B.S., 1961) and the University of Pennsylvania (M.A., 1963). He also studied at West Chester State College and the University of Oslo, Norway. He is a co-author of *A Manual for Direct Action* (1965).

From 1958 until 1961, Lakey was a part-time worker for the leftist-pacifist American Friends Service Committee. In 1959 and 1960, he was a high-school teacher in Oslo, Norway. From 1963 until 1965, he was executive director of the leftist-pacifist Friends Peace Committee. Since 1965, he has been a sociol-

ogy instructor at Upland Institute in Chester, Pennsylvania.

Lakey has been affiliated with the ultra-leftist-pacifist Committee for Nonviolent Action; the ultra-leftist-pacifist Fellowship of Reconciliation; and the War Resisters League, a group of conscientious objectors who describe themselves as anarchists, democratic socialists, and independent radicals. (The WRL agitates for unilateral disarmament, for U.S. diplomatic recognition of Red China, and on behalf of the Black Panthers. The WRL is affiliated with the War Resisters International, which has always been saturated with Communists and Socialists.) Lakey has been affiliated with the leftist-oriented Ad Hoc Faculty Committee on Vietnam. He was a member of the Norman Thomas 80th Birthday Committee, a tribute to the patriarch of the Socialist Party.

BEATRICE LAMB was born on May 12, 1904 in Morristown, New Jersey, daughter of Florence Shelton and Mahlon Pitney. She married Horace Lamb. She is an alumna of Bryn Mawr College (B.A., 1927) and Columbia University (M.A., 1956). She also pursued graduate studies at the Geneva School of International Studies. She is the author of *Introduction to India* (1960); *India: A World in Transition* (1963); *India* (1965); and *The Nehrus of India: Three Generations of Leadership* (1967). She is co-author of *The United Nations* (1946).

From 1928 until 1936, Mrs. Lamb was with the leftist-oriented League of Women Voters as secretary of the national staff (1928-1933) and pamphleteer (1928-1936). From 1945 until 1949, she was editor of *United Nations News*. In 1949 and 1950, she received a grant for travel and study in India from the leftist-pacifist Carnegie Endowment for International Peace. In 1955 and 1956, she was a lecturer at the radical New School for Social Research. In 1958, she was a lecturer at the Scarsdale (New York) Adult School. From 1960 until 1964, she was a lecturer in the division of general education at New York University. In 1964 and 1965, she was a lecturer at New York University's School of Education. As a professional lecturer and author, Mrs. Lamb for more than two decades has been an apologist for the ultra-leftist regimes in India.

A. WILLIAM LARSON was born on October 18, 1920 in Brooklyn, son of Florence Grandeman and Carl Larson. He married Barbara Slawson. He is an alumnus of Dartmouth College (B.A., 1941) and Syracuse University (J.D., 1948).

From 1949 until 1953, Larson was counsel for Kemper Insurance Company in New York City. From 1953 until 1960, he was vice president of the Martin E. Segal Company. Since 1960, he has been president and director of Woodward and Fondiller, Inc. Since 1968, he has been vice-president and director of the Stony Brook Foundation.

In 1968, Larson was a delegate to the Democratic National Convention.

Larson is affiliated with the ultra-radical Americans for Democratic Action; the ultra-leftist American Civil Liberties Union; the leftist African-American Institute; the leftist-oriented United Nations Advisory Committee of the Unitarian-Universalist Association; and Freedom House, a center for anti-anti-Communism.

CHRISTOPHER LASCH was born on June 1, 1932 in Omaha, son of Zora Schaupp and Robert Lasch. He married Nell Commager. He is an alumnus of Harvard University (B.A., 1954) and Columbia University (M.A., 1955; Ph.D., 1961). He is the author of *The American Liberals and the Russian Revolution* (1962); *The New Radicalism in America* (1965); and *The Agony of the American Left* (1969). In 1955 and 1956, he was an Erb fellow. In 1956, he was a Gilder fellow. In 1960, he was a Social Science Research Council fellow.

From 1956 until 1959, Lasch was an instructor in history at Williams College. In 1960 and 1961, he was an assistant professor of history at Roosevelt University. From 1961 until 1966, he was at the University of Iowa as an assistant professor (1961-1964), associate professor (1964-1965), and professor (1965-1966) of history. Since 1966, he has been a professor of history at Northwestern University.

Lasch is a Socialist. He is a member of the New Left. He has participated in the Socialist Scholars Conferences, annual get-togethers of Marxian Socialists and their fellow-travelers. He was affiliated with the leftist Committee to Defend the [Chicago] Conspiracy.

ERNEST W. LEFEVER was born on November 12, 1919 in York, Pennsylvania, son of Katie Roth and Calvin Lefever. He married Margaret Briggs. He is an alumnus of Elizabethtown College (A.B., 1942) and Yale University (B.D., 1945; Ph.D., 1956). He is the author of *Ethics and United States Foreign Policy* (1957); *Arms and Arms Control* (1962); *Crisis in the Congo* (1965); and *Uncertain Mandate: Politics of the UN Congo Operations* (1967). He is co-author of *Profile of American Politics* (1960). He is editor of *The World Crisis and American Responsibility* (1958).

From 1952 until 1954, Lefever was an international affairs specialist for the leftist-oriented National Council of Churches. In 1955 and 1956, he was a research associate in the School of Advanced International Studies of The Johns Hopkins University. In 1956 and 1957, he was a political science instructor at the University of Maryland. From 1957 until 1959, he was a research analyst and the acting chief of the foreign affairs division of the Library of Congress. In 1959 and 1960, he was a staff consultant on foreign relations to U.S. Senator Hubert H. Humphrey. In 1960 and 1961, he was a research associate at the leftist-oriented Washington Center of Foreign Policy Research of The Johns Hopkins University. From 1958 until 1963, he was a consultant to the leftist-oriented Council on Religion and International Affairs. From 1961 until 1964, he was a research analyst for the international studies division of the Institute for Defense Analyses, a part of the Establishment's think factory system. Since 1964, he has been on the senior staff of the foreign policy studies division at Brookings Institution. He has lectured at the U.S. Foreign Service Institute, at the Salzburg [Austria] Seminar in American Studies, at the National Defense College of Japan, and at the School for International Service at American University. He has been a consultant to the U.S. Disarmament Agency. He was a consultant to President John F. Kennedy's Task Force on Arms Control. He was a consultant to the international affairs division of the leftist-oriented Ford Foundation.

CAROL LEIMAS was born on September 12, 1931 in New York City, daughter of Lillian Segall and Reuben Chauls. She married Irwin Leimas. She is an alumna of Syracuse University (B.A.,

1952). As a Fulbright fellow, she studied at the University of Paris.

From 1953 until 1956, Mrs. Leimas was a research assistant for the defamatory Anti-Defamation League. In 1956 and 1957, she was a research assistant for the U.S. National Organizations on the United Nations, the main propaganda arms for the UN. From 1957 until 1960, she was an inquiry specialist for the leftist-oriented World Affairs Center. From 1960 until 1967, she was director of the information-reference department of the Foreign Policy Association, a bulwark of leftist internationalism. Since 1969, she has been the United Nations representative of the leftist-oriented American Association of University Women. She has been a member and director of the leftist-oriented League of Women Voters in New York City.

ARTHUR J. LELYVELD was born on February 7, 1913 in New York City, son of Dora Cohen and Edward Lelyveld. He was married to and divorced from Toby Bookholtz. He is married to Teela Stovsky. He is an alumnus of Columbia University (A.B., 1933) and Hebrew Union College (M.H.L., 1939). In 1939, he was ordained a rabbi. He is the author of *Atheism Is Dead: A Jewish Response to Radical Theology* (1968).

Lelyveld served as a rabbi for congregations in Hamilton, Ohio (1939-1941) and Omaha, Nebraska (1941-1944). From 1944 until 1948, he was with the Committee on Unity for Palestine as executive director (1944-1946) and national vice-chairman (1946-1948). From 1946 until 1956, he was with the B'nai B'rith Hillel Foundation in New York City as associate national director (1946-1948) and national director (1948-1956). From 1956 until 1958, he was executive vice-chairman of the

American-Israel Cultural Foundation in New York City. Since 1958, he has been rabbi of the Fairmount Temple in Cleveland, Ohio. He has also been national vice-president of the American Jewish League for Israel and president of the American Jewish Congress. From 1941 until 1946, he was secretary of the Joint Rabbinical Committee on Conscientious Objectors. From 1941 until 1943, he was president of the Jewish Peace Fellowship.

In the 1950's, Lelyveld was very active in the National Committee to Secure Justice for Morton Sobell ("Communist front"). He has been a member of the Institute for American Democracy, an anti-anti-Communist witch-hunting offshoot of the defamatory Anti-Defamation League. He has been an official of the National Association for the Advancement of Colored People, the fountainhead of Negro agitation for more than half a century. His opposition to the Vietnam War has been demonstrated by his affiliations with the ultra-left in such organizations as Negotiation Now!; Clergy and Laymen Concerned About Vietnam; the National Citizens Committee for the Amendment to End the War; and the National Committee for a Political Settlement in Vietnam. He has supported the Hanoi-inspired People's Peace Treaty.

GAYLORD C. LeROY was born on September 28, 1910 in Aspinwall, Pennsylvania. He is an alumnus of Oberlin College (A.B., 1930) and Harvard University (A.M., 1931; Ph.D., 1935). He is the author of *Perplexed Prophets: Six Nineteenth-Century British Authors* (1953) and *Marxism and Modern Literature* (1967).

From 1934 until 1938, LeRoy was an instructor at the University of Maine.

From 1938 until 1946, he was at the University of Hawaii as an instructor (1938-1940) and assistant professor of English (1941-1946). Since 1946, he has been at Temple University as assistant professor of English (1946-1953), associate professor (1953-1960), and professor (1960 to the present).

LeRoy has been affiliated with the ultra-leftist-pacifist World Fellowship. He has been a participant in the annual ultra-leftist Socialist Scholars Conferences. He has been on the faculty of the Center for Marxist Education. He was a sponsor of the ultra-leftist National Student Strike for Peace.

JULIUS LESTER was born on January 27, 1939 in St. Louis, Missouri, son of Julia Smith and W.D. Lester. He married Joan Steinau. He is an alumnus of Fisk University (B.A., 1960). He is the author of *Look Out, Whitey! Black Power Gon' Get Your Mama!* (1968); *To Be a Slave* (1968); and *Search for the New Land: History as Subjective Experience* (1969). He is co-author with Pete Seeger, the Communists' favorite folk singer, of *The 12-String Guitar as Played by Leadbelly* (1965). Since 1964, he has been associate editor of *Sing Out.* Since 1964, he has been a contributing editor of *Broadside of New York.* He has also been a contributor to *Sounds & Fury.*

Lester has had a varied career as a professional musician and singer, recording artist, folklorist, and writer. He has been a columnist for the Communist weekly, *Guardian.* From 1966 until 1968, he was director of the Newport (Rhode Island) Folk Festival, which featured the country's far-left folk singers. From 1966 until 1968, he was employed by the ultra radical Student Nonviolent Coordinating Committee. From 1968 until 1970, he conducted a program on

WBAI-FM Radio entitled "The Great Proletarian Cultural Revolution." He has taught a course in black history at the radical New School for Social Research. He was a prominent member of the Sing-In for Peace Committee.

Lester is equally at home with racist agitators and leftists. In 1967, he made illegal trips to North Vietnam and Communist Cuba. In 1967, as field secretary for SNCC, he wrote that to "resist is to make the President [Lyndon B. Johnson] afraid to leave the White House because he will be spat upon wherever he goes to tell his lies." In the February 24, 1968 issue of the *Guardian*, he wrote: "The government has made extensive preparations for the coming summer. If necessary they'll hire somebody to go throw a rock through the window of a ghetto store. Any way you go, there is going to be violence this summer . . . . Faced with the prospect of extermination, blacks are arming themselves, and saying thereby, if you are marked for death, just don't die without knowing that some honky is going to be buried the same day you are. And preferably, two or three . . . . For those who read this and can only view it as extreme paranoia, reflect on the history of this country — the rape of Africa for black slaves, the extermination of the Indian, the atomic bomb dropped on Hiroshima and Nagasaki, the war in Viet Nam. America's history shows that its capacity to murder is unfathomable. Hitler is held up to us as the example supreme of a madman, but only so that attention will be drawn away from our own madness and insanity. Blacks are taking up arms to respond to this madness. It is not the role of whites to argue against this."

Lester, as a racist agitator and leftist, has received appropriate recognition from the Far Left. In Pandora's column,

"AC/DC," in the *Guardian* of May 4, 1968, Lester was given a well-deserved tribute: "It seems to be Julius Lester's function at this time in his life to be the medium through which black militancy addresses itself to whites. His articles in the *Guardian, Sing Out!* and other publications strike me as that carefully thought-out opening to the white left which many on this side of the tracks seem unable to tune in on. Some seem to feel their personal outrage at some remark or position is more important than the dynamic which is essential if a revolutionary bridge is ever to be built in this generation. For those who have trouble listening to words, especially, I recommend Julius Lester, singer and songwriter. His new record album, 'Departures' (Vanguard), picks up where his last LP left off. No, you won't get from Julius Lester what you could get from The Supremes or Otis Redding or Aretha Franklin. But if you listen carefully (and think about it, too) you might be able to understand the nature of the dialogue now taking place within Black America much more clearly. For here is the black man who has rejected our word, 'Negro,' who does not hesitate to flaunt us [*sic*] with the 'nigger' now turned into revolutionary, the new black man who demands to be accepted only on his own terms — and who ultimately does not care if you accept him or not, because he knows he is on the side of destiny . . . ."

WILLIAM E. LEUCHTENBURG was born on September 28, 1922 in Ridgewood, New York, son of Lauretta McNamara and William Leuchtenburg. He married Jean McIntire. He is an alumnus of Cornell University (B.A., 1943) and Columbia University (M.A., 1944; Ph.D., 1951). He is the author of *Flood Control*

Politics (1953); *The Perils of Prosperity: 1914-1932* (1958); *Franklin D. Roosevelt and the New Deal: 1932-1940* (1963); *New Deal and Global War* (1964); *The Great Age of Change* (1964); and *Franklin D. Roosevelt and the Supreme Court* (1967). He is a contributor to *Times of Trial* (1958); *Change and Continuity in Twentieth-Century America* (1964); *Freedom and Reform* (1967); and *The Comparative Approach to American History* (1968). He is the editor of *Theodore Roosevelt: The New Nationalism* (1961); *Woodrow Wilson: The New Freedom* (1961); *Walter Lippmann: Drift and Mastery* (1961); *An American Primer* (1966); *Franklin D. Roosevelt: A Profile* (1967); and *The New Deal: A Documentary History* (1968). He has contributed articles to *American Heritage, Current History, Dictionary of American Biography, Nation,* and *New Leader.*

In 1942 and 1943, Leuchtenburg was a cartographer for the U.S. Geological Survey. In 1943 and 1944, he was with the ultra-leftist Liberal Party as Queens County director and state youth director in New York. In 1945, he was the assistant editor of the American Labor Conference for International Affairs. In 1945 and 1946, he was the New England field representative of the National Council for a Permanent Fair Employment Practices Commission. In 1947, he was an economics instructor at New York University. From 1947 until 1949, he was with the ultra-radical Americans for Democratic Action as a national field representative and state director in Massachusetts. From 1949 until 1951, he was at Smith College as an instructor in government (1949-1950) and assistant professor (1950-1951). In 1951 and 1952, he was an assistant professor of history at Harvard University. Since 1952, he has been at Columbia University as a research associate (1952-1954), associate professor (1954-1959), and professor of American history (1959 to the present). In 1956, he was a visiting professor at the Salzburg [Austria] Seminar in American Studies. In 1961 and 1962, he was a fellow at the Center for Advanced Study in the Behavioral Sciences. In 1962 and 1964, he was an election analyst for the National Broadcasting Company. In 1965, he was a fellow at the University of Michigan's Seminar on Methods in Historical Analysis. Since 1964, he has been an adviser to the Social Security Administration. In 1965 and 1966, he was a consultant to the leftist-oriented Ford Foundation. From 1959 until 1961, he was on the board of governors of the Bureau for Applied Social Research. Since 1965, he has been on the board of governors of the Center for Research and Education in American Liberties, and a member of the advisory committee on oral history for the John F. Kennedy Memorial Library. In the 1950's and 1960's, he was on the national board of the ultra-radical Americans for Democratic Action.

DENISE LEVERTOV was born on October 24, 1923 in Ilford, England, daughter of Beatrice Spooner-Jones and Paul Levertoff. She married Mitchell Goodman. She came to the United States in 1948 and was naturalized in 1955. She is the author of *The Double Image* (1946); *Here and Now* (1957); *Overland to the Islands* (1958); *With Eyes at the Back of Our Heads* (1959); *The Jacob's Ladder* (1961); *O Taste and See* (1964); *The Sorrow Dance* (1967); *Guillevic, Selected Poems* (1969); and *Relearning the Alphabet* (1970). She has contributed to anthologies, including *The*

New American Poetry, Penguin Contemporary American Poetry, Poet's Choice, Today's Poets, Poets of Today, America, and *New Poets of England.*

In 1964, Levertov-Goodman taught the craft of poetry at the Poetry Corner of New York City's YMHA. In 1964 and 1965, she was an associate scholar at Radcliffe College's Institute for Independent Study. In 1965 and 1966, she was a visiting lecturer at Drew University. In 1965 and 1966, she was a writer-in-residence at the City College of New York. In 1966 and 1967, she was a visiting lecturer at Vassar College. In 1969, she was a visiting lecturer at the University of California at Berkeley. In 1969 and 1970, she was a visiting lecturer at Massachusetts Institute of Technology. In 1970 and 1971, she was a writer in residence at Kirkland College. In 1962, she held a Guggenheim fellowship. In 1965, she held a grant from the National Institute of Arts and Letters.

In 1965, Levertov-Goodman organized the ultra-leftist Writers' and Artists' Protest in Vietnam. She has been affiliated with the leftist Poets for Peace; the National Committee to Abolish the House Un-American Activities Committee ("to lead and direct the Communist Party's 'Operation Abolition' campaign"); the 1971 People's Peace Treaty, a leftist project; the ultra-leftist American-Korean Friendship and Information Center; and the leftist-oriented Read-In for Peace in Vietnam.

DAVID LEVIN was born on November 21, 1924 in ·York, Pennsylvania, son of Rose Braufman and Louis Levin. He married Patricia Marker. He is an alumnus of Harvard University (A.B., 1947; A.M., 1949; Ph.D., 1954). He is the author of *History as Romantic Art* (1959); *What Happened in Salem?* (1950

and 1960); and *In Defense of Historical Literature* (1967). He is the editor of Cotton Mather's *Bonifacius: An Essay Upon the Good* (1967); P.A. Bates' *Faust* (1969); and *Jonathan Edwards: A Profile* (1969).

From 1948 until 1952, Levin was a teaching fellow at Harvard University. Since 1952, he has been at Stanford University as an English instructor (1952-1955), assistant professor (1955-1959), associate professor (1959-1964), and professor (1964 to the present). In 1956 and 1957, he was a Fulbright exchange lecturer at the Universities of Strasbourg and Toulouse. Since 1960, he has been general editor of Harbrace Sourcebooks for Harcourt, Brace & World, Inc. In 1962 and 1963, he was a fellow at the Center for Advanced Study in Behavioral Sciences at Stanford University. In 1968 and 1969, he was a senior fellow of the National Endowment of the Humanities.

Levin is a member of the leftist-oriented American Association of University Professors; the ultra-leftist American Civil Liberties Union; and the National Association for the Advancement of Colored People, the fountainhead of Negro agitation for more than half a century.

ROBERT JAY LIFTON was born on May 16, 1926 in Brooklyn, son of Ciel Roth and Harold Lifton. He married Betty Kirschner. He is an alumnus of New York Medical College (M.D., 1948). He also studied at Cornell University. He is the author of *Thought Reform and the Psychology of Totalism: A Study of 'Brainwashing' in China* (1961 and 1967); *Death in Life: Survivors of Hiroshima* (1968); and *Revolutionary Immortality: Mao Tse-tung and the Chinese Cultural Revolution* (1968). He is the editor of *The Woman In America* (1965). He has contributed articles to *American Scholar, Daedalus, New Republic,* and *New York Review of Books.*

From 1949 until 1951, Lifton was a psychiatric resident at the Downstate Medical Center of the State University of New York. In 1954, he was a research associate at the Asia Foundation. In 1954 and 1955, he was a member of the faculty at the Washington School of Psychiatry. From 1956 until 1961, he was at Harvard University as a research associate in psychiatry and an associate in East Asian studies. Since 1961, he has been at the Foundations Fund for Research in Psychiatry at Yale University as an associate professor of psychiatry (1961-1967), and a professor of psychiatry and a fellow at Branford College (1967 to the present). In 1954, he held a fellowship from the Asia Foundation. In 1954 and 1955, he held a study grant, in Hong Kong and Washington, D.C., from the Washington School of Psychiatry. In 1956 and 1957, he held a fellowship from the leftist-oriented Ford Foundation. From 1958 until 1961, he held a fellowship from the Foundations Fund for Research in Psychiatry. From 1962 until 1964, he was a consultant to the National Institute of Mental Health.

Lifton has been affiliated with the ultra-leftist-pacifist National Committee for a Sane Nuclear Policy; the leftist-pacifist Voters Peace Pledge; and the People's Peace Treaty, the pet 1971 project of the ultra-left. In 1969, he supported the radical-leftist demonstrators who paraded under the banner, Vietnam Moratorium. He has been closely affiliated with the leftist-dominated Veterans for Peace in Vietnam. On May 25, 1971, he described his experiences in weekly meetings with members of Veterans for Peace at a New York City storefront. Said Lifton: "These men feel the need to tell the truth about what is going on, about our general lack of sensitivity to indiscriminate killing. Voicing their protest is a combination of a political impulse and a psychological need. To the extent the public can understand the truth, the veterans feel expunged of their guilt feelings about the brutalizing they have undergone. They use the phrase 'becoming human again.' These men are reacting to the emotions that all veterans feel, even though most simply choose to move offstage. The others are not joining chauvinistic organizations like the American Legion, so one can conclude that the message of anti-war veterans has some meaning for all veterans in our society."

Lifton described public protest as a healthy activity for Vietnam veterans, although many veterans still remained deeply alienated, he said, because they had "a strong and disturbing feeling of having been victimized and betrayed by their own country." He predicted that some veterans would seek outlets for a pattern of violence to which they had become accustomed, others would undergo periodic depressions and disabling psychosomatic disorders, and others would hold onto racist ideas or the need to victimize people. Lifton said that psychiatrists such as himself, who had participated in the talk sessions with Vietnam Veterans Against the War, "believe that they themselves derive considerable help in coming to terms with their own guilt for the violence in which the nation has involved itself." As a result of his own experiences, Lifton has concluded that "it is difficult to make into heroes the men who have fought in this filthy, ambiguous war."

LINDBECK

JOHN M. LINDBECK was born on July 8, 1915 in Kikungshan, China, son of American citizens Magda Hallquist and John Lindbeck. He was married to the late Nancy Gantt and the late Dorothea Wehrwein. He is married to Anne Jackson. He is an alumnus of Gustavus Adolphus College (A.B., 1937) and Yale University (B.D., 1940; Ph.D., 1948). He also studied at the Harvard-Yenching Institute as a Rockefeller Foundation fellow.

In 1944 and 1945, Lindbeck was a lecturer at the School of Military Government at Princeton University. From 1948 until 1952, he was at Yale University as assistant professor of political science (1948-1949), assistant professor of Far Eastern studies (1949-1952), director of undergraduate Far Eastern area studies (1950-1951), faculty research fellow in the humanities (1951-1952), and lecturer in the Institute of Far Eastern Languages (1948-1952). From 1952 until 1958, he was a public affairs advisor in the Chinese affairs division of the Department of State. In 1958 and 1959, he was at Columbia University as the deputy director of a research project on men and politics in modern China. From 1959 until 1967, he was at Harvard University as research fellow in Chinese studies (1959-1967), associate director of the East Asian Research Center (1959-1967), field researcher in Hong Kong (1961-1962), and lecturer in government (1963-1967). Since 1967, he has been director of Columbia University's East Asian Institute. He has been a visiting lecturer at the Foreign Service Institute, the Army War College, and the Bernadotte Institute. He has been a consultant to the Department of State, the Department of Health, Education and Welfare, and two think factories, RAND Corporation and the Institute for Defense Analyses.

Lindbeck is a long-time member of the Council on Foreign Relations, the informal supra-State Department of the United States. He has been on the board of directors and has been vice-president of the National Committee on U.S.-China Relations, one of the more important branches of the Red China lobby.

GEORGE N. LINDSAY JR. was born on October 20, 1919 in New York City, son of Eleanor Vliet and George Lindsay. He married Mary Dickey. He is an alumnus of Yale University (B.A., 1941; LL.B., 1947). In 1947, he was admitted to the New York bar.

Since 1947, Lindsay has been with the legal firm of Debevoise, Plimpton, Lyons & Gates as an associate (1947-1954) and partner (1955 to the present). Since 1964, he has been on the advisory council of African affairs of the Department of State. In 1965, he was co-director for research in the New York City mayoralty campaign of his brother, John V. Lindsay. Since 1963, he has been with the leftist-oriented Planned Parenthood-World Population Council as treasurer and member of the executive committee (1963-1965), chairman of the board (1965-1968), and honorary vice-chairman (1969 to the present). Since 1968, he has been on the board of overseers of the Center for New York City Affairs at the radical New School for Social Research. Since 1968, he has been on the board of directors of the leftist-oriented African-American Institute. Since 1961, he has been a member of the Council on Foreign Relations, the informal supra-State Department of the United States.

SEYMOUR LIPSET was born on March 18, 1922 in New York City, son of Lena Lippman and Max Lipset. He married Elsie Braun. He is an alumnus of the City College of New York (B.S., 1943) and Columbia University (Ph.D., 1949). He is the author of *Agrarian Socialism* (1950); *Political Man: Social Bases of Politics* (1960); and *The First New Nation: The U.S. in Historical and Comparative Perspective* (1963). He is co-author of *Union Democracy* (1956); *Social Mobility in Industrial Society* (1959 and 1966); and *The Politics of Unreason* (1970). He is editor of Harriet Martineau's *Society in America* (1962); M. Ostrogorskii's *Democracy and the Organization of Political Parties* (1964); *Social Structure Mobility and Economic Development* (1966); and *Politics and Social Science* (1969). He is co-editor of *Class, Status, and Power* (1953); *Labor and Trade Unionism* (1960); *Culture and Social Character* (1961); *Sociology: Progress of a Decade* (1961); *The Berkeley Student Revolt* (1965); *Social Structure and Social Mobility in Economic Growth* (1966); *Class, Status, and Power in Comparative Perspective* (1966); *Elites in Latin America* (1967); *Students and Politics* (1967); *Party Systems and Voter Alignments* (1967); *Revolution and Counterrevolution* (1968); and *Students in Revolt* (1969). He has contributed articles to *Commentary, Encounter, New York Times Magazine, New Republic*, and *Reporter*.

In 1945 and 1946, Lipset held a fellowship from the Social Science Research Council. From 1946 until 1948, he was a lecturer in sociology at the University of Toronto. From 1948 until 1950, he was at the University of California at Berkeley as assistant professor (1948-1950), research associate and instructor in industrial relations (1948-1950), and assistant professor (1949-1950). From 1950 until 1956, he was at Columbia University as assistant professor of sociology (1950-1954), associate professor (1954-1956), research associate in the Bureau of Applied Social Research (1951-1954), and assistant director of the Bureau of Applied Social Research (1954-1956). In 1951 and 1959, he was a lecturer at the Salzburg [Austria] Seminar on American Studies. In 1953, he was a visiting professor at the Free University of Berlin. In 1955 and 1956, he was a fellow at the Center for the Advanced Study in the Behavioral Sciences. From 1956 until 1966, he was at the University of California at Berkeley as associate professor of sociology (1956-1957), professor of sociology (1957-1966), research associate in the Institute of International Studies (1956-1966), and director of the Institute (1962-1966). Since 1966, he has been at Harvard University as a professor of government and social relations and a research associate in the Center for International Affairs. In 1960 and 1961, he was a Ford research professor at Yale University. He has been a consultant to the leftist-oriented Fund for the Republic since 1958, and to the defamatory Anti-Defamation League since 1959.

In 1968, Lipset and his co-author Earl Raab received the Myrdal Award of $10,000 from Harper & Row. (The award was named in honor of the Swedish Socialist Gunnar Myrdal, as one of the latest tributes reserved exclusively for the Left.)

In 1969, Lipset was associated with Negotiation Now!, an ultra-leftist-pacifist group which called for the United States to propose at the perennial peace talks in Paris an immediate cease-fire in Vietnam. In recent years, he has been associated with the ultra-leftist Cesar

Chavez and his Citizens for Farm Labor. For the past quarter of a century, Lipset has been one of the best known critics of the anti-left. His chief bugbear has been the rightwing extremists whom Lipset has found to be legion throughout American history.

WILLIAM W. LOCKWOOD was born on February 24, 1906 in Shanghai, China, son of American citizens Mary Town and William Lockwood. He married Virginia Chapman. He is an alumnus of DePauw University (A.B., 1927) and Harvard University (A.M., 1929; Ph.D., 1950). In 1956 and 1957, he held a fellowship from the leftist-oriented Ford Foundation. In 1961 and 1962, he was a Fulbright research scholar in Japan. In 1965 and 1966, he held a McCosh faculty fellowship. He is the author of *The Economic Development of Japan* (1954). He is the editor of *The State and Economic Enterprise in Japan* (1965) and *The United States and Communist China* (1965).

From 1929 until 1934, Lockwood was at Bowdoin College as instructor (1929-1932) and assistant professor (1932-1934). From 1935 until 1961, he was associated with the American Institute of Pacific Relations as research secretary (1935-1940), executive secretary (1941-1943), and trustee (1946-1953 and 1955-1961). In 1940 and 1941, he was executive secretary of the American Committee for International Studies at Princeton, New Jersey. In 1941, he was a consultant to the U.S. Office of Export Control. In 1943, he was assistant chief of the Far East division of the research and analysis branch in the Office of Strategic Services. In 1946, he was with the Department of State as assistant chief in the division of Japanese and Korean Economic Affairs. Since 1946, he has been at Princeton University's Woodrow Wilson School of Public and International Affairs as assistant director (1946-1957), associate professor (1949-1954), and professor of politics and international affairs (1955 to the present). From 1953 until 1955, he was a consultant to the leftist-oriented Ford Foundation.

Lockwood's affiliations have included *Amerasia*, a Communist-controlled magazine; the American League Against War and Fascism ("subversive and Communist"); the American-Russian Institute ("a 'Communist-controlled' organization which was intimately linked with the Institute of Pacific Relations"); the National People's Committee Against Hearst ("subversive and Communist"); and the ultra-leftist-pacifist Fellowship of Reconciliation. He has been a member of the Council on Foreign Relations, the informal supra-State Department of the United States.

In the 1951-1952 Institute of Pacific Relations hearings of the Senate Internal Security Subcommittee, Lockwood was a key witness. He testified that he had been attracted to the IPR because he had an aversion to Communism and all its works and because of his belief that totalitarianism in any form was a threat to every ideal in American life and every hope of betterment in the rest of the world. Said Lockwood: "The truth is, in my opinion, that the Institute of Pacific Relations has never been subverted to Communist ends. From fairly extensive knowledge of its operations I believe it has remained true to its principles of nonpartisan investigation and free discussion. If the Communists tried to use it to further their designs, then on the record they failed . . . . I should like to make three points more explicitly concerning the record of the Institute of Pacific

Relations. These are fundamental to the committee's investigation, as I understand its purpose. The first is the wide and diversified character of the institute's associations, necessary to the conduct of its work. The second is the support and participation it has enjoyed generally from scholars and men of affairs in all Pacific countries, except those behind the iron curtain. The third concerns the actual character of its publications and its conferences which, far more than associations alone, provide the real criterion by which it should be judged . . . . Only by the narrowest and most partisan selection of facts can it be made to appear that the participation of Communists or Communist sympathizers bulks significantly in the record."

Lockwood's defense of the IPR's integrity and his denial of Communist and pro-Communist influences were in the sharpest contrast to the eventual findings of the Senate Internal Security Subcommittee. The SISS heard sworn testimony in which many IPR'ers were identified as Communists and many as collaborators with the Soviet Union's intelligence apparatus. Many were identified as writers for Communist Party publications, while others were the subjects of action by agencies of the U.S. Government, or by foreign non-Communist governments, on grounds involving loyalty or national security. The SISS concluded: "The Institute of Pacific Relations has not maintained the character of an objective, scholarly and research organization. The IPR has been considered by the American Communist Party and by Soviet officials as an instrument of Communist policy, propaganda and military intelligence. The IPR disseminated and sought to popularize false information including information originating from Soviet and Communist sources. A small core of officials and staff members carried the main burden of IPR activities and directed its administration and policies. Members of the small core of officials and staff members who controlled IPR were either Communist or pro-Communist. There is no evidence that the large majority of its members supported the IPR for any reason except to advance the professed research and scholarly purposes of the organization. Most members of the IPR, and most members of its board of trustees, were inactive and obviously without any influence over the policies of the organization and the conduct of its affairs. IPR activities were made possible largely through the financial support of American industrialists, corporations, and foundations, the majority of whom were not familiar with the inner workings of the organization. The effective leadership of the IPR often sought to deceive IPR contributors and supporters as to the true character and activities of the organization. Neither the IPR nor any substantial body of those associated with it as executive officers, trustees or major financial contributors, has ever made any serious and objective investigation of the charges that the IPR was infiltrated by Communists and was used for pro-Communist and pro-Soviet purposes. The names of eminent individuals were by design used as a respectable and impressive screen for the activities of the IPR inner core, and as a defense when such activities came under scrutiny . . . . The effective leadership of IPR worked consistently to set up actively cooperative and confidential relationships with persons in Government involved in the determination of foreign policy . . . . It was the continued practice of IPR to seek to place in Government posts both persons associated with IPR and other persons selected by the effective leadership of IPR. The IPR possessed close organic relations with the State Department through interchange of personnel, attendance of State Department officials at IPR conferences, constant exchange of information and social contacts . . . . The effective leadership of the IPR used IPR prestige to promote the interests of the Soviet Union in the United States. A group of persons operating within and about the Institute of Pacific Relations exerted a substantial influence on United States far eastern policy. The IPR was a vehicle used by the Communists to orientate American far eastern policies toward Communist objectives . . . . The net effect of IPR activities on United States public opinion has been such as to serve international Communist interests and to affect adversely the interests of the United States."

Lockwood was evidently not impressed by the conclusions of the SISS, despite the fact that the IPR hearings were among the most extensive ever held by a congressional committee. He remained a trustee of the IPR until it finally removed itself from the United States to Canada in 1961.

ROBERT H. LOUNSBURY was born on June 15, 1921 in New York City, son of Elsa Cook and Orlando Lounsbury. He was married to and divorced from Nancy Rausch. He is an alumnus of Princeton University (A.B., 1943) and Yale University (LL.B., 1949).

From 1946 until 1949, Lounsbury was an assistant instructor in Spanish and law at Yale University. He was admitted to the New York bar in 1950. From 1950 until 1953, he was an assistant in the Office of the Director of the Central Intelligence Agency. From 1953 until 1956, he was an associate in the legal firm of Cravath, Swaine & Moore in New York City. From 1956 until 1960, he was an attorney with the IBM Corporation. From 1960 until 1967, he was general counsel for the Kennecott Copper Corporation. Since 1967, he has been general counsel and vice president of Eltra Corporation.

Lounsbury has been extremely active in the Democratic Party since 1956. He was executive director of National Businessmen for Harriman (1956); delegate to the New York County Democratic Judicial Conference (1957 and 1966); member of the Lehman, French, Vanden Heuvel, and Akers congressional campaign committees; member of the finance committee in the Lehman-for-U.S. Senate campaign; secretary of the businessmen's division of the Citizens for Harriman and Hogan (1958); member of the steering committee of the Democratic Forum (1960 to the present); vice chairman of the finance committee of the New York State Democratic Committee (1960-1964); alternate delegate-at-large to the Democratic National Convention (1964); co-chairman of the New York County Citizens for Johnson-Humphrey-Kennedy (1964); assistant campaign manager in the Ryan-for-Mayor Committee (1965); campaign chairman for Robert J. Schwartz' congressional candidacy (1965-1966); member of National Businessmen for Humphrey-Muskie (1968); and finance co-chairman of New York Citizens for Kennedy (1968).

Lounsbury has been a member of the Council on Foreign Relations, the informal supra-State Department of the United States. He has been a member of the U.S. committee of the leftist-oriented Inter-American Association for Freedom and Democracy. He has been very active with the ultra-radical Americans for Democratic Action as chairman of the political action committee of the New York ADA (1965-1966 and 1968 to the present) and member of the board of the national ADA (1966).

DAVID R. LUCE was born on February 22, 1927 in Boston, Massachusetts, son of Agnes Foote and Stanford Luce. He married Maria Hebenstreit. He is an alumnus of Dartmouth College (A.B., 1950) and the University of Michigan (M.A., 1952; Ph.D., 1957).

From 1957 until 1959, Luce was an instructor in philosophy at the University of Arkansas, and in 1959 and 1960, at the University of Minnesota. In 1960, he was a visiting assistant professor at the University of Minnesota and the University of Chicago. Since 1960, he has been at the University of Wisconsin as assistant professor (1960-1967) and associate professor (1967 to the present) of philosophy.

Luce is a long-time active official of the ultra-leftist American Civil Liberties Union. He is affiliated with the leftist-oriented American Association of University Professors. He has been a member of the National Committee to Abolish the House Un-American Activities Committee ("to lead and direct the Communist Party's 'Operation Abolition' campaign").

RICHARD D. LUNT was born on October 24, 1933 in New Haven, Connecticut, son of Pearl Collins and Herbert Lunt. He is married to Ruth Bainton. He is an alumnus of Oberlin College (B.A., 1955) and the University of Mexico (M.A., 1959; Ph.D., 1962). He is the author of *The High Ministry of Government: The Political Career of Frank Murphy* (1965).

Since 1961, Lunt has been at the

Rochester Institute of Technology serving successively as instructor, assistant professor and associate professor of history. He is affiliated with the leftist-racist Congress of Racial Equality.

SALVADOR E. LURIA was born on August 13, 1912 in Turin, Italy, son of Ester Sacerdote and David Luria. He married Zella Hurwitz. He came to the United States in 1940 and was naturalized in 1947. He is an alumnus of the University of Torino (M.D., 1935).

From 1935 until 1938, Luria served in the Italian Army. From 1938 until 1940, he was a research fellow at the Curie Laboratory and the Institute of Radium in Paris. From 1940 until 1942, he was a research assistant at Columbia University. From 1943 until 1950, he served successively as an instructor, assistant professor, and associate professor of bacteriology at Indiana University. From 1950 until 1959, he was a professor of bacteriology at the University of Illinois. Since 1959, he has been a professor of microbiology at Massachusetts Institute of Technology. Since 1965, he has been a nonresident fellow at the Salk Institute for Biological Studies. He has been a visiting lecturer at the University of Colorado, Columbia University, the University of Notre Dame, and the National Institute of Health. He has held Guggenheim fellowships at Vanderbilt University, Princeton University, and the Pasteur Institute in Paris.

Luria has been affiliated with the leftist-pacifist American Friends Service Committee; the leftist-pacifist Civil Defense Letter Committee; the leftist-pacifist National Committee for a Sane Nuclear Policy; the leftist-pacifist Educational Committee to Halt Atomic Weapons; the leftist-pacifist Committee of Responsibility; the leftist-pacifist Inter-

University Committee for a Public Hearing on Vietnam; the leftist-pacifist Voters' Peace Pledge Campaign; and the People's Peace Treaty, the pet 1971 project of the ultra-left. He has also been affiliated with the leftist-oriented Ad Hoc Committee for an Open Letter on Vietnam and the leftist-pacifist Ad Hoc Faculty Committee on Vietnam.

In 1969, Luria was a co-winner of the Nobel Prize in medicine and physiology. He gave a large share of his $25,000 prize money to several anti-war groups. He has been a leading figure in the Federation of American Scientists, a group of bleeding-heart leftwing-pacifists. He joined with other members of the FAS in 1970 to encourage the physical attack by leftists upon the Instrumentation Laboratory at Massachusetts Institute of Technology. Luria has been especially vocal in his opposition to biological warfare, U.S. participation in the Vietnam War, and the U.S. space program. In his hysterical enthusiasm, he has justified his leftist posture by saying: "Money needed for the ghettos, medical research, and substandard housing are victims of the war in Vietnam and our overgrown defense program."

DON M. MANKIEWICZ was born on January 20, 1922 in Berlin, Germany, son of American citizens Sara Aaronson and Herman Mankiewicz. He married Ilene Korsen. He is an alumnus of Columbia University (B.A., 1942). He is the author of *See How They Run* (1960); *Trial* (1955); and *It Only Hurts A Minute* (1967). His motion picture scripts include "Trial" (1956) and "I Want to Live" (1959). Mankiewicz has written television plays for "Playhouse 90," "Profiles in Courage," "Studio One," "Kraft Theatre," "Armstrong Theatre," and "DuPont Theatre."

From 1946 until 1948, Mankiewicz was a reporter for *New Yorker* magazine. Since 1948, he has been a free-lance writer. Since 1969, he has been an instructor at New York University's Institute of Film and TV. Since 1948, he has been active in Democratic Party politics in New York State and on a national level. In 1950, he was on the campaign staff for U.S. Senate candidate Herbert Lehman; in 1952 and 1956, on that of presidential candidate Adlai Stevenson; and in 1964, on that of senatorial candidate Robert F. Kennedy. In 1952, he was a Democratic-Liberal candidate for the New York State Assembly. Since 1953, he has been vice-chairman of the Nassau County Democratic Committee. He has been at the Democratic National Convention as an alternate delegate (1960) and delegate (1968). His work in the Democratic Party has been done exclusively for leftwing candidates.

FRANK F. MANKIEWICZ was born on May 16, 1924 in New York City, son of Sara Aaronson and Herman Mankiewicz. He married Holly Jolley. He is an alumnus of the University of California at Los Angeles (A.B., 1947); Columbia University (M.S., 1948); and the University of California at Berkeley (LL.B., 1955).

From 1948 until 1952, Mankiewicz worked as a journalist in Washington, D.C., and in Los Angeles. In 1951 and 1952, he was a civil rights director for the defamatory Anti-Defamation League in Los Angeles. In 1955, he was admitted to the California bar, and from 1955 until 1961, he practiced law in Beverly Hills. From 1962 until 1966, he was with the Peace Corps as director in Lima, Peru (1962-1964), and as Latin

American regional director (1964-1966). In 1965, he reaped a harvest of bad publicity for the Peace Corps when he consulted with Carl Oglesby and Paul Booth, leaders of the ultra-radical Students for a Democratic Society, and asked their advice on how to recruit New Left activists into the Peace Corps. From 1966 until 1968, he was press assistant to Robert F. Kennedy. At the time of his appointment to the Kennedy staff, *Human Events* commented on a then recently delivered Mankiewicz speech: "On June 18 Mankiewicz stunned an audience at California State College at Los Angeles with a commencement address indirectly condemning any 'toughness' LBJ has displayed in his foreign policy and glorifying the beatnik-leftists for taking to the streets. Americans, he claimed, have 'an extraordinary willingness to assign extreme and irrelevant political labels to those who want fundamental change.'

"Echoing left-wing sentiment, Mankiewicz said that when an underdeveloped nation seeks to establish policies which exist in the United States – such as free public schools, Medicare or civil rights – U.S. foreign policy makers view such a nation as 'dangerously irresponsible, untimely, revolutionary and probably Communist.' (This statement has drawn a horse laugh from anti-Communist diplomats who recall how the State Department supported both Castro and Mao Tse-tung, precisely because they were for Socialistic measures.)

"Continuing his strange speech, Mankiewicz asserted that one law which emerges from the 'ludicrous nature of our stance toward the world is this: If you call a man a "Communist" often enough and loud enough, he will become one.' (He did not cite even one example bearing out this contention.)

"The Peace Corps was viewed by Mankiewicz as the nation's 'only saving remnant of a commitment to [the] revolution for dignity and recognition.' He pictured the small percentage of beatnik-leftists as the 'students who take seriously from the campus the ideas they have learned in the classroom, and seek to apply them to the problems of our time – poverty, discrimination, injustice.' If that 'slice of campus society which takes ideas seriously and is willing to conduct its policies in the streets of the nation and the world can strengthen and grow,' he said, 'then there is a chance – a narrow chance but one worth trying – that the ancient revolutionary ideas that are the basis of our society can once again inspire and light the world.' "

After the death of Robert F. Kennedy, Mankiewicz kept busy in a variety of ways. In the summer of 1968, he worked as a correspondent for NBC News, covering the Republican and Democratic National Conventions. After leaving the network's staff, he worked in the presidential campaign of leftist Senator George McGovern. In December 1968, Mankiewicz along with other leftists became a member of the board of directors of the Center for Community Change, which was funded with $3.5 million by the leftist-oriented Ford Foundation. In February 1969, it was revealed that the Ford Foundation had granted $15,692 to Mankiewicz for a study on the effects of Peace Corps community development projects in Latin American and Caribbean countries. In 1968, Mankiewiez and veteran journalist Tom Braden began a syndicated column which from the beginning was carried in major liberal newspapers throughout the country. The partners also conducted a five-day-a-week news commentary on WTOP-TV in Washington, D.C. As a columnist and commentator, Mankiewicz has not only adopted the liberal position on major public issues, but also remains, as in the past, an ardent apologist for the New Left.

JULIUS MARK was born on December 25, 1898, son of Ida Tanur and David Mark. He married Margaret Baer. He is an alumnus of Hebrew Union College (B.H.L., 1917) and the University of Cincinnati (A.B., 1921). In 1922, he was ordained a rabbi. He is the author of *Behaviorism and Religion* (1930); *The Rabbi Meets Some Big Dilemmas* (1956); and *Reaching for the Moon* (1959).

From 1922 until 1926, Mark was a rabbi in South Bend, Indiana. From 1926 until 1948, he was rabbi of Vine Street Temple in Nashville, Tennessee. From 1948 until 1968, he was senior rabbi at Congregation Emanuel in New York City and, since 1968, rabbi emeritus. Since 1949, he has been professor of homiletics and practical theology at Hebrew Union College.

Mark is a member on the Eastern board of directors of the defamatory Anti-Defamation League. He is a long-time member of the Foreign Policy Association, a bulwark of leftist internationalism. He is a long-time member of the Council on Foreign Relations, the informal supra-State Department of the United States.

IRVING L. MARKOVITZ was born on August 9, 1934 in McKeesport, Pennsylvania. He is an alumnus of Brandeis University (B.A., 1956); Boston University (M.A., 1958); and the University of California at Berkeley (Ph.D., 1967). In 1957 and 1958, he held an African Affairs fellowship at Boston University From 1964 until 1966, he held a Foreign Area fellowship from the Social Science Research Council and the American Council of Learned Societies. He is the author of *Leopold Senghor and the Politics of Negritude* (1968). He is the editor of *African Politics: Basic Issues and Problems* (1968).

From 1959 until 1962, Markovitz was at the University of California at Berkeley as a teaching assistant in political science (1959-1960), head teaching assistant (1960-1961), and research assistant (1961-1962). In 1962 and 1963, he was a visiting assistant professor at New York University. Since 1966, he has been at Queens College as a lecturer (1966-1967) and assistant professor (1967 to the present). In 1968 and 1969, he held a faculty research grant at the City University of New York.

Markovitz has participated in the annual ultra-leftist Socialist Scholars Conferences.

CHARLES B. MARSHALL was born on March 25, 1908 in Catskill, New York, son of Alice Beeman and Caleb Marshall. His second wife is Betty O'Brien. He is an alumnus of the University of Texas (B.A., 1931; M.A., 1932) and Harvard University (Ph.D., 1939). In 1934 and 1935, he held a fellowship from the leftist-pacifist Carnegie Endowment for International Peace. He is the author of *The Limits of Foreign Policy* (1954); *The Exercise of Sovereignty* (1965); *The Cold War: A Concise History* (1965); and *Crisis Over Rhodesia: A Skeptical View* (1967).

From 1925 until 1931, and from 1934 until 1938, Marshall worked for newspapers in El Paso and Austin, Texas, and in Detroit, Michigan. From 1938 until 1942, he was an instructor and tutor in government at Harvard and Radcliffe Colleges. From 1947 until

1950, he was a staff consultant for the Foreign Affairs Committee of the House of Representatives. From 1950 until 1953, he was on the policy planning staff of the Department of State. From 1955 until 1957, he was an adviser to the prime minister of Pakistan. Since 1957, he has been with the leftist-oriented Washington Center for Foreign Policy Research as research associate (1957 to the present) and acting director (1969 to the present). Since 1965, he has been with The Johns Hopkins School of Advanced International Studies as visiting professor (1965-1966), professor (1966-1967), and Paul H. Nitzi professor of international politics (1967 to the present). In 1958 and 1959, he was a visiting scholar at the leftist-pacifist Carnegie Endowment for International Peace. He is a long-time member of the Council on Foreign Relations, the informal supra-State Department of the United States. He has served as a high official of the Foreign Policy Association, a bulwark of leftist internationalism.

ERNEST R. MAY was born on November 19, 1928 in Fort Worth, Texas, son of Rachel Garza and Ernest May. He married Nancy Caughey. He is an alumnus of the University of California (A.B., 1948; M.A., 1949; Ph.D., 1951). In 1958 and 1959, he held a Guggenheim fellowship. From 1959 until 1961, he held a faculty resident fellowship from the Social Science Research Council. In 1963 and 1964, he held a fellowship at the Center for Advanced Study in the Behavioral Sciences. He is the author of *The World War and American Isolation: 1914-1917* (1959); *The Ultimate Decision: The President as Commander-in-Chief* (1960); *Imperial Democracy: The Emergence of America as a Great Power*

(1961); *From Imperialism to Isolationism: 1898-1919* (1964); *Anxiety and Affluence: 1945-1965* (1966); and *American Imperialism: A Speculative Essay* (1968). He is co-author of *A History of the United States* (1964); *The Progressive Era and World War, Boom and Bust* (1964); and *Land of the Free* (1966). He has contributed articles to *Foreign Affairs, New Republic,* and *Saturday Review.*

In 1950 and 1951, May was a lecturer in history at Los Angeles State College. From 1952 until 1954, he was a member of the history section of the Joint Chiefs of Staff. Since 1954, he has been at Harvard University: instructor (1954-1956), assistant professor (1956-1959), associate professor (1959-1963), and professor (1963 to the present) of history; Allston Burr Senior Tutor in Kirkland House (1960-1966); and dean of Harvard College (1969 to the present). Since 1967, he has been with the Institute of Politics as a member (1967 to the present), and is now acting director (since 1969). He has been a consultant to the U.S. Air Force and two of the Establishment's think factories -- RAND Corporation and the Institute for Defense Analyses. He is a member of the Council on Foreign Relations, the informal supra-State Department of the United States. As dean of Harvard College, despite his appeasement gestures, he was pushed around by black militant students in a 1969 campus uprising. Politically he has been closely affiliated with the Kennedy dynasty.

JEAN MAYER was born on February 19, 1920 in Paris, France, son of André and Jeanne Eugénie Mayer. He married Elizabeth Van Huysen. He came to the United States in 1946 and is a naturalized citizen. He is an alumnus of the University of Paris (B. Litt., 1937; B.S., 1938; M. Sc., 1939; D. Sc., 1950) and Yale University (Ph.D., 1948). From 1946 until 1948, he held a Rockefeller Foundation fellowship at Yale. He is the author of *Overweight: Causes, Cost, and Control* (1968).

In 1948, Mayer was an adviser on nutrition with UNESCO. In 1948 and 1949, he was a research associate in pharmacology at George Washington University's Medical School and a member of the nutrition division in the Food and Agriculture Organization. Since 1950, he has been at Harvard University: assistant professor (1950-1956), associate professor (1956-1965), and professor (1965 to the present) of nutrition; lecturer on the history of public health (1961 to the present); and member of Harvard's Center of Population Studies (1968 to the present). In the past decade, he has been a consultant to the United States Government, the Food and Agricultural Organization, and the World Health Organization. In 1969, he was a founder of the leftist-oriented National Council on Hunger and Malnutrition in the United States and served six months as chairman of the Council.

In 1969, President Richard Nixon appointed Mayer as his special consultant on nutrition. Mayer took a leave of absence from Harvard to organize a three-day White House Conference on Food, Nutrition and Health, which was held in December 1969. Although three thousand persons were invited to participate in the Conference, it proved to be little more than a forum for such rabble rousers as Jesse Jackson, Fannie Lou Hamer, and Ralph D. Abernathy. In keeping with the tradition of farcical White House conferences, a 625-page report was issued, recommending a variety of socialist measures including a minimum annual income of $5500 for a family of four, a nationalized health and disability insurance program, a widely expanded school lunch program subsidized by the federal government, a massive food stamp program subsidized by the federal government, a 50 per cent increase in Social Security payoffs, and compulsory enrichment of basic foods. In 1970, Mayer returned to his duties at Harvard, but he also helped to plan the nutrition program for the 1970 White House Conference on Children and Youth, a fiasco completely dominated by leftists from campuses and elsewhere.

Mayer has been affiliated with the leftist-oriented Ad Hoc Committee for an Open Letter on Vietnam; the leftist-pacifist Committee of Responsibility; the leftist-loaded Citizens Crusade Against Poverty; the leftist-oriented Sex Information and Education Council of the United States; and the leftist-loaded Population Crisis Committee.

JOHN G. McCARTHY was born on June 16, 1909 in Methuen, Massachusetts, son of Ann Rochefort and Andrew McCarthy. He married Lily Lambert. He is an alumnus of Williams College (A.B., 1930) and Harvard University (M.B.A., 1932; LL.B., 1935). In 1937, he was admitted to the Massachusetts bar.

From 1935 until 1940, McCarthy was assistant secretary and an assistant to the general counsel of Johnson & Johnson. From 1940 until 1943, he was vice-president of Atlantic Diesel Corporation. From 1948 until 1953, he was vice-president of the Motion Picture Association of America and vice-president of the Motion Picture Export Association. From 1953 until 1957, he was president of International Affiliates. From 1957 until 1960, he served as the U.S. Minister for Economic Affairs to

NATO and the Organization for European Cooperation. Since 1960, he has been president of the Television Program Export Association.

McCarthy is a long-time member of the Council on Foreign Relations, the informal supra-State Department of the United States. He has served on the national council of the Foreign Policy Association, a highly effective pro-Communist vehicle.

MARY McCARTHY was born on June 21, 1912 in Seattle, Washington, daughter of Therese Preston and Roy McCarthy. She was married to and divorced from Harold Johnsrud, Edmund Wilson, and Bowden Broadwater. She is married to James West. She is an alumna of Vassar College (A.B., 1933). She is the author of *The Company She Keeps* (1942 and 1957); *The Oasis* (1949); *Cast A Cold Eye* (1950); *The Groves Of Academe* (1952); *A Charmed Life* (1955); *Sights and Spectacles: 1937-1956* (1956); *Venice Observed* (1956 and 1961); *Memories of a Catholic Girlhood* (1957); *The Stones of Florence* (1959 and 1963); *On the Contrary: Articles of Belief, 1946-1961* (1961); *Mary McCarthy's Theatre Chronicles: 1937-1962* (1963); *The Group* (1963); *The Humanist In The Bathtub* (1964); *Vietnam* (1967); *Hanoi* (1968); and *Birds of America* (1971). She has contributed to *Encounter, Harper's, New Yorker,* the *New York Review of Books,* and *Observer.*

From 1933 until 1935, Mary McCarthy was a book reviewer for the leftwing publications *Nation* and *New Republic.* In 1936 and 1937, she was an editor with Covici, Friede. From 1937 until 1948, she was a drama critic with the ultra-leftist *Partisan Review.* From 1945 until 1946, she was an instructor in literature at Bard College. In 1948, she was an English instructor at Sarah Lawrence College. In 1949 and 1950, and in 1959 and 1960, she held Guggenheim fellowships. In 1957, she received a grant-in-literature from the National Institute of Arts and Letters.

Mary McCarthy has described herself as a libertarian socialist. In recent years, her leftist sympathies have been expended mostly on her opposition to United States involvement in the Vietnam War. On March 30, 1971, *National Review Bulletin* reported: "About one second after the State Department rescinded its ban on travel to Red China, Mary McCarthy was reported engaged in trying to get herself a Peking visa, and using as intermediary Wilfred Burchett, the Australian Communist who is the main foreign correspondent for the Maoist *Guardian.*"

PAUL N. McCLOSKEY JR. was born on September 29, 1927 in San Bernardino, California, son of Vera McNabb and Paul McCloskey. He married Caroline Wadsworth. He is an alumnus of Stanford University (B.A., 1950; LL.D., 1953).

Since 1954, McCloskey has maintained a law practice in Palo Alto. In 1967, he was elected to the 90th Congress representing the Eleventh District of California. He campaigned as a Republican; his primary opponent was Shirley Temple Black. During his campaign, he received heavy support from Democrats as he stressed his anti-Vietnam War views, called for the admission of Red China to the United Nations, and urged a reduction in penalties for the use of marijuana. Prior to his congressional campaign, McCloskey's career as a Republican had been rather irregular. In 1960, he had been co-chairman of

Young Lawyers for Nixon-Lodge. In 1962 and 1966, he had campaigned for Republican candidates. In 1964, however, he supported Democrat Pierre Salinger for the U.S. Senate and at the same time declined to endorse Republican Barry Goldwater, who was running for the presidency. He also supported Democrat Wilson Riles against Republican Max Rafferty in the 1970 campaign for the office of California Superintendent of Public Instruction. In 1970, he refused to support the incumbent U.S. Senator George Murphy, a Republican, who was defeated by Democrat John V. Tunney.

In the Congress, McCloskey, who was re-elected in 1968, has compiled one of the most liberal voting records of all House Republicans. On domestic issues, he has been a consistent supporter of welfare legislation. He has been a vigorous opponent of the House Internal Security Subcommittee, a role shared with the extreme leftists of both parties. He has voted against the anti-ballistic missile defense program. He has voted against the continuance of aid to Free China. He has voted against appropriations for military research and construction. He has further endeared himself to the liberal-leftists in and out of Congress by defending the ultra-leftist Associate Justice William O. Douglas of the Supreme Court, and insisting that campus riots have been due primarily to the Vietnam War.

McCloskey has joined such far-out leftists as U.S. Senators George McGovern, Birch Bayh, and Harold Hughes in Members of Congress for Peace Through Law. The group has called for admission of Red China to the UN; the withdrawal of U.S. diplomatic recognition of Free China; and the extension of such recognition to Red China. The group has also called for the placing of Free China under the control of the United Nations Trusteeship Council.

Opposition to the Vietnam War has been McCloskey's main preoccupation since he entered Congress. In 1968, he expressed the opinion that South Vietnam "is better suited to Ho chi Minh's Communism than to Democracy." He described the barbaric Ho chi Minh as "a great national patriot." In 1969, he was one of the few Republicans to endorse the anti-war demonstrations conducted by the ultra-leftist Vietnam Moratorium Committee.

During the Nixon Administration's first two years, McCloskey's opposition to the Vietnam War and the conduct of the Nixon Administration placed him in the forefront of the Congressional doves. In the spring of 1971, he took part in the Washington, D.C., demonstrations led by the ultra-leftist Vietnam Veterans Against the War. He told the radical group: "It was an honor to walk with you this morning." As a result of his action, the California Republican Assembly took the unusual step of censuring him for "siding with radical groups on the left to promote violence," and urged him to join another Party. It was also in 1971 that the National Young Republican Leadership Training School ousted him from the ranks of its participants because of his "ill-advised and halfwitted attacks" on President Nixon. The Young Republicans had reference to McCloskey's suggestion that the Congress should begin a dialogue concerning the possibility of impeaching Nixon. The more Nixon relaxed the American war effort, the more vituperative McCloskey became. He had arrived at the point where he was calling President Nixon, American diplomats, and American military leaders liars and enemies of the Constitution. In his opinion, they were waging illegal and genocidal war against innocent people. The climax came when McCloskey announced his intention to run for the presidency.

McCloskey did not lack support when he made his campaign announcement. He had the immediate political allegiance of the ultra-leftist Allard Lowenstein, a one-term Democratic Congressman from New York, whose claim to fame was his 1968 leadership of the dump-Lyndon Johnson movement. Liberal fatcats were ready with their open purses. They included Cyrus Eaton, Norton Simon, Martin Peretz, Jack Dreyfus Jr., Stewart Mott Jr., Alan Miller, Ellsworth Carrington, Robert Meyerhoff, Sam Rubin, and Martin Fife. Further support was available from John Gardner and his leftist-liberal Common Cause group and Harold Willens and his extreme leftist Business Executives Move for Vietnam Peace. When he was asked about his anti-Nixon candidacy, McCloskey said: "I really have only one great goal, and that's what I first went to Congress for – to preserve our clean air and water and help keep California the loveliest place in the world. But I can't do anything about that or anything else until we get this war ·over. So if there's no other way to do that but go into the primaries, then I'll go into the primaries."

JOSEPH M. McDANIEL JR. was born on March 1, 1902 in Baltimore, son of Georgia Katzenberger and Joseph McDaniel. He married Eileen Driver. He is an alumnus of The Johns Hopkins University (A.B., 1924; Ph.D., 1930). He is the author of *Introduction to Social Sciences* (1939).

In 1928 and 1929, McDaniel was a professor of economics at the University of Delaware. From 1930 until 1942, he served successively as an assistant profes-

sor, associate professor, and professor of economics at Dartmouth College. From 1947 until 1951, he was at Northwestern University as a professor of business administration (1947-1951) and dean of the school of commerce (1950-1951). Since 1951, he has been associated with the leftist-oriented Ford Foundation as assistant to the president (1951-1953), secretary (1953-1967), and consultant (1967 to the present).

McDaniel is a long-time member of the Council on Foreign Relations, the informal supra-State Department of the United States. He is chairman of the board of the leftist-oriented Ford Fund for Adult Education.

WILLIAM A. McGIRT was born on May 4, 1923 in Wilmington, North Carolina, son of Delia Inman and William McGirt. He is an alumnus of Duke University (A.B., 1943). He is the author, under the pseudonym of Will Inman, of *Lament and Psalm* (1960); *I Am the Snakehandler* (1960); *A River of Laughter* (1961); *Honey in Hot Blood* (1962); *108 Verges Unto Now* (1964); *Selected Poems from 108 Prayers for J. Edgar* (1965); *108 Tales of a Po' Buckra From the Lower Cape Fear* (1965); *A Congress of the Winds* (1966); and *Black Power: A Search for Umbra Within* (1966). He is a contributor to *Where Is Vietnam?: American Poets Respond* (1967).

McGirt is the editor of *Kauri*, a poetry newsletter. He has been an artist-in-residence at American University. He has described himself as a "Democratic revolutionary socialist." In 1966, he signed an advertisement in the Communist *National Guardian*, indicating that he would refuse to pay a federal income tax because of the United States involvement in the Vietnam War. He has been affiliated with the Emergency Civil Liberties Committee ("Communist front" – "subversive"). He was a member of the War Resisters League, a group of conscientious objectors who describe themselves as anarchists, democratic socialists, and independent radicals, and who agitate for unilateral disarmament, for U.S. diplomatic recognition of Red China, and on behalf of the Black Panthers.

VERNON McKAY was born on October 8, 1912 in Independence, Kansas, son of Myrtle Pierson and Peter McKay. He married Lila Buck. He is an alumnus of Baker University (A.B., 1933); Syracuse University (M.A., 1934); and Cornell University (Ph.D., 1939). He is the author of *Africa in World Politics* (1963). He is co-author of *Southern Africa and the United States* (1968). He is editor and co-author of *African Diplomacy: Studies in the Determinants of Foreign Policy* (1966). He is editor of *Africa In the United States* (1969). He is a contributor to *Africa Today* (1955); *Africa in the Modern World* (1955); *The United States and Africa* (1958); and *Historical Literature* (1961).

From 1936 until 1945, McKay was at Syracuse University as instructor (1936-1940) and assistant professor (1940-1945) in history. From 1945 until 1948, he was a research associate on Africa for the Foreign Policy Association, working under the direction of the extreme leftist Vera Micheles Dean, who had made the FPA a highly effective pro-Communist vehicle. From 1948 until 1956, he was with the Department of State as foreign affairs officer (1948-1955) and deputy director of the Office of Dependent Area Affairs (1955-1956). Since 1956, he has been at The Johns Hopkins University as profes-

sor of African Studies and director of the Program of African Studies in the School of Advanced International Studies. He has been a lecturer at the University of Stellenbosch, the University of Witwatersrand, and Northwestern University. He has been a consultant to the leftist-pacifist Carnegie Corporation and the leftist-oriented Ford Foundation. He was a recipient of travel grants from the Carnegie Corporation, The Johns Hopkins School of Advanced International Studies, and the Ford Foundation.

From 1960 until 1966, McKay was affiliated with the leftist-oriented U.S. National Commission for UNESCO as a member of the commission (1960-1966) and a member of its executive committee (1961-1963). He is a long-time member of the Council on Foreign Relations, the informal supra-State Department of the United States. He is a trustee of the leftist-oriented African-American Institute. In 1965, he contributed to *Apartheid and United Nations Collective Measures*, published by the leftist-pacifist Carnegie Endowment for International Peace. The document was a blueprint for the application of military and economic sanctions by the United Nations against South Africa as part of an international pro-Communist drive against that Republic. In 1966, McKay in testimony before the House Subcommittee on Africa reiterated his desire for sanctions against South Africa.

STEWART MEACHAM is a graduate of Davidson College. He received a bachelor of divinity degree from Union Theological Seminary in 1934. He served as a Presbyterian pastor in Birmingham, Alabama. He worked for eight years at the National Labor Relations Board in Washington, D.C. Immediately after World

War II, he was a labor adviser in Korea with the American occupation forces. He was an assistant to Jacob Potofsky, a radical Socialist and president of the Amalgamated Clothing Workers of America. He was a director of the Sidney Hillman Foundation, which gives awards annually to leftwingers in mass communications.

From 1951 until 1955, Meacham worked in India for the Methodist Board of Missions. The June 1959 issue of *News and Views* described Meacham's experiences in India: "All of this took place in buildings labeled as houses of worship in Houston. The moderator was one Stewart Meacham, director of the American Friends Service Committee's international affairs program, graduate of Union Theological Seminary, former assistant to the President of the Amalgamated Clothing Workers, and former Methodist missionary to India.

"Meacham was expelled by the Indian Government. He sought to disrupt a missionary conference in Landour in August 1953 where he was accused by fellow missionaries and pastors of 'following the Communist Party line.' He defended the Communist thesis, 'From each according to his ability, to each according to his need,' and further defended Communist leaders in the World Council of Churches.

"The Rev. Alton Shirey, pastor of the Champion Hill Presbyterian Church, Cullendale, Arkansas, reported March 10, 1954 that he knows Meacham to be a communist.

"In a letter dated January 18, 1954, Rev. Shirey stated: 'I have heard that you recently had a "run in" with Stewart Meacham in India. I know him well. We were students at Louisville Presbyterian Seminary at the same time. Then we were both Socialists. I later became

converted to premillennialism, while he became converted to communism. He has gone to India to prepare the way for communism to take over in that vast country. Frankly, I consider Stewart Meacham one of the most dangerous men I know anything about today.' "

In the late 1950's, Meacham was executive director of World Literacy, a functional committee of the ultra-leftist National Council of Churches. In the late 1950's, Meacham also became the peace education director of the American Friends Service Committee [AFSC], a position which he still holds. The AFSC, beginning in the early 1930's, became a vital part of the Communist movement in the United States and abroad. In 1954, the House Special Committee to Investigate Tax-Exempt Foundations and Comparable Organizations reported that the AFSC "organized the Student Peace Service Committee, which assisted in the organization of the Youth Committee Against War, which brought together: the American Student Union [cited as a Communist front]; the War Resisters League [part of the War Resisters International Council of International Anti-Militarist Groups, whose avowed purpose was to work 'for the supercession of capitalism and imperialism by the establishment of a new social and international order']; the Fellowship of Reconciliation; the Young Peoples Socialist League; the Farmers Union; the Independent Communist Labor League; the Methodist Federation for Social Service [Youth Section]; the American Youth Congress; and other leftwing groups."

When Meacham went to work for AFSC, it was almost totally committed to leftist political affairs. In December 1957, the AFSC published its recommended program for United States foreign policy: "(1) Cancel our nuclear weapons tests. (2) Start [unilateral] disarmament by gradual steps. (3) Share our resources more fully. (4) Consider the problems of men more important than the promotion of alliances. (5) Strengthen the United Nations as an inclusive and responsible agency for peace. (6) Seek ways to bring men together across the Iron and Bamboo curtains."

In May 1959, in full-page newspaper advertisements, the AFSC presented its hysterical views of nuclear warfare: "*What else but madness* is it when we seek comfort in the calculation that one-half rather than three-fourths of our population would die in an all-out nuclear war? *What else but madness* is it when our hope for security lies in terror? *What else but madness* is it when each of two powerful countries insists that all agreements be to the sole advantage of it alone? *What else but madness* is it when we think that rearming Germany with nuclear weapons is a step toward peace?"

In 1961, the AFSC – through its lobbying arm, the Friends Committee on National Legislation – adopted as its legislative program: "*World Disarmament*. Conclusion of a Nuclear Test Ban Treaty. Resume negotiations leading to a treaty calling for the permanent abolition of nuclear testing. Resume General Disarmament Negotiations. Make a greater, more intensified effort to reach agreement with the Soviet Union and [Red] China on immediate next steps toward world disarmament under United Nations inspection and control. Prevent the Transfer of Nuclear Weapons to NATO Commands . . . . *World Law*. Strengthen the International Court of Justice by removing the United States' 'self-judging' reservation ["disputes with regard to matters which are essentially within the domestic jurisdiction of the United States of America as determined by the United States"]. *World Economic Development*. Appropriate more funds on a long-term basis for U.N. and U.S. economic aid and technical assistance programs. Strengthen and improve the 'Food for Peace' program to use America's $7 million plus surplus agricultural products more creatively. Establish an International Youth Service Corps to provide an opportunity for young men and women to serve abroad in an international program to improve living standards and increase friendship around the world." [Since 1943, when the Friends Committee on National Legislation was organized, it has lobbied on problems affecting American Indians, race relations, and "civil rights." It has worked for the benefit of the United Nations. It has promoted extremely liberal immigration laws and more liberal laws for the benefit of conscientious objectors, with concomitant efforts to oppose military training.]

In 1959, Meacham wrote for the AFSC a booklet, "Labor and the Cold War," which reflected the ultra-leftist posture of the AFSC on national defense, nuclear warfare, nuclear testing, disarmament, and foreign policy. He showed a mastery for leftist clichés. He was in complete command of the hysterical horror stories about nuclear warfare and nuclear testing that were a regular part of the leftists' litany in the 1950's and 1960's. He revealed all the pet hates that certified him as an anti-anti-Communist, as he found the opportunity to be splenetic about Chiang Kai-shek, Korea's Syngman Rhee, Vietnam's Bao Dai, Cuba's Batista, Spain's Franco, and the Dominican Republic's Trujillo. According to Meacham, American foreign policy has failed the people of organized labor in nine particulars: (1) It has delivered power over the economy into the hands of the Pentagon and those who make the decisions in the larger corporations; (2) It has projected us into rapid technological change without adequate social controls; (3) It has crippled both labor and the consumer in the exercise of their rightful economic powers in the market place; (4) It has exposed the people of the world to radioactive poison; (5) It has magnified the destructive powers of war and brought war perilously close; (6) It has delivered us into the embrace of irresponsible allies, and alienated our natural friends; (7) It has stimulated the harsh tendencies of the communist countries and silenced voices of moderation; (8) It has diverted funds and energy from the constructive tasks of world development into military build-ups which are irrelevant to the needs of the underdeveloped lands; and (9) It has degraded our moral purposes.

Meacham wanted a return to "the crusading spirit and idealism of the New Deal period [which] began to drain out of the union movement as the economy began to shift over and adapt to the requirements of war."

Meacham's feverish anti-militarism, his ultra-leftist pacifism, his obsession with unilaterial disarmament, his total commitment to socialism at home and abroad, and his brazen anti-Americanism were all evident in his 1959 booklet, and he has maintained them consistently down to the present time. In the bibliography of his booklet, he listed exclusively leftist sources for his views on economy, labor, warfare, disarmament, and foreign policy: Joseph A. Beirne, A.A. Berle Jr., J.D. Bernal, Estes Kefauver, Henry Kissinger, Sidney Lens, C. Wright Mills, Gunnar Myrdal, Harvey

O'Connor, Linus Pauling, John Swomley, James Warburg, the National Planning Association, and the American Friends Service Committee.

Meacham was a close associate of Abraham J. Muste, who spent decades in the vanguard of Communist projects while posing as a high-minded pacifist. Meacham was a national committeeman of Omaha Action Against Nuclear Missiles and a member of the executive committee of Polaris Action, two of Muste's unilateral disarmament projects. Meacham participated in Muste's Church Peace Mission at Evanston, Illinois. The CPM was loaded with Communist fronters who were calling for "peaceful" resistance to Communism and for unilateral disarmament by the United States.

In 1960, Meacham participated in a rally to support the "first amendment defendants," a collection of Communists who refused to answer questions in congressional investigative hearings. They included Carl Braden, Pete Seeger, Harvey O'Connor, and Willard Uphaus.

Meacham was on the executive council of the Highlander Folk School, a center for pro-Communist activities, run by Communists and fellow travelers. He has been a member of the Methodist Federation for Social Action ("With an eye to religious groups, the Communists have formed religious fronts such as the Methodist Federation for Social Action").

Meacham has been affiliated with the Emergency Civil Liberties Committee ("To defend the cases of Communist lawbreakers, fronts have been devised making special appeals in behalf of civil liberties and reaching out far beyond the confines of the Communist Party itself. Among these organizations [is] the ... Emergency Civil Liberties Committee. When the Communist Party itself is under fire these fronts offer a bulwark of protection"); the ultra-leftist Committee to Defend the Panthers; the Citizens Committee for Constitutional Liberties ("created, dominated, and controlled by members and officials of the Communist Party"); Veterans of the Abraham Lincoln Brigade ("subversive and Communist"); the ultra-leftist-pacifist Committee for Nonviolent Action; the ultra-leftist-pacifist Voters' Peace Pledge; the ultra-leftist Committee to Defend the [Chicago] Conspiracy; the Student Mobilization Committee to End the War in Vietnam, dominated by Communists and fellow travelers; the ultra-leftist November 8 Mobilization Committee; the leftist-oriented Sex Information and Educational Council of the United States; the National [and New] Mobilization Committees to End the War in Vietnam, under control of Communists, Trotskyite Communists, and fellow travelers; the National Conference for New Politics, a classic united-front third-party movement largely controlled by the Communist Party; the ultra-leftist-pacifist National Committee for a Sane Nuclear Policy; the People's Peace Treaty, a Hanoi-inspired project undertaken by the ultra-left in America; and the ultra-leftist Peace and Justice Fund.

Meacham was an endorser of the ultra-leftist Freedom and Peace Party. He has often petitioned to abolish anti-Communist congressional investigative committees. He has always been a leader in David Dellinger's "Mobe" complex, which has been a rallying point in recent years for ultra-leftist demonstrations against the Vietnam War. He is on the coordinating committee of the Communist-controlled Peoples Coalition for Peace and Justice. He was a signer of "Declaration of Conscience," which said, in part: "We hereby declare our con-scientious refusal to cooperate with the U.S. Government in the prosecution of the war in Vietnam. We encourage those who can conscientiously do so to refuse to serve in the armed forces and to ask for discharge if they are already in." He was a leader in the Communist-controlled National Coalition Against War, Racism and Repression.

In 1968, Meacham was a participant at the Communist-controlled Hemispheric Conference to End the Vietnam War. In 1968, he went to Hanoi with Vernon Grizzard and Anne Scheer to receive three American pilots who had been held as prisoners of war by the North Vietnamese. The participation by Meacham and the publicity surrounding the release of the POWs made a propaganda coup for the Communists.

In 1968, Meacham went to Moscow at the invitation of the so-called Soviet Peace Committee, a governmental propaganda unit in the Soviet Union's perennial "peace" movement. Meacham's fellow travelers from America included Fay Knopp, his fellow-representative from the American Friends Service Committee; Homer Jack from the ultra-leftist Unitarian-Universalist Association; Richard J. Barnet, co-director of the ultra-leftist Institute for Policy Studies; Sanford Gottlieb, executive director of the ultra-leftist-pacifist National Committee for a Sane Nuclear Policy; Anci Koepel of the ultra-leftist Women Strike for Peace; Sidney Lens, a leading leftist radical leader of the midwest; Bruce Nelson of the ultra-leftist-pacifist Resistance; Robert Rothstein, a member of the ultra-leftist-pacifist Resist; and, Naomi Marcus of the ultra-leftist Women's International League for Peace and Freedom. The junket by the Americans was one more move by leftist Americans who periodically go through the ritual of a "dialogue" with "peace-loving" Communists in order to prove that a dialogue is better than war to resolve differences between the United States and the Soviet Union. In the 1968 "confrontation" between the American peaceniks and the Soviet Peace Committee, it was carefully explained to the world that the meeting's purpose was to discuss continuing U.S.-Soviet Union relations in the wake of the Soviet Union's invasion of Czecho-Slovakia. The impression was given that the handful of American "peace" leaders were, in reality, spokesmen for the American people and quasi-official spokesmen for the United States Government. The Americans went through the motions of insisting that they wanted to discuss the Czecho-Slovakian slaughter and administer some mild knuckle-rapping to their Soviet friends. The Soviet officials were not about to be chastised even mildly and excluded Czecho-Slovakia from the discussions. They did this in the following exchange between Meacham and Yuri Zhukov, who served as moderator during "three days of substantive talks."

Meacham: "We see the agenda in four main areas . . . [including] youth and resistance movements in the United States and broad problems of dissent throughout the world [and] problems of intervention – relationships between small and great powers, the primary example being the relationship of European security to Czechoslovakia."

Zhukov: ". . . In our private talks you can deal with any questions you please . . . . That applies to the question you mention about Czechoslovakia. As you are aware, the Czechoslovak Government announced in the U.N. that what is happening in Czechoslovakia is an internal problem of Czechoslovakia and is not for discussion outside. It would be strange indeed if we were to discuss the problems without the presence of Czechs here at all and it would be difficult for us to pass judgment on the affairs taking place. If you are interested, you can visit people at *Pravda*, journalists who were in Czechoslovakia during the events. . . . We should concentrate our efforts here on the struggle for peace . . . ."

Meacham: ". . . It is not possible when peace is the problem to divide internal problems from common problems. For instance, not only in the U.S. but also in Socialist countries there are also new impulses working among the young people . . . ."

Zhukov: "The question is quite clear . . . if we are dealing with problems of the youth movement, then we should deal with the Soviet Youth Committee . . . . I repeat my offer to introduce you to my colleagues in *Pravda*. Here we will not discuss the problem."

In another exchange between Zhukov and Meacham, Zhukov impressed upon Meacham that the meeting was to concentrate on "peace matters," not Czecho-Slovakia, and Meacham acted his part perfectly as a participant in a genuine debate.

Zhukov: "Every international meeting should take up the questions it is supposed to deal with. We are representatives of the peace movement and will speak on matters of peace . . . . We have no right to deal with other questions and we will not deal with them. If you are interested in a question not bound by the framework of the peace movement, I repeat the offer for you to meet with people who are competent to deal with these questions . . . . If you wish to discuss international questions dealing with the community of Socialist nations, you can meet with one or another representatives of the Socialist nations. Regarding our own opinion of Czechoslovakia, I will arrange a meeting with our correspondents who were on the scene in Czechoslovakia. But to discuss Czechoslovakia here in the framework of the peace movement is irrelevant and we will not discuss it here."

Meacham: "I appreciate your frankness in responding, because being frank we can remain friends even though we don't see things in the same way. We might take advantage of your invitation to talk to the people at *Pravda*. We will let you know. We hope you will appreciate that we have a different view of what is pertinent to peace. If we attempt to strain out of our mind nonpeace issues, then we can't speak our mind, and we wouldn't want you to sit here and listen to a dialogue without inner reality . . . . So, not wanting to press you against your will to engage in the kind of dialogue we want to engage in, but not assured of and not wanting to be pressed into your anticipated dialogue, I wonder if we could discuss other formats in which we could engage in the next few days."

The point that Zhukov put across in their exchange was that war and not peace was his business and should be Meacham's business. It was all good propaganda as the Soviet official lectured the Americans, whose "peace" credentials were impeccable in the eyes of the liberal-leftists at home, on what constitutes a legitimate agenda for "peace" promoters.

Meacham proved to be the perfect stooge for Zhukov. On one occasion, he gave Zhukov the opportunity to explain that the Soviet Peace Movement was beyond the pale of Communist discipline:

Meacham: "We realize there are many differences between the S.P.C. [Soviet Peace Committee] and the American peace movement, differences in structure, responsibility, and relationship to government. It is not surprising that to develop dialogue and discussion between these two entities would not be without difficulty.

"If we were a quasi-governmental organization representing our government with certain views, this might make it easier in some ways for us to approach the situation of discussion and dialogue. We are grateful that the S.P.C. arranged for us to meet with responsible people whose range lies outside the S.P.C. We would like to accept this offer and particularly to discuss these issues with high officials of the Communist party if this could be arranged . . . ."

Zhukov: "A clarification, please. The S.P.C. is not a quasi-governmental body. It is a public movement which involves hundreds of thousands of people who are selflessly engaged in activity. It is outside ideological framework. I myself am a Communist party member, but in the S.P.C. I am sitting opposite and holding debates with my ideological enemies — for instance, the representatives of churches. These are ideologies incompatible. But we have come together on the struggle for peace and we cooperate. Therefore it is not right to talk about quasi-governmental organizations and we cannot call the people officials who are in these organizations. We reaffirm our willingness to establish contact for you with other public organizations. As to meetings with top Communist party officials, this is not within our competence. Inter-party contacts are something different, and so far it is only with the American Communist party that our party has contact in the U.S."

Meacham: "I didn't describe the S.P.C. as a quasi-governmental organization. I merely said that if we had such a status, it would make it easier .... As a Quaker, I don't know of any ideology that can make a man my enemy. One of the things we feel strongly about is there is not only truth in every other person, even those with whom we disagree, but it is truth we desperately need to acquire. Therefore we have an ideology to remain open and not turn ourselves off."

In the phony debate, Meacham acquiesced in Zhukov's points: (1) A Communist Party member and official (he is employed by the Party's *Pravda*), such as himself, could speak in public without adhering to the Party line. (2) Hundreds of thousands of peaceniks were running around loose in the Soviet Union, exercising freedom of speech. (3) Church officials were allowed freedom of speech in the Soviet Union. (4) The Soviet Peace Committee was independent of the government.

At the Moscow meeting, Sanford Gottlieb of the American delegation seemed anxious to show that in the U.S. and the U.S.S.R. there were hard-liners and soft-liners, and because the U.S. had hard-liners, the U.S.S.R. had to have them, and vice versa. A Soviet delegate disagreed and insisted that only the U.S. had hard-liners. Gottlieb accepted that without rebuttal. Meacham found an answer in psychology and agreed that U.S. hard-liners, at least, were guilty of reacting to Soviet hard-liners, but he didn't seem sure about the reverse being true. But whatever his doubts, he pointedly placed the U.S. on or above the U.S.S.R.'s plane of guilt: "Psychological forces . . . influence both groups, causing each to project its own fears and ascribe them to the other, thereby seeing in the other the very characteristics which motivated its own conduct. By this process each group justifies actions which provide the opposite group with justifica-

tion for acting in the same way. I have seen precisely this process actively at work in the State Department .... Is it possible – and maybe it is not – for us to discuss how to break out of the interplay of fears which creates madness and prevents us from being what we should be in this world, and break this mirror-image pattern?"

It was Zhukov, however, who really had the final word in the Moscow meeting when he was allowed by the American delegation to portray the Russians as the true peacemongers in the midst of the "cold war": "It is said Americans and Russians are very much alike. It is true. We are frank and direct, ready to defend our convictions. At the same time we are quite different people. We grew up in different societies and convictions. Moreover, we have different information media .... In our information or press media, we are doing everything to counter forces of the cold war. We scrupulously avoid any sort of insults, any sort of crude statements against leaders of countries who are opposed to us . . . ."

In the late 1960's, Meacham built up a strong relationship with North Vietnamese officials, as did so many other leaders involved in David Dellinger's "Mobe" complex. Many of the "peace" demonstrations, in which Meacham was a leader, were undertaken after Mobe leaders conferred with North Vietnamese officials abroad.

In January 1970, Meacham and three other Hanoi favorites (Dellinger, Cora Weiss, and Richard Fernandez) announced the formation of the Committee of Liaison with Families of Servicemen Detained in North Vietnam. The Committee was formed at the request of the North Vietnamese in order that the American "peaceniks" would be granted a monopoly as liaison between American prisoners of war and their families. It was and remains an insidious plot to exploit for the advantage of the "peaceniks" the miseries of the POWs and their families. In practice, letters from POWs were and are delayed in delivery to their families. The families were and are harassed by Meacham and his cohorts who have made strenuous efforts to have the families participate in their "peace" demonstrations. The entire project has resulted in the Committee of Liaison serving as a major propaganda arm in the United States for the North Vietnamese regime.

DAVID MECHANIC was born on February 21, 1936 in New York City, son of Tillie Penn and Louis Mechanic. He married Margaret Newton. He is an alumnus of the City College of New York (B.A., 1956) and Stanford University (M.A., 1957; Ph.D., 1959). He is the author of *Students Under Stress: A Study in the Social Psychology of Adaptation* (1962); and *Medical Sociology: A Selective View* (1968). He is co-author of *The Social Psychology of Organizations* (1963). He is a contributor to *New Perspectives in Organization Research* (1964) and *Community Psychiatry* (1966).

From 1956 until 1958, Mechanic was a research assistant at the Institute for Advanced Study in the Behavioral Sciences. In 1959 and 1960, he held a postdoctoral fellowship at the National Institute of Mental Health in Chapel Hill, North Carolina. Since 1960, he has been at the University of Wisconsin as an assistant professor (1960-1962), associate professor (1962-1965), professor (1965 to the present), and chairman of the sociology department (since 1968). In 1965 and 1966, he was a special

fellow at the National Institute of Health in London. In 1965 and 1967, he was a visiting professor at the University of Washington in Seattle. He has been a consultant to the National Institute of Mental Health and the U.S. Department of Health, Education and Welfare. Away from the campus, he has been involved in leftist-political causes concerned with pacifism and civil rights agitation.

AUGUST MEIER was born on April 30, 1923 in New York City, son of Clara Cohen and Frank Meier. He is an alumnus of Oberlin College (A.B., 1945) and Columbia University (A.M., 1949; Ph.D., 1957). He is the author of *Negro Thought In America: 1880-1915* (1963). He is the co-author of *From Plantation to Ghetto* (1966). He is co-editor of *Negro Protest Thought In the Twentieth Century* (1966); *The Making of Black America* (1969); and *Black Nationalism In America* (1969). He has contributed articles to the *Journal of Negro History*, the *Journal of Southern History, Crisis, Phylon,* and *New Politics.* Since 1966, he has been general editor of the Negro in American Life Series for Atheneum Publishers.

From 1945 until 1949, Meier was an assistant professor of history at Tougaloo College. In 1951 and 1952, and in 1956 and 1957, he was secretary for the Newark branch of the National Association for the Advancement of Colored People, the fountainhead of Negro agitation for more than half a century. In 1952, he held an advanced graduate fellowship from the American Council of Learned Societies. In 1953, he was a research assistant to President Charles S. Johnson of Fisk University. From 1953 until 1956, he was an assistant professor of history at Fisk University. From 1957 until 1964, he served successively as assistant professor and associate professor at Morgan State College. From 1964 until 1967, he was a professor of history at Roosevelt University. Since 1967, he has been at Kent State University as professor of history (1967-1969) and university professor (1969 to the present).

Meier has been a long-time member of the ultra-radical Americans for Democratic Action. He has served the ADA as chairman of the Baltimore chapter, as a member of the ADA's national board, and as a member of the ADA's executive committee. From 1960 until 1963, he was active in the ultra-radical Student Nonviolent Coordinating Committee. In 1963 and 1964, he was active in the leftist-racist Congress of Racial Equality. He is a long-time member of the ultra-leftist American Civil Liberties Union.

JACK MENDELSOHN was born on July 22, 1918 in Cambridge, Massachusetts. He is an alumnus of Boston University (B.A., 1939) and Harvard University (S.T.B., 1945). In 1945, he was ordained a Unitarian Universalist minister. He is the author of *Why I Am a Unitarian* (1960); *God, Allah and Ju Ju* (1962); *Why I Am a Unitarian Universalist* (1964); *The Forest Calls Back* (1965); and *The Martyrs: Sixteen Who Gave Their Lives for Racial Justice* (1966).

Mendelsohn has served Unitarian or Unitarian Universalist ministries in Rockford, Illinois (1947-1954); Indianapolis (1954-1959); Boston (1959-1969); and, since 1969, Chicago. During his ten years at the Arlington Street Church in Boston, Mendelsohn became one of the most active leftists in the ranks of Massachusetts clergy. He worked tirelessly with pacifists, conscientious objectors, civil rights agitators, and leftwing internationalists. He was affiliated with the National Association for the Advancement of Colored People (the fountainhead of Negro agitation for more than half a century); the ultra-leftist Massachusetts Civil Liberties Union; the leftist-internationalist International Institute of Boston; the *New England Free Press*, a leftwing newsletter; and the World Affairs Council, a pivotal agency in a complex of one-world, leftist, and pacifist groups. The Arlington Street Church, under his direction, became a popular forum for a steady stream of national and international leftists.

THOMAS C. MENDENHALL II was born on June 14, 1910 in Chicago, son of Dorothy Reed and Charles Mendenhall. He married Cornelia Baker. He is an alumnus of Yale University (B.A., 1932; Ph.D., 1938) and Oxford University, where he was a Rhodes scholar (B.A., 1935; B. Litt., 1936). He is the author of *The Shrewsbury Drapers and the Welsh Wool Trade in the Sixteenth and Seventeenth Centuries* (1953). He is the co-author of *The Quest for a Principle of Authority in Europe: 1715 to the Present* (1948); *Ideas and Institutions In European History: 800-1715* (1948); *The Dynamic Force of Liberty in Modern Europe: Six Problems in Historical Interpretation* (1952); *Foundations of the Modern State: Four Problems in Historical Interpretation* (1952); and *Problems in Western Civilization* (1956).

From 1937 until 1959, Mendenhall was at Yale University as a history instructor (1937-1942), assistant professor (1942-1946), associate professor (1946-1959), assistant to the provost (1942-1950), director of the foreign area studies (1944-1946), master of Yale's Berkeley College (1950-1959), and director of the Office of Teacher Training (1958-1959). Since 1959, he has been at

Smith College as president and professor of history. In 1956, he was a research fellow of the Huntington Library at San Marino, California.

Mendenhall has been affiliated with the leftist-oriented International Movement for Atlantic Union and the National Council for Civic Responsibility, an election year's drive in 1966 by the Democrat Party against anti-Communists. In 1970, he joined with other leftist college heads to urge a "stepped-up timetable for withdrawal from Vietnam."

MATTHEW S. MESELSON was born on May 24, 1930 in Denver, son of Ann Swedlow and Hyman Meselson. He is an alumnus of the University of Chicago (Ph.B., 1951) and California Institute of Technology (Ph.D., 1957).

From 1957 until 1960, Meselson was at California Institute of Technology as a research fellow. Since 1960, he has been on Harvard's faculty, and from 1964 to the present he has been a professor of biology.

Meselson has been an active member of the Federation of American Scientists, a bleeding-heart group, members of which are generally affiliated with a variety of radical one-world and/or pacifist organizations. He has been an official of the Council for a Livable World, an ultra-leftwing pacifist and political pressure group making an especial appeal to the scientific community. He has been a member of the ultra-leftist Pugwash group. He has been affiliated with the leftist-pacifist Educational Committee to Halt Atomic Weapons; the leftist-oriented Ad Hoc Committee for an Open Letter on Vietnam. and the leftist-pacifist Ad Hoc Faculty Committee on Vietnam. In 1971, he participated in the Runnymede Project, a leftist-oriented conference run by anti-war students of the Massachusetts Institute of Technology. In 1966, he originated a petition which was circulated in the leftist scientific community urging President Lyndon Johnson to halt the use of non-lethal chemical weapons against enemy troops and food crops in Vietnam. In 1969, he participated in a leftist-oriented demonstration at Massachusetts Institute of Technology against the alleged misuse of science and technology by the U.S. Government.

WILLIAM R. MILLER was born on July 3, 1927 in Waterloo, New York, son of Mildred Hollister and Roy Miller. He married Edith Meyer. He is an alumnus of the radical New School for Social Research (B.A., 1964). He is the author of *Nonviolence: A Christian Interpretation* (1964) and *The World of Pop Music and Jazz* (1965).

In 1952 and 1953, Miller was a copyboy for *Time* magazine. In 1954, he was a copy editor for W.W. Norton & Company, a publishing house. In 1955, he was a reporter for *Forbes* magazine. From 1956 until 1961, he was managing editor of *Fellowship* magazine, published by the ultra-leftist-pacifist Fellowship of Reconciliation. Since 1962, he has been managing editor of the *United Church Herald.*

Miller is an official of the ultra-leftist-pacifist Fellowship of Reconciliation. He is an official of the leftist-oriented New York Committee to Abolish Capital Punishment. He is a member of the ultra-leftist American Civil Liberties Union. He is a member of the leftist-racist Congress of Racial Equality.

KATHARINE MURRAY MILLETT was born on September 14, 1934 in St. Paul, Minnesota. She married Fumio

Yoshimura. She is an alumna of the University of Minnesota (B.A., 1956) and Columbia University (Ph.D., 1970). She also attended St. Hilda's College at Oxford University. She is the author of *Sexual Politics: A Surprising Examination of Society's Most Arbitrary Folly* (1970), originally written as her doctoral dissertation at Columbia.

In 1958, Kate Millett – as she is known – was an English instructor for one semester at the University of North Carolina. From 1959 until 1961, she worked as a bank employee and kindergarten teacher in New York City. From 1961 until 1963, she studied art at the University of Tokyo. In 1963, she became a political activist and involved herself in the so-called peace movement. She joined the leftist-racist Congress of Racial Equality. In 1966, she joined the National Organization for Women and became chairman of NOW's education committee. In 1968, while studying at Columbia University, she taught English at Barnard College. In this period, she became a well-known agitator in such causes as abortion reform, women's liberation, and student rights. Her activities led to her dismissal, but by 1970 she was being hailed in national publications as the "principal theoretician" and "new high priestess" of the women's liberation movement. In 1971, she was a part-time sociology teacher at Bryn Mawr College. In 1971, she was affiliated with the ultra-leftist National Peace Action Coalition. In 1971, she endorsed the People's Peace Treaty, a notorious leftist project.

PATSY MINK was born on December 6, 1927 in Paia, Maui, Hawaii, daughter of Mitama Tateyama and Suematsu Takemoto. She married John Mink. She is an alumna of the University of Hawaii (B.A., 1948) and the University of Chicago Law School (J.D., 1951). She also studied at Wilson College in Pennsylvania and the University of Nebraska. She was admitted to the Hawaii bar in 1952.

From 1953 until 1965, Mrs. Mink had a private law practice in Honolulu. From 1952 until 1956, and from 1959 until 1962, she lectured on business law at the University of Hawaii. In 1955, she was attorney for the territorial legislature.

Since 1954, Mrs. Mink has been active in the Democratic Party. From 1954 until 1956, she was the founding president of the Young Democrats of Oahu. From 1956 until 1958, she was state president of the Young Democrats of Hawaii. From 1957 until 1959, she was vice-president of the National Young Democrats of America. In 1960, she was a delegate to the Democratic National Convention and a member of the platform committee.

In 1956, Mrs. Mink was elected to the Hawaii House of Representatives. In 1958 and 1962, she was elected to the Hawaii Senate. In 1960, she was an unsuccessful candidate for Congress. Since 1965, she has been a member of the U.S. House of Representatives.

Before Mrs. Mink went to Congress, she had earned a reputation as a leftist in Hawaii. She was a favorite candidate of the Communist-dominated International Longshoremen's & Warehousemen's Union. She was a staunch anti-anti-Communist. She allied herself with leftwing-pacifists. She was a member of the ultra-radical National Association for the Advancement of Colored People. She was a member of the leftist-internationalist American Association for the United Nations.

In the Congress, Mrs. Mink has been on the leftist side of all important domestic and foreign issues. She has been especially interested in promoting heavy federal expenditures on education, poverty programs, housing programs, Social Security payoffs, programs for the elderly, and other socialistic issues. She once expressed her contempt for free competition as "the law of the jungle." She has had a consistent pro-labor voting record. She has been sympathetic to anti-war demonstrators. She has been one of the most conspicuous doves in the Congress on the matter of the Vietnam War. She has often resorted to the leftist-liberal argument that expenditures for the military are depriving the American people in their war on poverty. Since she first came to Congress, Mrs. Mink has worked to promote trade between the United States and the Soviet bloc. And she has offered the ultra-liberal rationale to justify her position: "The expansion of East-West trade could strengthen America's leadership in international affairs, not only economically, but politically and morally."

STEPHEN MINOT was born on May 27, 1927 in Boston, Massachusetts, son of Elizabeth Chapman and William Minot. His second wife is Virginia Stover. He is an alumnus of Harvard University (A.B., 1953) and The Johns Hopkins University (M.A., 1955). He is the author of *Chill of Dusk* (1964) and *Three Genres: The Writing of Fiction, Poetry, and Drama* (1965). He has written radio scripts for the Voice of America. He has contributed short stories to *Atlantic Monthly, Redbook, Kenyon Review,* and the *Virginia Quarterly.*

From 1955 until 1958, Minot was at Bowdoin College as an instructor in English (1955-1957) and assistant professor (1957-1958). In 1958 and 1959, he was a visiting assistant professor of English at the University of Connecticut. Since 1959, he has been at Trinity College serving successively as a visiting lecturer, assistant professor, and associate professor of English.

Minot has been affiliated with the ultra-leftist American Civil Liberties Union; the National Association for the Advancement of Colored People, the fountainhead of Negro agitation for more than half a century; the ultra-leftist National Committee for an Effective Congress; and the leftist-oriented American Veterans Committee. He has been an official of the leftist-internationalist United World Federalists.

NEWTON MINOW was born on January 17, 1926 in Milwaukee, Wisconsin, son of Doris Stein and Jay A. Minow. He married Josephine Baskin. He is an alumnus of Northwestern University (B.S., 1949; LL.B., 1950). He is the author of *Equal Time: The Private Broadcaster and the Public Interest* (1964). He was a contributor to *As We Know Adlai* (1967).

In 1950, Minow was admitted to the Illinois and Wisconsin bars. In 1950 and 1951, he practiced law in Chicago. In 1951 and 1952, he was a law clerk to Chief Justice Fred M. Vinson of the Supreme Court of the United States. In 1952 and 1953, he was administrative assistant to Adlai E. Stevenson, the liberal governor of Illinois. From 1953 until 1961, he practiced law in Chicago; from 1955 until 1961, he was a partner in Adlai E. Stevenson's law firm. From 1961 until 1963, he was chairman of the Federal Communications Commission. From 1963 until 1965, he was vice-president and general counsel of *Encyclopaedia Britannica.* Since 1965, he has practiced law in Chicago, and has also been on the board of directors of the

RAND Corporation, one of the Establishment's major think factories.

In 1952 and 1956, Minow was a principal aide in Adlai E. Stevenson's presidential campaigns. In 1960, he was secretary and general counsel of the National Business and Professional Men and Women for Kennedy-Johnson and the Chicago area chairman of Citizens for Kennedy. During the 1960 campaign, Minow attempted vainly to persuade his old friend Adlai Stevenson to endorse John F. Kennedy before the start of the Democratic National Convention. For his efforts, Minow was rewarded with the chairmanship of the Federal Communications Commission. Two months after assuming the FCC post, he virtually threatened television broadcasters with federal censorship and interference unless they met his personal cultural standards. Although the FCC lacked authority to interfere directly with television programming, and despite Minow's protestations that he detested censorship or interference with free speech, he told the Senate Committee on Interstate and Foreign Commerce: "I do think that the Commission has a role in elevating and encouraging better programs, and I am determined to do something about it."

In 1962, Minow's liberal big brotherism was put to a test when the American Broadcasting Company televised a program entitled "The Political Obituary of Richard M. Nixon." The program, moderated by the liberal Howard K. Smith, had as its star performer Alger Hiss, who had been convicted of perjury after a congressional committee investigated his associations with the Communist espionage apparatus. Before and after Hiss was provided a forum, there were waves of protest from the general public on the ground that Hiss, whose loyalty was in serious doubt, should not be given free-dom to castigate Richard M. Nixon, who had a part in bringing Hiss to justice. James C. Hagerty, who was ABC's news chief, defended the Hiss appearance by saying: "In addition to the program itself, a more fundamental issue, in my opinion, is presented. That issue deals with the basic American principle of freedom of the press, the exchange of free ideas, free speech, free assent and dissent. Pressure in advance to force the cancellation of a program, and pressure after it by economic means to punish or intimidate, threatens not only the very existence of freedom of the press, but free enterprise as well. It must be resisted." Minow, who had said the people own the air and who talked about "elevating and encouraging better programs," concurred with Hagerty's views "most emphatically." When two regular sponsors of ABC programs tried to cancel their contracts with the network because of the Hiss appearance, Minow paraded his liberalism in defense of those who had foisted the convicted perjurer Hiss upon the American viewing public. In his statement, Minow said: "Whether this particular program was in good taste is for the public to decide. The real issue transcends this particular program. The basic issue is the freedom and responsibility of broadcast journalism. To be responsible, broadcast journalism on all the networks and stations must be free. This means freedom not only from government censorship, but also from threatening pressure groups and from those few, fearful advertisers who seek through commercial reprisals to influence the professional judgment of broadcast newsmen."

The Hiss incident and the failure of Minow's tortured logic to appease the general public brought Minow's career as head of the FCC to a premature halt. His resignation was accepted by President Kennedy with the customary "regret."

Minow has been affiliated with the leftist-liberal Chicago Council on Foreign Relations and the leftist-oriented Roger Baldwin Foundation. He is a long-time director of the leftist-oriented National Educational Television.

RICHARD M. MONTAGUE was born on September 20, 1930 in Stockton, California, son of Frances McKay and Edgar Montague. He is an alumnus of the University of California at Berkeley (A.B., 1950; M.A., 1953; Ph.D., 1957). He is co-author, with Donald Kalish, a colleague and notorious leftist, of *Logic: The Techniques of Formal Reasoning* (1964).

Since 1955, Montague has been at the University of California at Los Angeles as acting instructor of philosophy (1955-1957), assistant professor (1957-1959), associate professor (1959-1963), and professor (1963 to the present). He has been affiliated with the National Committee to Abolish the House Un-American Activities Committee ("to lead and direct the Communist Party's 'Operation Abolition' campaign").

LUCILE MONTGOMERY was born on June 18, 1911 in Williamston, North Carolina, daughter of Mary Woodard and Cushing Hassell. She was married to and divorced from Thomas Harris. She is married to Kenneth Montgomery. She is an alumna of Salem College (B.A., 1930). She also studied at the University of North Carolina and New York School of Social Work.

From 1931 until 1933, Mrs. Montgomery was a teacher in a junior high school in North Carolina. In 1933, she was a director of women's work for the Civil Works Administration in Washington. In 1934, she was a county administrator for the North Carolina Emergency Relief Administration. In 1935 and 1936, she was a case worker for the Travellers Aid Society in Washington, D.C.

For more than twenty years, Mrs. Montgomery has been deeply involved in radical projects and has provided generous financial support to a host of leftists and leftist organizations. From 1949 until 1954, she was vice-president of the leftist-oriented League of Women Voters in Winnetka, Illinois. In 1962 and 1963, she was a founding member and vice-president of the leftist-oriented Voters for Peace in Chicago. From 1964 until 1967, she was director of workshops in South Carolina, Georgia, Tennessee, and Mississippi, where racial agitators were conducting voter registration drives. In 1965 and 1966, she was chairman of a leftist-oriented Committee for Independent Political Action in Chicago. From 1966 until 1968, she was a director and a member of the convention steering committee of the National Conference for New Politics, which was largely dominated by Communists. In 1968, she was the organizer in Illinois of the leftist-pacifist Jeannette Rankin Brigade. In 1968, she was a member of the radical caucus of the Coalition for an Open Convention. She has also been affiliated with the leftist-oriented Poor People's Development Foundation and the Highlander Research and Education Center.

PAUL MOORE JR. was born on November 15, 1919 in Morristown, New Jersey, son of Fanny Hanna and Paul Moore. He married Jennie McKean. He is an alumnus of Yale University (B.A., 1941) and General Theological Seminary (S.T.B., 1949). He is the author of *The*

Church Reclaims the City (1964).

In 1949, Moore was ordained to the ministry of the Protestant Episcopal Church. From 1949 until 1957, he was a minister at Grace Church in Jersey City. From 1957 until 1964, he was dean of Christ Church Cathedral in Indianapolis. From 1964 until 1970, he was suffragan bishop of Washington, D.C. Since 1970, he has been Bishop Coadjutor of the Episcopal Diocese of New York.

In 1963, Moore participated in the leftist-dominated March on Washington. In 1965, he picketed the White House to protest the alleged lack of federal protection for civil rights demonstrators in Selma, Alabama. In 1966, as co-chairman of the Coalition of Conscience, Moore was the leader of a boycott in the District of Columbia in an effort to promote Home Rule. To justify the blackmail operation, Moore said: "We are sorry this kind of militancy is necessary to bring to people the right to vote. But all other methods have failed. We have tried lobbying, polite talk and even picketing and demonstrations. I want to make it crystal clear that this is not a black and white issue. There are a number of district residents who are white and who clearly support this issue. But the business community has been using the money of the community to fight against justice and citizenship for the people who live in the community." When Bishop Moore and his associates were warned that any demand for contributions in the face of a boycott could result in fines and jail sentences, he retreated hastily by saying: "This was never the intention of the movement. Rather, the intent is to gather the names of businessmen who are in favor of the vote for the District of Columbia on a petition, and to ask them to send telegrams to the authorities stating their positions. Those who state their positions to this effect, will have a sticker in their window. Naturally, voluntary contributions will be welcome from them, or anyone else, for that matter."

Despite Moore's apparent about-face, the blackmailing boycott continued and Moore drew severe criticism from his fellow clergy in Washington, including the Dean of the Washington Cathedral and the Bishop of Washington. As a consequence, Moore made an extended and a strategic trip to Europe.

Earlier in 1966, Moore had been a leader of militant demonstrations in Mississippi. The Commission on the Delta Ministry, of which he was chairman, conducted a forcible demonstration at the Greenville Air Force Base in Mississippi. The demonstrators, who called themselves "The Poor People's Conference," were evicted by Air Force police, under the direction of the Department of Justice. Moore flew to the scene and issued a statement: "The Delta Ministry, the Mississippi Freedom Democratic Party, and the Freedom Labor Union called a conference of poor people last weekend at Edwards, Mississippi. At the conference, the people decided to go to the Air Force Base at Greenville, and stay there until the federal government would pay attention to the requests they had been making continuously over the last two years." The requests mentioned by Moore were actually demands by the trespassers for federal housing, federal food handouts, and federal job training.

In 1967, Moore, as a leader of the ultra-leftist Clergy and Laymen Concerned about Vietnam, participated in demonstrations outside the White House. Moore and his cohorts issued a statement to President Lyndon Johnson in which they said that increased American involvement in the Vietnam War had strengthened the will of the Communists to resist, had made the world suspicious of the United States, and had jeopardized new alliances that the United States might be creating. The members of the group said they would support young men who decide "that they cannot condone the war by their personal involvement," and criticized "the discrepancy between what we are told by our Government and what we discover is actually taking place." They suggested four points to be observed by President Johnson in attempting to get peace negotiations started: (1) the United States should assure the Communists that it is genuinely ready to negotiate and does not expect to gain diplomatically what could not be won militarily; (2) the bombing of North Vietnam should be halted; (3) the National Liberation Front, the political arm of the Viet Cong, should be accepted at the peace talks; and (4) the role of the United Nations and other agencies, such as the International Control Mission, in ending the war and maintaining peace should be increased.

In 1971, Moore was still carrying the leftist banner against U.S. involvement in Vietnam. Writing in the *New York Times* he declared that 75 per cent of the American people were convinced of the "uselessness if not the moral depravity of the Vietnam War." On the Vietnamization policy, he said that "substituting brown bodies for white . . . [is] perhaps the most cynical and immoral policy of all." In other parts of his polemic he said, "When the state wages illegal war against the will of the majority, the claims by which the state are traditionally honored by the church come into question. Has our state ceased to be a democratic instrument of peace and justice?" – "The health of a democracy can be judged by its debonair tolerance for dissent. A sick state, lacking in confidence, quivers at the sight of opposition. Is our government verging on paranoia, the most dangerous of psychoses?"

Moore's opposition to the Vietnam War has also been expressed through the leftist-oriented National Peace Action Coalition and the leftist-oriented Clergy Committee for the Moratorium. He has also endorsed the People's Peace Treaty, a Hanoi-inspired document which became the pet 1971 project of the ultra-left. He has also been a member of the leftist-pacifist Committee of Responsibility. For many years, he has been chairman of the "Committee of 100" of the ultra-leftist NAACP's Legal Defense and Education Fund.

WILLIAM E. MORAN JR. was born on January 8, 1916 in Herkimer, New York, son of Esther Henry and William Moran. He married Phyllis Duffy. He is an alumnus of Syracuse University (A.B., 1937; LL.B., 1940). He is the co-author of *Handbook on African Economic Development* (1964). He is editor of *Population Growth: Threat to Peace?* (1969).

From 1940 until 1945, Moran was an agent of the Federal Bureau of Investigation. From 1945 until 1949, he was employed successively by the Department of State and the Atomic Energy Commission. From 1949 until 1952, he was assistant director of the Economic Cooperation Administration's mission to Belgium. In 1952 and 1953, he was chief of the Dependent Overseas Territories Branch of the Economic Cooperation Administration and Mutual Security Agency. From 1953 until 1957, he was director of the African division of the Foreign Operations Agency. From 1957 until 1959, he was deputy director of the International Cooperation Administration's mission to Morocco. From 1959 until 1962, he was head of the African program at Stanford Research Institute. From 1962 until 1966, he was dean of the School of Foreign Service at Georgetown University. From 1966 until 1968, he was vice-president and executive director of the International Economic Policy Association. Since 1968, he has been president of the leftist-oriented Population Reference Bureau.

Moran is affiliated with the leftist-loaded Population Crisis Committee; the pacifist Catholic Association for International Peace; the Council on Foreign Relations, the informal supra-State Department of the United States; and the National Conference on the United States and China, a part of the Red China lobby.

EDWARD P. MORGAN was born on June 23, 1910 in Walla Walla, Washington, son of Pansy Paddock and Arthur Morgan. He was married to and divorced from Jane Stolle. He is married to Katharine Sohier. He is an alumnus of Whitman College (B.A., 1932). He pursued graduate studies at the University of Washington. He is the author of *Clearing the Air* (1963). He is a contributor to *This I Believe*, Vol. II (1954); *Candidates: 1960* (1959); and *The Press in Washington* (1966). He is co-editor of *This I Believe*, Vol. I (1952). He has contributed articles to *Atlantic, Esquire, New York Times Magazine, Saturday Evening Post*, and leftist publications including *New Republic, Progressive,* and *Reporter.*

From 1932 until 1934, Morgan was a reporter for the *Seattle Star*. From 1934 until 1943, he was a correspondent for the United Press. From 1943 until 1946, he was a roving correspondent for the *Chicago Daily News* foreign service.

From 1946 until 1948, he was an associate editor and foreign correspondent for *Collier's* weekly. From 1948 until 1950, he was a free-lance journalist in Paris. In 1950, he collaborated with the leftist Edward R. Murrow in producing *This I Believe* for the Columbia Broadcasting System's station WCAU in Philadelphia. From 1951 until 1954, he was with CBS as a newscaster and news director on radio and television. From 1955 until 1967, he was a news commentator for the American Broadcasting Company. From 1957 until 1967, his program, *Edward P. Morgan and the News*, was sponsored by the AFL-CIO. Despite his strenuous denials, Morgan devoted much of his broadcasting time to propagandizing for organized labor. Since 1966, he has produced a newspaper column for the Newsday Syndicate. Since 1967, he has been a senior correspondent for the Public Broadcasting Laboratory of the leftist-liberal National Education Television Network.

Morgan's broadcasts and writings have reflected his left-of-center views. He has garnered the usual awards given to deserving leftists, including the Sidney Hillman Foundation award, the George Foster Peabody award, the Overseas Press Club award, the Alfred I. duPont award, and the Headliner award. He has also been cited by the leftist-oriented National Education Association and the leftist Workers Defense League. He is a member of the ultra-leftist American Civil Liberties Union.

JOSEPH P. MORRAY was born on December 17, 1916 in Vienna, Illinois, son of Halloween Parker and Kenneth Morray. He married Marjorie Kuh. He is an alumnus of the United States Naval Academy (B.S., 1940) and Harvard University (LL.B., 1948). He also studied at the University of Illinois, St. John's College in Maryland, and the University of Paris. He is the author of *Pride of State: A Study in Patriotism and American National Morality* (1959); *From Yalta to Disarmament* (1961); *Cuba and Communism* (1961); and *The Second Revolution in Cuba* (1962). He is the translator of Ché Guevara's *Guerrilla Warfare* (1968). For research in Cuba (1960) and for research on disarmament (1963), he received grants from the Louis M. Rabinowitz Foundation.

From 1942 until 1944, Morray was an assistant naval attaché at Asunción, Paraguay. In 1949 and 1950, he was a teaching fellow at Harvard Law School. In 1950 and 1951, he practiced law in San Francisco. From 1951 until 1954, he was an assistant naval attaché in Madrid, Spain. From 1957 until 1960, he was at the University of California at Berkeley as a visiting professor of law (1957-1969) and visiting associate professor of speech (1959-1960). In 1961 and 1962, he was a visiting professor of political science at the University of Havana in Cuba, where he also served as a correspondent for the Communists' weekly *National Guardian.* From 1965, he was a professor of sociology at the University of Chile.

Morray has earned a reputation as a noted Marxist scholar. He is easily recognized as an apologist for the Soviet Union, Communist Cuba, and North Vietnam. The Communist Party has noted that Morray's defense of the Marxist movement in the United States, in his *Pride of State,* has been more effective than any defense offered by the Communist Party itself. In 1962, Morray helped to direct the Marxist school in San Francisco. In 1961, while on Castro's payroll, he was affiliated with the Cuban Congress of Artists and Writers. In 1966,

he sponsored the Aptheker Dinner Program on the Second Anniversary of the American Institute for Marxist Studies, a tribute to the Communist Party's chief theoretician in the United States. Morray has been affiliated with the National Committee to Abolish the House Un-American Activities Committee ("to lead and direct the Communist Party's 'Operation Abolition' campaign"); the East Bay Community Forum ("Communist front"); and *New World Review* ("Communist magazine").

LLOYD N. MORRISETT was born on November 2, 1929 in Oklahoma City, son of Jessie Watson and Lloyd Morrisett. He is married to Mary Pierre. He is an alumnus of Oberlin College (B.A., 1951) and Yale University (Ph.D., 1956). He also pursued graduate studies at the University of California at Los Angeles. From 1953 until 1956, he held a National Science Foundation fellowship at Yale.

From 1956 until 1958, Morrisett was at the University of California as an education instructor (1956-1957) and assistant professor (1957-1958). In 1958 and 1959, he was a member of the staff of the leftist-oriented Social Science Research Council. From 1959 until 1969, he was with the leftist-pacifist Carnegie Corporation as executive assistant (1959-1961), executive associate (1961-1963), assistant to the president (1963-1965), and vice-president (1965-1969). From 1965 until 1969, he was also vice-president of the Carnegie Foundation for the Advancement of Teaching, a source of great financial benefits for the ultra-leftist Establishment in education. Since 1969, he has been president of the Markle Foundation. He is a resident member of the Council on Foreign Relations, the informal supra-State Department of the United States.

ARTHUR D. MORSE was born on December 27, 1920 in Brooklyn, son of Henrietta Mensher and Frank Moskowitz. He married Joan Berend. He is an alumnus of the University of Virginia (B.A., 1941). He is the author of *Schools of Tomorrow – Today* (1960). He is a contributor to *Freedom and Public Education* (1953); *Prose for Professionals* (1961); and *While Six Million Died* (1968).

In 1945 and 1946, Morse was public relations director for Parents' Institute. From 1946 until 1954, he was a freelance writer for national magazines. From 1954 until 1959, he was a reporter and director for Edward R. Murrow's "See It Now" programs on CBS-TV. Since 1960, he has been with CBS Reports as producer-writer (1960-1964) and executive producer (1964 to the present).

Through his work with "See It Now," CBS Reports, and various documentaries, Morse has made unmistakable liberal-leftist contributions which have brought him awards traditionally offered to the Left – the George Foster Peabody award, the National School Bell award, the Sherwood award from the Fund for the Republic, the Educational Writers Association award, and the Sidney Hillman Foundation award.

J[OHN] BROOKE MOSLEY was born on October 18, 1915 in Philadelphia, Pennsylvania, son of Bertha Urwiler and John Mosley. He married Betty Wall. He is an alumnus of Temple University (B.A., 1937) and Episcopal Theological School (B.D., 1940). He was ordained to the ministry of the Protestant Episcopal Church as a deacon in 1940 and as a priest in 1941. He contributed to *The Challenge of Reunion* (1963).

In 1938, Mosley was a volunteer worker with the American Friends Service Committee on the Delta Cooperative Farm in Clarksdale, Mississippi. From 1940 until 1944, he served successively as an assistant pastor and a pastor at St. Barnabas Church in Cincinnati. From 1944 until 1948, he was director of the department of social relations of the Episcopal Diocese of Washington, D.C. From 1948 until 1953, he was dean of St. John's Cathedral in Wilmington, Delaware. From 1953 until 1968, he served the Diocese of Delaware as Bishop Coadjutor (1953-1955) and Bishop (1955-1968). From 1968 until 1970, he was deputy for overseas relations for the Episcopal Executive Council. Since 1970, he has been president of Union Theological Seminary in New York.

Mosley has been an active official of the leftist-oriented World Council of Churches. He was a member of the ultra-leftist National Peace Action Coalition. He is affiliated with the ultra-leftist Clergy and Laymen Concerned about Vietnam. His most important leftist-pacifist expression on Vietnam was made in 1967 when he said: "Those in high places pay lip service to the democratic principle of dissent but seem to favor it mostly when it is not practiced. Thus Selective Service becomes a device to punish young men who dissent; thus the President of the United States states that a hero's death in Vietnam has been caused not by the grievous miscalculations of the government but by those who would correct the miscalculations of the government. We can expect an increase of such attacks on dissenters as the fever of war increases and positions harden. Dissent is always costly. But for a growing number of citizens, it is required. Many of us add our voice to the voices . . . urging a reappraisal of our policy in Vietnam. Each day it grows more difficult to reconcile our allegiance to God with support of the foreign policy of the United States Government . . . . Those who approve of the destruction we heap upon the Vietnamese often argue that we have a right to use harsh measures because the enemy is also harsh, but we are obliged to live by our own moral standards, not by theirs."

STEWART MOTT was born on December 4, 1937 in Flint, Michigan, son of Ruth Rawlings and Charles Mott. He is an alumnus of Columbia University (B.A., 1961; B.A. Litt., 1962).

In 1963 and 1964, Mott was an English instructor at Eastern Michigan University. He has been a director of the Michigan National Bank since 1964, the United States Sugar Corporation since 1965, and Compo Industries since 1968. He has been a partner and director of Rubin Realty Company since 1968 and of Peerage Properties since 1968. In 1965, he was founder and has since been president of Spectemur Agendo.

Mott, a multi-millionaire, is heir to a fortune in General Motors stock. In recent years, he has become one of the nation's better known radicals through his leftist political activism and his financial contributions to leftist organizations and causes.

Since 1967, Mott has been a member of the executive committee of the leftist-oriented Planned Parenthood-World Population Council. Since 1967, he has been a member of the leftist-oriented Population Crisis Committee. Since 1968, he has been on the board of directors of the leftist-oriented Urban

League of New York City. He has been a trustee of the leftist-oriented Roger Baldwin Foundation (since 1967), the ultra-leftist National Committee for an Effective Congress (since 1968), and the Socialist-oriented Center for the Study of Democratic Institutions (since 1968). In 1968, he was founder and has since been chairman of the leftist-liberal Coalition for a Republican Alternative. In 1967, he contributed $365,000 to political candidates, including Nelson Rockefeller of New York and Eugene McCarthy of Minnesota in their unsuccessful campaigns to obtain the presidential nomination. In 1968, he was the chief fund-raiser for the leftist Senator Ernest Gruening of Alaska. He has been a financial supporter of the leftist Senator George McGovern of North Dakota. In 1969, he was co-chairman of the First National Convocation on the Challenge of Building Peace, held under the auspices of the leftist-oriented Fund for Education in World Order. He has been a generous financial supporter of the ultra-leftist *Ramparts* magazine. He is on the national council of the National Emergency Civil Liberties Committee ("subversive" – "Communist front"). He is affiliated with the ultra-leftist American Civil Liberties Union; the leftist-pacifist National Council to Repeal the Draft; the leftist-pacifist National Citizens Committee for the Amendment to End the War; the leftist-pacifist National Committee for a Political Settlement in Vietnam; and the leftist-pacifist Business Executives Move for Vietnam Peace. He endorsed the Hanoi-inspired People's Peace Treaty, the pet 1971 project of the ultra-left.

BILL D. MOYERS was born on June 5, 1934 in Hugo, Oklahoma, son of Ruby Johnson and John Moyers. He married Judith Davidson. He is an alumnus of the University of Texas (B.J., 1956) and Southwestern Baptist Theological Seminary (B.D., 1959). In 1956 and 1957, he attended the University of Edinburgh in Scotland as a graduate student. He is the author of *Listening to America: A Traveler Rediscovers His Country* (1971). He is the co-author of *ABM* (1969), which was financed in great part by U.S. Senator Edward M. Kennedy, and was a dovish attack against the anti-ballistic missile program.

From 1957 until 1959, while studying at Southwestern Theological Seminary, Moyers held rural pastorates and was director of information at the seminary. In 1959 and 1960, he was an aide to U.S. Senator Lyndon B. Johnson. In 1960, he was executive assistant to Mr. Johnson during the latter's vice-presidential campaign. From 1961 until 1964, he was with the Peace Corps as associate director (1961-1963) and deputy director (1963-1964). From 1963 until 1967, he was a special assistant to President Johnson. He was assigned the responsibility of organizing and developing a great deal of legislation in Mr. Johnson's Great Society Program. He helped in the preparation of Presidential messages to Congress. Mr. Johnson sought his advice on foreign policy and national security matters. From 1965 until 1967, he served as White House press secretary. From 1967 until 1970, he was publisher of *Newsday*, a Long Island publication.

Moyers has described himself as a "very pragmatic liberal." This was exemplified when he urged Peace Corpsmen to "pursue the ideals of a Joan of Arc with the political prowess of an Adam Clayton Powell. Whatever you say about Joan, her purpose was noble. And whatever you say about Adam, his politics is effective."

Moyers attracted an exorbitant amount of publicity and attention when he served as President Johnson's press secretary. Of the position he said: "My job is to make sure that the President's viewpoint is known. In Washington, the press generally tends to write its opinion of a matter and then to seek out facts for it." One way in which Moyers saw to it that the President's viewpoint was known was to plant questions with reporters before a news conference began. He explained that he did this to make certain that some reporters would ask the President questions for which he had prepared answers and would bring up topics upon which he wanted to expatiate. In the view of Moyers: "It's to serve the convenience of the President, not the convenience of the press, that presidential press conferences are held." In the course of Moyers' tenure as press secretary, there were repeated instances of reporters who, being called into a confrontation with the President, Moyers, or some other White House aide, had written stories unappreciated by the President. Moyers was especially impatient with reporters who anticipated some presidential act or decision. He had a curious rationalization for his stand: "It's very important for a President to maintain up until a moment of decision his options, and for someone to speculate days or weeks in advance that he's going to do thus and thus, is to deny the President the latitude he needs in order to make, in the light of existing circumstances, the best possible decision."

Moyers is a trustee of the Rockefeller Foundation, a pillar of the liberal Establishment. He is a nonresident member of the Council on Foreign Relations, the informal supra-State Department of the

United States. In 1971, he attended a Bilderberg Conference, an annual get-together of the world's political and economic power magnates. Since 1971, he has been associated with the leftist-liberal Public Broadcasting Service.

FORREST D. MURDEN JR. was born on March 10, 1921 in Norfolk, Virginia, son of Irene Stavro and Forrest Murden. He is an alumnus of the College of William and Mary (A.B., 1941) and the Fletcher School of Law and Diplomacy at Tufts University (M.A., 1942). He also studied at the National University of Mexico and Oxford University. He is the author of *Economic Cooperation* (1954) and *Underdeveloped Lands: Revolution of Rising Expectations* (1956). He is co-author of *Our Stake in World Trade* (1954).

In 1946 and 1947, Murden was an instructor in government and economics at the College of William and Mary. From 1948 until 1951, he was at Columbia University as a fellow (1948-1950), university liaison officer to the United Nations (1949-1950), and lecturer on foreign trade (1950-1951). From 1954 until 1957, he was an assistant to Henry Ford II. From 1957 until 1959, he was manager of public relations for Ford Motor Company and Ford International. From 1959 until 1961, he was government relations counsellor for the Standard Oil Company of New Jersey. Since 1962, he has been president of Murden & Company of New York City.

Murden has been affiliated with the leftist-oriented American Association for the United Nations; the leftist-oriented United States Committee for UNICEF; the leftist-oriented International Movement for Atlantic Union; and the leftist-oriented United Nations Association of the U.S.A. He is a long-time consultant to the ultra-leftist Ford Foundation. He is a long-time member of the Council on Foreign Relations, the informal supra-State Department of the United States.

RALPH NADER was born on February 27, 1934 in Winsted, Connecticut, son of Rose Bouziane and Nadra Nader. He is an alumnus of Princeton University's Woodrow Wilson School of Public and International Affairs (A.B. 1955) and Harvard University (L.L.B., 1958). He has been admitted to the Connecticut bar (1958), the Massachusetts bar (1959), and the bar of the Supreme Court of the United States. He is the author of *Unsafe at Any Speed: The Designed-In Dangers of the American Automobile* (1965).

From 1960 until 1963, Nader practiced law in Hartford, Connecticut. From 1961 until 1963, he lectured in history and government at the University of Hartford. In 1964, the Assistant Secretary of Labor, Daniel P. Moynihan, hired Nader as a $50-a-day consultant. It was Nader's job to produce a study calling for the federal government to take more responsibility for promoting auto safety. In May 1965, Nader left the Department of Labor to write his own book on auto safety, and in November of that year, *Unsafe at Any Speed* was published. The book was an attack upon the automobile industry with particular emphasis on the alleged lack of safety in the Chevrolet Corvair. In February 1966, Nader testified before a U.S. Senate Subcommittee on Executive Reorganization. Connecticut's Senator Abraham Ribicoff, a long-time friend of Nader, was chairman of the subcommittee. Nader delivered a scatter-gun indictment against the automobile industry. At the time, his testimony did not receive a great deal of publicity. However, on March 6, 1966, newspapers throughout the country carried a story of Nader's complaints that the automobile industry had hired private detectives to investigate him. A few days later, a spokesman for General Motors confessed that his company had begun a routine investigation of Nader. He explained that GM suspected that Nader might have some connection with damage suits filed against GM because of defects in the Chevrolet Corvair, the principal target of Nader's book. Two weeks later, the president of General Motors, James M. Roche, admitted to the Ribicoff subcommittee, in a nationally televised hearing, that there had been some harassment of Nader, and Roche took the opportunity to publicly apologize to Nader. In November 1966, Nader filed suit against GM and a private detective for $26 million, alleging invasion of privacy and harassment. In 1970, the case was settled out of court, and GM paid Nader $425,000, probably the largest sum ever paid for damages in such a suit. Of far more significance to Nader was the fact that the publicity surrounding the GM-Nader dispute caused his *Unsafe at Any Speed* to become one of the best-selling books of 1966 and 1967. (GM in its bumbling way had accomplished for Nader what he had been unable to do for himself. Automobile safety was not a new interest to him. In 1958, he had written "American Cars: Designed for Death," published in the *Harvard Law Record.* In 1964, *Fact* magazine published "American Cars Are Death-Traps," written by the magazine's editor, Ralph Ginsburg, and researched by Nader.)

Once Nader's clash with GM had been publicized he became a national celebrity, and he immediately began to exploit his recognition. He became a self-appointed crusader for all American consumers. He did not content himself with a fight for automobile safety. Somewhere along the line, he announced that his ultimate goal was nothing less than the qualitative reform of the industrial revolution. He became the idol of the liberal press. He was portrayed ad infinitum as living a monastic, spartan existence. One bleeding heart after another wrote of Nader's 16-hour-a-day, 18-hour-a-day, and even 20-hour-a-day work regimen. His office was drab, his clothes were drab, his diet was drab, his virtues were many, and his vices were nonexistent. He was the subject of feature stories in *Time, Newsweek, Progressive, Nation, New Republic,* the *Washington Post, National Observer*, the *New York Times, Esquire, Coronet,* the *New York Post*, and the *Wall Street Journal*, and he even arrived in *Who's Who in America.* Along the way, he received the annual award from the League for Industrial Democracy, one of the most prestigious socialist tributes given in America. In the June 1971 issue of *Esquire* magazine, Gore Vidal wrote a lengthy article suggesting Nader would be the best possible Democratic nominee in the 1972 presidential campaign. Julius Duscha, in the *New York Times* magazine (March 21, 1971), wrote: "Although Nader is usually tagged simply as a 'consumer advocate' by the newspapers, he is much more than that. He is an ombudsman; a symbol to all the little people of the world; a one-man court of last resort that receives an average of 1,500 letters a week from the helpless; an inspiration to college students; the man who turned the phrase 'public-interest law' into a whole new concept of the legal profession."

In Washington, D.C., Nader has set up three organizations: the Center for the Study of Responsive Law, the Public

Interest Research Group, and the Center for Auto Safety. Each organization has a paid staff that is augmented by volunteers recruited in the summertime. The volunteers are generally recruited from law schools and colleges. The Nader operation has been financed from such sources as the Marshall Field, the Carnegie, the New World, Taconic, and the Jerome Levy Foundations; the Aaron Norman and Philip M. Stern Family Funds; and Gordon Sherman of Midas International. In 1971, Nader began soliciting funds through the use of advertisements in newspapers and through pleas in the mail. The ads and mailings were issued under Public Citizens, Inc., a tax-exempt group formed by Nader.

Nader has expanded his interest far beyond auto safety. His targets are many, and they include pesticides, herbicides, meat and poultry inspection, consumer credit, detergents, diet soft drinks, drugs, mouth washes, property taxes, supermarkets, banks, the fishing industry, deodorants, the mining industry, the plight of American Indians, air pollution, natural gas pipelines, X-ray radiation, and noise pollution.

Nader and his co-workers (Nader's Raiders) have made special efforts to investigate and harass the Federal Trade Commission, the Interstate Commerce Commission, the Food and Drug Administration, the Department of Agriculture, and various agencies within the Department of Health, Education, and Welfare, the Department of Labor, and the Department of the Interior.

In December 1971, Nader broadened his line of attack to include the entire Congress. He announced this phase of his work in a speech delivered in Washington. Excerpts were reprinted in the form of an article in the *New York Times* (December 23, 1971): "Congress has

been a continuous underachiever. It would be difficult to overstate the extent of abdication to which Congress has been driven by external and internal forces. Contrary to its pre-eminent constitutional authority and constitutional stature as the branch of Government closest to the people, it has been reduced to a puny twig through which flows the allocation of a massive taxpayer treasure chest of over $200 billion in appropriations, largely at the beck and call of executive branch and special interest advocacy and pressure. It reacts to the executive far more than it initiates.

"In the more important Congressional hearings and deliberations secrecy is rampant, contributing to the great difficulty of the populace in establishing performance standards and specific accountabilities. More critical is the process of entrance to the national legislature — wracked with obstacles and expenses for those who wish to contend on the merits and the issues.

"What does the public know of Congress? Not much. There is, to be sure, a widespread cynicism about 'politicians' along with a feeling that nothing can be done about them beyond mere endurance. At times, a reading of postures toward the Congress leads to the conclusion that three major attitudes prevail — that it is something to be manipulated by interest groups or bureaucracy, something to be ridiculed or something to be ignored either because it is an ornament, or that it is hopelessly beyond reach. Nothing remotely compares with the Congress as the hope of reclaiming America.

"Accordingly, we are launching what is probably the most comprehensive and detailed study of Congress since its establishment. The nonpartisan Congress project will enlist the assistance of hundreds of citizens covering nearly every Congressional district. If information is the currency of democracy, it is time to apply that principle to the sinews of citizenship involvement with their representatives in Congress. Who is to say that our Congressmen and Senators would not welcome the participation of the people?"

By the end of 1971, seventeen books and major reports were or were about to be published. Nader was co-author of several, and he wrote introductions to at least six of the published books. On August 8, 1971, the *New York Times Book Review* featured on its front page – a position much sought-after by authors and publishers – five of the Ralph Nader Study Group Reports: *The Chemical Feast: The Food and Drug Administration,* by James S. Turner; *The Interstate Commerce Omission,* by Robert Fellmeth; *Vanishing Air: Air Pollution,* by John C. Esposito; *The Water Lords: Industry and Environmental Crisis in Savannah, Georgia,* by James M. Fallows; *Old Age: The Last Segregation: Study Group Report on Nursing Homes,* by Claire Townsend; and *One Life – One Physician: The Medical Profession's Performance in Self-Regulation,* by Dr. Robert McCleery.

Nader does not depend entirely upon published books and reports to promote his crusade. He frequently testifies before congressional committees. He lectures at university and college campuses and before the type of groups usually encountered on the lecture circuit. Julius Duscha, writing in the *New York Times* magazine, described another Nader tactic to gain headlines: "In dealing with governmental bureaucracy, Nader has perfected a familiar Washington tactic which drives administrators up walls. Through a friend working in an agency,

Nader will find out that a long-pending decision favorable to one of his causes is about to be made public. He then will write a letter to the administrator in charge demanding to know why this decision has not been made for lo! these many months. Copies of the letter go to Nader's many friends in the Washington press corps, and when, within a few days, the governmental decision is dutifully announced, Nader gets credit for once again cracking open the bureaucracy."

There can be no disputing the fact that Nader has made "consumerism" a national byword. It is also indisputable that Nader in his crusade is working for statism. If he had his way, government – especially the federal government – would have its regulatory powers increased to a totalitarian level in just about all parts of American social and economic life. Occasionally, he does encounter a perceptive critic such as Thomas R. Shepard Jr., formerly publisher of *Look* magazine. On May 7, 1971, in a speech delivered at the annual meeting of the Better Business Bureau of Eastern Massachusetts, Mr. Shepard said: "Take Ralph Nader, for example. Some businessmen persist in regarding Mr. Nader simply as a defender of the common man – as a crusader for fair play in business. Well, he may be, but he is one thing more. Mr. Nader is a staunch advocate of the nationalization of industry. What is my source for that statement? The best source. Mr. Nader himself.

"Last September, in a speech in Providence, R.I. – and I quote now from an Associated Press report – 'Ralph Nader proposed that corporations that abuse the public interest should be transferred to public trusteeship.'

"The syllogism is inescapable. Ralph

NADER

Nader says corporations that abuse the public interest should be taken over by the government. According to Ralph Nader, virtually all corporations abuse the public interest. Therefore, all corporations should be taken over by the government.

"More recently, in an interview for the *New York Times* Mr. Nader called for federal chartering of all corporations, with the government empowered to set production standards, prescribe marketing procedures and hire and fire executives. He called the process 'popularization of the corporation.' Well, I call it nationalization of industry. By any name, it would mark the end of free enterprise, and make no mistake about that.

". . . And then we have the situation involving the American Advertising Federation and the Council of Better Business Bureaus. For more than a year now, these two organizations, spurred on by such progressive leaders as AAF President Howard Bell and Whirlpool Corp. Chairman Elisha Gray, have been working on ways to help advertisers police their own output. The programs they have come up with seem to be exactly what the consumerists say they want — self-regulation that would make government controls unnecessary.

"But, of course, the consumerists don't want self-regulation. On the day the AAF announced plans for its ad-screening project, one of Ralph Nader's associates, Mrs. Aileen Cowan, summarily rejected them. She said nothing short of government intervention would be acceptable. In other words, Nader's Raiders have decided to go for broke. Why let free enterprise remain free when the public has been primed for something much more drastic?

"All right, then, we know the nature of the threat. What do we do about it? As I think I have demonstrated, there is nothing to be gained in cooperating with the Ralph Naders of America. They are intransigent. They are against free enterprise. They are the enemy."

In October 1968, the first issue of *Mayday*, a four-page weekly tabloid, was published in Washington, D.C. Its editors were three well-known radicals: Andrew Kopkind, James Ridgeway, and Robert Sherrill. Its consulting editor was Ralph Nader. Kopkind, the spokesman for *Mayday,* said: "We all like the repertorial focus, but it's going to be an example of 'advocate journalism,' an assertive, muckraking, analytical weekly. The title is a triple pun that we hope will appeal to different constituencies. *Mayday* is the international distress signal, a call by radicals to take to the streets and a reference to springtime for the counterculture love generation." Five months after it began publishing, *Mayday* was retitled *Hard Times.* The tabloid featured writings of Nader as well as those of such radicals as the Belgian Marxist Ernest Mandel, the British Socialist Robin Blackburn, and Norm Fruchter and Todd Gitlin of the ultra-radical Students for a Democratic Society. Early in 1970, Nader's name disappeared from the masthead of *Hard Times.* No public explanation was given, but it is reasonable to assume that his association with the Marxist tabloid was an unnecessary hindrance to his crusade. He has made no disavowal of the tabloid's philosophy, however; nor has he expressed any regrets that he appeared on its masthead and in its pages for more than a year.

In early 1972, Nader endorsed the presidential candidacy of the leftist-pacifist U.S. Senator George McGovern. Nader expressed his admiration for McGovern's "concern for the poor" and his extreme pacifist approach to disarmament.

ALFRED C. NEAL was born on June 23, 1912 in Kentfield, California, son of Belle Klutts and Joseph Neal. He married Marguerite Stephenson. He is an alumnus of the University of California (A.B., 1934) and Brown University (Ph.D., 1941). He also studied at the leftist London School of Economics. He is the author of *Industrial Concentration and Price Inflexibility* (1942). He is co-author of *Modern Economics* (1948) and *The New England Economy* (1951). He is author and editor of *Introduction to War Economics* (1942).

From 1937 until 1943, Neal was at Brown University as an instructor in economics (1937-1940) and assistant professor (1942-1943). From 1943 until 1945, he was an economist with the Office of Price Administration. From 1946 until 1956, he was with the Federal Reserve Bank of Boston as research director (1946-1948), vice-president (1948-1951), and first vice-president (1951-1956). In 1953 and 1954, he was director of research for the Commission on Foreign Economic Policy. Since 1956, he has been president of the Committee for Economic Development, the major propaganda arm of the Council on Foreign Relations, in the important work of socializing the American economy. From 1964 until 1967, he was a member of the President's Public Advisory Committee for Trade Negotiations. Since 1965, he has been a member of the business leadership advisory council of the Office of Economic Opportunity. He is a long-time board member of the Council on Foreign Relations, the informal supra-State Department of the United States, and a long-time member of the Atlantic Council, an organization which stresses the need for closer cooperation, especially economic, between the United States and the socialist nations of Western Europe.

ARYEH NEIER was born on April 12, 1937 in Berlin, Germany. In 1947, he came to the United States and he is a naturalized American. He married Yvett Celton. He is an alumnus of Cornell University (B.S., 1958).

From 1958 until 1963, Neier worked as executive secretary of the Socialist League for Industrial Democracy. Since 1963, he has been with the ultra-radical New York Civil Liberties Union as a field organizer (1963-1965) and executive director (1965-1971). Since 1971, he has been executive director of the ultra-radical American Civil Liberties Union.

WILLIAM L. NEUMANN was born on March 4, 1915 in Buffalo, New York, son of Elizabeth Boller and William Neumann. He married Doris McGlone. He is an alumnus of New York State Teachers College (B.S., 1938) and the University of Michigan (M.A., 1939; Ph.D., 1948). He is the author of *Genesis of Pearl Harbor* (1945); *Recognition of Governments in the Americas* (1947); *Making the Peace: 1941-1945* (1950); *America Encounters Japan: Perry to MacArthur* (1963); and *After Victory: Churchill, Roosevelt and Stalin* (1967). He is the co-author of *Isolation and Security* (1957) and *Issues and Conflicts* (1959).

From 1941 until 1945, Neumann was a conscientious objector and served in Civilian Public Service Camps. In 1946 and 1947, he was a lecturer at Howard University. In 1948 and 1949, he was an assistant professor of history at the University of Hawaii. From 1949 until 1951, he was executive secretary of the

Foundation for Foreign Affairs and editor of *American Perspective.* In 1952 and 1953, he was a consultant on foreign affairs to the Republican Policy Committee of the U.S. Senate. From 1951 until 1953, he was an associate professor of history at the University of Maryland. Since 1954, he has been at Goucher College as an associate professor of history (1954-1958) and professor and chairman of the American studies program (1958 to the present). He has been a visiting professor at the University of Virginia, the University of Wisconsin, the University of Rhode Island, The Johns Hopkins University, and Morgan State College. He has held fellowships from the Volker Foundation, the leftist Social Science Research Council, and the leftist Rockefeller Foundation. Since 1962, he has been a member of the international conference and seminar program of the leftist-pacifist American Friends Service Committee.

Neumann is affiliated with the leftist-oriented American Association of University Professors; the ultra-leftist American Civil Liberties Union; the ultra-leftist-pacifist Fellowship of Reconciliation; the ultra-leftist-pacifist National Committee for a Sane Nuclear Policy; and the American Forum for Socialist Education, which is under Communist "inspiration and domination." He has written for A.J. Muste's *Liberation,* a Socialist publication. In 1961, Neumann was the leader of a group of American historians who urged President-elect John F. Kennedy to extend diplomatic recognition to Red China and East Germany.

ROBERT P. NEWMAN was born on January 26, 1922 in Hannibal, Missouri, son of Naomi Anderson and Paul Newman. His second wife is Dale Reaves. He is an alumnus of the University of Redlands (B.A., 1942); Oxford University (B.A., 1949; M.A., 1952); and the University of Connecticut (Ph.D., 1956). He also studied at the University of Chicago. He is the author of *Recognition of Communist China?* (1961); *The Pittsburgh Code for Academic Debate* (1962); and *Evidence* (1968). He is co-author of *A Handbook of Debate* (1967).

In 1949 and 1950, Newman was an instructor in speech at Smith College. From 1950 until 1952, he was an instructor in speech at the University of Connecticut. Since 1952, he has been at the University of Pittsburgh as an assistant professor of speech (1952-1956), associate professor (1956-1962), and professor and director of the William Pitt Debating Union (1962 to the present). From 1957 until 1959, he was a communications consultant to the Bell Telephone Company of Pennsylvania. He has been a visiting lecturer at Knox College Summer School in Jamaica, West Indies. He has been a visiting professor at the University of Hawaii.

Newman has been an official of the leftist American Association of University Professors, and a member of the ultra-leftist American Civil Liberties Union and the Foreign Policy Association, a bulwark of leftist internationalism.

HAROLD L. NIEBURG was born on November 26, 1927 in Philadelphia, Pennsylvania, son of Emma Dubinsky and Samuel Nieburg. He married Janet Withey. He is an alumnus of the University of Chicago (Ph.B., 1947; A.M., 1952; Ph.D., 1961). He is the author of *Nuclear Secrecy and Foreign Policy* (1964) and *In the Name of Science* (1966). He has contributed articles to

American Behavioral Scientist, American Political Science Review, Bulletin of Atomic Scientists, Science, and *World Politics.*

In 1953 and 1954, Nieburg was an instructor in political science at San Antonio College. From 1956 until 1959, he was an assistant professor of political science at Illinois State University. In 1960 and 1961, he was associate director of the Center for Government Programs at the University of Chicago. From 1961 until 1963, he was an assistant professor of political science at Case Institute of Technology. Since 1963, he has been at the University of Wisconsin in Milwaukee as an associate professor (1963-1967) and professor (1967 to the present) of political science. In 1960 and 1961, he held a Danforth Foundation fellowship. In 1962 and 1963, and in 1965 and 1966, he held fellowships from the leftist Rockefeller Foundation.

Nieburg is affiliated with the leftist-oriented American Association of University Professors and the ultra-radical American Civil Liberties Union.

KARL H. NIEBYL was born on June 30, 1906 in Prague, Czecho-Slovakia. He is a naturalized American. He is married. He is an alumnus of the University of Frankfurt (M.A., 1932) and the University of Wisconsin (Ph.D., 1936). He also attended the Institute of Technology in Hanover, Germany, the University of Paris, the University of Berlin, and the radical London School of Economics.

In 1935 and 1936, Niebyl was a research assistant at the University of Wisconsin. From 1936 until 1940, he served successively as an instructor and assistant professor of economics at Carleton College in Minnesota. In 1940 and 1941, he was an adviser on monetary and fiscal policies to the Consumer Division of the Office of Price Administration. (He was fired from the OPA "because of the confidential nature of the work in this office and the unsatisfactory report of the character investigation of Mr. Niebyl.") From 1941 until 1943, he was an associate professor of economics and chairman of the graduate department of economics at Tulane University. In 1946, he was a professor of economics at the University of Texas. In 1946 and 1947, he was a professor of economics at Black Mountain College in North Carolina. From 1947 until 1953, he was a professor of economics and chairman of the economics department at Champlain College of the State University of New York. In 1953 and 1954, he was chairman of the department of economics and business administration at Muskingum College in Ohio. From 1954 until 1965, he was an economist, financial consultant, and partner of Economic Research Associates in New York City. From 1956 until 1965, he was a lecturer at the radical New School for Social Research. Since 1964, he has been at Temple University as a visiting professor of economics (1964-1966) and professor (1966 to the present).

In 1957, Niebyl testified before the Senate Internal Security Subcommittee during an investigation of the scope of Soviet activity in the United States. He pleaded protection of the Fifth Amendment when asked about membership in the Communist Party, his associations with Communists, his attendance at the Communist Party's Chicago Workers School, his affiliation with the Communist Party's Abraham Lincoln School of Chicago, and his affiliation with the Communist Party's *Science and Society* quarterly. In 1966, he sponsored the Herbert Aptheker Dinner Program, a tribute to the Communist Party's chief theoretician on the occasion of the Second Anniversary of the American Institute for Marxist Studies. He has been affiliated with the ultra-leftist American Society for the Study of the German Democratic Republic. He has participated in the annual ultra-leftist Socialist Scholars Conferences.

HENRY E. NILES was born on January 20, 1900 in Baltimore, son of Mary Waters and Alfred Niles. He married Mary Howard. He is an alumnus of Johns Hopkins University (A.B., 1920). He is co-author of *The Office Supervisor* (1960).

From 1923 until 1930, Niles was assistant manager of the Life Insurance Sales Research Bureau in Hartford, Connecticut. In 1930 and 1931, he was associated with the firm of Woodward, Fondiller & Ryan. From 1931 until 1939, he was a member of the firm of Henry E. Niles & M.C.H. Niles. In 1942 and 1943, he was advertising director for the Maryland National Bank and a management consultant for the Office of Price Administration. Since 1940, he has been with the Baltimore Life Insurance Company as superintendent of agencies (1940), secretary (1940-1942), vice-president (1943-1957), president (1957-1965), and chairman of the board (1965 to the present).

Niles has been affiliated with the ultra-leftist United World Federalists; the leftist-pacifist National Coalition for a Responsible Congress; the leftist-pacifist National Citizens Committee for the Amendment to End the War; the leftist-pacifist Individuals Against the Crime of Silence; and the leftist-pacifist Citizens Committee to End the War. In 1962, he was a member of the advisory council of the Peace Research Institute, one of the most prestigious organizations in the entire leftist-pacifist movement. Since 1967, Niles has been the head of Business Executives Move for Vietnam Peace. The organization was launched on February 8, 1967, with a half-page advertisement in the *Washington Post*, which was in the form of an open letter to President Lyndon Johnson. It said, in part: "We, the undersigned American business executives, most of whom have served at least once in the Armed Services of the United States, protest against the escalation of the war in Vietnam. We believe that this war is against our national interest and world interest. We feel this on moral and practical grounds." In the fall of 1967, Niles' organization had its first national meeting, and since that time BEMVP has become one of the most active of all the pacifist groups in the country. (Within Niles' own family, his daughter Alice has been an active pacifist since at least 1949. His son-in-law, Staughton Lynd, is one of America's better-known revolutionary pacifists.

ANN LANE NUCHOW was born on July 27, 1932 in New York City, daughter of Elizabeth Brown and Harry Lane. She married William Nuchow. She is an alumna of New York University (M.A., 1957) and Columbia University (Ph.D., 1968).

From 1958 until 1960, Mrs. Nuchow was managing editor of *Challenge* magazine. In 1961 and 1962, she was on the faculty at Hunter College. In 1962 and 1963, she was on the faculty at Brooklyn College. In 1963 and 1964, she was an assistant to John Hope Franklin while he was writing his *History of Civil Rights in the United States*. In 1965 and 1966, she was on the faculty of Sarah Lawrence College. Since 1967, she has been on the history faculty at Douglass College.

Mrs. Nuchow has been a contributor to the ultra-radical *Studies on the Left.* She is a founder of and participant in the annual ultra-leftist Socialist Scholars Conferences.

HARVEY O'CONNOR was born on March 29, 1897 in Minneapolis, son of Jessie Kenney and James O'Connor. He married Jessie Lloyd (whose father, William B. Lloyd, was a founder of the Communist Party in the United States.) O'Connor is the author of *Mellon's Millions* (1933); *Steel-Dictator* (1935); *The Guggenheims* (1937); *The Astors* (1941); *History of the Oil Workers International Union* (1950); *The Empire of Oil* (1955); *World Crisis in Oil* (1961); and *Revolution in Seattle* (1963).

From 1919 until 1924, O'Connor was the labor editor for the *Seattle Daily Union Record.* From 1924 until 1927, he was assistant editor of the *Locomotive Engineers Journal.* From 1927 until 1930, he was bureau manager for the Federated Press, a Communist news service. From 1935 until 1937, he was managing editor of *People's Press,* a Communist Party publication. In 1937 and 1938, he was editor of *Ken,* a leftist magazine. From 1937 until 1944, he was vice-chairman of the ultra-leftist Chicago Civil Liberties Committee. From 1945 until 1948, he was publicity director and editor for the Oil Workers International Union.

In 1939, O'Connor was identified as a member of the Communist Party by Benjamin Gitlow, the Communist Party's former secretary-general, who was testifying under oath before the Committee on Un-American Activities. In 1954, O'Connor was cited for contempt by the Senate Government Operations Committee. He was tried and convicted, but the U.S. Court of Appeals reversed the con-

viction. In 1958, he was cited for contempt and indicted for refusing to respond to a subpoena issued by the House Committee on Un-American Activities. In 1965, the Department of Justice dismissed the indictment.

O'Connor has contributed to such Communist publications as *New Masses, Daily Worker, Sunday Worker, Science and Society, Champion, Fight, Voice of Labor, March of Labor,* and *Equality.* From 1934 until 1936, he was on the executive committee of the ultra-leftist Pittsburgh Civil Liberties Committee. Since 1955, he has been with the Emergency Civil Liberties Committee ("Communist front" – "subversive") as chairman (1955-1963) and member of the executive committee (1963 to the present). He was an instructor at the Abraham Lincoln School in Chicago ("an adjunct of the Communist Party"). He has been affiliated with the International Labor Defense ("legal arm of the Communist Party"); the National Committee to Aid Striking Miners Fighting Starvation ("Communist front"); the John Reed Club ("Communist front"); the All-America Anti-Imperialist League ("Communist front"); the League of American Writers ("subversive and Communist"); the American League for Peace and Democracy ("subversive and Communist"); the American Peace Mobilization ("subversive and Communist"); the Emergency Peace Mobilization ("Communist front"); the China Aid Council ("Communist-controlled"); the National Federation for Constitutional Liberties ("under Communist Party domination and headed by responsible Party functionaries"); the Citizens Committee to Free Earl Browder ("Communist"); the Friends of the Soviet Union ("to propagandize for and defend Russia and its system of government" –

"directed from Moscow"); the Citizens Victory Committee for Harry Bridges ("Communist front"); the National Council of American-Soviet Friendship ("subversive and Communist" – "specializing in pro-Soviet propaganda"); the Joint Anti-Fascist Refugee Committee ("subversive and Communist"); the League for Mutual Aid ("Communist enterprise"); the Consumers' National Federation ("Communist front"); the Council for Pan-American Democracy ("Communist front"); Herbert Aptheker's American Institute for Marxist Studies; the Conference for Legislation in the National Interest ("Communist front"); the American Committee for the Protection of Foreign Born [Americans] ("subversive and Communist"); the Communist-run Hemispheric Conference to End the War in Vietnam; the Fair Play for Cuba Committee (subsidized by Castro); the ultra-leftist-pacifist World Fellowship; the Committee of First Amendment Defendants ("Communist front"); and the American Forum for Socialist Education (under Communist "inspiration and domination").

RICHARD M. OHMANN was born on July 11, 1931 in Cleveland, son of Grace Malin and Oliver Ohmann. He married Carol Burke. He is an alumnus of Oberlin College (B.A., 1952) and Harvard University (M.A., 1954; Ph.D., 1960). He is the author of *Shaw: The Style and the Man* (1962). He is co-author of *The Logic and Rhetoric of Exposition* (1963). He is editor of *The Making of Myth* (1962). He is co-editor of *Inquiry and Expression* (1958). He has contributed articles to *Commonweal* and the ultra-leftist *Partisan Review*. Since 1966, he has been editor of *College English.*

From 1954 until 1961, Ohmann was at Harvard University as a university fellow (1954-1958) and a junior fellow in the Society of Fellows (1958-1961). Since 1961, he has been at Wesleyan University in Connecticut, as an assistant professor of English (1961-1963), associate professor (1963-1966), professor (1966 to the present), associate provost (1966-1969), and acting provost (1969 to the present). In 1964 and 1965, he held a Guggenheim fellowship. Since 1966, he has been a consultant to Random House, Inc., and Alfred A. Knopf, Inc.

Ohmann has been affiliated with the ultra-leftist American-Korean Friendship and Information Center. Since 1967, he has been an official of RESIST. This anti-war, anti-draft agency issued a "New Call to Resist Illegitimate Authority" to support those who resist by refusing to register for the draft or submit to induction; by impeding the operations of draft boards and induction centers; by expressing anti-war views while in the armed forces, or refusing to obey "illegal or immoral" orders, or absenting themselves without leave; by conducting rent and workers' strikes, boycotts, and similar direct actions aimed at ending "exploitation" in the fields, in factories, and in housing; and by organizing against harassment by police, the FBI, the courts, and Congress. RESIST organizes sit-ins, strikes, and demonstrations at schools and universities in order to end alleged racist practices and direct complicity with militarism. RESIST serves as a clearing-house for information about anti-war and anti-draft groups. It also grants funds to these groups.

ALIDA O'LOUGHLIN was born on May 21, 1930 in The Hague, Holland, daughter of Wilhelmina Olijslag and Sieger Kolk. She was married to and divorced from Francis O'Loughlin. She is an alumna of the University of Massachusetts (M.A., 1953).

From 1962 until 1964, Mrs. O'Loughlin was a French instructor at the Lesley-Ellis School in Cambridge, Massachusetts. Since 1963, she has been with the leftist-internationalist Experiment in International Living as executive secretary of the Boston office (1963-1964) and director (1964 to the present). Since 1967, she has been vice-president and member of the steering committee of the United Nations Association of Greater Boston, part of the most prestigious leftwing propaganda agency for the UN in this country. She is a member of the World Affairs Council, a pivotal agency in a complex of one-world, leftist, and pacifist groups. She is a member of the National Association for the Advancement of Colored People, the fountainhead of Negro agitation for more than half a century.

WILLIAM C. OLSON was born on August 19, 1920 in Denver, Colorado, son of Frances Murray and Albert Olson. He married Mary Matthews. He is an alumnus of the University of Denver (A.B., 1942) and Yale University (M.A., 1951; Ph.D., 1953). He is the co-author and editor of *The Theory and Practice of International Relations* (1970).

From 1947 until 1949, Olson was a staff officer with the Social Science Foundation of Denver. From 1953 until 1961, he served successively as an assistant professor and associate professor of government at Pomona College and Claremont Graduate School. In 1959 and 1960, he was a senior member of St. Antony's College at Oxford University. From 1961 until 1965, he was chief of the foreign affairs division in the legislative reference service of the Library of Congress. Since 1964, he has been at

Columbia University as visiting professor (1964-1965), associate dean of the School of International Affairs (1965 to the present), and research associate in the Institute for War and Peace Studies (1965 to the present). Since 1967, he has been associate director of the humanities and social sciences for the leftist-oriented Rockefeller Foundation. From 1962 until 1964, he was a lecturer in international politics at the School for Advanced International Studies at The Johns Hopkins University.

Since 1959, Olson has been affiliated with the leftist-oriented Experiment in International Living as trustee (1959-1965) and chairman of the advisory council (1965 to the present). In 1968, he signed the Declaration of Atlantic Unity, a leftist-internationalist statement. He is a nonresident member of the Council on Foreign Relations, the informal supra-State Department of the United States. He is a member of the leftist-oriented Washington Institute of Foreign Affairs.

WAYNE A. O'NEIL was born on December 22, 1931 in Kenosha, Wisconsin, son of Kathryn Obremeyer and Leslie O'Neil. He married Donna Carr. He is an alumnus of the University of Wisconsin (B.A., 1956; M.A., 1957; Ph.D., 1960). He is the author of *Kennels and Transformations* (1965).

In 1960 and 1961, O'Neil was an instructor in English at Duke University. In 1961, he was in Iceland as a Fulbright fellow. From 1961 until 1964, he was an assistant professor of English at the University of Oregon. In 1964 and 1965, he was at Massachusetts Institute of Technology on a grant from the American Council of Learned Societies. From 1965 until 1968, he was at Harvard University as an associate professor of linguistics and education (1965-1967) and professor (1967-1968). Since 1968, he has been a lecturer in education at Harvard University and a professor of the humanities at Massachusetts Institute of Technology.

O'Neil has been affiliated with the leftist-oriented Ad Hoc Faculty Committee on Vietnam; the leftist-oriented Ad Hoc Committee on the Vietnam War; and the ultra-leftist American-Korean Friendship and Information Center. Since 1967, he has been a regional organizer for National Resistance, an ultra-leftist-pacifist group which supports "an end to racism, imperialism, and economic exploitation in this country and around the world." National Resistance opposes the entire Selective Service System and supports those "who refuse, out of conscientious, philosophical, and/or political beliefs, to cooperate in any manner with the Selective Service System and who share a desire for radical change in this nation."

HAROLD ORLANS was born on July 29, 1921 in New York City. He is an alumnus of the City College of New York (B.S.S., 1941) and Yale University (Ph.D., 1949). In 1948 and 1949, he was a Social Science Research Council fellow at the radical London School of Economics, and in 1949 and 1950, he was a Fulbright scholar at the same institution. He is the author of *The Effects of Federal Programs on Higher Education* (1962) and *Contracting for Atoms* (1967).

In 1950 and 1951, Orlans was a visiting lecturer in sociology and anthropology at the University of Birmingham in England. In 1951 and 1952, he was a senior information officer for *Social Survey*. From 1952 until 1954, he was research associate at the Institute for

Research in Human Relations. From 1954 until 1959, he was a social science analyst and section chief at the National Science Foundation. In 1959 and 1960, he was director of studies for the leftist-oriented White House Conference on Children and Youth. Since 1960, he has been a member of the senior staff at Brookings Institution, a unique think factory which has influenced internationalist trends in the federal government for the past fifty years. Since 1962, he has been a member of the Federation of American Scientists, a bleeding-heart group, members of which are generally affiliated with a variety of radical one-world and/or pacifist organizations.

JACOB OSER was born on April 4, 1915 in New York City, son of Sophie Kantor and Solomon Oser. He married Kathleen Johnson. He is an alumnus of the University of Illinois (B.S., 1935) and Columbia University (M.A., 1947; Ph.D., 1950). He is the author of *Must Men Starve?: The Malthusian Controversy* (1956); *The Evolution of Economic Thought* (1963); and *Promoting Economic Development with Illustrations from the Experience of Kenya* (1967). He is co-author of *Economic History of Modern Europe* (1953).

From 1948 until 1956, Oser was an economics teacher at Harpur College of the State University of New York. Since 1956, he has been a professor of economics at Utica College of Syracuse University. In 1963, he held a fellowship from the leftist-oriented Ford Foundation.

Oser is affiliated with the National Association for the Advancement of Colored People, the fountainhead of Negro agitation for more than half a century, and with the leftist-racist Congress on Racial Equality.

CHARLES E. OSGOOD was born on November 20, 1916 in Somerville, Massachusetts, son of Ruth Egerton and Merrill Osgood. He married Cynthia Thornton. He is an alumnus of Dartmouth College (B.A., 1939) and Yale University (Ph.D., 1945). He is the author of *Method and Theory in Experimental Psychology* (1953); *An Alternative to War or Surrender* (1962); and *Perspective in Foreign Policy* (1966). He is co-author of *The Measurement of Meaning* (1957). In 1962, his "Reciprocal Initiative" was the longest article contributed to the notorious *Liberal Papers,* edited by James Roosevelt. Osgood suggested in his theory of reciprocal initiative that the United States initiate disarmament by dismantling a nuclear striking base near the Soviet Union. Such a gesture, he claimed, would prove the sincerity of the United States Government's desire for peace, and subsequently public opinion would force the Soviet Union to reciprocate by reducing its nuclear power "for reasons of good sense – even if not of goodwill."

From 1942 until 1945, Osgood was an instructor in psychology at Yale University. In 1945, he was a research associate in the Office of Scientific Research and Development. In 1945 and 1946, he was a statistician with the Navy Department and an instructor at Yale University. From 1946 until 1949, he was an assistant professor of psychology at the University of Connecticut. Since 1949, he has been at the University of Illinois as an associate professor of psychology (1949-1952), professor of psychology (1952 to the present), director of the Institute of Communications Research (since 1957), and professor of communications and psychology at the Institute (also since 1957). In 1954 and 1955, he was a Guggenheim fellow. In 1958 and 1959, he was a fellow at the Center for Advanced Study in the Behavioral Sciences. In 1964 and 1965, he was a visiting professor at the University of Hawaii. In 1966, the chairman of the U.S. Senate Foreign Affairs Committee, J. William Fulbright, had Osgood "psychoanalyze" United States foreign policy in a well-publicized leftist propaganda stunt.

In 1966, Osgood was affiliated with the Committee on Free Elections in the Dominican Republic, a lobbying effort on behalf of Communist Juan Bosch. Osgood has been affiliated with the leftist-pacifist Student Peace Union; the leftist-pacifist Ad Hoc Faculty Committee on Vietnam; the leftist-pacifist Voters' Peace Pledge; and the ultra-leftist-pacifist National Committee for a Sane Nuclear Policy.

ROBERT E. OSGOOD was born on August 14, 1921 in St. Louis, Missouri, son of Harriet Johnson and Harold Osgood. He married Gretchen Anderson. He is an alumnus of Harvard University (B.A., 1943; Ph.D., 1952). He is the author of *Ideals and Self-Interest in America's Foreign Relations* (1953); *Limited War* (1957); *NATO: The Entangling Alliance* (1962); and *Alliances and American Foreign Policy* (1968). He is co-author of *Force, Order, and Justice* (1967). He has contributed articles to *American Political Science Review, Confluence, New Republic,* and *Social Forces.*

From 1952 until 1961, Osgood was at the University of Chicago as a research associate at the University's Center for the Study of American Foreign and Military Policy (1952-1961), and as assistant professor (1956-1958), associate professor (1958-1961), and professor (1961) of political science. Since 1961, he has been at The Johns Hopkins University's School of Advanced International Studies as professor of American diplomacy. Since 1961, he has been at the leftist-oriented Washington Center of Foreign Policy Research as associate director (1961-1965) and director (1965 to the present). In 1959, he was the NATO visiting professor at the University of Manchester (England). In 1957 and 1961, he was a lecturer at the Salzburg [Austria] Seminar in American Studies. He has also lectured at the Army, Navy, and Air War Colleges. He has been an adviser to the Department of State on Foreign Relations (1963-1966) and on Europe (1966 to the present).

Since 1967, Osgood has been on the advisory committee of the leftist-oriented Atlantic Institute. He is a nonresident member of the Council on Foreign Relations, the informal supra-State Department of the United States.

FRANK PACE JR. was born on July 5, 1912 in Little Rock, son of Flora Layton and Frank Pace. He married Margaret Janney. He is an alumnus of Princeton University (A.B., 1933) and Harvard University (LL.B., 1936). He was admitted to the Arkansas bar in 1936.

From 1936 until 1942, Pace practiced law in Arkansas. From 1936 until 1938, he was an assistant district attorney in Arkansas. From 1938 until 1940, he was the general attorney for the Arkansas Revenue Department. In 1946, he was an assistant to the Attorney General of the United States. From 1946 until 1948, he was an executive assistant to the Postmaster General. From 1948 until 1950, he was with the Bureau of the Budget as assistant director (1948-1949) and director (1949-1950). From 1950 until 1953, he was Secretary

of the Army. Since 1964, he has been president and chief executive officer of International Executive Service Corps. In 1968, President Lyndon Johnson appointed Pace as chairman of the newly formed Public Broadcasting Corporation, a quasi-private, federally financed "educational" TV operation, created by the 1967 Public Broadcasting Act.

Pace has served as chairman of the board of General Dynamics Corporation and Canadair, Lt. He has been a director of American Fidelity Life Insurance Company, Nation-Wide Securities Company, Colgate-Palmolive Company, Continental Oil Company, and Time, Inc. He is a long-time resident member of the Council on Foreign Relations, the informal supra-State Department of the United States. He has served on the board of directors of the leftist-oriented Atlantic Council of the United States.

LESLIE PAFFRATH was born on May 10, 1915 in New York City, son of Alice Gray and John Paffrath. He married Adrianne Knight. He is an alumnus of Union College (A.B., 1939).

In 1939 and 1940, Paffrath was a staff trainee at the Institute of Public Administration in New York City. In 1940, he was a special assistant in the State Comptroller's office of New Hampshire. In 1941, he was acting executive director of the State Council for Civilian Defense in New Hampshire. In 1941 and 1942, he was senior administrative assistant in the U.S. Regional Office of Civilian Defense in New England. From 1946 until 1949, he was director of the New Hampshire State Planning and Development Commission, located in New York City. From 1950 until 1959, he was secretary of the leftist-pacifist Carnegie Endowment for International Peace. Since 1959, he has been president of the Johnson Foundation in Racine.

Paffrath has been affiliated with the United Nations Association of the United States, the most prestigious left-wing propaganda agency for the UN in this country. He is a long-time nonresident member of the Council on Foreign Relations, the informal supra-State Department of the United States. He has been a member of the leftist-pacifist Commission to Study the Organization of Peace. He has been a member of the international affairs committee, and of the general committee of the department of international affairs, of the leftist-oriented National Council of Churches. In 1965, he was secretary-general of the leftist-loaded International Convocation on Pacem in Terris. In 1968, he was a founding member of the leftist-loaded World Assembly for Human Rights. In 1964, he was an American delegate to the Red-loaded Fourth Dartmouth Conference in Leningrad.

NORMAN D. PALMER was born on June 25, 1909 in Hinckley, Maine, son of Gertrude Dunbar and Walter Palmer. He married Evelyn Kalal. He is an alumnus of Colby College (B.A., 1930) and Yale University (M.A., 1932; Ph.D., 1936). He is the author of *The Irish Land League Crisis* (1940); *The Indian Political System* (1961); and *South Asia and United States Policy* (1966). He is the co-author of *Fundamentals of Political Science* (1942); *International Relations: The World Community in Transition* (1953, 1957, and 1968); *The Idea of Colonialism* (1958); *Major Governments of Asia* (1958 and 1963); *Leadership and Political Institutions in India* (1959); *Sun Yat-sen and Communism* (1957); *The United States and the United Nations* (1964); and *Problems of Defense of South and East Asia* (1969).

From 1933 until 1947, Palmer served successively as instructor, assistant professor, and associate professor of history and government, and as department chairman, at Colby College. Since 1947, he has been at the University of Pennsylvania as associate professor of political science (1947-1951), professor of political science (1951 to the present), chairman of the political science department (1949-1952), chairman of the international relations department (1959-1966), and member of the Foreign Policy Research Institute (1955 to the present). In 1950, he was a visiting professor at the School of Advanced International Studies. In 1952 and 1953, he was a Fulbright professor of international affairs and political science at the University of Delhi. From 1954 until 1959, he was the coordinator for the University of Pennsylvania-University of Karachi project. In 1959 and 1960, he was a fellow at the leftist-pacifist Carnegie Endowment for International Peace. In 1961, he was a visiting professor at Swarthmore College. In 1961 and 1962, he was a research fellow at the Council on Foreign Relations. In 1966 and 1967, he was a senior specialist at the East-West Center in Honolulu, and also was a research fellow in India for the American Institute for Indian Studies, and a visiting professor at Bombay University. Since 1949, he has been a contributing editor to *Current History*; since 1957, a member of the editorial board of *Orbis*; and since 1968, a consultant to the Department of State.

Palmer is a long-time nonresident member of the Council on Foreign Relations, the informal supra-State Department of the United States. He is a long-time member of the Foreign Policy Association, a bulwark of leftist-internationalism; of the leftist-internationalist

PARSONS

World Affairs Council; and of the leftist American Veterans Committee.

HOWARD L. PARSONS was born on July 9, 1918 in Jacksonville, Florida. He is an alumnus of the University of Chicago (B.A., 1942; Ph.D., 1946).

In 1946 and 1947, Parsons was a visiting assistant professor and director of religious activities at the University of Southern California. From 1947 until 1949, he was an instructor at the University of Illinois in Galesburg. From 1949 until 1957, he was an assistant professor of philosophy at the University of Tennessee. From 1957 until 1965, he was at Coe College as an associate professor (1957-1960), professor (1960-1965), and chairman of the department of philosophy and religion (1959-1965). Since 1965, he has been Bernhard Professor of Philosophy and department chairman at the University of Bridgeport.

Since 1964, Parsons has been a member of the board of the American Institute for Marxist Studies. He is a member of the board of the National Council of American-Soviet Friendship ("subversive and Communist" – "specializing in pro-Soviet propaganda"). He is chairman of the ultra-leftist American-Korean Friendship and Information Center. In 1962, he promoted the Communist Party's World Youth Festival at Helsinki. He has been a writer for *New World Review*, a Communist publication. In 1966, he was chairman of the Aptheker Dinner Program, a tribute to the Communist Party's best-known theoretician. He has been affiliated with the National Committee to Repeal the McCarran Act ("Communist front" – "subversive"); the National Committee to Abolish the House Un-American Activities Committee ("to lead and direct the Communist Party's

'Operation Abolition' campaign"); the ultra-leftist American Society for the Study of the German Democratic Republic; the ultra-leftist Fort Hood Three Defense Committee; the leftist-oriented Ad Hoc Committee for an Open Letter on Vietnam; the National Assembly for Democratic Rights ("created, dominated, and controlled by members and officials of the Communist Party"); and the leftist-racist Southern Conference Educational Fund. He has been an instructor at the New York School for Marxist Studies. He joined in a tribute to the Communist Party's *Daily World*, saying that it "deserves the support of all who cherish peace, democracy and social progress."

MARTHA PATE was born on November 27, 1912 in Louisville, daughter of Gertrude Lasch and Robert Lucas. She was married to the late Maurice Pate. She is an alumna of Goucher College (A.B., 1933); George Washington University (A.M., 1935); and the University of London (Ph.D., 1940). She is co-author of *Religious Faith and World Culture* (1951).

From 1941 until 1944, Mrs. Pate was associate professor of philosophy and religion and dean of students at the University of Richmond. From 1944 until 1946, she was associate dean at Radcliffe College. From 1946 until 1950, she was president of Sweet Briar College. In 1961 and 1962, she was with the leftist-oriented Institute of International Education as the director for the office of university and college relations. Since 1963, she has been chairman and a member of the board of directors for the college and school division of the United Negro College Fund. From 1948 until 1950, she was on the national selections committee for Fulbright Scholarships. In

540

1948 and 1949, she was a U.S. delegate to Communist-dominated UNESCO conferences. Since 1970, she has been a member of the U.S. National Advisory Commission on International Education and Cultural Affairs.

Mrs. Pate has been on the board of directors of the Foreign Policy Association, a bulwark of leftist-internationalism. Since 1969, she has been a trustee of the leftist-oriented Fund for Theological Education. Since 1968, she has been a trustee of the leftist-pacifist Council on Religion and International Affairs. She has been affiliated with the leftist-internationalist Fund for Peace.

HUGH B. PATTERSON was born on February 8, 1915 in Cotton Plant, Mississippi, son of Martha Wilson and Hugh Patterson. He married Louise Heiskell. He attended Henderson State Teachers College.

From 1933 until 1936, Patterson was with the sales department of Smith Printing Company of Pine Bluff, Arkansas. From 1936 until 1938, he was assistant to the sales manager of the Democrat Printing & Lithographing Company of Little Rock, and from 1940 until 1942, he was promotion manager of the same firm. In 1938 and 1939, he was with the sales department of the Art Metal Construction Company of New York City. In 1939 and 1940, he was planning and production manager for the Rufus H. Darby Company of Washington, D.C. Since 1946, he has been with the *Arkansas Gazette*, serving successively as national advertising manager, assistant business manager, and since 1948, publisher. He is vice-president and treasurer of the Gazette Publishing Company.

Patterson has been a long-time member and official of the Foreign Policy Association, a bulwark of leftist internationalism. He has also been a long-time official of the World Affairs Council, a pivotal agency in a complex of one-world, leftist, and pacifist groups, which has become a major propaganda arm for the United Nations.

BURTON PAULU was born on June 25, 1910 in Pewaukee, Wisconsin, son of Sarah Murphy and Emanuel Paulu. He married Frances Brown. He is an alumnus of the University of Minnesota (B.A., 1931; B.S., 1932; M.A., 1934) and New York University (Ph.D., 1949). He also studied at Northern State Teachers College in South Dakota. In 1953 and 1954, he was a Fulbright senior research scholar. In 1958 and 1959, and in 1964 and 1965, he received grants from the ultra-leftist Ford Foundation. He is the author of *British Broadcasting: Radio and Television in the United Kingdom* (1956) and *British Broadcasting in Transition* (1961).

Since 1938, Paulu has been at the University of Minnesota as manager of the University's radio station KUOM (1938-1957) and director of radio and television, with the rank of professor (1957 to the present). In 1943 and 1944, and in 1947 and 1948, he worked as an instructor and assistant director of the summer radio workshop at New York University. He has also been a visiting lecturer at the University of Southern California and Los Angeles State College. In 1944 and 1945, he was a member of the radio division of the Red-loaded Office of War Information. In 1958, he was a member of the five-man U.S. delegation of radio and television broadcasters visiting the Soviet Union to study Soviet broadcasting. He is a long-time member and has been president of the leftist-oriented National

Association of Educational Broadcasters.

DEAN G. PEERMAN was born on April 25, 1931 in Mattoon, Illinois, son of Irene Monen and Staley Peerman. He is an alumnus of Northwestern University (B.S., 1953) and Yale University's Divinity School (B.D., 1959). He pursued graduate studies at Cornell University. He is co-author of *Pen-ultimates* (1963) and *Frontline Theology* (1967). He is co-editor of *New Theology No. 1* (1964); *New Theology No. 2* (1965); *New Theology No. 3* (1966); *New Theology No. 4* (1967); *New Theology No. 5* (1968); and *A Handbook of Christian Theologians* (1965).

From 1954 until 1956, Peerman was a conscientious objector and worked as a psychiatric aide in a hospital. Since 1959, he has been with *Christian Century* magazine as copy editor (1959-1961), associate editor (1961-1964), and managing editor (1964 to the present).

Peerman is a member of the ultra-leftist-pacifist Fellowship of Reconciliation; the ultra-leftist American Civil Liberties Union; and the National Association for the Advancement of Colored People, the fountainhead of Negro agitation for more than half a century.

DeVERE E. PENTONY was born on September 10, 1924 in Manchester, Iowa, son of Amber Davis and Joseph Pentony. He married Isabel Hoag. He is an alumnus of the University of Iowa (B.A., 1949; M.A., 1951; Ph.D., 1955). He is the author of *U.S. Foreign Aid* and *The Underdeveloped Lands* (1960); and *Soviet Behavior in World Affairs, China: The Emerging Red Giant*, and *Red World in Tumult* (1962).

In 1954 and 1955, Pentony was a teacher at the Longfellow School for Boys in Bethesda, Maryland. In 1956

and 1957, he was an instructor at the State University of Iowa. Since 1958, he has been at San Francisco State College as an associate professor of international relations (1958-1961), professor and chairman of the department of international relations (1961-1966), and dean of the School of Behavioral and Social Sciences (1966 to the present). From 1962 until 1966, he was a consultant to and lecturer for the Peace Corps. He is affiliated with the leftist-oriented American Association for University Professors. He is a member of the ultra-leftist American Civil Liberties Union.

WILLIAM F. PEPPER was born on August 16, 1937 in Yonkers, New York. He is an alumnus of Columbia University (B.A., 1959; M.A. 1960).

In 1969, the Senate Internal Security Subcommittee was examining the spectrum of the New Left. In the course of the examination, the subcommittee focused its attention upon the National Conference for New Politics and its executive director, William F. Pepper. At the time of the investigation, William F. Pepper had recently founded the Glenrock Community School in Ossining, New York. The school was described as a small private school for exceptionally gifted boys.

In 1967, the Yonkers (New York) Police Department's Intelligence Unit had cause to investigate William F. Pepper. Detective William E. Grogan testified before the Senate Internal Security Subcommittee on the results of that investigation. In the course of his testimony, Grogan said: "Very early in our investigation of Mr. Pepper, we became aware of an article printed in the January 1967 issue of *Ramparts* magazine with the title 'Children of Vietnam' – photographs and text by William F.

Pepper . . . . Because of his anti-draft activities, and his activist position against the policy of the United States in Vietnam, we thought that Mr. Pepper should be looked into. After a preliminary investigation we began to maintain an active file on Mr. Pepper and all of his activities . . . . As we have investigated Mr. Pepper, we find that Mr. Pepper, either by omission or commission, has made statements contrary to fact. Mr. Pepper has listed himself on many applications as having degrees and attending schools which he has not attended and degrees which he does not possess. During our investigation we have come across a criminal complaint made against Mr. Pepper for carnal abuse of . . . two young male children . . . . Mr. Pepper has in the past led a Freedom March which he listed as the Westchester Independent Democratic Assembly, which was comprised of high school students. Mr. Pepper listed this Westchester Democratic Assembly as a political organization; however, in checking the files of the New York State Department of State he has never filed any type of papers which would support this claim . . . . He has claimed to be a nephew of the now Congressman, former Senator Claude Pepper. However, in attempting to check this, we have been informed there is a letter from Congressman Pepper which states that he has absolutely no relation to William Francis Pepper . . . . I have here a brochure which was put out by Mr. Pepper on the faculty and professional staff of the Glenrock Community, Inc. Mr. Pepper in his own dossier out of this brochure lists himself as being a recipient of the Charles Heyden Memorial Scholarship while attending Columbia Teachers College in New York City. A check with that college discloses that they have no knowledge of a Charles Heyden Memorial Scholarship nor has there ever been such a scholarship issued out of Columbia University. Mr. Pepper lists himself as attending the graduate faculties and teachers college of study. The records of that particular unit of Columbia College indicate that he has never been in attendance there. Mr. Pepper lists himself as attending the London School of Economics and Political Science in 1960. He did attend that school, but not as a registered student. He was allowed only to attend the class and not to take any tests or receive any diplomas . . . . Mr. Pepper lists himself as a doctoral candidate through the New School for Social Research. A check with the New School for Social Research in New York City indicates that Mr. Pepper was only a candidate for admission to that school, never a candidate for a Ph.D. or doctorate. Mr. Pepper lists himself as a member of the faculties of Mercy College, Fairleigh Dickinson University, City University of New York, and Pratt Institute. Mr. Pepper is, in fact, only a part-time teacher one night a week at Fairleigh Dickinson University on the Teaneck campus . . . . Mr. Pepper was on the faculty of Mercy College. He was listed as an instructor of political science and an LL.B. candidate at Fordham University. Mr. Pepper took a leave of absence from Fordham University and was not readmitted . . . . Our check with Fordham University officials shows that Mr. Pepper was not readmitted, due to a complaint being filed against him by Mrs. Adaila Cann, residing at 32 Rockland Avenue in Yonkers . . . . Mrs. Cann complained to Fordham University that Mr. Pepper was not of fit moral character to attend this particular section of their college [and our investigation showed it was for that reason that he was not readmitted] . . . . Mr. Pepper goes on to state that he is a free-lance photographer, journalist and author, published in American and foreign press, and a lecturer on over forty college and university campuses. The only published work of Mr. Pepper we were able to find at this time is the *Ramparts* magazine article, and it is believed that in the cases of all the forty college and university campuses he was invited there by not the faculty but student groups . . . . Mr. Pepper is presently in violation of the Federal draft law by at least one committed felony. Mr. Pepper wrote to the draft board and got an exemption on a student deferment. The letter that he wrote to the draft board stated that he was attending Howard University as a law candidate. We have a letter . . . from Howard University stating that Mr. Pepper was never accepted by them as a law candidate . . . . Mr. Pepper attended the Pennsylvania Law School for one year, and when he applied for a law candidacy at Fordham University, he was not given credit for the year at Pennsylvania. He lists himself as the baseball coach for the city of Yonkers PAL, which is the police athletic league. The police athletic league has absolutely no record whatsoever of Mr. Pepper being a baseball coach . . . . Mr. Pepper has participated in anti-Vietnam War rallies in Sheep's Meadow, Central Park, and in Nassau County, Long Island."

In 1966, Pepper went to South Vietnam where he spent a little less than six weeks. His adventures there were chronicled in the *Yonkers Herald Statesman*. On April 6, 1966, Archie Wilson wrote: "A Yonkers teacher is in Viet Nam today on a different kind of mission. His interests are not military or political – they deal with people. William F. Pepper of 63 Cumberland Drive, a political science instructor at Mercy College in

Dobbs Ferry is in the Gia Dinh province of Viet Nam on 'a multi-faceted assignment.' He has taken a month's leave of absence from the college to gather information for a national magazine article. Mr. Pepper's subject is displaced persons, a problem he feels has become more acute with the war's intensification. He's a representative of the 'People to People' movement. As such, he'll negotiate the transfer of athletic and recreational equipment to Viet Nam while investigating the feasibility of human exchange programs. He plans to apply for permission to enter mainland China and visit Hugh Francis Redmond, a Yonkers man imprisoned there for 15 years.

"After spending a morning visiting civilian hospitals in Viet Nam, Mr. Pepper said, 'My God, what tragedies have fallen upon these innocents.' He arranged for living accommodations in a religious institution and is 'gambling this will provide an immunity not available to Americans.' The institution is in an area infested with Viet Cong and lies outside the capital district. Mr. Pepper wrote: 'There are now 18 American civilians who are prisoners of the Cong. They are everywhere and into everything. They control the roads and force travelers to pay road taxes. Americans who are captured bring high ransom figures and are prize bait.'

"He wrote: 'The greatest setback since the full entrance of the U.S. into the Viet Nam conflict appears about to break in the government forces . . . . Reliable sources high in the U.S. military command are extremely worried about the loss of five northern provinces, commonly known as the Corps One area . . . . It is feared that a Viet Cong capital may soon be established in the north at Hue, the old imperial capital. This would follow, or occur simultaneously with the secession or absorption of the five provinces from the Republic of South Viet Nam.

"Mr. Pepper said the large-scale anti-government and anti-American demonstrations coupled with a general strike in Da Nang indicate 'a coordinated military, political and psychological enemy pattern that American authorities secretly fear is to be followed by a takeover.' In his remaining three weeks in Viet Nam, Mr. Pepper intends to work closely with the Social Ministry of South Viet Nam and the Catholic Relief Services Agency. He'll be living in Da Nang and Hue where the problems are most intense. How does he pay his way? 'I teach English three hours a week.' "

On May 4, 1966, Pat Leisner wrote: "A man with a mission – Yonkers teacher William F. Pepper – said today he will ask federal support to promote American adoption of Vietnamese children. Mr. Pepper, who just returned from Southeast Asia, said Vietnamese Social Welfare Minister Lieng agreed to negotiate terms for a blanket release of children from stricken areas. Now an American referral agency must be set up to receive the children.

"Completing a five-week study tour of civilian conditions in war-torn areas, Mr. Pepper estimates a cumulative total of 993,000 displaced persons, most of whom are women and children. Through Catholic Relief Services (CRS) he hopes to appear before Sen. Edward Kennedy's subcommittee on refugees in Washington. He will evaluate the Vietnamese problems and point up the accomplishments of voluntary agencies. Although the Vietnamese ministry is opposed to foreign adoptions, unbearable living standards have forced consideration of an alternative.

"Mr. Pepper, of 63 Cumberland Drive, said it is common to see children scarred by mosquito bites for lack of something so basic as screening or netting to protect them. He said disease is rampant for lack of soap and first aid supplies. He said the Vietnamese diet contains practically no protein, only nuoc mon, a fish source, and its transportation and distribution are limited."

In the May 4, 1966 issue of the *Yonkers Herald Statesman*, an anonymous dispatch read: "A great number of the uncommitted Vietnamese choose to pay service to the Viet Cong rather than fight, William F. Pepper, a political science teacher just back from five weeks in Viet Nam, said today. When not traveling between cities and villages, Mr. Pepper lived at the Sancta Maria orphanage in Gia Dinh province, a Viet Cong controlled area. He taught English to the children, but was warned that to continue the lessons would be considered a hostile act. To remain in the area he was indirectly advised to pay a standard tax to guarantee his security.

"The Viet Cong infiltrate a village, indoctrinating its inhabitants, promising security from the American enemy. These villagers believe in a 'liberation' army. They are willing to accept the word of another Asian who speaks the language and knows the customs. 'Sympathy to the Viet Cong is not generated by fear as Secretary Rusk says,' Mr. Pepper said. 'You cannot sustain sympathy for a long period of time by terror.'

"Politically we are in bad shape, Mr. Pepper said. How can we compete against Viet Cong who are of the same racial and cultural background and at least speak the language if not the specific dialect? Freedom means little to most South Vietnamese. 'They want to be left alone to farm, and couldn't care less under whom,' he said. Among the 1½ million Catholics exists a pro-American spirit. The Buddhists range from 'friendly' in the south, to militant anti-Americans. The Confucianists 'associate discomfort with both sides,' said Mr. Pepper. He emphasized that too often these distinctions are not recognized.

"Mr. Pepper said we 'suffer today from the fact that France produced a small Western-oriented urbanized elite leadership. France suffered from it, Diem suffered from it and we are suffering from it.' The educated few, he said, are alienated from village life. There are not enough schools: 5,200 primary, when the need is for 10,000; 500 secondary, where 2,000 are needed. 'Even the children who go to school often receive only two hours instruction a day with anywhere from 60 to 100 students in a classroom.'

"Mr. Pepper applied for permission to enter mainland China to visit Hugh Francis Redmond, a Yonkers man imprisoned there for 15 years. Saigon indicated permission would be granted by the State Department, he said. If so, he will probably negotiate privately through a neutral source such as Switzerland. Within the next six months he may return to Viet Nam as field coordinator to establish a settlement of 10,000 refugees. The land has already been given for the project."

Pepper did not make a personal appearance before the Senate Subcommittee on Refugees, but he did submit a rather lengthy statement together with a very ambitious list of proposals which would allegedly alleviate the plight of refugees in Vietnam. Along with his statement, he submitted a vita which included his alleged credentials as an expert on the refugee problem: "William F. Pepper, Executive Director of the New Rochelle Commission on Human Rights, Instructor in Political Science at Mercy College in Dobbs Ferry, New York, and Director of that college's Children's Institute for Advanced Study and Research spent between five and six weeks this spring (1966) in Viet-Nam as a Free Lance Correspondent accredited by the Military Assistance Command in that country, and the Government of Viet-Nam. During that period in addition to travelling, he lived in Sancta Maria Orphanage in Gia Dinh Province and in the main 'shelter area' in Qui-Nhon, for a shorter period of time. His main interests were the effects of the war on women and children, the role of the American Voluntary Agencies there and the work of the military in civil action.

"His visits took him to a number of orphanages – among them, An Lac; Go-Vap; Don Bosco; Hoi Duc Anl; Bac Ai – hospitals: Cho-Ray; Holy Family; Phu My; Saigon-Cholon (central hospital) and shelters in Saigon, Cholon, Qui-Nhon and outer Bingh-Dinh. He interviewed, frequently, more than once, the following Cabinet Ministers of South Viet-Nam: Dr. Nguyen Ba Kha, Minister of Health; Dr. Tran Ngoc Ninh – Minister of Education; Mr. Tran Ngoc Lieng – Minister of Social Welfare; Dr. Nguyen Thuc Que – High Commission for Refugees.

"In addition, he conferred with the leaders of the Voluntary Agency Community, and the USAID Coordinator for Refugee Affairs Mr. Edward Marks, as well as the USAID child welfare specialist, Mr. Gardner Monroe. Sessions were also held with Mademoiselle E. La Mer of UNICEF and Mr. Pierre Baesjous of UNESCO. At the present time he has a book in preparation and has authored a number of newspaper articles since returning."

The climax of Pepper's Vietnam trip was his published article in the ultra-radical *Ramparts* magazine in January 1967. In August 1967, Pepper was once more in the limelight when he organized a New York City chapter of the National Conference for New Politics, of which he was the executive director. The NCNP was organized in 1965 by such radicals as Julian Bond, Simon Casady, and Stokely Carmichael. By 1967, when Pepper was the NCNP's executive director, the national council of the NCNP included such radicals as Donna Allen, Ronnie Dugger, W.H. (Ping) Ferry, Erich Fromm, Dick Gregory, Nat Hentoff, Hallock Hoffman, H. Stuart Hughes, Martin L. King Jr., Irving Laucks, Sidney Lens, Herbert Marcuse, Carey McWilliams, Stewart Meacham, Robert Scheer, Benjamin Spock, and Arthur Waskow. In an interview, Pepper said: "We aren't a bunch of liberal do-gooders; we are revolutionary." He said that the 1967 NCNP convention aimed at affiliating with the hundreds of anti-war committees and leftist-oriented "single-issue and multi-issue" groups that had sprung up throughout the country.

Pepper has been affiliated with the leftist-pacifist Committee of Responsibility; the leftist-pacifist American Friends Service Committee; Vietnam Summer: a Nationwide Peace-In, a leftist-pacifist project; and the Student Mobilization Committee to End the War in Vietnam, dominated by Communists and fellow-travelers. In 1968, he was a founder of the Freedom and Peace Party, dominated by Communists.

MORTON J. PERLIN was born on December 14, 1934 in Chicago, son of Jean Feinboldt and Sam Perlin. He married Charlotte Weiss. He is an alumnus of the University of Florida (A.B., 1955; LL.B., 1962).

Since 1962, Perlin has practiced law in Florida. Since 1963, he has been active in the Democratic Party as president of the Young Democrats in Hollywood (1963-1965), executive vice-president of the Young Democratic Clubs of Florida (1966-1967), and treasurer of the leftist-oriented Conference of Concerned Democrats in Florida (1967 to the present). In 1968, he was the Florida coordinator for the presidential campaign of Eugene J. McCarthy, and was a delegate to the Democratic National Convention.

Perlin is associated with the ultra-leftist American Civil Liberties Union, the ultra-leftist-pacifist National Committee for a Sane Nuclear Policy, and the ultra-radical Americans for Democratic Action.

NATHAN PERLMUTTER was born on March 2, 1923 in New York City, son of Bella Finkelstein and Hyman Perlmutter. He married Ruth Osofsky. He is an alumnus of New York University (LL.B., 1949). He also studied at Georgetown University and Villanova College. He is the author of *How to Win Money at the Races* (1964). He has contributed articles to the *Florida Historical Quarterly, Frontier, Commentary, Midstream, National Jewish Monthly,* and such leftist publications as *Nation, New Leader,* and *Progressive.*

From 1949 until 1964, Perlmutter was a civil rights and human relations education executive of the defamatory Anti-Defamation League in Denver (1949-1952), Detroit (1952-1953), New York City (1953-1956), and Miami (1956-1964). Since 1964, he has been an executive of the American Jewish Committee in New York City.

Perlmutter is a member of the ultra-leftist American Civil Liberties Union and the leftist-oriented International League for the Rights of Man.

CHANNING E. PHILLIPS was born on March 23, 1928 in Brooklyn, son of Dorothy Fletcher and Porter Phillips. He married Jane Nabors. He is an alumnus of Virginia Union University (B.A., 1950) and Colgate Rochester Divinity School (B.D., 1953). He pursued graduate studies at Drew University. In 1952, he was ordained to the ministry of the United Church of Christ.

From 1956 until 1958, Phillips was an instructor at Howard University. Since 1956, he has been at the Lincoln Temple of Washington as pastor (1956-1961) and senior minister (1961 to the present). Since 1967, he has been president of the Housing Development Corporation, a rehabilitation agency funded in part by the Office of Economic Opportunity. In 1968, at the Democratic National Convention, he was chairman of the delegation from the District of Columbia and a member of the convention's platform committee. Since 1968, he has been a member of the Democratic National Committee, and in 1969, he was a member of the rules reform committee of the DNC.

In 1964, Phillips attended the Democratic National Convention as a supporter of the leftist-racist Mississippi Freedom Democratic Party. In 1965, he participated in the racist demonstrations and marches in Selma, Alabama. He has been affiliated with the ultra-leftist American Civil Liberties Union; the leftist American Committee on Africa; the leftist-racist Black United Front; the Student Mobilization Committee to End the War in Vietnam, which is dominated by Communists and fellow travelers; the Committee of National Inquiry, a black leftist political group; the leftist-pacifist National Council to Repeal the Draft; the leftist-oriented National Religious Committee Opposing ABM; and the ultra-leftist National Peace Action Coalition.

In 1968, the District of Columbia Democratic delegates were originally pledged to support the presidential candidacy of Robert F. Kennedy. After Kennedy's death, the delegation went to the Democratic National Convention in support of Phillips as a favorite-son candidate. During the proceedings of the convention, Phillips became the favorite-son candidate of the Black Caucus and received 67½ votes for the presidential nomination. After the convention, Phillips granted an exclusive interview to the Communist Party's *Daily World.* He talked about his nomination and explained: "We meant it to be more than symbolic. When it started out as a favorite-son move from Washington, D.C., it was symbolic but then the black caucus was organized and it went beyond that. It was a way of rallying Negroes into a bloc, just like the labor bloc or the southern bloc. We think it can be demonstrated that this bloc has the power to grant or deny an election. This is the power of the swing vote. Hopefully, we will be in a position to negotiate with others whose interests are compatible with ours to form a coalition. But before that can happen I think there must be a pretty honest examination by these other forces of where they are headed, how seriously they take the political movement." Phillips was rather critical of some who were carrying the banner of "New Politics." He reflected: "People want to punish the Democratic Party. I thought the convention was very oppressive to the spirit. But it is interesting to note that all the protest was directed at the Democratic Party, while most have given up on the Republican Party. The reason for this concentration of protest on the Democratic Party is that people still have hope for a change in the Democratic Party." For his part, Phillips with some misgivings supported the Democratic presidential candidate Hubert H. Humphrey, whom Phillips described as the candidate most likely to be responsive to pressure for radical changes on behalf of the poor.

As the first black man ever to receive votes for a presidential nomination by either major party, Phillips was lionized by the liberal media. However, in the summer of 1968, Phillips had suffered some loss of popularity as a result of an incident involving two white policemen who were shot – one fatally. Three citizens were charged with homicide. The Black United Front unanimously adopted a resolution which had been drafted by Phillips. It "resolved that: The methods of self-defense by the family charged with the alleged slaying of the honky cop is justifiable homicide, in the same sense police are allowed to kill black people and call it justifiable homicide." Phillips later enlarged upon the resolution and charged that the police were a "colonial" force in the black community.

In April 1969, Phillips, in an address to Georgetown University students, warned – or threatened – that violence from ghetto-based Negroes was inevitable in Washington, but that it could be constructive if it were directed to areas of the city, such as Georgetown, "where the decision-makers live." Phillips denied that he condoned violence and insisted that he only wanted to channel the anger of frustrated Negroes to make it effective. Less than a month later, at a World Council of Churches meeting in London, he was harshly critical of the "capitalist system" and said that the Christian Church should aid and abet the only power available to oppressed blacks – the power of violence.

CHRISTOPHER H. PHILLIPS was born on December 6, 1920 in The Hague, Holland, son of American citizens Caroline Drayton and William Phillips. He married Mabel Olsen. He is an alumnus of Harvard University (A.B., 1943).

In 1947 and 1948, Phillips was a reporter for the *Beverly* [Mass.] *Evening Times.* From 1949 until 1953, he was a member of the Massachusetts Senate. From 1953 until 1957, he was with the Department of State as a deputy assistant secretary for international organization affairs and as a special assistant to the assistant secretary for United Nations affairs. In 1957 and 1958, he was a U.S. Civil Service Commissioner and vice chairman of the U.S. Civil Service Commission. From 1958 until 1961, he was a U.S. representative to UNESCO. From 1961 until 1965, he was with the Chase Manhattan Bank as its representative to the United Nations and as manager of the bank's Canadian division. From 1965 until 1969, he was president of the U.S. council of the International Chamber of Commerce. Since 1969, he has served as the U.S. deputy representative to the United Nations Security Council with the rank of ambassador. In 1952 and 1960, he was a delegate to the Republican National Convention.

Phillips is a member of the Council on Foreign Relations, the informal supra-State Department of the United States. He has served as director of the leftist-oriented United States Committee for UNICEF. He is a member of the United

549

Nations Association of the United States, the most prestigious leftwing propaganda agency for the UN in this country. He is a member of the leftist Republicans for Progress.

GERARD PIEL was born on March 1, 1915 in Woodmere, New York, son of Loretto Scott and William Piel. He was married to the late Mary Bird. He is married to Eleanor Jackson. He is an alumnus of Harvard University (A.B., 1937). He is the author of *Science in the Cause of Man* (1961).

From 1938 until 1940, Piel was an office boy at Time, Inc. From 1940 until 1945, he was science editor of *Life* magazine. From 1945 until 1946, he was assistant to the president of the Henry J. Kaiser Company. In 1947, along with Dennis Flanagan and Donald H. Miller Jr., Piel organized a management partnership. In 1948, the partners purchased *Scientific American.* They were financed by Lessing Rosenwald of Sears, Roebuck; John Hay Whitney; Frasier McCann of the Woolworth fortune; Bernard Baruch; Gerard Swope of General Electric; and Royal Little of Textron.

Since 1948, Piel has been the publisher of *Scientific American*, and the magazine has been notorious as a forum for the most extreme leftists in the scientific community. It has been a paramount feature of Piel's policy to downgrade the need for secrecy in scientific work conducted under the auspices of the federal government's defense and security programs. He has consistently opposed what he calls "the fallacy of national security through secrecy" and he has insisted that enemy scientists will ultimately discover anything that American scientists discover. In a 1958 address before a gathering of the ultra-radical Americans for Democratic Action, he said: "In our

obsession with secrecy during the past fifteen years we have surely disrupted the work of American scientists but we have not prevented scientists in other countries from discovering the secrets we were trying to hide." At no time did Piel encourage better and more efficient counter-espionage measures to prevent the leakage of secrets. As a matter of fact, Piel and his *Scientific American* have been very strong supporters of Pugwash Conferences and other international meetings of American and Red-bloc scientists, at which secrecy is practically non-existent.

Piel is a member of the Council on Foreign Relations, the informal supra-State Department of the United States. He has been a long-time official of the ultra-leftist American Civil Liberties Union. He has served on the executive committee of the leftist-oriented National Citizens Committee Concerned About Deployment of the ABM. He has served as a trustee of the Institute for Policy Studies, which is nothing less than a leftist propaganda agency for disarmament. He is a member of the leftist-pacifist Business Executives Move for Peace in Vietnam.

ALAN J. PIFER was born on May 4, 1921 in Boston, Massachusetts, son of Elizabeth Parrish and Claude Pifer. He married Erica Pringle. He is an alumnus of Harvard University (B.A., 1947). In 1947 and 1948, he studied at Emmanuel College of Cambridge University in England as Lionel de Jersey fellow from Harvard.

From 1948 until 1953, Pifer was executive secretary of the United States Educational Commission in the United Kingdom, administering the Fulbright program of fellowships and educational exchanges. Since 1953, he has been with the Carnegie Corporation, one of the world's wealthiest and most influential centers of leftist-pacifist endeavors. Within the Carnegie complex, Pifer has served successively in the Carnegie Corporation as executive assistant (1953-1957), executive associate (1957-1963), vice-president (1963-1965), acting president (1965-1967), and president (1967 to the present); and in the Carnegie Foundation for the Advancement of Teaching as vice-president (1963-1965), acting president (1965-1967), and president (1967 to the present). Under Pifer's leadership, the Carnegie Corporation has placed its well-financed leftist imprint upon educational television. Pifer appointed the well-known leftist Clark Kerr to head a Carnegie commission to "study" the future of higher education, a thinly-veiled ploy by Pifer to recommend federal planning and federal financing as a means of controlling the nation's institutions of higher learning.

While serving as a top official of the Carnegie Corporation, Pifer has been a consultant and adviser to the Department of Health, Education and Welfare, the Department of State, the U.S. Office of Education, and UNESCO. He has long been a trustee of the leftist African-American Institute. He is a member of the Council on Foreign Relations, the informal supra-State Department of the United States.

JOHN N. PLANK was born on July 22, 1923 in Dayton, Ohio, son of Grace Ganssle and Laurance Plank. He married Eleanor Bent. He is an alumnus of Harvard University (A.B., 1949; Ph.D., 1959) and Haverford College (M.A., 1953). He is the editor of *Cuba and the United States: Long Range Perspectives* (1967).

In 1953 and 1954, Plank was director of a project for community development in El Salvador for the leftist-pacifist American Friends Service Committee. From 1955 until 1963, he was at Harvard University as a teaching fellow in government (1955-1958), a Doherty fellow (1957-1958), an instructor in government (1959-1961), an assistant professor (1961-1962), a Bliss fellow (1960-1961), a visiting professor (1962), and a research associate in the Center for International Affairs (1959-1963). In 1959, he was a visiting assistant professor in government at Northwestern University. In 1962 and 1963, he was a professor of Latin American affairs at the Fletcher School of Law and Diplomacy at Tufts University. In 1963 and 1964, he was director of the Office of Research and Analysis for the American Republics in the Department of State's Bureau of Intelligence and Research. Since 1964, he has been a senior fellow in foreign political studies at the Brookings Institution. Since 1959, he has served as a consultant to various foundations, associations, and government agencies.

Plank is a long-time nonresident member of the Council on Foreign Relations, the informal supra-State Department of the United States. He is a long-time member of the leftist-pacifist American Friends Service Committee. He has been a long-time member of the leftist-oriented Inter-American Association for Democracy and Freedom.

E[MIL] RAYMOND PLATIG was born on March 29, 1924 in Clayton, New Jersey, son of Freda Schuman and Raymond Platig. He married Miriam Philips. He is an alumnus of Albion College (A.B., 1948); Emory University (M.A., 1949); and the University of

Chicago (Ph.D., 1957). He is the author of *Our American Foreign Policy* (1956); *The United States and World Affairs* (1965); *International Relations Research: Problems of Evaluation and Advancement* (1967); and *The United States and the Soviet Challenge* (1967).

From 1949 until 1951, Platig was an instructor in history at Millsaps College. In 1951 and 1952, he was at the University of Chicago, holding a faculty fellowship from the socialistic Ford Foundation's Fund for the Advancement of Education. From 1953 until 1961, he was at the University of Denver, serving successively as an assistant professor and associate professor of international relations. In 1956 and 1957, and 1960 and 1961, he held grants from the Rockefeller Foundation, a pillar of the leftist-liberal Establishment. From 1961 until 1966, he was director of studies for the Carnegie Endowment for International Peace, which has long labored to subvert America's nationalist interests in favor of a collectivist one-world. Since 1966, he has been with the Department of State as director of the Office of External Research. He is a nonresident member of the Council on Foreign Relations, the informal supra-State Department of the United States. Since 1966, he has been on the leftist-oriented advisory committee on international affairs of the United Presbyterian Church.

T[HOMAS] ALEXANDER POND was born on December 4, 1924 in Los Angeles, son of Florence Alexander and Arthur Pond. He married Barbara Newman. He is an alumnus of Princeton University (A.B., 1947; A.M., 1949; Ph.D., 1953).

From 1951 until 1953, Pond was an instructor in physics at Princeton University. From 1953 until 1962, he was at Washington University in St. Louis, serving successively as assistant professor and associate professor of physics. Since 1962, he has been at the State University of New York at Stony Brook as professor of physics (1962 to the present), chairman of the physics department (1962-1967), and executive vice-president (1968 to the present).

From 1949 until 1951, Pond was secretary of the leftist-oriented Scientists Committee on Loyalty and Security Problems. From 1960 until 1962, he was a member of the Scientific Advisory Committee of the leftist-oriented Greater St. Louis Committee on Nuclear Information. He is a member of the Federation of American Scientists, a bleeding heart group, members of which are generally affiliated with a variety of radical one-world and/or pacifist organizations.

CHARLES O. PORTER was born on April 4, 1919 in Klamath Falls, Oregon, son of Ruth Peterson and Frank Porter. He married Priscilla Galassi. He is an alumnus of Harvard University (B.S., 1941; LL.B., 1947). In 1948, he was admitted to the Oregon bar. He is co-author of *The American Lawyer* (1954) and *The Struggle for Democracy In Latin America* (1961).

In 1947 and 1948, Porter was a law clerk in the United States Court of Appeals at San Francisco. From 1948 until 1951, he was assistant to the director of the American Bar Association's Survey of the Legal Profession. From 1951 until 1956, he practiced law in Eugene, Oregon. From 1957 until 1961, he served in the U.S. House of Representatives. In 1961, he served as a White House consultant in the Food-for-Peace program. Since 1961, he has practiced law in Eugene. In 1960, 1964, and

1968, he was a delegate-at-large from Oregon to the Democratic National Conventions. In 1966, he was unsuccessful in his attempt to regain a seat in the Congress. He was supported in his campaign by the National Conference for New Politics, a classic united front third-party movement largely controlled by the Communist Party. In 1968, he was the Oregon chairman of Democrats working to promote a presidential-vice-presidential ticket of Robert F. Kennedy and J. William Fulbright.

During Porter's four years in the Congress of the United States, he became notorious for his persistent advocacy of United States support of any and all leftist and socialist regimes throughout Latin America. Fidel Castro was an especial favorite of Porter, who described Castro as a champion of a people's revolution. Five months after Castro's Communist takeover of Cuba, Porter wrote to a congressional colleague: "No one in the State Department believes Castro is a Communist, or a Communist sympathizer, nor does any other responsible person who wants to get his facts straight." Porter's role as a stooge and apologist for Castro was the main factor in his failure to obtain a third term in the House of Representatives in the election of 1960. His defeat, however, did not discourage him from further pro-Castro blatancy. In December 1960 and January 1961, he urged the United States to cede its Guantanamo Naval Base to the dictatorship of Communist Cuba. In 1961, he collaborated with the leftist Robert J. Alexander in writing *The Struggle for Democracy in Latin America*, a paean to Castro and other Communists and Socialists on the Latin American scene. And in 1963, he went to Castro's Cuba on assignment from *Look* magazine, a publication which paid periodic tribute to Cuba's Communist regime.

It was also during Porter's congressional years that he became preoccupied with Red China. In 1959, he applied to the Department of State for permission to visit Red China, asserting: "A member of Congress has a right to go anywhere in the world to do his duty as a U.S. legislator as he sees it, except in time of war or emergency. Any other policy would seem to be an unconstitutional breach of the separation of powers." Porter's application for a passport was denied and he failed to get relief from the decision in the U.S. District Court of Appeals. In a speech on the floor of the House, Porter made it clear that his planned visit to Red China was for the purpose of promoting trade relations between the United States and Mao Tse-tung's barbaric regime.

In 1963, Porter returned to his prepossession with Red China. He organized the Committee for a Review of Our China Policy with the purpose of sponsoring an American trade delegation to a Red Chinese trade fair which was scheduled to be held in Canton in October 1963. Porter hoped that such a move would result in the opening of trade relations between the United States and Red China. In an effort to promote his proposal, Porter addressed the World Trade Association of the San Francisco Chamber of Commerce. He told his audience: "We're trading with every Communist nation in the world, except China and Cuba. There isn't any opposition to what we want to do. What stops people is the political fear that a cry of 'soft on Cuba' would be followed by a cry of 'soft on China.' " Porter's audience was cool toward his proposals and no trade mission went to Red China at that time. Later he admitted: "My own

553

liberal tendencies were too much for the people involved." As recently as the spring and summer of 1971, Porter attempted to promote a visit to Red China by a delegation of 250 American men and women as a means of opening up U.S.-Red China trade. He was joined in his 1971 effort by such notable leftists as ex-Senator Wayne Morse of Oregon, ex-Senator Ernest Gruening of Alaska, and Columbia University professor O. Edmund Clubb, one of the earliest members of the Red China lobby.

Porter's adherence to the Left has also been marked by his vigorous opposition to the House Committee on Un-American Activities. He became an early member of the National Committee to Abolish the House Un-American Activities Committee, which was established in the summer of 1960 "to lead and direct the Communist Party's 'Operation Abolition' campaign," and which within a year of its inception had seven of its national leaders identified under oath as Communists. On November 14, 1964, the *People's World*, the west coast daily of the Communist Party, noted with approval that Porter had become the founder and chairman of an Oregon Ad Hoc Committee to Abolish HUAC. The Communists' obvious delight with Porter's work was evident when they printed his group's mailing address along with mention that contributions were being sought.

In his other leftist activities, Porter has been affiliated with the leftist-globalist World Parliament Association; the leftist-oriented Public Affairs Institute; and the leftist American Committee on Africa. He was a member of the Norman Thomas 80th Birthday Anniversary Committee, an ultra-leftist group that paid tribute to the patriarch of the Socialist Party.

On the matter of the Vietnam War, Porter's leftist stance was perhaps best expressed in a letter he wrote to the *Washington Post* in 1966. He said: "It is high time that the President and the Congress moved to eliminate war profiteering here at home and not just in Saigon. The sacrifices in blood by our young men in Vietnam must, at the very least, be matched by sacrifices in treasure by Americans, young and old, at home. Whether you believe, as I do, that this is an illegal, unconstitutional and immoral war, you should agree with me that profits at home in the United States should not be tied to a larger and longer war in Asia. No one should have a selfish stake in extending the conflict in time or space.

" 'Peace scares' cause momentary sags in the stock market. This is wrong. Appropriate legislative steps should be taken immediately to establish bodies like the World War II Renegotiation Board to tax away all war profits. If our sons can be sent to battle to be wounded or to die, the folks at home can forego enriching themselves. Besides, the Great Society domestic program for education, conservation, pollution control and the war against poverty needs these funds. To keep faith with our servicemen, the President should take immediate steps, by executive order and through the Congress, to eliminate the profits from this and every war."

KEITH R. PORTER was born on June 11, 1912 in Yarmouth, Nova Scotia, son of Josephine Roberts and Aaron Porter. He married Elizabeth Lingley. He is an alumnus of Acadia University (B.S., 1934) and Harvard University (A.M., 1935; Ph.D., 1938).

In 1938 and 1939, Porter was a National Research Council fellow at

Princeton University. From 1939 until 1961, he was with the Rockefeller Institute as a research assistant (1939-1945), associate (1945-1950), associate member (1950-1956), and member (1956-1961). From 1961 until 1969, he was a professor of biology at Harvard University. Since 1969, he has been chairman of the molecular, cellular, and developmental biology department at the University of Colorado.

Porter is a member of the Federation of American Scientists, a bleeding heart group, members of which are affiliated with a variety of radical one-world and/or pacifist organizations.

KENNETH W. PORTER was born on February 17, 1905 in Sterling, Kansas, son of Catherine Wiggins and Ellis Porter. He married Georgina MacDonald. He is an alumnus of Sterling College of Kansas (A.B., 1926); the University of Minnesota (M.A., 1927); and Harvard University (Ph.D., 1936). He is the author of *John Jacob Astor: Business Man* (1931); *Relations Between Negroes and Indians Within the Present Limits of the United States* (1933); *Pilate before Jesus, and Other Biblical and Legendary Poems* (1936); *The Jacksons and the Lees: Two Generations of Massachusetts Merchants, 1765-1844* (1937); *The High Plains: Poems* (1938); *No Rain from These Clouds: Poems, 1927-1945* (1946); and *The Negro on the Frontier* (1969). He is a co-author of *Christ in the Breadline: Poems for Christmas, Lent and Other Holy Days* (1932 and 1933) and *A History of Humble Oil and Refining Company: A Study in Industrial Growth* (1959). He has contributed to *Dictionary of American Biography, Dictionary of American History, American Oxford Encyclopedia, New Century Cyclopedia of*

Names, and *World Book Encyclopedia.*

In 1926 and 1927, Porter was an assistant in the history department at the University of Minnesota. From 1927 until 1931, and from 1934 until 1936, he was a research assistant in business history at Harvard University's Graduate School of Business Administration. From 1936 until 1938, he was an assistant professor of history and political science at Southwestern College in Kansas. From 1938 until 1948, he was at Vassar College as an instructor of history (1938-1942) and assistant professor (1942-1948). From 1948 until 1951, he was a research associate and special director of research at the Business History Foundation in Houston, Texas. In 1951 and 1952, he was a visiting professor at the University of Oregon. In 1952 and 1953, he returned to his positions at the Business History Foundation in Houston. In 1954, he was a Fulbright lecturer at the University of Melbourne in Australia. In 1955, he was a senior associate at the Business History Foundation in Cambridge, Massachusetts. From 1955 until 1958, he was a professor of history at the University of Illinois. Since 1958, he has been a professor of history at the University of Oregon.

Porter is a Socialist. He is a member of the Socialist League for Industrial Democracy and the ultra-leftist American Civil Liberties Union, and is affiliated with the leftist-oriented American Association of University Professors.

ROBERT O. PREYER was born on November 11, 1922 in Greensboro, North Carolina, son of Mary Richardson and William Preyer. He has been married to and divorced from Renée Haenel. He is married to Kathryn Turner. He is an alumnus of Princeton University (A.B.,

1945) and Columbia University (M.A., 1948; Ph.D., 1954). He is the author of *Bentham, Coleridge and the Science of History* (1958). He is a co-author, and the editor, of *Victorian Literature* (1966).

From 1948 until 1953, Preyer was an instructor at Smith College. Since 1954, he has been at Brandeis University as assistant professor (1954-1958) and associate professor (1958-1963) of English, and professor of English and chairman of the department of English and American literature (1963 to the present). In 1951 and 1952, he was a visiting instructor at Amherst College. In 1956 and 1957, he was a visiting professor at Freiburg University in Germany.

Preyer has been a member of the National Committee to Abolish the House Un-American Activities Committee ("to lead and direct the Communist Party's 'Operation Abolition' campaign"). He is a member of the ultra-leftist American Civil Liberties Union and the National Association for the Advancement of Colored People, the fountainhead of Negro agitation for more than half a century.

DON K. PRICE was born on January 23, 1910 in Middlesboro, Kentucky, son of Nell Rhorer and Don Price. He married Margaret Gailbreath. He is an alumnus of Vanderbilt University (A.B., 1931) and Oxford University (B.A., 1934; B. Litt., 1935). He is the author of *Government and Science* (1954) and *The Scientific Estate* (1965). He is editor and co-author of *The Secretary of State* (1960). He is a contributor to *City Manager Government in the United States* (1940); *United States Foreign Policy: Its Organization and Control* (1952); and *The Political Economy of American Foreign Policy* (1955).

From 1930 until 1932, Price was a reporter and editor with the *Nashville Evening Tennessean.* From 1932 until 1935, he was a Rhodes scholar at Oxford University. From 1935 until 1937, he was a research assistant with the Home Owners Loan Corporation. From 1937 until 1939, he was a staff member of the leftist-oriented Social Science Research Council. (He has been on the board of directors of the SSRC from 1949 until 1952 and from 1963 to the present.) Intermittently from 1939 until 1953, he was with the leftist-oriented Public Administration Clearing House as an editorial assistant and writer (1939-1941), assistant director (1941-1943), and associate director (1946-1953). In 1945 and 1946, he worked for the U.S. Bureau of the Budget, and in 1947 and 1948, for the Hoover Commission on the Organization of the Executive Branch of the Government. In 1952 and 1953, he was deputy chairman of the Research and Development Board of the Department of Defense. From 1946 until 1953, he lectured on political science at the University of Chicago, and in 1953, at New York University. From 1953 until 1958, he was with the socialistic Ford Foundation as associate director (1953-1954) and vice-president (1954-1958). Since 1958, he has been at Harvard University's Graduate School of Public Administration (renamed in 1966 the John Fitzgerald Kennedy School of Government) as professor of government and dean. From 1959 until 1961, he was a consultant to President Dwight Eisenhower. From 1961 until 1963, he was a special adviser to John F. Kennedy. From 1963 until 1969, he was a consultant to President Lyndon B. Johnson.

Price has been a long-time nonresident member of the Council on Foreign Relations, the informal supra-State Department of the United States. In 1967 and 1968, he was president of the leftist-oriented American Association for the Advancement of Science. He has been a trustee of the leftist-pacifist Carnegie Endowment for International Peace. He has been a trustee of the RAND Corporation, one of the Establishment's most important think factories. He is a long-time member of the board of trustees of the Twentieth Century Fund, which in its half-century history has been a financial boon to leftwing researchers in the fields of economics, political science, and sociology. He was a member of the National Council for Civic Responsibility, an election year's drive in 1964 by the Democratic Party against anti-Communists.

ORESTE PUCCIANI was born on April 7, 1916 in Cleveland, Ohio, son of Eugenie Williams and Ettore Pucciani. He is an alumnus of Western Reserve University (B.A., 1939) and Harvard University (M.A., 1940; Ph.D., 1943). He is the author of *The French Theatre Since 1930* (1954). He is the translator of Racine's *Phaedra* (1961). He is co-author of *Langue et Langage* (1967); *Langue et Langage: le manuel du professeur* (1967); and *Langue et Langage au Laboratoire* (1967).

From 1943 until 1948, Pucciani was at Harvard University as an instructor in Romance languages. In 1946 and 1947, he was in France and Italy as a Sheldon traveling fellow from Harvard University. Since 1948, he has been at the University of California at Los Angeles as assistant professor (1948-1954), associate professor (1954-1960), and professor (1960 to the present) of French, and chairman of the French department (1961-1966). He is a member of the leftist-oriented American Association of University Professors. He was a member of the National Committee to Abolish the House Un-American Activities Committee ("to lead and direct the Communist Party's 'Operation Abolition' campaign").

LUCIAN W. PYE was born on October 21, 1921 in Shansi Province, China, son of American citizens Gertrude Chaney and Watts Pye. He married Mary Waddill. He is an alumnus of Carleton College (B.A., 1943) and Yale University (M.A., 1949; Ph.D., 1951). He is the author of *Guerrilla Communism in Malaya* (1956); *Politics, Personality and Nation-Building: Burma's Search for Identity* (1962); *Aspects of Political Development* (1966); *Southeast Asia's Political Systems* (1967); and *The Spirit of Chinese Politics: A Psychocultural Study of the Authority Crisis in Political Development* (1968). He is the editor of *Communications and Political Development* (1963). He is co-editor and a contributor to *Political Culture and Political Development* (1965). He is a contributor to *Nationalism and Progress in Free Asia* (1956); *The Politics of the Developing Areas* (1960); *The Emerging Nations* (1961); *Political Decision-Makers* (1961); *The Role of the Military in Underdeveloped Countries* (1962); *The New Nations: The Problem of Political Development* (1963); *Federalism in the Commonwealth* (1963); *Studying Politics Abroad* (1964); *The Internal War* (1964); *World Pressures on American Foreign Policies* (1964); *Foreign Policy in the Sixties* (1965); *Political Parties and Political Development* (1966); *Modernization: The Dynamics of Growth* (1966); *Communication and Change in the Developing Countries* (1966); *Contemporary Political Science* (1967); and *Post-Primary Education and Politi-*

QUIGG

cal and Economic Development (1969).

From 1949 until 1952, Pye was at Washington University in St. Louis as an instructor (1949-1951) and assistant professor (1951-1952) of political science. In 1951 and 1952, he was a research associate in international relations at Yale University. From 1952 until 1956, he was a research associate at Princeton University's Center for International Studies. In 1956, he was a visiting lecturer at Columbia University. Since 1956, he has been at Massachusetts Institute of Technology as assistant professor (1956-1957), associate professor (1957-1960), and professor (1960 to the present) of political science, and as senior staff member at the Center for International Studies, which is subsidized by the Central Intelligence Agency (1956 to the present). In 1959 and 1960, he was a visiting associate professor at Yale University. Since 1963, he has been chairman of the committee on comparative politics of the leftist-oriented Social Science Research Council. Since 1961, he has been an adviser to the Department of State's Agency for International Development. In 1963, he was a fellow at the Center for Advanced Study in the Behavioral Sciences.

Pye is a long-time nonresident member of the Council on Foreign Relations, the informal supra-State Department of the United States. He has long been affiliated with the United Nations Association of the United States, the most prestigious leftwing propaganda agency for the UN in this country. In 1966, as a member of the UN Association's panel on Red China, he recommended membership in the United Nations for Mao Tse-tung's regime. He has been a member of American Friends of Vietnam, a front of the Socialist-lined International Rescue Committee.

PHILIP W. QUIGG was born on October 30, 1920 in New York City, son of Eleanor Wisner and Murray Quigg. He is an alumnus of Princeton University (A.B., 1943). He is the editor of *Africa: A Foreign Affairs Reader* (1964).

In 1946 and 1947, Quigg was a reporter for the Macy newspapers in Westchester County, New York. From 1947 until 1955, he was at Princeton University as editorial administrator (1947-1951) and editor (1951-1955) of the *Princeton Alumni Weekly*. Since 1955, he has been editor of *Foreign Affairs*, the quarterly journal of the Council on Foreign Relations, the informal supra-State Department of the United States. He is a member of the CFR.

VICTOR RABINOWITZ was born on July 2, 1911 in Brooklyn. He is an alumnus of the University of Michigan (A.B., 1931; LL.B., 1934). In 1935, he was admitted to the New York bar and was subsequently admitted to the bar of the United States Supreme Court and other federal court bars. Since 1935, he has practiced law in New York City.

In 1951, 1955, and 1960, Rabinowitz testified before the Senate Internal Security Subcommittee, and on every occasion when he was asked about his affiliations with and membership in the Communist Party he invoked the Fifth Amendment in refusing to answer. He and his legal partners have had as clients a long succession of Communist and/or Soviet agents and/or fellow-travelers, including Frederick Vanderbilt Field, Steve Nelson, Dashiell Hammett, Alpheus Hunton, W.L. Ullman, Joanne Grant, Judith Coplon, and Paul Robeson. They have defended the Communist government of Cuba; the Communist-dominated Distributive, Processing, and Office Workers of America; the Ameri-

558

can Communications Association; and the Federation of Architects, Engineers, Chemists and Technicians.

Since the founding of the National Lawyers Guild, Rabinowitz has been a member, and has served as an official in various capacities, including president, of the NLG ("the foremost legal bulwark of the Communist Party, its front organizations, and controlled unions"). He has served for many years as a top official of the Emergency Civil Liberties Committee ("Communist front" – "subversive"). In 1950, he signed an *amicus curiae* brief in behalf of eleven Communist leaders who were on trial at that time. In 1962, he supported the Communist-run World Youth Festival at Helsinki. He was an official of the subversive Fair Play for Cuba Committee, which was subsidized by Fidel Castro. He was an official of the Friends of British Guiana, a Communist Party operation on behalf of Cheddi Jagan. He wrote for the Communist weekly, *National Guardian.* He wrote for the Marxist-oriented *Studies on the Left*, a publication of Students for a Democratic Society.

Rabinowitz has been affiliated with the National Council of American-Soviet Friendship ("subversive and Communist" – "specializing in pro-Soviet propaganda"); the Jefferson School of Social Science ("adjunct of the Communist Party"); the International Workers Order ("subversive and Communist"); the Red-loaded International Committee to Defend Eldridge Cleaver; the Conference for Legislation in the National Interest ("Communist front"); the Red-loaded Steering Committee Against Repression; the Radical Education Project, an ultra-leftist program of the Students for a Democratic Society; the American Committee for Protection of Foreign Born [Americans] ("subversive and Commu-

nist"); the ultra-leftist National Peace Action Coalition; the ultra-radical Student Nonviolent Coordinating Committee; and the Aptheker Dinner Program Committee, a tribute to the American Institute for Marxist Studies and America's best-known Communist Party theoretician.

In recent years, Rabinowitz has been president of the Louis M. Rabinowitz Foundation, which has supported the Southern Conference for Human Welfare ("Communist front"); the ultra-radical Student Nonviolent Coordinating Committee; and the ultra-leftist Socialist Scholars Conferences. In 1967, the Rabinowitz Foundation subsidized *Where It's At*, by Jill Hamberg, Paul Boothe, Mimi Feingold, and Carl Wittman. The book, widely distributed by Students for a Democratic Society, the National Council of Churches' Department of Social Justice, and other radical groups, is a research guide for revolutionary community organizing.

FRANCIS B. RANDALL was born on December 17, 1931 in New York City, son of Mercedes Moritz and John Randall. He married Laura Rosenbaum. He is an alumnus of Amherst College (B.A., 1952); Columbia University (M.A., 1954; Ph.D., 1960). In 1952 and 1953, he held a fellowship from the American Council of Learned Societies. From 1954 until 1956, he held a fellowship from the ultra-leftist Ford Foundation. He is the author of *Stalin's Russia: An Historical Reconsideration* (1965) and *N.G. Chernyshevskii* (1967). He is co-author of *Essays in Russian and Soviet History* (1963). He is the editor of *Problems in Russian History* (1968).

From 1952 until 1954, Randall was a fellow at Amherst College. From 1956 until 1959, he was an instructor in history at Amherst College. From 1959 until 1961, he was at Columbia University as an instructor (1959-1960) and assistant professor (1961) of history. Since 1961, he has been a member of the social science faculty at Sarah Lawrence College. In 1965, he was a Fulbright fellow in India. In 1967 and 1968, he was a visiting professor at Columbia University.

Randall has described himself as a radical or revolutionary. In 1961, he was a so-called Freedom Rider. He has been affiliated with the leftist-oriented American Association of University Professors. He was a participant in Read-In for Peace in Vietnam, a leftist-pacifist program.

GUY H. RANER JR. was born on November 7, 1919 in Vicksburg, Mississippi, son of Caroline Campbell and Guy Raner. He married Jane Law. He is an alumnus of the University of Missouri (B.J., 1942) and the University of Southern California (M.A., 1956). He also studied at the University of Mississippi, the University of California at Los Angeles, and San Fernando Valley State College.

Since 1946, Raner has been a government and history teacher at Canoga Park High School in the Los Angeles school district. In 1968, he was an unsuccessful candidate for the California State Assembly. Since 1968, he has been a member of the California Democratic State Central Committee.

Raner is a member of the ultra-radical Americans for Democratic Action; the National Association for the Advancement of Colored People, the fountainhead of Negro agitation for more than half a century; and the United Nations Association for the United States, the most prestigious leftwing propaganda agency for the UN in this country.

ANATOL RAPOPORT was born on May 22, 1911 in Lozovaya, Russia, son of Adel Rapoport and Boris Rapoport. He came to the United States in 1922 and became a naturalized American citizen in 1928. He married Gwen Goodrich. He is an alumnus of the University of Chicago (Ph.D., 1941). He is the author of *Science and the Goals of Man* (1950); *Operational Philosophy* (1953); *Fights, Games, and Debates* (1960); *Strategy and Conscience* (1964); and *Two-Person Game Theory* (1966). He is co-author of *Prisoner's Dilemma: A Study in Conflict and Cooperation* (1965).

In 1946 and 1947, Rapoport was an instructor in mathematics at the Illinois Institute of Technology. From 1947 until 1954, he was an assistant professor of mathematical biology at the University of Chicago. In 1954 and 1955, he was an assistant professor at the Center for Advanced Study in Behavioral Sciences at Stanford University. Since 1955, he has been at the University of Michigan as a professor of mathematical biology and associate professor at the University's Mental Health Research Institute.

Rapoport has been affiliated with the ultra-leftist-pacifist National Committee for a Sane Nuclear Policy; the ultra-leftist Fort Hood Three Defense Committee; the National Committee to Secure Justice in the Rosenberg Case ("Communist front"); Honorary Sponsors of the Committee to Free Morton Sobell, a convicted atom spy; the leftist-pacifist Voters Peace Pledge; the leftist-oriented Ad Hoc Committee for an Open Letter on Vietnam; the leftist-pacifist Committee of Responsibility; the leftist-oriented

Inter-University Committee for Debate on Foreign Policy; the leftist-oriented Inter-University Committee for a Public Hearing on Vietnam; the Student Mobilization Committee to End the War in Vietnam, dominated by Communists and fellow-travelers; and the leftist-pacifist Federation of American Scientists. He sponsored the leftist-dominated March on Washington for Peace in Vietnam.

ANTON REFREGIER was born on March 20, 1905 in Moscow, Russia, son of Valentina Beserkirsky and Anton Refregier. He came to the United States in 1920 and became a naturalized American in 1930. He married Lila Kelly. He studied sculpture in Paris and painting in Munich. From 1920 until 1925, he studied at the Rhode Island School of Design.

Refregier has held visiting professorships at the University of Arkansas, Stanford University, the Cleveland School of Fine Arts, and Bard College. He has been a sculptor, painter, muralist, designer, and decorator. His art work has been done for private businesses, magazines, and U.S. postoffices. He has lectured, in recent years, in Stockholm, Moscow, Sofia, Berlin, and Bucharest.

Shortly after Refregier became an American citizen, he began his life-time association with the far Left in America and elsewhere. In 1932, he wrote a pamphlet, "Tom Mooney," for the International Labor Defense. The ILD "was the American section of the International Red Aid, which had its headquarters in Moscow and which was the parent organization of the various Communist defense organizations" and, essentially, "the legal defense arm of the Communist Party of the United States."

In 1965, Refregier's book *An Artist's Journey* was issued by International Publishers, an "official publishing house of the Communist Party in the United States" and a medium through which "extensive Soviet propaganda is subsidized in the United States."

In 1930, the year Refregier gained American citizenship, his name appeared on a list of persons affiliated with the John Reed Club who signed a protest against alleged anti-Communist propaganda (*New York Times*, May 19, 1930). The John Reed Clubs have been cited as organizations "whose affiliation with the Communist Party is clear beyond dispute."

In the Communist Party's *New Masses* (April 2, 1940), the name of Anton Refregier, mural painter, appeared on a letter to President Franklin Roosevelt protesting "the badgering of Communist leaders."

The name of Anton Refregier, mural painter, appeared on a list of persons requesting President Franklin Roosevelt to exert his influence to end an attack on the freedom of the press, with specific reference to *New Masses*. ("*New Masses*, a weekly publication, . . . was an officially controlled organ of the [Communist] Party which dealt principally with problems in the arts and sciences from the Party's point of view.")

In the Communist Party's *Daily Worker* (September 16, 1941) the signature of Anton Refregier, member of the United American Artists ("Communist front"), appeared on a letter to President Franklin Roosevelt urging help to the Soviet Union.

Refregier called for an American Artists Congress, which was cited as subversive by the California Committee on Un-American Activities.

Refregier sponsored the Artists' Front to Win the War, a "Communist front."

Refregier sponsored the American Peace Mobilization, "formed in the summer of 1940 under the auspices of the Communist Party and the Young Communist League as a 'front' organization designed to mold American opinion against participation in the war against Germany."

Refregier has been a sponsor of the National Council of American-Soviet Friendship ("subversive and Communist" – "specializing in pro-Soviet propaganda").

On June 17, 1941, Refregier contributed to a book of drawings, *Winter Soldiers*, in defense of certain Communist teachers. In 1959, he collaborated with old-time Communist Walter Lowenfels in *Song of Peace*, published by Roving Eye Press.

In May 1965, Refregier returned to the United States from a visit to the Soviet Union and the Communist satellites in East Europe. The Communist Party's *Worker* (May 18, 1965) announced that he was to speak about his journey at the Philadelphia Social Science Forum, an adjunct of the Philadelphia School of Social Science and Art ("subversive").

Refregier was a sponsor of the leftist-oriented National Teach-In on the Vietnam War. He is a member of the Soviet-controlled World Peace Council, sponsor of the anti-American World Peace Conferences.

OSCAR K. RICE was born on February 12, 1903 in Chicago, son of Thekla Knefler and Oscar Rice. He married Hope Sherfy. He is an alumnus of the University of California (B.S., 1924; Ph.D., 1926). From 1927 until 1929, he was a National Research Council fellow at the California Institute of Technology. In 1929 and 1930, he was a research fellow at the University of Leipzig. He is the author of *Electronic Structure and Chemical Binding* (1940) and *Statistical Mechanics, Thermodynamics and Kinetics* (1967).

In 1926 and 1927, Rice was an associate in chemistry, and in 1935 and 1936, a research associate in chemistry, at the University of California. From 1930 until 1935, he was an instructor in chemistry at Harvard University. Since 1936, he has been at the University of North Carolina as associate professor (1936-1943), professor (1943-1959), and Kenan professor (1959 to the present) of chemistry. In 1946 and 1947, he was the principal chemist at Clinton Laboratories, Oakridge, Tennessee. In 1957, he was the Reilly lecturer in chemistry at the University of Notre Dame.

Rice has been affiliated with the National Committee to Abolish the House Un-American Activities Committee ("to lead and direct the Communist Party's 'Operation Abolition' campaign"); the ultra-leftist American Civil Liberties Union; the National Committee to Secure Justice in the Rosenberg Case ("Communist front"); and the leftist-pacifist Federation of American Scientists.

MILDRED ROBBINS was born on August 9, 1922 in New York City, daughter of Isabella Zeitz and Samuel Elowsky. She married Louis Robbins. She is an alumna of New York University (B.A., 1942).

Since 1957, Mrs. Robbins has been with the leftist-oriented National Council of Women of the United States as representative at the United Nations (1957-1964), first vice-president (1959-1964), president (1964-1968), and honorary president (1968 to the present). Since 1961, she has been with the leftist-oriented U.S. National Organizations at the UN as secretary and vice-president of the conference group (1961-1964), vice-chairman and secretary (1962-1964), chairman of the hospitality and information service (1960-1966), and member of the executive committee (1961 to the present). Since 1960, she has been on the executive committee of the leftist-oriented International Council of Women. Since 1967, she has been a member of the women's advisory committee on poverty of the Office of Economic Opportunity. In 1956, she was co-chairman of Volunteers for Adlai Stevenson in New York City. Since 1969, she has been vice-chairman of the task force of the National Democratic Committee.

Mrs. Robbins has been affiliated with the leftist-internationalist Internal Movement for Atlantic Union; the National Council for Civic Responsibility, an election year's drive in 1964 by the Democratic Party against anti-Communists; and the United Nations Association of the United States, the most prestigious leftwing propaganda agency for the UN in this country.

JOSEPH W. ROBINSON was born on June 16, 1908 in St. Paul, Minnesota, son of Emma Weston and Joseph Robinson. He was married to the late Jeanne Keever. He is an alumnus of Stanford University (A.B., 1930; M.A., 1931; Ph.D., 1936). He also studied at Harvard University, the University of Wisconsin, the University of Chicago, and the University of California at Los Angeles. He is the author of *The Roots of International Organization* (1968). He is co-author of *Royal Commissions of Inquiry* (1937) and *General International Organization: A Source Book* (1956).

From 1932 until 1965, Robinson was

an instructor in government at Stanford University. In 1935, he was an instructor in government at the University of Idaho. From 1937 until 1947, he was at Purdue University as an instructor (1937-1939), assistant professor (1939-1942), associate professor (1942-1946), and professor (1946-1947) of government. Since 1947, he has been at Whittier College as professor of political science and chairman of the department of political science and international relations. In 1970, he was director of Whittier College in Copenhagen. Since 1950, he has been a member of the executive committee of the University of Southern California's Institute of World Affairs. In 1964 and 1968, he was a visiting professor at the University of Southern California. Since 1961, he has been an instructor at the University of California Extension.

Robinson is a long-time nonresident member of the Council on Foreign Relations, the informal supra-State Department of the United States. He has been a member of the leftist American Association for the United Nations. He has been a member of the leftist-pacifist Commission to Study the Organization of Peace, the research arm of the leftist-internationalist United Nations Association of the United States.

ARNOLD A. ROGOW was born on August 10, 1924 in Harrisburg, Pennsylvania, son of Mary Hilelson and Morris Rogow. He was married to and divorced from Kathleen Cremin. He is married to Patricia Evans. He is an alumnus of the University of Wisconsin (A.B., 1947) and Princeton University (A.M., 1950; Ph.D., 1953). In 1951 and 1952, he held a fellowship from the leftist-oriented Social Science Research Council. In 1954 and 1955, he held a fellowship from the leftist-oriented Center for Advanced Study in the Behavioral Sciences. In 1965 and 1966, he held a Guggenheim fellowship. He has also received research grants from the ultra-leftist Ford Foundation and its Fund for the Republic. He is the author of *The Labour Government and British Industry, 1945-1951* (1955) and *James Forrestal: A Study of Personality, Politics and Policy* (1964). He is the editor of *Government and Politics: A Reader* (1961) and *The Jew in a Gentile World: An Anthology of Writings About Jews, by Non-Jews* (1961). He is co-author of *Power, Corruption, and Rectitude* (1964).

From 1952 until 1958, Rogow was at the State University of Iowa as an instructor (1952-1954) and assistant professor (1955-1958) of political science. In 1958 and 1959, he was an assistant professor of political science at Haverford College. From 1959 until 1966, he was at Stanford University as an associate professor (1959-1964) and professor (1964-1966) of political science. Since 1966, he has been a graduate professor of political science at the City University of New York.

Rogow has been affiliated with the American Committee for Protection of Foreign Born [Americans] ("one of the oldest auxiliaries of the Communist Party in the United States") and the National Committee to Abolish the House Un-American Activities Committee ("to lead and direct the Communist Party's 'Operation Abolition' campaign"). He signed a Communist-supported petition on behalf of Carl Braden and Frank Wilkinson, who were imprisoned for contempt of Congress. He was a long-time member of the national council of the Emergency Civil Liberties Committee ("Communist front" – "subversive").

He petitioned President John F. Kennedy to pursue a hands-off policy vis-à-vis Communist Cuba.

Rogow's book on Forrestal (Secretary of Defense in the Truman Administration) was not so much a biography as it was a diatribe against an anti-Communist American patriot, whose plunge to death from a window at the Bethesda Naval Hospital indicated murder rather than suicide. Rogow's publishers came close to admitting his extreme bias against Forrestal when they wrote in the book's advertising material: "Besides recreating the man who was Forrestal, Arnold A. Rogow brings out into the open one of the most urgent questions of our troubled times: What can we do about men in positions of great power who crack under the stress of high office? A dedicated opponent of Communism, Forrestal distrusted Stalin and the Soviet system, even when under the pressures of 'peaceful coexistence' following World War II. His fight for . . . military preparedness often met with bitter opposition and malignant accusations. Why is it that men in high government office are not allowed to have mental illnesses? If those who worked with Forrestal knew he suffered from more than 'operational fatigue,' why was medical care withheld? What if the atom bomb should come into the hands of a madman? Arnold Rogow . . . captures the living suspense of a fantastic career – and poses a frightening question about the men who hold the reins of power."

In a review of Rogow's book in *National Review* (April 7, 1964), M. Stanton Evans made some pertinent observations concerning Rogow's excursion into psychoanalysis: "Rogow begins by noting the variant interpretations given Forrestal's death and the cloud of mystery within which they flourish. But he does nothing to dispel the confusion. Instead, he sets out to establish Forrestal's problem as one of mental illness, and to trace all his triumphs and failures to a common origin in his unhappy childhood. Forrestal's mother, we are told, was strict, domineering and a religious zealot. As any good Freudian knows, such a background was bound to make Forrestal 'insecure,' eager to prove his independence and his toughness. The problem is thus easily resolved, since Forrestal's drive for success, his fabulous endurance, his suspicion of Moscow and his ultimate collapse may all be referred unerringly to 'early psychic deprivation.'"

Mr. Evans cited a number of the Freudian clichés employed by Rogow: "Did Forrestal understand why he worked sixteen hours a day? . . . this fatal flaw in his personality . . . perhaps uncertain of his masculinity . . . to be militant was to be masculine . . . all his life Forrestal had difficulty relating to and accepting authority . . . a taut personality . . . ." But as Evans observed, Rogow offered "precious little evidence" that the clichés had a real basis in Forrestal's life.

For Rogow, the undeniable anti-Communism of Forrestal was proof positive that Forrestal was mentally ill. Rogow, the political scientist turned psychoanalyst, argued: "It is difficult to avoid the conclusion that Forrestal's personality needs and policy recommendations were closely related. The Cold War, no matter how inevitable, provided him with an arena for the play of transference and projection. Anxieties and insecurities, regardless of personal source, could become focused on Soviet behavior and be partially appeased by a stubborn insistence on a 'tough' foreign and military policy. Suspicions of all sorts readily attached themselves to real or alleged Communist conspiracies at home and abroad, and fear directed at the Soviet Union could appear to be wholly sane and rational. Until the last few months of his life, Forrestal could impress almost everyone as a 'reasonable' man because it was 'reasonable,' in the context of the Cold War, to feel anxious, insecure, suspicious, and fearful. Above all, it was 'reasonable' to appear 'tough,' to warn against compromises and concessions, and to talk of 'forcing the issue' and the necessity of 'showdown.'"

Mr. Evans observed: "In thus arguing Professor Rogow obviously follows the lead of such pioneers as the Overstreets, Richard Hofstadter, and the compilers of *The Authoritarian Personality*, who have made it their business to brand departures from Liberal orthodoxy as a sign of mental illness. But he has gone his predecessors one better by attaching the theory to a particular historical figure, a dangerous business even when the circumstances seem favorable. On the one hand, there is the juicy fact that Forrestal did suffer a mental breakdown; on the other, there is the embarrassment that all his suspicions about Communism have been vindicated by history. Professor Rogow avoids the difficulty by speaking of Communist machinations as if they were phenomena in Forrestal's mind rather than objective realities (while the names Laurence Duggan, Lauchlin Currie, and Harry Dexter White appear in the book, no mention is made of their identification as members of the Soviet *apparat* in the American government; Alger Hiss, a Forrestal contemporary in the New and Fair Deals who also made headlines in 1949, is not mentioned at all)."

Mr. Evans was one of the few reviewers who recognized that Rogow had oriented his book to "the lurid thesis of anti-Communism-as-sickness," and he concluded that "the real question to which Professor Rogow ought to have addressed himself is not why Forrestal perceived a danger which was there, but why so many other people did not perceive it – and apparently do not perceive it to this day."

THEODOR ROSEBURY was born on August 10, 1904 in London, England, son of Emily Dimesets and Aaron Rosebury. He is a naturalized American. He was married to Lily Aaronson. His second wife is Amy Loeb. He is an alumnus of the University of Pennsylvania (D.D.S., 1928). He also studied at the City College of New York, New York University, and Columbia University. He is the author of *Experimental Air-Borne Infection* (1947); *Peace or Pestilence* (1949); *Microorganisms Indigenous to Man* (1962); and *Life on Man* (1969). He is a contributor to *Agents of Disease and Host Resistance* (1935); *Dental Science and Dental Art* (1938); and *Bacterial and Mycotic Infections of Man* (1948-1965).

From 1930 until 1951, Rosebury was at Columbia University's College of Physicians and Surgeons as instructor (1930-1935), assistant professor (1935-1944), and associate professor of bacteriology (1944-1951). Since 1950, he has been at the School of Dentistry of Washington University in St. Louis as professor of bacteriology (1950-1967) and professor emeritus (1967 to the present). From 1943 until 1946, he was with the U.S. War Department as a civilian bacteriologist (1943-1945) and consultant (1945-1946).

On December 17, 1952, John D. Hickerson, Assistant Secretary of State for United Nations Affairs, testified be-

fore the Senate Internal Security Subcommittee and presented a list of forty individuals formerly "employed by the United Nations . . . [who were subject to adverse comment], on the grounds that the Department [of State] believed them to be Communists or under Communist discipline, with three on moral grounds." On this list was Theodor Rosebury, with the following comment by Mr. Hickerson: "(a) According to information supplied by the United Nations, he was employed by the United Nations in June 1950 and was terminated September 18, 1950. (b) His name was submitted on or about June 16, 1950. Adverse comment was made on or about August 23, 1950."

On March 24, 1952, the Senate Internal Security Subcommittee heard testimony from William B. Reed with regard to the subversive character of the American Association of Interns and Medical Students. Dr. Theodor Rosebury spoke at the convention of this organization held in Chicago in December 1947.

For a number of years, Rosebury held posts in the Communist-controlled American Association of Scientific Workers. He became a member of AASW in 1940. He was chairman of the New York branch of AASW from 1941 until 1944, president of the executive committee in 1944 and 1945, and national president from 1949 until 1952.

In 1946, 1947, 1948, and 1949, Rosebury was registered in New York City as a voter on the American Labor Party roster ("Communist dissimulation extends into the field of political parties forming political front organizations such as the . . . American Labor Party. The Communists are thus able to present their candidates for elective office under other than a straight Communist label").

ROSEN

According to the *New York Times* of August 8, 1955, Rosebury was the signer of a statement asking President Eisenhower to reconsider prosecution of alleged Communists under the Smith Act.

The *New York Herald Tribune* of March 12, 1948 stated that Theodor Rosebury, then associate professor of bacteriology at Columbia University, participated in a press conference and rally at the Hotel New Yorker in New York City on March 12, 1948, the purpose of which was to defend Dr. Edward U. Condon, former director of the National Bureau of Standards, who had been cited by the House Committee on Un-American Activities as "one of the weakest links in the forces protecting our atomic security."

The Communist Party's *Daily Worker* (January 19, 1948) carried the announcement that the Coordinating Committee on Civil Liberties had released a statement calling for the reinstatement of a New York school teacher who had been suspended because of his alleged Communist Party membership. Rosebury was listed as a signer of the statement.

The Communist Party's *Daily Worker* (December 10, 1951) carried an "Appeal for Amnesty," which was an appeal in behalf of Communist Party leaders who had been convicted under the Smith Act. Rosebury, then of Washington University, was listed as a signer.

Rosebury appeared as a sponsor of the Conference for Legislation in the National Interest, according to press releases of the organization, issued on March 28 and April 3, 1956. The CLNI was under "complete domination by the Communist Party." It was established early in 1956 and its "major function . . . was a conference at the Manhattan Center in New York on April 7, 1956, for the purpose of generating wide popular support for legislation endorsed by the [Communist] Party and its auxiliaries. Although the organizers of the conference stated that it would be concerned with 'civil rights, social security, health, education, labor, and civil liberties,' which it designated as 'the chief unresolved problems before Congress,' the conference concentrated most of its vigor against the Government's security program.' "

The Communist Party's *Daily Worker* (October 1, 1953) announced a list of "80 notables" who sponsored a conference called by the American Committee for Protection of Foreign Born [Americans] ("one of the oldest auxiliaries of the Communist Party in the United States") for repeal of the McCarran-Walter Act. Rosebury was on the left and he was also named on a letterhead of the ACPFB, dated July 20, 1956, as a sponsor.

Rosebury has been affiliated with the Cultural and Scientific Conference for World Peace ("a Communist front set up to mobilize American intellectuals in the field of arts, sciences and letters as a propaganda forum for Soviet foreign policy and Soviet culture"); the Jefferson School of Social Science ("adjunct of the Communist Party"); the Joint Anti-Fascist Refugee Committee ("subversive and Communist"); Progressive Citizens of America ("subversive"); the National Council of the Arts, Sciences and Professions ("a Communist front used to appeal to special occupational groups"); the leftist-oriented Physicians for Social Responsibility; the leftist-oriented National Teach-In on the Vietnam War; and *Soviet Russia Today* ("Communist-controlled publication").

SUMNER M. ROSEN was born on June 17, 1923 in Boston, Massachusetts.

He is an alumnus of Harvard University (A.B., *c.* 1948) and Massachusetts Institute of Technology (Ph.D., 1959). From 1954 until 1956, he held a fellowship from the ultra-leftist Ford Foundation. He is the co-author of *Labor in Developing Economies* (1962); *The Negro and the American Labor Movement* (1968); and *The Dissenting Academy* (1968).

From 1956 until 1960, Rosen was an assistant professor of economics at Northeastern University. In 1960 and 1961, he was a research associate in the industrial union department of the AFL-CIO. In 1961 and 1962, he was a research fellow at the Center for Middle East Studies at Harvard University. From 1962 until 1965, he was at Simmons College as an assistant professor (1962-1964) and associate professor (1964-1965) of economics. From 1965 until 1968, he was a director of education for the American Federation of State, County & Municipal Employees. Since 1968, he has been a research associate professor in the School of Education at New York University. In 1962, he was a guest lecturer at Brandeis University. In 1963, he was a lecturer for the U.S. Department of Labor.

Rosen has been an official of the leftist American Veterans Committee. He has been affiliated with the leftist-pacifist Massachusetts Political Action for Peace (PAX); the leftist-pacifist Turn Toward Peace; the National Committee to Abolish the House Un-American Activities Committee ("to lead and direct the Communist Party's 'Operation Abolition' campaign"); the ultra-leftist American Civil Liberties Union; the Radical Education Project, an adjunct of the ultra-leftist Students for Democratic Action; the National Conference for New Politics, a classical united front third party movement largely controlled by the Communist Party; the Student Mobilization Committee to End the War in Vietnam, dominated by Communists and fellow-travelers; the leftist-oriented Ad Hoc Committee for an Open Letter on Vietnam; and the leftist-pacifist Ad Hoc Faculty Committee on Vietnam. In 1962, he was active in the senatorial campaign of the ultra-leftist-pacifist H. Stuart Hughes.

MORRIS H. RUBIN was born on August 7, 1911 in New York City, son of Leah Abrahamson and Jacob Rubin. He married Mary Sheridan. He is an alumnus of the University of Wisconsin (B.A., 1934).

From 1929 until 1934, Rubin was a reporter for the *Portland* [Me.] *Evening Express*. In 1934, he was a special correspondent for the *Milwaukee Journal*. From 1934 until 1938, he was a political writer for the *Wisconsin State Journal* and a special correspondent for the *New York Times* and *Time* magazine. From 1938 until 1940, he was an aide to Wisconsin's Governor Philip F. LaFollette. From 1940 until 1946, he was an aide to U.S. Senator Robert M. LaFollette Jr. of Wisconsin. Since 1940, he has been editor of *The Progressive*, one of the nation's most durable leftist-liberal publications.

As a collegian, Rubin was a leader of the Socialist Student League for Industrial Democracy. He is a long-time member and a long-time high official of the ultra-leftist American Civil Liberties Union and the ultra-radical Americans for Democratic Action.

WILLIAM RUDER was born on October 17, 1921 in New York City, son of Rose Rosenberg and Jacob Ruder. He married Helen Finn. He is an alumnus of the City College of New York (B.S.S.,

1942). He is co-author of *The Business-man's Guide to Washington* (1964).

From 1946 until 1948, Ruder was on the public relations staff of Samuel Goldwyn Productions in Hollywood. Since 1948, he has been president of Ruder & Finn, Inc., a public relations firm. In 1961 and 1962, he was Assistant Secretary of Commerce. He has lectured at the Harvard Graduate School of Business and has been a consultant to the Department of State and an adviser to the Office of Economic Opportunity.

Ruder has been a member of the leftist-internationalist International Movement for Atlantic Union; the National Council for Civic Responsibility, an election year's drive (in 1964) against anti-Communists by the Democrat Party; and the United Nations Association of the United States, the most prestigious leftist propaganda agency for the UN in this country.

KENNETH RUSH was born on January 17, 1910 in Walla Walla, Washington, son of Emma Kidwell and David Rush. He married Jane Smith. He is an alumnus of the University of Tennessee (A.B., 1930) and Yale University (LL.B., 1932).

From 1932 until 1936, Rush was associated with the legal firm of Chadbourne, Stanchfield & Levy. In 1936 and 1937, he was an assistant professor at Duke University's Law School. In 1936, and from 1937 until 1969, he was with Union Carbide Corporation as a counsel (1936 and 1937-1949), vice-president (1949-1961), executive vice-president (1961-1966), president (1966-1969), director (1958-1969), chairman of the general operating committee (1965-1969), and member of the executive committee (1966-1969). Since 1969, he has been U.S. Ambassador to West Germany.

Rush is a long-time member of the Council on Foreign Relations, the informal supra-State Department of the United States. He has been an official and long-time member of the Foreign Policy Association, a bulwark of leftist-internationalism. He has been on the board of directors of the leftist-oriented Institute of International Education. He has been a member of the industries advertising committee of the leftist-oriented Advertising Council.

DANKWART A. RUSTOW was born on December 21, 1924 in Berlin, Germany, son of Anna Bresser and Alexander Rustow. He has been married and divorced. He is a naturalized American. He is an alumnus of Queens College (B.A., 1947) and Yale University (M.A., 1949; Ph.D., 1951). He also studied at the University of Istanbul. In 1949 and 1950, he held a fellowship from the leftist-oriented Social Science Research Council. In 1951 and 1952, he held a fellowship from the leftist-oriented Fund for the Advancement of Education. In 1965 and 1966, he held a Guggenheim fellowship. He is the author of *The Politics of Compromise: A Study of Parties and Cabinet Government in Sweden* (1955); *Politics and Westernization in the Near East* (1956); *Modernization and Political Leadership* (1967); and *A World of Nations* (1967). He is co-editor of *Political Modernization in Japan and Turkey* (1964). He is a contributor to *Modern Political Parties* (1956); *Islam and the West* (1957); *Foreign Policy in World Politics* (1958); *The Politics of Developing Areas* (1960); *Modern Political Systems* (1963); *The Military in the Middle East* (1963); *Islam and International Relations* (1965); *Political Culture and Political Development* (1965); and *Political Parties* *and Political Development* (1966).

From 1950 until 1952, Rustow was an associate professor of political science at Oglethorpe University. From 1952 until 1959, he was at Princeton University as assistant professor (1952-1957) and associate professor (1957-1959) of politics; staff member of the Near Eastern Studies Program (1952-1959); research associate in the University's Center of International Studies (1955-1959): and field researcher in Turkey and other Near Eastern countries (1953-1954 and 1958-1959). Since 1959, he has been at Columbia University as associate professor (1959-1963) and professor (1963 to the present) of international social forces. From 1961 until 1963, he was on the senior staff of the Division of Foreign Policy Research of the Brookings Institution. Since 1962, he has been a consultant to the Department of State. Since 1963, he has been a consultant to RAND Corporation, the notorious think factory. From 1965 until 1967, he was a consultant to the Twentieth Century Fund, which has had a long history of financing leftists and leftist causes. He has been a visiting lecturer or professor at Hunter College, American University in Beirut, Columbia University, Yale University, The Johns Hopkins University's School of Advanced International Studies, the leftist London School of Economics, Massachusetts Institute of Technology, New York University, the University of Istanbul, and the University of Heidelberg.

Rustow has been an official of the leftist-oriented Social Science Research Council. Since 1960, he has been a member of the Council on Foreign Relations, the informal supra-State Department of the United States.

EDWARD E. SAMPSON was born on December 4, 1934 in Chicago. He is an alumnus of the University of California at Los Angeles (B.A., 1956) and the University of Michigan (Ph.D., 1960). He is the author of *Approaches, Contexts, and Problems of Social Psychology* (1964).

From 1957 until 1960, Sampson was an assistant in social psychology at the University of Michigan. Since 1960, he has been at the University of California at Berkeley as an assistant professor of psychology (1960-1966) and associate professor (1966 to the present).

In 1964, Sampson was a leader of Psychologists for Political Freedom, supporting the Free Speech Movement led by leftist Mario Savio and Bettina Aptheker on the Berkeley campus. In 1967, he belonged to Professionals for Peace, an ultra-leftist anti-Vietnam War group. He sponsored a number of leftist-compiled anti-Vietnam War advertisements. He took part in anti-draft demonstrations at the Oakland induction center and demanded that he be arrested and punished in the same manner as the New Left students who initiated the demonstrations. In 1968, he took part in a "Vietnam Commencement" at Berkeley, during which leftist students and faculty members honored conscientious objectors. He signed a statement, issued by the demonstrators, which said: "Our war in Vietnam is unjust and immoral. As long as the United States is involved in this war, I will not serve in the armed forces." On a CBS-TV broadcast in 1969, he claimed that he had made a comparison study of ROTC cadets and draft resisters. He alleged that he found cadets to be "conventionally moral" and resisters had "principled morality." On the Berkeley campus, he supported a lecture series on racism given by the arch-racist Eldridge Cleaver, leader of the Black Panthers.

RONALD SANTONI was born on December 19, 1931 in Arvida, Quebec, son of Phyllis Tremaine and Fred Santoni. He married Marguerite Kiene. He is an alumnus of Bishop's University (B.A., 1952); Brown University (M.A., 1954); and Boston University (Ph.D., 1961). He also pursued graduate studies at the University of Paris and Yale University. He is editor of *Religious Language and the Problem of Religious Knowledge* (1968). He is co-editor of *Social and Political Philosophy* (1963). He is contributor to *Current Philosophical Issues: Festschrift In Honor of C.J. Ducasse* (1966).

From 1958 until 1961, Santoni was an assistant professor of philosophy at the University of the Pacific. In 1961 and 1962, he was a research fellow at Yale University. From 1962 until 1964, he was an assistant professor of philosophy at Wabash College. Since 1964, he has been at Denison University as associate professor (1964-1968) and professor (1968 to the present) of philosophy, and acting chairman of the philosophy department (1966-1967).

Santoni has been affiliated with the ultra-leftist American Civil Liberties Union; the National Association for the Advancement of Colored People, a fountainhead of Negro agitation for more than half a century; the ultra-leftist-pacifist National Committee for a Sane Nuclear Policy; the leftist-internationalist American Association for the United Nations; the leftist-oriented Episcopal Society for Cultural and Racial Unity; and the leftist-oriented Universities Committee on Problems of War and Peace.

IRVING SARNOFF was born on May 25, 1930 in New York City.

Sarnoff has been located in California since about 1946. In 1951 and 1952, he served in the U.S. Army for about one year and received an honorable discharge.

On September 5, 1958, Sarnoff testified before the House Committee on Un-American Activities and pleaded the Fifth Amendment when asked about his Communist Party affiliations. It is known that he was active in the American Youth for Democracy ("subversive and Communist") and the Labor Youth League ("Communist organization"). In 1956, he was a labor director of the Los Angeles County Labor Youth League and a member of the national executive committee of the Labor Youth League. In 1957, he was a delegate to the California State Labor Youth League convention. In 1957, he was a delegate to three Communist Party conventions: the Los Angeles County Convention, the California State Convention, and the Southern California District Convention. He is a long-time member and sometime official of the District Council of the Communist Party in Southern California.

Sarnoff has been affiliated with the ultra-leftist American-Korean Friendship and Information Center; the ultra-leftist GI Civil Liberties Defense Committee; the ultra-leftist People's Coalition for Peace and Justice; the ultra-leftist American Society for the Study of the German Democratic Republic; the Communist-dominated Peace Action Council of California; the ultra-leftist Community for New Politics in Berkeley; the ultra-leftist Spring Mobilization Committee; the ultra-leftist National Mobilization Committee to End the War in Vietnam; and the Emergency Conference Committee, an ultra-leftist call to the United Nations to impose sanctions against the United States until the United States ratifies the Genocide Treaty. He has been a leader in so-called peace demonstrations in Los Angeles. He has worked closely with the radical leftist Black Congress in Los Angeles. He has been a fund raiser for Black Panther leader Huey Newton.

In 1968, Sarnoff attended the Communist-operated Hemispheric Conference to End the Vietnam War. In 1969, he participated in the ultra-leftist National Anti-War Conference in Cleveland, and that same year he participated in the Stockholm Conference on Vietnam as a member of the ultra-leftist International Liaison Committee. In June 1969, Sarnoff attended the World Peace Assembly in East Berlin as a representative of the Communist Party and the Peace Action Council. Prior to the Assembly, he flew to Moscow and East Berlin in May to plan propaganda details for the June conference. He travelled on the Soviet Union's Aeroflot and all expenses were provided for by the East German Government. In 1970, he attended the Communist-operated World Peace Council in British Columbia, and he helped to initiate a similar meeting in Africa for later in 1970. In 1971, he attended the Communist-operated World Peace Council in Budapest, Hungary. En route to Budapest, Sarnoff and his fellow-travelers from the United States met in Paris with North Vietnamese officials, to discuss future strategy and tactics to be employed by the ultra-leftists in the United States in their anti-Vietnam War campaign.

ROBERT SCHEER was born on April 4, 1936 in New York City, son of Ida Kuran and Frederick Scheer. He married Anne Weills. He is an alunnus of the City College of New York (B.A., 1958). In 1959, he was a Maxwell fellow in public administration at Syracuse University's Maxwell School of Government. In 1961, he was a fellow at the Center for Chinese Studies at the University of California at Berkeley. He is the author of *How the United States Got Involved in Vietnam* (1965). He is co-author of *Cuba: Tragedy of Our Hemisphere* (1961).

In 1960, Scheer was an instructor in American government at the City College of New York. In 1960, he was a teaching assistant in economics at the University of California at Berkeley. When he took the position at Berkeley, he also began a long association with the ultra-leftist Center for the Study of Democratic Institutions. From 1965 until 1969, he was with the ultra-leftist *Ramparts* magazine as foreign editor (1965-1966), managing editor (1966-1967), vice-president of the Ramparts Corporation (1967-1969), and editor-in-chief (1968-1969).

In 1956 and 1960, Scheer was active in the ultra-radical Americans for Democratic Action, working in the presidential campaigns of Adlai Stevenson. Once Scheer settled in Berkeley, he began to build up a most impressive list of ultra-leftist credentials. He was an active member of the Fair Play for Cuba Committee, and it was as such that he wrote *Cuba: Tragedy in Our Hemisphere* – a defense of Fidel Castro which he retitled *Cuba: An American Tragedy*. On the Berkeley campus, he was active in the Free Speech Movement led by Mario Savio and Bettina Aptheker. He was an early and active supporter of the leftist-radical labor leader Cesar Chavez, who gained tremendous national publicity with the appearance of his autobiographical article in the July 1966 issue of *Ramparts* magazine. In 1965, Scheer became very active on and off campus in leftist-dominated anti-Vietnam War projects. In 1965, he wrote *How the United States Got Involved in Vietnam* under a grant from the ultra-leftist Center for the Study of Democratic Institutions. It was this work which attracted the attention of Warren Hinckle, president of *Ramparts*. It was Hinckle who hired Scheer as foreign editor of the magazine, which was instituting a leftist campaign against U.S. involvement in the Vietnam War. Scheer was so extreme in his attitude as to equate the position of the United States in Vietnam with that of the Soviet Union in Hungary. Said Scheer: "In Eastern Europe, Soviet communism became involved in a ludicrous situation that presents it with continued instability and turmoil and has stained the ideology of communism. Writing about Hungary, Albert Camus created the phrase 'socialism of the gallows' to describe the low point of an ideology that claimed to lead a civilization. But must we not also speak of the United States' involvement in Viet Nam in terms of 'a democracy of the gallows'?"

In 1966, Scheer became a candidate for Congress in California's Democratic primary. His candidacy was supported by the Communist Press and by Californians for Liberal Representation. In his campaign literature, he described his campaign workers: "On the committee there are socialists, liberal Democrats, radicals, Communists, reformers, and people who have never before participated in politics. We are agreed that our differences are less important than the need to work together on this campaign." Scheer's campaign coordinator was Carl Bloice, a member of the Communist Party and a staff writer for *People's World*, the Communist weekly on the West Coast. Bloice was also publications director for the Communist-controlled W.E.B. DuBois Clubs and a member of the National Committee of the Communist Party. (Although Scheer did say that he disagreed with Bloice's politics, he nevertheless hinted during the course of his campaign that he would join the Communist Party if the W.E.B. DuBois Clubs were subjected to continuing harassment.)

When Scheer's campaign for Congress was unsuccessful, he kept his workers together under the name of Community for New Politics. Bloice was not only coordinator for Scheer's organization, he was also a contributor to the CNP's occasional newsletter.

In 1967, Scheer – in the guise of a journalist – travelled to Prague, Czecho-Slovakia, where he met with the Communist-controlled International Union of Students. He also met with representatives of the National Liberation Front and the Viet Cong. At that time it was Scheer's position that "Americans should re-evaluate the entire concept of foreign policy, especially since it is based on the theory of the international Communist conspiracy . . . such a conspiracy simply does not exist."

In 1968, Scheer made at least two visits to Communist Cuba to attend meetings sponsored by Castro's regime. In the same year, under Scheer's direction, *Ramparts* magazine carried "The Diary of Ché Guevara," purportedly an authentic production of Communist Cuba's No. 2 hero.

In 1969, Scheer was one of eleven American radicals, calling themselves the U.S. People's Anti-Imperialist Delegation, who travelled to North Korea and North Vietnam at the invitation of the Vietnam Committee of Solidarity With the American People. Eldridge Cleaver, the Black Panther leader, and Scheer were the spokesmen for the group.

(Scheer's attacks upon the policies of the U.S. Government were so vehement that they were recorded and broadcast over Radio Hanoi.)

In 1969, Scheer was a candidate for Congress with the support of the National Conference for New Politics, a classic united-front third-party movement, largely controlled by the Communist Party. Eventually, the NCNP evolved into the Peace and Freedom Party and Scheer became a PFP candidate. (On one occasion Scheer said: "People realize that if [the government] gets the Panthers, it gets everybody — like the Jews in Germany." Scheer's fellow candidate on the Peace and Freedom ticket was Black Panther leader Eldridge Cleaver. In July 1969, Scheer accompanied Black Panther leaders to the Pan-African Cultural Festival in Algiers.)

Scheer's affiliations have included the New School in San Francisco, which he helped to found in company with a group of ultra-radicals. He was very active in the Communist-saturated Vietnam Day Committee. He has been a member of the ultra-leftist International Committee to Defend Eldridge Cleaver and of the ultra-leftist Soledad Brothers Defense Committee, and also of the Student Mobilization Committee to End the War in Vietnam, a group dominated by Communists and fellow-travelers. He has been closely affiliated with the ultra-leftist Students for a Democratic Society.

IVAN H. SCHEIER was born on January 7, 1926 in Plattsburgh, New York, son of Melba Gottlob and Joel Scheier. He is an alumnus of Union College (A.B., 1948) and McGill University (M.A., 1951; Ph.D., 1953). He is co-author of *The Meaning and Measurement of Neuroticism and Anxiety* (1961).

From 1953 until 1955, Scheier was at George Washington University in the Human Resources Research Office as a research associate in psychology. From 1955 until 1960, he was at the University of Illinois as a research associate in psychology. From 1959 until 1963, he was associate director and test editor at the Institute for Personality and Ability Testing in Champaign, Illinois. Since 1963, he has been in Boulder, Colorado, as consulting psychologist to the Boulder County Juvenile Court (1963 to the present) and director of the Boulder County Juvenile Delinquency Project (1966 to the present).

Scheier has been affiliated with the National Association for the Advancement of Colored People, a fountainhead of Negro agitation for more than half a century; the ultra-leftist American Civil Liberties Union; the ultra-leftist National Committee for a Sane Nuclear Policy; and the leftist-oriented Urban League.

RALPH SCHOENMAN was born on October 16, 1935 in New York City, son of Helen Benedek and Theodore Schoenman. He married Susan Goodricke. He is an alumnus of Princeton University (B.A., 1958) and London University (M.S., 1960). He is the author of *Death and Pillage in the Congo: A Study of Western Rule* (1965). He is co-editor of *War Crimes in Vietnam* (1966). He is editor of *Bertrand Russell: Philosopher of the Century* (1967).

From 1960 until 1967, Schoenman was personal secretary to Bertrand Russell, the British Marxist and pacifist agitator. He was director of the Bertrand Russell Peace Foundation. He was an errand boy for Russell, carrying messages from Russell to such leftist leaders as Chou En-lai, Nikita Khrushchev, Ho chi Minh, Fidel Castro, Achmed Sukarno,

Gamal Abdel Nasser, Indira Gandhi, and Sirimavo Bandaranaike. On many occasions, on Russell's behalf, he met with leaders of the National Liberation Front and the Viet Cong. With Russell, he established the Committee of 100, which organized massive civil disobedience demonstrations in Britain. With Russell, he recruited leftists from around the world to participate in a so-called war crimes tribunal, which was nothing less than a Communist forum directed against United States involvement in Vietnam.

Sometime in 1967, Russell dismissed Schoenman. In 1968, Schoenman was expelled from Britain as an undesirable alien. Since that time, Schoenman, who describes himself as a revolutionary Marxist, has been a free-lance lecturer in the United States. The content of his lectures is indistinguishable from that of lectures by official leaders of the Communist Party.

HOWARD SCHOMER was born on June 9, 1915 in Chicago, son of Daisy Aline and Frank Schomer. He is married to Elsie Swenson. He is an alumnus of Harvard University (B.S., 1937) and Chicago Theological Seminary (D.D., 1954). In 1941, he was ordained to the Congregationalist ministry. He is the editor of *The Oppression of Protestants in Spain* (1955). Since 1959, he has been editor-at-large for *Christian Century* magazine.

From 1941 until 1945, Schomer worked for the leftist-pacifist American Friends Service Committee. From 1946 until 1955, he was co-minister of the Reformed Church in Le Chambon-sur-Lignon, France, and coordinator of the American Congregational Christian Interchurch Aid to Europe. From 1946 until 1951, he was an instructor in history at the International Christian College in

Cevenol, France. From 1959 until 1967, he was president of the Chicago Theological Seminary. Since 1967, he has been executive director of the specialized ministries department in the division of overseas ministries of the leftist-oriented National Council of Churches.

Schomer is a long-time member of the ultra-leftist-pacifist Fellowship of Reconciliation. From 1959 until 1963, he was president, and from 1963 until 1965, vice-president, of the International Fellowship of Reconciliation. He has been affiliated with the ultra-leftist-pacifist National Commitee for a Sane Nuclear Policy; the ultra-leftist American Civil Liberties Union; the National Committee to Abolish the House Un-American Activities Committee ("to lead and direct the Communist Party's 'Operation Abolition' campaign"); the ultra-leftist Clergy and Laymen Concerned About Vietnam; the leftist-pacifist Student Peace Union; the leftist-pacifist International Committee of Conscience on Vietnam; and the leftist-oriented Inter-University Committee for a Public Hearing on Vietnam.

ROBERT JAY SCHWARTZ was born on October 2, 1917 in New York City, son of Helene Morvay and Joseph Schwartz. He married Josephine Diaz. He is an alumnus of the City College of New York (B.S.S., 1940); Columbia University (M.A., 1942); and American University (Ph.D., 1957). He is the author of *Obstacles to Foreign Investments* (1957).

From 1946 until 1953, Schwartz was chief of the international statistics division of the U.S. Treasury Department. From 1953 until 1962, he was vice-president of the Amalgamated Bank of New York. From 1962 until 1966, he was vice-president of the Israel Discount

Bank, Ltd., in New York City. Since 1966, he has been senior pension fund advisor for Bache & Company. He has lectured at the City College of New York, American University, Howard University, Fairleigh Dickinson College, and the Foreign Service Institute. In 1965, he was an unsuccessful candidate for Congress.

Schwartz is a long-time member of the national board of the ultra-radical Americans for Democratic Action. He is a long-time member of the national board of the ultra-leftist-pacifist National Committee for a Sane Nuclear Policy.

STEPHEN M. SCHWEBEL was born on March 10, 1929 in New York City, son of Pauline Pfeffer and Victor Schwebel. He is an alumnus of Harvard University (B.A., 1950) and Yale University (LL.B., 1954). In 1950 and 1951, he was a Frank Knox Memorial fellow at Trinity College in England. In 1955, he was admitted to the New York bar. He is the author of *The Secretary-General of the United Nations* (1952).

As a high-school student, Schwebel began what has amounted to a lifelong career as a propagandist for the United Nations. In his senior year, he was appointed first national president of United Nations Youth. As a freshman at Harvard, he founded the Harvard United Nations Council and served as its chairman from 1946 until 1948. From 1947 until 1949, he conducted, together with a fellow student, a weekly pro-United Nations radio program, *This World This Week*, in Boston. From 1948 until 1950, he was national chairman of the Collegiate Council for the United Nations. In 1947, he was a delegate to the leftist-dominated UNESCO's national conference in Philadelphia. In 1948 and 1949,

he testified before the Senate Foreign Relations Committee as a representative of the Collegiate Council on the North Atlantic Treaty and submitted proposals for "strengthening" the United Nations charter. In 1948, he was a member of the United Nations delegation at the third plenary assembly of the World Federation of United Nations Associations. In 1949, he was an administrative aide to United Nations Secretary-General Trygve Lie. In 1949 and 1950, he was on the national board of directors and the executive committee of the leftist American Association for the United Nations. In 1950 and 1951, he was president of the International Student Movement for the United Nations. From 1950 until 1953, he was the American director of the World Federation of United Nations Associations. From 1958 until 1961, he was a trustee of the Trust for Education on the United Nations.

From 1954 until 1959, Schwebel was associated with the law firm of White & Case in New York City. From 1959 until 1961, he was an assistant professor of law at Harvard Law School. From 1961 until 1967, he was with the Department of State as assistant legal adviser for United Nations affairs (1961-1966) and special assistant to the assistant secretary of state for international organizational affairs (1966-1967). Since 1967, he has been executive director and executive vice-president of the American Society of International Law. Since 1967, he has been a professor of international law at the School of Advanced International Studies at The Johns Hopkins University. He has served as a legal adviser to the United States delegation at several General Assemblies of the United Nations. Since 1967, he has been a consultant to the Department of State. He has served as the Department of State's special representative on Micronesian claims. In 1964, he was chairman of the U.S. delegation to the first session of the United Nations Special Committee on Principles of International Law. From 1966 until 1968, he was the United States representative on the advisory committee of the United Nations Program for Assistance in Teaching, Study, Dissemination, and Wider Appreciation of International Law. He has lectured at Indian universities under the auspices of the Department of State. From 1966 until 1968, he lectured at the U.S. Naval War College. In 1967, he was visiting lecturer at the Dag Hammarskjöld Institute in Uppsala, Sweden.

Schwebel is a nonresident member of the Council on Foreign Relations, the informal supra-State Department of the United States. He is a trustee of the leftist-oriented Washington Institute of Foreign Affairs. For thirteen years, he was on the executive committee of the Commission to Study the Organization of Peace, the research arm of the leftist-internationalist United Nations Association of the United States.

MARY SCOVILLE was born on May 14, 1909 in Fulton, Missouri, daughter of Marian Marquess and Raymond Branch. She married Merrill Scoville. She is an alumna of Western College for Women (B.A., 1930) and the University of Chicago (M.A., 1934). She also pursued graduate studies at the University of Cincinnati and the University of North Carolina. She is the author of *Women and Wealth* (1934).

From 1932 until 1938, Mrs. Scoville was an assistant professor of economics and sociology at Western College for Women. From 1938 until 1940, she was an instructor in economics and sociology at Wellesley College. From 1941 until 1950, she was an assistant professor of social service administration at the University of Chicago. In 1950 and 1951, she was director of research for Edwin Shields Hewitt & Associates in Chicago. In 1958 and 1959, she was a psychiatric caseworker in the Mental Health Clinic of the Will County Health Department in Joliet, Illinois. Since 1959, she has been a caseworker for the Family Service Agency of Will County.

From 1940 until 1950, Mrs. Scoville was on the advisory committee of the leftist-oriented Consumers Union. In 1970, she was affiliated with the leftist-oriented White House Conference on Children and Youth. She has been an official and a long-time member of the leftist-oriented League of Women Voters. She has been affiliated with the ultra-leftist Center for the Study of Democratic Institutions. She is a member of the National Association for the Advancement of Colored People, a fountainhead of Negro agitation for more than half a century; and the United Nations Association of the United States, the most prestigious leftist propaganda agency for the UN in this country.

PAUL SEABURY was born on May 6, 1923 in Hempstead, New York, son of Maude Harris and Adam Seabury. He married Marie-Anne Phelps. He is an alumnus of Swarthmore College (B.A., 1946) and Columbia University (Ph.D., 1953). He is the author of *The Wilhelmstrasse: A Study of German Diplomacy Under the Nazi Regime* (1954); *Power, Freedom and Diplomacy* (1963); *The Balance of Power* (1965); *The Rise and Decline of the Cold War* (1967); and *The Game of Croquet* (1968). He is co-author of *U.S. Foreign Policy: Perspectives and Proposals* (1969).

From 1947 until 1953, Seabury

served successively as a lecturer and instructor at Columbia University. In 1951, he was a guest lecturer at the Free University of Berlin. From 1953 until 1965, he was at the University of California at Berkeley: assistant professor, associate professor, and professor of political science (1953-1965); assistant dean of the College of Letters and Science (1963-1964); and vice-chairman of the political science department (1964-1965). In 1966 and 1967, he was at the University of California at Santa Cruz as professor of government and provost. Since 1967, he has been at the University of California at Berkeley as professor of government (1967 to the present) and chairman of the faculty at the College of Letters and Science (1967-1969). In 1956, he was a visiting fellow at Princeton University's Center of International Studies. In 1957, he was a visiting professor at Hamline College. In 1961 and 1962, he was a visiting research professor and a Guggenheim fellow at Brookings Institution. In 1965 and 1966, he was a research scholar at Harvard University's Center for International Affairs. Since 1963, he has been a consultant to the State Department, and since 1967, he has been vice-chairman of the Department of State's Board of Foreign Scholarships.

Seabury is a long-time nonresident member of the Council on Foreign Relations, the informal supra-State Department of the United States. He has been a top official and long-time member of the ultra-radical Americans for Democratic Action.

ERIC SEVAREID was born on November 26, 1912 in Velva, North Dakota, son of Clare Hougen and Alfred Sevareid. He was married to and divorced from Lois Finger. He is married to Belen Marshall. He is an alumnus of the University of Minnesota (B.A., 1935). He also studied at the leftist London School of Economics and the Alliance Française. He is the author of *Not So Wild a Dream* (1946); *In One Ear* (1952); *Small Sounds in the Night* (1956); and *This is Eric Sevareid* (1964). He is editor of *Candidates: 1960* (1959).

During his college days, Sevareid was a leading campus leftist. He was a founder of the Jacobin Club, a student group that rallied against fascism and caused the abolition of compulsory ROTC training at the University of Minnesota. (Writing in *Look* magazine, September 5, 1967, Sevareid said: "... As a college kid in the thirties, I was a hollering 'activist' and even voted for that Oxford oath — 'I will not fight for flag or country.'")

As a collegian, Sevareid was a part-time reporter for the *Minneapolis Journal* and the *Minneapolis Star.* In 1936 and 1937, he was a full-time reporter for the *Minneapolis Journal.* In 1937, after a layoff from the newspaper, he went to Europe to study. In 1938 and 1939, he was in Paris working as a reporter and city editor for the Paris edition of the *New York Herald-Tribune.* He also worked briefly for the United Press as Paris night editor. In 1939, the leftist Edward R. Murrow recruited Sevareid as a radio reporter for the Columbia Broadcasting System. During the next year, he worked in France and London. From 1941 until 1943, he was assigned to the CBS News Bureau in Washington, D.C. In 1943, he worked for a few months as a correspondent in the China-Burma-India theatre. In 1944 and 1945, he returned to Europe as a correspondent, working in Yugoslavia, France, Germany, and England. In 1945, he returned to the United States and reported on the founding conference of the United Nations. From 1946 until 1959, he worked in the CBS News Bureau in Washington, D.C. From 1959 until 1961, he was a roving European correspondent for CBS. From 1961 until 1964, he worked for CBS in New York City and was the moderator for CBS television programs, including *Town Meeting of the World, The Great Challenge, Years of Crisis,* and *Where We Stand.* Since 1948, he has participated in CBS News coverage of presidential elections and national conventions. Since 1964, he has been based in Washington, D.C., and he has been a regular commentator on *CBS Evening News with Walter Cronkite.* For many years he has written a syndicated weekly column on world affairs and he has contributed articles to a variety of national magazines. He has received just about every award that leftist journalists can expect, including the Sidney Hillman Foundation award, the George Foster Peabody award, the George Polk Memorial award, the Overseas Press Club award, and the One World award. In 1967, for a brief time, he entertained the thought of running for the U.S. Senate from his native North Dakota, as a Democrat.

As was the case with many of Edward R. Murrow's protegés, Sevareid came into national prominence through his unceasing attacks upon Senator Joseph R. McCarthy when the Senator was upsetting the entire Left and the liberal Establishment. And Sevareid since the McCarthy days has frequently reminded his listeners and his readers — as he attacks the right — of what a scourge was McCarthyism, which he has described as "that most frightening of all things, ignorance empowered."

Jack Gould of the *New York Times* once described Sevareid as "CBS's com-mentator in charge of significance." In one of his most famous articles ("The Final Troubled Hours of Adlai Stevenson," *Look* magazine, November 30, 1965), Sevareid wrote: "Adlai didn't make me feel powerful, but he made me feel importantly alive, and he made me feel trusted. There was something else, of no meaning to anybody but me; I am cursed with a somewhat forbidding Scandinavian manner, with a restraint that spells stuffiness to a lot of people. But Adlai saw through all that unfortunate facade. He knew that inside I am mush, full of a lot of almost bathetic sentimentality about this country, the Midwest, Abraham Lincoln, and the English language." There can be little doubt about Sevareid's devotion to the English language. His writings and his radio and television commentaries are certainly readable and listenable. But, in fact, his smooth-flowing prose does not conceal either his leftist bias or his lack of scholarship. He is prone to deal in generalities and he frequently relies upon "consensus" — of mysterious origin and highly questionable accuracy — to prove a particular point. For example, in discussing one of his favorite bogies — the military-industrial complex — Sevareid wrote: "It has become clear that the world's condition just before, during, and just after World War II represented an episode in history, a special confluence of events, unlikely of repetition. Peace and freedom are both highly divisible and will remain so, as they have through most of human history, coexisting with war and tyranny. There is a growing consensus about this throughout the world, the American military establishment, apparently, excepted. They still want to maintain force levels and worldwide bases predicated on readiness for one major crisis in Europe, one major crisis in Southeast Asia, and one minor crisis somewhere else – and simultaneously. We must re-predicate on the basis of one major necessity in Europe and one minor necessity somewhere else. That is the maximum foreseeable in world realities, certainly the maximum that the general American will, purse and stomach can endure. Our reach has exceeded our grasp." In these profound sentences, written in 1969, Sevareid exceeded his usual grasp. He employed the device of a growing world consensus. He apparently had insight as to what the entire American military establishment thought about the divisibility of peace and freedom. And he knew with certainty what the "general American will" would tolerate in the matter of military preparation and intervention.

In this same piece, "American Militarism: What Is It Doing To Us?" (*Look* magazine, August 12, 1969), Sevareid wrote: "When you approach Washington, D.C., from the southwest, coming from Virginia, there is a brief moment on the crest of the highway in which you glimpse a bizarre panorama: the five sides of the Pentagon are elided in your vision and appear as two massive concrete arms outstretched to enfold the heart of the national city, everything from the Capitol dome to the White House to the temple of Abraham Lincoln captured within their embrace. It is an optical illusion, haunting in its symbolism ever since a great American, Gen. George Marshall, built the Pentagon in World War II. It is no longer symbolistic only. Throughout the Federal city, among congressmen, the press, citizens' groups, the other agencies of Government, a strangling sensation of claustrophobia has set in. It affects a wide range of American traditions and human values, from money-consciousness to in-dividual conscience and the condition of the national spirit. 'A nation's budget ... tells what a society cares about and what it does not care about,' remarked Sen. J. William Fulbright a couple of years ago. This nation has spent around a thousand billion dollars on arms and men-in-arms since the end of World War II, the last foreign war, and perhaps the only foreign war in which our vital interests and national security were indisputably at issue." The passage is a typical Sevareid product. He animates the Pentagon. He discovers that thousands, perhaps tens of thousands, of Washingtonians are falling prey to a "strangling sensation of claustrophobia." He exhumes a quotation from the renowned leftist Fulbright and converts the quotation into an infallible axiom. He dismisses the Korean War and Vietnam War as perhaps less than vital to our national interests. And he ignores how much of the arms expenditures and how many of the men-in-arms were made necessary as a prudent preparation for defense of the national security.

In another passage, Sevareid wrote: "Now, world Communism is not only split, it is hopelessly fragmented. The anti-Communist nations around the fringes of China are, most of them, much stronger than they were [around the time of the deep split between Russia and China and the establishing of the credibility of the American nuclear deterrent in the Cuban missile crisis] and more self-confident; on the whole, less worried about China than we were. It is the same for the free nations of Europe in respect to the Soviet Union. East or west, they are anything but 'dominoes' about to fall with a click. And the Russians and Chinese are no more able than we to manipulate lastingly the politics of the small states of Asia, Latin

America and Africa." Fortunately for Sevareid's reputation, he did not attempt to substaniate any one of the statements in this passage, which contains about as many errors of fact as phrases.

In an earlier *Look* magazine article, "The World Still Moves Our Way" (July 9, 1968), Sevareid had displayed his deprecation of Communism and the intentions of Communist leaders: "Communism already appears irrelevant, essentially passé. The more the Communist regimes educate their people, the more complex their life will become. They will struggle with the complexities the Western world confronts already, and they will discover that authoritarian direction from the top cannot cope with them. Only the essentially liberal society can manage twentieth-century life, even in practical terms. They will learn, as we have always known, that the effective, the lasting revolution lies in the West, particularly in America."

Sevareid once wrote: "There is a type of intellectual who always thinks in large categories and all-inclusive definitions. His specters are fully fleshed and complete – 'police state' or 'garrison state.' This is no more accurate than to speak of America as an 'intellectual state' or a 'television state.' We are too big, too diverse and pluralistic to fit these simple-minded concepts; but we are closer to becoming a 'bureaucracy state' than anything else." The observation is obviously applicable to Sevareid himself, who has written of "the historic ambivalence in the American mind." He has written that "Americans are the most natural workers-together in the world. We say we live by the system of individual enterprise, while we are the supreme cooperative society." – "Americans, of course, are not spiritually geared to the past but to the future."

– "People nowhere except in the U.S. have a collective will." – "We [Americans] have always had a high tolerance level for violence."

Sevareid, ever-striving for a moderate image, has denounced Negro militants from time to time, but he has also attempted to glorify the upheaval which has plagued the United States for more than a decade: "We live in the midst of the negro revolution; relatively peaceable as it is, it is the first true people's revolt." (1965) – "The Negro passion of today is a revolution within the continuing American revolution, and the one absolute certainty about it is that it is going to succeed, however long and distracting the agony for everyone. It will succeed not only because it has justice with it (justice has been suppressed before) but because there is a deep evangelical streak in the American people, a true collective conscience, and it has been aroused." (1968) – "The Negro passion of our day seems to be the closest thing to a true people's revolution that this country has experienced."

Perhaps one of the most revealing insights as to Sevareid's frame of reference was present in a commencement address he delivered in 1965 at Luther College in Iowa. He said: "There was a time when young men and women who wanted to live at the cutting edge of history had to make their chief relationship that with religion. Now that is much more a private matter. There was a time when the nexus between educated individual and society was the arts in its various forms. Now he must relate to science and to politics to understand his time on earth and to affect the growing points of reality. I can use the next few minutes to best effect if I try to talk to you about the politics of this age in a few of its more fundamental aspects.

They involve all of you profoundly.

"Five great minds above all other, I would think, made the social realities of today — Darwin, Marx, Freud, Einstein, and John Maynard Keynes; with Gandhi possibly a sixth; Lenin a seventh; Mao Tse-tung possibly the eighth. Political conservatives instinctly resist the fact that society, including government, responds to the laws of Darwin, not those of Newton. That what is fixed is only change; that all is growth and development and sometimes a jungle growth. I do not know that Marx would have written what he did and set in motion what he did had he not preceded Freud and Einstein and Keynes . . . .

"Marx did not appreciate the profound hold of free institutions in those few countries that have a long tradition of them. He was, of course, unable to know and Lenin apparently unable to sense that the scientific revolution would be so fundamental that given adequate resources and know-how, virtually any country under any political system can, at least hypothetically, provide an abundant material life for its people, the great aim of Communism. Lenin as well as Marx preceded the writings of Keynes and did not, of course, grasp what a flexible political system such as ours and those of west Europe could do to prevent poverty and the degrading of the middle class by the instruments of taxation, central deficit spending, interest rates and the rest of the modern tools of government finance. What Mao Tse-tung has contributed to the current messy world scene is the theory and practice of limited, extremely flexible warfare — for what he calls the wars of liberation." In only a few minutes, Sevareid had described a change of relationship between individuals and religion; rejected all absolutes; disregarded any and all contribu-

tions to today's social realities by religious leaders, technologists, philanthropists, inventors, statesmen, educators, and for that matter, any American; alleged that humanitarianism was the great aim of Communism; omitted Mao Tse-tung's major contributions to genocidal warfare against Tibetans and Chinese; and completely misrepresented the effects of Keynesianism upon poverty and the middle class.

If there is a conspicuous virtue in Sevareid's writings, it is that he reassures his readers — but not always in the same context. Before Mr. Nixon's election, he wrote: "But this is not It — this is not our Armageddon, not the great day of judgment on America. For America is change, and the changes have come, often enough, in convulsive spasms. This country is the vast experimental laboratory in human relations for the twentieth century; it is, in a sense, defining and creating the twentieth century for much of the world." After Mr. Nixon's election he wrote: "This is indeed a critical period, but we don't stand at Armageddon, the great, the final day of judgment, on America. Most of the continuous upheaval is of a positive, not a negative, nature in its impulse. A basically healthy society is trying, for one thing, to cleanse itself of the one serious, chronic virus in its blood stream, which is racism."

Before Mr. Nixon's inauguration, Sevareid wrote: "This nation is not going to go isolationist in the old-fashioned sense: we could not even if we would. But, of iron necessity, the heaviest concentration of the new Administration is going to be on our domestic affairs. Even some of our friendliest allies abroad are urging this course upon us." After Mr. Nixon's inauguration, he wrote: "We are not about to 'go isolationist.' We could not if we wished. Our people know that while pride goeth before a fall, in this kind of world, purity precedeth paralysis. We will not reform the world of man by our domestic example alone, however shining it might become."

Occasionally, a statement of Sevareid's defies any rational analysis, as was the case when he described Jack Ruby, the murderer of Lee Harvey Oswald, as that "pathetic, lost, little creature."

ROGER L. SHINN was born on January 6, 1917 in Germantown, Ohio, son of Carrie Buehler and Henderson Shinn. He married Katharine Cole. He is an alumnus of Heidelberg College (A.B., 1938); Union Theological Seminary (B.D., 1941); and Columbia University (Ph.D., 1951). He is the author of *Beyond This Darkness* (1946); *Christianity and the Problem of History* (1953); *The Sermon on the Mount* (1954 and 1962); *Life, Death, and Destiny* (1957); *The Existentialist Posture* (1959); *The Educational Mission of Our Church* (1962); *Moments of Truth* (1964); *Tangled World* (1965); and *Man: The New Humanism* (1968). He is co-author of *We Believe* (1966), and co-author and editor of *The Search for Identity: Essays on the American Character* (1964). He is editor of *Restless Adventure: Essays on Contemporary Expressions of Existentialism* (1968). He is a contributor to *Saturday Review* and *Christian Century*.

From 1947 until 1949, Shinn was an instructor in philosophy and religion at Union Theological Seminary. From 1949 until 1954, he was at Heidelberg College in Ohio as associate professor (1949-1951) and professor (1951-1954) of philosophy and religion, and chairman of the department of philosophy (1949-1954). From 1954 until 1959, he was at Vanderbilt University's Divinity School as professor of theology (1954-1957), and professor of Christian ethics (1957-1959). Since 1959, he has been at the Union Theological Seminary as professor of Christian ethics (1959), the William E. Dodge Jr. professor of applied Christianity (1960 to the present), and dean of instruction (1963 to the present). Since 1962, he has been adjunct professor of religion at Columbia University. Since 1959, he has been on the editorial board of *Christianity and Crisis*.

Shinn has been affiliated with the leftist American Veterans Committee; the ultra-radical Americans for Democratic Action; the leftist-oriented American Association for the United Nations; the leftist Committee to Defend the [Chicago] Conspiracy; and the National Committee to Repeal the McCarran Act ("Communist front" – "subversive").

MULFORD Q. SIBLEY was born on June 14, 1912 in Marston, Missouri, son of Erna Quickert and William Sibley. He married Marjorie Hedrick. He is an alumnus of the Central State College of Oklahoma (A.B., 1933), the University of Oklahoma (A.M., 1934), and the University of Minnesota (Ph.D., 1938). He is the author of *The Political Theories of Modern Pacifism* (1944). He is the co-author of *Conscription of Conscience* (1952). He is a contributor to and editor of *Introduction to Social Science: Personality, Work, Community* (1953) and *Unilateral Initiatives and Disarmament* (1962). He is editor and author of *The Quiet Battle* (1963). He has contributed articles to *New Republic, New Politics*, and the *American Socialist*. Since at least 1962, he has been an associate editor of David Dellinger's Socialist magazine, *Liberation*.

From 1938 until 1948, Sibley was an instructor and assistant professor of political science at the University of Illinois. Since 1948, he has been on the political science faculty at the University of Minnesota as associate professor (1948-1957) and professor (since 1957). He has been a visiting professor at Stanford University, Cornell University, and the State University of New York. In 1959 and 1960, he held a Rockefeller Foundation fellowship in political philosophy. In 1961, University of Minnesota alumni of the College of Science, Literature and the Arts voted him the college's outstanding teacher of the year.

On and off campus over the past two decades, Sibley has achieved a great deal of notoriety by his leftwing activities. He has been a delegate to national conventions of the Socialist Party. He has served as chairman of the Twin Cities branch of the Socialist Party. In 1957, he helped to organize the American Forum for Socialist Education and later served as vice president of the organization. On the University of Minnesota campus, he has been a faculty advisor to the leftwing-pacifist Student Peace Union.

In pursuit of his leftwing-pacifism, Sibley has been an activist in the American Friends Service Committee, the Fellowship of Reconciliation, the Committee for Nonviolent Action, and the War Resisters League. His other affiliations on the far left include the Fair Play for Cuba Committee; the Student Mobilization Committee; the Fort Hood Three Defense Committee; the National Mobilization Committee to End the War in Vietnam; and the National Committee to Repeal the McCarran Act ("a Communist front" – "subversive"). He has petitioned on behalf of convicted Communist Party leaders and he worked for the abolition of the House Committee on Un-American Activities. He has been a vocal supporter of student rioters, draft-card burners, and those who aid and abet draft evaders.

Sibley's views, as expressed in his writings, leave little doubt as to his total commitment to the Left. On December 3, 1963, in a letter to the editor of the University of Minnesota *Daily*, he wrote: "We need students who challenge the orthodoxies. American culture is far too monolithic for its own good. Personally, I should like to see on the campus one or two Communist professors, a student Communist Club, a chapter of the American Association for the Advancement of Atheism, a Society for the Promotion of Free Love, a League for Overthrow of Government by Jeffersonian Violence, an Anti-Automation League, and perhaps a Nudist Club. No university should be without individuals and groups like these. If we don't sow seeds of doubt and implant subversive thoughts in college, where, in heaven's name (if there be a heaven), will they be implanted? And if they are never sown, moral and intellectual progress may be even more doubtful than many of us think."

In an article in the January issue of *Annals* of the American Academy of Political and Social Science titled "Ethics and the Professional Patriots," Sibley wrote: "Whether from the viewpoint of morality or that of utility, world citizenship is an imperative in our day." Considered a stumbling block to world citizenship, the professional patriot was scorned by Sibley: "He [the professional patriot] cannot be open to the view that communism may have a considerable measure of validity, for he has already placed the emotion-laden slogans of anti-communism beyond the pale of critical inquiry." For his part, Sibley was obviously infatuated with a simplistic and fantastic estimate of Communism: "And, of course, the ideal of Karl Marx, as we all know, is one in which an individual contributes what he can to the community and receives in accordance with his needs, in a society in which all bureaucracy, all armies, all police, and the 'state' are abolished." ("Anonymity, Dissent and Individual Integrity," AAPSS *Annals*, July 1968.)

LELLA SMITH was born on April 11, 1935 in Abington, Pennsylvania, daughter of Frances Heacock and James Smith. She is an alumna of Goucher College (B.A., 1956). She pursued postgraduate studies at Santiniketan University in India and at Oxford University in England.

In 1956 and 1957, Lella Smith was a librarian at the United Nations. From 1957 until 1959, she was an editorial assistant on *New Yorker* magazine. In 1960 and 1961, she was an administrative assistant of the leftist-pacifist American Friends Service Committee. From 1962 until 1965, she was a national fund-raiser for the leftist-pacifist Women's International League for Peace and Freedom. (She was national director of the WILPF from 1966 until 1969.) In 1965 and 1966, she was a program consultant to the Washington, D.C., Commissioner's Council on Human Relations. Since 1967, she has been a program analysis officer in the Community Relations Service of the Department of Justice. She is a consultant to the leftist-pacifist American Friends Service Committee and to the leftist African-American Institute.

HUGH H. SMYTHE was born on August 19, 1913 in Pittsburgh, Pennsylvania, son of Mary Barnhardt and William Smythe. He married Mabel Murphy.

He is an alumnus of Virginia State College (A.B., 1936); Atlanta University (M.A., 1937); and Northwestern University (Ph.D., 1945). He pursued graduate studies at Fisk University, the University of Chicago, and Columbia University. He is the co-author of *Negro Land Grant Colleges Social Studies Project* (1944); *The New Nigerian Elite* (1960); and *Educating the Culturally Disadvantaged Child* (1966). He is a member of the editorial boards of the *Journal of Human Relations* (1954 to the present); *Africa Today* (1955 to the present); and *Sociological Abstracts* (1956 to the present.)

In 1937, Smythe was an assistant instructor at Morehouse College. In 1938, he was a field researcher and an administrative assistant for the American Youth Commission of the American Council on Education. In 1938 and 1939, he was an instructor and research assistant at Fisk University. From 1939 until 1941, he was a Rosenwald fellow at the University of Chicago. In 1942, he was a research associate at Atlanta University. In 1944, he was a professor of sociology at Morris Brown College. In 1945 and 1946, he was a professor of anthropology and sociology at Tennessee State College. From 1947 until 1949, he was deputy director of special research for the ultra-radical National Association for the Advancement of Colored People. In 1949 and 1950, he was director of research for W.B. Graham & Associates in New York City. From 1951 until 1953, he was visiting professor of sociology and anthropology at Yamaguchi National University in Japan. Since 1953, he has been professor of sociology at Brooklyn College. From 1965 until 1967, he was U.S. Ambassador to Syria. From 1967 until 1969, he was U.S. Ambassador to Malta. In 1961 and 1962, he was social affairs officer of the U.S.

SOCOLAR

Mission to the United Nations. In 1963 and 1964, he was Fulbright professor at Chulalongkorn University in Thailand and adviser to the National Research Council of the Thai Government.

Smythe has been affiliated with the ultra-leftist American Civil Liberties Union; the National Association for the Advancement of Colored People, the fountainhead of Negro agitation for more than half a century; the leftist American Committee on Africa; and the leftist-oriented U.S. National Commission for UNESCO.

SIDNEY J. SOCOLAR was born in Baltimore, Maryland. He is an alumnus of The Johns Hopkins University (A.B., 1943; M.A., 1944; Ph.D., 1945). He also pursued graduate studies at the University of Chicago.

On June 9, 1953, when Socolar was an instructor in the physical sciences at the University of Chicago, he testified before the Senate Internal Security Subcommittee. He answered questions about his education, saying that he had been on the faculties of Pennsylvania State College, the University of Illinois, and the University of Chicago; that in 1945 and 1946 he had been a researcher in chemistry at Johns Hopkins University; and that in 1946 and 1947 he had held a post-doctoral fellowship at Pennsylvania State College.

Socolar pleaded the First and Fifth Amendments when asked: "When you were an undergraduate at Johns Hopkins University and with particularity during the years 1942 and 1943, were you a member of the Young Communist League?" – "Did you join the Communist Party in 1943?" – "Have you remained a member of the Communist Party from 1943 down to date?" – "Were you a member of [the] executive committee of the executive district committee of the Communist Party during the year 1944, while you were doing postgraduate work at Johns Hopkins University?" – "Do you know a gentleman named Phillip Frankfeld . . . district organizer of the Communist Party of Baltimore?" – "Do you know a member of the Johns Hopkins faculty named Owen Lattimore?"

Socolar testified that during World War II, he received a deferment of service in the Armed Forces. He was employed by Johns Hopkins University in research on radiation and radiation detection. He had access to classified information.

Socolar pleaded the First and Fifth Amendments when asked if he had been a member of the Communist Party when he was deferred from the Armed Services and was working with classified materials. He made the same plea when asked: "Were you a member of the Communist Party when you were at the University of Illinois?" – "Were you a member of the Communist Party when you came to the University of Chicago faculty?" – "Have you attended secret meetings of the Communist Party while you have been here in Chicago?" – "Are you presently a member of the Communist Party?" – "Did you attend the Civil Rights Congress in the year 1949?" – "Have you been a member of the faculty-graduate committee for peace at the University of Chicago?"

After 1953, Socolar was never again mentioned in any congressional investigative committee's report or hearings until he, like so many other dormant radicals, emerged as a sponsor of the leftist-oriented National Teach-In on Vietnam in 1965, by which time he was in the biophysics department at Columbia University.

EMILE E. SOUBRY was born on March 18, 1896 in London, England, son of Alice Fowler and Stephen Soubry. He married Jennie Bennett. He attended Acton Commonwealth College. He came to the United States in 1941. He became a United States citizen in 1948.

From 1911 until 1941, Soubry was with the Anglo-American Oil Company, Ltd., and its successor organization, the Esso Petroleum Company, Ltd., and eventually became chairman of the board of directors. From 1943 until 1961, he was with the Standard Oil Company of New Jersey as foreign marketing coordinator (1943-1951), vice-president (1951-1958), executive vice-president (1958-1961), director (1949-1961), and member of the executive committee (1955-1961).

Soubry has been a long-time resident member of the Council on Foreign Relations, the informal supra-State Department of the United States. He has been a long-time official of the Foreign Policy Association, a pivotal agency for pro-Communist, one-world propaganda; of the World Affairs Council, where corporation executives, educators, civic leaders, and journalists are brainwashed in briefings extolling the glories of pacifism, internationalism, anti-anti-Communism, anti-Americanism, and, most of all, the United Nations; and of the United Nations Association of the United States, the most prestigious left-wing propaganda agency for the UN in this country.

CARL B. SPAETH was born on May 3, 1907 in Cleveland, Ohio, son of Elizabeth Villwock and Charles Spaeth. He married Sheila Grant. He is an alumnus of Dartmouth College (A.B., 1920); Oxford University in England, where he was a Rhodes scholar (B.A., 1931;

B.C.L., 1932); and Yale University (LL.B., 1933).

In 1933 and 1934, Spaeth was a professor of law at Temple University. From 1935 until 1939, he was an associate professor of law at Northwestern University. In 1939 and 1940, he was an associate professor of law at Yale University's Law School. In 1940, he was vice-president, director, and general counsel of the Cia de Fomento Venezolano in Caracas, Venezuela. From 1940 until 1942, he was assistant coordinator for Inter-American Affairs in the Office of Emergency Management. From 1942 until 1944, he was the U.S. Member of the Emergency Advisory Comitee for Political Defense in Montevideo, Uruguay. From 1944 until 1945, he was chief of the River Plata Division of the Department of State. In 1945, he was an assistant diplomatic adviser to UNRRA. In 1945 and 1946, he was a special assistant to the assistant secretary of state for American Republics Affairs. From 1946 until 1962, he was dean of the Law School at Stanford University. Since 1962, at Stanford, he has been the William Nelson Cromwell professor of law. In 1952 and 1953, he was director of the division of overseas activities for the ultra-leftist Ford Foundation.

Spaeth is a long-time nonresident member of the Council on Foreign Relations, the informal supra-State Department of the United States. He was a member of the National Council for Civic Responsibility, an election year's drive (1964) against anti-Communists by the Democratic Party.

KENNETH M. STAMPP was born on June 12, 1912 in Milwaukee, Wisconsin, son of Eleanor Schmidt and Oscar Stampp. He was married to and divorced from Katharine Mitchell. He is married to Isabel M. Macartney-Filgate. He is an alumnus of the University of Wisconsin (B.S., 1935; M.A., 1937; Ph.D., 1942). He is the author of *Indiana Politics During the Civil War* (1949); *And the War Came: The North and the Secession Crisis* (1950); *The Peculiar Institution* (1946); and *The Era of Reconstruction, 1865-1877* (1965). He is co-author of *The National Experience* (1963), editor of *The Causes of the Civil War* (1959), co-editor of *A Reconstruction Reader* (1969), and a contributor to *Problems in American History* (1952).

In 1941 and 1942, Stampp was an instructor in history at the University of Arkansas. From 1942 until 1946, he was at the University of Maryland as an assistant professor (1942-1945) and associate professor (1945-1946) of history. Since 1946, he has been at the University of California at Berkeley as assistant professor (1946-1949), associate professor (1949-1951), and professor (1951-1957) of history; research professor in humanities (1965); and Morrison Professor of American history (1967 to the present). He has been a visiting professor at Harvard University, the University of Wisconsin, and the University of Colorado. He held Guggenheim fellowships in 1952 and 1953, and 1967 and 1968. In 1967 and 1968, he was a Fulbright lecturer at the American Institute of the University of Munich. In 1960, he was a Commonwealth Fund lecturer in American history at the University of London. In 1961 and 1962, he was the Harmsworth professor of American history at Oxford University. He has been the American history editor for Thomas Y. Crowell Company, publishers.

Stampp has supported leftist anti-Vietnam War projects. He has been affiliated with the National Committee to Abolish the House Un-American Activities Committee ("to lead and direct the Communist Party's 'Operation Abolition' campaign"); the ultra-radical American Civil Liberties Union; and the National Association for the Advancement of Colored People, the fountainhead of Negro agitation for more than half a century.

ROBERT B. STEWART was born on November 30, 1908 in Matewan, West Virginia, son of Elmira Stewart and William Stewart. He married Charlotte Fuller. He is an alumnus of the University of Kentucky (A.B., 1931; A.M., 1932); the Fletcher School of Law and Diplomacy at Tufts University (M.A.L.D., 1937); and Harvard University (Ph.D., 1938). He also studied at Morehead State Teachers College in Kentucky. In 1936 and 1937, he held a fellowship from the leftist-pacifist Carnegie Foundation while studying international law in Europe. He is the author of *Treaty Relations of the British Commonwealth of Nations* (1939).

From 1938 until 1945, Stewart was with the U.S. Department of State as a British Commonwealth specialist in the division of European affairs and assistant chief in the division of British Commonwealth affairs. In 1945, he was assistant executive secretary, working under Alger Hiss, at the San Francisco organizing conference of the United Nations. Since 1945, he has been at the Fletcher School of Law and Diplomacy as dean (1945-1965) and professor of international relations (1945 to the present). He has been a visiting lecturer on government at Harvard University. In recent years he has been a consultant to the Department of State.

Stewart is a long-time nonresident member of the Council on Foreign Relations, the informal supra-State Department of the United States. He is a long-time member of the leftist-globalist Atlantic Union Committee and the leftist-globalist International Movement for Atlantic Union.

DONALD B. STRAUS was born on June 28, 1916 in Middletown, New Jersey, son of Edith Abraham and Percy Straus. He married Elizabeth Allen. He is an alumnus of Harvard University (A.B., 1938; M.B.A., 1940).

In 1942 and 1943, Straus was chief of personnel for the Civil Aeronautics Board. From 1946 until 1953, he was vice-president of Management-Employee Relations, Inc., a consulting firm. From 1948 until 1953, he was executive director of the labor relations panel of the Atomic Energy Commission. From 1953 until 1961, he was vice-president of the Health Insurance Plan of Greater New York. Since 1963, he has been president of the American Arbitration Association.

From 1946 until 1951, Straus was an official of the Institute of Pacific Relations ("a vehicle used by the Communists to orientate American far eastern policies toward Communist objectives"). He was a sponsor of the Committee for a Democratic Far Eastern Policy ("a Communist-controlled organization"). He has been a trustee of the leftist-pacifist Carnegie Endowment for International Peace. He is a long-time member of the Council on Foreign Relations, the informal supra-State Department of the United States. He is a member of the United Nations Association of the United States, the most prestigious left-wing propaganda agency for the UN in this country.

JOHN M. SWOMLEY JR. was born on May 31, 1915 in Harrisburg, Pennsylvania, son of Florence Forsyth and John

Swomley. He married Marjie Carpenter. He is an alumnus of Dickinson College (A.B., 1936); Boston University (M.A., 1939; S.T.B., 1940); and the University of Colorado (Ph.D., 1959). He is the author of *The Military Establishment* (1964). He was a contributor to *Peace and Power* (1960). His monographs include *Militarism in Education* (1949); *America, Russia and the Bomb* (1950); and *Church, State and Education* (1964). From 1944 until 1957, he was editor of *Conscription News.* He is a contributing editor of *Fellowship, Progressive,* and *Christian Century.*

From 1940 until 1944, Swomley served successively as youth secretary and associate secretary of the ultra-leftist-pacifist Fellowship of Reconciliation. From 1944 until 1952, he was executive director of the leftist-pacifist National Council Against Conscription. From 1953 until 1960, he was executive secretary of the ultra-leftist-pacifist Fellowship of Reconciliation. In 1956, he was ordained to the Methodist ministry. Since 1960, he has been professor of social ethics at the St. Paul School of Theology in Kansas City, Missouri.

Swomley has been affiliated with the ultra-leftist Clergy and Laymen Concerned About Vietnam; the ultra-leftist Fort Hood Three Defense Committee; the Student Mobilization Committee to End the War in Vietnam, dominated by Communists and fellow-travelers; the leftist-pacifist National Council to Repeal the Draft; the leftist-pacifist Student Peace Union; the leftist-pacifist Committee of Correspondence; and the leftist-pacifist Church Peace Mission. He petitioned for amnesty for Communists imprisoned under the Smith Act. He signed a leftwing manifesto in favor of total world disarmament. He was a member of the Norman Thomas 80th Birthday Committee, a tribute to the patriarch of the Socialist Party. His book, *The Military Establishment*, received a highly favorable review in the *New Times* of Moscow.

VELMA TATE was born on September 7, 1913 in Aurora, Illinois, daughter of Elsie Collins and Marshall Young. She is divorced. She attended Blackburn College. She is the author, under the pseudonym Valerie Taylor, of *Hired Girl* (1952); *Whisper Their Love* (1957); *The Girls in 3-B* (1959); *Stranger on Lesbos* (1960); *Unlike Others* (1963); *Return to Lesbos* (1963); *A World Without Men* (1963); *Journey to Fulfillment* (1964); and, under the pseudonym Francine Davenport, *Secret of the Bayou* (1966). Under the pseudonym Nacella Young, she has contributed to religious and popular periodicals including *Catholic Home Journal, Christian Century,* and *Ladies Home Journal.*

Since 1959, Velma Tate has been on the staff of *Specialty Salesman Magazine.* Since 1961, she has owned and operated her own editorial agency.

Velma Tate is a member of the ultra-radical American Civil Liberties Union; the leftist-racist Congress of Racial Equality; and the leftist-pacifist Women's International League for Peace and Freedom.

ARLO TATUM was born on February 21, 1923 in Prairie City, Iowa, son of Clio Grover and Elmer Tatum. He married Shirley Carton. He attended William Penn College (1939-1941). He is co-author of *Guide to the Draft* (1968). He is editor of *Handbook for Conscientious Objectors*, 6th through 12th editions (1964-1971).

From 1941 until 1943, Tatum was in federal prison for failure to register for the draft. In 1949, he was again sentenced to federal prison for failing to register for the draft. After his second prison term, he worked for about a year for the leftist-pacifist American Friends Service Committee. From 1953 until 1955, he was executive secretary of the War Resisters League in New York City. (The WRL is a group of conscientious objectors who describe themselves as anarchists, democratic socialists, and independent radicals. They agitate for unilateral disarmament, for U.S. diplomatic recognition of Red China, and on behalf of the Black Panthers. The WRL is affiliated with the War Resisters International, which has always been saturated with Communists and Socialists.) From 1955 until 1962, Tatum was general secretary in London, England, for War Resisters International. Since 1962, he has been national secretary of the Central Committee for Conscientious Objectors.

In the *New York Times* (June 14, 1971), Israel Shenker reported on an interview he had with Tatum. Said Tatum: "We're winning a higher percentage of conscientious objection cases, winning cases we wouldn't have won in World War II, simply because courts are more sensitive to due process of law . . . . Many judges are very concerned about the war, and they have trouble sending a kid to prison because he believes in what the judge does . . . . Conscientious objection has become an accepted, honorable position in the minds of hundreds of thousands of people who are not themselves conscientious objectors. It's won the respect it ought to have had all along.

"I don't believe in conscription in a democratic society. If the cause is right and the method is right, you don't have to threaten people with prison to get them to fight . . . . The Government is there to serve the people, and not the people to serve the government. The first is a definition of democracy, and the other a definition of totalitarianism."

The CCCO has its national headquarters in Philadelphia and regional offices in Chicago and San Francisco. Its personnel dispense technical information and free counseling about the draft. Since 1952, it has been publishing the *Handbook for Conscientious Objectors*, and by mid-1971, 350,000 copies had been sold. (The *Handbook* received its biggest single boost when the writer of the syndicated column "Dear Abby" told her readers that the best source of information about the draft was the CCCO's *Handbook*. She also conveniently afforded the address of Tatum's group.)

The CCCO's other publications include a *Draft Counselor's Manual,* which describes methods of attaining deferment and provides information on Canada as an evaders' haven; *Advice for Conscientious Objectors in the Armed Forces*, which by mid-1971 had sold 19,000 copies; and *Attorney's Guide to Selective Service and Military Case Law,* for lawyers who cooperate with the CCCO. The CCCO also has a program to encourage visits to draft evaders in federal prisons.

GEORGE E. TAYLOR was born on December 13, 1905 in Coventry, England, son of Sarah Chapman and Thomas Taylor. He came to the United States in 1928. In 1943, he became a naturalized American citizen. He was married to the late Roberta White. His second wife is Florence Kluckhohn. He is an alumnus of the University of Birmingham, England (A.B. and M.A., 1928). He pursued graduate studies at Harvard University and The Johns Hopkins University, where he was a Commonwealth Fund fellow. He is the author of *The Struggle for North China* (1941); *America in the New Pacific* (1942); *Changing China* (1942); and *The Philippines and the United States: Problems of Partnership* (1964). He is the co-author of *Atlas of Far Eastern Politics* (1942); *The Phoenix and the Dwarfs* (1944); and *The Far East in the Modern World* (1956 and 1964).

From 1930 until 1932, Taylor was a fellow at the Harvard-Yenching Institute in China. From 1933 until 1936, he was a lecturer in European history and political science at the Central Political Institute in Nanking, China. In 1936 and 1937, he was an extension lecturer at the University of London, where he held a Leverhulme fellowship. From 1937 until 1939, he was a tutor in history at Yenching University in Peiping, China. In 1941 and 1942, he held a fellowship from the Rockefeller Foundation, a pillar of the liberal Establishment, at the Institute of Pacific Relations, "a vehicle used by the Communists to orientate American far eastern policies toward Communist objectives." From 1942 until 1945, he was with Elmer Davis' Red-lined Office of War Information. From 1946 until 1969, he was at the University of Washington in Seattle as director of the University's Far Eastern and Russian Institute and professor of Far Eastern history and politics.

Taylor is a long-time nonresident member of the Council on Foreign Relations, the informal supra-State Department of the United States. He is also a member of the United Nations Association of the United States, the most prestigious leftwing propaganda agency for the UN in this country. In 1966, Taylor testified before the Senate Foreign Relations Committee. He told the

Committee that it would be safest to proceed on the premise that there is no conceivable world community into which we could ever persuade the Chinese Communists to enter and participate. He was of the opinion that you can't live with the Chinese Communists and it is useless to try. He favored the containment of Chinese aggression. He warned that the Chinese Communists, if they had a favorable opportunity, would not hesitate to declare war on the United States. Eight months after Taylor testified so sensibly on the nature and intentions of the Chinese Communists, he was on a UN Association panel which recommended that the U.S. promote Red China's membership in the U.N.

KENNETH W. THOMPSON was born on August 29, 1921 in Des Moines, Iowa, son of Agnes Rorbeck and Thor Thompson. He married Lucille Bergquist. He is an alumnus of Augustana College (A.B., 1943) and the University of Chicago (M.A., 1948; Ph.D., 1950). He is the author of *Christian Ethics and Dilemmas of Foreign Policy* (1959); *Political Realism and the Crisis of Foreign Policy* (1960); *American Diplomacy and Emergent Patterns* (1962); and *The Moral Issue in Statecraft* (1966). He is co-author of *Principles and Problems of International Politics* (1951); *Man and Modern Society* (1953); and *Conflict and Cooperation Among Nations* (1960). He is a contributor to *Toynbee and History* (1956); *Reinhold Niebuhr: His Religious, Social and Political Thought* (1956); *Isolation and Security* (1957); *Foreign Policy in World Politics* (1958); *Nuclear Weapons and the Conflict of Conscience* (1963); and *Foreign Policies in a World of Change* (1964). He is a contributor to various publications, including *The Reporter* and *World Politics*.

From 1948 until 1953, Thompson was at the University of Chicago as a lecturer in social science (1948) and assistant professor of political science (1951-1953). From 1948 until 1955, he was at Northwestern University as instructor in political science (1948-1951) and associate professor of political science and chairman of the international relations committee (1951-1953). He has been a visiting lecturer at Duke University, New York University, Rice University, and Macalester College. Since 1953, he has been with the Rockefeller Foundation, a pillar of the liberal Establishment, as a consultant on international relations (1953-1955), assistant director (1955-1957), associate director (1957-1960), director for social sciences (1960-1961), and vice-president (1961 to the present). Since 1957, he has been a seminar associate at Columbia University. Since 1960, he has been a member of the department of international affairs of the leftist-oriented National Council of Churches. He is a long-time member of the Council on Foreign Relations, the informal supra-State Department of the United States. He is a member of the leftist-pacifist Council on Religion and International Affairs, and he was active in its predecessor organization, the Church Peace Union. He is a trustee and chairman of the educational policy committee of the Union Theological Seminary, which has produced hordes of leftist clergymen. Since 1956, he has been a contributing editor to the leftist-oriented *Christianity and Crisis*.

LORENA TINKER was born on December 3, 1921 in Butler, Pennsylvania, daughter of Irene Shanor and John McGregor. She married Leonard Tinker Jr. She is an alumna of Scarritt College (B.A., 1943); Northwestern University

(M.A., 1944); and Iowa State University (Ph.D., 1969).

From 1960 until 1964, Mrs. Tinker was an instructor in psychology at Grand View College in Des Moines. In 1963 and 1964, she was a visiting lecturer in the department of psychology at Drake University. From 1966 until 1968, she was a clinical psychologist in the department of psychiatry at the College of Osteopathic Medicine. In 1968 and 1969, she was a professor in the department of education at the University of Missouri. Since 1970, she has been a research associate at the George Warren Brown School of Social Work at Washington University in St. Louis.

From 1944 until 1968, Mrs. Tinker was a member of the ultra-radical National Association for the Advancement of Colored People, the fountainhead of Negro agitation for more than half a century. From 1963 until 1965, she was a member of the leftist-racist Congress of Racial Equality. Since 1964, she has been a member of the leftist-pacifist Women's International League for Peace and Freedom. Since 1942, she has been a member of the ultra-leftist-pacifist Fellowship of Reconciliation. In 1965 and 1966, she was a member of the ultra-leftist-pacifist National Coordinating Committee to End the War in Vietnam. In 1967 and 1968, she was a member of the leftist-pacifist Committee of Responsibility. She is a member of the ultra-leftist American Civil Liberties Union. Her other leftist-pacifist affiliations include the Des Moines Peace Research Committee; Iowans for Peace in Vietnam; and the Independent Peace Party of Iowa.

BEVERLEE TRACY was born *c.* 1922 in Bennett, Iowa, daughter of Ethel Meumann and Harry Carl. She was married to Joseph Scolaro. She is mar-ried to Alan Tracy. She is an alumna of Augustana College (B.A., 1944) and the University of Iowa (M.S.W., 1957).

From 1952 until 1963, Mrs. Tracy was with the Scott County [Iowa] Department of Social Welfare as caseworker (1952-1955) and supervisor (1955-1963). From 1963 until 1966, she was executive director of the Family and Children's Service in Davenport, Iowa. From 1966 until 1968, she was assistant professor at Augustana College. Since 1968, she has been chairman of the department of social welfare at Marycrest College. Since 1971, she has been on the faculty of the School of Social Work at the University of Iowa.

Mrs. Tracy is a member of the National Association for the Advancement of Colored People, the fountainhead of Negro agitation for more than half a century; the ultra-leftist American Civil Liberties Union; the ultra-leftist-globalist United World Federalists; the leftist-oriented Catholic Interracial Council; and the pacifist Quad-Citizens for Peace.

DAVID F. TRASK was born on May 15, 1929 in Erie, Pennsylvania, son of Ruth Miller and Hugh Trask. His second wife is Elizabeth Brooks. He is an alumnus of Wesleyan University (B.A., 1951) and Harvard University (A.M., 1952; Ph.D., 1958). He is the author of *The United States in the Supreme War Council: American War Aims and Inter-Allied Strategy, 1917-1918* (1961); *General Tasker Howard Bliss and the Sessions of the World, 1919* (1966); and *Victory Without Peace: American Foreign Relations in the Twentieth Century* (1968). He is the compiler, with others, of *A Select Bibliography for Students of History* (1958). He is the co-author of *A Bibliography for the Study of United*

States-Latin American Relations Since 1810 (1968).

From 1956 until 1958, Trask was an instructor in political economy at Boston University. From 1959 until 1962, he was at Wesleyan University as instructor (1958-1959) and assistant professor (1959-1962) of history. From 1962 until 1966, he was at the University of Nebraska as assistant professor (1962-1963) and associate professor (1963-1966) of history. Since 1966, he has been at the State University of New York at Stoney Brook as associate professor (1966-1967) and professor (1967 to the present).

Trask is affiliated with the ultra-leftist American Civil Liberties Union; the National Association for the Advancement of Colored People, the fountainhead of Negro agitation for more than half a century; and the United Nations Association of the United States, the most prestigious leftwing propaganda agency for the UN in this country.

DAVID B. TRUMAN was born on June 1, 1913 in Evanston, Illinois, son of Jane Mackintosh and Malcolm Truman. He married Elinor Griffenhagen. He is an alumnus of the University of Chicago (M.A., 1936; Ph.A., 1939). He is the author of *Administrative Decentralization* (1940); *The Government Process* (1951); and *The Congressional Party* (1959). He is a contributor to *The Pre-Election Polls of 1948* (1949).

From 1939 until 1941, Truman was an instructor at Bennington College in Vermont. From 1941 until 1944, he was an instructor at Cornell University. In 1946 and 1947, he was a lecturer in government at Harvard University. From 1947 until 1951, he was an associate professor of political science at Williams College. From 1950 until 1969, he was at Columbia University as visiting associate professor of government (1950-1951), professor of government (1951-1969), dean (1963-1967), and vice-president and provost (1967-1969). Since 1969, he has been president of Mt. Holyoke College. In 1955 and 1956, he was a Guggenheim fellow. In 1956 and 1957, he was a visiting lecturer at Yale University.

Truman is a long-time nonresident member of the Council on Foreign Relations, the informal supra-State Department of the United States, and the Foreign Policy Association, a pivotal agency for pro-Communist, one-world propaganda. In 1970, he joined 78 other college heads in a widely publicized, dovish appeal to President Nixon urging a "stepped-up timetable for withdrawal from Vietnam."

BARBARA W. TUCHMAN was born on January 30, 1912 in New York City, daughter of Alma Morgenthau and Maurice Wertheim. She married Lester Tuchman. She is an alumna of Radcliffe College (B.A., 1933). She is the author of *The Lost British Policy* (1938); *Bible and Sword* (1956); *The Zimmerman Telegram* (1958); *The Guns of August* (1962); *The Proud Tower* (1966); and *Stilwell and the American Experience in China: 1911-1945* (1971).

From 1933 until 1935, Mrs. Tuchman was a research and editorial assistant for the Institute for Pacific Relations in New York City and Tokyo. (The IPR was "a vehicle used by the Communists to orientate American far eastern policies toward Communist objectives.") From 1935 until 1937, she was a staff writer and foreign correspondent for the leftist *Nation* magazine, which at the time was owned by her father. In 1937, she reported on the Spanish Civil War from Madrid. After leaving Spain, she went to London, where for a brief time, she was a staff writer for the leftist magazine, *The War In Spain.* In 1939, she was a correspondent in the United States for the leftist British journal, *New Statesman and Nation.* From 1943 until 1945, she was a writer and editor for Elmer Davis' Red-lined Office of War Information. Since 1945, Mrs. Tuchman has been a free-lance author. She has written articles for *Atlantic Monthly, Nation, Esquire, Pacific Affairs, Foreign Affairs, Christian Science Monitor, New Republic,* and *American Heritage.* Of her books, *The Guns of August, The Proud Tower,* and *Stilwell and the American Experience in China* have received deserved praise from the liberal left.

Mrs. Tuchman is undeniably on the left. In 1968, she was a fund-raiser for the ultra-leftist National Committee for an Effective Congress. She sought funds for Senators Fulbright, Church, Morse, McGovern, and Nelson, who, according to her solicitation letter, could "go down before racists, isolationists, cops and bomb zealots or, at best, standpat nonentities." She was fearful that "arch conservatives, drum-beating war candidates and extremist right-wing organizations" might gain a stranglehold on all important legislation.

JOHN V. TUNNEY was born on June 26, 1934 in New York City, son of Mary Lauder and Gene Tunney. He married Mieke Sprengers. He is an alumnus of Yale University (B.A., 1956) and the University of Virginia (LL.B., 1959). He also studied at the Academy of International Law, The Hague, Netherlands. In 1959, he was admitted to the New York bar.

In 1959 and 1960, Tunney practiced law in New York City. From 1960 until 1963, he was in the U.S. Air Force, assigned to legal work in the Advocate General's Office. While in the Air Force, he spent most of a 30-day leave touring Latin America with Edward M. Kennedy, who had been his roommate in Virginia University's Law School. (From at least 1960, Tunney could have been considered a full-fledged member of the Kennedy dynasty.) In 1961 and 1962, also while in the Air Force, he taught business law at the Riverside campus of the University of California. In 1963, he resumed the practice of law in Riverside. From 1965 until 1971, he was in the U.S. House of Representatives. In Congress, he was an outstanding liberal on domestic issues. On matters of foreign policy, especially U.S. involvement in the Vietnam War, he supported President Johnson; but in 1969, with the advent of Richard M. Nixon into the White House, he became one of the House's most dovish members.

In 1970, Tunney won an outstanding victory in the race for the U.S. Senate against the incumbent, Republican George Murphy, a conservative in both domestic and foreign policy. Tunney's leftist-liberalism was so strong that he received more than adequate financial support from organized labor and two of the nation's most extreme leftist political pressure groups, the National Committee for an Effective Congress and the Council for a Livable World. Such support was deserved by Tunney. He had voted consistently for the welfare state. He had supported the ultra-leftist labor agitator Cesar Chavez. He had consistently advocated governmental handouts for education, housing, poverty programs, medical programs, and Social Security payoffs. In the Senate he has joined with the dovish forces. He voted against the supersonic transport. He voted for the

McGovern-Hatfield Amendment, calling for the total withdrawal of U.S. forces from Vietnam by the end of 1971. Tunney argued that the withdrawal would lead to the conversion of defense industries to peacetime production, and that such a conversion would help solve problems of unemployment and environmental pollution. He has followed the extreme left in the Senate in their everlasting battle against the cloture process. He has been a member of the leftist Democratic Study Group. In 1969, he supported the ultra-leftist Vietnam Moratorium demonstrations. In 1971, he endorsed the ultra-leftist National Peace Action Coalition demonstrations.

LYNN TURGEON was born on August 26, 1920 in Mitchell, South Dakota, son of Margie Fellows and Edgar Turgeon. He married Livia Racko. He is an alumnus of the University of California at Berkeley (A.B., 1942; M.A., 1948) and Columbia University (Ph.D., 1959). He is the author of *The Contrasting Economics* (1963).

From 1950 until 1957, Turgeon was an economic consultant to the RAND Corporation. In 1955 and 1956, he held a fellowship from the ultra-leftist Ford Foundation at Columbia University. Since 1957, he has been at Hofstra University as assistant professor (1957-1963), associate professor (1963-1969), and professor (1969 to the present) of economics.

Turgeon has been affiliated with the leftist-oriented Ad Hoc Committee for an Open Letter on Vietnam; the leftist-pacifist Ad Hoc Faculty Committee on Vietnam; and the Socialist Scholars Conferences, annual get-togethers of Marxian Socialists and their fellow-travelers. In recent years, he has been active in the American Society for the Study of the

German Democratic Republic. The Society, which he helped to found, is supported by Communists and well-known fellow travelers, who have launched a propaganda campaign urging the United States Government to extend diplomatic recognition to the Communist regime in East Germany.

MAURICE B. VISSCHER was born on August 25, 1901 in Holland, Michigan, son of Everdena Bolks and Johannes Visscher. He married Janet Pieters. He is an alumnus of Hope College (A.B., 1922) and the University of Michigan (Ph.D., 1925; M.D., 1931). He pursued graduate studies at University College in London, England.

From 1922 until 1925, Visscher was an assistant in physiology at the University of Minnesota. In 1925 and 1926, on leave of absence as an assistant professor from Minnesota, he was a national research council fellow at University College in London. In 1926 and 1927, he was a fellow at the University of Chicago. From 1927 until 1929, he was a professor of physiology at the University of Tennessee's College of Medicine. From 1929 until 1931, he was a professor of physiology and pharmacology at the University of Southern California. From 1931 until 1936, he was professor of physiology and chairman of the physiology department at the University of Illinois. Since 1936, he has been at the University of Minnesota as chairman of the department of physiology (1936-1938), professor of physiology (1936-1960), distinguished service professor (1960-1967), and regents professor of physiology (1967 to the present).

Visscher has been affiliated with the ultra-leftist-pacifist National Committee for a Sane Nuclear Policy; the National Committee to Abolish the House Un-

American Activities Committee ("to lead and direct the Communist Party's 'Operation Abolition' campaign"); the Mid-Century Conference for Peace ("aimed at assembling as many gullible persons as possible under Communist direction and turning them into a vast sounding board for Communist propaganda"); the Committee of One Thousand ("Communist created and controlled front organization"); the National Council of the Arts, Sciences and Professions ("Communist front"); and the leftist-pacifist Voters Peace Pledge. Since 1950, he has been a member of the Federation of American Scientists, a bleeding heart group, members of which are generally affiliated with a variety of radical one-world and/or pacifist organizations.

GEORGE WALD was born on November 18, 1906 in New York City, son of Ernestine Rosenmann and Isaac Wald. He was married to and divorced from Frances Kingsley. He is married to Ruth Hubbard. He is an alumnus of New York University (B.S., 1927) and Columbia University (M.A., 1928; Ph.D., 1932). He is the co-author of *General Education in a Free Society: Twenty Six Afternoons of Biology* (1962).

In 1932 and 1933, as a fellow of the National Research Council, Wald studied at the Kaiser Wilhelm Institute in Berlin, the University of Zurich, and the University of Heidelberg. In 1933 and 1934, he was associated with the department of physiology at the University of Chicago. Since 1934, he has been at Harvard University as a tutor of biochemistry (1934), instructor (1935-1939), faculty instructor (1939-1944), associate professor (1944-1948), professor (1948-1968), and Higgins professor of biology (1968 to the present). In 1956, he was a visiting professor in

biochemistry at the University of California at Berkeley. From 1954 until 1956, he was chairman of the divisional committee on biology and medical sciences of the National Science Foundation. In 1963 and 1964, he held a Guggenheim fellowship and was an overseas fellow at Churchill College of Cambridge University, England.

On March 4, 1969, university scientists throughout the United States held a day-long strike. They deserted their laboratories, classrooms, and lecture halls and took to the political platforms. At Massachusetts Institute of Technology, more than a thousand faculty members and students listened to George Wald deliver a speech — "A Generation In Search of a Future." It was a highly emotional indictment of the Vietnam War, the Selective Service System, nuclear weapons, and war in general. The Communists thought so much of Wald's speech that they reprinted more than a page of excerpts from it in the *Daily World.* Said Wald: "The aftermath of that speech has taken up my whole life." In the course of the speech, Wald said: "I think the Vietnam War is the most shameful episode in the whole of American history." He also said: "Our government has become preoccupied with death, with the business of killing and being killed." In November 1970, Wald showed the effects of the adulation that was showered upon him after he publicly joined the ranks of the leftist-pacifists. He said at the time: "All the Administration's forces of repression are turned against the schools. We are isolated. We are in a completely defenseless position. If we need anything now, it is a base in the outside community."

In March 1971, Wald returned to this same theme when he was instrumental in setting up the Labor University Alliance, a political pressure group of students, faculty members, and labor leaders who are opposed to the war in Vietnam and the United States "military-oriented" economy. Said Wald: "The main point is that there has been no real communication among these three groups, that each represents a focus of power and influence. Academic people have the illusion that labor unions are interested only in such matters as wages, hours and working conditions, whereas in fact almost all labor unions cover the whole spectrum of social and political interests.

"The hope is that the academic community, which has knowledge and expertise, but lacks a broad base in the outside community and any real political muscle, will forge a working arrangement with labor unions who could use our research, expertise and articulateness."

Wald found many bases in the outside community. He became affiliated with the leftist-pacifist National Council to Repeal the Draft, which had as its theme: "The draft has effectively abolished the freedom of American men between the ages of eighteen and twenty-six." His other affiliations included the leftist-pacifist American Friends Service Committee; the ultra-leftist Committee to Defend the Black Panthers; the leftist-oriented Ad Hoc Committee for an Open Letter on Vietnam; the leftist-pacifist Ad Hoc Faculty Committee on Vietnam; the ultra-leftist National Peace Action Coalition; the leftist-pacifist Educational Committee to Halt Atomic Weapons; the leftist-pacifist Civil Defense Letter Committee; the leftist-oriented Inter-University Committee for Debate on Foreign Policy; and the leftist-pacifist Federation of American Scientists. He supported the ultra-leftist Vietnam Moratorium demonstrations throughout 1969. He endorsed the Hanoi-inspired People's Peace Treaty, the pet 1971 project of the ultra-left.

ERIC WALDMAN was born on September 21, 1914 in Vienna, Austria, son of Sophie Blau and Leo Waldman. In 1938, he came to the United States. In 1943, he became a naturalized American citizen. He married JoAnn Lowden. He is an alumnus of the University of Vienna (Ph.D., 1938) and George Washington University (B.A., 1951; M.A., 1952; Ph.D., 1955). In 1958, 1964, and 1965, he held research grants from the German Government. In 1960, he was an advanced research fellow in Germany under the auspices of the North Atlantic Treaty Organization. In 1960 and 1961, and from 1964 until 1966, he held Marquette University research grants. In 1961 and 1962, he held a Fulbright senior research grant, and in 1965, he held a Fulbright travel grant. He is the author of *The Spartacist Uprising* (1958); *The Goose Step Is Verboten – The German Army Today* (1964); and *Notstand und Demokratie* (1968). He is a contributor to *Contemporary Political Ideologies* (1961); *Meet Germany* (1963); and *Soviet Foreign Relations and World Communism* (1965). He is a contributing editor of *Dictionary of Political Science* (1964).

From 1952 until 1955, Waldman was a lecturer at George Washington University and a research analyst at Columbia University. From 1955 until 1966, he was at Marquette University as an assistant professor (1955-1958), associate professor (1958-1962), and professor (1962-1966) of political science; chairman of the political science department (1958-1962); and director of the University's Institute of German Affairs (1957-1966). Since 1966, he has been professor of political science at the

University of Calgary in Canada. In 1965, he was a visiting professor at the University of Marburg.

Waldman has been a member and official of the ultra-leftist-globalist United World Federalists. He has been a member and official of the World Affairs Council, a pivotal agency in a complex of one-world, leftist, and pacifist groups. He is a member of the ultra-leftist American Civil Liberties Union.

BROOKS R. WALKER was born on January 2, 1935 in Gunnison, Colorado, son of Letha Brooks and Robert Walker. He married Sandra Fraser. He is an alumnus of the University of Colorado (B.A., 1956) and Harvard Univeristy (S.T.B., 1959). He is the author of *The Christian Fright Peddlers* (1964).

In 1959 and 1960, Walker was an assistant minister of the North Shore Unitarian Society in Plandome, New York. Since 1960, he has been minister of the Emerson Unitarian Church in Canoga Park, California.

Walker has been active in the leftist-oriented department of social responsibility of the Unitarian-Universalist Association. Since 1963, he has been on the advisory committee for radio station KPFK, operated by the ultra-leftist Pacifica Foundation. He has been an officer of the leftist-oriented Southern California Friends of Free Radio. He has been a member of the leftist-oriented Southwest Liberal Religious Educators Association. He has been a member of the leftist-internationalist American Association for the United Nations.

FREDERICK CHAMPION WARD was born on December 29, 1910 in New Brunswick, New Jersey, son of Helen Eshbaugh and Clarence Ward. He married Duira Baldinger. He is an alumnus of Oberlin College (B.A., 1932; A.M., 1935) and Yale University (Ph.D., 1937).

From 1938 until 1945, Ward was at Denison University as an instructor (1938-1940), assistant professor (1940-1942), and associate professor (1942-1945) of philosophy and psychology. From 1945 until 1958, he was at the University of Chicago as assistant professor (1945-1947) and associate professor (1947-1950) of philosophy, professor of the humanities (1950-1958), dean of the college (1947-1954), and William Rainey Harper professor of the humanities (1955-1958). Since 1954, he has been with the ultra-leftist Ford Foundation as educational consultant in India (1954-1958), director of the Middle East and Africa programs (1958-1963), deputy vice-president for international programs (1963-1966), and vice-president for education and research (1966 to the present).

Ward has been a long-time member of the Council on Foreign Relations, the informal supra-State Department of the United States. He is a long-time member of the ultra-radical National Association for the Advancement of Colored People.

ROBERT PENN WARREN was born on April 24, 1905 in Guthrie, Kentucky, son of Anna Penn and Robert Warren. He was married to and divorced from Emma Brescia. He is married to Eleanor Clark. He is an alumnus of Vanderbilt University (B.A., 1925); the University of California (M.A., 1927); and Oxford University in England, where he was a Rhodes scholar (B. Litt., 1930). He also pursued graduate studies at Yale University. He is the author of *John Brown: The Making of a Martyr* (1929); *Thirty-Six Poems* (1936); *Night Rider* (1939); *Eleven Poems on the Same Theme*

(1942); *At Heaven's Gate* (1943); *Selected Poems, 1923-1943* (1944); *All the King's Men* (1946); *Blackberry Winter* (1946); *The Circus in the Attic, and Other Stories* (1948); *World Enough and Time* (1950); *Brother to Dragons* (1953); *Band of Angels* (1955); *Segregation: The Inner Conflict in the South* (1956); *Promises: Poems 1954-1956* (1957); *Remember the Alamo!* (1958); *Selected Essays* (1958); *The Cave* (1959); *The Gods of Mount Olympus* (1959); *You, Emperors and Others: Poems 1957-1960* (1960); *The Legacy of the Civil War* (1961); *Wilderness: A Tale of the Civil War* (1961); *Flood: A Romance for Our Time* (1964); *Who Speaks for the Negro?* (1965); *Selected Poems New and Old: 1923-1966* (1966); *Incarnations: Poems 1966-1968* (1968); and *Audubon: A Vision* (1969). He is the co-author of *Modern Rhetoric* (1949, 1958, and 1961) and *Fundamentals of Good Writing* (1950 and 1956). He is a contributor to *I'll Take My Stand* (1930) and *Who Owns America? A New Declaration of Independence* (1936). He is the editor of *A Southern Harvest: Short Stories by Southern Writers* (1937) and *Faulkner: A Collection of Critical Essays* (1966). He is co-editor of *An Approach to Literature* (1936); *Understanding Poetry* (1938 and 1960); *Understanding Fiction* (1943 and 1959; published in shorter version as *Scope of Fiction*, 1960); *Anthology of Stories from "Southern Review"* (1953); *Short Story Masterpieces* (1954 and 1958); *Six Centuries of Great Poetry* (1955); and *A New Southern Harvest* (1957). He has contributed to numerous publications, including *American Review, American Scholar, Botteghe Oscure, Fugitive, Harvard Advocate, Holiday, Mademoiselle, New York Times Book Review, Poetry, Saturday Review, Sewanee Review, Southern Review, Virginia Quarterly Review, Yale Review,* and such leftist publications as *Nation* and *New Republic.*

In 1930 and 1931, Warren was assitant professor of English at Southwestern College in Tennessee. From 1931 until 1934, he was an acting assistant professor of English at Vanderbilt University. From 1934 until 1942, he was at Louisiana State University as assistant professor (1934-1936) and associate professor (1936-1942) of English. From 1942 until 1950, he was professor of English at the University of Minnesota. Since 1950, he has been at Yale University as professor of play writing (1950-1956) and professor of English (1961 to the present). He has been a visiting lecturer at the University of Iowa. He has been a staff member of writers' conferences at the University of Colorado and Olivet College. In 1944 and 1945, he held the chair of poetry at the Library of Congress.

In light of his Southern birth and his unmistakable liberal bias, Warren is a modern-day scalawag. In much of his writings, especially in recent years, he has been a glorifier of and apologist for some of the most outrageous Negro agitators in the country. His efforts on behalf of the liberal left have not gone unrewarded. He has received a Guggenheim fellowship, Pulitzer Prizes, the *New York Herald Tribune* Van Doren award, Screen Writers Guild Award, and an award from the ultra-leftist Sidney Hillman Foundation. He is affiliated with the ultra-radical National Association for the Advancement of Colored People. He has been affiliated with the Freedom House Bookshelf Committee composed of the most brazen-faced leftists in the literary and academic world.

STANLEY A. WEIGEL was born on December 9, 1905 in Helena, Montana, son of Jennie Hepner and Louis Weigel. He married Anne Kauffman. He is an alumnus of Stanford University (A.B., 1926; J.D., 1928). In 1928, he was admitted to the California bar.

From 1928 until 1962, Weigel practiced law in San Francisco. Since 1952, he has been an occasional lecturer at Stanford University's Law School. Since 1962, he has been a justice of the United States District Court in San Francisco.

Weigel has been affiliated with the ultra-leftist Ford Foundation; the ultra-leftist United World Federalists; the leftist-internationalist World Affairs Council of Northern California; and the ultra-radical American Civil Liberties Union.

JACOB J. WEINSTEIN was born on June 6, 1902 in Stephin, Poland, son of Shaindel Weinstein and Benjamin Weinstein. In 1907, he was brought to the United States. He was naturalized in 1925. He married Janet Harris. He is an alumnus of Reed College (A.B., 1923) and Hebrew Union College (M.H.L., 1929). In 1929, he was ordained a rabbi.

Weinstein has served as rabbi for congregations in Austin, Texas (1929-1930), San Francisco (1930-1932), and Chicago (since 1939). In 1932 and 1933, he was an adviser to Jewish students at Columbia University. From 1933 until 1935, he was director of the Adult School for Jewish Studies in New York City. From 1935 until 1939, he was director of the School for Jewish Studies in San Francisco. Since 1933, he has been on the editorial board of *Jewish Frontier*. During the administrations of Presidents Kennedy and Johnson, he was a member of the Presidential Committee on Equal Employment Opportunity. In the 1960's, he was vice president and president of the Central Conference of American Rabbis.

Weinstein has been affiliated with the American Committee for Protection of Foreign Born [Americans] ("subversive and Communist" – "one of the oldest auxiliaries of the Communist Party in the United States"); American Youth for Democracy ("subversive and Communist"); the National Council of American-Soviet Friendship ("subversive and Communist" – "specializing in pro-Soviet propaganda"); the Civil Rights Congress ("Communist front" – "subversive and Communist"); the Committee for Citizenship Rights ("to protect Communist subversion from any penalties under the law"); Consumers Union ("subversive and un-American"); the Council for Pan-American Democracy ("subversive and Communist" – "Communist front"); *Fight* ("a Communist front publication"); the Harry Bridges Defense Committee ("Communist front"); the Joint Anti-Fascist Refugee Committee ("subversive and Communist"); the Medical Bureau to Aid Spanish Democracy ("series of Communist enterprises which have dealt with Spain and the Spanish Civil War"); the National Committee to Secure Justice for Morton Sobell ("Communist campaign"); the National Religion and Labor Foundation ("Communist front"); the Open Letter in Defense of Harry Bridges ("Communist front"); the People's Institute of Applied Religion ("subversive and Communist"); the National Committee to Secure Justice in the Rosenberg Appeal ("Communist front"); the Spanish Refugee Appeal ("subversive" – "Communist front"); the National Committee to Repeal the McCarran Act ("a Communist front" – "subversive"); the National Committee to Abolish the House Un-American Activities Committee ("to lead and direct the Communist Party's 'Operation Abolition' campaign"); and the Chicago Ad Hoc Com-

WELCOME

mittee of Welcome for the [Red] Dean of Canterbury. He participated in such Communist Party projects as the *Freedomways* Tribute to W.E.B. du Bois, the du Bois Centennial Celebrations, the fight against renewal of the Dies Committee in 1943, and the protest against the deportation of Harry Bridges in 1943 and the conviction of Communist Party leaders in 1949. He has also been affiliated with such ultra-leftist-pacifist groups as the Fellowship of Reconciliation, the National Committee for a Sane Nuclear Policy, the National Coordinating Committee to End the War in Vietnam, and Clergy and Laymen Concerned About Vietnam.

In 1965, after traveling to Vietnam with other radical clergymen, Weinstein proclaimed that military power would never settle the war and demanded that the United States cease bombing raids against North Vietnam as a "demonstration of good faith." A few months later, he signed a Fellowship of Reconciliation fund-raising appeal which read, in part: "To the people and government of the United States: The horrors that your planes and massive firepower are inflicting on the people of Viet Nam are beyond moral or political justification." Weinstein and his fellow-travelers tendered no similar condemnation to the people and government of North Vietnam for their atrocious history of aggression against South Vietnam and its allies, including the United States.

VERDA FREEMAN WELCOME was born *c.* 1912 in Lake Lure, North Carolina, daughter of Docia Proctor and John Freeman. She married Henry Welcome. She is an alumna of Morgan State College (B.S., 1939) and New York University (M.A., 1943). She received a diploma from Cappin State Teachers

College in 1932. She pursued postgraduate studies at Columbia University.

From 1934 until 1945, Mrs. Welcome was a teacher in the public schools of Baltimore. From 1959 until 1962, she was a member of the Maryland House of Delegates. Since 1963, she has been a member of the Maryland Senate.

Mrs. Welcome has been affiliated with the leftist-oriented League of Women Voters; the leftist-pacifist Women's International League for Peace and Freedom; the ultra-radical National Association for the Advancement of Colored People; and the ultra-radical Americans for Democratic Action.

DONALD A. WELLS was born on April 17, 1917 in St. Paul, Minnesota, son of Ultima Johnson and Harry Wells. He married June Mickman. He is an alumnus of Hamline University (B.A., 1940) and Boston University (S.T.B., 1943; Ph.D., 1946). He also studied at the University of Minnesota. In 1943, he was ordained to the ministry of the Methodist Church. He is the author of *God, Man and the Thinker: Philosophies of Religion* (1962) and *The War Myth* (1967). He is a contributor to *Exploration in Human Potentialities* (1966).

From 1942 until 1946, Wells held pastorates in Boston and Weston, Massachusetts. In 1945 and 1946, he was a therapist at the Bedford, Massachusetts Mental Hospital. From 1946 until 1948, he was an assistant professor of philosophy at Oregon State College. From 1948 until 1969, he was at Washington State University as assistant professor (1948-1953), associate professor (1953-1957), and professor (1957-1969) of philosophy, and chairman of the philosophy department (1948-1969). Since 1969, he has been chairman of the philosophy department at the University of Illinois.

Wells has been a counselor for conscientious objectors. He is a member of the ultra-radical American Civil Liberties Union. He is a member of the ultra-leftist-pacifist Fellowship of Reconciliation.

ALAN F. WESTIN was born on October 11, 1929 in New York City, son of Etta Furman and Irving Westin. He married Bea Shapoff. He is an alumnus of the University of Florida (A.B., 1948) and Harvard University (LL.B., 1951; Ph.D., 1965). In 1959 and 1960, he held a grant from the Rockefeller Foundation, a pillar of the liberal Establishment. He has also held grants from the ultra-leftist Fund for the Republic and the New World Foundation. He is the author of *The Anatomy of a Constitutional Law Case* (1958); *The Supreme Court: Views from Inside* (1961); *The Uses of Power: Seven Cases in American Politics* (1961); *An Autobiography of the Supreme Court* (1963); and *Freedom Now! The Civil Rights Struggle in America* (1964). He is a co-author of *The Third Branch of Government* (1962); *The Centers of Power* (1963); *Power and Order: Seven Cases in World Politics* (1963); *Politics and Government in the United States* (1965); and *Politics in Europe: Five Cases in European Government* (1965). He is the editor of Charles Beard's *The Supreme Court and the Constitution* (1962). He is a contributor to *Foundations of Freedom in the American Constitution* (1958); *The Radical Right* (1963); *Mr. Justice* (1964); and *Quarrels That Have Shaped the Constitution* (1964). He has contributed articles to the *New York Times, Harper's, American Heritage, Saturday Review,* and such leftist publications as *New Republic, Nation,* and *New Leader.*

From 1957 until 1959, Westin was an assistant professor of government at Cornell University. In 1960 and 1961, he was a visiting associate professor of political science at Yale University. Since 1959, he has been at Columbia University as associate professor of public law and government (1959 to the present), lecturer in the University's Law School (1962), lecturer in the University's Teachers College (1962-1964), and director of the Center for Research and Education in American Liberties (1965 to the present). In 1958, he was a lecturer at the Salzburg [Austria] Seminar in American Studies. In 1959, he was the Sidney Hillman lecturer at Brandeis University.

Westin has been a long-time member of the national board of directors of the ultra-radical American Civil Liberties Union. He has long been on the civil rights committee of the defamatory Anti-Defamation League, in which position he has shown a strong hostility toward anti-Communists. In 1958, he received an award from the ultra-leftist Sidney Hillman Foundation.

URBAN WHITAKER JR. was born on May 19, 1924 in Colony, Kansas, son of Gladys Fackler and Urban Whitaker. He married Jean Knox. He is an alumnus of Occidental College (A.B., 1946) and Washington University in Seattle (Ph.D., 1954). In 1947 and 1948, he studied at the College of Chinese Studies in Peking. In 1955, he held a fellowship from the ultra-leftist Ford Foundation. In 1960 and 1961, he held a fellowship from the Rockefeller Foundation, a pillar of the liberal Establishment. He is the author of *Nationalism and Internationalism* (1961); *Politics and Power, A Text in International Law* (1964); and *The World and Ridgeway* (1968). He is the editor of *Foundations of U.S. China Policy* (1959); *Nationalism and International Progress* (1960 and 1962); *Propaganda and International Relations* (1960 and 1962); and *Democracies and International Affairs* (1961). He has contributed articles to *Western Political Quarterly, Frontier,* and such leftist publications as *Nation, Progressive,* and *War/Peace Report.*

Since 1954, he has been at San Francisco State College as instructor (1954-1956), assistant professor (1956-1958), associate professor (1958-1962), and professor (1962 to the present) of international relations, and dean of undergraduate studies (1969 to the present). From 1958 until 1961, he was co-director of the International Studies Project of the leftist-pacifist Carnegie Corporation. In 1968, he was an unsuccessful candidate for Congress. Since 1968, he has been a member of the California Democratic State Committee. In 1964, he was an active supporter of the radical students involved in the Free Speech Movement demonstrations at the University of California's Berkeley campus.

Whitaker has been affiliated with the National Committee to Abolish the House Un-American Activities Committee ("to lead and direct the Communist Party's 'Operation Abolition' campaign"). He was a long-time member and national official of the American Association for the United Nations, and he is on the board of directors of its successor, the United Nations Association of the United States. The AAUN and the UNAUS have served as propaganda organizations for the United Nations, for one-worldism, for disarmament, and for admission of Red China to UN membership. Since 1965, he has been a member of the board of directors of the leftist-pacifist Commission to Study the Organization of Peace, the research arm of the UNAUS.

FRANCIS O. WILCOX was born on April 9, 1908 in Columbus Junction, Iowa, son of Verna Gray and Francis Wilcox. He was married to the late Genevieve Byrnes. He is married to Virginia Sullivan. He is an alumnus of the University of Iowa (A.B., 1930; A.M., 1931; Ph.D., 1933) and the University of Geneva (Ph.D., 1935). He is a graduate of the Institute of International Studies at Geneva. He was a fellow at The Hague Academy of International Law. He is the author of *The Ratification of International Conventions: A Study of the Relationship of the Ratification Process to the Development of International Legislation* (1935). He is a co-author of *Proposals for Changes in the United Nations* (1955), and a co-editor of *Recent American Foreign Policy: Basic Documents, 1941-1951* (1952).

From 1931 until 1933, Wilcox was a teaching assistant in political science at the University of Iowa. In 1933 and 1934, he was a fellow of the leftist-pacifist Carnegie Endowment for International Peace. From 1935 until 1942, he was at the University of Louisville as assistant professor (1935-1937) and associate professor (1937-1939) of political science, and chairman of the division of social science (1939-1942). In 1941, he was a visiting professor at the University of Michigan. From 1941 until 1943, he was a consultant for the American Council on Education. In 1942, he was associate chief of the division of inter-American activities in the Office of the Coordinator of Inter-American Affairs, who was Nelson A. Rockefeller. In 1943, he was chief of the program services section of the Office of Civilian Defense.

In 1943 and 1944, he was an international relations analyst in the Bureau of the Budget. From 1945 until 1947, he was the chief international relations analyst for the Library of Congress. From 1947 until 1955, he was chief of staff of the Senate Foreign Relations Committee. From 1955 until 1961, he was an assistant secretary of state for international organizational affairs. From 1946 until 1952, he lectured on international organizations and American foreign relations at the School of Advanced International Studies of The Johns Hopkins University. Since 1961, he has been dean of the School of Advanced International Studies.

Wilcox is a long-time nonresident member of the Council on Foreign Relations, the informal supra-State Department of the United States. For more than a decade, he has been an official of the Foreign Policy Association, a pivotal agency for pro-Communist, one-world propaganda.

HAROLD WILLENS was born on April 26, 1914 in Chernigov, Russia, son of Bertha Heskin and Sam Willens. He became a United States citizen in 1924. He married Grace Silverman. He is an alumnus of the University of California at Los Angeles (B.A., 1944).

From 1932 until 1935, Willens was a grocery clerk in Los Angeles. From 1935 until 1944, he was a food specialties broker in Los Angeles. From 1946 until 1949, he was a textile broker. Since 1949, he has been president of the Factory Equipment Supply Corporation of Los Angeles, which he founded. He also founded the Wilshop Corporation of Los Angeles, and has been its president since 1954.

Since 1963, Willens has been an official of the ultra-leftist Center for the Study of Democratic Institutions. He has been on the board of directors of the ultra-leftist Fund for the Republic. He is on the board of trustees of the leftist-internationalist Fund for Peace, which has been associated with the ultra-leftist Pugwash group. He has been affiliated with the leftist-oriented Fund for Education in World Order; the Institute for American Democracy, an anti-anti-Communist witch-hunting offshoot of the defamatory Anti-Defamation League; and the ultra-radical American Civil Liberties Union. Since 1967, he has been national co-chairman of the leftist-pacifist Business Executives Move for Vietnam Peace. In 1968, he was national chairman of Businessmen for Eugene McCarthy, in McCarthy's attempt to gain the presidential nomination. Willens, who has been vehemently opposed to United States involvement in the Vietnam War, has also been closely associated with the extremely dovish California Congressman Paul McCloskey.

HAYDN WILLIAMS was born on August 21, 1919 in Spokane, Washington, son of Kathryn Williams and Robert Williams. He married Margaret Gregory. He is an alumnus of the University of California at Berkeley (A.B., 1946) and the Fletcher School of Law and Diplomacy at Tufts University (A.M., 1947; Ph.D., 1958).

From 1941 until 1943, Williams was employed by Pan Am World Airways. From 1949 until 1952, he was assistant professor, professor, and associate dean at the College of Business Administration of the University of Washington in Seattle. From 1952 until 1958, he was at the Fletcher School of Law and Diplomacy as assistant dean and assistant professor (1952-1953), and associate dean and associate professor

(1954-1958). From 1958 until 1964, he was with the Department of Defense as a deputy assistant secretary for National Security Council affairs and plans (1958-1961) and a deputy assistant secretary for international security affairs (1961-1964). Since 1964, he has been president of the Asia Foundation in San Francisco.

Williams has been affiliated with the leftist-internationalist World Affairs Council of Northern California. He is a long-time nonresident member of the Council on Foreign Relations, the informal supra-State Department of the United States. He is a long-time member of the leftist-internationalist U.S. Commission on UNESCO.

HARPER H. WILSON was born on June 18, 1909 in Springfield, Massachusetts. He is an alumnus of Springfield College (B.S., 1932); Clark University (A.M., 1939); and Wisconsin University (Ph.D., 1947). He has written several books in the area of political science.

In 1942 and 1943, Wilson was an economic analyst with the War Production Board. Since 1947, he has been at Princeton University as assistant professor (1947-1950), associate professor (1950-1962), and professor (1962 to the present) of political science.

Wilson has been affiliated with the National Committee to Abolish the House Un-American Activities Committee ("to lead and direct the Communist Party's 'Operation Abolition' campaign"); the Emergency Civil Liberties Committee ("Communist front" – "subversive"); the ultra-leftist Medical Aid to [Castro's] Cuba Committee; the National Committee to Repeal the McCarran Act ("Communist front" – "subversive"); the National Committee to Secure Justice in the Rosenberg Case ("Communist front"); the American Forum for Socialist Education, under Communist inspiration and domination; and the Honorary Sponsors of the Committee to Free Morton Sobell, the convicted atom spy. He is an active participant in the Socialist Scholars Conferences, annual get-to-gethers of Marxian Socialists and their fellow-travelers.

MARSHALL WINDMILLER was born on June 29, 1924 in Sacramento, California, son of Gladys Hook and Louis Windmiller. He married Myra Bailey. He is an alumnus of the University of the Pacific (B.A., 1948) and the University of California at Berkeley (M.A., 1954; Ph.D., 1964). He pursued graduate studies at the Sorbonne University of Paris. From 1952 until 1954, he held fellowships from the ultra-leftist Ford Foundation. He is the author of *Five Years on Free Radio* (1965). He is the co-author of *Communism in India* (1959). He has contributed articles to *Canadian Dimension, St. Louis Post-Dispatch, Tribune* (London), *Motive,* and such leftist publications as *Nation, Progressive, Ramparts,* and *Review of International Affairs.*

From 1954 until 1959, Windmiller was a resident political scientist at the University of California at Berkeley. Since 1959, he has been at San Francisco State College as assistant professor (1959-1964), associate professor (1964-1968), and professor (1968 to the present) of international relations, and director of the International Relations Center (1964 to the present).

Windmiller has been a regular foreign affairs commentator on radio station KPFA, operated by the ultra-leftist Pacifica Foundation. He has contributed articles to the *People's ·World,* a west coast Communist daily. He has been

WITHERS

associated with the Marxian Socialist labor agitator Cesar Chavez. He has been affiliated with the National Association for the Advancement of Colored People, the fountainhead of Negro agitation for more than half a century; the ultra-leftist American Civil Liberties Union; the Castro-subsidized Fair Play for Cuba Committee; the leftist-pacifist Women Strike for Peace; the East Bay Community Forum, a Communist front; the leftist-pacifist Vietnam Day Committee in California, the Radical Education Project, operated by the ultra-leftist Students for a Democratic Society; the ultra-leftist Community for New Politics in Berkeley; and the leftist-oriented Inter-University Committee for Debate on Foreign Policy.

HENRY S. WINGATE was born on October 8, 1905 in Talas, Turkey, son of Jane Smith and Henry Wingate. He married Ardis Swenson. He is an alumnus of Carleton College (B.A., 1927) and the University of Michigan (J.D., 1929).

From 1929 until 1935, Wingate was associated with the well-known legal firm of Sullivan & Cromwell in New York City. Since 1935, he has been with the International Nickel Company of Canada as assistant secretary (1935-1939), secretary (1939-1952), director (1942 to the present), vice-president (1949-1954), president (1954-1960), and chairman of the board (1960 to the present). Since 1935, he has been with the International Nickel Company, Inc., as assistant to the president (1935-1954), director (1944 to the present), president (1954-1960), and chairman of the board and chief executive officer (1960 to the present). He has been a director of the Bank of Montreal, the Morgan Guaranty Trust Company, American Standard, Inc., the U.S. Steel

Corporation, the Canadian Pacific Railway, and J.P. Morgan and Company.

Wingate is a long-time member of the Council on Foreign Relations, the informal supra-State Department of the United States; and the Foreign Policy Association, a pivotal agency for pro-Communist, one-world propaganda.

WILLIAM WITHERS was born on December 21, 1905 in St. Louis, Missouri, son of Margaret Mathews and John Withers. He married Irma Rittenhouse. He is an alumnus of Columbia University (A.B., 1926; A.M., 1928, Ph.D., 1932). He is the author of *The Retirement of National Debts* (1932); *Current Social Problems* (1936); *Financing Economic Security* (1939); *The Public Debt* (1945); *Public Finance* (1948); *The Social Foundations of Education* (1955); *The Economic Crisis in Latin America* (1964); and *Business in Society* (1966). He is a contributor to the *Encyclopedia of Social Sciences, American Economic Review, School and Society, Annals, Journal of Commerce,* and such leftist publications as *Nation* and *New Leader.*

From 1927 until 1929, Withers was an instructor in economics at Lehigh University. From 1929 until 1931, he was an instructor in economics at New York University. From 1931 until 1937, he was at Columbia University as a research associate (1931-1932) and assistant professor of education (1935-1937) in the University's Teachers College, and chairman of the social science department in the University's New College (1932-1937). Since 1937, he has been at Queens College as assistant professor (1937-1940), associate professor (1940-1951), and professor (1951 to the present) of economics.

In 1945 and 1946, Withers was vice-chairman of the ultra-leftist Liberal

Party of New York State. He was an official of the Union for Democratic Action, whose guiding genius was Louis Fraina, one of America's first Communists. He has been an official of the Socialist League for Industrial Democracy. He was a consultant to the Redladen Federal Council of Churches. He has been a member of the leftist Workers Defense League.

ROBERT K. WOETZEL was born on December 5, 1930 in Shanghai, China, son of Eva Gumprich and Kurt Woetzel. He married Sheila Barry. He is an alumnus of Columbia University (A.B., 1952); Oxford University in England (Ph.D., 1958); and the University of Bonn (J.D.,1959). He also studied at The Hague Academy of International Law. He is the author of *The International Control of Space* (1960); *The Nuremberg Trials in International Law* (1960 and 1962); and *The Philosophy of Freedom* (1967).

In 1956, Woetzel was a legislative assistant in the U.S. House of Representatives. From 1956 until 1959, he was an associate of the director of the Institute of International Law at the University of Bonn. From 1959 until 1963, he was at Fordham University in the graduate faculties of the arts and sciences as an assistant professor of public law and government. In 1960 and 1961, he was a consultant to the leftist-pacifist Carnegie Endowment for International Peace. From 1960 until 1963, he was an associate professor of international law at New York University. In 1961 and 1962, he was a visiting professor at the Seminary of the Immaculate Conception. In 1963 and 1964, he was a scholastic novice in the Society of Jesus. From 1964 until 1966, he was a staff member at the ultra-leftist Center for the Study

of Democratic Institutions. In 1964 and 1965, he was a visiting professor at the Old Mission Theological Seminary in Santa Barbara. Since 1966, he has been a professor of international politics and law at Boston College. He is a member of the ultra-radical American Civil Liberties Union.

LEON WOFSY was born on November 23, 1921 in Stamford, Connecticut, son of Rose and Isadore Wofsy. (Leon has described his father as having been a radical Socialist. When Isadore died in 1964, he was eulogized in the Communist Party's monthly journal, *Political Affairs*. The eulogist described Isadore Wofsy: "As a lad of sixteen, having just emigrated from his native Latvia to New Rochelle, New York, in 1910, he joined the local branch of the Socialist Party. His earnestness, his willingness to perform the required Jimmy Higgins tasks, and his unquenchable thirst for knowledge, won the admiration of his co-members. The then editor of *Printer's Ink* readily helped the young immigrant to learn the language of his adopted country. When, three years later, he went to Connecticut, he was already a dedicated socialist, having determined to give his all to the cause of human freedom, to the abolition of the exploitation of man by man. It was logical, therefore, that once the Socialist Party was irreparably split after World War I, he should become a charter member of the Communist Party, firmly adhering to its Marxist principles until the very end.")

In March 1964, Leon Wofsy applied for a faculty position at the university of California at Berkeley. He provided a résumé of his previous employment: chemist for the May Chemical Company in Newark, New Jersey (November 1942-January 1943); U.S. Army (January 1943-September 1943); chemist for Pyridium Corporation in New York (September 1943-May 1944); executive of American Youth for Democracy (May 1944-May 1949); executive of the Labor Youth League (May 1949-May 1956); unemployed (May 1956-July 1956); chemist for Armstrong Rubber Company in West Haven, Connecticut (August 1956-August 1957); teacher at North Branford (Connecticut) Junior High School (September 1957-January 1958); laboratory assistant at Sterling Chemical Laboratories at Yale University (January 1958-August 1958); graduate student at Yale University (September 1958-May 1961); post-doctoral chemist at Yale University (June 1961-August 1961); and assistant research bacteriologist and associate professor at the University of California at San Diego (September 1961-June 1964). Since July 1964, Wofsy has been at the University of California in Berkeley as, successively, assistant professor and professor of bacteriology.

In the 1965 Report of California's Senate Fact-Finding Subcommittee on Un-American Activities, further details of Wofsy's career were provided: "He finished high school at New Haven, then attended City College of New York in 1942. While he was a high school student in New Haven he was also active in the American Student Union, a Communist-dominated organization, and at New York City College in 1941 he was president of the Marxian Cultural Society, a section of the Young Communist League, and in 1942 he was an officer of American Youth for Democracy in New York. Having majored in science, Wofsy worked as a chemist for about a year and a half after leaving college, and then became a full-time Communist functionary, specializing in its youth division. From 1937, certainly through the next eighteen years, he was one of the most active and important Communist officials in the United States." (Wofsy served American Youth for Democracy as executive secretary in New York and as AYD's national educational director. In 1948, he applied for a passport to attend a meeting of the Soviet-controlled World Federation of Democratic Youth. The government denied him the passport on grounds that he was a subversive individual. In a 1947 Report, the House Committee on Un-American Activities said of AYD: "Cited as a front formed in October 1943 to succeed the Young Communist League and for the purpose of exploiting to the advantage of a foreign power the idealism, inexperience, and craving to join which is characteristic of American college youth. Its 'high-sounding slogans' cover 'a determined effort to disaffect our youth and to turn them against religion, the American home, against the college authorities, and against the American Government itself.' " In 1956, the Senate Internal Security Subcommittee said: "As part of Soviet psychological warfare against the United States, Communist fronts seek to paralyze America's will to resist Communist aggression by idealizing Russia's aims and methods, discrediting the United States, spreading defeatism and demoralization . . . . Specializing in this field . . . have been such organizations as . . . the American Youth for Democracy.")

In 1948, American Youth for Democracy was dissolved and Wofsy became National Youth Director for the Communist Party. In 1949, he was one of eight Communist Party leaders who went to Chicago for the purpose of planning a new Communist youth organization. At a meeting, presided over by Wofsy, the Labor Youth League was established as the successor to American Youth for Democracy.

Wofsy explained the basic aims and objectives of the Labor Youth League: "The Labor Youth League stands against the big business tycoons whose system exists by war and human misery. It opposes Wall Street's preparations for a third world war. It opposes reaction's drive to fascism. It opposes all efforts to militarize America's young people and to poison their minds. It combats every form of chauvinism, war mongering, white supremacy, religious bigotry, anti-semitism, labor-baiting and anti-communism.

"The Labor Youth League strives for friendship between the United States of America and the USSR as the cornerstone of lasting peace. It also builds friendship and solidarity with the democratic youth of all nations, united in their determination for peace and in their hatred for imperialism and colonial oppression.

"The Labor Youth League calls on youth to defend, support and build the trade unions. It calls for a vigorous defense of the economic rights and interests of working youth, threatened by mounting unemployment and developing economic crisis. It opposes every kind of special exploitation of young workers, whether through wage discrimination, speed-up, or child labor.

"Because of the very nature of our organization, we will develop the warmest fraternal relations with the Communist Party which is leading party of the American working class. No one can learn about Marxism, without getting to know how and by whom Marxist policies are applied from day to day in the interests of our country and its people. We know that our young people will have much to learn from the Communist Party, from Foster, and from the heroic twelve on trial. Our fraternal relations with the Communist Party are, of course, not in contradiction to, but a further expression of the independence of our organization for the Communists are on principle against control of the youth. Those whose Marxist outlook makes them the best friends and teachers of the young people have no reason to fear the independence of youth. No doubt, witch-hunters will try to distort the character of our organization, to distort the fact that thousands of non-Communist youth will join in building and leading our organization."

In September 1964, a student demonstration took place on the campus of the University of California at Berkeley. In the months that followed, there were more demonstrations and, before they had run their course, Berkeley became the site of a full-fledged student rebellion — one of the most serious ever to have taken place on an American campus up to that time.

In 1965, California's Senate Fact-Finding Subcommittee on Un-American Activities devoted most of its Report to the Senate on the background, circumstances, organizations, and personalities related to the rebellion. The Subcommittee explained: "It is the responsibility of this subcommittee to ascertain the causes of these disturbances and to report the extent to which they were inspired or influenced by subversive elements. We do this realizing that there is an unfortunate trend at present for the extreme right to see Communists everywhere, and for the extreme left to pretend that they no longer exist. We have conducted investigations of subversive infiltration at the University of California and at other educational institutions throughout the state since 1941.

From the inception of the most recent troubles at Berkeley we have had both overt and covert agents in this area who have provided us with a flow of information on a day-to-day basis. In addition we have obtained statements from university administrators, faculty members, Regents, and students; we have obtained all documents we believe material to the subject, we have studied the newspaper accounts, magazine articles, TV and radio programs that seemed important . . . ."

In its 1965 Report, the Subcommittee devoted some attention to Leon Wofsy and other individuals with a background of Communist Party activities. Wofsy was of special interest for many reasons. He had moved from the University of California's San Diego campus to the Berkeley campus just prior to the beginning of the student rebellion. The Subcommittee considered him as unquestionably "the top expert in the field of organizing Communist youth movements." The Subcommittee reflected on Wofsy's long-time experiences on the California scene: "Leon Wofsy made many trips to California in connection with his duties as national director for the young Communist movement in the United States. He lectured at Communist schools, to groups of important party members, to youth leaders, and the usual array of Communist front organizations. He has been a resident of California continuously since September of 1961 . . . . He arrived at Berkeley in September of 1964, just in time for the commencement of the demonstrations."

The Subcommittee noted that, when Wofsy obtained his faculty position at the University, he declared that he became disenchanted with Communism and left the Communist movement in 1956. The Subcommittee conceded the possibility "that Leon Wofsy, after a period of intensive devotion to Communist activity since he was a teenager in high school, was one of those who left the party." But the Subcommittee wanted to be reassured about Wofsy's sincerity.

The Subcommittee wondered just how much University officials knew about Wofsy before he was hired: "It is possible that the officials of the state university who assumed the responsibility of employing this former director of Communist youth activities throughout the entire country, and whose whole life from the time he was a high school student until he was a mature man was devoted to the Communist cause, had some confidential information that his statement about becoming disenchanted with Communism and breaking away from the movement was sincere and truthful. It is, of course, common knowledge that in many instances such statements are made to naive persons for the purpose of securing a well-paying job as an undercover subversive agent so that subversive activities may be pursued at taxpayers' expense . . . .

"Mr. Wofsy has only been on the Berkeley campus a short period of time, but he has nonetheless aligned himself with a group of colleagues some of whom have exhibited considerable sympathy for the Free Speech Movement in general and its radical leadership in particular.

"We do not know, either, whether Mr. Wofsy saw fit to explain to those university officials who assumed the responsibility of accepting his story and giving, him a job, that there was a great deal more to his Communist background than simply the work he did for American Youth for Democracy and the Labor Youth League as set forth in his form number 1501. If he made a full disclosure to these officials, and a full disclosure to the appropriate agency of our government, we will be most happy to make that fact as public as we have made public Mr. Wofsy's Communist background in the foregoing account. Until that time it is perfectly plain that we have nothing more than his simple statement to the effect that he became disenchanted with Communism and left the movement in 1956.

"For approximately twenty years Leon Wofsy played a role of ever-increasing importance in the American Communist Party, until he was making reports directly to its National Executive Committee and was considered sufficiently reliable and indoctrinated to be placed in charge of its National Youth Movement. We know that he made an involuntary appearance before a legislative committee in Washington in 1955, and on that occasion when he was interrogated about his experiences in the Communist Party, he responded by seeking refuge behind the Fifth Amendment."

In the course of its Report, the Subcommittee directed some attention to the role of the University's President, Clark Kerr, in the student rebellion. The Report included a review of Kerr's early contacts with many Communists, some of whom came to work at the Berkeley campus in the Institute of Industrial Relations, which Kerr once headed, or elsewhere on the campus while Kerr was either Chancellor or President. The Subcommittee explained why Kerr's name was brought into the "rebellion" story: "We are fully aware that some readers will criticize us for what they consider to be red-baiting and witch-hunting, and implying all sorts of dark motives by bringing this background into the open – but it is, we believe, an indispensable

part of this report, and has a direct and pertinent bearing on the innovations that characterized Kerr's administration, both as Chancellor at Berkeley and later as President of the University. The tolerance of the radical student groups, the opening of the campus to Communist officials, the reluctance to curb the activities of the most brash and defiant student rebels, and the obvious distaste for adequate security precautions, speak for themselves."

President Kerr took such serious exception to the Subcommittee's 1965 Report that he compiled a lengthy analysis in which he attempted to refute general and detailed items, including much that the Subcommittee had to say about Wofsy.

Kerr wrote that the 1965 Report noted that the University had only Wofsy's word that he had become disenchanted with Communism and left the Communist movement in 1956. Kerr brought up the point that the Subcommittee offered no evidence to contradict Wofsy.

In its 1966 Report, the Subcommittee reacted to Kerr's criticism. It pointed out that Kerr himself worried about the truth of Wofsy's declaration. In conference with the University's Chancellor, Edward W. Strong, on May 30, 1964, Kerr had said the Wofsy case held "considerable risk in view of the long record of Communist Party activity and commitment." Kerr had suggested that, in order to forestall future criticism, Strong and he should draft a "carefully-written letter making known our concern about reported past activities which Wofsy had acknowledged, to make clear that we regard these as necessarily terminated in the interest of pursuing a scholarly career."

The Subcommittee uncovered a letter

written by Wofsy to Dr. Sanford E. Elberg, professor of bacteriology at Berkeley, when Wofsy was seeking the job at Berkeley as associate professor of bacteriology. In the letter, Wofsy wrote: "As you may know, I turned down an associate professorship at the State University of New York because of objections to the Feinberg Law, New York's version of the 'loyalty oath.' Although I disagree with such 'oaths' as a criterion for academic appointment, the California oath is far less objectionable to me. I signed it in 1961 when I came to La Jolla and accept the fact that it is one of the requirements for working in the California system.

"The California Oath presents me with no problems of principle or conscience, but any system with such a provision does confront me with certain risks and some insecurity. I was for a very considerable period in my youth publicly identified with and very active in radical organizations, and was personally before the House Un-American Committee and the McCarran Subversive Activities Control Board in 1954 .... "

The Subcommittee interpreted the Wofsy-Elberg letter as conveying "the impression that he [Wofsy] had engaged in radical activities only as a youth and that his appearance before the House Committee on Un-American Activities was accompanied by no especially significant occurrences. He neglected to state that he was national director for the youth section of the Communist Party for several years, and that what he referred to as his 'youth' lasted until he was thirty-five years of age. He also used the Communist derogatory term for the House Committee on Un-American Activities by calling it the 'Un-American Committee.' " (The Subcommittee dis-

covered that in conversation with Chancellor Strong, Kerr had stated that Wofsy "apparently did not invoke the fifth amendment when brought before the HUAC and the McCarran Board in 1954." And, in a conversation with Vice Chancellor Alex Sherriffs, Kerr states that "Wofsy had not taken the fifth amendment and had been frank [at least to a point] about his past activities.")

The truth is that Wofsy, when he did testify before HCUA on March 16, 1955, had invoked the Fifth Amendment fifty-three times. The invocations came when Wofsy was asked about his Communist Party membership; the offices he held in the Communist Party; his speeches on behalf of the Communist Party; his activities in the Labor Youth League and American Youth for Democracy; his affiliations with the United May Day Committee, the Civil Rights Congress, and the World Federation of Democratic Youth; his authorship of articles in Communist Party publications; and his difficulties in trying to obtain a passport to attend a Communist meeting.

The Subcommittee discovered that Chancellor Strong, who had approved Wofsy's appointment to the Berkeley faculty, withdrew his approval when he learned the truth about Wofsy's background. Strong wrote to Kerr on June 8, 1964: "Now that we have from published documents a fuller account of Dr. Leon Wofsy, I withdraw my signature from the form submitted requesting his appointment as Associate Professor of Bacteriology .... He invoked the First and Fifth Amendments when questioned by a Congressional committee about Communist Party activities, but he makes no mention of this in his letter to Dean Elberg. The letter is also secretive in stating that his participation in left-wing activities took place in his youth.

Until age 35 at least he was in a national leadership role in Communist Party activities."

On June 25, Strong received a call from Roger Stanier, a Berkeley professor and a friend of Wofsy. Stanier had learned that Strong and Dean William Fretter were going to interview Wofsy. Strong made notes of his conversation with Stanier: ". . . He asked what questions I would ask . . . if I wanted a recantation from Wofsy with respect to his past activities . . . . Stanier said that Wofsy, if called before the HUAC again, would probably again refuse to answer questions about Party membership and activities. I remarked that the Chancellor was not a Congressional committee. I stood with the AAUP (American Association of University Professors) in its 1956 policy that questions could properly be asked and an individual could be expected to respond when record of past activities gave rise to questions about the fitness of the individual to be appointed to a faculty position. Roger took no exception to this statement of position . . . ."

When Strong and Fretter completed their interview with Wofsy, they submitted separate résumés to President Kerr. They said that Wofsy was cooperative and frank, that he explained that his father had been a radical Socialist, that he was raised in a family of Marxists, and that it was almost inevitable that his thinking should be oriented toward Communism. Wofsy told them that he still retained radical views but that he had no intention of rejoining the Communist Party. What Wofsy did not tell his interviewers was equally as important as what he told them, if not more so. He did not mention that his father had been a high functionary of the Communist Party for decades, and his mother an

active Communist, so that neither of his parents could be hidden behind the weasel term "Marxist." He did not offer proof to Strong and Fretter that he had ever left the Communist Party. As a matter of fact, Strong and Fretter confronted Wofsy with evidence that he had not left the Party in 1956 as he had claimed. They produced an article from the Communist Party's *Daily Worker* of June 6, 1956, which reported that Wofsy had been granted a leave of absence "to take on other responsibilities in the people's movement." The article read as follows: "The National Council of the Labor Youth League issued the following statement at the conclusion of its meeting recently in New York:

" 'The main order of business dealt with the needs of youth and the coming elections. A program of activity was discussed to help every League club across the country play an influential among the young people in the communities and campuses. A document entitled The Needs of Youth and the Challenge of Peace was issued for discussion in and around the League. Based on these discussions, this program to meet the needs of youth will be edited and published sometime this summer for wide distribution among all those concerned with the problems of Young America. After seven years of outstanding leadership, Leon Wofsy, national chairman of our organization, was granted a leave of absence pending the next national convention. The gratitude and affection of the entire League was expressed to him as he left to take on other responsibilities in the people's movement.' "

Strong and Fretter were in agreement that Wofsy was surprised, concerned, and resentful when confronted with the official word of the Communist Party that he had only taken a leave of absence in 1956. And, for those aware of such things, as Wofsy was, the article indicated that Wofsy, a young, disciplined, and active Party functionary, was – according to the article – assigned to a new job in the Communist movement ("the people's movement"), but in a less conspicuous position than he had held as national chairman of the Labor Youth League. But neither Strong nor Fretter appreciated the subtleties. Strong reversed his position and Wofsy's appointment was approved.

Kerr is no longer President and Strong is no longer Chancellor at Berkeley. Wofsy is still there and is now a full professor. In recent years, he has been associated with the hard-core Left on the west coast in the Peace Action Council, a united front conglomerate dominated by Communists.

ROBERT P. WOLFF was born on December 27, 1933 in New York City, son of Charlotte Ornstein and Walter Wolff. He married Cynthia Griffin. He is an alumnus of Harvard University (A.B., 1953; M.A., 1954; Ph.D., 1957). He is the author of *Kant's Theory of Mental Activity* (1963); *Political Man and Social Man* (1966); *The Poverty of Liberalism* (1968); and *The Ideal of the University* (1969). He is a co-author of *A Critique of Pure Tolerance* (1965). He is the editor of *Kant: A Collection of Critical Essays* (1967); *Ten Great Works of Philosophy* (1969); and *The Essential Hume* (1969).

From 1958 until 1961, Wolff was an instructor in philosophy at Harvard University. From 1961 until 1963, he was an assistant professor of philosophy at the University of Chicago. In 1963 and 1964, he was a visiting lecturer at Wellesley College. Since 1964, he has been at Columbia University as an associate professor (1964-1969) and professor (1969 to the present) of philosophy.

Wolff has been affiliated with the ultra-leftist-pacifist National Committee for a Sane Nuclear Policy; the leftist Committee to Defend the [Chicago] Conspiracy; the ultra-radical American Civil Liberties Union; and the Emergency Civil Liberties Committee ("Communist front" – "subversive"). He has been an active participant in the Socialist Scholars Conferences, annual get-togethers of Marxian Socialists and their fellow travelers. In 1970, he was one of six Socialist Scholars to bring suit "in Federal Court in Brooklyn . . . to restrain Secretary of State William P. Rogers and Attorney General John N. Mitchell from barring a Belgian Marxist [Ernest Mandel] from visiting the United States." Less than a year previously, Mandel had urged the total destruction of the United States government and America's social structure.

DONALD B. WOODWARD was born on December 17, 1905 in Clayton, Indiana, son of Sarah Bosley and Alvin Woodward. He was married to Jean Davis. His second wife is Ethel Hutcheson. He is an alumnus of Indiana University (A.B., 1928). He is a co-author of *Primer of Money* (1932); *Inflation* (1933); and *Prosperity: We Can Have It If We Want It* (1945).

From 1927 until 1929, Woodward worked for the *Wall Street Journal.* From 1929 until 1932, he was financial editor of *Business Week.* From 1933 until 1940, he was an economist with Moody's Investors Service. In 1933, he was a member of the research staff of the National Recovery Administration. In 1939, he was a consultant to the board of governors of the Federal Reserve System. From 1939 until 1941, he was an instructor in bank investments at Columbia University. From 1942 until 1944, he was a consultant to the Treasury Department. In 1947 and 1948, he was a consultant to the Department of State. From 1940 until 1953, he was with the Mutual Life Insurance Company of New York City as research assistant to the president (1940-1946), second vice-president (1946-1952), and vice-president for research (1952-1953). From 1953 until 1961, he was a director and economist for Richardson Merrill, Inc. Since 1961, he has been a partner in A.W. Jones & Company.

Woodward is a long-time member of the Council on Foreign Relations, the informal supra-State Department of the United States; and the Foreign Policy Association, a pivotal agency for pro-Communist, one-world propaganda.

STEPHEN J. WRIGHT was born on September 8, 1910 in Dillon, South Carolina, son of Rachel Eaton and Stephen Wright. He married Rosalind Person. He is an alumnus of Hampton Institute (B.S., 1934); Howard University (M.A., 1939); and New York University (Ph.D., 1943).

From 1934 until 1936, Wright was a high-school teacher in Maryland. From 1936 until 1938, he was a high-school principal in Maryland. From 1939 until 1944, he was at North Carolina College as director of student teaching (1939-1941) and acting dean of men and chairman of the department of education (1942-1944). From 1944 until 1953, he was at Hampton Institute as director of the division of education (1944-1945), professor of education (1945-1953), and dean of the faculty (1945-1953). From 1953 until 1957, he was president of Bluefield State College

in West Virginia. From 1957 until 1966, he was president of Fisk University. Since 1966, he has been president of the United Negro College Fund.

Wright is a trustee of the leftist-oriented World Foundation and the leftist-oriented Institute of International Education. He has been a national official of the ultra-radical Amerian Civil Liberties Union, and of the Foreign Policy Association, a pivotal agency for pro-Communist, one-world propaganda. He has been affiliated with the United Nations Association of the United States, the most prestigious leftwing propaganda agency for the UN in this country.

MELVIN L. WULF was born on November 1, 1927 in New York City, son of Vivian Hurwitz and Jacob Wulf. He married Deirdre Howard. He is an alumnus of Columbia University (B.S., 1952; LL.B., 1955). In 1957, he was admitted to the New York bar.

From 1958 until 1962, Wulf was assistant legal director, and since 1962 legal director, of the American Civil Liberties Union, that motley collection of defenders of subversion, crime, and licentiousness. He is a member of the National Lawyers Guild ("the foremost legal bulwark of the Communist Party, its front organizations, and controlled unions"). He is a member of the ultra-left National Peace Action Coalition. He has supported the Hanoi-inspired People's Peace Treaty, the pet 1971 project of the ultra-left.

[GREGORY] JEROME WYCKOFF was born on March 17, 1911 in Jersey City, son of Villette Waldron and George Wyckoff. He married Marjorie Morrison. He is an alumnus of Trinity College in Connecticut (B.S., 1931) and Columbia

University (M.A., 1940). He is the author of *Story of Geology* (1960) and *Marvels of the Earth* (1964). He is co-author of *Sky Observer's Guide* (1959) and *Pocket Science Guide* (1966).

Since 1940, Wyckoff has been a senior editor, specializing in science, for Artists and Writers Press. He is affiliated with the National Association for the Advancement of Colored People, the fountainhead of Negro agitation for more than half a century; the leftist-racist Congress of Racial Equality; and the ultra-leftist-globalist United World Federalists.

THEODORE O. YNTEMA was born on April 8, 1900 in Holland, Michigan, son of Mary Loomis and Douwe Yntema. He was married to Kathryn van der Veen. His second wife is Virginia Payne. He is the author of *A Mathematical Reformulation of the General Theory of International Trade* (1932). He is a co-author of *Jobs and Markets* (1946).

From 1923 until 1949, Yntema was at the University of Chicago as an instructor in accounting (1923-1930), professor of statistics (1930-1944), and professor of business and economic policy (1944-1949). In 1929 and 1930, he was an acting associate professor of statistics at Stanford University. In 1934 and 1935, he was an economic consultant to the National Recovery Administration. From 1942 until 1949, he was research director, and from 1961 until 1966 was chairman, of the research and policy committee of the Committee for Economic Development, the major propaganda arm of the Council on Foreign Relations, in the important work of socializing the American economy. From 1949 until 1965, he was with the Ford Motor Company as vice-president for finance (1949-1961) and chairman of the finance committee (1961-1965). Since 1966, he has been a visiting professor at the University of Chicago and Oakland University.

Yntema is a director of the leftist-pacifist Carnegie Endowment for International Peace. He is a nonresident member of the Council of Foreign Relations, the informal supra-State Department of the United States. He is a member of the leftist-pacifist Business Executives Move for Vietnam Peace.

HENRY T. YOST JR. was born on January 22, 1925 in Baltimore, son of Martha Minsker and Henry Yost. He married Martha Thomas. He is an alumnus of The Johns Hopkins University (A.B., 1947; Ph.D., 1951).

Since 1951, Yost has been on the faculty at Amherst College, and since 1965 he has been a professor of biology. Since 1959, he has been on the science advisory board of the leftist-oriented Consumers Union. Since 1960, he has been on the executive committee of the leftist-pacifist Massachusetts PAX. He has been affiliated with the leftist-oriented Ad Hoc Committee for an Open Letter on Vietnam; the leftist-pacifist Ad Hoc Faculty Committee on Vietnam; and the leftist-oriented Ad Hoc Committee on the Vietnam War. He is a member of the leftist-pacifist Federation of American Scientists.

QUENTIN D. YOUNG appeared before the House Committee on Un-American Activities on October 3 and 4, 1968, during the course of hearings on "Subversive Involvement in Disruption of [the] 1968 Democratic Party National Convention." He proved to be an obstreperous, voluble, and argumentative witness. When asked if he were a Communist, he pleaded the First, but not the Fifth, Amendment.

On June 14, 1970, the Senate Internal Security Subcommittee, in the course of its hearings on "Extent of Subversion in the 'New Left,' " printed the following information on Young: "Dr. Quentin Young has an extensive history of association with the S.D.S. He was involved in making arrangements for medical and first aid treatment for any casualties that would result from the demonstration during the S.D.S. Weatherman riots of October 8-11, 1969. On December 5, 1969, a subpoena was issued commanding him to appear at the Commission office on December 12, 1969. He was accompanied by his attorney, Ira A. Kipnis, 10 South LaSalle Street, Chicago. Dr. Young resides at 1418 East 55th Street, Chicago, with his wife and five children. Two of his children, Barbara and Michael, are known to be S.D.S. members at Kenwood High School in Chicago. He was born in Chicago on September 5, 1923; holds Social Security Number 353-05-3515 and an Illinois Doctor's License Y510-704-3253. He has his office at 1512 East 55th Street and is a resident doctor at Michael Reese Hospital in Chicago.

"He has been associated with the Medical Committee for Human Rights since July, 1964, at which time, he performed emergency medical service for civil rights workers in the Mississippi Summer Voters Registration Drive. Upon completion of that movement the Medical Committee for Human Rights remained as an organization and developed nationally to pursue programs of 'ending discriminatory practices in health services and in obtaining health services in poor areas of the urban and rural areas.' It is a voluntary organization consisting of physicians, Registered Nurses, medical students and social workers. Dr. Young uses his medical office as a mailing address for the Medical Committee on Human Rights although the national office for this Committee is in New York City.

"Twice a month, the Chicago members of this Committee meet at the Trinity Episcopal Church, 125 East 26th Street, Chicago, telephone 842-7545. Dr. Young said that several days prior to the October 8-11, 1969 Chicago demonstration, his Committee held one of its regular meetings. Daniel Green of the S.D.S. Weatherman Faction appeared at the meeting to ask for possible first aid assistance in the event of violence at the forthcoming riots. The assistance was promised. Subsequently, Young arranged to establish three mobile stations in the Loop area. Each station was equipped with first aid material. A total of about fifty volunteer doctors, nurses, medical students and laymen manned the three stations. Young told us that none of these volunteers participated in any way in the riots, pursuant to the prearranged agreement he had with Green. Young said he was at one of these stations. According to him, there were no serious injuries brought to either his station or any of the other two stations.

"Young was questioned whether he had given any contributions to the S.D.S. Weatherman but he denied it. He did admit that he made a financial contribution to the Revolutionary Youth Movement II, but refused to furnish us the amount, claiming 'it's none of your business.'

"In 1967-1968 Dr. Young was a member of the Advisory Board of the Student Health Organization. On June 30, 1969, Sgt. Joseph Grubisic testified before U.S. Senator John McClellan's

Permanent Sub-Committee on Investigations. He said that Dr. Quentin Young was a member of the Committee for Independent Political Action (CIPA), 1903 West Howard Street, Chicago. On January 15, 1966 CIPA held a mass meeting at McCormick Place. According to Sgt. Grubisic's testimony, in addition to Dr. Young, some of the other sponsors of that mass meeting were Lucy Montgomery, Paul Booth, Lee Webb, Rennie Davis (the convicted 'Conspiracy 7' defendant in the federal court trial in Chicago), Todd Gitlin (a S.D.S. leader), Sidney Lens and Jack Spiegel of the Chicago Peace Council.

"During the 'Conspiracy 7' trial in federal court, defendant Abby Hoffman failed to appear in court a few days during the trial. Dr. Young testified on December 26, 1969 that he was Hoffman's physician and determined his patient was suffering from chronic bronchitis.

"On February 19, 1970, Dr. Young and Dr. Al Klinger had a conference with Dr. Murray Brown, Chicago Health Commissioner. Dr. Young and Dr. Klinger claimed that the reason the Black Panther Party had not applied for a license to conduct a health clinic was that it would lead to 'constant harassment' by city officials. Previously a clinic conducted by the Black Panther Party located at 3850 West 16th Street had been served with a summons charging operators of the clinic of dispensing drugs without a license.

"On October 3-4, 1968, Dr. Young testified, pursuant to the service of a subpoena, before the U.S. House of Representatives Committee on Un-American Activities. He was questioned concerning the fact that he had paid $1,000 of the $1,500 due on the rent of the National Mobilization Office located at 407 Dearborn Street. (We have since obtained a copy of the check which was dated April 1, 1968, signed Quentin D. Young, Trustee, on the National Bank of Hyde Park in Chicago.)

"At first, Dr. Young said that he had loaned Rennie Davis $1,000 and was repaid in 48 hours. Later when confronted with a check he said 'If you are interested in the details, they were renting an office, and he said, could I lend $1,000 for 48 hours. Normally, I wouldn't do it, but they said they couldn't make it without it, and I lent them the money.' It was pointed out to him that the check was made out to Sudler and Company, a Realtor and Rennie Davis. Dr. Young said this was the nature of the request made to him by Davis, 'The exact circumstances, as I recall, is Davis was out of the City. He called me and asked if I could make the thing out to the Realtor. As I have testified, I have no intentions to conceal the fact. When asked, I responded immediately. The check was made out to the person to whom it was received by since Mr. Davis was not around to receive it.'

"Dr. Young refused to answer a question as to whether he attended a mass meeting of the Communist Party at the Ashland Building Auditorium in Chicago on October 10, 1948. The Committee Counsel also asked Young the following question: 'On July 14-16, 1967, the Radical Education Project of S.D.S. staged a conference on "Radicals in the Professions," in Ann Arbor, Michigan. An account of this conference published in the *National Guardian* of August 5, 1967, in describing what took place at the conference reported: "the political importance of the health profession was highlighted by Quentin Young of the Medical Committee for Human Rights who points out that by 1975, one out of every 10 persons entering the work force will be in health, a 10 per cent that is also the largest unorganized sector of the working class." Dr. Young, I hand you a reproduction of the *National Guardian* account referred to and I ask you: Did you speak at the conference in the manner indicated in the *National Guardian* as so marked?' Dr. Young admitted the statement ascribed to him. Dr. Young denied being a member of the S.D.S., but said that those who were members were entitled to their political opinions.

"On September 14, 1955 Royal W. France of New York City and Mr. Laurent B. Frantz of California filed in the Supreme Court of the United States a motion and brief for leave to file brief as *amici curiae*, supporting the Communist Party in the case of the Communist Party of the United States versus the Subversive Activities Control Board. Under questioning by Committee Counsel, Dr. Young admitted he was one of the many persons who signed the brief.

"He was also asked, 'During the time you have known Rennie Davis, has he ever discussed his theory of how to change this country, and specifically his plans concerning Chicago, that is, aside from the seeking of your help as an official of the Medical Committee for Human Rights?' Dr. Young avoided the question with irrelevant remarks and never did answer it."

On June 10, 1970, Ronald L. Brooks, an agent of the Illinois Crime Investigating Commission, shed further light on Quentin Young's background. Brooks, who was investigating the New Left, testified before the Senate Internal Security Subcommittee. He said that it had been ascertained that 18-year-old Ethan Young, who was in the first Venceremos

contingent to go to Communist Cuba, was the son of Quentin Young. Brooks submitted an account of Ethan Young's experiences which appeared in the June 1970 *Hyde Park-Kenwood* [Illinois] *Voices*, under the by-line of Patricia Bach: "Last December, Ethan Young, 4923 Greenwood, along with some 200 other persons, mostly students from all over the United States, traveled to Cuba to help in that country's 10-million-ton sugar cane harvest. The group, known as the Venceremos Brigade, took its name from Cuba's *Patria o muerte, venceremos* – 'Our country of death, we will win.'

"Many speakers also addressed the camp, including the Cuban minister of health, ambassador from North Vietnam and the Provisional Revolutionary Government of South Vietnam, soldiers from the National Liberation Front and Vietnamese students studying in Cuba.

"Young was particularly impressed with the Vietnamese. 'They've been subjected to so much but still really treasure life,' he said. Some Vietnamese soldiers also helped cut cane. Young explained, 'They recognize the Cuban struggle as the same as their struggle over oppression.'

"Fidel Castro visited the camp on Christmas Day and worked in the fields with a special brigade, Young said, as a security precaution. But in the evening, he spoke to the entire camp. 'A dynamite cat!' Young exclaimed. 'He rapped about the United States and the kind of struggle we would have to undertake here and how it's going to take a while. Cuba supports it – that is morally.' Admittedly Castro is a charismatic leader but, Young said, 'He is trying to accentuate the role of the people. All he is there for is to educate, advise and act as an example. Castro believes he acts as the revolutionary consciousness of the people.'

"After six weeks of cutting cane, the brigade spent the last two weeks touring Cuba, visiting schools, factories and universities. The group also toured the Isle of Pines, where experimental youth camps are located. 'These camps were experimenting in communism. That is, they've wiped out money and have tried to build a work-force based on the will to benefit the common good.'

"Young believes most Cubans support the revolution. 'The government is set up to serve the people with its own eventual destruction in mind. The country is highly mobilized. Everyone is working on common goals in the stages of the revolution. Their most immediate goal is completion of the 10-million-ton harvest of sugar by July. Although Castro recently announced that the goal won't be reached, Cuba has produced more sugar this year than ever before in history,' Young said. 'The sugar harvest is only one step in wiping out underdevelopment, paving the way for a socialist industrialized society. They don't intend to create a society that will be socialist in name only – one where the state owns the means of production but the people don't really participate in controlling those means of production. They already participate,' Young pointed out.

"Young believes Cuba's prime goal is 'development of the socialist man, who can, in fact, live for the development of the common good. This is what really impressed me most.' He said it means developing persons who can sustain a classless egalitarian society and build communication between people. But Young also thinks Cuba is not the ideal society yet. Its two major social problems, he says, are the existence of male chauvinism and attitudinal racism. But he believes the country is working to correct them. He said institutional rac-ism does not exist there. 'Cuba doesn't have the system to sustain attitudinal racism so it, too, is dying out.'

"Young sees Cuba's main problem as the 'immediate threat of the United States, which tries to undermine Cuba in different ways. The whole blockade really hurts the country. It creates a heavy shortage of meat and other things that necessitates food rationing. Some Cubans aren't ready to make sacrifices like that and they generally split to the United States.'

"Young said Cubans are 'very aware of the risks in trying to establish a socialist society 90 miles away from the biggest imperialist power, but they're prepared to go to any length to keep Cuba independent and develop a socialist country.' Cuba, he believes, 'is trying to be an example first to Latin America and then to the whole world. They recognize their revolution won't survive unless it spreads throughout Latin America, that it will take united Latin American power to stand up both as a socialist structure and against the imperialist structure.'

"As a result of working, meeting and talking with Cubans while a member of the Venceremos Brigade, Young feels more committed to 'furthering the revolution.' 'Essentially what I see myself working for in the future is socialism in the United States. It will have to be a different kind of socialism because of the differences in our society,' he said. 'Exactly how it is going to emerge, I'm still not sure,' he admitted, 'but that's what I'll be working for.' "

WILLIAM S. YOUNGMAN was born on May 25, 1907 in Boston, Massachusetts, son of Helen Yerxa and William Youngman. He married Elsie Perkins. He is an alumnus of Harvard University (A.B., 1929; LL.B., 1932). He has been

ZAHN

admitted to the Massachusetts bar (1934), the bar of the Supreme Court of the U.S. (1939), the bar of the District of Columbia (1941), and the New York bar (1951).

In 1932 and 1933, Youngman was law secretary to Judge Learned Hand in New York City. From 1933 until 1938, he was with a law firm in Boston. In 1939 and 1940, he was in Washington, D.C., as counsel to the National Power Policy Commission and chief counsel in the power division of the Public Works Administration. In 1940 and 1941, he was general counsel for the Federal Power Commission. From 1941 until 1945, he was with China Defense Supplies, Inc., as executive vice-president and director (1941-1942) and president (1942-1945). From 1944 until 1947, he was general counsel in the United States for the National Resources Commission of China. From 1941 until 1949, he was a partner in the legal firm of Corcoran & Youngman. From 1949 until 1968, he was president of C.V. Starr & Company. From 1952 until 1969, he was chairman of the board of the Home Assurance Company of Pennsylvania. From 1958 until 1967, he was chairman of the board of the American International Assurance Company of Hong Kong. From 1958 until 1968, he was chairman of the board of the Philippine American Life Insurance Company. From 1959 until 1968, he was chairman of the board of the American International Underwriters Corporation.

Youngman is a long-time member and official of the Foreign Policy Association, a bulwark of leftist-internationalism. He is a long-time resident and/or nonresident member of the Council on Foreign Relations, the informal supra-State Department of the United States.

GORDON C. ZAHN was born on August 7, 1918 in Milwaukee, son of Dorothy Spoehr and Charles Zahn. He is an alumnus of the College of St. Thomas (B.A., 1949) and Catholic University (M.A., 1950; Ph.D., 1953). He also pursued graduate studies at Harvard University. He is the author of *German Catholics and Hitler's Wars* (1962); *In Solitary Witness – The Life and Death of Franz Jägerstüffer* (1964); *War, Conscience, and Dissent* (1967); and *The Military Chaplaincy* (1969). He is editor of *Readings in Sociology* (1958). He is a contributor to *Morality and Modern Warfare* (1960) and *Breakthrough to Peace* (1962). In 1952 and 1953, he held a fellowship from the leftist-oriented Social Science Research Council. In 1956 and 1957, he was a Fulbright research fellow in Germany. In 1961, he was in Austria on a grant from the American Philosophical Society. In 1964 and 1965, he was at the University of Manchester in England as a Simon senior research fellow.

From 1953 until 1967, he served successively as an assistant professor, associate professor, and professor of sociology at Loyola University in Chicago. Since 1967, he has been professor of sociology at the University of Massachusetts.

In World War II, Zahn was a conscientious objector. Since 1955, he has been a consultant to the defamatory Anti-Defamation League. He has been affiliated with the leftist-pacifist National Council to Repeal the Draft; the leftist-pacifist Voters Peace Pledge; the leftist-pacifist Ad Hoc Faculty Committee on Vietnam; the leftist-oriented Catholic Interracial Council; the ultra-leftist-pacifist Fellowship of Reconciliation; the leftist-pacifist American PAX Association; and the ultra-leftist-pacifist National Committee for a Sane Nuclear Policy.

622

REGINALD H. ZALLES was born on December 20, 1910 in Washington, D.C., son of Arcadia Calderon and Jorje Zalles. He is an alumnus of Williams College (A.B., 1932) and Harvard University (M.A., 1948).

From 1935 until 1940, Zalles was on the faculty of the Henry George School in New York City and Boston. In 1939 and 1940, he was director of the Free Market Institute in Boston. From 1949 until 1951, he was director of the Massachusetts Council of the CIO. Since 1949, he has been with the ultra-radical Americans for Democratic Action as executive secretary of the Massachusetts chapter of the ADA (1949-1951); chairman of the Boston chapter of the ADA (1950); chairman of the Montgomery County, Maryland, chapter of the ADA (1955); chairman of the Washington, D.C., chapter of the ADA (1959); national executive secretary of the ADA (1951-1953); secretary of the ADA's national board (1956-1963); and national treasurer of the ADA (1963 to the present).

ARNOLD S. ZANDER was born on November 26, 1901 in Two Rivers, Wisconsin, son of Anna Scheuer and Arnold Zander. He married Lola Dynes. He is an alumnus of the University of Wisconsin (B.S.,1923; M.S., 1929; Ph.D., 1931).

In 1923 and 1924, Zander was a draftsman for the Wisconsin Telephone Company. In 1924 and 1925, he was a bridge draftsman for the Baltimore & Ohio Railroad. From 1925 until 1927, he was a structural steel draftsman for the Manitowoc Shipbuilding Corporation. From 1927 until 1929, he was a faculty assistant at the University of Wisconsin. In 1929, he was secretary for the League of Wisconsin Municipalities. From 1930 until 1934, he was principal examiner for the Wisconsin State Civil Service Department in the Bureau of Personnel. From 1933 until 1935, he was executive secretary of the Wisconsin State Civil Service Employees Union. From 1936 until 1966, he was president of the American Federation of State, County and Municipal Employees, which he founded. Since 1966, he has been president emeritus. Since 1968, he has been a visiting lecturer at the University of Wisconsin. He has served on the board of the AFL-CIO.

Zander has been a long-time member of and has served as president of the ultra-leftist-globalist United World Federalists. He is a long-time member of and has served on the national board of the ultra-radical Americans for Democratic Action. He has been affiliated with the Workers Defense League, a leftwing group defending political undesirables who are subject to deportation.

INDEX OF ORGANIZATIONS

INDEX OF BIOGRAPHIES

633

634

635